JUST BEYOND YOUR IMAGINATION

FROM APRIL 15 TO DECEMBER 10*, ONE OF THE BEST VALUES UNDER  THE BOSS PACKAGE GIVES YOU OUR TROPICAL SUN.

· 1ST NIGHT FREE WITH A 5 NIGHT MINIMUM STAY.
· TRANSFERS FROM AIRPORT TO HOTEL INCLUDED.
· CONTINENTAL BREAKFAST INCLUDED DAILY.
· COMPLIMENTARY DINNER AND DANCING AT AN AUTHENTIC BAJAN PARTY.

CALL YOUR AAA TRAVEL AGENT OR 1-888-BARBADOS.

*BLACKOUT DATES ARE JUL 20 - AUG 9

-BARBADOS OFFERS SUMMER SAVINGS-BARBADOS OFFERS SUMMER SAVINGS-

CARIBBEAN
INCLUDING BERMUDA

An annual catalog of selected travel information prepared to enhance the travel experience of our members.

1999 EDITION

PUBLISHED BY:

AAA PUBLISHING
1000 AAA DRIVE
HEATHROW, FL 32746-5063

SEND WRITTEN COMMENTS TO:

CARIBBEAN EDITOR
AAA EDITORIAL SERVICES
BOX 59, 1000 AAA DRIVE
HEATHROW, FL 32746-5063

FOR ADVERTISING RATES AND CIRCULATION INFORMATION CALL:

(407) 444-8280

The publisher is not responsible for changes that occur after publication.

Printed in the USA by Quebecor Printing, Buffalo, NY

Printed on recyclable paper. Please recycle whenever possible.

Stock #1002

CONTENTS

PRACTICAL INFORMATION

USING YOUR TRAVELBOOK 4

PLANNING YOUR TRIP 5

CUSTOMS INFORMATION 19

ABOUT LODGINGS & RESTAURANTS 23

FOR YOUR INFORMATION

TEMPERATURE CHART 16

THE AAA DIAMONDS 27

LODGING CLASSIFICATIONS 30

SAMPLE LODGING LISTING 28

LANGUAGE TIPS 285

INDEXES

INDEX TO TOWNS AND AREAS 289

BED & BREAKFAST LODGINGS 292

COUNTRY INNS* 292

HISTORICAL LODGINGS & RESTAURANTS* 293

RESORTS 294

*MAY INCLUDE BED AND BREAKFAST PROPERTIES

Caribbean TravelBook

Islands

Anguilla 33
Antigua and Barbuda 36
Aruba 46
The Bahamas 57
Barbados 77
Bermuda 91
Bonaire 108
Cayman Islands 112
Curaçao 124
Dominica 131
Dominican Republic 135
Grenada 147
Guadeloupe 153
Jamaica 159
Martinique 184
Puerto Rico 190
St. Barthélemy 211
St. Eustatius and Saba 217
St. Kitts and Nevis 219
St. Lucia 226
St. Martin/St. Maarten 234
St. Vincent and The Grenadines 243
Trinidad and Tobago 248
Turks and Caicos Islands 255
Virgin Islands, British 259
Virgin Islands, U.S. 264
Other Ports of Call 282

Maps

Caribbean Islands 10
Anguilla 34
Antigua 37
Aruba 48
The Bahamas 60
New Providence Island 64
Barbados 79
Bermuda Island 94
Bonaire 110
Grand Cayman 114
Curaçao 125
Dominica 132
Dominican Republic and Haiti 137
Grenada 148
Guadeloupe 155
Jamaica 162
Martinique 186
Puerto Rico 192
San Juan 198
St. Barthélemy 213
St. Kitts and Nevis, Saba and St. Eustatius 220
St. Lucia 227
St. Martin/St. Maarten 236
St. Vincent 245
Trinidad and Tobago 249
Virgin Islands, British 261
Virgin Islands, U.S. 266

Using Your TravelBook

The primary purpose of this TravelBook is to make your trip as enjoyable as possible. From planning your mode of travel to seeing the sights and selecting your accommodations and restaurants, the book offers the most recent information available. However, since the material must be prepared several months prior to publication, changes will sometimes occur after the book is printed.

No attraction, hotel, resort or restaurant pays for a listing; they are listed on the basis of merit alone after approval by a AAA field inspector or a designated AAA representative. Attractions of particular or unusual interest are preceded by a star (★). A detailed explanation of the selection of dining and lodging facilities appears in the *About Lodgings & Restaurants* section.

In most cases, islands are listed in alphabetical order rather than according to geographical location or political affiliation; however, St. Kitts and Nevis, Antigua and Barbuda, and Trinidad and Tobago are listed as units because these three twin-island groupings are independent nations. The Bahamas, Cayman Islands, St. Eustatius and Saba, Turks and Caicos Islands, British Virgin Islands and U.S. Virgin Islands also are listed as island groups. References to individual islands within the French West Indies, Leeward Islands, Netherlands Antilles and Windward Islands can be found in the Index to Towns and Areas at the back of the *What To See* section. Though English is widely spoken throughout the islands, many locals will appreciate your attempt to converse in their first language. See the *Language Tips* section for Dutch, French and Spanish translations of commonly used expressions and words.

The descriptive material about each island begins with information about its history, government and economy; shopping; food and drink; sports and amusements; excursions and sightseeing; and transportation. Such information as the local currency and exchange rate, immigration requirements, holidays and sources of further information is contained in the *Things To Know* box. Points of interest are listed under the nearest community, and operating schedules are given at the end of most listings. Exact admission prices are not always stated because of currency fluctuation. Communities are keyed to the island maps by means of coordinates (A-3, for example) following the place name.

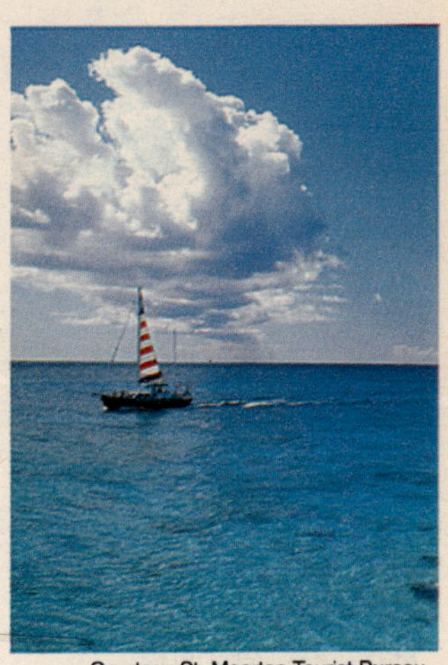

Courtesy St. Maarten Tourist Bureau

Travel Advisories

The U.S. Department of State issues Consular Information Sheets, Travel Warnings and Public Announcements concerning serious health or security conditions that might affect U.S. citizens. They can be obtained at U.S. embassies and consulates abroad, regional passport agencies in the United States and from the Overseas Citizens Services, Bureau of Consular Affairs, Room 4811, U.S. Department of State, Washington, DC 20520-4818; phone (202) 647-5225.

Consular Information Sheets provide information about entry requirements, currency regulations, health conditions, security, political disturbances, areas of instability and drug penalties. A Travel Warning is issued when the situation in a country is dangerous enough for the Department of State to recommend that Americans not travel there. Public Announcements are a means of releasing information to travelers about short-term conditions which might pose security risks to Americans traveling abroad.

In addition, travelers are urged to remain abreast of regional events and to contact their AAA travel agent or air or sea carrier for the latest updates.

In AAA publications you will find advertisements for accommodations, restaurants and attractions. Only operations inspected and approved by a AAA field inspector may advertise, but be assured the purchase of advertising in AAA publications has no effect on our ratings or inspections. In addition, you might find advertising for various travel-related products, services and specific areas. Acceptance of advertising for any product, service or area does **not** imply endorsement by AAA. These advertisements provide more information that might be helpful in selecting what to see and where to stay.

To help AAA maintain the best possible service, members are encouraged to report both pleasant and unpleasant experiences from their visits to the Caribbean; write AAA Member Comments, Mail Stop 61, 1000 AAA Dr., Heathrow, FL 32746-5063.

PLANNING YOUR TRIP

The islands of the Caribbean region stretch east and south from the Gulf of Mexico and Florida to the northern coast of South America—a span of more than 2,000 miles (3,200 km). The hundreds of islands within this arc are divided into the Bahamas (and the adjacent Turks and Caicos Islands) and the Greater and Lesser Antilles. The Greater Antilles include the largest islands: Cuba, Jamaica, Puerto Rico and the island of Hispaniola, which contains Haiti and the Dominican Republic. The Lesser Antilles encompass the remaining arc of smaller isles as well as several islands off the coast of Venezuela. Major groupings within the Lesser Antilles include the Virgin Islands and the Windward and Leeward Islands. The term Antilles derives from "Antillia," a mythical island supposedly discovered by Columbus. The leeward and windward expressions have nautical beginnings: Sailors call the direction from

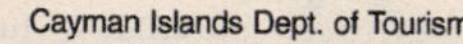
Cayman Islands Dept. of Tourism

which the wind is coming windward and the direction to which the wind is blowing leeward. Bermuda is not a Caribbean island at all, but is located in the Atlantic Ocean 568 miles (914 km) east of Cape Hatteras, N.C.

According to geologists the Caribbean archipelago is a portion of a once unbroken bridge that joined North and South America. Through unknown events some of the land sank, and what remains are the peaks of a submarine volcanic mountain range. Others speculate these mountains are the remnants of the legendary lost continent of Atlantis. A few of the Caribbean islands, as well as Bermuda, are coral formations.

The easterly trade winds maintain the region's even temperatures and carry seeds and spores to the islands, where they germinate and thrive. The trade winds also were responsible for depositing Columbus at what he thought was the "back door" of India, but was probably San Salvador in the Bahamas.

Columbus continued onward to Cuba and Hispaniola. Although the great golden treasures he envisioned never fully materialized, he did meet the Arawaks and the Caribs, whom he mistook for East Indians. His return to Spain with charts, a small amount of gold and tales of great fortunes to be made gained him financing for three more visits. On the heels of Columbus came such *conquistadores* as Hernando Cortés and Francisco Pizarro seeking their share of the territory and gold. Mining operations and sugar plantations requiring

large work crews were started. Native Indians became laborers but refused to work by force. As their numbers diminished, a license was arranged permitting the importation of 4,000 African slaves—an agreement that was to have far-reaching effects on the New World.

Ships with holds laden with the produce of the Caribbean opened the door on yet another occupation. Buccaneers, pirates, smugglers and freebooters proliferated, using the islands' numerous caves and inlets as shelter and for ambush. The result was many years of terror, bloodshed and territorial feuding. As Spanish supremacy in the region weakened, England, France, the Netherlands and the United States all added their cultural marks to the Caribbean.

The islands' diversity of races and traditions generates an aura of romance and mystery. Though bathed by the same sea, each isle has a distinctive past. But whatever the process of evolution, the vitality and beauty of the islands and their residents are the keynote for the visitor.

Every year the number of travelers to the region increases, and every year new hotels and resorts arise on such well-known vacation spots as the Bahamas and Bermuda as well as on islands little known to tourists until a few years ago. Interisland flights and the more leisurely cruise ships have gained popularity. Sightseeing also has increased, aided largely by the availability of rental vehicles. Swimming, sailing, fishing, scuba diving, snorkeling, golf, tennis and other outdoor sports are major draws. The islands of the Caribbean, the Bahamas and Bermuda offer enough variety to please any visitor's tastes.

WHERE TO GO

If you are undecided about where to go, read the various chapters and look over the descriptions of AAA-approved accommodations. If language barriers are a concern, keep in mind that English is spoken at most large resorts and in most shops and restaurants.

Consider your priorities and interests: If you do not care for water sports, sunbathing or having lots of time on your hands, choose one of the more developed islands that offers plenty of shopping, sightseeing, dining and nightlife. On the other hand, if you want to "get away from it all" there are still some islands that have yet to be "discovered" and commercialized. On such islands modern conveniences might be rather sparse but privacy is abundant.

The local currency exchange rate also might influence your decision. Check the *Things To Know* boxes for the governing rates at press time. Exchange rates can fluctuate significantly, so you should always check them with a financial institution prior to departure.

Unfortunately, because of the varying economic conditions on most islands, the contrast between luxury resorts and poverty-ridden villages can be a harsh reality. You might want to investigate the political and social climate of an island before planning your trip.

A AAA travel agent can answer your questions, plan an itinerary and make your reservations. At the same time, the agent can arrange for you to be met on arrival, book you on sightseeing expeditions and reserve a chauffeur-driven or rental car.

CLIMATE AND CLOTHING

Much of the Bahamas and all of the Caribbean islands lie below the Tropic of Cancer, the northern limit of the tropics, and therefore enjoy a mild climate year round. There is no "wrong" season to visit the Caribbean and the Bahamas; choose the time most convenient for you. The main season varies from island to island and hotel to hotel but generally runs from mid-December to mid-April. The off-season is late spring, summer and fall, except in Bermuda, which is much farther north, where the off-season spans November to mid-March.

Most islands are subject to a rainy season—sometime between June and November—but its effect on the vacationer is minimal. Hurricane season also is June through November. For average monthly temperatures and rainfall *see the Climate Chart.*

The best rule to follow when packing for any trip, whether by plane or ship, is to first include everything that seems absolutely indispensable and then repack, taking only half as much as you would have originally planned. Another rule is to not take anything you would hate to lose, such as expensive jewelry or unneeded credit cards. Remember to pack toiletries, film and extra eyeglasses, as they are often more expensive on the islands. Be sure to pack prescription medicines, in their original containers, and other essentials in your carry-on luggage.

When deciding what clothes to take to the Caribbean, keep in mind the climate, the islands you will visit and where you plan to stay. Clothing made from artificial fibers can be uncomfortable in the heat, though for some the convenience of no-iron clothes might outweigh this disadvantage. A good compromise is a cotton-synthetic blend that is both cool and wrinkle free.

In general, colorful, lightweight sport and resort-style clothes are appropriate all year throughout the islands. A lightweight wrap for cool evenings should be added for the Bahamas, Bermuda, the Cayman Islands, the Dominican Republic and Jamaica. In fact, it is always wise to pack a sweater, no matter how tropical the climate. In Bermuda, silks and lightweight woolens are comfortable during the day from mid-December to late March. For the most part, cocktail dresses and jackets and ties are not required for evening wear in the Caribbean except at resorts and large hotels on some of the more developed islands.

When packing for a cruise follow the same general rules. Formal clothes—dinner jackets and long dresses—are suitable for such highlights as the captain's dinner or the captain's cocktail parties. For regular dinners, most passengers change from their daytime attire to more sophisticated garb. Cruises are an excellent opportunity to wear high fashion outfits and styles that you might be uncomfortable wearing at home.

For shore visits or strolling around the deck, any type of vacation or outdoor clothing is appropriate. Swimwear, however, should be worn only at the beach or pool, not in public areas. Bathing *au naturel* or topless is fashionable at some beaches in the French West Indies, but is still an unwelcome

trend on most of the other islands. Some of the people in the more conservative countries are offended by revealing clothes, especially if they are worn in the daytime.

GETTING THERE

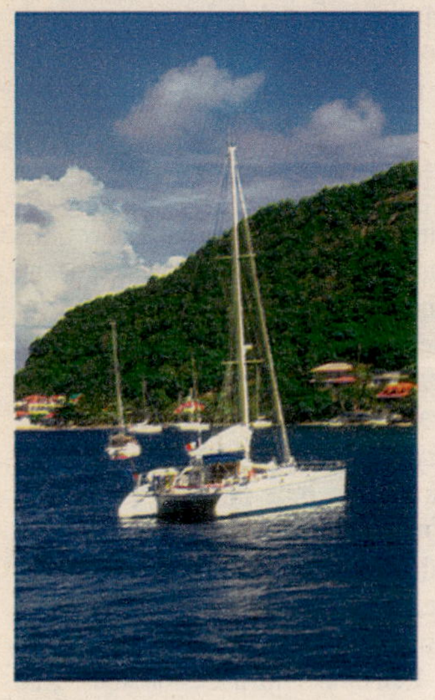

Travel to the islands is by plane, cruise ship or charter boat. Planned excursions tailored to fit your schedule and pocketbook are abundant; the mode of transportation you select is a matter of personal preference. However you choose to travel, a AAA travel agent can make all the necessary arrangements.

BY AIR: Air transportation has made the weekend, 1- or 2-week vacation as practical as it is delightful. Many excursion fares, some with stopovers, are available. Most Caribbean destinations can be reached in a matter of hours from major cities and often in a matter of minutes from Miami. Some islands do not have direct air service; check with a AAA travel agent about access to these smaller destinations. Also consult your travel agent for group fares, special packages, seasonal rates and current schedules. Most offices can make plane reservations and obtain tickets.

Air travel in the Caribbean requires some special considerations. Many island governments require visitors to complete a tourist card and perhaps a customs declaration form before entering their country. These forms are provided by your air carrier and should be completed while en route. Allow about an hour to clear customs and immigration upon arrival. *Keep your copy of the tourist card; it must be returned when you depart.* Though no Caribbean island requires a passport of U.S. visitors, using one will expedite matters. See your destination's *Things To Know* box for specific immigration requirements.

On departure day you should arrive at the airport 2 hours before your flight leaves. This will ensure enough time to obtain seat assignments, check luggage, reconvert unused unspent currency, pay departure taxes and clear emigration and security checkpoints before boarding. Allow another hour when you land to claim your luggage and clear customs and immigration. Allow at least 90 minutes to make a connecting flight.

BY SEA: Other than owning and operating your own vessel, there are two ways to visit the Caribbean via the bounding main: by charter boat *(see Charter Tips)* and by cruise ship *(see Cruise Tips)*.

BY AIR AND SEA: Try a combination air *and* sea vacation. Some cruise lines will fly you from their departure point to one of the balmy Caribbean islands where you can relax and unwind for a few days; then you can return by luxury cruise ship—or cruise to the Caribbean and return by air. Many cruise lines will pay part of your airfare to and from their departure point as part of the full cruise package.

CHARTER TIPS

Sailing on a charter boat from the mainland United States to any of the islands is possible, though the time and money required makes this an unfeasible option for many vacationers.

Instead, most people fly to a major island and start their sailing adventure there. The waters around the Virgin Islands and St. Vincent and the Grenadines are considered the best for sailing in the Caribbean.

Chartering a boat means renting it for a specified period of time, during which you can do whatever you want—sail the entire time, hop from island to island or stay in the marina. In most cases when you charter a boat it becomes your home, where you will live, eat and sleep. The only travelers on board will be you, your party and perhaps a crew.

There are two basic types of charter cruises. The bareboat charter is for the experienced sailor; you sail the boat yourself and provide your own meals. The crewed-boat charter is for those with limited or no sailing experience, in which so a skipper and crew are provided.

If you are interested in a sailing vacation, consult a charter broker. Most work on a commission basis, so the consultation is free. Information on brokers is available from your AAA travel agent.

When selecting a broker ask for a recommendation. Almost all brokers inspect the boats they represent; make sure this is the case with the broker you choose. Before you meet with the broker, define your priorities—the length of your vacation, the amount of time you want to spend at sea, the amount of money you want to spend, the number of persons who will be traveling, the type of crew you need and the season you will be sailing. Though sailing in the Caribbean is good all year, it is best from January to March. Rainy season and hurricane season extend from June through November.

The average charter runs 10 to 14 days and should be no more expensive than staying at a resort and dining out at restaurants. The fee includes all meals, liquor and other activities that take place on board. If you have special dietary needs, inform your broker or travel agent during the planning stages. On-shore meals are not included.

Sailing the Caribbean on a chartered boat is a very independent vacation—the itinerary, style and atmosphere are set by you. If you charter a large yacht, the atmosphere will almost always be formal. The crew will be uniformed and the only communication with them will be through the captain. However, the larger the vessel, the larger the bill; most people opt for smaller boats—about 50 feet in length. The atmosphere on a smaller boat is naturally more casual, but it is up to you to set the tone. Tipping is a standard practice; 15 percent of the charter fee is considered reasonable. Give the tip to the captain, who will divide it among the crew.

Depending on your experience, you may help sail the boat, but the captain is always the final authority. If children are aboard, keep them under control both for their own safety

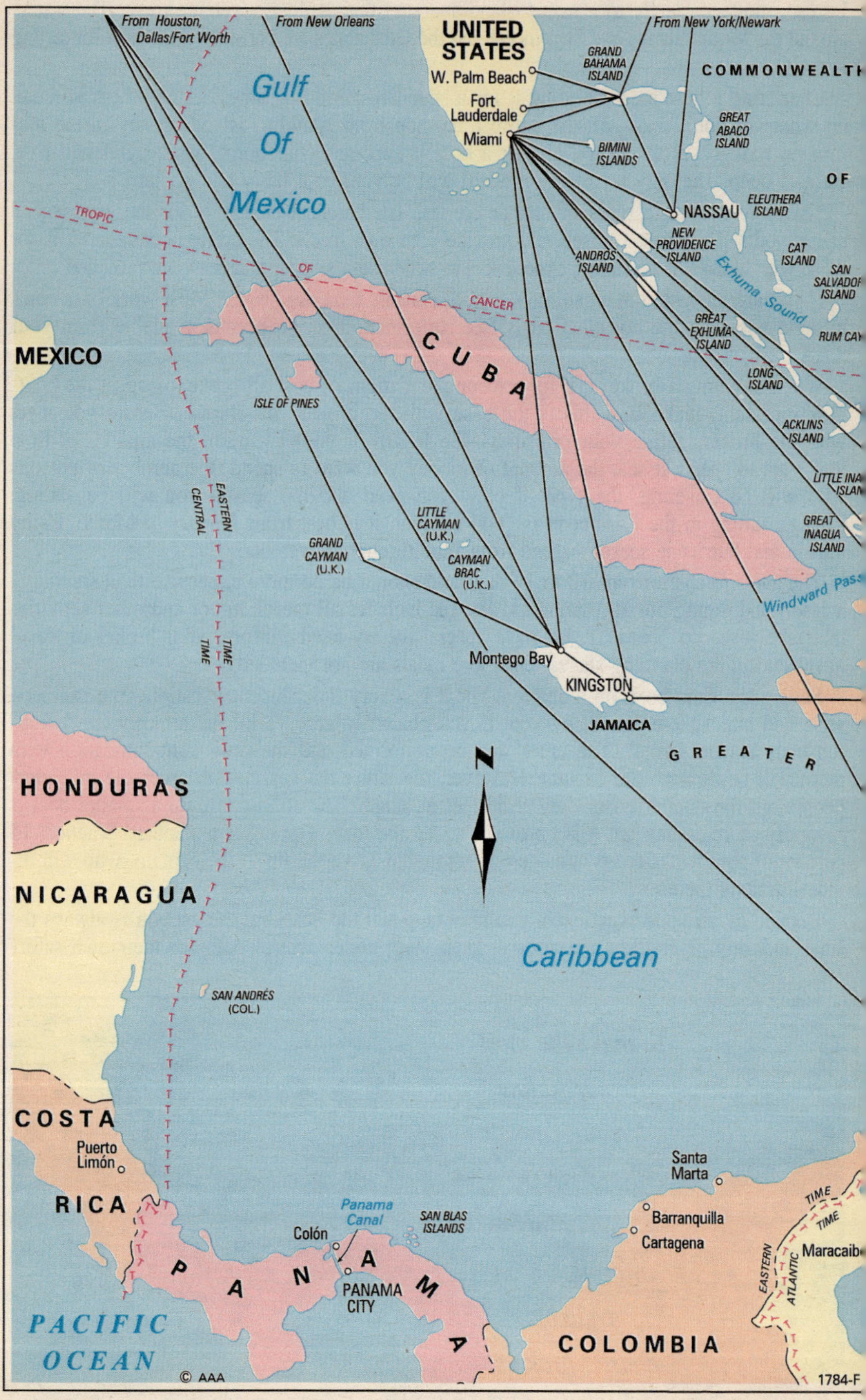

From Houston, Dallas/Fort Worth
From New Orleans
From New York/Newark
UNITED STATES
GRAND BAHAMA ISLAND
COMMONWEALTH
W. Palm Beach
Fort Lauderdale
Miami
GREAT ABACO ISLAND
OF
BIMINI ISLANDS
NASSAU
ELEUTHERA ISLAND
Gulf
Of
Mexico
NEW PROVIDENCE ISLAND
Exhuma Sound
ANDROS ISLAND
CAT ISLAND
SAN SALVADOR ISLAND
TROPIC
OF
CANCER
GREAT EXHUMA ISLAND
RUM CAY
MEXICO
C U B A
LONG ISLAND
ISLE OF PINES
ACKLINS ISLAND
LITTLE INA ISLAND
LITTLE CAYMAN (U.K.)
GRAND CAYMAN (U.K.)
CAYMAN BRAC (U.K.)
GREAT INAGUA ISLAND
EASTERN
CENTRAL
TIME
TIME
Windward Pass
Montego Bay
KINGSTON
JAMAICA
G R E A T E R
N
HONDURAS
Caribbean
NICARAGUA
SAN ANDRÉS (COL.)
COSTA
Puerto Limón
Santa Marta
RICA
Barranquilla
Panama Canal
SAN BLAS ISLANDS
Cartagena
TIME
TIME
Colón
Maracaib
P A N A M A
EASTERN
ATLANTIC
PANAMA CITY
PACIFIC OCEAN
COLOMBIA
© AAA
1784-F

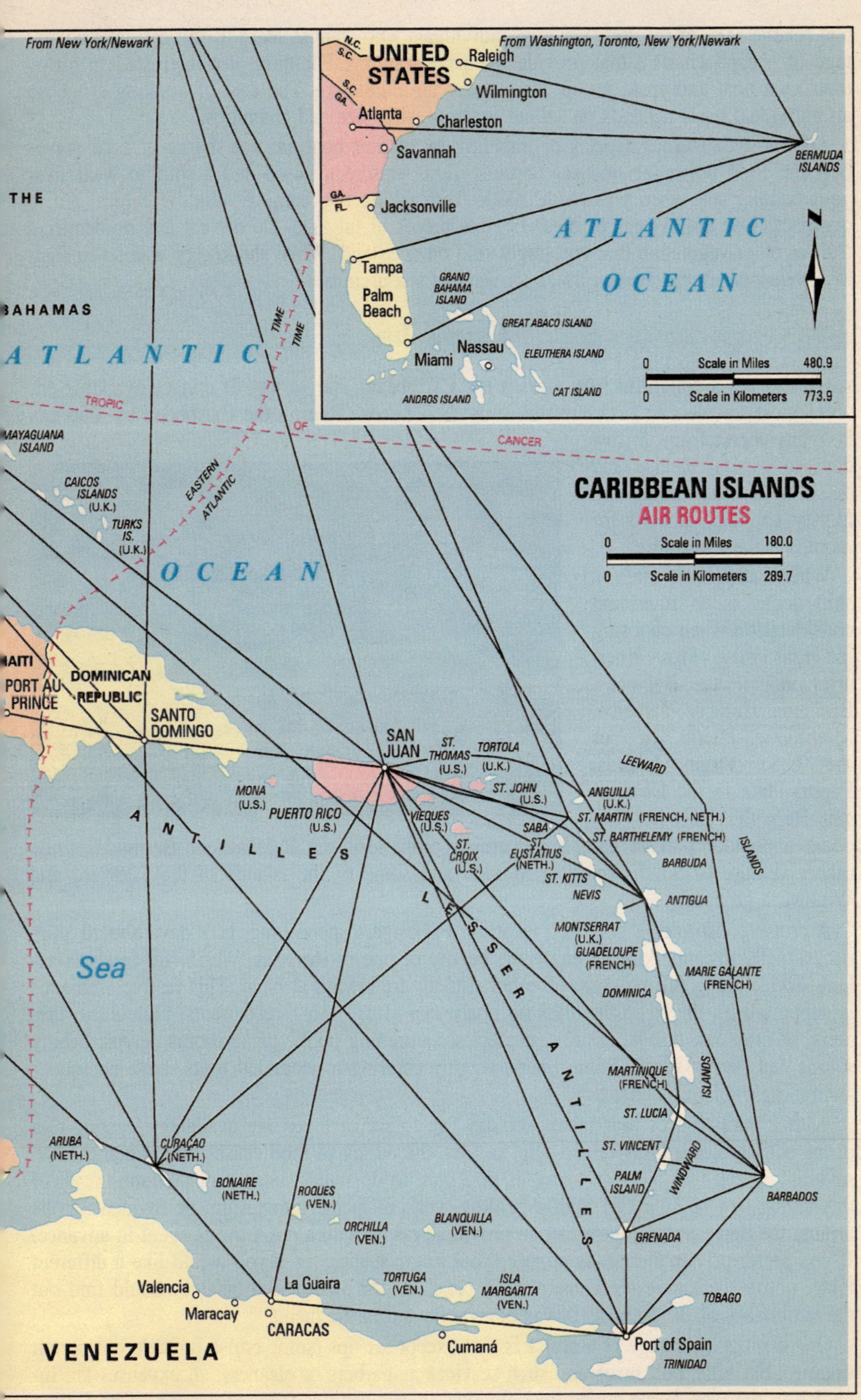
From New York/Newark
From Washington, Toronto, New York/Newark
N.C.
S.C.
UNITED STATES
Raleigh
Wilmington
S.C.
GA.
Atlanta
Charleston
Savannah
GA.
FL.
Jacksonville
ATLANTIC
OCEAN
N
Tampa
Palm Beach
GRAND BAHAMA ISLAND
GREAT ABACO ISLAND
Miami
Nassau
ELEUTHERA ISLAND
0   Scale in Miles   480.9
0   Scale in Kilometers   773.9
ANDROS ISLAND
CAT ISLAND
THE
BAHAMAS
ATLANTIC
MAYAGUANA ISLAND
TROPIC
OF
CANCER
CAICOS ISLANDS (U.K.)
EASTERN ATLANTIC
TIME
TIME
CARIBBEAN ISLANDS
AIR ROUTES
0   Scale in Miles   180.0
0   Scale in Kilometers   289.7
TURKS IS. (U.K.)
OCEAN
HAITI
PORT AU PRINCE
DOMINICAN REPUBLIC
SANTO DOMINGO
SAN JUAN
ST. THOMAS (U.S.)
TORTOLA (U.K.)
LEEWARD
MONA (U.S.)
PUERTO RICO (U.S.)
VIEQUES (U.S.)
ST. JOHN (U.S.)
ANGUILLA (U.K.)
ST. MARTIN (FRENCH, NETH.)
SABA
ST. BARTHELEMY (FRENCH)
ISLANDS
A N T I L L E S
ST. CROIX (U.S.)
ST. EUSTATIUS (NETH.)
ST. KITTS
NEVIS
BARBUDA
ANTIGUA
L E S S E R
MONTSERRAT (U.K.)
GUADELOUPE (FRENCH)
Sea
MARIE GALANTE (FRENCH)
DOMINICA
A N T I L L E S
MARTINIQUE (FRENCH)
ISLANDS
ST. LUCIA
ARUBA (NETH.)
CURAÇAO (NETH.)
ST. VINCENT
WINDWARD
BONAIRE (NETH.)
ROQUES (VEN.)
PALM ISLAND
BARBADOS
ORCHILLA (VEN.)
BLANQUILLA (VEN.)
GRENADA
Valencia
La Guaira
TORTUGA (VEN.)
ISLA MARGARITA (VEN.)
TOBAGO
Maracay
CARACAS
Cumaná
Port of Spain
TRINIDAD
VENEZUELA

and for the sake of the crew's sanity. Individuals who want to learn to sail can take advantage of special charters that provide intensive training. For those not interested in hiring their own boat and crew, group charters are an alternative. The cost of booking space on an individual basis depends on sailing location, ship size and amenities.

The most dangerous aspects of traveling by charter boat are not sharks or tidal waves but sun, food poisoning and sea urchins. Take sunscreen lotion and a shirt to wear over your bathing suit when you swim. Aside from taking two bathing suits, be careful not to overpack. Use duffel bags or other flexible pieces of luggage. Do not eat any unidentified fruit or other vegetation that you might find on an island. When shelling or wading in shallow water, wear sneakers as protection against sea urchins.

CRUISE TIPS

Cruises are a delightful way to visit the Caribbean. The variety of cruises available enables most travelers to find one that suits their needs. Touring the Caribbean by ship can last anywhere from a few days to several weeks, and those with the time and money can stay aboard for months if they so desire.

Where and how often a ship docks is an important consideration when choosing the right cruise. Most itineraries include the Bahamas, Bermuda, Curaçao, Jamaica, Martinique, Puerto Rico or the U.S. Virgin Islands. Puerto Plata in the Dominican Republic also has become a popular port of call. Some cruises only visit the Bahamas or Bermuda, while others venture to South America, Mexico and some of the islands of the Leeward and Windward groups.

A cruise constitutes a compact vacation. Passengers spend long, lazy days aboard ship, occasionally disembarking to enjoy the beauty of one of the isles. Wonderful food, excellent service and a full program of entertainment are always at hand. This festive ambiance is supported by the basic facilities on board any cruise ship—restaurants, nightclubs, theaters, health spas, discos, casinos, nurseries, swimming pools, game rooms, shops, beauty salons and barber shops. Some liners, usually catering to extended tours, have an indoor swimming pool and a chapel.

With a minimum of four meals per day (up to six or seven are available) feasting is a prime activity aboard any cruise ship. In fact, the outlay of food ceases only when the last midnight snack tray is taken away. If you plan to do much sunning or swimming, all of this eating can be balanced with a healthy workout in the gymnasium or frequent strolls around the deck. Special diets can be provided; check with a AAA travel agent in advance. If you prefer private dining, as opposed to a group seating, or if you would like a different table, notify the maitre d'. Those with a penchant for a particular cuisine should find out the nationality of the crew, as this is often reflected in the menu.

One distinct advantage of a cruise is that except for tips (some cruise lines do not permit tipping), bar bills, port taxes and such services as barbers or cleaners, all expenses are included in the fare. Some cruise lines include air connections from anywhere in the United

States in their one-payment package; others offer air supplements to the cruise price. In most cases passengers who make their air arrangements through the cruise line are met by representatives who provide transportation to the ship for both passenger and luggage. Many cruise packages also include free parking.

Frequent ports of departure include Miami, Port Everglades at Fort Lauderdale, Port Canaveral at Cape Canaveral, Tampa and New York. Cruises also depart from Boston, Baltimore and Norfolk.

It is best to follow the standard tipping policy accepted on the majority of cruise lines. A couple on a 1-week cruise can expect to pay about $100 in tips. Tips are usually given on the last day of the cruise or at the end of the week, depending on the length of the voyage. The crew members who should receive tips at the end of the cruise are the cabin steward, the dining room waiter and the busboy; it is up to them to divide tips among any assistants. The current "rule" is $3 per person per day for the cabin steward and waiter, and $1.50 per person per day for the busboy.

Discretionary rewards also should be given to wine stewards and deck stewards. It is best to tip bartenders, cleaners and barbers when services are rendered. Also tip the maitre d', half at the start of the trip and half at the end of the trip, to ensure satisfactory table seating.

Prices vary with the length of the cruise, the season and the accommodations. Cruises from Florida to the Bahamas are usually the least expensive, not only because they are short but because this standard route simplifies operations for the captain and crew. Because less time is spent in the cabin, shorter cruises tend to emphasize activities more than luxurious accommodations. Seven-day cruise packages, often available at promotional rates, can be very economical.

The high or expensive season for cruising the Caribbean runs from late December to Easter, though there are times within the season when rates might be reduced. For instance, the 2 weeks after New Year's are often available at a lower rate. Off-season rates are considerably less—sometimes half of what you might pay during the high season.

Cabins are an important variable affecting price. The more luxurious quarters are generally on the top deck. However, the cabins at the waterline or deck level have less side to side motion, while the cabins in the center of the ship have less back and forth sway. All ships have stabilizers to help minimize motion. The number of people in a cabin also affects the price. Cruises are most expensive for singles without roommates. Information on sharing a room is available from a AAA travel agent. Keep in mind that, unlike what you might have been led to believe from watching "Love Boat" on television, cabins aboard cruise ships are generally quite small.

Prospective cruise passengers should contact a AAA travel agent, who is particularly familiar with the various cruise lines and can match clients' needs, interests and personalities with the many types of cruises available.

Check with your local AAA club for complete information on rates and dates of departure. Most club

Courtesy St. Maarten Tourist Bureau

offices can reserve your cabin and obtain tickets. For information on what to pack for your trip, *see Climate and Clothing*.

INTERISLAND TRAVEL

Island hopping is enjoyable and simple. Although almost all of the Caribbean islands are accessible by air or seaplane, a more exotic way to travel is by sailboat. These leisurely cruises to other islands usually include beverages and a meal. Mail boats, though not as glamorous, often take on passengers for a nominal fee. Ferries also connect several islands. Information on these services can be obtained at most hotels, tourist bureaus and shops.

INTRAISLAND TRAVEL

Driving conditions on the islands range from good to poor. Most roads are not as well maintained as in the United States, and some are narrow and meandering, making it difficult to stay to one side. As well, in some areas domestic animals are known to roam the roads freely. Where road signs exist they are usually in the native tongue, so studying a phrase book or translation dictionary in advance is helpful. On most of the islands driving is on the left side of the road.

Given the confusion of other tourists and the independent driving nature of some locals, defensive driving is a must. It might be best to first monitor the driving conditions on the island before going out on your own. You might decide to leave the driving to the cabbies and bus operators.

RESERVATIONS

Have AAA make your reservations early. When you obtain your transportation and hotel reservations, plan any excursions you want to make. If you wish, you also can arrange to be met on arrival and escorted to your hotel.

HEALTH AND SAFETY

The sun's rays are intense in the Caribbean. Just an hour in the Caribbean sun can result in a painful sunburn and even illness to the unwary visitor. Be sure to bring plenty of suntan lotion or sunscreen; the higher the sunscreen rating the more it protects the skin from the most harmful rays. A good pair of sunglasses and a lightweight hat give added protection.

Some other common-sense precautions include taking an extra pair of glasses or contact lenses and extra quantities of prescription medicines, along with a letter from your physician stating the nature of your ailment and the recommended dosage. Keep prescription medicines in their original containers. Persons with physical conditions that might require emergency care should carry a card or tag identifying the condition.

Even the strongest constitution can sometimes be caught off guard by the excitement of travel or by culinary exploration. Reasonable precautions will usually eliminate serious risks, but should they fail, see a doctor. Medical services are generally excellent on the more developed islands, and your hotel desk or travel agent can refer you to a reliable physician or clinic. Emergency medical treatment also is available on cruise ships.

Rain is the main source of fresh water on many islands; sparse rainfall means scarce water. Even on islands where water is distilled from the sea, the supply is limited and should be used sparingly. Tap water and water served in restaurants and bars is generally safe; if in doubt, abstain or drink bottled water, beverages made with boiled water, canned or bottled carbonated beverages, beer or wine. If the water quality is unknown, avoid ice, containers that have held water, and such foods as fruit or vegetables that might have been rinsed in contaminated water.

Where mosquitoes abound, use a repellent, wear clothing that covers your arms and legs and stay in well-screened areas. Mosquitoes bearing malaria, yellow fever and other infections exist in very limited regions. In the Caribbean the risk of malaria is present only in Haiti and in areas of the Dominican Republic bordering Haiti. Other countries with a malaria risk are Colombia, Panama and Venezuela. Travelers to any of these areas are urged to check with their physician or local health department to determine the advisability of taking a preventative drug.

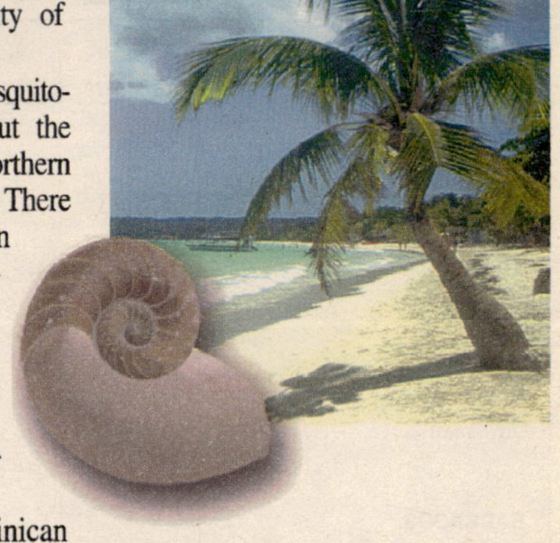

Cases of dengue (breakbone) fever, also a mosquito-borne infection, have been reported throughout the Caribbean (except the Cayman Islands), northern South America, Central America and Mexico. There are no preventative medical measures other than wearing insect repellent, and treatment is limited to relieving the symptoms. A few cases of yellow fever have occurred in Trinidad and Tobago. Inoculations for yellow fever are available; most of the islands require vaccination certificates for yellow fever *only* of those travelers arriving from infected countries.

Hepatitis B is highly prevalent in the Dominican Republic and Haiti. A Hepatitis B vaccination is recommended for those traveling to these areas. Hepatitis A is found in rural areas. Schistosomiasis is a skin infection that exists in Antigua, the Dominican Republic, Guadeloupe, Martinique, Puerto Rico and St. Lucia. Islands at risk of rabies include Cuba, Dominican Republic, Grenada, Puerto Rico and Trinidad and Tobago.

The Centers for Disease Control and Prevention in Atlanta recommends that before traveling, visitors should make sure that all immunizations are current (the tetanus/diphtheria vaccine should be boosted every 10 years). It also is recommended that travelers receive either an immune serum globulin or the hepatitis A vaccine. The center has a hot line offering international health requirements and recommendations for foreign travelers. A touch-tone phone is needed for the service, which is available daily 24 hours; phone (404) 332-4559.

Carefully assess the risk potential of recreational activities on the islands. Sports equipment that you rent or buy might not meet U.S. safety standards. Unless you are certain that scuba diving equipment, for example, is safe, do not use it. Be especially careful when out on excursions: Should you need it, help might not be readily available.

Many pools and beaches on the islands do not have lifeguards, so take heed when swimming. Undertows can be treacherous; be sure to inquire about such conditions before entering the water. Do not dive into unknown waters; hidden rocks, coral formations and shallow depths can cause serious injury or death.

Familiarize yourself with the local laws and customs of the islands you are visiting; remember, you are subject to *their* laws. It is wise to leave a copy of your travel itinerary with family or friends at home and to phone or register in person with the U.S. embassy or consulate upon your arrival. If you get in trouble, contact the U.S. consul.

You can take various precautions to avoid being victimized by thieves. Travel light and do not leave luggage unattended in public places. It also is a good idea to leave expensive jewelry, clothing and unnecessary credit cards at home. Be sure not to travel with all of your money, credit cards and travelers checks in one place. Consider leaving valuables in your hotel safe or safe deposit box.

You should be alert at all times, especially in crowds. Secure your wallet carefully, perhaps in a front pocket, or wear a money belt; carry your purse diagonally across your chest. When-

Temperature Averages / Rainfall
(Temperatures are in Fahrenheit, rainfall in inches)

	JAN.	FEB.	MAR.	APR.	MAY	JUNE	JULY	AUG.	SEPT.	OCT.	NOV.	DEC.
ANGUILLA	78 / 1.8	76 / 1	78 / 1.8	78 / 5	78 / 4.8	78 / 1	78 / 4	80 / 2	80 / 2	80 / .8	78 / 10	78 / 2.6
ANTIGUA	78 / 1.8	76 / 1	78 / 1.8	78 / 5	78 / 4.8	78 / 1	78 / 4	80 / 2	80 / 2	80 / .8	78 / 10	78 / 2.6
ARUBA, Oranjestad	79.5 / 1.9	79.8 / .7	80.6 / .4	81.5 / .5	82.7 / .5	83.1 / .6	83.1 / .8	83.8 / .7	84 / 1.1	83.6 / 2.6	82.2 / 3.8	80.4 / 3.2
BAHAMAS, Nassau	71 / 1.4	70.5 / 1.5	72.5 / 1.4	75 / 2.5	77.5 / 4.6	80.5 / 6.4	81.5 / 5.8	82.5 / 5.3	81.5 / 6.9	79 / 6.5	75.5 / 2.8	73 / 1.3
BARBADOS, Bridgetown	76.5 / 2.6	76 / 1.1	77.5 / 1.3	79 / 1.4	80 / 2.3	80.5 / 4.4	80 / 5.8	80.5 / 5.8	80.5 / 6.7	79.5 / 7	79 / 8.1	77 / 3.8
BERMUDA, Hamilton	63 / 4.4	62.5 / 4.7	62.5 / 4.8	65 / 4.1	70 / 4.6	75 / 4.4	79 / 4.5	80 / 5.4	78 / 5.2	74 / 5.8	68.5 / 5	65 / 4.7
BONAIRE, Kralendijk	79.8 / 2	79.8 / 1	80.6 / .8	80.9 / .6	82 / .7	82.2 / .7	82 / 1	82.5 / 1.1	82.7 / 1.3	83.1 / 2.7	82.4 / 4.7	80.6 / 3.5
CAYMAN ISLANDS	78 / 1.8	78 / 1.4	79 / 1.0	80 / 1.6	83 / 7.4	85 / 9.6	85 / 7.0	85 / 6.4	84 / 8.8	83 / 11	82 / 5	81 / 2.8
CURAÇAO, Hato	79.2 / 2.3	79.2 / 1.2	79.9 / .7	81 / .8	82 / .8	82.6 / .9	82.4 / 1.2	83.1 / 1.4	83.7 / 1.4	82.9 / 3.4	81.9 / 4.8	80.2 / 4
DOMINICA, Roseau	76 / 5.2	76 / 2.9	77.5 / 2.9	78.5 / 2.4	80.5 / 3.8	81.5 / 7.7	80.5 / 10.8	81 / 10.3	81.5 / 8.9	80.5 / 7.8	79 / 8.8	77.5 / 7.8
DOMINICAN REPUBLIC, Santo Domingo	75 / 2.4	75.5 / 1.4	75.5 / 1.9	77 / 3.9	78.5 / 6.8	79.5 / 6.2	80 / 6.4	80.5 / 6.3	80 / 7.3	79.5 / 6	78 / 4.8	76 / 2.4
GRENADA, St. George's	77 / 3	77.5 / 3	77.5 / 1	80 / 2	81 / 6	80 / 12	80 / 10	80 / 10	81 / 6	80.5 / 6	79.5 / 8	78 / 7
GUADELOUPE, Camp Jacob	70.5 / 9.2	69.5 / 6.1	70 / 8.1	72 / 7.3	73.5 / 11.5	74.5 / 14.1	74.5 / 17.6	75.5 / 15.3	75.5 / 16.4	74.5 / 12.4	73.5 / 12.3	71.5 / 10.1

Temperature Averages / Rainfall
(Temperatures are in Fahrenheit, rainfall in inches)

	JAN.	FEB.	MAR.	APR.	MAY	JUNE	JULY	AUG.	SEPT.	OCT.	NOV.	DEC.
JAMAICA, Kingston	76.5 / .9	76.5 / .6	77 / .9	78.5 / 1.2	79.5 / 4	81.5 / 3.5	81.5 / 1.5	81.5 / 3.6	81 / 3.9	80.5 / 7.1	79 / 2.9	78 / 1.4
MARTINIQUE, Fort-de-France	76 / 4.7	76.5 / 4.3	77 / 2.9	78.5 / 3.9	80 / 4.7	80 / 7.4	80 / 9.4	80.5 / 10.3	81 / 9.3	80 / 9.7	79 / 7.9	77.5 / 5.9
PUERTO RICO, San Juan	75 / 4.3	75 / 2.7	75.5 / 2.9	77 / 4.1	79 / 5.9	80 / 5.4	80 / 5.7	80.5 / 6.3	80.5 / 6.2	80 / 5.6	78.5 / 6.3	76.5 / 5.4
ST. BARTHÉLEMY	73 / 9.6	72 / 6	71 / 8.4	72 / 7	73 / 11.2	75 / 10.2	75 / 18	76 / 15	75 / 16	75 / 12.8	74 / 12.8	73 / 10.2
ST. EUSTATIUS, Oranjestad	77.3 / 2.7	77.5 / 1.8	78.3 / 1.9	79.5 / 2.1	80.8 / 3.6	82 / 3.4	82 / 4	82.4 / 4.6	82 / 5.3	81.3 / 4.8	79.9 / 5.2	78.1 / 3.5
ST. KITTS, La Guerite	75.5 / 4.1	75.5 / 2	76.5 / 2.3	78 / 2.3	79.5 / 3.8	80.5 / 3.6	81 / 4.4	81 / 5.2	81 / 6	80 / 5.4	79 / 7.3	77.5 / 4.5
ST. LUCIA, Soufrière	75.5 / 5.3	76 / 3.6	76.5 / 3.8	79 / 3.4	80.5 / 5.9	81 / 8.6	80.5 / 9.3	81 / 10.6	80.5 / 9.9	79.5 / 9.3	78 / 9.1	76.5 / 7.8
ST. MAARTEN, Philipsburg	77.2 / 2.6	77.4 / 1.8	77.9 / 1.6	78.9 / 2.4	80.9 / 4	82.5 / 3.1	82.5 / 3.2	82.7 / 4.3	82.4 / 5.5	81.8 / 5	80.4 / 5.5	78.4 / 3.3
ST. VINCENT	76 / 5	77 / 4	78 / 4	78 / 3	78 / .6	78 / 9	78 / 9	78 / 11	78 / 10	77 / 9	76 / 9	76 / 8
TRINIDAD, Port of Spain	76 / 2.3	76.5 / 1.2	77 / 1.4	78.5 / 1.3	79.5 / 2.8	79 / 6.4	78.5 / 7.8	79 / 7.6	79.5 / 6.9	79.5 / 5.6	78.5 / 6.5	77.5 / 4.7
TURKS & CAICOS	77 / 2.2	77 / 1.6	78 / 1.0	78 / 1.6	80 / 2.8	81 / 1.8	82 / 1.8	84 / 2	83 / 3.2	82 / 4	82 / 4.6	81 / 2.8
VIRGIN ISLANDS, BRITISH	78 / 4	78 / 3	78 / 3	80 / 4	82 / 6	82 / 5.2	82 / 6	82 / 6	82 / 6	82 / 6	80 / 6	78 / 5
VIRGIN ISLANDS, U.S.	76.1 / 1.5	76.7 / 1.9	76.6 / 2.2	78 / 2.6	80 / 4.1	81.6 / 2.8	81.8 / 3.2	81.9 / 5.5	81.2 / 7.6	80.9 / 7.1	79 / 7.5	77.4 / 2.9

shopping, keep just a small amount of spending money readily available; do not display the entire contents of your wallet. Try to conceal your camera when not in use. Do not venture into unfamiliar areas, especially when you are alone and certainly not at night.

Visitors are often approached on the street by locals offering a variety of products and services that are best obtained through more reputable outlets. In most cases a polite "No, thank you" will suffice, but the more persistent vendor will require several similar responses. It is best to display a pleasant but assertive manner in such situations. Avoid prolonged discussions and do not answer questions that might reveal where you are staying or what your plans are. Accept rides from only licensed taxi or tour operators.

ELECTRICITY

Typical U.S. electric shavers, hair dryers and travel irons operate on 110- to 120-volt, 60-cycle alternating current. However, some islands use 210-230 volt, 50-cycle AC electricity, which will burn out most U.S. appliances. On other islands, 110- to 127-volt, 50-cycle AC current is used. At 50 cycles U.S. electric appliances operate at slower than normal speeds and damage to an appliance can occur. A converter plug is necessary in the French West Indies, where European plugs are used. Check the *Things To Know* boxes for the electric current used locally.

While some U.S. department stores do sell electric items for use overseas, be sure to check the voltage requirements before you purchase; do not be misled by a salesperson who offers you an "adapter" that only enables you to plug the appliance into the wall socket. A transformer is needed to convert high-voltage current for use with U.S. appliances.

In some parts of the Caribbean, cellular phone service is available to visitors; for additional information contact Boatphone at (800) 262-8366.

SIGHTSEEING TOURS

Sunning, swimming, surfing and skin diving are all part of a Caribbean vacation, but to make your pleasure complete add another "S"—sightseeing. Each island has its own scenic attractions, quaint villages and exotic countryside. To miss them is to miss some of the islands' charm and history. For information on self-guiding or guided tours, see *Excursions and Sightseeing* under the individual islands.

Car rentals are available on the major islands; rental information is listed under *Transportation*. Rates, subject to change, are shown in U.S. currency. Third-party insurance is included; full coverage is usually offered for a moderate daily charge. To avoid disappointment, make reservations well in advance through a local AAA club. Arrangements for guided tours can be made through a AAA travel agency, your hotel activities desk or your ship's cruise director.

Customs Information

Each Caribbean nation has its own immigration requirements; these are summarized in the *Things To Know* boxes. You should carry documentary proof of citizenship—a birth certificate or affidavit of birth and photo ID such as a driver's license, or a passport. Though most of the islands do not require a passport of U.S. citizens, using one will expedite your way through immigration. A AAA travel agent can assist you with the passport application procedure. Be aware that when returning to the United States from your island destination, a voter's registration card is no longer accepted as proof of U.S. citizenship by U.S. Customs.

Before you leave, make sure you have the required travel documents. It also is a good idea to make two photocopies of your documents, leaving one copy at home and carrying the other separately. If the original documents become lost during your trip, U.S. consulates will usually accept photocopies as proof of possession and issue temporary documents to you.

Pets taken to the islands are subject to each island's public health department's regulations, and pets taken out of the United States are subject to U.S. Public Health and Department of Agriculture requirements on return. Also check with state, county and municipal authorities about restrictions on importing pets, and make arrangements well in advance. Consult the "Pets, Wildlife, U.S. Customs" booklet available at your local U.S. Customs Office or by writing U.S. Customs, P.O. Box 7407, Washington, DC 20044.

If you plan to carry more than $10,000 in currency or negotiable instruments in or out of the United States, you must file form CF 4790 with U.S. Customs at the port of exit and at the port of entry. Forms are available from your local U.S. Customs Office or by writing U.S. Customs at the above address. They also can be obtained at U.S. international airports and all other ports of entry.

Customs regulations for U.S. residents are contained in "Know Before You Go," a pamphlet published by the U.S. Customs Service. Obtain a copy from your local U.S. Customs Office or write to the above address.

Courtesy St. Maarten Tourist Bureau

Returning To The United States

Exemptions: Any articles you acquire abroad and bring back to the United States must be declared to U.S. Customs. This requirement includes any repairs made to articles taken abroad and any gifts, such as wedding or birthday presents, you received while abroad. It is wise to register articles of foreign manufacture, such as cameras or watches, at any customs office *before* leaving the United States. It is easier to register items that have serial numbers, but unnumbered items such as jewelry also can be registered if a sales receipt, insurance policy or appraisal can be produced or if the item can be taken to a U.S. Customs Office so inspectors can see the item to be registered.

Returning residents of the United States are allowed a duty-free exemption for articles accompanying them. The exemption is $600 if you are returning from a CBERA (Caribbean Basin Economic Recovery Act) country; for nations not eligible, the exemption is $400. CBERA countries include: Antigua and Barbuda, Aruba, the Bahamas, Barbados, Belize, the British Virgin Islands, Costa Rica, Dominica, the Dominican Republic, El Salvador, Grenada, Guatemala, Guyana, Haiti, Honduras, Jamaica, Montserrat, Nicaragua, the Netherlands Antilles, Panama, St. Kitts and Nevis, St. Lucia, St. Vincent and the Grenadines, and Trinidad and Tobago.

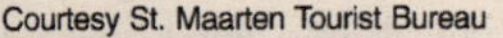

Courtesy St. Maarten Tourist Bureau

To receive the duty-free exemption, you must have been out of the country a minimum of 48 hours and have not used the exemption within the preceding 30-day period. The 48-hour minimum does not apply to U.S. residents returning from the U.S. Virgin Islands. For the U.S. Virgin Islands, the duty-free allowance is $1,200, of which no more than $600 may have been acquired elsewhere in the Caribbean.

The exemption, based on fair retail value, applies to articles that are *not intended for sale* but are for personal use or are bona fide gifts *(see the following section on Gifts)*. Returning residents who do not meet the 48-hour or 30-day time requirements may bring back up to $200 worth of items for personal or household use free of duty and tax.

High-quality merchandise from all over the world is usually featured in most duty-free shops. Prices are generally about the same as you would expect to pay in the country of origin. Do not be misled, however, by the words "duty free." This simply means that the local merchant has been exempted from his own country's taxes. All duty-free goods that return with you to the United States are still subject to U.S. import duties if you exceed your personal exemption.

DUTIES: A flat rate duty of 10 percent is applied to the next $1,000 worth of merchandise in excess of the maximum customs duty-free exemption. The flat-rate provision and duty-free exemptions may not be exercised more than once every 30 days. Assessment of merchandise is based on the fair retail value in the country of origin; remember to retain sales slips for proof of value. Keeping purchases and sales slips in a carry-on bag speeds the customs declaration procedure.

Members of a family residing in the same household and traveling together can make a joint declaration, combining their individual articles for application of the flat-rate duty. Any merchandise that exceeds the flat-rate duty on $1,000 worth of goods is dutiable at the various rates that apply to particular articles.

The United States and the following countries have entered into an agreement entitled the Caribbean Basin Initiative (CBI). These countries are Antigua and Barbuda, Aruba, the Bahamas, Barbados, Belize, the British Virgin Islands, Costa Rica, Dominica, the Dominican Republic, El Salvador, Grenada, Guatemala, Guyana, Haiti, Honduras, Jamaica, Montserrat, Nicaragua, the Netherlands Antilles, Panama, St. Kitts and Nevis, St. Lucia, St. Vincent and the Grenadines, and Trinidad and Tobago.

Some articles made in and purchased in these countries are accorded a free rate of duty and not counted against your exemption or flat rate. In addition, if you arrive directly from a CBI country, you may be entitled to a $600 exemption. Please check with the nearest Customs office for more information.

Articles acquired abroad and sent home by you or by the store where you purchased them do not qualify as accompanied baggage and are therefore subject to duty and taxes. You do not have to declare these items, as they cannot be included on the customs exemption. However, articles you purchase in the U.S. Virgin Islands and send home may be applied to your $1,200 exemption if the items are properly declared and processed.

If requested, you must present all sales receipts to U.S. Customs upon returning to the United States. *Do not* accept the friendly shopkeeper's offer to give you a sales slip showing a price lower than that actually paid. Customs inspectors are experts at spotting fraudulent receipts. If you understate an article's value or misrepresent an article on your declaration, you might have to pay a penalty in addition to the duty. Under certain circumstances the article might be seized and then forfeited if the penalty is not paid. Keep a record of what you spend for merchandise as you spend it.

GIFTS: Gifts not exceeding $100 ($200 from U.S. Virgin Islands) in total fair retail value where acquired may be sent duty free to persons in the United States, provided only one such package is received by the same person in one day. Gifts for more than one person may be mailed in the same package, provided each gift is individually wrapped and labeled with the name of the recipient. If any article in the consolidated gift package is subject to duty and tax, or if the total value of all articles exceeds the gift allowance, no article will be exempt from duty and tax. Duty cannot be prepaid; it is collected by the United States Postal Service in the form of postage-due stamps.

You may not send gifts to yourself, nor may persons traveling together send gifts to each other. The gift allowance does not include alcoholic beverages, tobacco products or perfume valued at more than $5 if it contains alcohol. Non-residents of the United States may not import liquor or cigarettes as gifts to anyone in the United States. All parcels must be marked *Unsolicited Gift,* and the nature of the gift and its estimated fair retail value must be noted on the outside wrapper.

RESTRICTED OR PROHIBITED ARTICLES: To prevent the introduction of plant and animal pests and diseases into the United States, an agricultural quarantine bans importation of certain fruits, vegetables, plants, livestock, poultry and meats. For details request the leaflet "Travelers' Tips" from APHIS, Department of Agriculture, 6505 Belcrest Rd., Hyattsville, MD 20782.

Endangered animal or plant species, and products made from them, cannot be exported or imported. This includes products made from elephant ivory, although articles made from antique ivory may be imported, provided they can be documented as being at least 100 years old. If you wish to purchase and bring back to the United States any articles made from fur, turtles, animal skins or products manufactured wholly or in part of any type of wildlife, write the U.S.

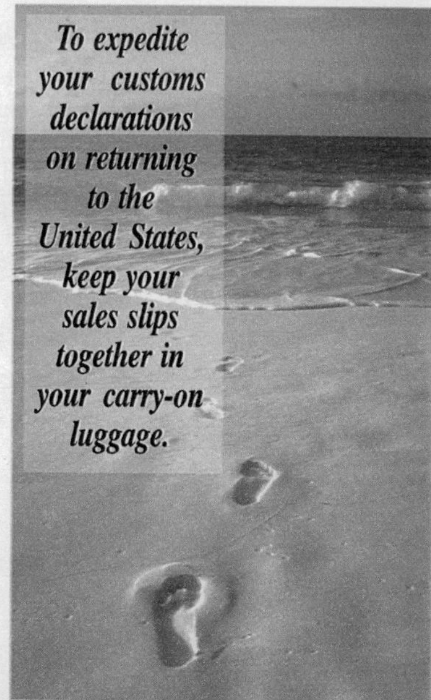

Fish and Wildlife Service, Office of Management Authority, Department of the Interior, Washington, DC 20240.

Certain articles considered injurious or detrimental to the United States also are prohibited; these include absinthe, liquor-filled confections, fireworks, lottery tickets and narcotics. There are stringent import restrictions on firearms and ammunition as well; consult the Bureau of Alcohol, Tobacco and Firearms, Department of the Treasury, Washington, DC 20220. Products originating in Angola, Burma, Iran, Iraq, Libya, North Korea, Republic of Yugoslavia (Serbia and Montenegro), Sudan and Cuba—and all items containing Cuban components—are subject to restriction and require a license. For further information consult the Office of Foreign Assets Control, Department of the Treasury, Washington, DC 20220.

If you require medicines containing habit-forming drugs or narcotics, keep them in their original containers and bring an authorizing prescription to avoid potential customs problems upon return to the United States. It is wise to pack medicines in your carry-on luggage.

Residents returning with foreign-made articles bearing a protected U.S. trademark are allowed one exemption per type of article. The goods must be intended for personal use and must not be sold within 1 year of importation. In the case of some trademarked items, greater quantities may be included in a personal exemption.

ALCOHOLIC BEVERAGES: A returning resident 21 years or older entitled to the $600 duty-free exemption may include 1 liter of alcoholic beverages (2 liters if returning from a Caribbean Basin Initiative country, provided 1 liter was produced in a CBI country). Persons of any age may bring back up to 100 cigars and 200 cigarettes. Travelers 21 years and older returning from the U.S. Virgin Islands may bring back 5 liters of alcoholic beverages, provided that 1 liter was produced there.

Travelers returning from the U.S. Virgin Islands also may include in their exemption 1,000 cigarettes, provided no more than 200 were acquired elsewhere, and 100 cigars. Liquor cannot be mailed to the United States. Laws concerning the importation of cigarettes and alcohol vary from state to state; check the importation requirements of your state of residence, as well as the state of entry.

AUTOMOBILES: Automobiles taken out of the country may be brought back duty free with a U.S. Customs certificate obtained before departure or with a tourist's state registration card. Unleaded fuel is usually not available in the Caribbean; if leaded fuel is used, catalytic converters on late-model cars will become inoperative and in most cases will fail to meet emission standards, requiring replacement in order to obtain entry back into the United States. For details contact the Environmental Protection Agency, Investigation/Imports Section (6405-J), Washington, DC 20460; phone (202) 233-9660.

About Lodgings and Restaurants

TRUST the AAA TravelBook for objective travel information. Each lodging and restaurant is listed on the basis of merit alone after careful evaluation, approval and rating by one of our full-time inspectors or, in rare cases, a designated representative. Annual lodging inspections are unannounced and conducted on site by random room sample.

An establishment's decision to advertise in the TravelBook has no bearing on its inspection, evaluation or rating. Advertising for services or products does not imply AAA endorsement.

All information in this TravelBook was reviewed before publication for accuracy at press time; however, changes inevitably occur between annual editions. We've included phone numbers in the listings so that you can confirm prices and schedules.

Guest Safety

Travelers are faced with the task of protecting themselves while in a strange environment. Although there is no way to guarantee absolute protection from crime, the experts—law enforcement officials—advise travelers to take a proactive approach to securing their property and ensuring their safety.

- Make sure the hotel desk clerk does not announce your room number; if so, quietly request a new room assignment.

- Ask front desk personnel which areas of town to avoid and what, if any, special precautions should be taken when driving a rental car (some criminals target tourists driving rental cars).

- Never open the door to a stranger; use the peephole and request identification. If you are still unsure, call the front desk to verify the identity of the person and the purpose of his/her visit.

- Carry money separately from credit cards or use a "fanny pack." Carry your purse close to your body and your wallet in an inside coat or front trouser pocket. Never leave luggage unattended, and use your business address, if possible, on luggage tags.

- Beware of distractions staged by would-be scam artists, especially groups of children that surround you or a stranger who accidentally spills something on you. They may be lifting your wallet.

- If using an automatic teller machine (ATM), choose one in a well-lit area with plenty of foot traffic, such as one at a grocery store. Machines inside establishments are the safest to use.

- Use room safes or safety deposit boxes provided by the hotel. Store all valuables out of sight, even when you are in the room.

- Law enforcement agencies consider card-key (electronic) door locks the most secure.

Due to unique conditions in Bermuda, the Bahamas and islands of the Caribbean, AAA does not require deadbolt locks on guest room entry and connecting room doors, secondary locks on sliding doors or viewports on guest room entry doors. Difficulty in obtaining hardware and individual styles of conducting business are some of the reasons why AAA delayed the implementation of its security requirements in these areas.

However, if a property listed in this publication met AAA's security requirements at the time of the inspection, the phrase "meets AAA guest room security requirements" appears in the listing. Field inspectors view a percentage of rooms at each property. Because it is not feasible for the inspectors to evaluate every room in every lodging establishment, AAA cannot guarantee that there are working locks on all doors and windows in all guest rooms.

Because of the highly specialized skills needed to conduct professional fire safety inspections, AAA inspectors cannot assess fire safety. However, guest rooms must be equipped with an operational, single-station smoke detector, and all public areas must have operational smoke detectors or an automatic sprinkler system.

The type of fire protection a lodging provides is identified with symbols (see the Safety features icon explanation on page 8). At each establishment whose listing shows these symbols, a AAA inspector has evaluated a sampling of the rooms and verified that this equipment is in place.

Access for Disabled Travelers

Qualified properties listed in this book have symbols indicating they are either *Fully Accessible or Semi-Accessible*. This two-tiered standard was developed to meet members' varying degrees of accessibility needs.

Fully Accessible properties meet the needs of those who are significantly disabled and primarily confined to a wheelchair. A fully accessible lodging will provide at least one guest room meeting the designated criteria. A traveler with these disabilities will be able to park and access public areas, including restrooms, check-in facilities and at least one food and beverage outlet. A *Fully Accessible* restaurant indicates that parking, dining rooms and restrooms are accessible.

Semi-Accessible properties meet the needs of those who are disabled but have some mobility and are not confined to a wheelchair. Such travelers would include the elderly, people using a cane or walker, or a disabled individual with good mobility but a limited arm or hand range of motion. A *Semi-Accessible* lodging will provide at least one guest room meeting the designated criteria. A traveler with these disabilities will be able to park and access public areas, including restrooms, check-in facilities and at least one food and beverage outlet. A *Semi-Accessible* restaurant indicates that parking, dining rooms and restrooms are accessible.

This symbol indicates a property with the following equipment available for Hearing Impaired travelers: TDD at front desk or switchboard; visual notification of fire alarm, incoming telephone calls, door knock or bell; closed caption decoder available; text telephone or TDD available for guest room use; telephone amplification device available, with shelf and electric outlet next to guest room telephone.

The criteria used by AAA do not represent the full scope of the Americans With Disabilities Act of 1990 Accessibility Guidelines (ADAAG); they are, however, consistent

> *AAA urges members with disabilities to always phone ahead to fully understand the accommodation's offerings. Some properties do not fully comply with AAA's exacting accessibility standards but may offer some property design standards that meet the needs of some guests with disabilities.*
>
> *AAA does not evaluate recreational facilities, banquet rooms or convention and meeting facilities for accessibility. Call a property directly to inquire about your needs for these areas.*

with the ADAAG. Members can obtain from their local AAA club the AAA brochure "Accessibility Criteria for Travelers With Disabilities," which describes the specific criteria pertaining to the *Fully Accessible* and *Semi-Accessible* standards.

The Americans With Disabilities Act (ADA) prohibits businesses that serve the public from discriminating against persons with disabilities who are aided by service animals. Some businesses have mistakenly denied access to their properties to persons with disabilities who use service animals. ADA has priority over all state and local laws, as well as a business owner's standard of business, that might bar animals from the premises. Businesses must permit guests and their service animal entry, as well as allow service animals to accompany guests to all public areas of a property. A property is permitted to ask whether the animal is a service animal or a pet, or whether a guest has a disability. The property may not, however, ask questions about the nature of a disability or require proof of one.

AAA urges members with disabilities to always phone ahead to fully understand the accommodation's offerings. Some properties do not fully comply with AAA's exacting accessibility standards but may offer some property design standards that meet the needs of some guests with disabilities.

AAA does not evaluate recreational facilities, banquet rooms or convention and meeting facilities for accessibility. Call a property directly to inquire about your needs for these areas.

MAKING RESERVATIONS

GIVE PROPER IDENTIFICATION

When making reservations, you must identify yourself as a AAA member. Give all pertinent information about your planned stay. Request written confirmation to guarantee: type of room, rate, dates of stay, and cancellation and refund policies. **Note:** Age restrictions may apply.

CONFIRM DEPOSIT, REFUND AND CANCELLATION POLICIES

Most establishments give full deposit refunds if they have been notified at least 48 hours before the normal check-in time. However, when making reservations, confirm the property's deposit, cancellation and refund policies. Some properties may charge a cancellation or handling fee. When this applies, "handling fee imposed" will appear in the listing. If you cancel too late, you have little recourse if a refund is denied. When an establishment requires a full or partial payment in advance, and your trip is cut short, a refund may not be given.

When canceling reservations, call the lodging immediately. Make a note of the date and time you called, the cancellation number if there is one, and the name of the person who handled the cancellation. If your AAA club made your reservation, allow them to make the cancellation for you as well so you will have proof of cancellation.

REVIEW CHARGES FOR APPROPRIATE RATES

When you are charged more than the rate listed in the TravelBook, under the option **Guaranteed Rates,** or you qualify for the **Senior Discount** and did not receive it, question the additional charge. If management refuses to adhere to the published rate, pay for the room and submit your receipt and membership number to AAA *within 30 days.* Include all pertinent information: dates of stay, rate paid, itemized paid receipts, number of persons in your party, the room number you occupied, and list any extra room equipment used. A refund of the amount paid in excess of the stated maximum will be made if our investigation indicates that unjustified charging has occurred.

GET THE ROOM YOU RESERVED

When you find your room is not as specified, and you have written confirmation of reservations for a certain type of accommodation, you should be given the option of choosing a different room or finding one elsewhere. Should you choose to go elsewhere and a refund is refused or resisted, submit the matter to AAA *within* 30 days along with complete documentation, including your reasons for refusing the room and copies of your written confirmation and any receipts or canceled checks associated with this problem.

LODGING RESERVATION AND DEPOSIT DEFINITIONS

RESERVATION: A temporary hold on lodgings, usually until 4 or 6 p.m. on the arrival date.

RESERVATION CONFIRMATION: Once the reservation process is complete, a "confirmation number" is assigned to the guest for future reference. When ample notice is given, a copy of the reservation details and confirmation number is mailed to the guest.

CREDIT CARD GUARANTEED RESERVATION: When reserved lodgings have been secured with a credit card number, the room will be held for the first night regardless of arrival time, but will be billed to the credit card if the guest fails to arrive at all (is a "no show"). Credit card guarantees usually pertain to the first night only.

RESERVATION DEPOSIT: These funds are collected from the guest in advance of arrival to secure reserved lodgings. A reservation deposit can be in the form of cash, check, money order, credit card transaction or other means to transfer funds. One or more days' payment may be required depending on the length of the stay.

PREPAID RESERVATION: Reserved lodgings that are fully paid in advance of arrival.

CANCELLATION POLICY: Published terms/conditions set by lodging by which the guest can cancel a reservation and recover all, or a portion of, the deposit/full payment. Sometimes a "service charge" or "handling fee" is levied regardless of how far in advance the reservation was cancelled.

CANCELLATION NUMBER: Upon receipt of a cancellation, it is customary for lodgings to assign a "cancellation number" that is given to the caller for future reference.

THE AAA DIAMONDS

Lodgings and restaurants are assigned ratings from one to five diamonds, which reflect the overall quality of the establishment or dining experience.

LODGINGS

AAA-RATED® lodgings are evaluated annually during unannounced visits by full-time inspectors. Properties must satisfy a set of minimum requirements that reflect the basic lodging needs members have identified. An increased number of diamonds reflects higher levels of quality in service and amenities.

The few lodgings with FYI in place of diamonds are included as an "informational only" service for members. It indicates that a property has not been rated for one or more of the following reasons: too new to rate; under construction; under major renovation; not inspected; or may not meet all AAA requirements.

◆ Properties meet all Listing Requirements. They are clean and well-maintained.

◆◆ Properties maintain the attributes offered at the one diamond level while showing noticeable enhancements in room decor and quality of furnishings.

◆◆◆ Properties show a marked upgrade in physical attributes, services and comfort. Additional amenities, services and facilities may be offered.

◆◆◆◆ Properties reflect an exceptional degree of hospitality, service and attention to detail, while offering upscale facilities and a variety of amenities.

◆◆◆◆◆ Property facilities and operations exemplify an impeccable standard of excellence while exceeding guest expectations in hospitality and service. These renowned properties are both striking and luxurious, offering many extra amenities.

RESTAURANTS

Diamond ratings are assigned based on conditions noted at the time of the evaluation. Food quality is the most critical to the overall rating, but other factors also are considered, such as service and atmosphere. Restaurants are classified by cuisine type. Some listings include additional information, such as the availability of a senior citizen menu, children's menu or "early bird specials," if offered at least 5 days a week. The dinner price range is approximate and includes a salad or appetizer, an entree, a vegetable and a non-alcoholic beverage for one person. Taxes and tip are not included. *Note: Major restaurant chains are not listed due to their widespread recognition.*

◆ Provides a simple, family or specialty meal in clean, pleasant surroundings. Food is basic and wholesome. Service is casual, limited or self-serve. Decor is informal.

◆◆ More extensive menus for family or adult dining. Food is prepared with standard ingredients. Service is attentive but may be informal, casual, limited or self-serve. The decor presents a unified theme that is comfortable but also may be trendy, casual or upbeat.

◆◆◆ An upscale or special family dining experience. Food is cooked to order and creatively prepared with quality ingredients. A wine list is available. A skilled, often uniformed staff provides service. The usually professional and inviting decor projects a trendy, upbeat, casual or formal atmosphere.

◆◆◆◆ A high degree of sophistication, thus creating an adult dining experience. Complex food is creatively presented. An extensive wine list is offered. The service staff, often formally attired, is professionally trained. The decor is distinctive, stylish and elegant; some establishments are casual while still offering refinement or formality.

◆◆◆◆◆ A memorable occasion—the ultimate in adult dining. Food shows the highest culinary skills, evident in all areas of preparation and presentation. An extensive wine list is available. A professional staff—often in formal attire—provides flawless and pampering service. The decor has classic details, often formal, and reflects comfort and luxury.

SAMPLE LODGING LISTING

(1)

(2)

POCO'S BEACH RESORT
Resort Hotel

12/20-3/20	$240-325	XP $40
12/1-12/19 & 3/21-11/30	$240-370	XP $40

(3)

Location: 5 mi w of Richards Sq at w end of Margene Beach. W Dressen Ave (PO Box 2401). Fax: 355/555-5255. **Terms:** F16; Reserv deposit, 21 days notice; BP; no pets. **Facility:** 207 rooms. Rates include all food, drinks & activities; exclusive of spa services. Honor bar, extra charge; 5 stories; interior/exterior corridors. **All Rooms:** free movies. **Cards:** AE, DS, MC, VI.

(4)

355/555-2300

(1) ◆◆◆ or ◆◆◆   The number of diamonds—not the color—informs you of the overall level of quality in a lodging's amenities and service. More diamond details on page 27.

Motel or Motel Diamond ratings are applied in the context of lodging type, or classification. See pages 30-31 for our Lodging Classifications.

or indicates our Official Appointment (OA) lodgings. The OA Program permits properties to display and advertise the or emblem. **We highlight these properties with red diamonds and classification**. OAs have a special interest in serving members like you. Some OA listings include special amenities such as free breakfast; early check-in/late check-out; free room upgrade or preferred room, such as ocean view or poolside (subject to availability); free local phone calls; and free daily newspaper. This does not imply that only these properties offer these amenities. The or sign helps traveling members find accommodations that want member business.

DISCOUNTS

[SAVE] is used to highlight Official Appointment properties that guarantee members a minimum 10% discount off the published rates.

[SAVE] appears in "icon row" below the listing and indicates that the following Show Your Card & Save® chain partners provide special values to our members: Choice Hotels, Days Inn, Hilton, Hyatt and La Quinta. Individual properties in these chains appearing in the TravelBook have been inspected and approved by AAA.

[S∅] identifies establishments offering a senior discount with either the Guaranteed Rates or Rates Subject to Change options (see below). Where [S∅] appears in "icon row," a minimum discount of 10% off the prevailing or guaranteed rates is available to members who are 60 or older.

[ASK] in "icon row" below the listing points out the many TravelBook properties that offer discounts to members even though the lodgings do not participate in a formal discount program. The [ASK] is another reminder to *ask* about available discounts when making your reservations.

NOTE: Discounts normally offered at some lodgings may not apply during special events or holiday periods.

② RATE LINES AND RATE OPTIONS

Rate Lines

Shown from left to right: dates the rates are effective, any meal plan included, the number of Persons/Beds allowed/provided, the rates charged, the extra person (XP) charge and any applicable family plan indicator. (See below for meal and family plan codes.)

Rate Options

If a lodging chooses not to offer a discount to our members, then it must select one of the following rate options:

Guaranteed Rates—The establishment guarantees our members will not be charged more than the maximum rates printed in the TravelBook.

Rates Subject to Change—Rates may vary for the life of the TravelBook but are guaranteed not to exceed a 15% increase on the printed rates.

Printed rates are based on rack rates and last room availability and are rounded to the nearest dollar. Rates do not include taxes and discounts. U.S. rates are in U.S. dollars; rates for Canadian lodgings are in Canadian dollars. Lodgings may temporarily increase room rates or modify policies during a special event.

ALWAYS VERIFY RATES AND DISCOUNTS

To obtain published rates or discounts, you must identify yourself as a AAA or CAA member and request them when making reservations. The SAVE or senior discounts may not be used in conjunction with other discounts. Show your card at registration and verify the room rate.

③ If applicable, the family plan indicator (F17=children 17 and under stay free; D17=discount for children 17 and under; F=children stay free; D=discounts for children) will be listed under **Terms**. The establishment may limit the number of children to whom the family plan applies. Any meal plan included in the rate (CP=Continental Plan of pastry, juice and another beverage; BP=Breakfast Plan of full breakfast; AP=American Plan of three meals daily; MAP=Modified American Plan of two meals daily; EP=European Plan, where rate includes room only) is also listed under **Terms**.

④

ⓐ — Pets allowed	ⓑ — Valet Parking	ⓚ — No Air Conditioning
ⓢ — Business	ⓐ — Laundry Service	ⓡ — Radio
ⓜ — Data Port/Modem Line	ⓧ — Fitness Center	ⓗ — Refrigerator
ⓟ — Pool	ⓡ — Recreation Facilities	ⓢ — Safe
ⓣ — Restaurant on Premises	ⓝ — No Cable TV	ⓢ — Roll-in Showers
ⓣ — Restaurant off Premises	ⓜ — Movies	ⓕ — Fully Accessible
ⓨ — Cocktail Lounge	ⓥⓒⓡ — VCR	ⓕ — Semi-Accessible
ⓝ — Nightclub	ⓒ — Coffe Maker in Room	ⓧ — Non-Smoking Rooms
ⓔ — Entertainment	ⓗ — Honor Bar	ⓗ — Hearing Impaired
ⓡ — 24 Hour Room Service	ⓜ — Microwaves	ⓓ — Smoke Detectors
ⓗ — Transportation to Airport	ⓣ — No Telephones	ⓢ — Sprinklers
ⓒ — Child Care	ⓚ — No Air Conditioning	

LODGING CLASSIFICATIONS

AAA inspectors evaluate lodgings based on classification, since all lodging types by definition do not provide the same level of service and facilities. Thus, hotels are rated in comparison to other hotels—and so on. A lodging's classification appears beneath its diamond rating in the listing.

APARTMENT (limited service)—Establishments that primarily offer transient guest accommodations with one or more bedrooms, a living room, a full kitchen and an eating area. Studio-type apartments may combine the sleeping and living areas into one room.

BED AND BREAKFAST (limited service)—Usually smaller establishments emphasizing a more personal relationship between operators and guests, leading to an "at home" feeling. Guest units tend to be individually decorated. Rooms may not include some modern amenities such as televisions and telephones, and may have a shared bathroom. Usually owner-operated, with a common room or parlor, separate from the innkeeper's living quarters, where guests and operators can interact during evening and breakfast hours. Evening office closures are normal. A continental or full, hot breakfast is served and is included in the room rate.

COMPLEX (service varies depending on type of lodgings)—A combination of two or more kinds of lodging classifications.

CONDOMINIUM (limited service)—Establishments that primarily offer guest accommodations that are privately owned by individuals and available for rent. These can include apartment-style units or homes. A variety of room styles and decor treatments as well as limited housekeeping service is typical. May have off-site registration.

COTTAGE (limited service)—Establishments that primarily provide individual housing units that may offer one or more separate sleeping rooms, a living room and cooking facilities. Usually incorporate rustic decor treatments and are geared to vacationers.

COUNTRY INN (moderate service)—Although similar in definition to a bed and breakfast, country inns are usually larger in size, provide more spacious public areas and offer a dining facility that serves at least breakfast and dinner. May be located in a rural setting or downtown area.

HOTEL (full service)—Usually high-rise establishments, offering a full range of on-premises food and beverage service, cocktail lounge, entertainment, conference facilities, business services, shops and recreational activities. Wide range of services provided by uniformed staff on duty 24 hours. Parking arrangements vary.

LODGE (moderate service)— Typically two or more stories with all facilities in one building, rustic decor. Located in vacation, ski, fishing areas, etc. Usually has food and beverage service.

MOTEL (limited service)— Low-rise or multistory establishment offering limited public and recreational facilities.

MOTOR INN (moderate service)— Single or multistory establishment offering on-premises food and beverage service. Meeting and banquet facilities and some recreational activities. Usually complimentary on-site parking.

RANCH (moderate service)— Often offers rustic decor treatments and food and beverage facilities. Entertainment and recreational activities are geared to a Western-style adventure vacation. May provide some meeting facilities.

RESORT—Geared to vacation travelers. It is a destination offering varied food and beverage outlets, specialty shops, meeting or conference facilities, entertainment, and extensive recreational facilities for special interests such as golf, tennis, skiing, fishing and water sports. Assorted social and recreational programs are typically offered in season, and a variety of package plans are usually available, including meal plans incorporated into the rates. Larger resorts may offer a variety of guest accommodations.

SUBCLASSIFICATIONS

The following are subclassifications that may appear along with the classifications listed above to provide a more specific description of the lodging:

SUITE—One or more bedrooms and a living room/sitting area which is closed off by a full wall.

EXTENDED STAY— Properties catering to longer-term guest stays. Will have kitchens or efficiencies. May have a separate living room area, evening office closure and limited housekeeping services.

HISTORIC—Accommodations in restored structures built prior to 1920, reflecting the ambiance of yesteryear and the surrounding area. Antique furnishings complement the overall decor of the property. Rooms may lack some modern amenities and may have shared bathrooms.

PREFERRED LODGING PARTNERS

Call the member-only toll-free numbers or your club to get these member benefits.

Choice Hotel brands
(800) 228-1222

- **SAVE** Save 10% at Sleep, Comfort, Quality and Econo Lodge
- **SAVE** Save 20% at Clarion Hotels and Clarion Carriage House Inns
- **SAVE** Guaranteed stay - If you're not satisfied with your stay, it's free

Days Inn
(800) 432-9755

- **SAVE** Guaranteed lowest rates available for dates of stay when booked in advance

Hilton Worldwide
(800) 916-2221

- **SAVE** Guaranteed lowest rates available for dates of stay when booked in advance

Hyatt Hotels
(800) 532-1496

- **SAVE** Guaranteed lowest rates available for dates of stay when booked in advance
- **SAVE** Receive second dinner entree at half-price in Hyatt dining room when staying at the hotel

La Quinta Inns
(800) 221-4731

- **SAVE** Guaranteed lowest public rate for dates of stay for standard room
- **SAVE** Children under 18 and spouse sharing room stay free
- **SAVE** Guaranteed stay - If you're not satisfied with your stay, it's free

Special rates and discounts may not apply to all room types. Not available to groups and cannot be combined with other discounts. Restrictions apply to stay guarantees. Valid AAA/CAA membership card must be presented at check-in. Offers good at time of publication; chains and offers may change without notice.

ANGUILLA

LONG AND NARROW Anguilla (An-GWIL-la), taking its name from the Spanish word for eel, lies about 5 miles (8 km) north of St. Martin and 60 miles (96 km) north of St. Kitts. Unlike the other Leeward Islands, low-lying Anguilla is of coral rather than volcanic formation. There are no big or concentrated villages on Anguilla. Instead, cottages and houses are sprinkled across the island. Island handicrafts can be found in The Valley, Anguilla's capital. Accommodations on the island include luxury hotels and resorts as well as small, low-key inns and guest houses.

HISTORY, GOVERNMENT AND ECONOMY

Christopher Columbus sighted Anguilla during his second voyage in 1493; it is not known whether he actually visited the island. English settlers from St. Kitts colonized Anguilla in 1650, and the island has remained a British territory ever since. In 1688 the island was attacked by a party of Irishmen who eventually settled there; their surnames are in evidence today. Anguilla repelled two attacks by the French in the 18th century. The island declared its independence from the Associated State of St. Kitts and Nevis and became a self-governing territory of the British Commonwealth in 1967. Their independence became official on Dec. 19, 1980.

It is said that the first seeds of the highly prized sea island cotton came from Anguilla. Today the island's economy is based on tourism and fishing.

SHOPPING

Anguilla has many small boutiques, specialty stores, art galleries and crafts shops. Some local trendy shops include the Arts and Crafts Center in The Valley; Beach Stuff, overlooking the scenic Road Bay and Sandy Ground; Cheddies' Carving Studio, on the island's west end, containing sculptures and carvings; Java Wraps, showcasing fashions made from cloth created on the island of Java; The Mariners' boutique, offering a variety of items; Malliouhana's, presenting an extensive selection of fine jewelry; and Oluwakemi's, featuring Afrocentric fashions and accessories. Elegant resort wear, casual summer fashions and accessories can be found at boutiques such as Caribbean Fancy, Images and Maleona's.

Fresh fruits and vegetables are available from roadside stands throughout the island. Shopping hours are generally Mon.-Sat. 8-5. Banking hours are Mon.-Thurs. 8-3, Fri. 8-5.

FOOD AND DRINK

Freshly caught lobster, crayfish, whelk, red snapper and yellowtail are several of the seafood delights that appear on tables in Anguilla. Local

---

THINGS TO KNOW

AREA: 35 square miles (91 sq km).

POPULATION: 9,700.

LANGUAGE: English.

CAPITAL: The Valley.

GOVERNMENT: Self-governing British Territory.

TIME ZONE: Atlantic.

UNIT OF CURRENCY: Eastern Caribbean dollar. $1 U.S.=2.37 Eastern Caribbean dollars.

ELECTRICITY: 110 volts, 60 cycles AC.

CARS: Local license ($7) required, valid for 3 months; drive on left.

IMMIGRATION REQUIREMENTS: Proof of U.S. citizenship (passport or or two other forms of official identification such as naturalization papers or birth certificate with a raised seal accompanied by a government-authorized photo identification card) and a return or through ticket are required. Departure tax $10 US from the airport; $2 US from the ferry.

FOR FURTHER INFORMATION:
Anguilla Tourist Board
P.O. Box 1388, Factory Plaza
The Valley, Anguilla, B.W.I.
(264) 497-2759, 497-2451 or (800) 553-4939

HOLIDAYS: Jan. 1; Good Friday; Easter Monday; Labour Day, May (1st Mon.); Whit Monday, May (8th Monday after Easter); Anguilla Day, May 30; Queen's Birthday, June; August Monday, Aug. (1st Mon. and following Thurs. and Fri.); Separation Day, Dec. 19; Dec. 25; Boxing Day, Dec. 26.

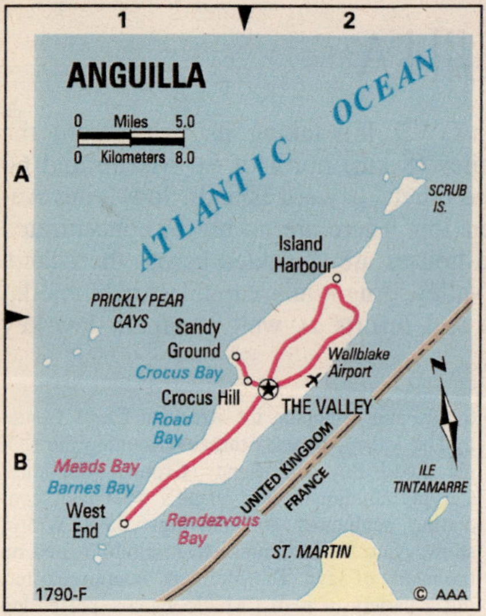

restaurants dish up specialties that reflect the ancestry of some of the island residents: Belgian, Italian, French and West Indian. The tantalizing fare includes stuffed crab, conch torta, grilled crayfish and Creole soups.

SPORTS AND AMUSEMENTS

Nightlife of the classic variety is somewhat limited on Anguilla. Most hotels offer nightly music, and several beach bistros can be found at Sandy Ground and Shoal Bay. Most recreation, however, is related to the island's white coral sand beaches, which offer many opportunities for swimming and shell collecting; swimming and sunbathing *au naturel* are prohibited. Some of the island's 33 beaches are accessible only by rough dirt roads or paths. The secluded atmosphere of these beaches, however, makes the visit worth the trouble. Popular beaches include those at Maunday's Bay, Rendezvous Bay and Shoal Bay. Visitors should note that in Anguilla it is considered rude to wear swimsuits in public places other than the beach.

The crystal-clear waters surrounding the island are excellent for snorkeling, scuba diving and fishing. Favorite snorkeling and diving spots are Little Bay, Cove Bay and Shoal Bay, the last distinguished by its undersea garden trail. Experienced divers can reach any of nine shipwreck sites. The Dive Shop in Sandy Ground, rents snorkeling equipment and conducts diving expeditions to such secluded spots as Little Bay and uninhabited Sandy Island. Anguillan Divers can take you to the hottest dive spots on the eastern part of the island. Hooked on Watersports makes arrangements for windsurfing and sailing in Cove Bay. Most hotels rent water sports equipment. Tennis also is popular on the island; most hotels and villas have courts.

Boats and guides for fishing trips can be hired at Sandy Ground and Island Harbour. Many islanders are fishermen by trade, and you can sample their succulent bounty at any local cafe or restaurant. Fish soup, sweet and sour conch, and lobster with lime butter are the primary delicacies.

Special events in Anguilla are Anguilla Day on May 30 and during August's Carnival Week. On both occasions, sailors race boats made in Anguilla. Carnival Week, which begins on the first Monday in August, features calypso contests, street dancing, the coronation of the Carnival Queen, sailboat races, beach barbecues and the Prince and Princess Show.

EXCURSIONS AND SIGHTSEEING

Sightseeing tours can be arranged through Bennie's Tours at Blowing Point and Malliouhana Tours in The Valley. Bennie's offers tours of the island and half- and full-day trips to Prickly Pear; Marigot, St. Martin; and Philipsburg, St. Maarten. Sandy Island Enterprises offers fishing trips and excursions to off-shore caves, nearby islands and secluded harbors.

Northwest of the capital in the Upper Valley is The Warden's Place, one of the oldest houses in Anguilla. Built in the 1780s on a plantation and restored in 1987, it now houses the KoalKeel Restaurant. The limestone blocks used to build its high foundation were carved from the cliffs of nearby Crocus Bay.

TRANSPORTATION

Connections to Wallblake Airport are through San Juan, St. Thomas, Antigua, St. Kitts and St. Maarten. Rental cars or taxis are necessary to get around the island, as beaches, stores and various accommodations are not within reasonable walking distance. A temporary driver's license is available for $7. Taxi rates are fixed, but agree on the fare in advance.

The island's main southern port is Blowing Point; ferries to Marigot, St. Martin, run about every 30 minutes from 7:30 a.m. to 5:00 p.m. and at 6:15 p.m. The ferry trip takes about 20 minutes. Travel documents are required, and a small tax is collected upon departure from both islands. Round-trip fare is about $20.

LODGINGS & RESTAURANTS

MEADS BAY

LODGINGS

LA SIRENA
◆◆ *Hotel*

12/15-3/31	$245-315	XP $35
12/1-12/14 & 11/1-11/30	$165-210	XP $35
4/1-10/31	$145-190	XP $35

Location: 8 mi s of international airport. (PO Box 200). Fax: 264/497-6829. **Terms:** F12; Reserv deposit, 30 day notice; handling fee imposed; 10% service charge. **Facility:** 25 rooms. Pathway to beach. Balcony. Intimate inn on landscaped grounds. Spacious modern rooms, some offer ocean view from the patio. 1- to 3-bedroom villas, $330-$530; $200-$320 off season. Cable TV avail on request; 3 stories, no elevator; exterior corridors; beach. **Recreation:** swimming, scuba diving, snorkeling & equipment. Fee: scuba equipment, windsurfing; bicycles. **All Rooms:** combo or shower baths. **Some Rooms:** 5 kitchens, color TV. **Cards:** AE, MC, VI.

(264/497-6827

MALLIOUHANA HOTEL
◆◆◆◆ *Resort Hotel*

12/18-3/31	$480-2100	XP $100
12/1-12/17, 4/1-5/31 & 11/1-11/30	$320-1450	XP $50
6/1-8/31	$240-1050	XP $25

Location: 7 mi w of airport. (PO Box 173). Fax: 264/497-6011. **Terms:** Open 12/1-8/31 & 11/1-11/30; reserv deposit, 30 day notice; 10% service charge; 7 night min stay, in season. **Facility:** 56 rooms. Spacious, luxurious rooms & villas on terraced hillside, Mediteranean inspired architecture on expansive white sand beach, breathtaking views. 3 two-bedroom units, 2 three-bedroom units. 3-bedroom villas for up to 6 persons, $1655-$2175 in season. 2-bedroom suites $690-$1400. For US reservations: (800)835-0796; 1-3 stories; exterior corridors; beach; 4 tennis courts (3 lighted); playground. **Services:** giftshop. Fee: massage. **Recreation:** swimming, snorkeling & equipment, waterskiing, windsurfing. Fee: charter fishing. Rental: boats.

(264/497-6111

RESTAURANTS

BLANCHARD'S
◆◆◆◆ *Continental*   **D** $21-$37

Location: 7 mi w of international airport. **Hours:** 7 pm-10 pm, 5/1-11/1 from 6:30 pm. Closed: Sun & 8/1-9/30. **Reservations:** suggested. **Features:** No A/C; casual dress; cocktails; a la carte. Candlelight open-air dining room overlooking garden pathway to sea. Innovative preparations of fresh local seafood, inspirations from the Caribbean, Asia & New Orleans. Specialty is whole roasted lobster. Extensive wine cellar. **Cards:** AE, MC, VI.

(264/497-6100

TOP OF THE PALMS
◆◆ *Ethnic*   **L** $6-$12 **D** $15-$24

Location: 8 mi s of international airport; in La Sirena. **Hours:** 7:30 am-10, 12:30-3 & 7-9:30 pm. **Reservations:** suggested. **Features:** No A/C; casual dress; children's menu; cocktails & lounge; a la carte. On open terrace overlooking pool. French Caribbean cuisine. 15% service charge. **Cards:** AE, MC, VI.

(264/497-6827

RENDEZVOUS BAY

LODGINGS

ANQUILLA GREAT HOUSE BEACH RESORT
◆◆ *Motor Inn*

12/18-3/31	$200-230	XP $50
12/1-12/17 & 9/22-11/30	$130-145	XP $50
4/1-9/21	$120-135	XP $50

Location: 5 mi s of international airport. (PO Box 157). Fax: 264/497-6019. **Terms:** Age restrictions may apply; reserv deposit, 14 day notice; handling fee imposed; 10% service charge; 5 night min stay, in season. **Facility:** 27 rooms. On white sand beach. Spacious, tastefully decorated rooms. 1 story; exterior corridors; beach. **Services:** giftshop. **Recreation:** swimming, fishing, snorkeling & equipment. Fee: windsurfing. **All Rooms:** shower baths. **Cards:** AE, DS, MC, VI.

(264/497-6061

SONESTA BEACH RESORT ANGUILLA
◆◆◆◆ *Resort Hotel*

12/23-1/2	$435-1025	XP $40
1/3-4/19	$350-825	XP $40
12/1-12/22 & 4/20-11/30	$200-550	XP $40

Location: 8 mi sw of airport. (PO Box 444). Fax: 264/497-6899. **Terms:** D12; Reserv deposit, 15 day notice, in season; 10% service charge; 7 night min stay, in season. **Facility:** 90 rooms. Quiet, secluded seaside location. Distinct Moroccan architecture. Spacious rooms with bright, tropical decor, deluxe appointments & private balcony. Closed 9/1-10/8. Meets AAA guest room security requirements. 1 two-bedroom unit, 1 three-bedroom unit. 4 whirlpool rms, extra charge; 3 stories, no elevator; interior/exterior corridors; beach; 2 lighted tennis courts; playground. **Services:** giftshop. Fee: massage. **Recreation:** swimming, sailboating, snorkeling & equipment, windsurfing. Fee: bicycles. **All Rooms:** combo or shower baths. **Some Rooms:** 2 kitchens. **Cards:** AE, MC, VI.

(264/497-6999

ANTIGUA AND BARBUDA

A T THE NORTHEASTERN CURVE of the West Indies, Antigua (an-TEE-ga) is one of 11 links in the chain of Leeward Islands. Its seascape alternates rocky coves with white, sunny beaches punctuated by gentle salt breezes. Christopher Columbus' first impression adequately describes this tropical paradise: "What beautiful lands the sun lights up in the distance..."

Antiguans are charming people, whose expressive English *patois* with its musical intonation enchants visitors. While engaged in daily affairs, the locals form a vivid tableau. Sitting around a *warri* board, taxi drivers play an ancient game while waiting for a fare. Dressed for school in distinctive uniforms that vary according to school and grade, Antiguan children add their smiles and colors to the scene. In equally vivid dress, members of Antigua's many steel bands parade during Carnival in St. John's, where the colorful activities contrast with the more traditionalist English atmosphere of the island's capital.

HISTORY, GOVERNMENT AND ECONOMY

Christopher Columbus named Antigua after the Santa Maria de la Antigua Church in Seville, Spain. Although Columbus visited the area in 1493, it is not known whether he actually set foot on Antiguan soil. An attempt to colonize the island was not made until almost a century and a half later, perhaps due to the unwelcoming population of Carib Indians.

Antigua became a British possession in 1632, when English planters from nearby St. Kitts successfully settled the area despite Carib resistance. In 1666 French raiders claimed the island, but the Treaty of Breda in 1667 restored the land to the British.

In 1674 Sir Christopher Codrington, a former governor of Barbados, established the first large sugar plantation on Antigua. Codrington's accomplishments encouraged other landowners to become involved in the sugar industry, and by the early 1700s the landscape was dotted with some 170 sugar mills; the ruins of many of these structures can be seen throughout the island. Because African slaves were imported to serve as laborers on the sugar plantations, Antigua became a key slave-trading post in the Caribbean.

THINGS TO KNOW

AREA: 108 square miles (280 sq km).

POPULATION: 67,000.

LANGUAGE: English and an English patois.

CAPITAL: St. John's.

GOVERNMENT: Independent. Member of the British Commonwealth of Nations.

TIME ZONE: Atlantic.

UNIT OF CURRENCY: Eastern Caribbean dollar. $1 U.S.=2.37 Eastern Caribbean dollars. U.S. currency is widely accepted.

ELECTRICITY: 110 volts AC and 220 volts DC, 60 cycles; voltage and current vary with location.

MINIMUM AGE FOR GAMBLING: 18.

CARS: Temporary permit ($12) required, valid for 90 days; drive on left.

IMMIGRATION REQUIREMENTS: A valid passport with an onward or return ticket are preferred for entry. However, an original birth certificate or naturalization papers accompanied by photo identification in the form of a valid driver's license and an onward or return ticket are acceptable. Departure tax $12 US.

PETS: No pets or other animals are allowed.

FOR FURTHER INFORMATION:

Antigua and Barbuda Department of Tourism
610 Fifth Ave., Suite 311
New York, NY 10020
(212) 541-4117 or (888) 268-4227

Antigua and Barbuda Department of Tourism
Nevis St. and Friendly Alley
St. John's, Antigua
(268) 462-0480

HOLIDAYS: Jan. 1; Good Friday; Easter Monday; Labour Day, May (1st Mon.); Whit Monday, May (8th Mon. after Easter); Caricom Day, July (1st Mon.); Carnival, Aug. (1st Mon. and Tues.); Independence Day, Nov. 1; Dec. 25; Boxing Day, Dec. 26.

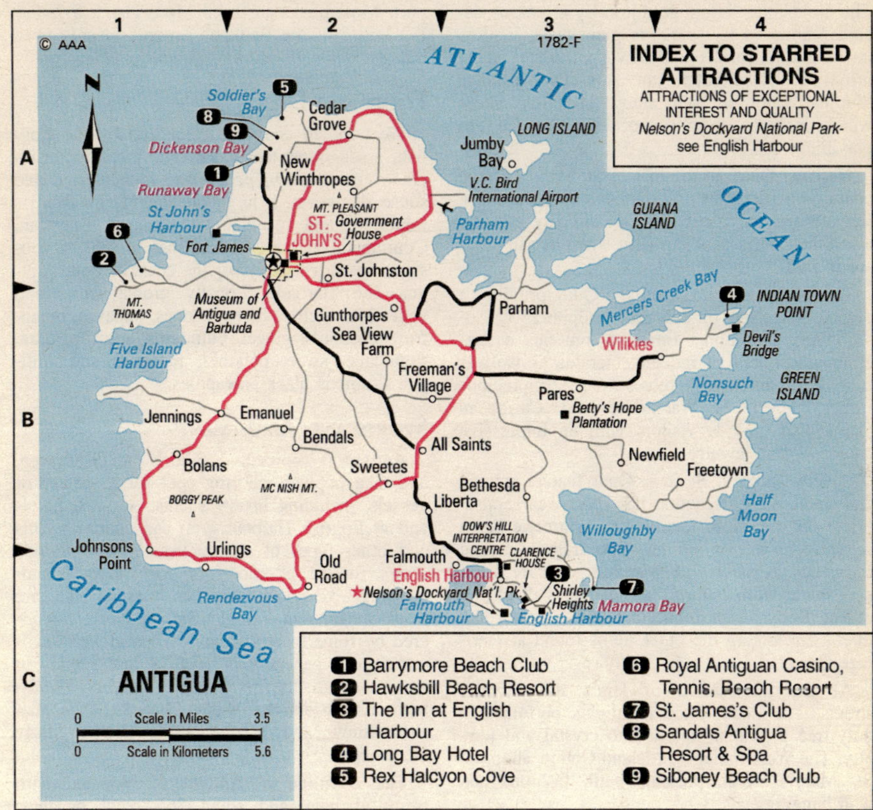

The economy suffered a severe blow when slavery was abolished in 1834, and a labor shortage ensued. Due to mounting pressure for a free trade market, sugar prices steadily declined and forced several plantations out of business. Three natural disasters in the mid-1800s—a hurricane, a fire and an earthquake—also contributed to the economic decline.

Antigua was granted status as an associated state of the United Kingdom as a result of the West Indies Act of 1967. This provision allowed Antigua to be self-governing with regard to internal matters, while the United Kingdom controlled defense and foreign affairs. On Nov. 1, 1981, Antigua graduated from its status as an Associated State of the British Commonwealth and became an independent country with Barbuda. The twin-island nation is governed by a prime minister and an upper and lower house.

Antigua's strategic position in the middle of the Antilles chain, as well as its natural harbors, made it the chief British naval base in the West Indies during the Napoleonic Wars and a prime U.S. base during World War II. The main sources of income for most islanders are tourism, light manufacturing and agriculture.

SHOPPING

The main shopping district is in St. John's between Redcliffe and Newgate streets, but numerous other shops are concealed in alleys and lanes. Popular buys are imports, straw handicrafts and sea island and silk-screened cottons. Antigua's duty-free shopping includes French perfumes, cashmeres, English tweeds, Irish linen, tobacco, pipes, English bone china, Swiss watches, jewelry, crystal and cameras. St. John's also has several jewelry stores where shoppers can find good buys on their favorite gemstones. Both locally produced rum and imported liquors sell at discounted prices.

Situated on lower Redcliffe Street, Redcliffe Quay consists of a charming collage of shops overlooking the waterfront. The area, which was once a slave compound, harbored warehouses for area merchants after slavery was abolished in 1834. Traditional architecture is accented by narrow alleys and picturesque courtyards interspersed with quaint shops and restaurants.

Shops in Redcliffe Quay include A Thousand Flowers, featuring women's silk, cotton and linen apparel fashioned in invigorating tropical colors.

The Goldsmitty offers gold jewelry in unique designs enhanced by sparkling gemstones. Visitors in the market for original artwork, colorful island prints or handicrafts can stop by Seahorse Studios. Children will enjoy The Toy Shop, which includes a variety of charming English playthings.

Heritage Quay, at the foot of St. Mary's Street, contains a pier that accommodates cruise ships. Reggae and calypso bands occasionally perform at a small band shell, usually when cruise ships are in port.

A modern complex, Heritage Quay provides a diverse selection of duty-free shopping. World-renowned Columbian Emeralds presents a dazzling assortment of radiant emeralds as well as sapphires, diamonds, rubies and semiprecious stones. Jeweller's Warehouse and Caribbean Gems also provide visitors with an impressive choice of fine jewelry.

Several shops at Heritage Quay feature apparel and accessories. Benetton has sportswear appropriate for the entire family. La Parfumerie has a splendid collection of duty-free fragrances and cosmetics. A medley of skin and hair-care products made from natural ingredients is displayed at The Body Shop. Tobacco products, liquor and linens are among the other items found at Heritage Quay.

At the intersection of High and Thames streets, The Scent Shop highlights perfumes at duty-free prices, in addition to crystal and jewelry. The West Indian Sea Island Cotton Shop, on St. Mary's street, presents batik fashions and wall hangings.

Geography buffs will delight in the selection of Caribbean maps and charts at the Map Shop on St. Mary's Street. A good place to find local crafts is the School for the Blind, on All Saints Road; visitors can choose from wicker and straw works including place mats, purses, hats and lamp shades. Kel-Print, at V.C. Bird International Airport, provides a variety of locally made and imported products.

Jolly Harbour, on the island's southwest coast, boasts an array of restaurants and shops overlooking a picturesque marina. Many of the shops feature beachwear, jewelry, perfume and souvenirs. Jacaranda offers island products including herbs, cosmetics and batik fashions. Arts and crafts with a Caribbean flair can be found at Seahorse Studios and Merry's Art Gallery. Visitors also can make arrangements for boat charters, car rentals and diving excursions.

Nelson's Dockyard in English Harbour also accommodates an extensive marketplace. Restaurants and shops are tucked away in the restored buildings of what was once the headquarters of the British Royal Navy.

Some shops have extended hours, but stores are generally open Mon.-Sat. 8-4. Many shops are open on Sundays when cruise ships are in port. Most banks are open Mon.-Thurs. 8-2, Fri. 8-2 and 3-4; the Bank of Antigua also is open Sat. 8-1.

FOOD AND DRINK

West Indian cookery, influenced by the English, graces most tables. Favorite local dishes include curry conch, *pepperpot*, fungee, rice and souse. However, a large portion of the food is imported, and resort hotels feature American, Continental and French cuisine. In season, lobsters are caught daily off the coast of both Antigua and Barbuda. Locally grown fruits and vegetables include herbs, eddoes, papayas, breadfruit, coconuts, ginger, pumpkins, soursop, okra, sugarcane, sweet potatoes, mangoes and Antigua's famous black pineapples.

SPORTS AND AMUSEMENTS

Antigua is known as a sailor's paradise/haven, and is a popular mooring spot for a variety of vessels, including luxury yachts. At most hotels and at English Harbour, you can charter yachts and other types of sailing vessels with trained crews for an afternoon or for longer island-hopping excursions. Smaller vessels also are available for rent. Antigua Sailing Week, considered by some to be *the* world's warm-water sailing regatta, generally is held the last Sunday in April through the first Saturday in May. The island also hosts the 9-day Nicholsons Annual Boat Show and Marine Trade Fair in early December.

The coastline of Antigua is indented with beautiful bays and some 365 coral beaches; swimmers, shell collectors and sunbathers need never visit the same beach more than once in a year. Those planning beach outings are advised to carry insect repellent; no-see-ums can be a nuisance, especially at dusk.

The beaches on the northwest coast are frequented by tourists due to the high concentration of resorts in the area. Popular northwest coast beaches include Dickenson Bay, a pretty white-sand beach bordered by several hotels and restaurants. Water sports enthusiasts will appreciate the multitude of operators offering rental equipment for scuba diving, windsurfing and other activities. The bay also is a departure point for glass-bottom boat and catamaran excursions.

The gentle surf of Runaway Bay also is perfect for water sports activities. Visitors can rent floats, kayaks, windsurfers and sailboats. Water skiing also can be arranged. Landlubbers can explore the area on horseback.

Deep Bay, also on the northwest coast, contains a sunken ship that can be explored by snorkelers and divers. The stately ruins of Fort Barrington rise high above the picturesque beach area bordering the bay. A path leads to the top of the fort; the hike can be strenuous, and only those in good physical condition should attempt it. Hikers who make the trek to the top will be rewarded with striking views of St. John's Harbour.

Half Moon Bay, on Antigua's southeast coast, derives its name from the coastline's shape. The crescent-shaped beach, enhanced by azure waters and cool breezes, is perfect for a pleasant stroll. Visitors like to climb the rocks at the north end of the shore. Surf conditions vary due to the bay's shape; visitors can experience crashing waves that present excellent opportunities for body surfing or gentle ripples ideal for swimming. Conveniences include parking and snack areas as well as facilities for horseback riding, diving and windsurfing.

Dark Wood Beach is situated on the island's southwest coast. The white-sand beach, surrounded by a hilly landscape, is punctuated by sailboats docked in crystal-blue water. Beach chairs can be rented at a small snack area, and shelters covered with palm fronds provide respite from the sun. On a clear day, visitors can see the island of Montserrat looming on the horizon. Morris Bay, off Antigua's south coast, is the site of the Curtain Bluff Resort. In this tranquil, secluded setting adorned by sweeping palms, a prominent bluff rises majestically from the sea.

The coral reefs and the remains of shipwrecks, where many multicolored fish gather, make snorkeling and scuba diving popular. Lessons and equipment for water skiing, scuba diving, snorkeling, sailing and deep-sea fishing are available at most resorts. Reputable dive operators include Dive Antigua, (268) 462-3483. Sea Sports, on the beach at Dickenson Bay, offers parasailing and water skiing; phone (268) 462-3355. Every Labour Day and Whit Monday, deep-sea and spear-fishing competitions are held.

Golf enthusiasts have two 18-hole courses on which to chase birdies: Cedar Valley Golf Club, (268) 462-0161; and Harbour Golf Club, (268) 464-9307. Tennis courts are available at most hotels. Fitness buffs can visit the National Fitness Centre off Old Parham Road, (268) 462-3681, or The Fitness Shack opposite Antigua Village in Dickenson Bay, (268) 462-5223. Temo Sports, (268) 463-6376 in Falmouth, and 463-9372 in English Harbour, has tennis and squash courts; reservations are recommended.

Horseback riding is an excellent means by which to explore the island's natural beauty. Popular facilities include Antigua Riding Stables at Pillar Rock Bay and St. James's Riding Stable at St. James's Club.

As in other English West Indian islands, cricket is the national obsession, and Antigua is home to some of the world's best cricketers. Tournaments between local district teams can be seen across the island on weekends. Spectators also enjoy netball (a women's game similar to basketball, only the hoop has no backboard), basketball, soccer and Thoroughbred racing in season.

Tennis tournaments held throughout the year attract many professionals. Men's and women's singles and doubles matches take place as well as a match that pits amateurs against the pros. Antigua Tennis Week is held at Curtain Bluff in early May and December.

Carnival is the island's most spectacular event. Inspired by the splendor of Queen Elizabeth's coronation and the desire for a yearly festival symbolizing freedom, the Antigua and Barbuda Tourist Board instituted the Antigua Carnival. Beginning the last week in July, Carnival commemorates the Antiguan people's emancipation in 1834.

For 10 days, including the first Monday and Tuesday in August, Carnival throngs revel from early evening until dawn to the pulsating strains of steel and brass band music. Holiday visitors join the community in the traditional "jump up," a kaleidoscope of singing, dancing and laughter from the early morning hours until the sun is high in the sky. Carnival City, in the Recreation Grounds at St. John's, presents talented entertainers amid magnificent sets.

Shirley Heights Lookout, which offers a spectacular view of English Harbour, is the site of 6 hours of non-stop entertainment on Thursday and Sunday beginning at 3 p.m. Visitors have the opportunity to mingle with residents, enjoy succulent barbecue and dance to the beat of reggae and steel bands. Year-round nightlife opportunities range from an evening at the theater to gambling in a casino or strolling on a beach. The island has many small nightclubs.

St. John's has just one cinema for English-language films, at the intersection of Cross and High streets, but many hotels offer movies in addition to floor shows and dancing. Art shows that feature local artists are held at galleries throughout the island. Harmony Hall, at Brown's Bay near the village of Freetown on the east coast, is a plantation-style house that overlooks the sea and contains a restored mill, an art gallery, a gift shop and a restaurant; the gallery is open daily 10-6.

The island has four casinos to tempt gamblers. King's Casino at Heritage Quay, (268) 462-1727, features slot machines, poker, blackjack, craps and roulette. Casinos also can be found at Harmony Hall, (268) 460-4120, the Royal Antiguan Hotel, (268) 462-3733, and the St. James's Club (electronic games only), (268) 460-5000.

Excursions and Sightseeing

Three-hour and all-day sightseeing cruises along Antigua's coast are available. *Jolly Roger* party cruises depart daily from Dickenson Bay; phone (268) 462-2064. *Coral Ark* cruises, departing from Heritage Quay pier, offer dancing and dining; phone (268) 461-6060. Wadadli Watersports, (268) 462-2980, provides catamaran cruises that include stops for snorkeling and swimming. Deep-sea fishing expeditions are possible on *Obsession,* a 45-foot Hatteras; phone (268) 462-3174.

Many other types of boat trips are available, including cocktail, barbecue and glass-bottom boat cruises. For more information inquire at your hotel, the Antigua and Barbuda Department of Tourism on Long Street in St. John's or the information booths at V.C. Bird International Airport, St. John's harbor and Heritage Quay pier.

Fig Tree Drive in southwestern Antigua winds inland through terrain similar to a rain forest and takes about 2 hours to explore by private car. Although this scenic drive is a bit bumpy, visitors are rewarded with views of old sugar mills and lush vegetation. Such tropical fruits as mangoes, oranges, guavas and pineapples grow alongside the road. Don't expect to see any figs—in Antigua, fig is the word for banana. Fig Tree Drive residents sell fruits and vegetables from stands in front of their homes. The road leading to Fig Tree Hill provides breathtaking views of fertile valleys and magnificent 1,320-foot (402-m) Boggy Peak.

Allow about a day to drive the coastal routes, taking time along the way to explore Nelson's Dockyard in English Harbour, the small fishing villages and such coastal archeological sites as Indian Creek and Mill Reef.

An excellent opportunity to mingle with Antiguans is at the open-air market held near "The Bridge" on Market Street in southern St. John's. Here you can bargain for fresh fish, fruits, vegetables and spices or simply enjoy the stimulating, colorful atmosphere. The market is open Mon.-Thurs. 8-4, Fri.-Sat. 5 a.m.-6 p.m. and Sun. 6 a.m.-10 a.m. Friday and Saturday are the best days to attend *(see St. John's).*

Another way to grasp the nature of the island and its people is to watch a game of *warri.* This ancient betting game is played on a board with 14 holes and a handful of seeds. Originally brought from Africa with the slave trade, it has remained a favorite pastime.

Air and sea excursions travel 36 miles (58 km) north to Barbuda, a sparsely populated coral island lined with white and pink sand beaches that run for miles. Reefs harbor tropical fish and lobster while hiding nearly 100 sunken wrecks. Barbuda's interior, notable for its wildlife, includes a large natural frigate bird sanctuary, one of two in the Western Hemisphere.

The only monument on Barbuda is the Martello Tower; although its origins are unknown, its design and location suggest that it was a lighthouse. Two hotels are in the main village of Codrington, which is named for the family who leased the island from the British Crown for "one fat pig per year if asked." Today most of the population lives here, leaving the rest of the island unspoiled.

A full-day excursion to Barbuda by air includes a tour of the bird sanctuary and Codrington as well as a barbecue picnic lunch with rum punch. Most hotels will make arrangements for the Barbuda day tour, which should be planned at least 24 hours in advance.

Transportation

Antigua's V.C. Bird International Airport, 6 miles (10 km) from St. John's, accommodates jet aircraft. Direct service is provided from New York City, Newark, N.J., and Miami. BWIA and American Airlines make frequent flights to Antigua from San Juan, Puerto Rico. LIAT services other island destinations. Many cruise ships include Antigua on their regular itineraries.

You can drive rented cars over most of Antigua's roads; however, use caution due to road conditions and left-hand driving. Be on the lookout for the occasional goat wandering absently across the road. It is probably best to rent a four-wheel-drive vehicle. The primary roads are navigable, but potholes are common. Although most of the island's roads are not marked, most hotels and the Antigua and Barbuda Department of Tourism provide a map that is easy to follow.

Signs throughout Antigua show arrows pointing toward major resorts and attractions: These can assist in determining direction. If you are planning to drive through St. John's, be sure to obtain a good map; even though most of the streets are well-marked, many of them are one-way.

Presentation of a valid U.S. license and $12 entitles you to a driver's license good for 90 days. Hertz, on All Saints Road, offers discounts to AAA members; phone (268) 462-4114, or 462-4115 in St. John's, 460-2617 in English Harbour, and 462-6450 at the airport. Other car rental agencies and scooter rental agencies are listed in the telephone directory. Taxis are readily available at major resorts and are plentiful throughout St. John's. Fares from the airport to hotels are listed at the airport, and range from $3 to $21 for four passengers and their luggage, depending upon the destination; for all other excursions round-trip fares are charged.

Attraction Admissions
Attraction admissions for this island are quoted in U.S. dollars.

POINTS OF INTEREST

See map page 37.

ENGLISH HARBOUR (C-2)

English Harbour is 15 miles (24 km) from St. John's on the south side of the island (pop. 6,000). Once an outfitting center for British warships, this harbor played host to the ships of Horatio Nelson, Sir Francis Drake and Walter Rodney. It suffered from neglect for many years until yachtsmen rediscovered its charm and natural beauty. Restored to its 18th-century appearance, the town is now one of the island's most popular tourist destinations.

CLARENCE HOUSE, on the winding road to Shirley Heights, was built in 1787 for Prince William Henry, the Duke of Clarence and later King William IV. It is now the governor-general's country house. Allow 30 minutes minimum. Guided tours are available Mon.-Sat. 9-4; hours may vary. Free. Phone (268) 460-1026.

DOW'S HILL INTERPRETATION CENTRE, near Shirley Heights, offers "Reflections of the Sun," a multimedia show which traces Antigua's history from prehistoric times to the present. Displays include a shell collection and 18th-century artifacts. A guided tour includes a visit to the Belvedere, an observation area that provides a panorama of Nelson's Dockyard National Park. The remains of a 1780s house and a gun platform also are on the grounds.

Allow 30 minutes minimum. Mon.-Fri. and holidays 9-5, Sat.-Sun. 9-6. Admission $4; ages 5-16, $2. MC, VI. Phone (268) 460-2777.

★NELSON'S DOCKYARD NATIONAL PARK, built 1743-94, is reputed to be the only existing Georgian dockyard. It was used by a number of British admirals, including Horatio Nelson, as the home port of the British Fleet during the Napoleonic Wars. The site also was used as a repair and maintenance station for ships. Several buildings have been restored. Fort Berkeley, the original British garrison, was built in 1704 and manned by more than 3,000 troops. Also noteworthy is the dockyard's marketplace.

The dockyard and adjacent 15-square-mile (39-sq-km) area were designated a national park in 1984; park boundaries extend inland from a line along the southern coastline from Mamora Bay to Carlisle Bay. The park's rolling hills afford memorable views of the dockyard and surrounding countryside. Food is available. Allow 1 hour minimum. Admission $2.50, under 16 free. MC, VI. Phone (268) 460-1053.

Admirals House is a small museum of artifacts. A painted bust of Horatio Nelson stands outside. Displays include naval buttons, maps, coins from the 1800s, telescopes, muskets, cannon balls, clay pipes, ships models and belongings of Nel-

son. A late 1700s sandbox tree next to the museum produces pods which once were used as ink blotters. Open daily 8-6.

SHIRLEY HEIGHTS, across the bay from Nelson's Dockyard, was named for Gen. Thomas Shirley, who became governor in 1781. This lovely rise, which affords a view of Antigua's southern coast, was the main lookout post in the days of Nelson. The ruins of Fort Shirley are visible. At the first sign of danger, the flag at Fort Shirley was raised to signal other forts on the island.

Approximately 60 structures were built on Shirley Heights 1781-1825, and visitors can see the remains of barracks, officers' quarters and powder magazines. An obelisk commemorates the men of the Dorset Regiment, many of whom died of yellow fever. Food is available. Daily 24 hours. Shirley Heights free.

GUNTHORPES (B-2)

POTTERIES are at Sea View Farm, a village in which potters live. Products range from primitive cooking pots, bowls and trays to figurines, vases, lamps and mugs.

PARES (B-3)

BETTY'S HOPE PLANTATION was once the largest sugar plantation on Antigua and also the seat of government 1689-1704. Founded in the 1650s, the plantation was taken over by the Codrington family in 1668 and remained in their possession for nearly 300 years. Two windmill towers and the walls and arches of the boiling houses and other structures are all that remain. The sugar plantation is in the process of being restored as a living-history museum that will depict life on a

sugar estate and explain sugar and rum production.

A visitor center has exhibits illustrating the history of the sugar industry in the West Indies. Visitor center open Tues.-Sat. 10-4. Free. Phone (268) 462-4930.

DEVIL'S BRIDGE is about 5 mi. (8 km) e. at Indian Town Point. This natural limestone arch was created by the erosive force of the Atlantic Ocean. Water rushes through crevices in the rock and spouts through blowholes in dramatic bursts. The force at which the ocean spray gushes from the blowholes is proportionate to the size of the waves. Archeologists have uncovered artifacts at nearby Indian Town, one of the first Arawak settlements on the island.

St. John's (A-2) pop. 33,000

Antigua's capital, St. John's has quaint shops and colonial homes above a landlocked harbor. Tempering St. John's 19th-century English atmosphere is a progressive spirit symbolized by modern architecture. The man-made harbor, completed in 1968, has made the island an important port of call for passenger and commercial vessels; cruise ships also dock at Heritage Quay.

Shops, banks and other businesses line High Street, which runs through the center of the city to the pier. The produce market in the southern part of town is divided into sections for fruits and vegetables, meat and fish. Vendors pay weekly or monthly rent for stalls, except on Saturdays when they pay according to the number of bundles they carry through the gates. Visitors enjoy watching this "weighing-in" process.

The beautiful St. John's Anglican Cathedral, at the intersection of Newgate Street and Church Lane, was originally built in 1683 and rebuilt in stone in 1745. However, an earthquake destroyed it nearly 100 years later, and it had to be reconstructed yet again. The cornerstone of the present building was laid in 1845. Island legend holds that the figures of St. John the Baptist and St. John the Divine at the south gate were taken from the masts of one of Napoleon's ships. The cathedral is open to the public for tours, except during religious services. Phone (268) 462-0820.

The Botanical Garden is near the intersection of Factory Road and Independence Avenue, behind the National Archives building. This small park's shaded benches and gazebo provide a quiet refuge from the bustle of activity in St. John's. The Museum of Marine Art, at Gambles Terrace, is a small facility containing fossilized bedrock, volcanic stones, petrified wood and a collection of more than 10,000 shells. Also displayed are artifacts from several English shipwrecks; for group tour information phone (268) 462-1228.

ANTIGUA RUM DISTILLERY, at Citadel, is the only distillery on the island. Annual production yields more than 180,000 gallons bottled under two labels. Guided tours are available by reservation. Daily 8-4. Free. Phone (268) 462-1072.

FORT JAMES, built in 1739 to guard St. John's harbor, is one of the many forts built by the British in the 18th century. Fear of French invasion prompted construction of the fort. A powder magazine, several cannons and the foundation of the fort's walls remain. Other forts include Fort George at Monks Hill, Fort Charles at Falmouth Harbour, Fort Shirley at Shirley Heights, Fort Berkeley at English Harbour and Fort Barrington at Deep Bay. Daily 24 hours. Free.

GOVERNMENT HOUSE, on Independence Ave., is the official residence and office of the governor-general of Antigua. The building has dignified colonial lines and is surrounded by beautiful grounds. The house is not open to the public on a regular basis. Tours are by appointment only; contact the Antigua and Barbuda Department of Tourism on Long Street. The house, which sustained hurricane damage in 1995, is temporarily closed for repairs. Phone (268) 426-0480.

MUSEUM OF ANTIGUA & BARBUDA, Long and Market sts., is housed in the Old Court House, built in 1750. Archeological exhibits trace the history of early inhabitants, colonists and slaves. Allow 30 minutes minimum. Mon.-Thurs. 8:30-4, Fri. 8:30-3, Sat. 10-2; closed holidays. Donations. Phone (268) 462-1469 or 462-4930.

LODGINGS & RESTAURANTS

DICKENSON BAY

LODGINGS

REX HALCYON COVE
◆◆◆   *Resort Hotel*

12/1-4/15 & 11/1-11/30	$190-380	XP $71-143
4/16-10/31	$130-315	XP $69-118

Location: 7 mi w of airport. (PO Box 251, ST. JOHN'S). **Fax:** 268/462-0271. **Terms:** F12; Check-in 4 pm; reserv deposit, 21 day notice; 10% service charge. **Facility:** 210 rooms. Very attractive setting, garden & sea views, most rooms with patios & balconies. For US reservations: (305)471-6170; 2-3 stories, no elevator; interior/exterior corridors; beachfront; beach; playground. Fee: 4 lighted tennis courts. **Services:** giftshop. Fee: massage. **Recreation:** swimming. Fee: fishing, sailboating, scuba diving, snorkeling & equipment, waterskiing, windsurfing. **All Rooms:** combo or shower baths. **Some Rooms:** color TV. **Cards:** AE, DI, DS, MC, VI.

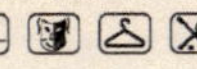

(268/462-0256

SANDALS ANTIGUA RESORT & SPA
◆◆◆   *Resort Hotel*

12/24-3/31	$3570-4900
12/1-12/23 & 4/1-11/30	$3255-4725

Location: 7.3 mi w of airport. (PO Box 147). **Fax:** 268/462-4135. **Terms:** Age restrictions may apply; reserv deposit, no refunds on cancellations; 3 night min stay. **Facility:** 191 rooms. All inclusive food, drink & activities; couples only. Excellent facilities & public areas. Piano bar. For US reservations: (305) 284-1300; 1-2 stories; exterior corridors; beach, saunas, steamrooms, whirlpools; 2 lighted tennis courts, tennis instructions. **Dining:** 4 restaurants, coffee shop; 7:30-11 am, 12:30-2:15 & 6:30-10 pm; cocktails. **Services:** giftshop. Fee: massage. **Recreation:** swimming, scuba diving/snorkeling & equipment, waterskiing, watersports, scuba instruction; spa facilities. Fee: island tours. **Cards:** AE, MC, VI.

((268)462-0267

SIBONEY BEACH CLUB
◆◆◆   *Apartment Motel*

12/20-4/14	$260-290	XP $30
12/1-12/19 & 4/15-11/30	$130-170	XP $30

Location: 7.5 mi w of airport. (PO Box 222). **Fax:** 268/462-3356. **Terms:** Reserv deposit, 42 day notice, 21 off season; handling fee imposed; 10% service charge. **Facility:** 12 rooms. Tranquil, beachfront 1-bedroom apartments. Balcony & patio. 3 stories, no elevator; exterior corridors; beachfront; beach. Fee: tennis privileges. **Dining:** Cocktails; also, Coconut Grove, see separate listing. **Recreation:** swimming. Fee: water sports. **All Rooms:** shower baths. **Some Rooms:** color TV. **Cards:** AE, MC, VI. **Special Amenities:** Early check-in/late check-out and free newspaper.

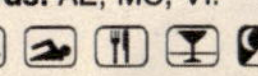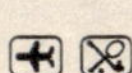

((268)462-0806

RESTAURANT

COCONUT GROVE
◆◆   *Seafood*   L $8-$15   D $18-$28

Location: 7.5 mi w of airport; in Siboney Beach Club. **Hours:** 7 am-10:30 pm. **Reservations:** suggested. **Features:** No A/C; casual dress; cocktails & lounge; a la carte. Beachside dining, well prepared island cuisine. Attractive, efficient staff. **Cards:** AE, MC, VI.

(268/462-1538

ENGLISH HARBOUR

LODGING

THE INN AT ENGLISH HARBOUR
◆◆◆   *Motor Inn*

12/15-3/15 & 4/25-5/3	$290-410
3/16-4/24	$200-320
12/1-12/14, 5/4-8/30 & 10/18-11/30	$140-210

Location: On road to Shirley Heights; 16 mi s of airport overlooking English Harbour. (PO Box 187, ST. JOHN'S). **Fax:** 268/460-1603. **Terms:** Open 12/1-8/30 & 10/18-11/30; reserv deposit, 14 day notice; 10% service charge. **Facility:** 28 rooms. English style. Pleasant rooms on hill overlooking bay or on secluded beach. Balconies. Country inn atmosphere. Fine pub & dining room. 1-2 stories; exterior corridors; beach. **Services:** giftshop. **Recreation:** swimming, boating, snorkeling & equipment, windsurfing. Fee: sailboating, scuba diving & equipment, waterskiing. **All Rooms:** combo or shower baths. **Cards:** AE, MC, VI.

(268/460-1014

RESTAURANTS

LE CAP HORN
◆◆ *French*
D $11-$21

Location: At entrance to Nelson's Dockyard. **Hours:** 6:30 pm-11 pm. **Reservations:** suggested. **Features:** No A/C; casual dress; cocktails & lounge; street parking; a la carte. Some classic dishes plus seafood & meat. Wood burning brick oven pizza. Outdoor covered dining area. Nighly specials. **Cards:** AE, MC, VI.

☎ 268/460-1194

THE TERRACE RESTAURANT
◆◆◆ *Continental*
L $10-$16 D $20-$30

Location: On road to Shirley Heights; 16 mi s of airport overlooking English Harbour; in The Inn at English Harbour. **Hours:** 7:30-10:30 am, 12:30-2:30 & 7-9 pm. Closed: 9/1-10/14. **Reservations:** suggested. **Features:** No A/C; cocktails & lounge; a la carte. Terrace overlooking harbour. Elegant, English style & atmosphere lunch served beachside. **Cards:** AE, DS, MC, VI.

☎ 268/460-1014

LODGING

🔺 SAVE ST. JAMES'S CLUB
◆◆◆ *Resort*

1/3-4/6	$500-640	XP $180
12/1-12/19 & 4/7-11/30	$430-540	XP $180
12/20-1/2	$395-510	XP $200-250

Location: 16 mi se of airport on Mamora Bay. (PO Box 63, ST. JOHN'S). Fax: 268/460-3015. **Terms:** F12; Reserv deposit, 45 day notice, in season; 7 day off season; handling fee imposed; package plans. **Facility:** 155 rooms. Large attractive rooms with balcony facing ocean or lagoon bay. 2- & 3- bedroom hillside villas & 3-bedroom hillside homes. 2-bedroom villas for up to 6 persons, $1170-$1250 in season; $810-$880 mid-season; $660-$730 off season. For US reservations: (212)486-2575; 1-3 stories; interior/exterior corridors; beach, whirlpool; 7 tennis courts (5 lighted), tennis instruction; boat dock; playground. **Dining:** 2 dining rooms, deli; patio dining; 7:30 am-10, noon-2:30 & 7-10 pm; $20-$40; cocktails; afternoon tea. **Services:** giftshop. Fee: massage. **Recreation:** swimming, boating, paddleboats, sailboating, snorkeling & equipment, waterskiing; casino, croquet. Fee: charter fishing, fishing. Rental: scuba equipment. **Some Rooms:** 50 kitchens. **Cards:** AE, DI, MC, VI. *(See color ad below)*

☎ (268)460-5000

LODGING

BARRYMORE BEACH CLUB
◆◆ *Apartment Motel*

12/15-4/14	$115-355	XP $20-30
12/1-12/14 & 4/15-11/30	$72-195	XP $20

Location: 2 mi nw from St John's on Runaway Bay. (PO Box 1774, ST. JOHN'S). Fax: 268/462-4140. **Terms:** F12; Reserv deposit, 21 day notice; 10% service charge. **Facility:** 32 rooms. White sand beach. Rooms & 1-to 2-bedroom apartments. 2-bedroom units, $295-$350 in season for up to 6 persons; exterior corridors; beach. **Recreation:** swimming. Fee: fishing. **All Rooms:** shower baths. **Some Rooms:** 16 kitchens. **Cards:** AE, DS, MC, VI.

☎ 268/462-4101

LODGINGS

HAWKSBILL BEACH RESORT
◆◆◆ *Hotel*

12/16-4/30	$375-450	XP $112-137
12/1-12/15 & 5/1-11/30	$276-325	XP $112

Location: 4 mi sw of St John's, via New Rd & Five Island Village. (PO Box 108). Fax: 268/462-1515. **Terms:** D12; Reserv deposit, 21 day notice; handling fee imposed; 10% service charge. **Facility:** 113 rooms. Relaxed atmosphere. Oceanfront & garden view rooms with balcony or patio, on series of 4 small sandy beaches. 1 beach, clothes optional. Terraced lawns & gardens. Villas. 1-2 stories; exterior corridors; beach; 1 tennis court. **Recreation:** swimming, paddleboats, snorkeling & equipment, windsurfing. Fee: waterskiing. **All Rooms:** shower baths. **Cards:** AE, MC, VI.

☎ 268/462-0301

ROYAL ANTIGUAN CASINO, TENNIS, BEACH RESORT
◆◆ **Resort Hotel**

12/21-4/15	$190-250	XP $30
12/1-12/20 & 4/16-11/30	$150-200	XP $30

Location: 3.5 mi w of St John's Harbor, via New Rd following coast; keep right at jct. (PO Box 1322). Fax: 268/462-3732. **Terms:** F17; Reserv deposit, 3 day notice; handling fee imposed; 10% service charge. **Facility:** 266 rooms. Overlooking lagoon. Tranquil beach area. Modern facilities. 1-bedroom cottages, $390 for 2 persons; $260 off season; 2-8 stories; interior/exterior corridors; beach; 8 tennis courts. **Services:** giftshop. Fee: massage. **Recreation:** swimming, charter fishing, sailboating, snorkeling, scuba & snorkeling equipment, windsurfing; hiking trails. Fee: scuba diving, waterskiing. **Cards:** AE, DI, MC, VI.

(268/462-3733

RESTAURANTS

BIG BANANA-PIZZAS ON THE QUAY
◆ *American*   L $5-$20   D $5-$20

Location: Downtown in Redcliffe Quay. **Hours:** 8 am-11 pm. Closed major holidays& Sun. **Features:** No A/C; casual dress; cocktails; a la carte. Indoor/outdoor cafe with pizza, salad & sandwiches. Daily lunch specials. Local flavors of conch & lobster salad. Live bands Fri & Sat nights. **Cards:** AE, DI, MC, VI.

(268/462-2621

CHEZ PASCAL
◆◆◆ *French*   L $18-$29 D $20-$38

Location: 4 mi sw, via New Road to Galley Bay Hill, following signs. **Hours:** 11 am-3 & 6-10 pm. **Reservations:** suggested. **Features:** No A/C; casual dress; cocktails; a la carte. Classic cuisine featured in new dining room opening onto patio. Spectacular ocean & lush forest view. Wine include high end Bordeaux. **Cards:** AE, DI, MC, VI.

(268/462-3232

HOME
◆◆◆ *Caribbean*   D $18-$25

Location: Just n in Upper Gambles, just e of Fort Rd. Gambles Terrace. **Hours:** 6:30 pm-10 pm. Closed: Sun, 6/1-7/15. **Reservations:** suggested. **Features:** No A/C; casual dress; cocktails; street parking; a la carte. Owner/chef serves Caribbean "haute cuisine" inspired by the freshest seafood & local produce in his childhood home. Warm hospitality. **Cards:** AE, MC, VI.   (268/61-7651

JULIAN'S
◆◆◆ *Continental*   D $19-$29

Location: Downtown at Corn Alley & Church Ln. PO Box 3007. **Hours:** 7 pm-10:30 pm. Closed major holidays, Mon & 6/1-6/30. **Reservations:** suggested. **Features:** cocktails & lounge; street parking; a la carte. Intimate dining in authentic West Indian building with courtyard. Classical modern cuisine prepared to order. Garden, balcony or main floor dining. **Cards:** AE, DS, MC, VI.

(268/462-4766

LE BISTRO
◆◆◆ *French*   D $20-$30

Location: 5 mi e, at Hodges Bay; 2 mi n of airport. **Hours:** 6:30 pm-10:30 pm. Closed: Mon. **Reservations:** suggested. **Features:** No A/C; casual dress; cocktails & lounge; a la carte. Spacious candelight dining room. Traditional French cuisine fused with island influences & local ingredients. Fresh fish & Caribbean lobster. No shorts permitted. **Cards:** AE, MC, VI.

(268/462-3881

WILLIKIES

LODGING

LONG BAY HOTEL
◆◆ *Hotel*

12/16-4/1	$375-425	XP $110
12/1-12/15, 4/2-5/27 & 10/21-11/30	$265-325	XP $110

Location: 12 mi e, on ne coast, 1.5 mi e of Willikies. (PO Box 442, ST. JOHN'S). Fax: 268/463-2439. **Terms:** Open 12/1-5/27 & 10/21-11/30; reserv deposit, 21 day notice; 10% service charge. **Facility:** 24 rooms. On point of land between sea & lagoon. Pleasant rooms with balcony 8 cottage units. Lovely remote setting, family operated since 1966. 6 housekeeping cottages, $255-$450, open all year, for up to 2 persons, meals included; 1-2 stories; exterior corridors; beach; 1 tennis court; boat dock. **Recreation:** swimming, fishing, sailboating, snorkeling & equipment, windsurfing. Fee: charter fishing, scuba diving, waterskiing. Rental: boats, scuba equipment. **All Rooms:** combo or shower baths. **Cards:** AE, MC, VI.

((268)463-2005

ARUBA

ARUBA IS THE SMALLEST and most westerly of the "ABC" (Aruba, Bonaire and Curaçao) islands. Just 15 miles (24 km) north of Venezuela, it has an exceptionally dry climate that is considered one of the most desirable in the Caribbean. Aruba's arid interior, marked by surreal, wind-bent divi-divi trees, sprawling stands of cactus and aloe vera, and

huge boulders strewn like marbles contrasts sharply with the more tropical, palm-lined southwest coast. It is perhaps as much the desert landscape as the active nightlife that gives Aruba the reputation as the Las Vegas of the Caribbean.

HISTORY, GOVERNMENT AND ECONOMY

Assessments of Aruba's worth have varied since 1499, when Alonso de Ojeda claimed the island for Spain. Because the Spaniards considered Aruba worthless, the native Arawak Indians were spared the annihilation their kinfolk faced on islands thought more valuable. The Dutch, who hardly considered the island prime real estate, took over in 1636.

During the Napoleonic Wars the British settled Aruba for a few years, but by 1816 the Dutch had returned to stay. Compared with other Caribbean islands, Aruba had a rather quiet history; the island was fought over only twice and suffered few pirate attacks.

Gold discovered on Aruba in 1824 attracted considerable investment, but a century later the mine was exhausted. A different sort of gold renewed interest in the island in 1924, when the Lago Oil and Transport Co. built a large refinery that brought one of the highest standards of living in the Caribbean.

This prosperity was furthered by the development of tourism, which became Aruba's primary industry when the refinery closed in 1985. (Coastal Corp. reopened the refinery in 1991.) Because of the focus on tourism and the number of resorts on the island, Arubans enjoy a very low unemployment rate. Consequently, an ordinance has been passed that prohibits the building of any new hotel or time-share resort since there are not enough workers to fill the jobs. Arubans are proud of their heritage and are concerned that

with the importation of additional workers the island's local flavor might be lost.

Aruba became a separate entity within the Kingdom of the Netherlands on Jan. 1, 1986; prior to that date it was a member of the Netherlands Antilles. The Kingdom of the Netherlands, which includes the Netherlands, the Netherland Antilles (Bonaire, Curaçao, St. Eustatius, St. Maarten and Saba) and Aruba, is responsible for the entire Kingdom's defense and foreign affairs while the government of each country performs autonomously.

SHOPPING

Aruba offers the finest in European luxury items, but it is always wise to check prices before leaving home, as not everything sells at a discount. Shops in Aruba do not charge sales tax on purchases. The main shopping district lies along Caya Gilberto François Croes Street in cosmopolitan Oranjestad. Such large stores as Little Switzerland, Aruba Trading Company, Bon Bini Bazaar, Penha and New Amsterdam Store sell perfumes, linens, jewelry, cameras, clothing, crystal and china.

Port of Call Market Place, at 17 L.G. Smith Blvd. just west of the harbor area, contains more than 30 shops that feature beachwear, jewelry, souvenirs and gift items. Seaport Market Place and Cinema, on L.G. Smith Boulevard across from the Government Executive Office, is situated on the waterfront next to a marina and Seaport Casino. The waterfront's more than 70 shops run the gamut from resortwear to island crafts.

Seaport Village Mall, adjoining the Sonesta Resort and the Crystal Casino, has entrances on Havenstraat and L.G. Smith Boulevard. The mall, where visitors can see caged exotic parrots and parakeets as well as the hotel's indoor boat lagoon, contains more than 80 shops and restaurants including Gucci, Cartier and Columbian Emeralds. In addition to designer fashions and such fine china as Royal Doulton and Wedgwood, Seaport Village also contains several souvenir and beachwear shops.

Holland Aruba Mall, off Havenstraat opposite Seaport Village, has a colorful assortment of shops featuring gift items, jewelry and souvenirs. Adjoining the Holland Aruba Mall in Plaza Daniel Ignacio Leo is Strada II, a small arcade of shops recognized by its Dutch Colonial architecture painted in pastels. The mall contains Aquarius, a shop specializing in trendy clothing for men and women as well as Fendi items. On the side of Strada II that runs along Schelpstraat is the Setar Teleshop, a facility for placing overseas phone calls.

Strada I is on Kazernestraat, across the street from Strada II and the Holland Aruba Mall. The two-story mall contains several shops, including Benetton. Both Strada I and Strada II complexes contain Sparky's, a perfumery.

Other stores specialize in imported items, such as Dutch pewter, Delft ware, Hummel figurines or liquor. Excluding hotel shopping arcades, which operate on different schedules, most stores in downtown Oranjestad are open Mon.-Sat. 8-6. Some stores also are open Sunday mornings and holidays when cruise ships are in port. Banking hours are Mon.-Fri. 8-noon and 1:30-4. The Caribbean Mercantile Bank at the airport is open daily 8-4.

FOOD AND DRINK

Restaurants catering to all tastes and budgets can be found in Oranjestad. A sampling of Dutch food might include *erwten soep,* a thick pea soup cooked with pork, ham and sausage. Local specialties include *funchi,* a cornmeal combination served with meat or fish; *soppi di pisca,* a fish soup that includes salted meats and coconut milk; pan bati, an Aruban pancake served with local dishes; and *keri keri,* a mixture of tomatoes, peppers, shredded codfish and herbs.

Other popular dishes include *keshi yena,* a Dutch cheese stuffed with meat, chicken or fish that is seasoned with raisins, olives, onions and tomatoes; and *pastechi,* pastries filled with cheese, meat, seafood or other ingredients. *Stoba* is a stew usually consisting of goat meat and vegetables. Another password to good eating is *rijsttafel,* or "rice table." This Dutch-Indonesian feast consists of rice accompanied by as many as 20 side dishes.

White snack trucks serving inexpensive and generous portions of local food can be found in Oranjestad after 10 p.m. Some of the locations where the trucks park are in front of the post office, at the Seaport Market Place and in front of the bus station in Oranjestad. As for liquid refreshment, sparse rainfall used to make drinking water scarce, but modern technology allows fresh water to be distilled from the sea.

SPORTS AND AMUSEMENTS

As on its sister islands, vegetation on Aruba is sparse. The dusty interior contains huge boulders

---

THINGS TO KNOW

AREA: 75 square miles (194 sq km).

POPULATION: 91,500.

LANGUAGE: Dutch, Spanish, English and Papiamento.

CAPITAL: Oranjestad.

GOVERNMENT: Autonomous member of the Kingdom of the Netherlands.

TIME ZONE: Atlantic.

UNIT OF CURRENCY: Aruba florin divided into 100 cents. $1 U.S.= approx. 1.79 Aruba florin.

ELECTRICITY: 110-120 volts, 60 cycles AC.

MINIMUM AGE FOR GAMBLING: 18.

CARS: U.S. license valid, must be 21; drive on right.

IMMIGRATION REQUIREMENTS: Proof of U.S. citizenship (birth certificate, affidavit of birth, naturalization papers with photo ID or passport) and return or through ticket are required. Departure tax is included in airline ticket price.

FOR FURTHER INFORMATION:
Aruba Tourism Authority
1000 Harbor Blvd., Ground Level
Weehawken, NJ 07087
(800) 862-7822
Aruba Tourism Authority
J.E. Irausquin Blvd. #172
Oranjestad, Aruba
Phone (297) 823777

HOLIDAYS: Jan. 1; Carnival Monday; Good Friday; Easter Monday; National Anthem and Flag Day, Mar. 18; Queen's Birthday, Apr. 30; Labor Day, May 1; Ascension Day; Dec. 25; Boxing Day, Dec. 26.

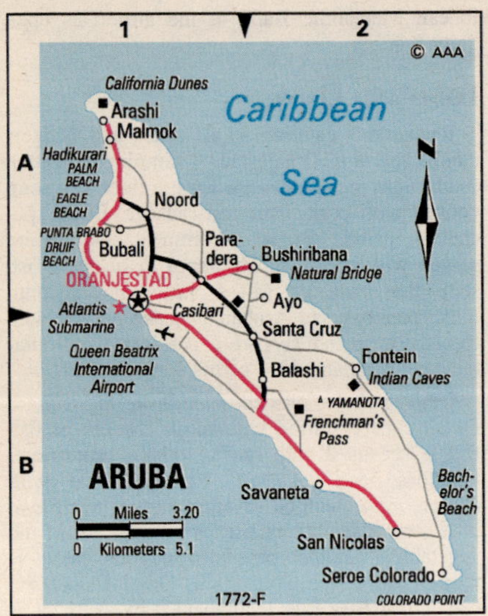

INDEX TO STARRED ATTRACTIONS

ATTRACTIONS OF EXCEPTIONAL
INTEREST AND QUALITY
Atlantis Submarine - see Oranjestad

---

and wind-bent divi-divi (watapana) trees. Recreational activities include hiking through Arikok National Park, cave exploring at Fontein and Guadirikiri caves, jeep tours of the interior and dune sliding at Boca Prins.

There is plenty to do along the coast. Seven miles (11 km) of uninterrupted beach stretch from Druif Beach to Eagle Beach and from Palm Beach to Malmok. The best swimming spots are Eagle and Palm beaches, due to the fact that the water is the calmest off the island's southwest coast. Druif Beach, south of Eagle Beach, also is a pleasant place to swim for those not averse to some slight wave action. There are only two white sand beaches on the north coast—Andicuri and Dos Playa. Although the scenery is beautiful, the north coast is not recommended for swimming, due to strong currents and large waves.

The beaches in the southeast section of the island beyond the oil refinery tend to be less populated than the southwest beaches. Baby Beach, at the island's southeast tip, is so named because it is perfect for small children and inexperienced swimmers. This is because the water remains shallow quite a distance from the shore, achieving depths no greater than 5 feet (1.5 m). It also is a popular beach for relaxing and picnicking. At Rodger's Beach, next to Baby Beach, swimmers can enjoy a little more surf. Bachelor's Beach also provides good swimming and snorkeling opportunities along with a little surf.

Trade winds that blow at a maximum speed of 27 knots (31 mph, 50 km/h) daily, with an average speed of 18 knots (21 mph, 34 km/h), make conditions perfect for windsurfing; the Aruba Hi-Winds Pro-Am Tournament takes place in June. The entire area of coast between Eagle and Palm beaches provides excellent windsurfing opportunities. Hadikurari, locally referred to as Fisherman's Hut, is a popular windsurfing spot north of Palm Beach just beyond the Aruba Marriot Resort and Casino.

North of Fisherman's Hut, the Malmok Beach area is a great place to learn how to windsurf since the water is only between 2 and 3 feet (.6 and .9 m) deep. There are many small hotels in this area which cater to windsurfers, and windsurfing lessons and equipment rental are readily available. Bachelor's Beach, north of Colorado Point, is an area famous for professional windsurfing. Skilled windsurfers also enjoy Boca Grandi, situated just north of the Bachelor's Beach area, and Dos Playa, on the north coast about a mile (1.6 km) north of Boca Prins.

Visibility in Aruba's clear waters can extend as far as 90 feet (27 m) and the water temperature is never under 70 F (21 C), making the area very desirable for snorkeling and scuba diving. A vessel often explored by divers is the *Antilla*, the wreckage of a World War II German freighter off the coast midway between Arashi and Malmok. Another cement cargo ship, the *Jane Sea*, lies near the Baracadera Reefs.

Arashi Beach, north of Malmok on the southwest coast, is frequented by both scuba divers and snorkelers. Spanish Lagoon, a reef off the southeast coast halfway between Oranjestad and San Nicolas, is a favorite with divers; snorkeling also is possible in this area. Commanders Bay, about 3 miles (5 km) east of Spanish Lagoon, is especially recommended for scuba diving.

Beautiful coral heads can be found at Little Lagoon, a good snorkeling reef easily accessible off the shallow channel of Baby Beach. Bird Reef, off Rodger's Beach, and the reefs off Bachelor's Beach, on the northeast coast, also are well-known snorkeling spots. Rental equipment for diving, windsurfing and water skiing is available throughout the island.

Fishing for blue and white marlin, kingfish, tuna, bonito and other game fish is best July through October. Also in abundant supply are sailfish, dolphin, amberjack, wahoo and barracuda. Boats for deep-sea fishing can be chartered at the Seaport Marina and Bali piers. Some yachts offer 2-hour coastal cruises, complete with snacks and beverages. Motorboats, small sailboats, pedalboats and sea jeeps (wave runners) can be rented for shorter periods of time at divers aquatic facilities.

As for non-aquatic recreation, most hotels and private clubs provide tennis courts and information about horseback riding. Those who would ather landsurf than windsurf can contact Aruba Sailcart at 23 Bushiri; phone (297) 35133. Bowling at the Eagle Bowling Palace on L.G. Smith Boulevard offers a good respite from the sun; phone (297) 35038. Drag races are held several times a year at Palo Marga, in the northeast section of the island; phone (297) 829085.

The Aruba Golf Club, (297) 842006, near San Nicholas has a nine-hole golf course. Tierra del Sol, (297) 860978, features an 18-hole desertlike golf course designed by Robert Trent Jones Jr. Miniature golf is offered at Adventure Golf, (297) 876625, on L.G. Smith Boulevard in front of La Cabana resort.

Aruba has an active nightlife: Hotel-casinos and various nightclubs and restaurants offer dancing and after-dinner entertainment. The island's resorts sponsor more than 50 themed-events that occur on a weekly basis, including folkloric, limbo and steel-band shows.

Casino gambling is a popular pastime in Aruba, with 11 casinos offering blackjack, roulette, baccarat, craps and slot machines. One of the most common games is Caribbean stud poker, which can be played by table or machine. Visitors to the casinos must be at least 18.

Among the most highly regarded establishments for casino gambling are Aruba Marriott Resort & Stellaris Casino, 101 L.G. Smith Blvd., open daily noon-4 a.m.; Crystal Casino, 82 L.G. Smith Blvd., open daily 24 hours; Hyatt Regency Aruba Beach Resort & Casino, 85 L.G. Smith Blvd., open daily noon-4 a.m.; and Royal Cabana Casino, 250 L.G. Smith Blvd., open daily 1 p.m.-7 a.m. Aruba's casinos are not as formal as those in Atlantic City or Las Vegas, and casual attire is acceptable.

The Royal Cabana Casino's Tropicana Showroom and the Alhambra Bazaar's Aladdin Theater present a variety of entertainment ranging from Broadway musicals to cabarets. For Las Vegas-style extravaganzas try the Americana Aruba Beach Resort & Casino. Dance revues with a Latin flair can be enjoyed at the Holiday Inn Aruba Beach Resort and Casino. The Stardust Showroom offers a Jean Ryan production, "Hot Ticket."

Some of the best local entertainment takes place at the Bonbini Festival, held every Tuesday evening at Fort Zoutman on Oranjestrad at 6:30 p.m. Concerts and folkloric shows also are performed at the Cultural Center at Vondellaan 2 in Oranjestad. Movies, usually American, are shown at the drive-in theater at Balashi and at the cinema at Seaport Market Place.

Aruba's version of New Orleans' Mardi Gras, Carnival is celebrated during February and March and enlists locals and tourists alike in parades, dances, contests and parties; the Grand Parade takes place the Sunday before Lent.

Aruba Holiday, available at hotel desks, publishes a schedule of events and entertainment.

Aruba's two English newspapers—*Aruba Today* and *The News*—are available free of charge at most hotels.

EXCURSIONS AND SIGHTSEEING

Aruba has good roads, though many are unmarked. However, the government has marked the roads to point the way to specific attractions. You might have to rely on word of mouth or try navigating by the divi-divi trees which always point southwest away from the trade winds; if you are lost, just remember that these trees blow in the direction of the resorts. The island is about 19.6 miles (30 km) long and 6 miles (10 km) wide at its broadest point and most of it can be toured by car.

For an adventurous excursion, drive into Aruba's *cunucu,* or countryside, where fields of cactuses and aloe vera are punctuated by wandering goats and colorful cottages. Old-style cunucu houses, which appear throughout the island, are characterized by such features as rain tanks, a necessity in the days before desalinization, wooden windows and doors, and chimneys once used for cooking. Huge rock formations mark the area around Casibari and Ayo, from which a road continues northeast to Andicuri near the Natural Bridge, an excellent place for shell collecting.

Visitors can view the entire island at Hooiberg, also nicknamed Haystack Mountain, between Santa Cruz and Ayo. Athletically inclined individuals may choose to climb the more than 600 steps that ascend to the mountain's top, which at 541 feet (165 m) is the island's second highest elevation. Yamanota, to the southeast at the center of the island, is Aruba's highest point at 617 feet (188 m). The panorama from its summit includes Frenchman's Pass on the south coast, where Indians defended their island against the French. The area is known for its wild parakeets.

At the island's northern tip, the California Lighthouse is on a cliff that offers a panorama of Arashi, Malmok, Palm and Eagle beaches. At this point, the difference can be observed between the calm southern coast and the northern coast with waves crashing against the shoreline. Although the lighthouse itself is not open, the area is worth a visit because of its captivating scenery. Visitors can see cactuses, boulders, roaming goats and the California Dunes, a collection of rolling sand dunes.

Because of its rugged landscape, Arikok National Park, directly across the island from Oranjestad, is best experienced in a jeep (jeeps are only permitted on jeep paths). The park abounds with such wildlife as parakeets, goats, butterflies, hares, iguanas and the wara-wara, a red-beaked eagle found throughout the ABC islands and Venezuela. Flora includes such rare species of trees as brazilwood, lignum vitae and kibrahacha. The park also contains the only divi-divi tree that grows straight up.

Indian symbols can be seen on some of the boulders at Arikok near San Fuego. A section of the park provides a sweeping view of the turbulent northeast coast and Boca Prins, white dunes covered with grassy sections that can be explored on foot.

Glass-bottom boats provide views of colorful fish, coral formations and shipwrecks during 90-minute trips from the Aruba Palm Beach Resort & Casino and the Holiday Inn Aruba Beach Resort & Casino to the California Lighthouse. Trimaran and catamaran sailing excursions, which offer snorkeling trips and sunset cocktail cruises, also are available.

Reputable ticket booking establishments include *Atlantis* Submarine *(see attraction listing under Oranjestad p. 50)*, DePalm Tours, Pelican Watersports, Red Sail Sports, Seaworld Explorer, Unique Sports of Aruba and Wave Dancer.

Some companies offer tours that cater to such specialized interests as wildlife or archeology. Information about excursions can be obtained at the Aruba Tourism Authority Public Relations Department in Oranjestad and at most hotels; phone (297) 823777.

Transportation

Queen Beatrix International Airport has direct flights from Atlanta, Baltimore, Houston, Miami, Newark, New York, Orlando, Puerto Rico and Tampa; interisland flights to the other "ABC" islands are available on ALM, the Dutch Antillean airline. Direct flights from Aruba to Brazil, Colombia and Venezuela also are available. In addition, Aruba is a port of call for cruise ships.

Most American car rental firms have branches on the island, and there also are several local companies. Hertz, 142 L.G. Smith Blvd., offers discounts to AAA members. Speed limits in Aruba are generally 25 mph (40 km/h) in town and 35 mph (60 km/h) on out-of-town roads.

Drivers should be aware that most of the traffic in Oranjestad is one-way, and vehicles approaching from the right have the right of way when there is no road sign posted. Driving is on the right side of the road. Use caution when traveling on wet roads; dirt and oil accumulate due to scarce rainfall, resulting in slippery conditions in the rain. If you are planning an excursion through Aruba's interior, make sure your vehicle is in good working order; roads are not paved and there are no repair facilities available.

Motorcycles and scooters also can be rented, but keep in mind that the island is deserted in certain areas and the terrain can be rough and hilly. Taxis also can be hired for sightseeing. If you choose to take a cab, check the fixed taxi rates beforehand; they are set by the government and are based on destination rather than mileage. To order a cab phone (297) 822116.

There is regular bus service from Oranjestad to Eagle and Palm beaches and other points throughout the residential areas of the island. The main bus terminal is on L.G. Smith Blvd., exit to Royal Plaza in downtown Oranjestad.

Buses run daily 5:40 a.m.-11:40 p.m. From Monday through Saturday the buses make scheduled stops 20 minutes before the hour, 10 minutes before the hour, on the hour and 25 minutes after the hour; after 7 p.m. buses only stop 20 minutes before the hour. On Sunday buses run on a reduced schedule, stopping 20 minutes before the hour.

Note: Part of L.G. Smith Boulevard, which runs in front of the high-rise hotels, has unofficially been changed to J.E. Irausquin Boulevard. Some street signs in the stretch of road between the Divi Tamarijn and the Aruba Marriott Resort and Casino may reflect this name change.

ATTRACTION ADMISSIONS

Attraction admissions for this island are quoted in U.S. dollars.

POINTS OF INTEREST

See map page 48.

ORANJESTAD (A-1) pop. 13,000

Oranjestad, which translates to "Orange City," derived its name from the House of Orange, the ruling family of the Netherlands. Dutch architecture in Oranjestad blends nicely with Caribbean colors: Dutch Colonial houses are painted green, blue, yellow and brown. This profusion of color is maintained by a local tenet that warns against coveting the color of a neighbor's house. Modern residences, broad boulevards and a park complement the city's charm.

Many shops in Oranjestad sell such fine products as crystal, china, linens, jewelry, cameras, watches and fashionable clothing. Caya Gilberto François Croes Street is the heart of the shopping district, and L.G. Smith Boulevard, which parallels the waterfront, has a houseboat restaurant and a colorful market that features fruit imported from Venezuela, souvenir stands and snacks.

ARCHEOLOGY MUSEUM, on Zoutmanstraat 1, contains artifacts from the Indians of Aruba. Exhibits feature the remains of stone tools dating from 2000 B.C., known as the preceramic period. Items that date from 500 A.D., which represents the ceramic period, include pottery, sling stones used for hunting and burial artifacts of the Dabajuroid Aruban Indians. Also displayed are skeletal remains excavated from an Indian burial site. Mon.-Fri. 7:30-noon and 1-4:30, Sat.-Sun. by appointment. Free. Phone (297) 828979.

ARUBA HISTORICAL MUSEUM is in the Willem III Tower in Fort Zoutman on Oranjestraat. Dominating the city's skyline, the tower was built in 1796 to protect the island from pirates. Historical displays in the museum include weights and measures, coins, furniture and antique tools. The Bon Bini Festival is held every Tuesday evening on the patio of the fort from 6:30-8:30; visitors can sample Aruban cuisine and enjoy the entertainment. Museum open Mon.-Fri. 9-noon and 1:30-4:30. Admission $1.15. Bon Bini Festival $1.30. Phone (297) 826099.

★*ATLANTIS* SUBMARINE departs from the marina opposite Seaport Village Mall. This 65-foot-long, 46-passenger submarine cruises at a maximum depth of 150 feet, offering excellent views of Barcadera Reef, marine life and coral formations. A 30-minute ferry ride transports passengers between the dock and the submarine for the 1-hour tour. Allow 2 hours minimum. Trips depart hourly Wed.-Mon. 10-3. Fare $65; 36 inches tall to age 12, $34. Under 36 inches tall are not permitted. Reservations are advised. AE, MC, VI. Phone (297) 836090 or (297) 825353

AYO, 1.9 mi. (3 km) s.w. of Andicuri, is a geological mystery; the origin of the rock formations has never been determined. Diorite boulders, each weighing several thousand tons, balance precariously on edge or on each other. Indian paintings can be seen on some of the rocks. Allow 30 minutes minimum. Open daily 24 hours. Free.

BALASHI, 3 mi. (5 km) s.e. of the airport, is the site of Aruba's early gold mining industry. Ruins of gold smelters remain in nearby Frenchman's Pass.

BUSHIRIBANA, across the island from Oranjestad, is the site of a deserted 19th-century gold mill. The ruin, also known as Pirate Castle, stands in a barren area with desertlike terrain that offers a picturesque view of the north coast. It is not recommended that visitors walk inside the ruin due to falling rocks.

CASIBARI, 2.5 mi. (4 km) e. of Oranjestad, is composed of diorite boulders that weigh thousands of tons. A climb to the top, made possible by ascending steps that wind through the conglomeration of rocks, is rewarded by a panorama of the southwest portion of the island. Only those in good physical condition should attempt the climb. The rock garden, at the base of the formation, is accented by beachgrape trees and contains boulders said to resemble certain animals. Open daily dawn-dusk. Free.

INDIAN CAVES, at Fontein, contain pre-Columbian petroglyphs. One particular graphic depicts a map of the caves. Near the Fontein cave is a Chinese garden. A cave containing pre-Columbian markings and impressive stalagmites and stalactites is located at nearby Guadirikiri; be advised that bats are present. Farther south, the Tunnel of Love is an underground cave that can be explored daily. Free guided tours are available at all three caves. A fee is charged for flashlights and helmets.

NATURAL BRIDGE, at Andicuri on the north coast, is a rock formation carved from coral cliffs by the continuous pounding of the sea. The bridge is more than 100 feet long and arches about 25 feet above sea level. There is a small beach area beyond the bridge that is good for picnicking or relaxing, but swimming is not recommended in this area.

NUMISMATIC MUSEUM, 7 Zuidstraat, displays various forms of currency from throughout the world dating from 221 B.C. to the present. Collections include Aruban Indian shell artifacts utilized for barter and trade; wampum, beads made of the interior of shells and used as money by North American Indians; currency from World Wars I and II, including inflation and occupation money as well as money used in concentration camps; and bills made of linen and silk. Mon.-Fri. 7:30-noon and 1-4. Donations. Phone (297) 828831.

PALM BEACH, 4 mi. (7 km) n.w. of Oranjestad, is known for its transparent water. Coral reefs, sea ferns and fish are visible at considerable depths. Buses run daily between Oranjestad and Palm Beach. Water sports equipment can be rented at most aquatic facilities along Palm Beach.

ST. ANNE CHURCH, in Noord, dates from 1776 and has an altar of carved oak. Since the altar was constructed for a church in Curaçao and shipped to St. Anne's by accident, the ceiling had to be cut to accommodate the structure. Adjoining the church is a cemetery with tombs painted in pastel colors and adorned with flowers and various mementos. The chapel of Alto Vista, established in 1750, is a few miles north.

WILHELMINA PARK, off L.G. Smith Boulevard, was created in 1955 in honor of the visit of Queen Juliana and Prince Bernhard of the Netherlands. A statue of Queen Mother Wilhelmina of the Netherlands, sculpted of white marble in Italy by Arnoldo Lualdi, dominates the plaza. The park is particularly beautiful when the tropical foliage is blooming in June, September and

October. Visitors can rest on benches shaded by palm trees.

SAN NICOLAS (B-2)

San Nicolas, 12 miles (19 km) southeast of Oranjestad, is Aruba's second largest city. Known as the island's Sunrise Side, San Nicolas was once a bustling company town when Lago Oil and Transport operated 1924-85. The refining of oil is again playing a part in Aruba's economy: In 1990 Coastal Corp. reopened the oil refinery. A Dutch marine camp is off Commanders Bay near the fishing village of Savaneta.

Charlie's Bar, in operation since 1941, once had a colorful reputation as a hangout for rowdy sailors and oil refinery workers. The establishment is known for its amazing variety of bric-a-brac. Pictures, business cards and license plates grace the walls of the bar while the hundreds of items hanging from the ceiling include hats, Frisbees, an inner tube, a life jacket and even shirts from the Boston Braves and Brooklyn Dodgers.

A section of San Nicolas' main street has been converted to a picturesque promenade with shops containing souvenirs, crafts and local snacks. There is a small natural bridge, not to be confused with the bridge at Andicuri, east of Seroe Colorado at the island's southern tip near Colorado Point. To view the bridge follow the road to its terminus, then hike approximately 200 feet (61 m) down old lava and coral formations.

LODGINGS & RESTAURANTS

ORANJESTAD—12,000

LODGINGS

AMERICANA ARUBA BEACH RESORT & CASINO
◆◆◆ *Resort Hotel*

12/20-4/18	$340-400	XP $50
12/1-12/19 & 4/19-11/30	$200-220	XP $50

Location: 7.6 km nw at Palm Beach. 83 J.E. Irausquin Blvd (PO Box 218, DUTCH CARIBBEAN). Fax: 297/8-63191. **Terms:** F12; Reserv deposit, 14 day notice; 11% service charge. **Facility:** 419 rooms. 2 hi-rise towers. Rooms with balcony. Attractive public areas. 9 stories; interior corridors; beachfront; beach; 2 lighted tennis courts. **Services:** giftshop. Fee: massage. **Recreation:** swimming, scuba diving, snorkeling. Fee: sailboating, scuba equipment. Rental: boats, paddleboats, snorkeling equipment. **Cards:** AE, DI, DS, MC, VI.

(297/8-64500

ARUBA MARRIOTT RESORT & STELLARIS CASINO
◆◆◆◆ *Hotel*

12/23-4/7	$335-500	XP $40
12/1-12/22, 4/8-4/24 & 10/1-11/30	$230-300	XP $40
4/25-9/30	$185-250	XP $40

Location: 10 km nw on Palm Beach. L.G. Smith Blvd 101. Fax: 297/8-60649. **Terms:** F18; Check-in 4 pm; reserv deposit, 14 day notice; 11% service charge. **Facility:** 413 rooms. Handsome guest rooms, public facilities & casino. All rooms with mini coolers. Attentive staff. Fine beach. All inclusive plans avail; 8 stories; interior/exterior corridors; oceanview; off site parking only; beach. **Services:** giftshop. Fee: massage. **Recreation:** swimming, charter fishing. Fee: boating, fishing, sailboating, scuba diving/snorkeling & equipment, waterskiing, windsurfing. Rental: paddleboats. **Cards:** AE, DI, DS, MC, VI.

(297/8-69000

AAA **SAVE** **ARUBA PALM BEACH RESORT & CASINO**
◆◆◆ *Hotel*

1/6-4/7	$195-495	XP $20
12/22-1/5	$220-395	XP $20
12/1-12/21 & 4/8-11/30	$125-375	XP $20

Location: 7.3 km nw at Palm Beach. J.E. Irausquin Blvd 79. Fax: 297/8-61941. **Terms:** F19; Check-in 4 pm; reserv deposit, 14 day notice, 7 day off season; 11% service charge; MAP avail; package plans. **Facility:** 186 rooms. Hi-rise hotel with nicely landscaped grounds. Meets AAA guest room security requirements. 13 apartments, $495; $375 off season; 8 stories; interior/exterior corridors; oceanfront; beach, wading pool; 2 lighted tennis courts. **Dining:** Restaurant, coffee shop; 7 am-11 pm; deli, 8 am-10 pm; $10-$25; cocktails. **Services:** giftshop. **Recreation:** swimming, scuba diving, snorkeling. Rental: scuba & snorkeling equipment. **Cards:** AE, CB, DI, DS, MC, VI.

((297)8-63900

ARUBA SONESTA RESORT AT SEAPORT VILLAGE
◆◆◆ *Hotel*

12/23-4/12	$240-330	XP $30
12/1-12/22 & 4/13-11/30	$145-235	XP $30

Location: In town, opposite the Port; adjacent to Seaport Village Mall. L.G. Smith Blvd #9. Fax: 297/8-3-4389. **Terms:** F12; Reserv deposit, 14 day notice; 11% service charge. **Facility:** 300 rooms. Contemporary, in town hotel connected to a shopping mall & conference center. Beautiful, secluded island beach avail. Launch every 10 minutes. 6 stories; interior corridors; 1 tennis court. **Services:** giftshop. **Recreation:** scuba diving. Fee: snorkeling, windsurfing. Rental: paddleboats, scuba equipment. **Cards:** AE, DI, DS, MC, VI.

(297/8-3-6000

ARUBA SONESTA SUITES AT SEAPORT VILLAGE
◆◆◆ *Apartment Hotel*

12/21-4/12	$300-400	XP $30
12/1-12/20 & 4/13-11/30	$205-305	XP $30

Location: In town; at Seaport Village. L.G. Smith Blvd 9. **Fax:** 297/8-25317. **Terms:** F12; Check-in 4 pm; reserv deposit, 14 day notice; 11% service charge. **Facility:** 250 rooms. On the southern shoreline of Aruba. In Seaport Village Complex Marina. All rooms with balcony, some with ocean view. Launch to beautiful, secluded island beach. 5 stories; interior corridors; beach; 1 tennis court. Fee: marina. **Services:** giftshop. **Recreation:** swimming, scuba diving, snorkeling. Fee: charter fishing, snorkeling equipment. Rental: boats, sailboats, scuba equipment. **All Rooms:** kitchens. **Cards:** AE, DI, DS, MC, VI.

(297/8-36000

BEST WESTERN BUCUTI BEACH RESORT
◆◆◆ *Motor Inn*

12/22-3/30	$200-260	XP $10
12/1-12/21 & 3/31-11/30	$120-155	XP $10

Location: 3.8 km w on Eagle Beach. J.E. Irausquin Blvd 55B (PO Box 1299). **Fax:** 297/8-25272. **Terms:** F12; Reserv deposit, 7 day notice; 11% service charge; BP, MAP avail. **Facility:** 63 rooms. Beachfront grounds. Beautiful white sandy beach. Balcony or patio, hairdryer & iron. Meets AAA guest room security requirements. 2-3 stories; interior corridors; beach. **Dining:** Restaurant; 7 am-10:30 pm; $7-$25; cocktails; mini market. **Recreation:** swimming; open air exercise room. **Some Rooms:** 5 kitchens. **Cards:** AE, DI, DS, MC, VI. **Special Amenities:** Free newspaper.

((297)8-31100

BEST WESTERN MANCHEBO BEACH RESORT HOTEL
◆◆◆ *Motor Inn*

12/20-4/17	$175-190	XP $15
12/1-12/19 & 4/18-11/30	$120-135	XP $15

Location: 3.6 km w. 55 J.E. Irausquin Blvd (PO Box 564, DUTCH CARIBBEAN). **Fax:** 297/8-33667. **Terms:** F16; Reserv deposit, 7 day notice, 3 day off season; 11% service charge; BP, MAP avail. **Facility:** 71 rooms. Beachfront grounds. Wide stretch of white sand beach. All rooms with ocean, pool or garden view. Meets AAA guest room security requirements. 1-2 stories; exterior corridors; beach. **Dining:** Dining room, coffee shop; 7 am-11 pm; Beach Bar & Grill 11:30 am-5 pm; $13-$30; cocktails. **Services:** giftshop. **Recreation:** swimming. **Cards:** AE, DI, MC, VI. **Special Amenities:** Free newspaper and preferred room (subject to availability with advanced reservations).

((297)8-23444

CARIBBEAN TOWN BEACH RESORT
◆◆ *Motor Inn*

12/22-4/5	$134-225	XP $10
12/1-12/21 & 4/6-11/30	$101-156	XP $10

Location: 2.4 km nw of airport terminal. L.G. Smith Blvd 2. **Fax:** 297/8-33208. **Terms:** F16; Reserv deposit, 3 day notice; 12% service charge; AP, BP, MAP avail. **Facility:** 63 rooms. Beach across road. Landscaped pool patio. Meets AAA guest room security requirements. 4 two-bedroom units. 1-2 stories; interior/exterior corridors. **Dining:** Coffee shop; 6 am-1 am; $4-$20; cocktails. **Recreation:** Fee: charter fishing. **Some Rooms:** 44 efficiencies. **Cards:** AE, DI, MC, VI. **Special Amenities:** Early check-in/late check-out and free room upgrade (subject to availability with advanced reservations).

((297)8-23380

COSTA LINDA BEACH RESORT
◆◆◆ *Suite Hotel*

12/21-1/1	$595
1/2-4/11	$489
12/1-12/20 & 4/12-11/30	$298

Location: 3.8 km w on Eagle Beach. 59 J.E. Irausquin Blvd (PO Box 1345, DUTCH CARIBBEAN). **Fax:** 297/8-36040. **Terms:** Check-in 4 pm; reserv deposit, 14 day notice, 7 day in summer; handling fee imposed; 11% service charge. **Facility:** 155 rooms. Beachfront grounds. Beautifully decorated 2-bedroom suites with Roman tub in master bedrooms, kitchen, living room & spacious balcony or terrace. Meets AAA guest room security requirements. 139 two-bedroom units, 16 three-bedroom units. Rates for up to 6 persons; 5 stories; exterior corridors; beach; 2 tennis courts (Fee: 2 lighted). **Services:** giftshop. **Recreation:** swimming, scuba diving, snorkeling. Rental: scuba & snorkeling equipment. **All Rooms:** kitchens. **Cards:** AE, DI, MC, VI

(297/8-38000

DIVI ARUBA BEACH RESORT
◆◆◆ *Complex*

12/19-1/1 & 2/6-2/26	$275-350	XP $25
1/2-2/5 & 2/27-4/9	$250-325	XP $25
12/1-12/18 & 4/10-11/30	$170-245	XP $25

Location: 3.2 km w on Druif Beach. 45 J.E. Irausquin Blvd. **Fax:** 297/8-34002. **Terms:** F12; Reserv deposit, 14 day notice; 11% service charge; BP, MAP avail. **Facility:** 203 rooms. Rooms with Spanish decor. All with balcony or patio. 1-3 stories, no elevator; exterior corridors; beachfront; beach; 1 tennis court. **Dining:** Dining room, restaurant; terrace dining; 7 am-11, noon-10 pm; $20-$33; cocktails; dancing, casino adjacent, 15% service charge. **Services:** giftshop. **Recreation:** swimming. Fee: windsurfing. **Some Rooms:** whirlpools. **Cards:** AE, DI, MC, VI. **Special Amenities:** Free room upgrade (subject to availability with advanced reservations). *(See color ad p 53)*

((297)8-23300

HOLIDAY INN-ARUBA BEACH RESORT & CASINO
◆◆◆ *Resort Hotel*

12/22-3/29	$190-250	XP $25
12/1-12/21 & 3/30-11/30	$100-140	XP $20

Location: 8 km nw; Palm Beach. 230 J.E. Irausquin Blvd. **Fax:** 297/8-6-5165. **Terms:** F18; Reserv deposit, 3 day notice; 11% service charge. **Facility:** 600 rooms. Beachfront grounds; rooms with balcony or terrace. Meets AAA guest room security requirements. 6 stories; interior corridors; beach; 4 tennis courts (Fee: 2 lighted). **Services:** giftshop. Fee: massage. **Recreation:** swimming, scuba diving, snorkeling. Fee: fishing, waterskiing. Rental: boats, scuba & snorkeling equipment. **Cards:** AE, DI, DS, MC, VI.

(297/8-6-3600

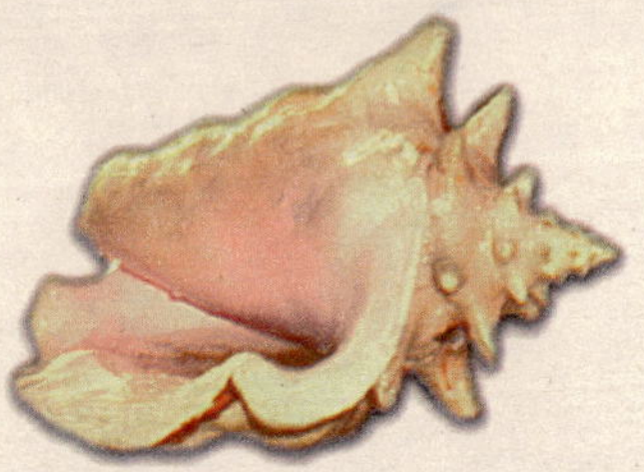

HYATT REGENCY ARUBA RESORT & CASINO
◆◆◆◆ *Resort Hotel*

All Year	$340-495	XP $30-60

Location: 7.8 km nw at Palm Beach. J.E. Irausquin 85. **Fax:** 297/8-6-5478. **Terms:** F18; Reserv deposit, 30 day notice; 11% service charge; MAP avail; package plans. **Facility:** 360 rooms. Beachfront hi-rise hotel. Beautifully appointed guest rooms. Extensive tropically landscaped pool & gardens. Meets AAA guest room security requirements. 9 stories; interior corridors; beach, sauna, whirlpools; 2 lighted tennis courts; playground. Fee: golf privileges. **Dining:** 4 restaurants, coffee shop; poolside dining; 7 am-2 am; $10-$30; cocktails; also, Las Ruinas del Mar, see separate listing. **Services:** giftshop. Fee: massage. **Recreation:** swimming, charter fishing, fishing, scuba diving, snorkeling. Fee: boating, windsurfing, banana boats, catamaran rides; video cassette player by request. Rental: paddleboats, sailboats, scuba & snorkeling equipment. **Some Rooms:** whirlpools. **Cards:** AE, CB, DI, DS, JC, MC, VI.

((297)8-6-1234

LA CABANA ALL SUITE BEACH RESORT & CASINO
◆◆◆ *Suite Hotel*

12/20-1/3 & 1/25-2/28	$520	XP $20
1/4-1/24 & 3/1-4/11	$475	XP $20
12/1-12/19 & 4/12-11/30	$300	XP $15

Location: 4 km w on Druif Beach. 250 L J Irausquin Blvd (PO Box 4273). **Fax:** 297/8-70844. **Terms:** F11; Check-in 4 pm; reserv deposit, 14 day notice, 3 in summer; handling fee imposed; 11% service charge. **Facility:** 803 rooms. Along tranquil powder white sand of Eaple Beach. Meets AAA guest room security requirements. 40 two-bedroom units, 20 three-bedroom units. 3-bedroom, $715-$855; $655 off season; 4-5 stories; interior/exterior corridors; oceanview; beach access; racquetball courts, 5 lighted tennis courts; playground. **Services:** giftshop. Fee: massage. **Recreation:** swimming, charter fishing; jogging. Fee: boating, fishing, sailboating, scuba diving/snorkeling & equipment, windsurfing. **All Rooms:** kitchens. **Cards:** AE, MC, VI.

(297/8-79000

RADISSON ARUBA CARIBBEAN RESORT AND CASINO

Hotel

12/21-1/3	$210-380	XP $45
1/4-4/14	$175-275	XP $45
12/1-12/20, 4/15-5/31 & 10/1-11/30	$130-205	XP $45
6/1-9/30	$120-185	XP $45

Under major renovation. **Location:** 7.6 km nw at Palm Beach. 81 J. E. Irausquin Blvd. Fax: 297/8-6-3260. **Terms:** F17; Reserv deposit, 3 day notice; 11% service charge; BP, MAP avail; package plans. **Facility:** 372 rooms. Beachfront. Rooms with balcony or patio. Ocean &/or garden view. Property closed for major renovations. Scheduled to open December, 1998; 6 stories; interior corridors; beach; 4 tennis courts (Fee: 4 lighted). **Dining:** 2 restaurants, coffee shop; 6:30 am-11 pm; $15-$50; cocktails; casino. **Services:** giftshop. **Recreation:** swimming, scuba diving, snorkeling; casino. Fee: fishing, scuba equipment, waterskiing, windsurfing. Rental: boats, sailboats, snorkeling equipment. **Cards:** AE, DI, DS, MC, VI. *(See color ad p 54)*

((297)8-6-6555

TAMARIJN ARUBA BEACH RESORT

Motor Inn

12/19-1/3 & 2/9-2/24	$500	XP $180-185
1/4-2/8 & 2/25-4/17	$320-400	XP $135-160
12/1-12/18 & 4/18-11/30	$300	XP $130-135

Location: 3.2 km w on Druif Beach. 41 J.E. Irausquin Blvd. Fax: 297/8-34002. **Terms:** Reserv deposit, 30 day notice; handling fee imposed; $11 service charge. **Facility:** 236 rooms. All rooms face beach, some with balcony. Casual atmosphere. 2 stories; exterior corridors; beach; 2 lighted tennis courts. **Dining:** 2 dining rooms, restaurant, coffee shop; 7 am-11, noon-3 & 6-10 pm; $13-$26; cocktails. **Services:** giftshop. **Recreation:** swimming, canoeing, sailboating, scuba diving/snorkeling & equipment, windsurfing, sunfish sailing, snorkeling lessons, beginning windsurfing boards. **Cards:** AE, DI, DS, MC, VI. **Special Amenities: Preferred room (subject to availability with advanced reservations).**

((297)8-23300

WYNDHAM ARUBA BEACH RESORT & CASINO

Resort Hotel

1/3-4/4	$229-266	XP $26
12/1-12/19, 4/5-5/1 & 10/16-11/30	$161-199	XP $26
5/2-10/15	$139-161	XP $26

Location: 7.2 km nw at Palm Beach. 77 J.E. Irausquin #77 Blvd (PO Box 363, DUTCH CARIBBEAN). Fax: 297/8-68217. **Terms:** F12; Open 12/1-12/19 & 1/3-11/30; 11% service charge. **Facility:** 444 rooms. Attractive pool & beach area. Meets AAA guest room security requirements. 14 stories; interior corridors; oceanfront; beach; 1 lighted tennis court. **Services:** giftshop. Fee: massage. **Recreation:** swimming, charter fishing. Fee: fishing, scuba diving/snorkeling & equipment, waterskiing, windsurfing; bicycles. Rental: boats, paddleboats. **Cards:** AE, DI, MC, VI.

((297)8-64466

RESTAURANTS

BUCCANEER RESTAURANT

Continental   **D** $12-$23

Location: 0.5 km e from Americana Aruba Beach Resort & Casino; 0.5 km s following signs. Gasparito 11-C. **Hours:** 5:30 pm-10 pm. Closed: 12/25 & Sun. **Features:** casual dress; children's menu; cocktails & lounge. Very popular dining in a ship's cabin with windows of saltwater aquariums. 15 % service charge. Reservations not accepted. **Cards:** AE, DI, MC, VI.

(297/8-66172

CHALET SUISSE RESTAURANT

Continental   **D** $18-$30

Location: 4.7 km w at Eagle Beach. 246 J. E. Irausquin Blvd. **Hours:** 6 pm-10:30 pm. Closed: 1/1 & Sun. **Reservations:** suggested. **Features:** semi-formal attire; children's menu; cocktails; a la carte. International cuisine with a Swiss touch. Featuring US prime meat & fresh seafood. Chef/owner. **Cards:** AE, DS, MC, VI.

(297/8-75054

CHEZ MATHILDE   *Historical*

French   **L** $18-$30 **D** $22-$40

Location: Downtown; one street inland from the Seaport shopping area. Havenstraat 23. **Hours:** 11:30 am-2:30 & 6-11 pm, Sun from 6 pm. Closed: 1/1 & 5/1. **Reservations:** required. **Features:** semi-formal attire; cocktails; entertainment; street parking; a la carte. Classic French cuisine served in romantic, elegant Arubian house circa 1870's. Intimate dining rooms, one with garden atmosphere. 15% service charge. **Cards:** AE, DI, MC, VI.

(297/8-34968

EL GAUCHO

Ethnic   **L** $16-$25 **D** $16-$25

Location: Downtown; 0.3 mi s of Seaport Village. St. Wilhelminastraat 80. **Hours:** 11:30 am-2 & 5:30-11 pm. Closed: 1/1, 12/25, 12/31 & Sun. **Reservations:** required; for dinner. **Features:** casual dress; cocktails; street parking. Excellent charcoal grilled churrasco steak, quality meat & fresh seafood capably served in cozy dining room with a touch of the Pampas. 15 years in operation. **Cards:** AE, DI, MC, VI.

(297/8-23677

LAS RUINAS DEL MAR

Continental   **D** $17-$30

Location: 7.8 km nw at Palm Beach; in the Hyatt Regency Aurba Resort & Casino. J. E. Irausquin Blvd 85. **Hours:** 5:30 pm-10:30 pm, Sun brunch 10 am-3 pm. **Reservations:** suggested. **Features:** children's menu; cocktails; a la carte. Mediterranean cuisine. Fine dining in replica of ruins of the Bushiribana Gold Mill. **Cards:** AE, CB, DI, JC, MC, VI.

(297/8-61234

L'ESCALE

Continental   **D** $22-$30

Location: Downtown; opposite the Port, adjacent to Seaport Village Mall; in Aruba Sonesta Resort at Seaport Village. **Hours:** 6:30 pm-11 pm. **Reservations:** suggested. **Features:** cocktails & lounge; entertainment; a la carte. Elegant atmosphere. Overlooking waterfront. 15% service charge. Late night lite menu, 11 pm-3 am, served in lounge. **Cards:** AE, DI, DS, MC, VI.

(297/8-36000

TUSCANY

Italian   **D** $16-$29

Location: 10 km nw on Palm Beach; in Aruba Marriott Resort & Stellaris Casino. L.G. Smith Blvd #101. **Hours:** 6 pm-11 pm. **Reservations:** required. **Features:** children's menu; cocktails; entertainment; a la carte. Excellent Northern Italian cuisine served in romantic, very well decorated dining room. **Cards:** AE, DI, DS, MC, VI.

(297/86-9000

ENJOYING SEPARATE VACATIONS. TOGETHER.

Abaco

She trails off. He sails off.

Eleuthera

He snoozes. She snorkels.

Grand Bahama Island

She bargains. He birdies.

Exuma

He dives. She tans.

Nassau/Paradise Island

They dance 'til dawn.

THE ISLANDS OF THE BAHAMAS

It Just Keeps Getting Better®

Call your local AAA or CAA travel agency • http://www.gobahamas.com

The Bahamas

THE SEMITROPICAL BAHAMAS, where turquoise waters flow along miles of white sand beaches, include more than 2,000 cays, islets and rocks. Of the approximately 700 islands, 22 of the largest ones are inhabited. Beginning 50 miles (80 km) from the Florida coast, The Bahamas form a 760-mile (1,223-km) arc through the Atlantic, creating a natural barrier across the eastern gateway to the Gulf of Mexico. The island of Bimini is closest to Florida, while the southernmost island, Inagua, is 60 miles (97 km) from Haiti.

The two most popular tourist destinations in The Bahamas are the city of Nassau/Paradise Island and Grand Bahama Island. The islands' capital, Nassau, on New Providence Island, is rich in colonial history and charm and offers varied opportunities for sports activities, shopping and sightseeing. Prestigious Paradise Island, a playground of the rich, is just across the bridge from Nassau. Freeport, the modern resort-residential complex on Grand Bahama Island, is more cosmopolitan and sports oriented than Nassau. Grand Bahama was developed more recently than Nassau and has become a favored resort, due in part to its nearness to Florida. About 80 percent of the people vacationing in The Bahamas are from the United States.

The Out Islands, known the world over for game fishing, scuba diving, sailing, pristine beaches and emerald-blue seas, extend as far as you can see. There are resorts in areas noted for their lack of commercial development, and where only the silver-top thatch palms and flamingoes claim residence. The principal Out Islands are Abaco, Eluthera and Exema. Abaco has naturally protected waters and dozens of offshore cays that make them a favorite with yachtsmen and fishing enthusiasts. Here there are excellent marinas, guides and boats for hire, and a championship golf course.

Just off the island of Eleuthera, with its picturesque little villages and exclusive resorts, are the charming settlements of Harbour Island, with its pink sandy beaches, and Spanish Wells, which in the old days served as a watering hole for Spanish galleons. The Exumas have many cays, most of which can be reached only by boat.

History, Government and Economy

The Bahamas claim the distinction of being Christopher Columbus' first New World discovery. In 1492 he stepped ashore on an island originally called *Guanahani* and renamed it San Salvador. The Arawak Indians, who then populated the islands, were soon sent by the Spaniards to labor in the mines and sugar mills of Cuba and Hispaniola. However, the Spaniards did not settle here, and in 1629 King Charles I of England granted the islands to Sir Robert Heath, attorney general of England.

A group of English merchants and pioneers from Bermuda, known as the Eleutheran Adventurers, then came seeking religious freedom.

They colonized Eleuthera in 1648 and attempted to establish the first republic in the New World. This attempt at colonization and other settlements which followed were, for the most part, unsuccessful. As a result, The Bahamas were soon overrun by pirates such as Blackbeard and Avery, who were finally routed in 1718 by Capt. Woodes Rogers, the first royal governor.

Another wave of immigration occurred after the American Revolution, when Loyalist refugees fled to The Bahamas, taking their slaves with them. England ruled until 1782, when Spain captured the islands; however, the Treaty of Versailles returned them to England once again in 1783.

Throughout The Bahamas' turbulent history their strategically positioned cays and islets played a vital role in international intrigues. Not only were The Bahamas a formidable hideout for pirates, but Confederate blockade runners during the American Civil War and bootleggers during America's Prohibition Era also exploited the islands' proximity to Florida in efforts to smuggle contraband into the United States.

From 1718 to 1969 a governor was appointed by the British Crown; after 1969 the appointment was made in consultation with The Bahamas Government. On July 10, 1973, the islands became an independent sovereign nation headed by a prime minister. Now a member of the British Commonwealth of Nations, the islands retain many legacies from the years of British rule, including the distinctive Bahamian accent and two popular spectator sports—cricket and rugby.

SHOPPING

Shoppers have a field day exploring the multitude of stores and boutiques lining the streets of Nassau and Freeport. Shops also are found just over the bridge on Paradise Island, at Cable Beach and at shopping malls in the outlying areas. Bay Street is the center of activity in Nassau, where the merchandise consists of imported European goods: perfumes, brass, leather goods, cameras, cashmere, candies, jewelry, china, porcelain, crystal, glass, figurines, linens and designer and sportswear fashions to name just a few. Duty-free prices, made available for the first time in 1992, make these items all the more attractive. Available at discount prices are the island's own liqueur, Nassau Royale, and local banana rums and coconut liqueurs.

Nassau's straw market on Bay Street specializes in island handicrafts made not only from straw but also from wood and a variety of shells, including conch and coconut. Items made from tortoiseshell are banned from importation into the United States under the Convention on International Trade in Endangered Species of Wild Fauna and Flora. Bargaining is expected in the straw market but not in Nassau's shops. Most shops are open Mon.-Sat. 9-5, Sun. noon-5. Banking hours are Mon.-Thurs. 9:30-3, Fri. 9:30-5.

Freeport's International Bazaar, a 10-acre (4-hectare) village of shops and restaurants, offers goods and cuisine representing many nations.

THINGS TO KNOW

AREA: 5,380 square miles (13,934 sq km).

POPULATION: 255,100.

LANGUAGE: English.

CAPITAL: Nassau.

GOVERNMENT: Independent sovereign. Member of the British Commonwealth of Nations.

TIME ZONE: Eastern. DST.

UNIT OF CURRENCY: Bahamian dollar, $1=1 Bahamian dollar. U.S. currency is widely accepted throughout the islands.

ELECTRICITY: 110-220 volts, 60 cycles AC; voltage varies with location.

MINIMUM AGE FOR GAMBLING: 21.

CARS: U.S. license valid for 3 months; drive on left.

IMMIGRATION REQUIREMENTS: Proof of U.S. citizenship (valid passport, original or certified copy of birth certificate and a government-authorized photo ID) and return or through ticket are required. Eight-month stay limitation.

Departure tax $15 US.

FOR FURTHER INFORMATION:
Bahamas Tourist Office
19495 Biscayne Blvd., #809
Miami, FL 33180
(305) 932-0051
(800) 422-4262
Bahamas Ministry of Tourism
P.O. Box N3701 Market Plaza, Bay Street
Nassau, New Providence, Bahamas
(242) 322-7501
Grand Bahama Tourist Office
International Bazaar
Freeport, Grand Bahama, Bahamas
(242) 352-8044

HOLIDAYS: Jan. 1; Good Friday; Easter Monday; Whit Monday (8th Monday after Easter); Labour Day, June (1st Fri.); Independence Day, July 10; Emancipation Day, Aug. (1st Mon.); Discovery Day, Oct. 12; Dec. 25; Boxing Day, Dec. 26.

Boutiques are found in some hotels, and handicrafts are sold in villages on the Out Islands.

FOOD AND DRINK

With the exception of fruit, vegetables and fish, most food is imported. Many restaurants and hotels feature European, Chinese, Polynesian, Japanese and American cuisines. But Bahamian specialties should not be overlooked: Dishes include peas and rice, lobster, grouper cutlets, fried jack, conch chowder and fritters, complemented by a variety of tropical fruits. Rum-raisin ice cream, guava duff or a coconut tart round off the meal. Tap water is usually safe to drink; bottled water is widely available. Milk is pasteurized.

Graycliff Manor in Nassau, reputedly built by a successful pirate, is currently as renowned for its jet-set clientele as for its cuisine. Buena Vista, also in a manor house, is another premier restaurant in Nassau. Café Martinique on Paradise Island is one of the most popular restaurants in The Bahamas.

Street vendors just off Bay Street in Nassau at Arawak Cay, provide an array of local specialties, including raw conch salad. The Bamboo Shack and Dirty's, on Nassau Street, serve a variety of take-out orders; cracked conch with hot sauce is a treat.

Prices for meals are slightly higher during the winter season, but most hotels in Nassau offer a modified American plan, which includes breakfast and dinner as an additional option. On the whole, native dishes are usually the least expensive. A 15-percent service charge is added automatically to the bill.

SPORTS AND AMUSEMENTS

Local and international yachting regattas, golf and tennis tournaments, cricket, rugby and squash are only a few of the activities available in The Bahamas. That golf ranks high in popularity is verified by the number of 18-hole public golf courses on New Providence Island, including Cable Beach Golf Course, South Ocean Golf and Beach Resort and Paradise Island Golf Course.

Grand Bahama Island boasts the most 18-hole courses, including those at The Bahamas Princess Resort and Country Club, the Fortune Hill Golf and Country Club and the Lucayan Golf and Country Club. Another 18-hole course is the Treasure Cay Golf Club on Great Abaco Island. Most hotels have tennis courts and information about bicycling and horseback riding.

Though landlubbers enjoy their share of activities, water sports captivate the majority of island travelers. The numerous coves along the beaches of New Providence Island create natural pools ideal for swimming and snorkeling. The 142-mile (227-km) underwater coral reef known for its "blue holes," freshwater springs that well to the surface, offers excellent scuba diving. Paradise Island boasts one of the finest beaches in The Bahamas. Fishing in The Bahamas is good, and light-tackle fishermen are amply rewarded.

Peterson Cay National Park, some 15 miles east of Freeport, offers excellent opportunities for snorkeling and diving in a pristine setting and is accessible by boat only.

The trade winds ensure fine sailing conditions all year; boats and equipment for sailing, parasailing, fishing, water skiing, windsurfing, snorkeling, scuba diving and spear fishing can be rented from charter firms at the major marinas and from the docks of many waterfront hotels. Hotels that offer parasailing are found in Nassau and Paradise Island, New Providence; Freeport and Lucaya, Grand Bahama Island; and Cockburn Town, San Salvador Island.

An informative publication for those interested in bareboat charters is the "Yachtsman's Guide to The Bahamas," available at many yachting supply stores, marinas and bookstores in The Bahamas. The 1- or 2-hour scuba diving lessons offered throughout the islands are usually not enough preparation for the sport; you should take a complete course in advance. One of the best places to learn diving is at the Underwater Explorers Society (UNEXSO), in the Grand Bahama's Port Lucaya area, home base of a prominent society of diving experts.

The Bahamas Ministry of Tourism publishes a series of "Sports Holiday" brochures covering in detail such activities as golf, tennis, scuba diving, snorkeling, fishing and boating. These brochures can be obtained from The Bahamas Ministry of Tourism, Market Plaza, Bay Street, P.O. Box N-3701, Nassau, Bahamas, or from The Bahamas Tourist Office *(see Things To Know box)*.

Those who prefer indoor recreation will find not only a bowling alley in Nassau, but also nightclubs and casinos on New Providence, Paradise Island and Grand Bahama. Hotel nightclubs and restaurants usually sponsor dancing and after-dinner entertainment. King & Knights II in New Providence specializes in native shows. The Out Island hotels occasionally feature calypso and steel-drum bands. First-run American films are shown in New Providence and Grand Bahama theaters.

Visitors in search of Lady Luck might find her at The Princess Casino in Freeport on Grand Bahama Island, the Paradise Island Casino on Paradise Island or the Nassau Marriott Crystal Palace Casino in Nassau.

Lively festivals and tournaments are held throughout the year. For the Junkanoo Parade, held December 26 and January 1, residents don colorful crepe paper costumes and start singing and dancing on Nassau's Bay Street at 4 a.m. Miniature versions of Junkanoo are held at various hotels year-round.

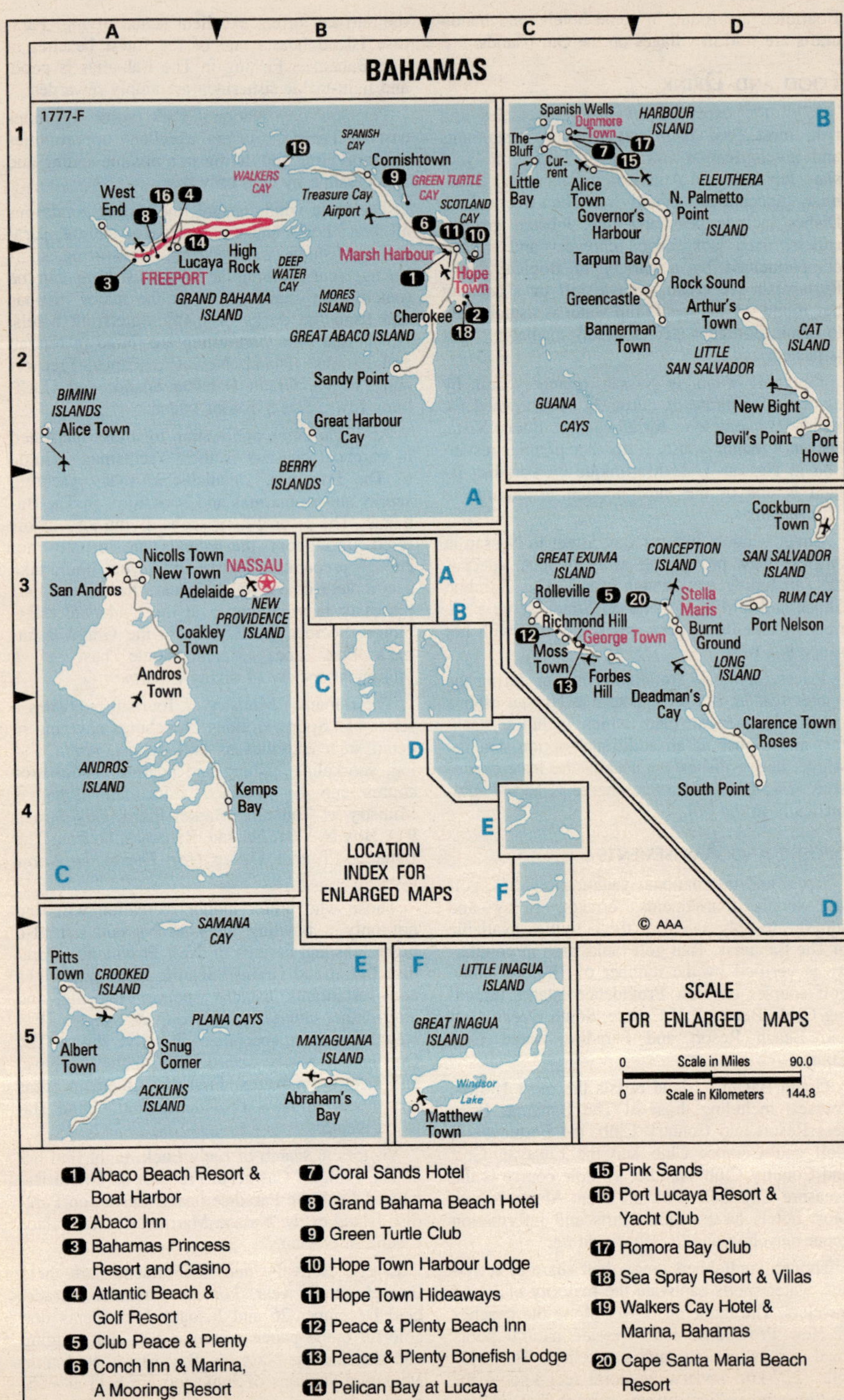

1 Abaco Beach Resort & Boat Harbor	**11** Hope Town Hideaways
2 Abaco Inn	**12** Peace & Plenty Beach Inn
3 Bahamas Princess Resort and Casino	**13** Peace & Plenty Bonefish Lodge
4 Atlantic Beach & Golf Resort	**14** Pelican Bay at Lucaya
5 Club Peace & Plenty	**15** Pink Sands
6 Conch Inn & Marina, A Moorings Resort	**16** Port Lucaya Resort & Yacht Club
7 Coral Sands Hotel	**17** Romora Bay Club
8 Grand Bahama Beach Hotel	**18** Sea Spray Resort & Villas
9 Green Turtle Club	**19** Walkers Cay Hotel & Marina, Bahamas
10 Hope Town Harbour Lodge	**20** Cape Santa Maria Beach Resort

EXCURSIONS AND SIGHTSEEING

Popular excursions include glass-bottom boat trips, which depart from the Prince George Dock in Nassau and the Lucayan Bay Hotel on Grand Bahama Island, or swimming and snorkeling cruises around Nassau Island and to Blue Lagoon Island aboard catamarans such as the *Tropic Bird* and *Calypso*. Several yacht trips depart from the Nassau Yacht Haven for excursions to nearby cays. Views of the underwater world around Nassau are offered daily aboard the *Seaworld Explorer*, a submarine that operates out of New Mermaid Marina.

East End Adventures offers all-day tours which include a 54-mile drive through pine forests and along deserted beaches with a hike to an inland blue hole and caverns and ending with a 6-mile speed boat ride to Sweeting's Cay. Phone (242) 373-6662.

The tour buses that leave from the major hotels are convenient and economical ways to tour Nassau Island. A pleasant 2-hour drive might include stops at such sites as the Queen's Staircase, Government House, Ardastra Gardens and forts Fincastle, Montagu and Charlotte.

TRANSPORTATION

Nassau and Grand Bahama islands are accessible by air from the East Coast and the Midwest on many major carriers. American Eagle, Bahamasair, Pan Am AirBridge (which flies amphibious planes), Delta, Continental Connection/ Gulfstream International, USAirways, USAirways Express and others depart daily from Miami. Direct commuter service to the Out Islands is available from Fort Lauderdale, Miami, Orlando and Palm Beach. Many cruise services travel from Miami, Port Everglades and Port Canaveral to Nassau and Freeport on a once- or twice-weekly basis.

Some of the large islands have bus service. Bicycles and motor scooters rent by the hour, day or longer. For more luxurious transportation, chauffeur-driven limousines can be hired in Nassau and Freeport. A quaint way to see the sites in Nassau is by horse-drawn carriage. Metered taxis are a convenient way to get around, and the rates are regulated. There are car rental agencies in Nassau and Freeport and on Andros, Eleuthera, Great Abaco and Great Exuma. Driving is on the left side of the road.

More than 260 miles (416 km) of good roads make for pleasant motoring from downtown Nassau to almost all parts of New Providence Island; road conditions on the Out Islands have improved since 1992. Automobiles can be taken duty free to Nassau for up to 6 months. A deposit covering duty charges (between 45 and 60 percent of the car's value plus 4 percent stamp tax), in the form of a customs bond executed by a local bank, is refunded if the vehicle is removed from the commonwealth before the end of this period (*also see Customs Information, Automobiles*). A U.S. driver's license is valid for 3 months.

Island-hopping is possible by both plane and boat. Bahamasair has regularly scheduled interisland flights from Nassau. If there is not a direct flight to the island of your choice, check with the charter companies listed in the telephone directory; information also is available at hotels on the Out Islands. Cruises are another excellent way to visit various islands. Traveling by mail boat, though it might lack some comforts, is an inexpensive way to island hop. Since departures are subject to change without notice, advance arrangements with the captain are recommended.

ATTRACTION ADMISSIONS
Attraction admissions for this island are quoted in U.S. dollars.

POINTS OF INTEREST

See maps on pages 60 and 64.

ANDROS ISLAND

The largest island in The Bahamas but one of the least populous, Andros (pop. 8,200) covers 2,300 square miles (5,957 sq km) replete with stands of virgin pine that often soar to more than 70 feet. The folklore of the Seminole Indians and slaves who once inhabited the island is alive and pervasive. Legend has it that miniature creatures called chickcharnies, a type of subtropical red-eyed leprechaun, nest in pine trees and exert both good and bad influence over daily events.

Chickcharnies are not the only ones attracted to Andros; outdoors enthusiasts appreciate the island's spectacular barrier reef that borders the eastern coast. Second in size only to Australia's Great Barrier Reef, Andros' barrier reef is ideal for diving and underwater photography. Blue holes, many of which have never been explored, abound in the sea floor and offer plentiful opportunities for divers. The Tongue of the Ocean, a depression in the ocean floor between Andros and Nassau, is the site of oceanographic research. A freshwater lake harbors waterfowl and provides hunting in season.

Fishermen also are drawn to Andros, as the surrounding waters provide many varieties of sea life. The island claims to be the world's premier spot for bonefishing. The Androsia Factory at Fresh Creek produces colorful batik with exquisite designs.

Bimini Islands

Westernmost of The Bahamas, North and South Bimini (pop. 1,600) and Cat Cay lie on the northwestern edge of the Grand Bahama Bank. Filled with marlin, sailfish, wahoo, kingfish, bonito and giant bluefin tuna, the waters surrounding the Biminis offer some of the best game fishing in the world. Ernest Hemingway's fishing trips in the Biminis inspired him to write his classic story "The Old Man and the Sea." Boats and accommodations are available on both islands; fishing clubs are on Cat Cay. Offshore waters beckon scuba divers with underwater caves, reefs and sunken ships.

Eleuthera Island

Eleuthera (pop. 10,600) has been a refuge for several groups seeking religious freedom since 1648, when the Eleutheran Adventurers established the first settlement here. These settlers gave the island its name, which is derived from the Greek word *eleutheros,* meaning "free."

Settlements at Governor's Harbour and Rock Sound have contributed to Eleuthera's development as a leading family-oriented resort. Its miles of secluded beaches and quiet atmosphere are its most appealing features. The main road runs the 110-mile (176-km) length of the island. A marina and a safe harbor are on the ocean side of Rock Sound.

The settlement of Current is popular among sportsmen. Also worth seeing is the pineapple plantation in Gregory Town. Ferries connect Eleuthera with Harbour Island and Spanish Wells.

Grand Bahama Island

Only 50 miles (80 km) east of Florida, Grand Bahama (pop. 41,000) is a major tourist destination. The fourth largest island of the group, Grand Bahama covers more than 530 square miles (1,373 sq km) and is known for excellent bonefishing, reef and deep-sea fishing. The island has three 18-hole golf courses, one nine-hole course and more than 30 tennis courts. Grand Bahama's hotels, Princess Casino and other nightspots have earned it the title of "New World Riviera."

The community of West End gained notoriety during America's Prohibition Era as a jumping-off place for rum runners to the United States. Public beaches include Barbary, Churchill and Taino beaches. The Underwater Explorers Society in the Lucayan Beach area has an 18-foot-deep diver training pool and rental equipment. "The Dolphin Experience," a program offered by UNEXSO, enables visitors to swim and interact with these marine mammals.

Freeport (A-2) pop. 16,000

The resort of Freeport offers shows with top-name entertainers and artists, the International Bazaar and the Princess Casino, distinguished as one of the Western Hemisphere's largest. Outdoor enthusiasts are lured by the area's many opportunities for fishing, sailing, snorkeling, swimming, golf and tennis. Horses are available at Pinetree Stables, off Freeport's East Sunrise Highway. Freeport International Airport and the International Bazaar have information centers, which are open Mon.-Sat. 9-6.

RAND NATURE CENTER, 3 mi. (4.8 km) n.e. of the International Bazaar on E. Settler's Way, is a national park of The Bahamas and comprises 100 acres of Bahamian pine forest complete with nature trails featuring native flora. This education center displays native reptiles and birds, a flock of Caribbean flamingos and a replica of a Lucayan Indian village. The center, home to more than 120 species of birds, is an ideal spot for birdwatching. Guided tours and guided bird walks are available.

Center open Mon.-Fri., 9-4, Sat. 9-1. Guided tours are offered Mon.-Sat. at 10. Guided bird walks are offered on the first Saturday of each month at 8 a.m. Admission $5; ages 5-12, $3. Phone (242) 352-5438.

Lucaya (A-1) pop. 41,000

Lucaya is a developed resort area with a well-manicured beach and streets lined with palms and flowering shrubs. One of the highlights is Port Lucaya, a complex of more than 70 shops and restaurants housed in 12 distinctly Bahamian buildings. During the evening many of the local hotels offer a variety of entertainment programs.

GARDEN OF THE GROVES, in the center of town, is an 11-acre (4-hectare) botanical garden with more than 5,000 species of flowers, shrubs, trees and exotic plant life. A chapel and museum also are on the grounds. Garden open Tues. and Thurs.-Fri. noon-4, Sat.-Sun. 1-4. Museum $7.95, children $4.95. Garden free. Phone (242) 373-5668.

LUCAYAN NATIONAL PARK, 24 mi. (38 km) e. on Grand Bahama Hwy., consists of 40 acres of land and one of the largest explored underwater cave system in the world. Ecological zones in the park include pineland with hardwood hammocks, rocky coppice, whiteland coppice, mangrove marshes and sand dunes. Hiking trails are available. A trail leading to Ben's Cave and Burial Mound Cave features boardwalk observation decks inside of the caves. Swimming in the caves is prohibited; diving requires special permits. Ben's Cave is closed to visitors during the summer months to protect the fruit bat nurseries. Picnicking and swimming are permitted. Daily 9-4. Admission $3, under 5 free. Tickets must be purchased in advance at the Rand Nature Center. Phone (242) 352-5438.

Great Abaco Island

Great Abaco (pop. 10,000) and its boomerang-shaped chain of cays lie south and east of Grand Bahama Island. The island contains extensive farming, resort and residential areas, although large regions are still undeveloped.

Reports of sunken treasure off the southwest tip of the island have brought Great Abaco fame and modern-day explorers. Two Nassau businessmen discovered several 17th-century Spanish coins and a 72-pound silver bar, which was identified as the personal property of King Philip IV of Spain and valued at $20,000.

Many residents, descendants of Loyalists who fled the American Colonies after the Revolution, have carried on the art of shipbuilding, which was introduced here centuries ago. Artisans at Man-O-War Cay continue to build some of the finest island boats with Abaco pine. The sailmaker's loft of the Alburys is worth a visit. Marsh Harbour is the main shopping area on the island as well as the bareboat charter center of the northern Bahamas.

The Abacos' resort potential is enhanced by many secluded, safe harbors along the cays. Such activities as sailing, bonefishing and hunting for wild boar can be arranged. Among the leading vacation spots are Treasure Cay, distinguished by a multimillion-dollar development; Elbow Cay, known for its much-photographed candy-striped lighthouse; the northernmost island of Walker's Cay, a sport fishing resort with one of the largest and best equipped marinas in The Bahamas; Hope Town, a top-rated diving center; and Green Turtle Cay, which exudes an early New England atmosphere.

The Memorial Sculpture Garden, downtown New Plymouth on Green Turtle Cay, displays 30 bronze busts of famous Bahamian citizens.

ALTON LOWE MUSEUM, 1 blk. from the docks on Green Turtle Cay, contains a fine collection of carved ships models and exhibits tracing the Abacos' history and development. Mon.-Sat. 9:45-11:45 and 1:30-5; closed holidays. Donations. Phone (242) 365-4094.

WYANNIE MALONE HISTORICAL MUSEUM, 1 blk. from the post office dock at Hope Town in Elbow Cay, is in a century-old white clapboard house. Displays include historical maps, ships models and items of everyday life. Allow 30 minutes minimum. Tours of the museum can be arranged on request. Sun.-Fri. 11-3, Sat. 10:30-2:30. Admission $1. Phone (242) 366-0033, 366-0088 or 366-0107.

Great Exuma Island

The Exumas consist of 365 islands, ranging from small, uninhabited dots on the map to the two largest islands, Great Exuma and Little Exuma. At the southernmost tip of the Exuma Cays, Great Exuma (pop. 4,000) is 100 miles (160 km) long. George Town, the principal settlement, is the site of the 3-day spring Out Island Regatta, whose participants constitute one of the area's few commercial sailing fleets. The flats on the island's west side offer excellent bonefishing.

A popular excursion follows the slave route from George Town to Rolleville, a village once owned by Loyalist Lord Rolle, who, upon his death, gave freedom, the land and the name of Rolle to all the tenants. The land may never be sold, but is passed down to each succeeding generation.

EXUMA CAYS LAND AND SEA PARK stretches from Wax Cay Cut in the north to Conch Cut in the south. A bird and marine life sanctuary, the park covers 176 square miles (456 sq km) and was one of the first to include underwater areas. This vast underwater preserve attracts snorkeling and scuba enthusiasts from around the world and is accessible only by boat. Mon.-Sat. 9-noon and 1-5, Sun. 9-1. Free. Phone (242) 359-1821.

Harbour Island

Harbour Island (pop. 1,200) almost encloses the northeast tip of Eleuthera, forming a harbor 6 miles (10 km) long and 3 miles (4.8 km) wide. The island boasts 3 miles (4.8 km) of pink sand beach, the color provided by particles of shell ground against the outer reefs by the force of the sea.

Harbour Island also claims one of the oldest settlements in The Bahamas, Dunmore Town. At the northern end of the island, the town retains an Old World charm through its many restored, brightly colored homes, whose carved shutters and verandas outlined in white create a gingerbread-cottage atmosphere. Many colonial houses were built during the latter part of the 19th century; Loyalist Cottage on Bay Street

Serving the
American traveler since 1902.

dates from 1790. A pink municipal building adds the finishing touch to this picturesque town. Snorkeling, scuba diving and bonefishing are popular.

LONG ISLAND

Long Island (pop. 3,100) is almost wholly within the tropic zone. The island covers 230 square miles (596 sq km), with a width of only a half-mile (.8 km) in some places. It also is one of The Bahamas' chief agricultural islands. According to legend, when Christopher Columbus landed here he found the inhabitants living in tent-shaped buildings and sleeping in nets stretched between posts. The latter idea, adopted by his sailors, evolved into the hammock.

Interesting sites include the ruins of Gray's Plantation in Grays and two impressive churches in Clarence Town. The Stella Maris Inn stands on the island's highest point and affords superb views. The waters off the coast of Long Island are ideal for scuba diving and fishing. Regular flights from Nassau are available.

NEW PROVIDENCE ISLAND

Home to a majority of the country's population, New Providence Island is the domain of the capital city, Nassau. A prime tourist destination, the island features all the amenities associated with The Bahamas—an array of water sports, golf, tennis, nightlife, casinos, international shopping and a colorful history. The 21-mile-long (34-km), 7-mile-wide (11-km) island also is

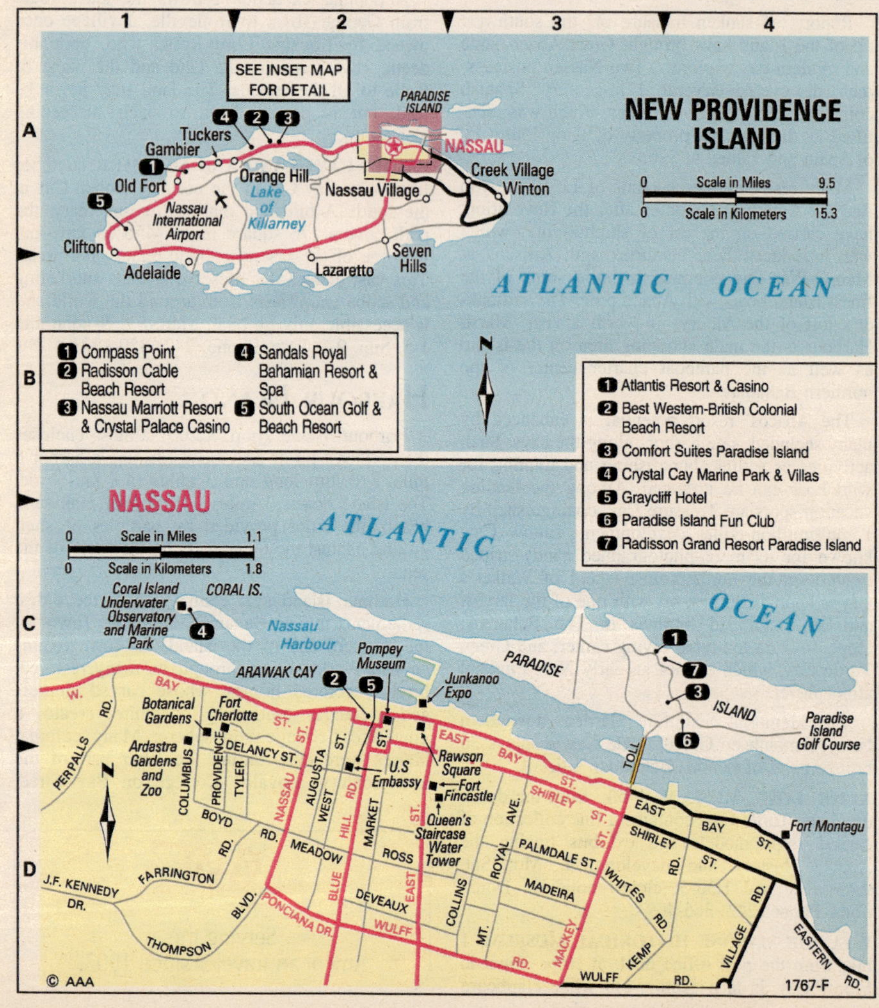

home to the popular resort areas of Paradise Island, linked to Nassau by a bridge, and to Cable Beach.

NASSAU (A-2) *pop. 284,000*

Capital and principal city of The Bahamas, Nassau is on the northeast coast of New Providence Island (pop. 172,200). This resort was a battleground for Spanish, British and French colonization efforts and a haven for buccaneers. It was here that the infamous pirate Blackbeard posted a lookout in his tower while he caroused around the islands. In 1718, a century after the first British colony was established, the British sent the first royal governor to The Bahamas. Nassau was named in 1729 for King William III of the House of Orange-Nassau.

There is always plenty to do in downtown Nassau: sightseeing by horse-drawn carriage, photographing the colorful buildings, dining, dancing or duty-free shopping. The focal point of Nassau is Bay Street, dominated by Parliament Square. Here are the two chambers of Parliament and the Supreme Court. Visitors can watch the proceedings of the House of Assembly when it is in session; arrangements must be made at the House office of the clerk of courts. To find out when the House will be in session, phone (242) 302-2081. Also in the square are the Garden of Remembrance, with its cenotaph honoring Bahamians who died in World Wars I and II, and the octagonal Nassau Public Library and Museum.

Nassau's 18th-century forts also are worth visiting. Of the three forts, only Fort Montagu at the eastern entrance to the harbor was confronted by invaders. High above the city, the Government House is host to tea parties held the last Friday of each month from January through August. A colorful changing of the guard ceremony takes place every other Saturday at 10 a.m.

Vibrant, sociable Nassau possesses almost every conceivable sports facility. Tennis courts and golf courses abound, as do local entrepreneurs marketing rentals or lessons for snorkeling, scuba diving, fishing and sailing. Nassau's many fine beaches include Cable, Montagu, Paradise and Western Esplanade.

The waters, noted for deep-sea and reef fishing, are most famous for giant blue marlin, but white marlin, tuna, wahoo, bonito and sailfish also are abundant. Nassau Yacht Haven on E. Bay Street is the charter and fishing headquarters. Sailing is popular in the bays and around the coral islands; local and international races are held by The Bahamas Sailing Association, Royal Nassau Sailing Club and the Nassau Yacht Club.

Brochures, maps and guides are available at information centers at the Nassau International Airport, Rawson Square and Prince George Wharf, where cruise ships dock.

ARDASTRA GARDENS AND ZOO, 5.5 acres on Chippingham Rd. near Fort Charlotte, contain more than 4,000 tropical and subtropical plants. Against this setting, a platoon of 40 flamingos drill and perform under the command of their trainer daily at 11, 2 and 4. The birds, usually a shy and easily frightened species, will stand while visitors snap pictures at close range. The zoo has more than 300 birds, mammals and reptiles. Open daily 9-5. Last admission 30 minutes before closing. Admission $7.50; ages 5-10, $3.75. Phone (242) 323-5806.

BOTANICAL GARDENS, 3 blks. off W. Bay St. on Chippingham Rd., showcases native plants and flowers on 18 acres of landscaped grounds. Two freshwater ponds with lilies and tropical fish, a cactus garden, and a grotto made of local quarry stones and conch shells add to the beauty of the gardens. Also featured are a children's playground and a replica of an Arawak Indian village. Open Mon.-Fri. 9-4:30, Sat.-Sun. 10-4:30. Admission $1; ages 5-12, 50c. Phone (242) 323-5975.

CRYSTAL CAY MARINE PARK, on Crystal Cay off W. Bay St., offers a variety of marine exhibits, such as a shark tank, sea turtle pool, stingray pool, reef tank and the Marine Gardens Aquarium, which contains 24 individual aquariums. Highlights include touching underwater creatures at the Marine Encounter Pool, observing various feeding habits of different fish and viewing the hundreds of living coral formations within the exhibits.

An offshore observation tower, reached by a bridge, provides three levels of sweeping views above and below the waterline. The coral reef environment 20 feet beneath the surface can be examined through windows in the underwater observatory level. The Pleasure Reef Snorkeling Trail allows visitors to view the marine life up-close.

Shuttle bus service is available to and from the Cable Beach, downtown and Paradise Island hotels; round-trip fare $3 per person. A ferry link to Woodes Rogers Walk, a boardwalk, also is available. Parking is on Arawak Cay; a bridge connects the parking lot to the marine park. Allow 1 hour minimum. Daily 9-6. Snorkeling trail daily 9:30-4. Admission $15; ages 3-11, $11. Combination ferry and admission $20; ages 3-11, $15. Round-trip bus transfers $4. Snorkeling rental equipment $12; ages 6-18, $10. AE, CB, DI, DS, MC, VI. Phone (242) 328-1036.

FORT CHARLOTTE, one of the largest Bahamian forts, commands the western entrance to the harbor. Lord Dunmore, the British governor of The Bahamas 1787-96, built the fort 1787-89 and named it for the wife of George III. The fort never fired a shot in hostility. Tours of the dungeon, with corridors cut out of solid rock, are available. Contact the Ministry of Tourism to arrange tours; phone (242) 322-7500. To the east of Fort Charlotte is the original guardhouse. Fort

daily 8:30-4:30. Tipping is suggested. Phone (242) 325-9186.

FORT FINCASTLE stands on Bennet's Hill behind the town and affords a fine view of the area. Built about 1793, the fort resembles a paddlewheel steamer.

JUNKANOO EXPO, on Prince George Wharf, showcases the elaborate costumes from recent Junkanoo parades. The vivid costumes, which can weigh up to 400 pounds, are made from such materials as cardboard, posterboard, aluminum, crepe and Styrofoam. A film of parade highlights also is shown. The parade, which also features musicians and native dancers, takes place on Dec. 26 and Jan. 1. Guided tours are available.

Allow 1 hour minimum. Open Tues.-Wed. and Fri.-Sun. 10-4 (also Tues. and Fri.-Sat. 4-7), Mon. and Thurs. 10-1; closed major holidays and July 10, Oct. 12 and Dec. 26. Admission $2; under 13, 50c. Phone (242) 356-2731.

PARADISE ISLAND, connected to Nassau by bridge (toll $2), boasts one of the finest beaches in the islands. The island also can be reached on one of the regularly scheduled boat trips, a good alternative when traffic jams the bridge. Tennis, golf, parasailing and horseback riding lure the sports minded, while the island's "strip," which includes a casino and cabaret theater, provides other entertainment.

The tiny island was privately owned for many years until Huntington Hartford, whose fortune came from the A&P supermarket chain, developed it as a resort, changing its name from Hog Island. A 14th-century French cloister, imported to The Bahamas by Hartford, presents a stark contrast to the glittering casinos and nightclubs. Versailles Gardens, on the grounds of the Ocean Club, consists of seven terraces including statues of missionary/explorer David Livingstone, United States president Franklin Roosevelt and various mythological figures.

POMPEY MUSEUM, W. Bay St., is housed in an 18th-century slave auction house. Displays include historical documents and local artifacts. An art gallery upstairs features paintings by local artist Amos Ferguson, whose Bahamian-style artwork consists of house paints and cardboard canvases. Allow 30 minutes minimum. Mon.-Fri. 10-4:30, Sat. 10-1; closed holidays. Admission $1; ages 8-12, 50c. Phone (242) 326-2566.

QUEEN'S STAIRCASE, Elizabeth Ave., is a flight of 66 steps cut from solid limestone by slaves. The stairs, named for Queen Victoria, lead to Fort Fincastle and the Water Tower.

SEA GARDENS, reached by boat from the Woodes Rogers Walk, are undersea gardens reached by glass-bottom boats from the Prince George Wharf adjoining Rawson Square. The round trip takes about 90 minutes. Gardens admission $15.

WATER TOWER, just e. of Fort Fincastle at the top of the Queen's Staircase, has cannon facings and a viewing deck. The highest point on the island, the 126-foot tower offers a view of Nassau and New Providence. Daily 9-5. Elevator fee 50c.

Spanish Wells Island

Spanish Wells, covering half a square mile (1.3 sq km), is the smallest inhabited island in The Bahamas. At the end of St. George's Cay near the northern tip of Eleuthera, it derived its name from the Spanish ships that once stopped here to replenish their water supply from the island's wells.

Several years after the Eleutheran Adventurers established a settlement a half-mile (.8 km) east on the island of Eleuthera, they moved to Spanish Wells because it was smaller and easier to defend. Loyalists fleeing the results of the American Revolution also settled here. Some of them attempted to establish a plantation economy. However, the original settlers would not tolerate slavery, so the idea was squelched. This attitude earned the Spanish Wellsians the hatred of their slave-trading sister islands. Relics of that era include some colorful New England-style homes and traces of the English dialect spoken by early settlers.

The lobster industry is the most important factor in an economy that depends primarily on the sea. Tomatoes, cucumbers, onions and pineapples provide supplemental income. Sailing and fishing are among the main attractions for tourists. Offshore a wide variety of shipwrecks and coral reefs provide scuba divers and snorkelers with a wealth of underwater adventures.

LODGINGS & RESTAURANTS

DUNMORE TOWN (HARBOUR ISLAND)

LODGINGS

CORAL SANDS HOTEL
◆◆ *Resort Complex*

12/21-4/26	$175-225	XP $20
12/1-12/20, 4/27-9/6 & 11/15-11/30	$130-165	XP $20

Location: Reached from N Eleuthera Airport by taxi & ferry. (PO Box EL 27023, DUNMORE TOWN). Fax: 242/333-2368. **Terms:** Open 12/1-9/6 & 11/15-11/30; reserv deposit, 21 day notice; 10% service charge. **Facility:** 23 rooms. Varied room styles & decors. Some units with private balcony overlooking the ocean & miles of coral sand beach. Provide a mix of king, double & twin-sized bed. 8 two-bedroom units. A/C avail upon request; 1-2 stories; exterior corridors; beach; 1 lighted tennis court. **Recreation:** swimming, canoeing, charter fishing, sailboating, snorkeling & equipment. Fee: bicycles. **All Rooms:** combo or shower baths. **Some Rooms:** 2 kitchens. **Cards:** AE, MC, VI.

(242/333-2350

PINK SANDS
◆◆◆◆ *Resort Cottage*

12/1-4/15	$650-750	XP $85-100
4/16-9/30 & 11/1-11/30	$375-425	XP $85-100

Location: Reached from N Eleuthera Airport via taxi & ferry. (PO Box 87, HARBOUR ISLAND). Fax: 242/333-2060. **Terms:** Open 12/1-9/30 & 11/1-11/30; reserv deposit, 14 day notice; handling fee imposed; $10 service charge. **Facility:** 26 rooms. Handsome individual & duplex cottages on 3 miles of pink beach. Excellent guest facilities. Beautifully decorated rooms. CD players all rooms. Closed 10/1-10/31. 4 two-bedroom units. 1 story; exterior corridors; oceanview; beach; 3 tennis courts (1 lighted). **Services:** giftshop. **Recreation:** swimming, charter fishing, fishing. Fee: snorkeling & equipment; bicycles. **Cards:** AE, MC, VI.

(242/333-2030

AAA **SAVE** **ROMORA BAY CLUB**
◆◆◆ *Resort Cottage*

12/16-4/21	$390
12/1-12/15 & 4/22-11/30	$240

Location: Reached from N Eleuthera Airport by taxi & ferry. (PO Box EL 27146, DUNMORE TOWN). Fax: 242/333-2500. **Terms:** Reserv deposit, 21 day notice; handling fee imposed; 10% service charge; AP avail, rates include breakfast & lunch daily; package plans. **Facility:** 38 rooms. Hillside units overlooking harbor; on lush tropical grounds. Most with balcony or patio. Bayside. Eclectic European decor. 4 two-bedroom units. 1-2 stories; exterior corridors; whirlpool, access to ocean beach; 1 tennis court. **Dining:** Dining room; 7:30 am-10:30, 12:30-3 & 7:30-9:30 pm; $20-$29; cocktails; dining room, see separate listing. **Services:** giftshop. **Recreation:** swimming, charter fishing. Fee: fishing, scuba diving/snorkeling & equipment, waterskiing, windsurfing; bicycles. Rental: paddleboats, sailboats. **All Rooms:** combo or shower baths. **Some Rooms:** 4 kitchens. **Cards:** AE, MC, VI. **Special Amenities: Free local telephone calls and free room upgrade (subject to availability with advanced reservations).** *(See color ad below)*

((242)333-2325

RESTAURANTS

THE LANDING RESTAURANT
◆◆ *Continental*   L $8-$14 D $15-$35

Location: Just above Town Dock; overlooking habor. Bay St. **Hours:** 8 am-10, noon-2 & 6-10 pm. Closed: Wed. **Reservations:** accepted. **Features:** No A/C; casual dress; children's menu; cocktails & lounge; a la carte. Mediterranean, Bahamian & Asian cuisine. Graceful setting. **Cards:** MC, VI.

(242/333-2707

PINK SANDS DINING ROOM
◆◆◆ *Nouvelle Continental*

Location: Reached from N Eluthera Airport via taxi & ferry; in Pink Sands. PO Box 87. **Hours:** 7 pm-9 pm. Closed: 10/1-10/31. **Reservations:** required. **Features:** No A/C; casual dress; cocktails & lounge; prix fixe. Eclectic Caribbean fusion cuisine, with Japenese influence. Excellent wine list. Romantic dining on moonlit terrace. 15% service charge. **Cards:** AE, MC, VI.

(242/333-2030

FREEPORT

LODGING

PELICAN BAY AT LUCAYA
◆◆◆ *Motor Inn*

All Year $110-130   XP $25
Location: 6 mi se of Freeport; adjacent to Unexso. (PO Box F-42654). Fax: 242/373-9551. **Terms:** F12; Reserv deposit, 7 day notice. **Facility:** 48 rooms. Cozy European inspired complex facing the marina; all rooms with patio or balcony. Attractive decor . Convenient to Port Lucaya marketplace & beach. $12 tax per person per day; 3 stories; exterior corridors; boat dock, marina. **Recreation:** charter fishing. **Cards:** AE, MC, VI.

(242/373-9550

RESTAURANTS

THE BRASS HELMET
◆ *American*   **L** $6-$11   **D** $6-$23
Location: Next to Port Lucaya Marketplace on second floor of the Underwater Explorers Society. Royal Palm Way. **Hours:** 7 am-9 pm. **Features:** No A/C; children's menu; carryout; cocktails; a la carte. Casual dining room filled with diving memorabilia. Distinct nautical atmosphere. Small outdoor patio area. Good menu selection. **Cards:** AE, DI, DS, MC, VI.

(242/373-2032

THE STONED CRAB
◆◆ *Seafood*   **D** $18-$34
Location: At Taino Beach. **Hours:** 5 pm-10 pm. **Reservations:** suggested. **Features:** Large casual restaurant featuring indoor & outdoor dining overlooking the beach. Nautical atmosphere. Hearty portions. **Cards:** AE, MC, VI.

(242/373-1442

FREEPORT
(GRAND BAHAMA ISLAND)

LODGINGS

ATLANTIC BEACH & GOLF RESORT
◆◆◆ *Hotel*

12/21-4/18 $144-205   XP $30
12/1-12/20 & 4/19-11/30 $120-185   XP $30
Location: 6 mi se of Freeport; on Lucaya Beach opposite Port Lucaya Marketplace. (PO Box F-42500, FREEPORT). Fax: 242/373-7481. **Terms:** F12; Reserv deposit, 3 day notice; $12 service charge. **Facility:** 175 rooms. Oceanfront hotel on lush landscaped grounds. Wide variety of room styles; size varies from compact to spacious multi-room & multi-level suites. Many with wonderful ocean views. Apartment style suites with kitchenettes $170-$330. $12 tax per person per day; 16 stories; interior corridors; putting green; beach; 4 tennis courts. Fee: 18 holes golf. **Services:** giftshop; area transportation. **Recreation:** swimming, snorkeling. Fee: sailboating, snorkeling equipment, waterskiing, windsurfing; bicycles. Rental: paddleboats. **All Rooms:** combo or shower baths. **Some Rooms:** 18 efficiencies. **Cards:** AE, DS, MC, VI.

(242/373-1444

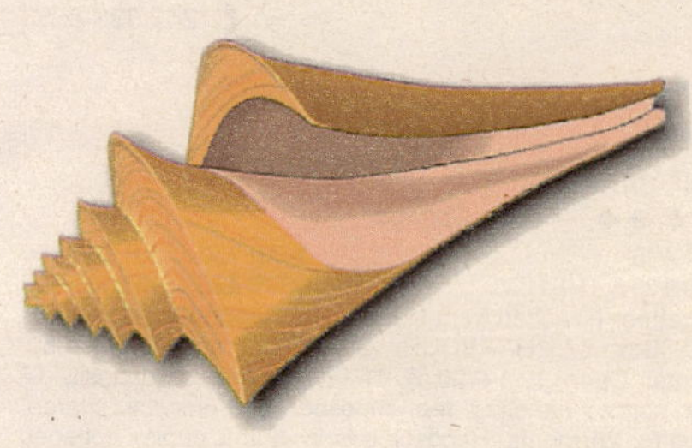

▲▲▲ BAHAMAS PRINCESS RESORT AND CASINO
◆◆◆ *Resort Complex*

12/21-4/18	$125-155	XP $30
12/1-12/20 & 4/19-11/30	$98-128	XP $30

Location: Opposite & adjacent to the International Bazaar. (PO Box F-40207, FREEPORT). Fax: 242/352-4485. **Terms:** F12; Reserv deposit, 4 day notice; package plans. **Facility:** 965 rooms. Sprawling facility. Wide variety of room sizes & decors, either in the high-rise tower or the low-rise country club buildings. 3-10 stories; interior/exterior corridors; 2 hot tubs; playground. Fee: 36 holes golf; 12 tennis courts (6 lighted). **Dining:** 5 dining rooms, 2 restaurants, 2 coffee shops; 6:30 am-3 am; $6-$28; cocktails; 15% service charge. **Services:** giftshop; area transportation, Xanadu Beach & Island Sea. Fee: massage. **Recreation:** rental mopeds. Fee: bicycles. **Cards:** AE, DI, DS, MC, VI. *(See color ad p 68)*

((242)352-6721

GRAND BAHAMA BEACH HOTEL
◆◆ *Motel*

All Year	$118-130	XP $30

Location: 6 mi se of Freeport; on Lucaya Beach opposite Port Lucaya Marketplace. (PO Box F-42496, LUCAYA). Fax: 242/373-8662. **Terms:** F12; Reserv deposit, 3 day notice. **Facility:** 244 rooms. Spacious pool deck, wide beach. Shared facilities with adjacent Atlantic Beach & Gulf Resort. $12 tax per person per day; 3 stories; interior corridors; putting green; beach; playground. Fee: 18 holes golf; 6 tennis courts. **Services:** giftshop; area transportation. Fee: massage. **Recreation:** swimming; sports court. Fee: boating, sailboating, snorkeling & equipment, waterskiing, windsurfing; bicycles. Rental: paddleboats. **Cards:** AE, DS, MC, VI.

(242/373-1333

▲▲▲ SAVE PORT LUCAYA RESORT & YACHT CLUB
◆◆◆ *Resort Hotel*

12/20-4/11	$100-135	XP $25
12/1-12/19 & 4/12-11/30	$80-110	XP $25

Location: 4 mi se of Freeport; adjacent to Port Lucaya Marketplace. Bell Channel Bay Rd (PO Box F-42452, FREEPORT). Fax: 242/373-6652. **Terms:** F12; Weekly rates; BP avail; package plans. **Facility:** 160 rooms. Pleasant tropical decor in guest rooms. First floor rooms with patio facing pool courtyard; second floor rooms with balcony facing the marina. 2 two-bedroom units. Tax $12 per person per night; 2 stories; interior/exterior corridors; beach access, whirlpool; playground. Fee: marina. **Dining:** Restaurant; 7 am-11:30 & 5:30-10 pm; $12-$25; cocktails; 15% service charge. **Services:** giftshop. **Cards:** AE, DS, MC, VI. **Special Amenities:** Early check-in/late check-out and free room upgrade (subject to availability with advanced reservations). *(See color ad below)*

((242)373-6618

RESTAURANTS

PIER ONE RESTAURANT
◆◆ *Seafood*   L $6-$24 D $15-$40

Location: At Freeport Harbour. 40567 Freeport Harbour. **Hours:** 10 am-4 & 5:30-10 pm. Closed: 12/25. **Reservations:** required; outdoor dining. **Features:** No A/C; casual dress; children's menu; carryout; cocktails; a la carte. Large dining room offering wonderful views of the harbour. Indoor & outdoor dining. Extensive menu selection. Shark feedings nightly 7 pm, 8 pm & 9 pm. **Cards:** AE, DI, MC, VI.

(242/352-6674

SILVANO'S ITALIAN RESTAURANT
◆◆ *Italian*   D $11-$28

Location: Facing International Bazaar. W Mall & Ranfurly Cir. **Hours:** 5:30 pm-11 pm. Closed: 12/25. **Reservations:** suggested. **Features:** cocktails; a la carte. Casual dining in a small, intimate dining room. Formally attired service staff. Offer seafood, meat & pasta dishes. 15% service charge. Call for Sun avail, off season. **Cards:** AE, MC, VI.

(242/352-5111

GEORGE TOWN
(GREAT EXUMA ISLAND)

LODGINGS

CLUB PEACE & PLENTY
◆◆ *Motor Inn*

12/16-4/30	$140-155	XP $26
12/1-12/15 & 5/1-11/30	$110-120	XP $26

Location: At the edge of George Town; 10 mi se of Exuma International Airport. (PO Box EX 29055, GEORGE TOWN). Fax: 242/336-2093. **Terms:** F12; Reserv deposit, 21 day notice. **Facility:** 35 rooms. On Elizabeth Harbor, at water's edge. Balcony. Three restaurants avail, free transportation between inn, beach & lodge. $19 tax per room per night; 1-2 stories; exterior corridors; beach access, small pool. **Services:** giftshop; area transportation. **Recreation:** swimming, snorkeling. Fee: windsurfing. Rental: snorkeling equipment. **All Rooms:** combo or shower baths. **Cards:** AE, MC, VI.

(242/336-2551

PEACE & PLENTY BEACH INN
◆◆◆ *Motor Inn*

12/21-4/30	$150-175	XP $26
12/1-12/20 & 5/1-11/30	$130-140	XP $26

Location: 1 mi nw of George Town; 9 mi se of Exuma International Airport. (PO Box EX 29055, GEORGE TOWN). Fax: 242/336-2253. **Terms:** Reserv deposit, 21 day notice, 14 day in summer. **Facility:** 16 rooms. Large rooms with balcony overlooking beach & ocean. Facilities of Club Peace & Plenty & Bone Fish Lodge avail. 1-2 stories; exterior corridors; beach; boat dock. **Dining:** Restaurant; 7 am-10:30, noon-2:30 & 6:30-9 pm; $15-$30; cocktails; 15% service charge. **Services:** area transportation, to George Town. **Recreation:** swimming, charter fishing, snorkeling, ferry boat service to private beach on Stocking Island. Fee: scuba diving. Rental: scuba & snorkeling equipment. **Some Rooms:** efficiency. **Cards:** AE, MC, VI.

((242)336-2250

PEACE AND PLENTY BONEFISH LODGE
◆◆◆ *Lodge*

12/1-7/31 & 10/1-11/30	$416

Location: 20 mi se of Exuma International Airport. (PO Box 29173, GEORGE TOWN). Fax: 242/345-5556. **Terms:** Open 12/1-7/31 & 10/1-11/30; reserv deposit, 60 day notice; handling fee imposed. **Facility:** 8 rooms. Peaceful peninsula location. Spacious rooms. Shared facilities with Peace and Plenty Inn and Club. Rates include transportation from airport, all meals, taxes & gratuities; 2 stories; exterior corridors. **Services:** area transportation. **Recreation:** charter fishing, fishing. Fee: bicycles. **Cards:** MC, VI.

(242/345-5555

Harbour Island

Restaurant

ROMORA BAY CLUB RESTAURANT
◆◆◆ *Continental*   **L** $12-$15 **D** $20-$29
Location: Reached from N Eleuthera Airport by taxi & ferry; at Romora Bay Club. **Hours:** 7:30 am-10:30, 12:30-3 & 7:30-9:30 pm. **Reservations:** suggested. **Features:** No A/C; cocktails; a la carte. Light luncheon menu. Pre fixe dinner selections. Elegant candlelit dining with choice of indoor or outdoor terrace seating. **Cards:** AE, MC, VI.

(242/333-2325

Hope Town
(Great Abaco Island)

Lodgings

ABACO INN
◆◆ *Cottage*
12/1-12/15 & 9/7-11/30	$105-195	XP $20
12/16-9/6	$120-195	XP $20

Location: On White Sound; 2.5 mi s of Hope Town Village. General Delivery. Fax: 242/366-0113. **Terms:** F6; Reserv deposit, 14 day notice; $15 service charge. **Facility:** 15 rooms. Informal, very pleasant setting. Cottage style units overlooking sound & ocean. Simple decor, well maintainded. 1 story; exterior corridors; oceanview; beach; boat dock. **Services:** giftshop; area transportation. **Recreation:** swimming, charter fishing, snorkeling & equipment; bicycles. Fee: fishing, sailboating. **All Rooms:** shower baths. **Some Rooms:** 2 kitchens. **Cards:** DS, MC, VI.

(242/366-0133

HOPE TOWN HARBOUR LODGE
◆◆ *Lodge*
12/1-9/6 & 11/1-11/30	$110-145
9/7-10/31	$65-85

Location: Just above harbor in, center of Hope Town. (General Delivery, HOPE TOWN). Fax: 242/366-0286. **Terms:** Reserv deposit, 14 day notice; handling fee imposed; 10% service charge; 3 night min stay, ocean view & pool rm. **Facility:** 20 rooms. Excellent location between ocean & harbor. Large freshwater pool. Rooms vary in size & decor. All well maintained. 2-bedroom cottage with full kitchen $1250 weekly for 4, $50 extra person up to 6 persons. Dining & pool bar closed 9/7-10/31; 3 stories, no elevator; exterior corridors; oceanview; beach; boat dock. **Recreation:** swimming, charter fishing, snorkeling. Fee: fishing, scuba diving, scuba & snorkeling equipment; bicycles. Rental: boats. **All Rooms:** shower baths. **Some Rooms:** kitchen. **Cards:** MC, VI.

(242/366-0095

HOPE TOWN HIDEAWAYS
◆◆◆ *Cottage*
12/16-9/15	$185	XP $20
12/1-12/15 & 9/16-11/30	$143	XP $20

Location: On Elbow Cay 6 mi ne from Marsh Harbour, airport taxi to ferry; request Hope Town Hideaways dock. 1 Purple Porpoise Pl. Fax: 242/366-0434. **Terms:** Reserv deposit, 60 day notice; handling fee imposed. **Facility:** 4 rooms. Idyllic, tropical setting with lush gardens & beautiful harbor views. Modern 2-bedroom villas with 2 bathrooms, large kitchen & spacious living room. Large, private sun decks. Rates for up to 4 persons, $260; $190 off season; 1 story; exterior corridors; beach access; boat dock. Fee: marina. **Services:** area transportation. **Recreation:** swimming, boating, fishing. **All Rooms:** kitchens. **Cards:** DS, MC, VI.

(242/366-0224

SEA SPRAY RESORT & VILLAS
◆◆◆ *Cottage*
All Year	$910-1500	XP $100

Location: 3.5 mi s of Hope Town Village, on White Sound. (General Delivery, HOPE TOWN). Fax: 242/366-0383. **Terms:** F14; Check-out 9 am; reserv deposit, 14 day notice; 3 night min stay. **Facility:** 7 rooms. Pleasant, modern cottages overlooking harbor & ocean. 4 two-bedroom units. Rates for up to 4 persons; 1 story; exterior corridors; oceanfront; beach. Fee: marina. **Services:** area transportation. **Recreation:** swimming, charter fishing, sailboating. Fee: scuba diving/snorkeling & equipment; bicycles. Rental: boats. **All Rooms:** kitchens, combo or shower baths. **Cards:** AE, MC, VI.

(242/366-0065

Restaurants

ABACO INN DINING ROOM
◆◆ *American*   **L** $5-$10 **D** $14-$30
Location: On White Sound; 2.5 mi s of Hope Town Village; in Abaco Inn. **Hours:** 8 am-10:30, noon-3 & 6:30-9 pm. **Features:** No A/C; casual dress; cocktails & lounge; a la carte. Patio & inside seating. Overlooking Atlantic Ocean. Very well prepared island & American cuisine. **Cards:** DS, MC, VI.

(242/366-0133

BOAT HOUSE RESTAURANT
◆◆ *Seafood*   **L** $5-$10 **D** $17-$21
Location: 3.5 mi s of Hope Town Village; on White Sound. **Hours:** 8 am-10, 11:30-2:30 & 6:30-8:30 pm. **Reservations:** accepted. **Features:** casual dress; children's menu; carryout; cocktails; a la carte. On the dock in White Sound. Excellent island cuisine, simple relaxed atmosphere. **Cards:** MC, VI.

(242/366-0359

CAP'N JACKS
◆ *Seafood*   **L** $5-$12 **D** $5-$23
Location: Hope Town harborfront. **Hours:** 8:30 am-10 & 11-9 pm. **Reservations:** required. **Features:** No A/C; casual dress; children's menu; cocktails & lounge; a la carte. Waterfront dining. Informal atmosphere & service. Very well prepared island & American cuisine. Check for availability late Aug, early Sept. Reservations needed by 4 pm for special dinner menu (posted at visitor center). **Cards:** MC, VI.

(242/366-0247

HARBOUR'S EDGE RESTAURANT
◆◆ *Continental*   **L** $7-$10 **D** $18-$22
Location: In center of Village; adjacent to town dock. **Hours:** 11:30 am-3 & 6-9 pm. Closed: Tues & mid Sept to mid Oct. **Features:** No A/C; casual dress; cocktails & lounge; a la carte. Open air deck overlooking Hope Town Harbor. Well prepared island & American cuisine. Casual & relaxed setting. **Cards:** MC, VI.

(242/366-0292

HOPE TOWN HARBOUR LODGE DINING ROOM
◆◆ *Continental*   L $5-$9   D $13-$28
Location: Just above harbor in center of Hope Town; in Hope Town Harbour Lodge. General Delivery. **Hours:** 8 am-10, 11:30-2:30 & 6:30-9 pm. Closed: 9/8-10/31; closed Mon for dinner. **Reservations:** suggested; for dinner. **Features:** No A/C; casual dress; cocktails & lounge; a la carte. Casual poolside dining for lunch & terrace overlooking harbor for dinner. Well prepared island & Continental cuisine. **Cards:** MC, VI.

(242/366-0286

MARSH HARBOUR (GREAT ABACO ISLAND)

LODGINGS

AAA SAVE **ABACO BEACH RESORT & BOAT HARBOR**
◆◆◆ *Resort Hotel*

All Year $185-500   XP $30
Location: 3.5 mi s from airport. (PO Box AB 20511, MARSH HARBOUR). Fax: 242/367-2819. **Terms:** F12; Reserv deposit, 14 day notice; $5 service charge; package plans; small pets only. **Facility:** 58 rooms. Extensive Marina. Very well furnished & decorated guest rooms & 2 bedroon 2 bath villas. Close to town but secluded in grove of trees. 6 two-bedroom units. 2-4 stories, no elevator; exterior corridors; oceanfront; beach, kayaks; 2 tennis courts; boat ramp. Fee: marina. **Dining:** Restaurant; 7 am-10:30, noon-2:30, 6-9:30 pm; $18-$28; cocktails; pool side dining from 10 am; beach beverage. **Services:** giftshop. **Recreation:** swimming, charter fishing, snorkeling, windsurfing; volleyball. Fee: sailboating, scuba diving, scuba & snorkeling equipment; bicycles. Rental: boats. **Some Rooms:** 6 kitchens. **Cards:** AE, DS, MC, VI.

((242)367-2736

CONCH INN & MARINA, A MOORINGS RESORT
◆◆ *Motor Inn*

All Year $90   XP $10
Location: On the harbourfront; 3 mi n from airport. Bay St (PO Box AB 20469, MARSH HARBOUR). Fax: 242/367-4004. **Terms:** F12; Reserv deposit; $5 service charge. **Facility:** 9 rooms. Bright, pleasant rooms at full service marina. Convenience store. 1 story; exterior corridors. Fee: marina. **Services:** giftshop. **Recreation:** charter fishing. Fee: boating, sailboating, scuba diving/snorkeling & equipment. **Cards:** MC, VI.

(242/367-4000

RESTAURANTS

CASTLE CAFE *Historical*
◆◆ *American*   L $5-$10
Location: S of center; 0.5 mi from Hope Town Ferry Dock. **Hours:** 11 am-5 pm, Wed happy hour 5 pm-7 pm. Closed: Sat & Sun; Sept-mid Nov. **Features:** No A/C; casual dress; carryout; cocktails & lounge. Very nice light menu & cocktails. Castle built by "The Out Island Doctor" in the 1940's. Commands a sweeping view of neighboring islands & Marsh Harbour. Gift shop. **Cards:** MC, VI.

(242/367-2315

CONCH INN CAFE
◆◆ *Seafood*   L $6-$11   D $15-$20
Location: On the harbourfront 3 mi from airport; in Conch Inn & Marina, A Moorings Resort. Bay St. **Hours:** 8 am-4 & 6-9:30 pm. Closed: for dinner Tues. **Features:** No A/C; casual dress; cocktails & lounge; a la carte. Informal waterfront dining. Full service marina. Island & Continental cuisine. **Cards:** MC, VI.

(242/367-4444

MANGOES
◆◆◆ *Seafood*   L $6-$11   D $17-$22
Location: Center; on waterfront. Bay St. **Hours:** 11:30 am-2:30 & 6:30-9 pm. Closed: Sun; 9/1-9/30. **Reservations:** suggested. **Features:** casual dress; children's menu; carryout; cocktails & lounge; a la carte. Attractive waterfront dining, complimentary use of dock for restaurant guests. Well prepared local & Continental cuisine. All day lighter menu/bar snacks avail. **Cards:** AE, MC, VI.

(242/367-2366

SAPODILLY'S
◆◆ *Seafood*   D $15-$26
Location: Across from waterfront in center. Bay St. **Hours:** 6:30 pm-9:30 pm; Sun bar service only. Closed: Sun for dinner. **Reservations:** suggested. **Features:** No A/C; casual dress; cocktails & lounge; entertainment; a la carte. Open sided rustic restaurant. Well prepared American & Bahamian dishes. Informal & friendly. **Cards:** MC, VI.

(242/367-3498

WALLY'S
◆◆◆ *American*   L $8-$11   D $18-$25
Location: In center; on waterfront. Bay St. **Hours:** 11:30 am-3 & 6-9 pm. Closed major holidays, Sun & Mon; mid Sept to late Oct. **Reservations:** suggested. **Features:** No A/C; casual dress; cocktails & lounge; a la carte. Attractive open air dining close to harbour. Pleasant service. Caribbean & American cuisine. **Cards:** AE, DS, MC, VI.

(242/367-2074

NASSAU

LODGING

GRAYCLIFF HOTEL
◆◆◆ *Historic Country Inn*

12/1-4/30 & 11/16-11/30 $235-365   XP $25
5/1-11/15 $155-290   XP $25
Location: Downtown; opposite Government House. W Hill St (PO Box N-10246). Fax: 242/326-6110. **Terms:** Reserv deposit, 7 day notice. **Facility:** 12 rooms. Secluded private setting with elegantly furnished rooms & suites in Manor House or Garden Courtyard. 2 stories; interior/exterior corridors. **All Rooms:** combo or shower baths. **Cards:** AE, CB, DI, DS, MC, VI.

(242/322-2796

RESTAURANTS

CAFE MATISSA
◆◆◆ *Italian*   L $9-$16   D $9-$29
Location: Downtown; across from the Supreme Court. Bank Ln. **Hours:** noon-3 & 6-10 pm. Closed: Sun, 9/1-9/30 & 12/24-12/30. **Reservations:** suggested. **Features:** cocktails; street parking; a la carte. Quaint European decor. Good selection of homemade pastas, seafood & Bahamian cuisine. **Cards:** AE, DS, MC, VI.

(242/356-7012

SEASHELLS
◆◆◆ *Continental* **L** $8-$12 **D** $16-$26
Location: Off w Bay St at the site of Crystal Cay Marine Park & Villas, auto access by narrow one way bridge. **Hours:** 11 am-3 & 6-11 pm. Closed: for lunch on Sun. **Reservations:** suggested. **Features:** cocktails. Elegant setting with indoor & outdoor patio dining offering spectacular ocean views. Varied menu with many cajun specialties. **Cards:** AE, DS, MC, VI.

NASSAU
(NEW PROVIDENCE ISLAND)

(See map page 64)

LODGINGS

ATLANTIS RESORT & CASINO
◆◆◆ *Resort Complex*

12/22-4/18	$195-360	XP $55
12/1-12/21 & 4/19-11/30	$125-275	XP $55

Location: On Paradise Island, reached by toll bridge from Nassau. Casino Dr (PO Box N-4777, NASSAU). Fax: 242/363-3524. **Terms:** F17; Reserv deposit, 14 day notice; $10 service charge. **Facility:** 1147 rooms. Expansive facility offering marine life stocked lagoons, underwater viewing tunnels, "Lazy River" tubing ride, extensive shops & entertainment. Meets AAA guest room security requirements. 3-12 stories; interior/exterior corridors; oceanfront; putting green; beach; playground. Fee: 18 holes golf; 9 lighted tennis courts. **Services:** giftshop. Fee: massage. **Recreation:** swimming, charter fishing; hiking trails. Fee: boating, canoeing, fishing, sailboating, scuba diving/snorkeling & equipment, waterskiing, windsurfing. Rental: paddleboats. **Cards:** AE, DI, DS, MC, VI. *(See color ad below)*

(242/363-3000

AAA SAVE **BEST WESTERN-BRITISH COLONIAL**
BEACH RESORT
◆◆ *Motel*

12/22-4/30	$134-194	XP $25
12/1-12/21 & 5/1-11/30	$94-144	XP $25

Location: Downtown; just w of Rawson Sq. 1 Bay St (PO Box N-7148, NASSAU). Fax: 242/322-2286. **Terms:** F12; Reserv deposit, 3 day notice; package plans. **Facility:** 174 rooms. Historic Spanish Colonial style hotel on own beach facing harbour. Rooms range in size from compact to more spacious. 3-6 stories; interior corridors; beach; 3 lighted tennis courts. **Dining:** Poolside cafe 7 am-3 pm. **Services:** giftshop. **Recreation:** swimming, paddleboats, sailboating, scuba diving, snorkeling, windsurfing; basketball, volleyball & shuffleboard. Fee: scuba & snorkeling equipment. **Cards:** AE, CB, DI, MC, VI. **Special Amenities: Free newspaper and free room upgrade (subject to availability with advanced reservations).**

((242)322-3301

AAA SAVE **COMFORT SUITES PARADISE ISLAND**
◆◆◆ *Motor Inn*

12/20-1/2	$195-240	XP $30
1/3-4/24	$185-225	XP $30
4/25-11/30	$150-195	XP $30
12/1-12/19	$140-185	XP $30

Location: On Paradise Island; reached by toll bridge from Nassau. Paradise Island & Casino Dr (PO Box SS 6202, NASSAU). Fax: 242/363-2588. **Terms:** F18; Reserv deposit. **Facility:** 150 rooms. Full use of the facilities at Atlantis Paradise Island Resort & Casino. 1-room suites with contemporary American appointments. 1-3 stories; interior corridors. **Dining:** Coffee shop; 7 am-10:30 & noon-3:30 pm; cocktails. **Cards:** AE, DI, DS, MC, VI. *(See color ad below)*

((242)363-3680

COMPASS POINT
◆◆◆ *Cottage*

12/15-4/15	$365
12/1-12/14 & 4/16-11/30	$235

Location: On Love Beach; 10 km w of Rawson Sq, 1.5 km w of airport on John F Kennedy. (PO Box CB-13842, NASSAU). Fax: 242/327-3299. **Terms:** Reserv deposit, 14 day notice; $5 service charge. **Facility:** 18 rooms. Brightly colored cottages facing the sea. Each with kitchen, private decks & rocking chairs. Upscale amenities. Fun, upbeat atmosphere. Oceanfront location. 2 two-bedroom units. 1 story; exterior corridors; oceanview; 1 lighted tennis court. **Services:** giftshop. **Recreation:** swimming, fishing, scuba diving, snorkeling, waterskiing. **All Rooms:** shower baths. **Some Rooms:** 9 efficiencies, 9 kitchens. **Cards:** AE, MC, VI.

(242/327-4500

▲▲▲ SAVE CRYSTAL CAY MARINE PARK & VILLAS
◆◆◆ **Cottage**

12/17-4/22	$550	XP $60
12/1-12/16 & 4/23-11/30	$425	XP $50

Location: Off W Bay St at site of Crystal Cay, auto access via narrow one way bridge. (PO Box N-7797, NASSAU). Fax: 242/323-3202. **Terms:** F12; Reserv deposit, 7 day notice; $5 service charge; weekly rates. **Facility:** 22 rooms. Secluded location. Bright 1-room suites, each with private pool & oceanfront patio. 1 story; exterior corridors; beach. **Dining:** Dining room; 11 am-3 & 6-11 pm; $16-$26. **Services:** giftshop; area transportation, to downtown & casinos. **All Rooms:** efficiencies. **Cards:** AE, DS, MC, VI. **Special Amenities: Early check-in/late check-out and free breakfast.** *(See color ad below)*

((242)328-1036

NASSAU MARRIOTT RESORT & CRYSTAL PALACE CASINO
◆◆◆ *Resort Hotel*

2/6-4/12	$169-305	XP $40
12/1-2/5 & 4/13-11/30	$129-255	XP $40

Location: On Cable Beach, 4.2 mi e of airport. (PO Box N-8306, NASSAU). Fax: 242/327-6818. **Terms:** F17; Reserv deposit, 3 day notice; $3 service charge. **Facility:** 1734 rooms. Large self-contained resort offering many activities & a variety of views. Large casino & "Vegas-style" shows. Somewhat futuristic public areas & tasteful rooms. 3 two-bedroom units, 867 three-bedroom units. 14 stories; interior corridors; oceanfront; beach. **Services:** giftshop. Fee: massage. **Recreation:** swimming, charter fishing. Fee: sailboating, snorkeling, windsurfing; bicycles. Rental: paddleboats, snorkeling equipment. **Some Rooms:** color TV. **Cards:** AE, DI, DS, MC, VI.

(242/327-6200

PARADISE ISLAND FUN CLUB
◆◆ *Resort Hotel*

All Year	$270-310	XP $90

Location: On Paradise Island; reached by toll bridge from Nassau. Harbour Dr (PO Box SS 6249, NASSAU). Fax: 242/363-3803. **Terms:** Reserv deposit, 14 day notice, 7 day in summer. **Facility:** 250 rooms. All inclusive facility located on the harbor-side of Paradise Island, overlooking downtown Nassau. Rates include tax, service charge, 3 meals & drinks; 12 stories; interior corridors; beach; 2 lighted tennis courts; boat dock. **Services:** giftshop. **Recreation:** swimming, charter fishing, scuba & snorkeling equipment; bicycles, sports court. Fee: scuba diving, snorkeling. **Cards:** AE, MC, VI.

(242/363-2561

▲▲▲ RADISSON CABLE BEACH RESORT
◆◆◆ *Resort Hotel*

12/19-1/3	$265-340	XP $45
1/29-4/26	$225-295	XP $45
1/4-1/28	$185-245	XP $45
12/1-12/18 & 4/27-11/30	$165-225	XP $45

Location: On Cable Beach; 5 mi w of Rawson Sq; 3.5 mi e of airport. (PO Box N-4914, NASSAU). Fax: 242/327-6987. **Terms:** F17; Reserv deposit, 21 day notice; handling fee imposed; monthly rates. **Facility:** 691 rooms. Oceanfront hotel. All units with small balcony or patio; many with views of the Atlantic Ocean. 1 time bellman charge, $5. All inclusive packages avail; 9 stories; interior corridors; beach, wading pool, whirlpools; racquetball courts, 18 tennis courts (5 lighted). Fee: 18 holes golf. **Dining:** 5 restaurants, cafeteria; 6 am-11:30 pm; $12-$42; cocktails; 15% service charge. **Services:** giftshop. **Recreation:** swimming, private beach-front water sports concession, sea kayaks; 3 squash courts. Fee: boating, canoeing, snorkeling & equipment. Rental: paddleboats. **Some Rooms:** whirlpools. **Cards:** AE, CB, DI, MC, VI. *(See color ad p 75)*

((242)327-6000

▲▲▲ SAVE RADISSON GRAND RESORT PARADISE ISLAND
◆◆◆ *Hotel*

12/20-1/2 & 2/1-4/24	$255-280	XP $35
1/4-1/31	$210-240	XP $35
4/25-11/30	$200-225	XP $35
12/1-12/19	$185-210	XP $35

Location: On Paradise Island, reached by toll bridge from Nassau. Casino Dr (PO Box SS 6307, NASSAU). Fax: 242/363-3900. **Terms:** F17. **Facility:** 360 rooms. Meets AAA guest room security requirements. All inclusive rates avail. $5 per person, per day energy surcharge; housekeeping gratuity; 13 stories; interior corridors; oceanfront; beach; 4 lighted tennis courts. **Dining:** 3 restaurants; 7 am-10:30 pm; poolside cafe also avail; $12-$33; cocktails; 15% service charge. **Services:** giftshop. Fee: massage. **Recreation:** swimming, scuba diving, snorkeling; beauty salon. Fee: waterskiing, windsurfing, charter fishing, parasailing, banana boats, jet skis; bicycles. Rental: sailboats, scuba & snorkeling equipment. **Cards:** AE, CB, DI, JC, MC, VI.

((242)363-3500

SANDALS ROYAL BAHAMIAN RESORT & SPA
◆◆◆ *Resort Hotel*

12/20-3/20	$560-800
12/1-12/19 & 3/21-11/30	$540-780

Location: 5 mi w of Rawson Sq at w end of Cable Beach. W Bay St (PO Box CB-13005, NASSAU). Fax: 242/327-6961. **Terms:** Age restrictions may apply; reserv deposit, 45 day notice; 2 night min stay. **Facility:** 196 rooms. Couples only. Elegant resort offering rooms in the manor house & upgraded garden suites with private verandas. Expansive beautiful public areas & grounds, Colonial architecture & Greco-Roman statuary. Rates include all food, drinks, activities, taxes & gratuities; exclusive of spa services; 6 stories; interior/exterior corridors; 18 holes golf; beach, heated pool, sauna; 4 lighted tennis courts. **Dining:** 6 restaurants; 7:30 am-3:30 am; cocktails; afternoon tea. **Services:** giftshop. Fee: massage. **Recreation:** swimming, charter fishing, sailboating, scuba diving/snorkeling & equipment, waterskiing, windsurfing; Full service spa. Misting pool. Private offshore recreational island. **Cards:** AE, DS, MC, VI.

☎ (242)327-6400

SOUTH OCEAN GOLF & BEACH RESORT
◆◆ *Resort Motor Inn*

12/19-1/3	$145-280	XP $25-35
1/4-4/7	$165-235	XP $25-35
12/1-12/18 & 4/8-11/30	$110-140	XP $30

Location: On sw end of island; 8.5 mi sw of airport. Adelaide Rd (PO Box N-8191, NASSAU). Fax: 242/362-4728. **Terms:** F12; Reserv deposit, 21 day notice, 7 day off season. **Facility:** 239 rooms. Lodge units with simple furnishings & compact bathrooms or upgraded oceanfront units in 3-story greathouse with Colonial ambiance & balcony or patio. Sprawling grounds. Remote peaceful setting. For US reservations 1-800-992-2015; 2-3 stories, no elevator; interior/exterior corridors; putting green; beach; 4 tennis courts (Fee: 4 lighted). Fee: 18 holes golf. **Services:** giftshop. Fee: area transportation. **Recreation:** swimming, charter fishing. Fee: sailboating, scuba diving, snorkeling, windsurfing. Rental: paddleboats, scuba & snorkeling equipment. **Cards:** AE, CB, DI, DS, MC, VI.

☎ 242/362-4391

RESTAURANTS

CAFE MARTINIQUE
◆◆◆ *French* — D $30-$39

Location: On Paradise Island, reached by toll bridge from Nassau; in Atlantis Resort & Casino. Casino Dr. **Hours:** 6:30 pm-10 pm. Closed: Sun. **Reservations:** required. **Features:** semi-formal attire; health conscious menu; cocktails & lounge; entertainment; valet parking; a la carte. Elegant dining rooms overlooking lagoon. Few American dishes. Patio dining, weather permitting. 15% service charge. Bustling atmosphere. Formal service. **Cards:** AE, MC, VI.

☎ 242/363-2222

▲▲▲ 'SUN AND —' RESTAURANT
◆◆◆   *French*   D $28-$40

Location: 4.8 mi e of Rawson Sq off Shirley St, just nw. Lakeview Dr. **Hours:** Open 12/1-8/1 & 10/1-11/30; 6:30 pm-9:30 pm. Closed major holidays, 4/2, 5/9, 12/26, Mon, 8/1-9/30 & Super Bowl day. **Reservations:** required; in season. **Features:** No A/C; semi-formal attire; children's menu; health conscious menu; cocktails & lounge; a la carte. Excellent variety of imaginative dishes incorporating local & International flavors. Features dessert souffles. Served in garden courtyard. 15% service charge. **Cards:** AE, DS, MC, VI.

(242/393-1205

TAMARIND HILL RESTAURANT
◆◆   *Ethnic*   L $6-$11   D $7-$26

Location: 2.5 mi e of Rawson Sq, off Shirley St. Village Rd. **Hours:** 1/2-5/31 noon-midnight, 6/1-12/31 4 pm-midnight. Closed: 1/1 & 12/25. **Reservations:** suggested. **Features:** No A/C; casual dress; cocktails; a la carte. Porch & patio dining with casual island atmosphere. Good mix of island seafood, pasta, chicken, pork & fajitas. Excellent selection of homemade dessert. 15% service charge. **Cards:** AE, MC, VI.

(242/393-1306

VESUVIO RISTORANTE
◆◆   *Italian*   D $14-$29

Location: Downtown on oceanfront, 0.5 mi w of Rawson Square. **Hours:** 6 pm-11 pm. Closed: 10/1-10/31. **Reservations:** accepted. **Features:** casual dress; cocktails & lounge; street parking; a la carte. Well prepared fresh local seafood, including a variety of conch dishes like Fettucine Bahamian. Wonderful Italian & pasta dishes also avail. **Cards:** AE, MC, VI.

(242/325-0324

STELLA MARIS (LONG ISLAND)

LODGING

CAPE SANTA MARIA BEACH RESORT
◆◆◆   *Cottage*

12/15-4/14	$245-370	XP $50
12/1-12/14 & 4/15-11/30	$195-295	XP $50

Location: 6 mi n from Stella Maris Airport at Cape Santa Maria (landing strip avail at resort). PO Box LI 30177 30117. Fax: 242/338-6013. **Terms:** F6; Reserv deposit, 30 day notice. **Facility:** 20 rooms. Peaceful setting. Fine beach & water sport facilities. Attractive cottages. 15% food & beverage service charge; room service charge, $6 per person per day; 1 story; exterior corridors; oceanfront; beach. **Recreation:** swimming, charter fishing, snorkeling & equipment; bicycles. Fee: fishing, scuba diving & equipment. **All Rooms:** combo or shower baths. **Cards:** AE, MC, VI.

(242/338-5273

WALKERS CAY (GREAT ABACO ISLAND)

LODGING

WALKERS CAY HOTEL & MARINA, BAHAMAS
◆◆   *Resort Hotel*

3/1-9/6	$140-160	XP $20
12/1-2/28 & 9/7-11/30	$100-120	XP $20

Location: Uppermost Island of Abaco chain. Pan Am Airbridge out of Ft. Lauderdale airport is the only scheduled transportation. (700 SW 34th St, FORT LAUDERDALE, FL, 33315). Fax: 242/353-1339. **Terms:** F12; Reserv deposit, 21 day notice. **Facility:** 63 rooms. On 100 acre private island. Large, simply furnished rooms with balcony. Airport accommodates charter & privately owned aircraft. Full service marina. Grocery & wholesale liquor store on property. 1 three-bedroom unit, 3 two-bedroom units. For US reservations: (954)359-1400. Villas, $250-$575; $200-$450 off season. Maids $1 per person, per night; 2 stories; interior/exterior corridors; beach; 2 tennis courts; playground. Fee: marina. **Services:** giftshop. **Recreation:** swimming; sports court. Fee: charter fishing, fishing, scuba diving/snorkeling & equipment. Rental: boats. **All Rooms:** shower baths. **Some Rooms:** color TV. **Cards:** AE, DI, DS, MC, VI.

(242/353-1252

BARBADOS

EASTERNMOST OF THE CARIBBEAN islands, Barbados is the "Little England of Eternal Summer." Meaning "the bearded ones," its name is said to have been given by a Portuguese discoverer because of the beardlike vines on the fig trees. With nearly 1,600 inhabitants per square mile, Barbados is one of the most densely populated countries in the Caribbean; the friendliness of its people is its foremost charm.

The silver sand beaches on the Caribbean side of the island contrast with the rugged Atlantic coastline. Roads commonly paved in coral are bordered by fields of cane, royal palms and rolling hills and terraces. Vivid tropical flowers, including fragrant oleander, frangipani, jasmine, cassia, bougainvillea, hibiscus and lady-of-the-night, lie in profusion along neat hedgerows. Scarlet flame trees and coral walls shelter the well-tended lawns of color-washed houses, and windmills of former sugar plantations dot the land, though the Morgan Lewis Sugar Mill is the only one with its arms and wheelhouses still intact.

Bridgetown, the capital, is representative of the island's heritage. Its typically English atmosphere is enhanced by names like Yorkshire and Windsor and by the ritual of afternoon tea, which occurs at "half after four."

HISTORY, GOVERNMENT AND ECONOMY

Once inhabited only by Arawak Indians, Barbados was discovered by the Portuguese in the 16th century. The English claimed it in 1625, and 2 years later the first settlers arrived. The island's population increased significantly during the mid-1600s as English immigrants fled the political unrest in their homeland and slaves were brought from Africa to work the sugar crops. The colony thrived early on as a result of the tobacco and cotton trade and became a prosperous sugar producer in the 17th and 18th centuries. During the struggle for European supremacy in the Caribbean, 35 forts were built along 25 miles (40 km) of coastline. The ruins of many are still visible.

Of all the islands in the West Indies, Barbados is the only one to have remained solely in the hands of its original settlers. This fact helps explain the island's stability and the British flavor that has remained constant over the centuries.

Since 1954 Barbados has had a ministerial system of government with a governor-general appointed by the Queen of Great Britain on recommendation of the Prime Minister, who heads the island's government. Barbados became an independent nation on Nov. 30, 1966. A coat of arms bearing the motto "Pride and Industry" speaks for the high literacy rate and prosperous economy; Barbados is one of the most economically stable Caribbean islands, with tourism, sugar production and light industry forming the basis of the economy.

SHOPPING

High-quality English clothing and Scottish and English fabrics are excellent buys in Barbados. Bridgetown tailor shops on Prince Alfred and Tudor streets offer made-to-measure clothing in a variety of materials ranging from sea island cotton to imported tweeds. Baskets, seashell trinkets, pottery, English china and silver, silks and Oriental objects and antiques also are popular purchases. Another leading commodity available at a very low price is Barbados rum. By shopping in the afternoon you can avoid the morning rush.

Most of the duty-free shopping in Bridgetown is concentrated on Broad Street. Cave Shepard, Barbados' largest department store, features Waterford, Wedgwood, Royal Doulton and Swarovski china and crystal, an extensive selection of cosmetics and fragrances, leather goods, jewelry, electronics, fashions and a liquor department. Harrison's is a department store that contains a vast assortment of luxury items including Lladro figurines, designer sweaters, jewelry and watches by Cartier, Fendi and Gucci.

Da Costa's Mall, also on Broad Street, houses several interesting boutiques including Louis L. Bayley & Sons, specializing in European jewelry, fine watches, camera equipment, china, crystal and silverware. Farther down the street is Mall 34, consisting of such shops as India House, which displays high quality merchandise from India and Europe, and the Royal Shop, with a wide selection of watches. Columbian Jewel is just beyond Mall 34.

Malls in the Hastings and Worthing area of Christ Church include Chattel House Village, Hastings Plaza, Keswick, Sandy Bank, Skyway Plaza and Quayside Centre. Sheraton Centre, one of the island's largest malls, is in Christ Church at Sargeants' Village.

Barbados is said to have some of the finest antiques in the West Indies. Reputable dealers include Antiquaria on Spring Garden Highway and Greenwich House Antiques at Greenwich Village, St. James.

Medford Craft Village, at Lower Barbarees Hill in St. Michael, specializes in such local handicrafts as pottery, wood carvings, batik and woven baskets. Shells, metal art, leather, coral and other island-made articles can be found at Pelican Village, on Princess Alice Highway near Deep Water Harbour. Temple Yard, south of Pelican Village in Bridgetown, is where members of the Rastafarian sect display crafts.

The Best of Barbados Shops, with several locations throughout the island, sell only products made or designed in Barbados. The shops have a wide assortment of local handicrafts and souvenirs including hand-painted tile, kitchen items, local prints, pottery and T-shirts. Earthworks Pottery atop Shop Hill in St. Thomas offers handmade pottery; phone (246) 425-0223.

Some stores feature in-bond departments, where certain merchandise has been set aside and marked with two prices. The higher price applies to buy-and-take purchases; the second in-bond price, usually considerably lower, applies to merchandise purchased in the store and delivered to the airport or pier. In-bond buys, discounted well below U.S. list prices, must be made at least 24 hours prior to departure. Shopping hours in Barbados are Mon.-Fri. 8-4, Sat. 8-noon. Banks are open Mon.-Thurs. 9-3, Fri. 9-1 and 3-5; some banks open at 8 a.m.

FOOD AND DRINK

In addition to fine Continental and curried dishes, Barbados has many island specialties. These include *bonavist*, small white beans often seasoned with pumpkin and herbs; *jug-jug*, a molded dish of chopped ham and salt beef or pork combined with green peas; *cou-cou*, a savory pudding made with cornmeal and okra; and Barbadian black pudding, similar to a sausage stuffed with seasoned grated sweet potatoes.

Other local foods are *pepperpot*, a spicy stew made with selected meats; and *conkies*, a steamed concoction of sweet potatoes, cornmeal, pumpkin, coconut, raisins and spices served in a

THINGS TO KNOW

AREA: 166 square miles (430 sq km).

POPULATION: 260,000.

LANGUAGE: English.

CAPITAL: Bridgetown.

GOVERNMENT: Independent nation within the British Commonwealth.

TIME ZONE: Atlantic.

UNIT OF CURRENCY: Barbados dollar. $1 U.S.=2.01 Barbados dollars. U.S. bills and travelers checks are accepted by most hotels.

ELECTRICITY: 110 volts, 50 cycles AC.

CARS: Local permit ($5) required; drive on left.

IMMIGRATION REQUIREMENTS: Proof of U.S. citizenship (birth certificate, naturalization papers with photo ID or passport) and return or through ticket are required. There is a 6-month limit on the stay. Departure tax about $12.50.

FOR FURTHER INFORMATION:
Barbados Tourism Authority
800 Second Ave., 2nd Floor
New York, NY 10017
(212) 986-6516 or (800) 221-9831
Barbados Tourism Authority
Harbour Road
Bridgetown, Barbados
(246) 427-2623

HOLIDAYS: Jan. 1; Errol W. Barrow's Birthday, Jan. 21; Good Friday; Easter Monday; Labour Day, May 1; Whit Monday (8th Monday after Easter); Kadooment Day, Aug. (1st Mon.); United Nations Day, Oct. (1st Mon.); Independence Day, Nov. 30; Dec. 25; Boxing Day, Dec. 26.

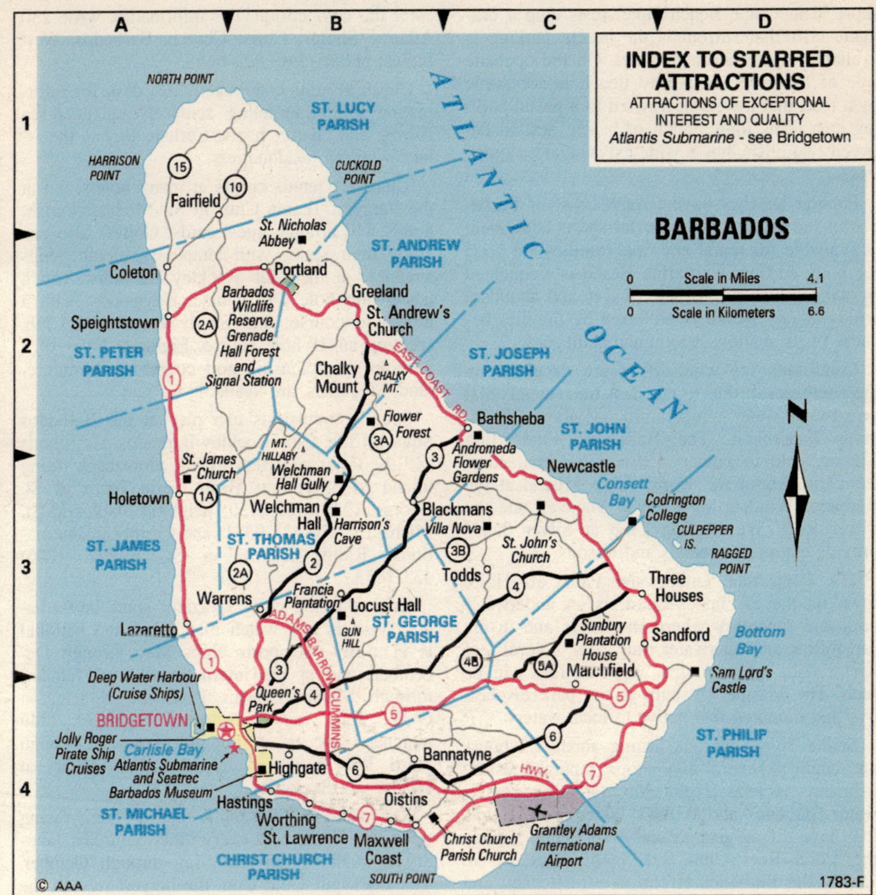

banana leaf. Roast suckling pig and native "flying fish" are favorite specialties. Fresh lobster and seafood are available. The fruits of Barbados are avocados, mangoes, guavas, bananas, breadfruit, golden apples, hog plums, gooseberries, cherries, pears, oranges, limes and grapefruit.

The island rum has a distinctive flavor; a 17th-century observer said of it, "The chief fuddling they make in the Island is Rum Bullion, alias Kill-Devil, and is made of sugar-cane distilled, a hot, hellish and terrible liquor."

Most hotels and resorts on Barbados include a 10-percent charge on the guest's bill to cover gratuities. However, in nightclubs and restaurants, tipping is at the discretion of the guest.

SPORTS AND AMUSEMENTS

Most major hotels have a beach or are near one, and all types of aquatic gear can be rented. Motorboats (for water skiing) and sailboats are available for hire at beach club resorts. Conditions are excellent for skiing in the tranquil waters off the west coast, while sailing is favorable on both the west and south coasts. In the path of the trade winds, the east coast beaches are considered dangerous for swimming but ideal for surfing, with the Soup Bowl at Bathsheba being the best area for this sport.

Popular west coast beaches include Mullins Beach near Speightstown, which features a good snorkeling reef just offshore, shaded areas, shower facilities and an open-air restaurant that provides a view of the bay. Paynes Bay, recognizable by the neighboring fish market, is a site where numerous water sports are indulged in. Visitors will enjoy the picturesque bay at Sandy Lane, with public access available on either side of the hotel.

Southeast coast beaches are not known for swimming amenities, but rather for their rugged beauty. Bottom Bay, north of Sam Lord's Castle, is a delightful cove with a white sand beach surrounded by cliffs and a coconut grove. At Crane Beach, pounding waves crash against the rocky shore. The Crane Beach Hotel rests atop a dramatic cliff that surrounds the beach; parking is available at the beach or hotel. On the opposite side of the hotel, Foul Bay Beach is accessible by a road that travels downward to a paved parking area. This long stretch of beach, nestled between two cliffs, has a wide expanse of seagrape trees.

Popular beaches on the south coast of Barbados include Accra, where water-sports equipment is available for rental and opportunities are good for body surfing. Casuarina Beach is frequented by windsurfers due to large waves and abundant winds. Sandy Beach is preferred by families because of its shallow lagoon and calm seas.

Conditions for windsurfing are excellent on the south coast, due to constant trade winds and year-round water temperatures of about 78 degrees Fahrenheit. The Barbados Windsurfing Classic, held in January, attracts top contenders from throughout the world. Club Mistral at the Barbados Windsurfing Club in Maxwell and the Silver Rock Windsurfing Club at Silver Sands provide equipment rentals and lessons.

The Folkestone Underwater Park, off Holetown on the St. James coast, is an underwater park and sanctuary where snorkelers and divers can follow an underwater trail along a coral reef where fish, sea anemones and sea fans can be seen. The Marine Museum at the park displays live and mounted fish native to local waters.

Scuba diving lessons lasting about 2.5 hours are taught at several dive shops; reputable establishments include Exploresub Barbados, Underwater Barbados and Willie's Watersports. Hotels that have diving gear available for rental include the Coral Reef Club and Sandy Lane in St. James; the Barbados Hilton in St. Michael; and Divi Southwinds and Sandy Beach in Christ Church.

Numerous shipwrecks in the waters around Barbados provide excellent diving opportunities. A large number of these wrecks are concentrated in Carlisle Bay, including *Sea Trek,* deliberately sunk in about 40 feet of water; *The Berwyn,* an old tugboat brimming with sea life less than 10 feet from the surface; and *The Fox,* a 120-foot schooner approximately 40 feet from the surface that is home to numerous crustaceans. *Friar's Craig* is a small vessel in the area of coast slightly east of the Hilton. The *Stavronikita,* a Greek freighter, was deliberately sunk by the Park and Beaches Commission in Folkestone Underwater Park.

January through June are the best fishing months; dolphin fish, kingfish, snapper, albacore, shark, barracuda and "flying fish" are plentiful. Fishing boats and guides can be hired for fishing excursions at most hotels or through the Barbados Game Fishing Club. The Barbados Game Fishing Club also sponsors an annual fishing contest the last week in April, and visitors may

enter the competition. For information write 230 Atlantic Shores, Christ Church, Barbados, West Indies; phone (246) 428-6668.

Check at your hotel's activities desk for information about snorkeling, scuba diving, deep-sea fishing and charter boats. Carlisle Bay is the island's sailing headquarters.

There are tennis courts at many hotels and at the Paragon Tennis Club in St. Michael Parish; hotels will arrange guest cards. Golfers also can enjoy their sport, with temporary memberships available at the Club Rockley Barbados, which has a nine-hole golf course; Heywoods, with a nine-hole course; and Sandy Lane Golf Club, sporting an 18-hole course. Eighteen holes of a 27-hole championship golf course at Westmoreland, St. James, are available for play.

Squash enthusiasts can play at the Barbados Squash Club, Club Rockley Barbados, Heywoods and the Pineapple Beach Club. Horseback riding inland is offered at Beau Geste Farm in St. George, (246) 429-0139; Brighton Stables in St. Michael, (246) 425-9381; and Caribbean International Riding Centre in St. Joseph, (246) 433-1453.

Cricket is the chief spectator sport in Barbados. Visitors can watch matches at the national level at several sports clubs May through December, and at the international level January through March. Queens Park and Kensington Oval, both in Bridgetown, regularly hold matches. Soccer is popular January through April. Polo is played July through February at Holder's in St. James.

The Garrison Savannah has a horse-racing track with races held every other Saturday, January through March and May through October. The Cockspur Gold Cup, the biggest race in the Caribbean, usually takes place in March; festivities and a parade accompany this exciting event. The Barbados Turf Club's race meetings, held five times a year, are joyous occasions with music, food booths and a general carnival atmosphere. Automobile races occur several times a year at Bushy Park in St. Philip.

Many discos, nightclubs and restaurants provide after-dinner entertainment. The limbo and calypso, danced to the haunting rhythm of steel bands, entertain spectators and participants alike. For those who would rather look at the stars than dance beneath them, the Barbados Astronomical Society offers a night of stargazing at the Harry Bayley Observatory in nearby Clapham every Friday from 8:30 to 10:30 (weather permitting). Although there are no casinos in Barbados, slot machines are permitted; there are arcades in Bridgetown and at some resorts.

Sunday and Thursday evenings from 6:30 to 10 the Barbados Museum *(see attraction listing p. 148)* presents the cultural show "1627 and All That Sort of Thing," a tour of the museum and an authentic Barbadian dinner. The Plantation

Restaurant stages two dinner shows: the "Plantation Tropical Spectacular II" on Saturday at 6 p.m. and the "Barbados by Night Calypso Cabaret Show" on Wednesday and Friday at 6:30 p.m.; phone (246) 428-5048.

The Ocean View Hotel in Hastings hosts a seasonal cabaret, with dinner served at 7 p.m. and curtain time at 9:30; for information phone (246) 427-7821. Marriott Sam Lord's hosts Bajan Fiesta Night, an evening of entertainment preceded by a food festival in a Barbadian village setting. Plays are presented by the Pinelands Creative Workshop, a group of amateur performers; phone (246) 429-5359.

Annual events include the Holetown Festival in February, a celebration which commemorates the arrival of English settlers in 1627. Activities include a parade of vintage cars, a street fair and arts and crafts. In April, the Oistins Fish Festival pays tribute to Barbados' fishing industry; a Coast Guard exhibition, boat races and a fishboning contest are among the events.

Barbadians eagerly anticipate the nonstop revelry of the Crop-Over Festival, which occurs from mid-July to early August. The event, an island-wide folk celebration in honor of the completion of the sugar cane harvest, is considered one of the Caribbean's most popular. It features calypso competitions, art shows, food, music, crafts, a costume parade and fireworks on Kadooment Day (a national holiday) and other entertainment. The folk music of Barbados is celebrated every year at the National Independence Festival of Creative Arts in November.

The *Barbados Advocate* and *The Nation* are Bridgetown's daily newspapers. *The Nation* also produces *The Sun on Saturday* and *The Sunday Sun*. The tourist publications *The Visitor* and *The Sun Seeker* contain entertainment information.

EXCURSIONS AND SIGHTSEEING

From mid-January to early April the Barbados National Trust provides tours of historic houses on Wednesday afternoons from 2:30-5:30. The $6 fee provides entry to some of Barbados' most attractive and interesting private homes. A different house is featured each Wednesday; residences highlighted may include Mullins Mill, Lancaster Great House, Leamington Pavilion, Porters Great House and Cluffs Plantation House. Villa Nova, a beautifully landscaped great house frequently on the tour, is an 18-room exclusive retreat.

The National Trust also sponsors free nature hikes every Sunday at 6 a.m. and 3:30. These informative walks offer insight into Barbados' history, environment and culture. For information about the historic house tours or the hikes phone the National Trust at (246) 436-9033.

Glass-bottom boats afford a fascinating view of sea life among the coral reefs of the west coast; the Folkestone Underwater Park and the old shipwrecks in Carlisle Bay are popular attractions. Luncheon and dinner cruises aboard the *Jolly Roger (see attraction listing p. 85)* depart from Bridgetown. The *Bajan Queen*, a Mississippi-style riverboat also departing from Bridgetown harbor, offers sunset dinner cruises; phone (246) 436-2149.

Snorkeling stops are included on the *Tiami*, (246) 427-7245, and *Heat Wave*, (246) 423-7871, catamarans that offer lunch and sunset cruises; the *Irish Mist*, (246) 436-9201, a catamaran featuring a calypso cruise and buffet lunch; and *Secret Love*, (246) 432-1972, a 40-foot yacht that sails along the coastline and provides a Barbadian buffet. The M/V *Harbour Master* offers a variety of cruises aboard the 4-deck-high boat complete with a ramp for beach landings and a semi-submersible chamber to view the underwater life; phone (246) 430-0900.

Cruises to neighboring islands can be arranged through Caribbean Safari Tours, Chantours Caribbean, Grenadine Tours and St. James Travel and Tours. Helicopter tours are available daily from Bajan Helicopters in Bridgetown.

Popular land excursions include a drive along the rugged Atlantic coast past such points of interest as Sam Lord's Castle, Codrington College, St. John's Church and the pottery works at Chalky Mount. Those touring Barbados will notice numerous chattel houses, made of wood and built up on rocks so they could be dismantled easily and moved to another location. Rum shops also contribute to the local flavor, serving as village meeting places where locals can exchange news.

About 850 feet (259 m) above sea level, Cherry Tree Hill in St. Andrew offers an excellent view of the hilly Scotland District, where cane fields stretch toward the coast. Mahogany trees on the hill's summit are a playground for monkeys, usually visible in the evening. For a small fee visitors can enter the Morgan Lewis Sugar Mill, about a mile (1.6 km) southeast of Cherry Tree Hill, and observe the machinery used to grind sugar cane in the 18th and 19th centuries. The window on the top level provides a glimpse of the surrounding countryside; phone (246) 422-7429.

St. Andrew's Parish Church dates from 1846; the previous building withstood the 1780 and 1831 hurricanes. The wooden altar, with stained-glass windows at its center, is surrounded by colorful floor tiles. St. Andrew also is home to Mount Hillaby, the highest point on the island at 1,115 feet (340 m); a narrow, winding road leads from the town of Hillaby to the summit. Nearby Turner's Hall Woods, a 50-acre (20-hectare) ecosystem containing many indigenous plant and animal species, is what remains of a dense tropical forest that once covered the island.

In St. Peter wild green monkeys frolic in their natural habitat in the Barbados Wildlife Reserve, where animals roam freely within 4 acres (1.6

hectares) of mahogany forest. Nearby Farley Hill National Park, which provides captivating views of the coast, contains lush gardens and the ruins of a sugar planter's estate. Sections of the park were filmed for the movie "Island In The Sun."

The Animal Flower Cave is in St. Lucy at the island's northern tip, one of the most scenic coastal areas in Barbados. Steps descend into a coral limestone cave that contains three rooms. This sea-sculptured formation obtains its name from the sea anemones that exist in the pools, one of which is deep enough to swim in. Use caution and wear sneakers since the steps are steep and the rocks can be slippery. A guide leads the way into the cave, which is sometimes closed due to high tides; for information phone (246) 439-8797.

Cove Bay is in St. Lucy on the east coast. The area provides a splendid panorama, but swimming is not possible in this area of wild natural beauty. Visitors can view the cove from the rocky cliffs that surround it and watch the tumultuous waves of the Atlantic crash against the shore. Towering above the cove is Pico Tenerife, a jagged rock formation that springs forth from the ocean to a height of 269 feet (82 m).

The East Coast Road, traversing the rolling hills and greenery of the Scotland district and the rocky east coast, provides spectacular sightseeing opportunities. The road travels past Bathsheba, a haven for surfers and identified by the huge boulders that protrude from the water. Cattlewash, a scenic stretch of coast punctuated by beach houses, took its name from the cattle that occasionally wander through the area. North of Cattlewash, Barclays Park is a popular spot for picnicking and recreation. The park overlooks a scenic stretch of coast lined with seagrape, hog plum and casuarina trees. Swimming is not recommended due to the strong current. A small restaurant in the 50-acre (20-hectare) park serves good Barbadian food.

Barbados' famed "Gold Coast" along the Caribbean is lined with luxury hotels that boast tranquil beaches of powdery sand. A tour through St. Thomas Parish in the center of the island usually includes the botanical garden at Welchman Hall Gully and Harrison's Cave. The parish also contains the 1799 Sharon Moravian Church, one of the few unaltered 18th-century structures on the island. St. Thomas and neighboring St. George are the only parishes without any coastal area.

Oistin is a picturesque fishing village in Christ Church Parish at the south end of the island. A fish market is held daily near the wharf where the fishing boats are docked. Several restored historic rum shops are in the area and can be visited. The Oistin Fish Fry, where visitors and locals can partake in freshly-cooked fish, takes place nightly.

Barbados has four lighthouses positioned on strategic areas of coastline. Ragged Point Lighthouse, in St. Philip at the island's eastern tip, is constructed of coral limestone and provides an outstanding view of the east coast and Pico Tenerife. South Point Lighthouse, at the island's southernmost point in Christ Church, is a cast-iron structure made in England and shipped to Barbados in 1851. Other lighthouses are at Harrison Point in St. Lucy and Needham's Point in St. Michael.

You can arrange to tour some of the large sugar factories, such as Portvale, Bulkeley and Corrington. The St. James Sugar Machinery Museum, next to the Portvale factory yard near Holetown, is open during the sugar-grinding season from February through June; phone (246) 432-0100.

Weekday tours and special luncheon tours are available at the Mount Gay rum distillery in Bridgetown on Spring Garden Highway; phone (246) 425-9066. "Where The Rum Come From" is a guided tour of the West India Rum Refinery, home of world-renowned Cockspur rum. The tour, which is held on Wednesday, includes a Barbadian buffet, entertainment provided by a steel band and complimentary rum drinks; for information phone (246) 435-6900. Banks Barbados Breweries, producers of Banks beer, conducts tours Tuesday and Thursday at 10 and 1; for reservations phone (246) 429-2113.

The Barbados Heritage Passport provides discounts to various places of historical and cultural interest. Sites include Andromeda Botanical Gardens, the Barbados Museum, the Bridgetown Synagogue, Codrington College, Francia Plantation, Gun Hill, Morgan Lewis Sugar Mill, St. Nicholas Abbey, Sunbury Plantation House, Villa Nova and Welchman Hall Gully. The passport, which can be purchased at hotels and National Trust properties, also offers discounts in shops and restaurants. For additional information phone (246) 426-2421 in Barbados, or (800) 221-9831 in the United States.

TRANSPORTATION

Daily non-stop flights from New York and Miami touch down at Barbados' Grantley Adams International Airport. Interisland flights connect Barbados with Trinidad, Grenada, St. Vincent, St. Lucia, Martinique and the islands to the north. Barbados also is a port of call for many cruise ships.

The roads from Bridgetown to the popular districts are good, and the Adams-Barrow-Cummins (ABC) Highway from the airport to Highway 2A at Warrens enables traffic to bypass Bridgetown, reducing travel time by about 50 percent. You can rent cars, minimokes (resembling small jeeps), scooters, bicycles, chauffeur-driven cars and limousines. You must present a valid U.S. driver's license to obtain a Barbados permit; the cost is $5 per year.

Driving is on the left side of the road. Speed limits are 35 mph (60 km/h) in most areas of the island, with the exception being 25 mph (40 km/h) in town and 50 mph (80 km/h) on the Spring Garden Highway. No car may be driven in Barbados without third-party insurance coverage.

Frequent bus service connects the parishes with Bridgetown. Transport Board buses, painted blue and trimmed in yellow, depart every half-hour from the three main terminals in Bridgetown: The Lower Green and Princess Alice Highway terminals provide transportation to destinations in the north part of the island and along the west coast, while the Fairchild Street terminal is for southbound travelers. There also is a Transport Board terminal in Speightstown.

Privately owned minibuses, mostly yellow with blue trim, travel shorter distances and therefore have faster turnaround times. The main minibus terminals are in Bridgetown at Probyn Street, River Road and Temple Yard. Even when at a designated stop, you must wave at the minibuses to get the driver to come to a halt. Buses run daily 6 a.m.-midnight; fare is $1.50 and exact change is required for the Transport Board buses.

Taxis are readily available in the Trafalgar Square area of Bridgetown; a taxi stand is next to a fountain that is adorned with dolphins. Check the fixed rates before taking a cab.

ATTRACTION ADMISSIONS
Attraction admissions for this island are quoted in U.S. dollars.

POINTS OF INTEREST

See map page 79.

BATHSHEBA (C-2)

A resort in St. Joseph's Parish 14 miles (23 km) from Bridgetown, Bathsheba has been called a miniature Cornish coast. The Flying Fish Fleet, purveyors of Barbados' national dish, arrives daily at Tent Bay. The outside verandah of the Atlantis Hotel is a popular spot for a typical Barbadian lunch, with Tent Bay and Bathsheba providing a scenic backdrop.

A drive up to 1,000-foot (305-m) Hackleton's Cliff offers an excellent view of a nature preserve, the island's eastern hills and Bathsheba's beaches. The nearby Cotton Tower is one of six signal stations built across Barbados by the British as part of the island's defense. Horse Hill, also in St. Joseph, provides a sweeping view of the east coast and Scotland district.

ANDROMEDA FLOWER GARDENS, .2 mi. (.4 km) off Hwy. 3 following signs, overlooking Bathsheba, contains individual gardens displaying such tropical flora as bougainvillea, hibiscus, orchids, palms and cactus, along with ferns, aroids, begonias and other plants. Giant boulders, lily ponds and a meandering stream enhance the landscape. Allow 1 hour minimum. Daily 9-5. Admission $5. Phone (246) 433-9261.

FLOWER FOREST, at Richmond Plantation, following signs from Bathsheba, covers 50 acres (20 hectares). Hillside trails wind among tropical trees and plants, including bamboo, banana, avocado, breadfruit, coconut, coffee, cocoa and Barbados cherry. Also on view are relics of the sugar industry. Food is available. Allow 1 hour minimum. Daily 9-5; closed Good Friday and Dec. 25. Admission $5; ages 5-16, $2.50. Phone (246) 433-8152.

BRIDGETOWN (B-4) pop. 97,000

Barbados' capital, Bridgetown is home port for many commercial vessels. The city was founded in 1629 and was the chief residential section during the island's settlement. The exuberance of its people and customs blend with a Victorian austerity typified by the Public Buildings that house Parliament.

A statue of Lord Nelson in Trafalgar Square was erected by planters in recognition of the British admiral, who saved their sugar profits from the French. St. Michael's Cathedral, on St.

Michael's Row, was rebuilt in 1831 of coral rock after the original was destroyed by hurricanes. George Washington is recorded as having attended services in the original cathedral in 1751; it is now one of the town's main attractions.

The Public Buildings are on Broad Street facing Trafalgar Square. The House of Assembly meetings, held in the east building's Public Gallery, usually can be observed Tuesday at noon; visitors must be appropriately dressed and cameras are not permitted. The gallery contains stained-glass windows that represent the sovereigns of England and a speaker's chair with intricate carvings.

The Careenage, in central Bridgetown alongside Wharf Street, is a picturesque harbor where pleasure craft are docked. The Chamberlain Bridge, one of two bridges that span the Careenage, contains the Independence Arch, erected in 1987 to commemorate the island's 21st anniversary as a self-governing nation. Next to the arch is an area of shops and restaurants that overlook the water, including an outdoor cafe. Fishing and sailing charters as well as scuba diving excursions can be arranged at the waterfront shops.

Off Broad Street, the center of activity for shoppers and strollers, visitors can find duty-free shops offering china, crystal, leather and fine jewelry. The city has many delightful side streets and marketplaces. The Fairchild Street market is a bustling center of activity, with merchants selling produce, snacks, clothing, shoes, newspapers and other items. Another colorful market can be found on Cheapside Street.

The Jewish Synagogue, on Magazine Lane, dates from 1654. Said to be one of the oldest synagogues in the Western Hemisphere, the structure was destroyed by a hurricane in 1933 and has been restored within the past 5 years. The adjoining cemetery has tombstones dating from the 1630s.

Situated on Bay Street, opposite the Prime Minister's office and next to Bayshore Beach, the Esplanade offers a nice view of Bridgetown's harbor area and Carlisle Bay. The small park, which was once a village of wooden houses, contains benches shaded by trees and a lovely gazebo. St. Patrick's Roman Catholic Cathedral, also on Bay Street, dates from 1839.

The Garrison Historic Area, just south of town, was a strategic military area housing British troops 1780-1905. The area contains several monuments and buildings of historical and architectural interest, including St. Ann's Fort and the 1804 Main Guard building with its prominent clock tower. The National Cannon Collection contains approximately 30 cannons, many dating from the mid-17th century. A British military cemetery, horse-racing track and the Barbados Museum also are in the area.

East of Bridgetown, in a residential area at the northern end of St. Barnabas Highway, is the Emancipation Statue of Bussa, "The Freed Slave." Commemorating the Emancipation of slavery in 1834, the statue depicts a slave standing with his chains broken and his hands to the sky in triumph. In 1816, Bussa purportedly led a revolt at Bayley's Plantation in St. Philip's Parish that was to be the largest revolt on the island.

Tourist information is available from the Barbados Tourism Authority's information booths. The booths, which are located at Deep Water Harbour inside the cruise ship terminals and at the airport, offer assistance with reservations, sightseeing tours and other services. The Barbados Tourism Authority's main office on Harbour Road also provides visitor information.

★*ATLANTIS* **SUBMARINE** departs from the Shallow Draft, in Deep Water Harbour. The 50-foot-long, 28-passenger submarine cruises at a maximum depth of 150 feet, offering excellent views of reefs, coral formations, marine life and a sunken ship. Fish feedings take place on the 5-7 p.m. dives. A 15-minute ferry ride transports visitors between the dock and the submarine for the 1-hour tour.

Allow 1 hour, 30 minutes minimum. Trips depart hourly Mon.-Sat. 9-7; closed 1 week in Sept. Fare $70; over 59, $62.50; ages 4-12, $34.75. Under 4 are not permitted. Reservations are advised. AE, DS, MC, VI. Phone (246) 436-8932 for information or 436-8929 for reservations.

Seatrec departs from the Shallow Draft Complex on Spring Garden Hwy. This 75-minute cruises allow visitors to snorkel Caribbean waters without getting wet. The semi-submersible tracking and exploration craft takes passengers 6 feet under water to view shore reefs through large viewing windows. Passengers may also remain on deck to take in the coastline view. Daily at 9, 11 and 1. Fare $35; under 13, $17.50. Reservations are advised. AE, DS, MC, VI. Phone (246) 436-8932 for information or 436-8929 for reservations.

BARBADOS MUSEUM, 2.5 mi. (4 km) s.e. in Garrison, St. Michael's Parish, faces a horse-racing track and occupies a former military prison. Exhibits depict the natural history of the Caribbean, Amerindian prehistory and the history of Barbados. The museum also has collections of ceramics, silver, maps and prints; period rooms from a Barbadian plantation house; a children's gallery; and a prisoner's cell as well as changing exhibits. Mon.-Sat. 10-6, Sun. 2:30-6. Admission $3.50. Phone (246) 427-0201.

CHRIST CHURCH PARISH CHURCH is 6 mi. (10 km) s.e. This Anglican church was the scene of considerable excitement during the 19th-century "Barbados Coffin Mystery." Coffins in the sealed Chase Vault were reportedly found in different positions each time the vault was opened. To stem the hysteria provoked by the strange incidents, the governor finally had the coffins buried elsewhere. Daily. Donations.

CODRINGTON COLLEGE is 15 mi. (24 km) n.e. of Bridgetown in St. John's Parish. The college was originally the plantation home of Christopher Codrington, a former governor. Founded in 1702, this is the oldest seminary in the Western Hemisphere. The wooded grounds offer a spectacular view of Consett Bay on the east coast. Daily. Grounds admission $2.50.

FRANCIA PLANTATION, in St. George Parish, is off Hwy. 3B between St. George Parish Church and Gun Hill Signal Station. Francia's grounds, accented by colorful gardens and terraced lawns, are on a wooded hillside overlooking the St. George Valley. Yams and sweet potatoes are among the vegetables grown on this working plantation.

The house contains many interesting antiques, including an 18th-century James McCabe bracket clock, a European chandelier with etched hurricane shades, a 1522 map of the West Indies and mid-19th-century furniture constructed by Barbadian craftsmen. Mon.-Fri. 10-4; closed public holidays. Admission $3. Phone (246) 429-0474.

GUN HILL, 6 mi. (10 km) n.e. in St. George's Parish, overlooks St. George Valley. During British occupation of the island, this hill was one of several points used to relay messages. A monument to Britain's supremacy is the lion carved on the side of a limestone cliff by British soldiers in 1868. The restored 19th-century Signal Station is open daily. Admission $4; under 12, 2. Phone (246) 429-1358.

HARRISON'S CAVE, 7 mi. (11 km) n.e. via Hwy. 2 in St. Thomas Parish following signs, offers narrated 20-minute tram rides through subterranean stream passages. A visitor center contains a handicraft shop and an exhibit of Arawak Indian artifacts found on Barbados. An introductory slide show depicts the discovery and development of the cave. Daily 9-4; closed Good Friday, Easter and Dec. 25. Trams depart every 15 minutes. Admission $7.50; ages 3-16, $3.75. Reservations are recommended. Phone (246) 438-6610 or 438-6611.

JOLLY ROGER **PIRATE SHIP CRUISES,** at Shallow Draft, offers 4-hour lunch and dinner cruises along the coast in a replica of a pirate ship. Music and swimming are featured. Lunch cruises depart Tues.-Fri. at 10 a.m.; dinner cruises depart Mon., Thurs. and Sat. at 5 p.m. Fare $57. Reservations are required. Phone (246) 436-6424 or 429-4545.

QUEEN'S PARK is off Constitution Rd. Opened as a park in 1909, the site was once the residence of the general who commanded British forces in the West Indies. Queen's Park House has a theater that presents local theater productions and an art gallery that features local works. The grounds contain a gazebo, a small collection of monkeys and birds, and a 1,000-year-old baobab tree. Park open daily dawn-dusk. Gallery open Tues.-Thurs. 10-8, Fri.-Sat. 10-6, Sun.-Mon. noon-8. Free. Phone (246) 427-2345.

ST. JAMES CHURCH, 6 mi. (10 km) n. on Hwy. 1 in the Holetown area of St. James Parish, survived the hurricane of 1831. The 1629 church contains a bell with the inscription "God Bless King William 1696." Other relics include hand-beaten silver pieces that date from the late 1600s and the original baptismal font with its mahogany cover. A graveyard where many of Barbados' early settlers are interred adjoins the church. Open daily dawn-dusk. Free. Phone (246) 432-1580.

ST. JOHN'S CHURCH, 11 mi. (18 km) n.e. on Hwy. 3B in St. John Parish, dates from the 17th century. On the edge of a cliff 825 feet (251 m) above sea level, the church affords a spectacular view of the eastern coast. Ferdinando Paleologus, an alleged descendant of Constantine the Great, is entombed in the churchyard. Daily. Donations. Phone (246) 433-5599.

SAM LORD'S CASTLE, 14 mi. (23 km) e. in St. Philip's Parish, is a Regency mansion built 1778-1844 by adventurer and planter Sam Lord. According to popular legend, Lord acquired his wealth by luring ships into what appeared to be a safe harbor, then plundering them when they wrecked. With his gain he built the finest residence on the island; it is now part of a hotel.

On Wednesday evenings a castle dinner is available which includes a cocktail party, a seven-course meal complemented by elegant china and crystal, and fine wines and champagne; reservations are required. Daily 9-5. Castle $1. Phone (246) 423-7350.

SUNBURY PLANTATION HOUSE, .7 mi. (1.2 km) w. of Six Cross Roads on Hwy. 5 in St. Philip Parish, was built in 1660 and is one of the oldest plantation houses on the island. Guides lead tours of the house, which is furnished with period pieces and antiques. The yam cellars contain collections of horse-drawn vehicles and an optometrist's artifacts. The surrounding plantation is still being worked.

Visitors can sample the gracious living of the plantation era during a special candlelight dinner offered Tuesday and Thursday; reservations are required. Allow 30 minutes minimum. Daily 10-4:30; closed Dec. 25. Admission $6; ages 5-12, $3. Phone (246) 423-6270.

WELCHMAN HALL GULLY, in St. Thomas Parish, is a 13-acre (5-hectare) tropical garden of fruit and spice trees. The gully is rimmed by cave-pocked cliffs inhabited by monkeys. A massive pillar formed by the joining of stalactites and stalagmites seems to support the rock cliff. With a diameter of more than 4 feet, the pillar is one of the largest in the world. Daily 9-5; closed Good Friday and Dec. 25. Admission $2.50; ages 6-12, $1.25. Phone (246) 438-6671.

CHALKY MOUNT (B-2)

A village of potters 18 miles (29 km) northeast of Bridgetown, Chalky Mount is in St. Andrew Parish. Built on a deposit of clay that looks like a man lying down with his hands on his chest, the formation has been nicknamed "Napoleon" by local residents. The area derives its name from the chalky texture of the clay. Panoramas of the Scotland district and the east coast are available from this area.

Craftsmen continue to use primitive potter's tools; their wares, made from native clay, are sold in the capital. Only three pottery businesses continue to operate in Chalky Mount; two of them are located in private homes. The third and largest, Chalky Mount Pottery, is open daily 8:30-5. Visitors can see potters in the process of molding clay using a "kick wheel," an antiquated instrument operated by simply kicking the wheel. A variety of articles are for sale, including plant pots, tableware, pitchers, jugs and cooking utensils.

ST. PETER

GRENADE HALL FOREST AND SIGNAL STATION, bordering the Barbados Wildlife Refuge and Farley Hill National Park, commands a panorama of the island and offers insight into its original role as part of a communications network that was unique in the Caribbean. The site was originally used by the Royal Artillery to communicate between island signal stations and the capital of Bridgetown. Visitors can explore a mile of coral pathways that wind through trees, shrubs, vines and herbs. Daily 10-5; closed Jan. 1 and Dec. 25. Admission, includes the Barbados Wildlife Reserve, $12; under 12, $6. Phone (246) 422-8826.

SPEIGHTSTOWN (A-2)

Speightstown, in St. Peter's Parish, is 12 miles (19 km) north of Bridgetown. This fishing village was once a shipping center known as Little Bristol. In 1663 Sir John Yeamans debarked from Speightstown on an expedition to colonize South Carolina; he later became the third governor of that colony. His house, St. Nicholas Abbey, is one of the oldest sugar plantation great houses still standing in the Caribbean. Also in the area are the remains of the Old Denmark, Orange and Dover forts. Six Men's Bay north of town is lined with cannons and old buildings once used for drying whale blubber.

ST. NICHOLAS ABBEY is 5.5 mi. (9 km) n.e. via Hwy. 1 following signs. Built about 1650 for a sugar planter, the house had as its second resident Sir John Yeamans, commissioned by King Charles II as lieutenant general and governor of South Carolina.

The present owner, whose family has owned the house since 1820, presents a film made by his father in 1934 depicting the sugar making process and other island scenes; the film is shown at 11:30 and 2:30. Visitors tour the ground floor, which is decorated with antique English and Barbadian furniture. Particularly noteworthy is a fine collection of early Wedgwood portrait medallions made 1771-1920. Mon.-Fri. 10-3; closed major holidays. Admission $2.50. Phone (246) 422-8725.

Lodgings & Restaurants

BRIDGETOWN

LODGINGS

ALMOND BEACH CLUB
◆◆ *Motor Inn*

12/18-3/31	$750	XP $100
12/1-12/17 & 4/1-11/30	$650	XP $100

Location: 11.4 km n on Hwy 1. Vauxhall, St. James. Fax: 246/432-2115. **Terms:** Age restrictions may apply; reserv deposit; handling fee imposed; $10 service charge; 3 night min stay. **Facility:** 161 rooms. Some beachfront units. 4 stories, no elevator; exterior corridors; beach; 1 lighted tennis court. **Recreation:** swimming, sailboating, snorkeling, waterskiing, windsurfing. **Cards:** AE, DI, DS, MC, VI.

 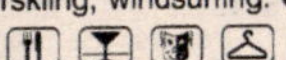 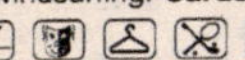 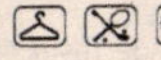 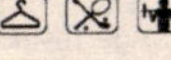

(246/432-7840

ALMOND BEACH VILLAGE
◆◆ *Resort Motor Inn*   *Rates Subject to Change*

12/18-3/31	$450-600	XP $100
12/1-12/17 & 4/1-11/30	$380-510	XP $100

Location: 24 km n on Hwy 1. St. Peter. Fax: 246/422-0617. **Terms:** D16; Reserv deposit, 21 day notice, in season; 14 day notice in summer; 10% service charge. **Facility:** 288 rooms. Beachfront, former sugar plantation with 30 acres of landscaped grounds. All rooms with patio or balcony, some with garden, pool or ocean view. 2-3 stories, no elevator; exterior corridors; 9 holes golf; beach; 5 lighted tennis courts; playground. **Services:** giftshop. **Recreation:** swimming, charter fishing, sailboating, snorkeling, waterskiing, windsurfing. **Fee:** scuba equipment. **Cards:** AE, DS, MC, VI.

(246/422-4900

BARBADOS HILTON
◆◆◆ *Hotel*

12/16-4/15	$238-285	XP $60
12/1-12/15 & 4/16-11/30	$157-187	XP $60

Location: Off Hwy 7, 2.8 km s. Nwedhams Pt, St Michael (PO Box 510). Fax: 246/436-8946. **Terms:** F; Reserv deposit, 14 day notice; 10% service charge. **Facility:** 184 rooms. On the site of Old Fort Charles, between the Caribbean Sea & Carlisle Bay. Extensive landscaped grounds. Meets AAA guest room security requirements. 2-6 stories; interior corridors; beachfront; beach; 4 tennis courts (Fee: 4 lighted). **Services:** giftshop. **Fee:** massage. **Recreation:** swimming, snorkeling. **Fee:** sailboating, scuba diving, waterskiing, windsurfing. **Cards:** AE, CB, DI, DS, JC, MC, VI.

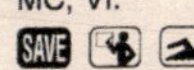       

(246/426-0200

COBBLER'S COVE HOTEL
◆◆ *Motor Inn*

1/3-4/11	$704-1891	XP $211
12/19-1/2	$605-1600	XP $75
12/1-12/18 & 10/1-11/30	$347-999	XP $112
4/12-9/30	$282-940	XP $106

Location: 18 km n on Hwy 1. Road View, St. Peter. Fax: 246/422-1460. **Terms:** Age restrictions may apply; reserv deposit, 30 day notice, 14 day in summer; 10% service charge. **Facility:** 40 rooms. Beachfront resort; nicely kept grounds. Units with living room, bedroom & private balcony or patio. Closed 9/1-10/15. Single rates in season, on request. 1 whirlpool rm, extra charge; 2 stories; exterior corridors; beach; 1 lighted tennis court. **Recreation:** swimming, sailboating, snorkeling, waterskiing, windsurfing. **Cards:** AE, MC, VI.

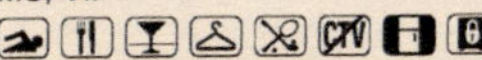   (246/422-2291

COCONUT CREEK HOTEL
◆◆ *Motor Inn*

12/19-1/2 & 2/1-3/1	$372
12/1-12/18, 1/3-1/31 & 3/2-4/23	$346
4/24-5/26, 7/22-8/31 & 10/7-11/30	$280
5/27-7/21 & 9/1-10/6	$268

Location: 8 km n on Hwy 1. St James. Fax: 246/432-0272. **Terms:** 10% service charge. **Facility:** 53 rooms. Landscaped grounds on low bluff above the sea. Many rooms with ocean view. 2-3 stories, no elevator; exterior corridors; beach. **Services:** giftshop. **Recreation:** swimming, paddleboats, snorkeling, waterskiing. **Fee:** sailboating, scuba equipment. **Cards:** MC, VI.

    (246/432-0803

COLONY CLUB HOTEL
◆◆◆ *Motor Inn*

1/2-3/30	$450-598	XP $114
12/1-1/1, 4/24-5/26 & 7/22-8/31	$334-432	XP $114
3/31-4/23	$428	XP $114
5/27-7/21 & 9/1-11/30	$322-408	XP $114

Location: 13 km n on Hwy 1. St. James (Porters, ST. JAMES). Fax: 246/422-0667. **Terms:** Reserv deposit, 21 day notice, 7 days off season; handling fee imposed; 10% service charge. **Facility:** 98 rooms. Beachfront. Swimming pools with waterfalls in tropical garden setting. 1-3 stories; beach; 2 lighted tennis courts. **Services:** giftshop. **Fee:** massage. **Recreation:** swimming, snorkeling, waterskiing, windsurfing. **Fee:** sailboating, scuba equipment. **Cards:** MC, VI.

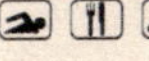  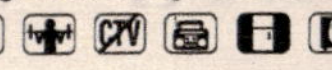   (246/422-2335

CORAL REEF CLUB
◆◆ *Complex*

12/16-1/9 & 1/24-3/3	$525-1020	XP $220
1/10-1/23 & 3/4-3/24	$460-900	XP $195
3/25-4/14	$390-680	XP $145
12/1-12/15 & 4/15-11/30	$315-455	XP $100

Location: 13 km n on Hwy 1. St James. Fax: 246/422-1776. **Terms:** D12; Age restrictions may apply; reserv deposit, 28 day notice, 14 day in summer; handling fee imposed; 10% service charge. **Facility:** 69 rooms. Beachfront. Variety of rooms, apartments & cottages. Closed 6/1-7/26. 10 two-bedroom units. 1-2 stories; exterior corridors; beach; 1 lighted tennis court. **Services:** giftshop. **Recreation:** swimming, charter fishing, snorkeling, windsurfing. **Fee:** sailboating, waterskiing. **Cards:** AE, MC, VI.

   (246/422-2372

CRYSTAL COVE
◆◆ *Complex*

12/24-1/2	$380-521	XP $95
12/19-12/23 & 1/3-4/23	$345-500	XP $95
12/1-12/18, 4/24-5/26 & 11/6-11/30	$310-400	XP $90
5/27-11/5	$300-380	XP $85

Location: 7.2 km n on Hwy 1. (Appleby, ST. JAMES). Fax: 246/432-8290. **Terms:** Reserv deposit, 3 day notice; 10% service charge. **Facility:** 88 rooms. Beachfront. Rooms & bi-level units in tropical garden. Setting by the swimming pools with waterfalls. Exterior corridors; beach; 2 lighted tennis courts. **Services:** giftshop. **Recreation:** swimming, snorkeling equipment, waterskiing, windsurfing. **Fee:** fishing, sailboating. **Rental:** scuba equipment. **Cards:** MC, VI.

(246/432-2683

DISCOVERY BAY HOTEL
◆◆ *Resort Motor Inn*

12/21-1/7	$290-390	XP $80
1/8-4/15	$260-360	XP $80
12/1-12/20 & 4/16-11/30	$185-265	XP $60

Location: 12 km n on Hwy 1. St James. Fax: 246/432-2553. **Terms:** D12; Reserv deposit, 21 day notice; 10% service charge. **Facility:** 88 rooms. Beachfront. Some rooms with ocean view. All have balcony or patio. 1 three-bedroom unit. 2-3 stories, no elevator; exterior corridors; beach; 2 tennis courts (1 lighted). **Recreation:** swimming, snorkeling. **Some Rooms:** kitchen. **Cards:** AE, DI, DS, MC, VI.

(246/432-1301

DIVI SOUTHWINDS BEACH RESORT
◆◆ *Apartment Motor Inn*

12/19-1/3 & 2/15-2/28	$200-245	XP $25
1/4-2/14 & 3/1-4/3	$185-220	XP $25
12/1-12/18 & 4/4-11/30	$110-155	XP $10

Location: 6.5 km s on Hwy 7; 11 km w of airport. Christ Church. Fax: 246/428-4674. **Terms:** F16; Reserv deposit; 10% service charge. **Facility:** 150 rooms. Extensive landscaped grounds. Spacious one & two bedroom units with garden or pool view, or oceanview units. 11 two-bedroom units. 2-5 stories; interior/exterior corridors; putting green; beach; 2 lighted tennis courts. **Services:** giftshop. **Recreation:** swimming. Fee: sailboating, scuba & snorkeling equipment. **Some Rooms:** 132 kitchens. **Cards:** AE, DI, DS, MC, VI.

(246/428-7181

▲▲▲ SAVE EDGEWATER INN
◆ *Motor Inn*

11/15-11/30	$125-195
12/1-5/15	$105-175
5/16-11/14	$85-145

Location: 22 km ne on Hwy 3, following signs. (St Joseph, BATHSHEBA). Fax: 246/433-9902. **Terms:** Reserv deposit, 60 day notice; package plans. **Facility:** 20 rooms. Located on a cliff with spectacular view of the Atlantic coastline. Modest rooms with dated mahogany furnishings. 2 stories; interior/exterior corridors; beach access. **Dining:** Restaurant; 7 am-9 pm; $15-$25; cocktails. **Services:** giftshop. **Recreation:** swimming; hiking trails. **All Rooms:** combo or shower baths. **Some Rooms:** color TV. **Cards:** AE, DI, DS, MC, VI. **Special Amenities: Free breakfast and free local telephone calls.**

((246)433-9900

GLITTER BAY
◆◆◆ *Motor Inn*

12/13-1/3 & 2/1-2/28	$475-615	XP $105
1/4-1/31 & 3/1-4/18	$430-525	XP $85
12/1-12/12 & 11/7-11/30	$300-365	XP $40
4/19-11/6	$235-275	XP $40

Location: 14.5 km n on Hwy 1. St. James. Fax: 246/422-3940. **Terms:** D12; Reserv deposit, 30 day notice, in season; 7 summer; 14 spring/fall; handling fee imposed; 10% service charge. **Facility:** 83 rooms. Landscaped grounds along beach. Spanish style buildings. All units with balcony or patio. 7 two-bedroom units. 4 stories; exterior corridors; beach; 2 lighted tennis courts. **Services:** giftshop. Fee: massage. **Recreation:** swimming, sailboating, snorkeling, waterskiing, windsurfing. Fee: scuba equipment. **Some Rooms:** 48 efficiencies. **Cards:** AE, DI, DS, MC, VI.

(246/422-5555

GRAND BARBADOS BEACH RESORT
◆◆ *Hotel*

12/16-4/14	$225-275	XP $40
12/1-12/15 & 4/15-11/30	$145-190	XP $30

Location: Off Hwy 7, 2.5 km e. Aquatic Gap, St Michael (PO Box 639). Fax: 246/429-2400. **Terms:** F12; Reserv deposit, 3 day notice; 10% service charge. **Facility:** 133 rooms. On Carlisle Bay. All rooms with balcony, most with view of the bay. 5 suites on pier; 7 stories; interior/exterior corridors; beach. **Services:** giftshop. **Recreation:** swimming, sailboating, snorkeling equipment, windsurfing. Fee: scuba equipment. **Cards:** AE, DI, DS, MC, VI.

(246/426-4000

ROYAL PAVILION
◆◆◆◆ *Motor Inn*

4/19-11/6	$275	XP $40
1/4-1/31 & 3/1-4/18	$525	XP $85
12/1-12/19 & 11/7-11/30	$365	XP $40
12/20-1/3 & 2/1-2/28	$615	XP $105

Location: 14.7 km n on Hwy 1. Porters, St. James. Fax: 246/422-3940. **Terms:** Age restrictions may apply; reserv deposit, 30 day notice, in season; 7 in summer, 14 spring/fall; handling fee imposed; 10% service charge. **Facility:** 75 rooms. Beachfront. Most rooms with patio or balcony facing the beach. Inviting public areas & landscaped grounds. 3 stories; exterior corridors; beach; 2 lighted tennis courts. **Services:** giftshop. Fee: massage. **Recreation:** swimming, sailboating, snorkeling, waterskiing, windsurfing. Fee: scuba diving & equipment. **Cards:** AE, DI, DS, MC, VI.

(246/422-5555

SAM LORD'S CASTLE RESORT
◆◆◆ *Resort Complex*

2/23-1/3 & 2/11-2/16	$240-275	XP $35
2/16-12/22, 1/4-2/10 & 2/17-4/18	$210-245	XP $35
2/1-12/15 & 4/19-11/30	$145-170	XP $35

Location: 22.5 km e on se coast; 10.5 km from airport. Long Bay, St. Philip. Fax: 246/423-5918. **Terms:** F12; Check-in 4 pm; reserv deposit; handling fee imposed; 10% service charge. **Facility:** 248 rooms. Overlooking the Atlantic Ocean. 19th century restored mansion. 234 rooms on the spacious grounds with patio or balcony, 14 mansion rooms. 2 suites $600-$700; $500-$600 off season; 2-4 stories; exterior corridors; beach; 6 lighted tennis courts. **Services:** giftshop. Fee: massage. **Recreation:** swimming. Rental: bicycles. **All Rooms:** combo or shower baths. **Some Rooms:** color TV. **Cards:** AE, MC, VI.
See color ad below)

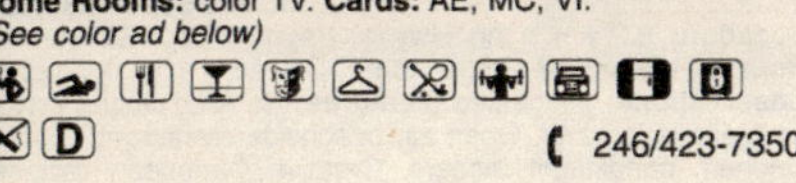

(246/423-7350

THE SANDPIPER
◆◆◆ *Motor Inn*

2/15-1/8 & 1/23-3/2	$490-1015
1/9-1/22 & 3/3-4/16	$405-835
2/1-12/14 & 11/16-11/30	$270-510
1/17-8/28 & 10/6-11/15	$235-445

Location: 12 km n on Hwy 1. St. James. Fax: 246/422-0900. **Terms:** Open 12/1-8/28 & 10/6-11/30; age restrictions may apply; reserv deposit, 21 day notice, 14 day in summer; handling fee imposed; 10% service charge. **Facility:** 45 rooms. Beachfront. Landscaped grounds. Units with patio or balcony. Closed 8/31-10/5. Meets AAA guest room security requirements. Rates for up to 4 persons; 2 stories; exterior corridors; beach; 2 lighted tennis courts. **Services:** giftshop. **Recreation:** swimming. **Cards:** AE, MC, VI.

((246)422-2251

SANDY BEACH ISLAND RESORT
◆◆ *Apartment Motor Inn*

12/16-4/5	$120-307	XP $25-30
12/1-12/15, 4/6-5/10 & 11/1-11/30	$90-183	XP $25
5/11-10/31	$85-167	XP $25

Location: 5.5 km s on Hwy 7; 11 km w of airport. Christ Church. Fax: 246/435-8053. **Terms:** F12; Reserv deposit, 14 day notice; handling fee imposed; 10% service charge. **Facility:** 128 rooms. On beach & lagoon. 1- & 2-bedroom housekeeping apartments, some 2-story duplex units. 9 two-bedroom units. 50 two-bedroom units, $270-$345 for up to 4 persons; $145-$170 off season. Suites for 4 persons avail. $190-$410; 3 stories, no elevator; exterior corridors; beach. **Recreation:** swimming. Fee: sailboating, snorkeling equipment, windsurfing. **Some Rooms:** 88 kitchens. **Cards:** AE, MC, VI.

(246/435-8000

SANDY LANE HOTEL
◆◆◆◆ *Resort Hotel*

12/19-1/8	$880-2390	XP $200
1/9-4/16	$695-2175	XP $200
4/17-11/30	$525-1010	XP $200
12/1-12/18	$485-940	XP $200

Location: 11 km n on Hwy 1. St. James (Sandy Lane, ST. JAMES). Fax: 246/432-2954. **Terms:** Reserv deposit, 14 day notice; handling fee imposed; 10% service charge. **Facility:** 120 rooms. Beachfront. Many rooms overlooking the ocean. Property will close from 4/25-9/19 for a major renovation. Meets AAA guest room security requirements. 2-4 stories; interior corridors; 18 holes golf, putting green; beach; 5 tennis courts (4 lighted). **Services:** giftshop. Fee: massage. **Recreation:** swimming, charter fishing, snorkeling equipment, waterskiing, windsurfing. Fee: sailboating. Rental: scuba equipment. **Cards:** AE, DI, MC, VI.

(246/432-1311

Retreat to a Legendary Landmark

Sam Lord's Castle, A Barbados Resort

Location: 72 lush acres featuring the pristine beaches of St. Philip's southeast shore on Cobbler's Reef. 20 minutes from Grantley Adams International Airport.

Accommodations: 248 guest rooms including 10 suites. Balconies/patios with pool or ocean views.

Restaurants & Lounges: The Wanderer, The Sea Grill, Oceanus Cafe, Sam's Place, and the Main Brace Lounge.

Banquets & Conferences: Conference Center with 5,184 square feet of flexible function space. Outdoor reception areas accommodate up to 1,000.

Features: 3 pools, whirlpool, 6 lighted tennis courts, private beach, fitness room, shuffleboard, nearby sailing, snorkeling, waterskiing, cruises, and horseback riding.

Rates:

Rack - European Plan
Per Room, Single/Double Occupancy

	Oceanview	Poolview
1/4/98 - 2/10/98	$245	$210
2/11/98 - 2/16/98	$275	$240
2/17/98 - 4/18/98	$245	$210
4/19/98 - 12/18/98	$170	$145
12/19/98-12/22/98	$245	$210
12/23/98 - 1/3/99	$275*	$240*
Extra Person	$35	$35

Rack - All-Inclusive
Per Room, Double Occupancy

	Oceanview	Poolview
1/14/98 - 2/10/98	$450	$415
2/11/98 - 2/16/98	$495	$455
2/17/98 - 4/18/98	$450	$415
4/19/98 - 12/18/98	$375	$335
12/19/98-12/22/98	$450	$415
12/23/98 - 1/3/99	$495	$455

Single, subtract $95; Triple, add $135.

Children under 12 stay and eat free when sharing room with parents.

* Includes Buffet breakfast daily. MAP-$50. FAP-$60 per person, per day plus 15% tax and 10% service. Tax and service charge — the 10% service charge and 7.5% value added tax must be added to the room rate (subject to change). 10% commission paid promptly.

Toll-Free Reservations in North America: (888) 765-6737 •
Telephone: (246) 423-7350 • Fax (246) 423-6361
Booking Codes: Amadeus WW BGISLC, Apollo/Galileo WW 78370, SystemOne WW BGISLC, Worldspan WW BGISL, Sabre WW 1346

RESTAURANTS

BAGATELLE GREAT HOUSE *Historical*
◆◆◆ *Caribbean*
Location: 11 km n on Hwy 2A. St. Thomas. **Hours:** 11:30 am-2:30 & 7-9:30 pm, Sat & Sun from 7 pm. **Reservations:** suggested; in season. **Features:** No A/C; casual dress; children's menu; cocktails & lounge; a la carte. An elegant 1645 mansion serving a unique French Caribbean cuisine. Shorts not permitted. **Cards:** MC, VI.

(246/421-6767

BOURBON STREET
◆◆ *Cajun* D $25-$45
Location: 5.7 km n on Hwy 1. St. James. **Hours:** 6 pm-10 pm. Closed: 12/25 & Mon 5/1-12/31. **Reservations:** suggested; in season. **Features:** No A/C; casual dress; cocktails; valet parking; a la carte. Casual, open-air terrace overlooking Caribbean Sea. Authentic Louisiana/Cajun cuisine. Late night "treats" after 10 pm. **Cards:** MC, VI.

(246/424-4557

AAA BROWN SUGAR
◆◆ *Ethnic* L $18 D $35
Location: Off Hwy 7, 2.5 km s. St Michael. **Hours:** noon-2:30 & 6-9:45 pm, Sat & Sun from 6 pm, Sun brunch noon-2:30 pm. Closed major holidays & lunch only. **Reservations:** suggested. **Features:** No A/C; casual dress; Sunday brunch; cocktails & lounge; a la carte. Converted home with veranda & garden terrace seating. Features Creole cuisine. 10% service charge. **Cards:** AE, DI, MC, VI.

(246/426-7684

CARAMBOLA RESTAURANT
◆◆◆ *Caribbean* D $25-$50
Location: 7 km n on Hwy 1. Derricks, St. James **Hours:** 6:30 pm-9:30 pm. Closed major holidays & Sun **Reservations:** required; in season. **Features:** No A/C; casual dress; cocktails; a la carte. Open-air dining with candle lit tables nestled along cliff side, overlooking Caribbean Sea Caribbean cuisine with a French flare. Thai cuisine also featured. Shorts not permitted. **Cards:** AE, MC, VI.

(246/432-0832

THE FATHOM'S
◆◆ *Seafood* L $15-$30 D $30-$50
Location: 8.2 km n on Hwy 1. Payne's Bay, St. James **Hours:** noon-3 & 6-10 pm. Closed: 1/1 & 12/25 **Reservations:** suggested. **Features:** No A/C; casual dress cocktails; a la carte. Open air, beachside restaurant. Casua lunches, candlelight dinners. Creative Caribbean recipes **Cards:** AE, MC, VI.

(246/432-2568

LA MAISON
◆◆◆ *Ethnic* D $25-$45
Location: 11 kn n on Hwy 1, Holetown, St James. Hwy 1 **Hours:** 6:30 pm-10 pm. Closed: Mon. **Reservations:** suggested. **Features:** No A/C; casual dress; cocktails & lounge a la carte. Open-air dining with the breeze of the ocean Fine French Caribbean cuisine. Shorts not permitted **Cards:** AE, MC, VI.

(246/432-1156

BERMUDA

VIEWED FROM THE AIR, Bermuda presents a kaleidoscope of pink beaches, blue-green ocean and patchwork isles. The mainland is a graceful chain of seven islands joined by roads and bridges; the colony comprises more than 150 isles. A closer view reveals well-ordered homes with white roofs and a profusion of flowers— Easter lilies, amaryllis, oleander, gladioli, hibiscus and poinsettias. Because Bermuda is the northernmost of the coral islands, limestone, the residual product of coral, is seen everywhere. The island is 650 miles (1,040 km) east of Cape Hatteras, N.C., and about a 2-hour flight from New York, Atlanta and other East Coast gateway cities.

Thanks to a mild climate and beautiful beaches, Bermuda's main business is tourism. However, Bermuda is *not* a tropical island, and the weather during December, January and February can be brisk enough to keep most people out of the water. The peak tourist season runs from spring until fall.

HISTORY, GOVERNMENT AND ECONOMY

Bermuda's discoverer and namesake, Juan de Bermúdez of Spain, is thought to have anchored off the islands as early as 1503. The first settlers, however, were Virginia-bound British colonists who were shipwrecked off St. George's Island in 1609. Some historians credit the event with providing Shakespeare with background for "The Tempest."

Although tourism, banking and international business are today's primary industries, Bermuda relied on shipbuilding as the mainstay of its economy 1684-1775. Vessels constructed of cedar were the basis of the island's flourishing economy until wooden ships were replaced by those made of steel during the late 1800s and tourism began to take on economic importance.

As a British colony Bermuda is administered by a governor appointed by the reigning British monarch; a cabinet appointed by the premier; a senate jointly formed by the governor, the premier and the opposition party; and a house of assembly elected by the citizens. The country's nine parishes are governed by separate advisory councils. The islands hold the distinction of being the oldest self-governing colony in the British Commonwealth. Bermuda's constitution, adopted in June 1968, provides for a large measure of self-government.

SHOPPING

Browsing for antiques and bric-a-brac is entertaining in itself. Shops in Hamilton have given Bermuda its reputation as the "Showcase of the British Commonwealth." Choice woolens, cashmeres, silver, English china, leather gloves and slacks, French perfumes, German cameras, Swiss watches, Swedish crystal and Italian leather can be purchased at great savings.

A.S. Cooper & Sons Ltd., on Front Street, sells Wedgwood china, and William M. Bluck and Co. deals in china and antiques. Archie Brown & Son, H.A. and E. Smith's and Trimingham's offer sweaters, tweeds and leather. The Calypso Shop on Front Street specializes in locally made play clothes, and the Irish Linen Shop features linens from Ireland, Italy and Switzerland. Perfumes can be found at Peniston Brown.

Fine selections of jewelry are displayed at Astwood Dickenson on Front Street and at Crisson's on Queen, Reid and Front streets in Hamilton and York Street in St. George's. The specialty shops composing The Emporium, entered from Front Street, allow visitors with limited time to purchase an array of interesting Bermudian items in one stop.

The Bermuda Perfumery and Gardens in Hamilton Parish *(see attraction listing p. 95)* welcomes visitors to observe the traditional creative processes employed by this native industry. Branch stores and specialty shops are tucked away in St. George's and Somerset as well as in several of the larger resort hotels throughout the island. Most stores are open Mon.-Sat. 9-5, and some have extended hours during the Christmas holidays and summer months. Banking hours generally are Mon.-Thurs. 9-4, Fri. 9-4:30.

FOOD AND DRINK

In Bermuda the lobster season extends from September through March. The delicacy is served steaming with melted butter or one of several rich sauces. Cassava pie filled with chicken and pork is a popular treat during the Christmas season. The secret of its unique flavor is the grated and baked root of the cassava plant. Favorite desserts are sweet potato pudding and *syllabub,* a guava jelly-cream-wine concoction.

Fruits and vegetables are grown locally, but meat is imported from the United States and Canada. Drinking water is distilled from sea water for hotels or collected on rooftops, and milk is pasteurized. All popular American drinks are available; meals in hotels are similar to those served in the United States. Reservations are suggested for lunch and dinner at the best restaurants. A tip of 15 percent, with extra allowance for special service, is customary. However, most hotels, restaurants, cottage colonies and guesthouses add a 15-percent gratuity to the accommodation or food bill. Most hotels and restaurants accept credit cards.

SPORTS AND AMUSEMENTS

Part of Bermuda's appeal is that it has something for everyone. Golf, tennis, horseback riding, fishing and water sports lure the athletically inclined, while shoppers can enjoy Hamilton's exclusive stores and civic activities. St. George's, the former capital, provides a journey into the past with its 17th-century architecture and narrow lanes. Lazy days are filled by sunning, sightseeing or browsing in out-of-the-way shops.

Bermuda ranks among the most sports-conscious countries of the world: More than 30 sporting clubs are found in an area of 22 square miles (57 sq km). The island's diverse activities include bowling, bridge, cricket, cycling, dog and horse shows, fishing, golfing, parasailing, sailing, swimming, scuba diving, tennis, racquetball, squash, table tennis, horseback riding, water skiing and windsurfing.

Soccer and cricket are the national sports—soccer matches are scheduled September through April, and cricket matches are held May through September. The Annual Cup Match, a national holiday, is a cricket match played between teams representing the island's east and west ends on the Thursday and Friday before the first Monday

---

THINGS TO KNOW

AREA: 21 square miles (54 sq km).

POPULATION: 60,000.

LANGUAGE: English.

CAPITAL: Hamilton.

GOVERNMENT: Self-governing British Colony.

TIME ZONE: Atlantic (Eastern plus 1 hour). DST.

UNIT OF CURRENCY: Bermuda dollar divided into 100 cents, $1 US=1 Bermuda dollar. Most shops, restaurants and hotels accept U.S. currency.

ELECTRICITY: 110 volt, 60 cycles AC.

CARS: Non-residents may not drive cars on Bermuda; rental cars are not available. Driving is on the left.

IMMIGRATION REQUIREMENTS: Proof of U.S. citizenship (birth certificate, naturalization papers or passport and photo ID) and return or through ticket are required. Three-week limit on stay; an extension can be obtained through the Immigration Office at the airport. Departure tax (included in airplane ticket price) does not apply to passengers who are in transit to another island or country.

FOR FURTHER INFORMATION:

Bermuda Department of Tourism
310 Madison Ave.
New York, NY 10017
(800) 223-6106

Bermuda Department of Tourism
43 Church St.
Hamilton, Bermuda
(441) 292-0023

Visitors Service Bureau
111 Front St., near ferry terminal
Hamilton, Bermuda
(441) 292-6384

HOLIDAYS: Jan. 1; Good Friday; Bermuda Day, May 24; Queen's Birthday, June (3rd Mon.); Cup Match/Somers Day, the Thurs. and Fri. before 1st Mon. in Aug.; Labour Day, Sept. (1st Mon.); Remembrance Day, Nov. 11; Dec. 25; Boxing Day, Dec. 26.

in August; most shops and eateries close during the event. Rugby also is popular; one major international tournament, the Easter Rugby Classic, is played on Easter and another, the World Rugby Classic, in mid-November.

Other sporting events include golf and tennis tournaments; yacht races on Saturday and Sunday; the Bermuda Game Fishing Tournament, held throughout the year; the International Open Badminton Tournament in April; water-ski shows throughout the summer; the Light Tackle Fishing Tournament in July; and the Bermuda International Triathlon in the fall. Summer is celebrated on Bermuda Day, May 24, with dinghy races in St. George's Harbour.

The beaches on the south shore are wild stretches of sand and surf. Horseshoe Bay is one of the most popular. Because Bermuda is not subject to strong ocean currents that stir up sediment, the waters are usually clear and excellent for snorkeling. In addition, more than 600 species of fish live in the surrounding waters. One of the most unusual underwater sports Bermuda offers is helmet diving, or underwater walking. It is an opportunity for nonswimmers and people who wear glasses to see the incredible variety of marine life in Bermuda's waters. Anyone from 5 to 85 can participate in the guided 3-hour tours departing from Flatts Village in Smith's Parish, daily May through October.

You can rent boats and equipment for snorkeling, scuba diving and spear fishing at many places on the island; spear fishing is not permitted within 1 mile (1.6 km) of the shore, and the importation and use of a spear gun in Bermuda is illegal. Since 1- or 2-hour scuba diving lessons are usually insufficient preparation for a novice, you should take a complete course in advance. Several operators offer snorkeling and scuba diving lessons on trips aboard glass-bottom boats.

The Department of Tourism at 43 Church Street in Hamilton provides information on trips for deep-sea, reef or shore fishing. Boats with tackle and bait can be chartered for both half- and full-day excursions; no license is required. Rentals and lessons for sailing vessels and windsurfing are abundant. Water skiing is best May through October and is permitted in Hamilton Harbour, the Great Sound, Castle Harbour, Mangrove Bay, Spanish Point, Ferry Reach, Ely's Harbour, Riddells Bay and Harrington Sound; the law requires that skiers be towed by a licensed skipper.

If you prefer to play on land, you can choose among golf, tennis, squash, bicycling or horseback riding. Public golf courses include the Ocean View Golf and Country Club, Devonshire Parish; Port Royal Golf Course, Southampton Parish; and St. George's Golf Club, St. George's Parish. Hotels offering use of their courses to visitors include the Belmont Hotel Golf and Country Club, Warwick Parish; Marriott's Castle Harbour Resort, Smith's Parish; and the Southampton Princess Hotel, Southampton Parish.

Many large hotels have tennis courts. The Bermuda Squash Racquets Club in Devonshire Parish is available to visitors; reservations are required. Bowlers can pursue their sport at the Warwick Lanes on Middle Road in Warwick Parish.

Bicycling is an engaging pastime, particularly on the Railway Trail, which runs along an old railroad line. The nature trail winds through three of the islands that make up Bermuda, beginning at Somerset and ending at St. George's, except for a 3-mile (4.8-km) section in and around Hamilton. The 18 miles (29 km) of trails are divided into seven sections, each with its own flavor and character. The trail also is a fine walking, moped and equestrian path. A free, 18-page trail guide is published by the Bermuda Department of Tourism (*see Things To Know box*). The guide includes a history of the trail, maps, descriptions of various sections of the path and historical photos.

The Spicelands Riding Centre in Warwick Parish offers a variety of programs, including trail rides, breakfast trail rides, evening rides and lessons; phone (441) 238-8212.

A special enticement for winter visitors is "November through March," appropriately held from November through March. Some of the events featured during this festival include a "skirling ceremony" performed by kilted pipers and dancers at Fort Hamilton; an open house of the official residence of the premier; guided tours of St. George's, Hamilton and Somerset; a historical review by the Gombey Dancers; and various golf tournaments.

The Bermuda Festival, which takes place in January and February in Hamilton, is an international gala of music, dance and drama. The Bermuda Regiment Band Beating of the Retreat provides pomp and ceremony as it is performed monthly on Wednesday at 8 p.m. in downtown Hamilton from May through October.

Several publications listing weekly events and entertainment are distributed at hotels and other establishments. Dancing and after-dinner entertainment are nightly fare at hotels and large cottage colonies. Calypso bands and local talent fill Hamilton nightclubs, some of which stay open until 3 a.m.

EXCURSIONS AND SIGHTSEEING

Excursions can be taken to almost any point on Bermuda by cycle, taxi, boat or bus. A blue flag on a taxi signifies that the driver has been approved as a qualified tour guide by the government. Excellent maps are available at the Department of Tourism at 43 Church St. in Hamilton. Some hotels will arrange escorted excursions.

INDEX TO STARRED ATTRACTIONS

ATTRACTIONS OF EXCEPTIONAL INTEREST AND QUALITY

Bermuda Aquarium, Museum and Zoo - see Hamilton Parish

1. Angel's Grotto
2. Ariel Sands
3. Astwood Cove
4. Aunt Nea's Inn at Hillcrest
5. Barnsdale Guest Apartments
6. Clear View Suites & Villas
7. The Elbow Beach Bermuda, A Rafael Resort
8. Fourways Inn Cottage Colony
9. Grape Bay Cottages
10. Greenbank & Cottages
11. Grotto Bay Beach Hotel & Tennis Club
12. Harmony Club
13. Lantana Colony Club
14. Loughlands Guest House
15. Marley Beach Cottages
16. Marriott's Castle Harbour Resort
17. Munro Beach Cottages
18. Oxford House
19. Palmetto Hotel & Cottages
20. Pompano Beach Club
21. The Princess Hotel
22. The Reefs
23. Rosedon Hotel
24. Rosemont
25. Royal Palms
26. The St. George's Club
27. Sky Top Cottages
28. Sonesta Beach Resort
29. Southampton Princess Hotel
30. Stonington Beach Hotel
31. Surf Side Beach Club
32. Whale Bay Inn
33. White Sands

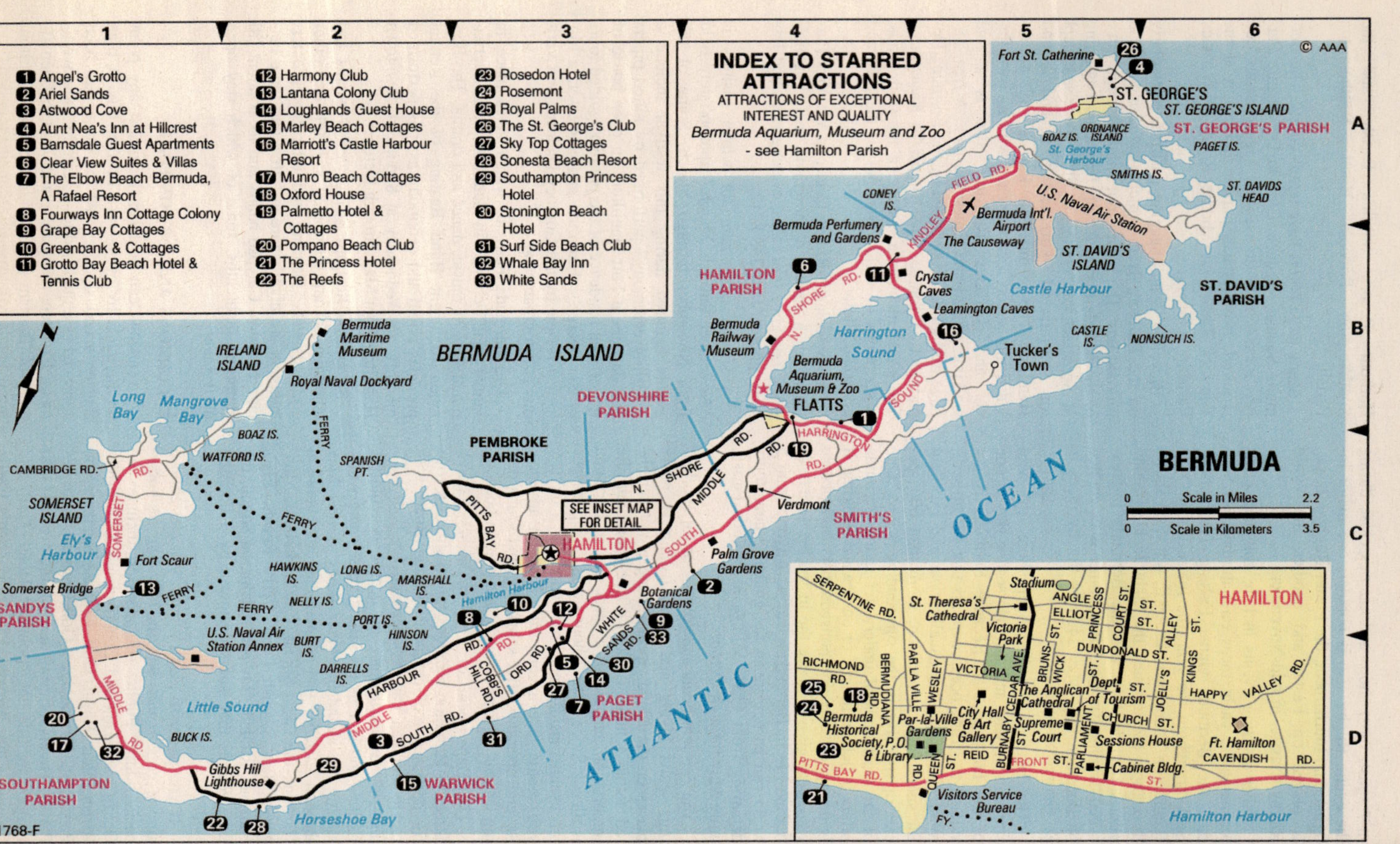

Bus tours operate from November through March. Three-hour tours include stops at the Crystal Caves, Devil's Hole—a natural pool containing large, captive fish— and the Bermuda Aquarium, Museum and Zoo *(see attraction listing p. 95)*. All-day bus tours to these areas also are offered. Horse and carriage tours are available.

Popular cruises include a 5-hour trip to Treasure Bay, Great Sound and Somerset, a 2-hour cruise aboard a glass-bottom boat to the sea gardens and a 3-hour catamaran cruise of Great Sound. Reservations can be made directly through the operator or arranged through a hotel activities desk. Ferries operate daily from Hamilton to the Bermuda Maritime Museum in Sandys Parish *(see attraction listing p.98)*.

TRANSPORTATION

Several air carriers provide daily service to Bermuda International Airport from Toronto, New York, Newark, Boston, Chicago, Philadelphia, Washington/Baltimore, Charlotte and Atlanta. Flights last from 2 to 2.5 hours.

Because law forbids the use of automobiles by non-residents, car-rental services are not available. Perhaps the most common and economical means of transportation in Bermuda is cycling. Mopeds and motor scooters can be rented for about $33 to $42 a day; required safety helmets are provided with a $20 deposit. For the hardier visitor, bicycles can be rented for about $10 to $15 a day; weekly rates also are available. Cycle rental operations are found throughout the island and at many of the large hotels. Riders should use caution, as roads in Bermuda are narrow, hilly, curving and banked in many spots by coral walls. Carriages with fringed tops also can be hired for sightseeing at $20 per half-hour.

Bus service, priced by zone, is available throughout the island; the central bus terminal is on Washington Street in Hamilton. Exact change, tokens or tickets are required; books of 15 tickets are available at substantial savings at the central terminal or at most sub-post offices throughout the island. Adult fare for up to three zones is $2.50 cash or $2.25 in tokens. The flat fare for ages 3 to 13 is $1. Transfer tickets are provided when changing buses.

Passenger ferries run daily between Hamilton, Paget, Warwick, Somerset and the Dockyard. The Hamilton-Paget-Warwick fare is $2.25 one way; the Hamilton-Somerset-Dockyard fare is $3.75 one way. Pedal bicycles can be carried on board at no charge, but motor-assisted cycles on the Hamilton-Somerset-Dockyard ferry cost $3.75 extra one way. Bus and ferry schedules, which include maps of routes and fare zones and sample fares, can be obtained at the bus and ferry terminals, tourism information centers and most hotels.

ATTRACTION ADMISSIONS
Attraction admissions for this island are quoted in U.S. dollars.

POINTS OF INTEREST
See map page 94.

PARISHES—When using a map of Bermuda it is often easier to find your destination if you know in which parish it is located. Therefore, the following points of interest are listed by parish.

DEVONSHIRE PARISH

PALM GROVE GARDENS, along South Shore Rd., is a private estate containing tropical birds and native and exotic trees and flowers. A pond has a floral map of Bermuda. Mon.-Thurs. 9-5; closed holidays. Free.

HAMILTON PARISH

★**BERMUDA AQUARIUM, MUSEUM AND ZOO,** in Flatts Village on North Shore Rd., exhibit most species of fish found in Bermuda waters as well as tropical birds, monkeys, turtles, seals and alligators. The North Rock Exhibit has two viewing tanks showcasing Bermuda's ocean resources and the underwater environment of the nearby North Rock coral reef. There also are a touch pool, discovery room and shark exhibit.

The Australasia Exhibit features the wildlife of Australia, New Guinea, Borneo and Malaysia. The museum includes sea coral, sea fans and a display about the geological development of Bermuda. A full-sized whale skeleton also is displayed. Self-guiding audio tours are available, and videotapes about Bermuda's marine life run continuously.

Allow 1 hour minimum. Daily 9-5; closed Dec. 25. Last admission 30 minutes before closing. Admission $8; ages 5-12, $4. Phone (441) 293-2727.

BERMUDA PERFUMERY AND GARDENS, 212 North Shore Rd. near Bailey's Bay, began production in 1935. The best time to visit the factory is April through August, when it is in full production. A nature trail winds through several gardens and a small section of lush jungle. Fragrances extracted from locally grown flowers are sold. Guided tours are available. Open Mon.-Sat. 9:15-5, Sun. 10-4, Apr.-Oct.; Mon.-Sat. 9-4:30, rest of year. Closed Jan. 1, Good Friday and holidays Nov.-Mar. Free. Phone (441) 293-0627.

BERMUDA RAILWAY MUSEUM, 37 North Shore Rd., contains memorabilia from the days of the Bermuda Railway, which operated 1931-48. The 21-mile (34-km) track no longer exists, but most of the roadbed is now part of the Railway Trail. Photographs, documents, equipment and a curiosity shop are contained in an old station house. Mon.-Sat. 10-4 (weather permitting). Closed holidays. Free. Phone (441) 293-1774.

CRYSTAL CAVES, Wilkinson Ave. on Bailey's Bay, has an underground lake and caves viewed from pontoon walkways. The 81 steps might be difficult for some; benches are available for resting. Food is available. Allow 30 minutes minimum. Guided tours daily 9:30-4:30, Apr.-Oct.; otherwise varies rest of year. Closed Good Friday, Remembrance Day and Dec. 24 to mid-January. Admission $5; ages 5-11, $2.50. Phone (441) 293-0640.

LEAMINGTON CAVES are near Crystal Caves on Harrington Sound Rd. Extensive stalactite formations and pools 60 feet underground are visible from well-lit passageways. The steep stairs might be difficult for some. Guided tours Mon.-Sat. 10-4, Feb.-Nov.; closed holidays. Admission $5; ages 5-11, $2.50. Phone (441) 293-1188.

Paget Parish

BOTANICAL GARDENS are on Berry Hill Rd. via Tee St. from South Shore Rd. On the property of Camden, the official residence of Bermuda's premier, the 36-acre (15-hectare) gardens display native and introduced flora identified by plaques and have several display houses and a garden for the blind. A visitor center offers educational displays and a videotape presentation. Food is available.

Allow 1 hour, 30 minutes minimum. Gardens open daily dawn-dusk. Display houses open Mon.-Fri. 8-3:45. Free tours are given Tues.-Wed. and Fri. beginning at 10:30. The premier's residence is open, except during official functions, Tues. and Fri. noon-2. Free. Phone (441) 236-4201.

Pembroke Parish

Hamilton (City) (C-3) pop. 4,000

Incorporated in 1793, Hamilton succeeded St. George's as capital in 1815. The city, overlooking Hamilton Harbour, is a latticework of pastel houses surrounded by tropical flowers. Whitewashed roofs, shuttered windows, arched doorways, Old World carriages and clusters of shops all enhance Hamilton's charm.

Self-guiding tours: A visitors' service bureau at 111 Front St. near the ferry terminal has brochures for self-guiding tours of the city. Phone (441) 295-1480.

THE ANGLICAN CATHEDRAL, on Church St., is built of native limestone and stones from around the world. Consecrated in 1911, the cathedral's special features include a marble altar, mosaics and stained-glass windows. Daily 8-4:45. Free.

BERMUDA HISTORICAL SOCIETY MUSEUM is in the public library at 13 Queen St. Displayed are china, silver, antique furniture, Bermudian coins, personal belongings of Admiral Sir George Somers and sketches and models of early Bermuda ships. Sommers was commander of the fleet carrying settlers to Virginia when it was shipwrecked off St. George's Island in 1609. Also featured is a collection of blue and white Canton porcelain and French silver spoons from 1727. Mon.-Sat. 9:30-3:30; closed holidays. Free. Phone (441) 295-2487.

THE CABINET BUILDING, on Front St., houses several government offices and the council chamber of the Senate, which is the upper house of the legislature. Mon.-Fri. 9-5; closed holidays. Free. Phone (441) 292-5501.

CITY HALL, on Church St., has ornamental fountains and a cedar interior. An art gallery contains collections of stamps and oil portraits of Queen Victoria and Prince Albert. The building's huge weather vane dominates the skyline. Mon.-Fri. 9-5; closed holidays. Free. Phone (441) 292-1234.

Bermuda National Gallery occupies two floors in City Hall. Paintings from the 15th through 19th centuries include works by Thomas Gainsborough, Bartolomé Murillo, Sir Joshua Reynolds and George Romney. The Masterworks Foundation features the Bermudiana Collection. Changing exhibitions also are displayed. Allow 1 hour minimum. Mon.-Sat. 10-4. Admission $3, under 16 free. MC, VI. Phone (441) 295-9428.

FORT HAMILTON, near Victoria and King sts., offers a view of Hamilton, Paget and Warwick parishes and the harbor. This well-preserved coral fortress was built during the American Civil War to prevent blockade running; the underground passageways and large cannons are noteworthy. A semitropical garden occupies the moat. Daily 9:30-5. Free. For more information phone the botanical gardens at (441) 236-5291.

PAR-LA-VILLE GARDENS, on Queen St. just off Front St., contains native flowers and plants in a formal arrangement. The Perot Post Office is in the gardens. Gardens open daily 24 hours. Post office open Mon.-Fri. 9-5; closed holidays. Free. For the post office phone (441) 292-9052.

ST. THERESA'S CATHEDRAL, Cedar Ave. and Elliott St., was built in 1931. The stained-glass windows from Canada enhance the Spanish-style architecture of this Roman Catholic church. Daily 7-6. Free. Phone (441) 292-0607.

THE SESSIONS HOUSE is entered from Reid St. Completed in 1819, this building accommodates the House of Assembly, which is the lower house of Bermuda's Parliament. Mon.-Fri. 9-12:30 and 2-5; closed holidays. Free. Phone (441) 292-7408.

VICTORIA PARK, Burnaby and Victoria sts., has a gazebo patterned after one in London designed for Queen Victoria. Daily 8 a.m.-dusk. Free.

St. George's Parish

St. George's (A-5) pop. 1,500

St. George's, on St. George's Island, is about 12 miles (19 km) northeast of Hamilton and is connected with the mainland by causeway. The town was once the seat of Bermuda's government, which was organized in 1612.

It would be difficult to find a more delightful storybook town. The quaintness of St. George's is reflected in the names of its narrow, twisting lanes: Old Maids Lane, Shinbone Alley, Featherbed Alley and One Gun Alley.

The Old State House on the town square dates from 1620. In April the governor of Bermuda makes his formal call on the Freemasons to collect the annual rent of one peppercorn for their use of the Old State House. It is open Wed. 10-4; phone (441) 272-2480.

Self-guiding tours: The visitor center at King's Square distributes a brochure outlining a self-guiding walking tour through St. George's. The center is open Mon.-Sat. 9-4. Phone (441) 297-1642.

THE BERMUDA NATIONAL TRUST MUSEUM is on Duke of York St. at King's Sq. Housed in the old Globe Hotel, built 1698-1700 and used as a Confederate headquarters during the U.S. Civil War, the museum chronicles the boom era of blockade running, when small steamships ran goods from St. George's to Confederate ports in the United States. A 12-minute videotape presentation gives an overview of Bermuda's history. Mon.-Sat. 10-4, Sun. 1-4; closed holidays. Admission $4, students with ID $2. Combination ticket with Tucker House and Verdmont $5. Phone (441) 297-1423.

CARRIAGE MUSEUM, Water St., displays 19th-century Bermudian carriages, harnesses and saddles. Mon.-Fri. 10-4; closed holidays. Free. Phone (441) 297-1367.

DELIVERANCE REPLICA, on Ordnance Island at King's Square, is a replica of the vessel built to carry the shipwrecked company of the *Sea Venture* to Jamestown, Va., in 1610. This saga of shipwreck and survival on Bermuda is thought to have been the basis of Shakespeare's play "The Tempest." A bronze sculpture of British admiral Sir George Somers also is here. A taped narration is given. Daily 9-6, Apr.-Oct.; otherwise varies rest of year. Closed Good Friday, Easter and Dec. 25-late Jan. Admission $3; under 12, $1. Phone (441) 297-1459.

FEATHERBED ALLEY PRINTERY, Featherbed Alley, contains a working replica of a 17th-century Gutenberg-style printing press. Mon.-Fri. 10-4; closed holidays. Admission (includes admission to St. George's Historical Society Museum) $4; under 12, $2. Phone (441) 297-0009.

FORT ST. CATHERINE, on Barry Rd. at Gates Bay, was begun in 1612 and completed in 1814. Alterations made 1822-66 remodeled the fort into its present shape. Exhibits in restored rooms and passageways include replicas of the British Crown Jewels and dioramas depicting key events in Bermuda's history. A videotape about forts in Bermuda runs continuously. Allow 30 minutes minimum. Daily 10-4:30. Last admission 30 minutes before closing. Closed Dec. 25. Admission $3, children $1.50. Phone (441) 297-1920.

KING'S SQUARE, center, is the site of the old Town Hall, which contains replicas of stocks, a pillory, a whipping post and a ducking stool. An art gallery on the northwest corner of the square displays works by local artists. Square open daily 24 hours. Art gallery Mon.-Sat. 10-5, mid-Feb. to mid-Jan.; Wed. and Sat. 10-5, rest of year. Free. For gallery information phone (441) 297-1833.

ST. GEORGE'S HISTORICAL SOCIETY MUSEUM, on Featherbed Alley between Duke of Clarence St. and Duke of Kent St., is in an 18th-century building of Bermuda limestone. The exhibits include Bermuda furniture, documents and pictures. Mon.-Fri. 10-4; closed holidays. Admission (includes Featherbed Alley Printery) $4; under 12, $2. Phone (441) 297-0423.

ST. PETER'S CHURCH, Duke of York St., is on the oldest Anglican church site in the Western Hemisphere. Bermuda's first governor, Richard Moore, erected a frame structure in 1612. In 1713-14 the church was rebuilt; additional work was done in 1815 and 1841.

Displayed are a large chalice, paten and two flagons, gifts of King William III. The churchyard is the scene of a Memorial Day service at the grave of U.S. Navy midshipman Richard Dale, who died here during the War of 1812. United States Marine and Navy honor guards and the Bermuda Regiment band participate in the annual commemorative ceremony. Open daily 9-5. Free. Phone (441) 297-8359.

SOMERS GARDEN, Duke of York St., contains two memorials to Adm. Sir George Somers, who established the first British settlement in 1609. Daily 8-4. Free.

TUCKER HOUSE, on Water St., was the 1775 residence of Henry Tucker, president of Bermuda's Governor's Council. During the U.S. Civil War, Joseph Rainey, former American slave and later the first black member of the U.S. House of Representatives, operated a barbershop at the house. China, silverware and antiques are displayed.

Allow 30 minutes minimum. Mon.-Sat. 10-4; closed holidays. Admission $3. Combination ticket with Bermuda National Trust Museum and Verdmont $5. Phone (441) 297-0545.

Sandys Parish

Sandys Parish is a popular picnicking area in rural Bermuda. Sightseers often arrive by ferry from Hamilton and return by bicycle via the Railway Trail. A visitors bureau on Somerset Road offers maps and brochures describing the Somerset area; it is open Mon.-Fri. 10-3.

FORT SCAUR, Somerset Rd. on Somerset Island, was built in the 19th century to protect the Royal Naval Dockyard in the event of an American invasion. The view from the fort is exceptional, and picnic facilities are available. Daily 9-4, May-Oct.; 10-4:30, rest of year. Closed Jan. 1 and Dec. 25-26. Free. Phone (441) 234-0908.

ROYAL NAVAL DOCKYARD, n. end of Ireland Island, supported British naval operations from the War of 1812 through World War II. Major construction of this "Gibraltar of the West" began in 1824, when British convicts toiled to build its major fortifications which include the Keepyard, Commissioner's House and Clock Tower Block. Twin 100-foot towers identify the Clock Tower Building, now a shopping mall; one clock tells the time and the other tracks the tides.

Today the dockyard features a dozen shops, restaurants, arts and crafts outlets and other attractions. Cruise ships dock April through November. Visitors can reach the island via a ferryboat from Hamilton. Buses leave Hamilton and the dockyard every 15 minutes. Open Mon.-Sat. 9-5, Sun. 11-3; closed Good Friday and Dec. 25. Free. Phone (441) 234-1709.

Bermuda Maritime Museum is in a powder magazine built in 1850. Exhibits depict Bermuda's nautical history, including its whaling industry and the Royal Navy. Artifacts date from the 16th century; highlighted is the "Tucker Treasure," artifacts salvaged from the 1609 wreck of the *Sea Venture.* Allow 1 hour minimum. Daily 9:30-4:30, May-Nov.; 10-4:30, rest of year. Closed Dec. 25. Last admission 30 minutes before closing. Admission $7.50; over 59, $6; ages 5-12, $3. Phone (441) 234-1418.

SOMERSET BRIDGE, Middle Rd., is believed to be the world's smallest hand-operated drawbridge. Its 18-inch draw allows the masts of sailboats to pass.

Smith's Parish

Bermuda's largest nature and wildlife reserve, Spittal Pond, is in Smith's Parish on South Road. The 34-acre (14-hectare) sanctuary harbors many species of waterfowl and plantlife. The best season for birdwatching is September through May. The North Nature Reserve at Mangrove Lake across from Pink Beach also preserves various examples of the island's fauna and flora. Both reserves are open daily.

VERDMONT, on Collector's Hill, is a restored house built about 1662 by Gov. William Sayles. The three-story mansion, which blends Bermudian and New England design elements, is furnished with antiques. The grounds offer ocean views and gardens with plants typical of the period. Allow 30 minutes minimum. Tues.-Sat. 10-4; closed holidays. Admission $3, students $2. Combination ticket with Bermuda National Trust Museum and Tucker House $5. Phone (441) 236-7369.

Southampton Parish

GIBBS HILL LIGHTHOUSE is on Lighthouse Rd. This cast-iron lighthouse was built in 1846 after 39 ships wrecked on the reefs west of the islands. The observation platform, reached by a 185-step climb, affords a magnificent view. A tearoom at the base of the lighthouse also is featured. Daily 9-4:30; closed Dec. 25. Admission $2.50. Phone (441) 238-0524.

Lodgings & Restaurants

Devonshire Parish

Lodging

ARIEL SANDS (AAA SAVE)
◆◆◆ *Complex*

5/1-10/31	$340-420	XP $35
12/1-3/31 & 11/1-11/30	$220-300	XP $35
4/1-4/30	$270-350	XP $35

Location: Adjacent to Palm Grove Garden. 34 South Shore Rd (PO Box HM 334, HAMILTON). Fax: 441/236-0087. **Terms:** Reserv deposit, 21 day notice; handling fee imposed; 10% service charge; MAP avail; package plans. **Facility:** 48 rooms. Oceanside setting. Attractive cottages & guest rooms, most with ocean views. All rooms with hair dryer, some with iron & ironing board. 2 two-bedroom cottage $680, 5/1-10/31; $550, 4/1-4/30; $430, 12/1-3/31 & 11/1-11/30; 1-2 stories; exterior corridors; oceanview; putting green; beach, wading pool, 2 pools, 1 saltwater, 1 freshwater heated; 3 tennis courts (2 lighted). Fee: tennis instructions. **Dining:** Restaurant; 8 am-10, noon-2:45 & 7-10 pm; Continental breakfast served until 11 am; $20-$26; cocktails; public by reservation only; afternoon tea. **Services:** Fee: massage. **Recreation:** swimming; spa with skin & beauty treatments. Fee: snorkeling equipment; golf instruction, motorbikes. **Cards:** AE, MC, VI. **Special Amenities: Free room upgrade and preferred room (each subject to availability with advanced reservations).**

((441)236-1010

Hamilton

Restaurant

LE FIGARO BISTRO AND BAR
◆◆ *French*   **L** $5-$14   **D** $13-$20

Location: Downtown, just e of Court St on Reid St. 63 Reid St HM19. **Hours:** noon-2:30 pm & 6-10:30 pm, Sat & Sun from 6 pm. **Reservations:** required. **Features:** casual dress; cocktails; street parking. Bustling new French bistro with turn of the century French posters hung on rag rolled walls; cozy, friendly, casual atmosphere; extensive, mouthwatering menu includes most classic bistro dishes. **Cards:** AE, MC, VI.

(441/296-4991

Hamilton Parish

Lodgings

CLEAR VIEW SUITES & VILLAS
◆ *Cottage*

All Year	$156-214	XP $24-40

Location: Off North Shore Rd at top of Crawl Hill. Sandy Lane CRO2. Fax: 441/293-0267. **Terms:** D12; Reserv deposit, 7 day notice. **Facility:** 30 rooms. Quiet patio units with commanding ocean view. Microwaves upon request. Very attractive art gallery on property. 1-2 stories; exterior corridors; 1 tennis court; playground. **Recreation:** swimming, fishing, snorkeling equipment. Fee: snorkeling. **All Rooms:** kitchens. **Cards:** AE, DI, MC, VI.

(441/293-0484

GROTTO BAY BEACH HOTEL & TENNIS CLUB
◆◆◆ *Resort*

4/16-10/31	$205-220	XP $50
12/1-4/15 & 11/1-11/30	$94-99	XP $50

Location: On Baileys Bay; near w end of the Causeway bridge. 11 Blue Hole Hill CRO4. Fax: 441/293-2306. **Terms:** F16; Reserv deposit, 14 day notice, 2 night dep req. **Facility:** 201 rooms. Lovely hillside setting on 21 landscaped acres. All rooms with bay view, balcony or patio. Children-friendly, waveless & shallow beach. Two caves to explore, one of which has swimming permitted. Hair dryer in all rooms. Service charge varies with meal plan; 3 stories; exterior corridors; beach; playground. Fee: 4 tennis courts (2 lighted). **Services:** giftshop. **Recreation:** swimming. Fee: scuba diving, snorkeling, waterskiing, windsurfing. Rental: boats, paddleboats, sailboats, scuba equipment. **Cards:** AE, MC, VI.

((441)293-8333

MARRIOTT'S CASTLE HARBOUR RESORT
◆◆◆ *Resort*

4/1-11/10	$229-289
12/1-3/31 & 11/11-11/30	$105-135

Location: In Tucker's Town. 2 Paynter's Rd HMCX (PO Box HM 841). Fax: 441/293-8288. **Terms:** Check-in 4 pm; reserv deposit, 14 day notice. **Facility:** 402 rooms. Beautiful country club location with spectacular view of Castle Harbour. Attractive guest rooms; excellent facilities. Service charge varies with meal plan; 8-10 stories; interior corridors; oceanfront; putting green; beach, heated pool. Fee: 18 holes golf; 6 tennis courts. **Services:** giftshop. Fee: massage. **Recreation:** swimming, snorkeling; jogging. Fee: scuba diving, scuba & snorkeling equipment; bicycles. Rental: boats, paddleboats. **Cards:** AE, CB, DI, JC, MC, VI.

(441/293-2040

Restaurants

SWIZZLE INN
◆ *Ethnic*   **L** $5-$15   **D** $6-$21

Location: On Blue Hole Hill, in Baileys Bay. 3 Blue Hole Hill CR04. **Hours:** 11 am-1 am. Closed: Mon 01/01-03/31. **Reservations:** accepted; 5 or more. **Features:** children's menu; carryout; cocktails & lounge; a la carte. Popular roadside pub; burgers, bangers, ale, dart board & pool table. English pub fare. Separate dining room. Live entertainment during summer season. Gift shop. **Cards:** AE, MC, VI.

(441/293-1854

TOM MOORE'S TAVERN (AAA)   *Historical*
◆◆◆◆ *Continental*   **D** $26-$36

Location: Walsingham Bay, off Harrington Sound Rd. 7 Walsingham Ln HSBX. **Hours:** 7 pm-10 pm. Closed: 12/25, may close early Jan to early Feb. **Reservations:** required. **Features:** formal attire; cocktails & lounge; a la carte. Bermuda's oldest restaurant. Carefully restored mid 17th-century home in lovely, peaceful setting. Graceful ambiance of handsome table settings, glowing woodwork & antiques. **Cards:** AE, MC, VI.

(441/293-8020

HAMILTON (PEMBROKE PARISH)

LODGINGS

OXFORD HOUSE
◆◆ *Bed & Breakfast*

3/16-11/30	$145	XP $38
12/1-3/15	$131	XP $36

Location: Between Pitts Bay & Richmond rds. 20 Woodbourne Ave HMBX (PO Box HM 374, HAMILTON). Fax: 441/295-0250. **Terms:** F3; Reserv deposit, 14 day notice; 10% service charge. **Facility:** 12 rooms. 1938 stylish Bermuda guest house. Very convenient to downtown Hamilton & restaurants. Interior/exterior corridors. **All Rooms:** combo or shower baths. **Cards:** AE, MC, VI.

(441/295-0503

THE PRINCESS HOTEL
◆◆◆ *Hotel*

4/18-11/13	$225-350	XP $40
11/14-11/30	$170-230	XP $30
12/1-4/17	$165-225	XP $30

Location: On Pitts Bay Rd. 76 Pitts Bay Rd HMCX (PO Box HM 837, HAMILTON). Fax: 441/295-1914. **Terms:** F16; Reserv deposit, 14 day notice; 9% service charge. **Facility:** 413 rooms. On edge of downtown, overlooking Hamilton harbor. Variety of facilities & services. Many rooms with balcony. Use of Southampton Princess facilities & restaurants. Meets AAA guestroom security requirements. Meets AAA guest room security requirements. 7 stories; interior/exterior corridors; oceanfront; putting green; heated pool. Fee: boat dock. **Services:** giftshop. Fee: massage, area transportation. **Recreation:** charter fishing, fishing, scuba diving. Fee: snorkeling, scuba & snorkeling equipment; bicycles. **All Rooms:** combo or shower baths. **Cards:** AE, CB, DI, JC, MC, VI.

((441)295-3000

ROSEDON HOTEL
◆◆◆ *Hotel*

4/1-11/30	$188-260
12/1-3/31	$138-198

Location: Opposite the Hamilton Princess Hotel. 57 Pitts Bay Rd (PO Box 290, HAMILTON). Fax: 441/295-5904. **Terms:** Reserv deposit, 14 day notice; 10% service charge; package plans. **Facility:** 43 rooms. Victorian style mansion & modern rooms over lush pool courtyard. 2 stories; interior/exterior corridors; heated pool, beach & tennis privileges at Stonington Beach. **Dining:** Afternoon tea. **Services:** area transportation, Stonington Beach Hotel. **All Rooms:** combo or shower baths. **Cards:** AE, MC, VI.

((441)295-1640

ROSEMONT
◆◆ *Bed & Breakfast*

4/1-11/30	$138-142	XP $20-25
12/1-3/31	$110-114	XP $12-15

Location: 0.5 mi w of downtown Hamilton on hill overlooking Hamilton Harbour above Hamilton Princess Hotel. 41 Rosemont Ave (PO Box HM 37, HAMILTON). Fax: 441/295-3913. **Terms:** F Facility: 37 rooms. Large studio efficiencies, most with fine view overlooking Hamilton Harbour. 1 two-bedroom unit. 3 deluxe suites, $220-$640 for 4-12 persons in season. Service charge $6 per person per day, in season. Service 5% single, 10% double off season; 3 stories, no elevator; exterior corridors. **All Rooms:** efficiencies, combo or shower baths. **Cards:** MC, VI.

((441)292-1055

ROYAL PALMS
◆◆◆ *Historic Country Inn*

4/1-11/15	$160-180	XP $25-40
12/1-3/31 & 11/16-11/30	$132	XP $25-30

Location: 0.3 mi from Pitts Bay Rd. 24 Rosemont Ave HM06 (PO Box HM 499, HAMILTON, HMCX). Fax: 441/292-1946. **Terms:** D16; Reserv deposit, 14 day notice; handling fee imposed; 10% service charge. **Facility:** 16 rooms. Small charming hotel with ambiance recalling Bermuda in an earlier time. Quiet residential setting. Handsome grounds. 2 stories; interior/exterior corridors. **All Rooms:** combo or shower baths. **Some Rooms:** 7 kitchens. **Cards:** AE, MC, VI.

(441/292-1854

RESTAURANTS

ASCOTS RESTAURANT
◆◆◆ *Continental*   L $8-$15 D $18-$29

Location: 0.3 mi from Pitts Bay Rd; in Royal Palms. 24 Rosemont Ave HMO6. **Hours:** noon-2:30 & 6:30-10 pm, Sat 6:30 pm-10 pm, Sun noon-2:30 & 6:30-10 pm. **Reservations:** suggested. **Features:** dressy casual; cocktails & lounge; a la carte. Attractive dining room in a gracious setting above downtown Hamilton. Varied menu, excellent food preparation & presentation. Attentive service. Terrace dining. Sun carvery, an English style carving lunch also, ala carte. **Cards:** AE, MC, VI.

(441/295-9644

THE BOMBAY INDIAN RESTAURANT
◆◆ *Indian*   L $12 D $14-$22

Location: Between King & Court sts, 3rd floor, Rego Building. 75 Reid St E HM12. **Hours:** noon-2:30 & 6:30-11 pm, Sat from 6:30 pm. Closed: Sun, & for lunch major holidays. **Reservations:** suggested; weekends. **Features:** dressy casual; carryout; cocktails & lounge; street parking; a la carte. Sophisticated Indian decor with ceiling fans & wicker peacock chairs. Very well prepared food; biryanis, tandoori specialties & curries of every variety. Luncheon buffet $11.95. 15% service charge. **Cards:** AE, MC, VI.

(441/292-0048

CHOPSTICKS
◆◆ *Chinese*   L $7-$11 D $13-$21

Location: Between King & Court sts. 88 Reid St HMI2. **Hours:** noon-2:30 & 5-11 pm, Sat, Sun & major holidays from 5 pm. Closed: 12/25. **Reservations:** suggested. **Features:** casual dress; carryout; cocktails; street parking; a la carte. Popular establishment serving a good variety of Oriental & Thai selections. Food prepared to order & diet restrictions respected. 15% service charge. **Cards:** AE, MC, VI.

(441/292-0791

FISHERMAN'S REEF
◆◆ *Seafood*   L $9-$22 D $18-$34

Location: Downtown; just off Front St on Burnaby St. 5 Burnaby Hill HMCX. **Hours:** noon-2:30 & 6-11 pm. Closed: 12/25. **Reservations:** suggested. **Features:** casual dress; early bird specials; health conscious menu; carryout; cocktails & lounge; a la carte. Attractive, conveniently located restaurant specializing in local seafood. Cool modern decor. Smart casual attire. 15% service charge. **Cards:** AE, DI, MC, VI.

(441/292-1609

FOURWAYS PASTRY SHOP
◆ *American* L $3-$11

Location: Downtown; at Reid St entrance to Washington Mall, just n of Front St. Reid St HMBX. **Hours:** 8 am-4:30 pm. Closed major holidays & Sun. **Features:** casual dress; health conscious menu items; carryout; street parking; cafeteria. Bake shop in center of Hamilton offering excellent fresh pastries, cakes, coffee, tea & sandwiches. **Cards:** MC, VI.

 (441/295-3263

THE GOURMET STORE
◆ *American* L $4-$13

Location: In Phoenix Ctr off Queen St, downtown Hamilton. 18 Queen St. **Hours:** 7 am-4 pm. Closed major holidays & Sun. **Features:** casual dress; health conscious menu items; carryout; minimum charge-$20; street parking. Very good selection of light meals, soups, sandwiches & pastries. Cool, comfortable surroundings. Table service. **Cards:** MC, VI.

 (441/295-4085

THE HARBOURFRONT RESTAURANT & BAR
◆◆◆ *Continental* L $7-$20 D $15-$27

Location: Between Par-La-Ville Rd & Queen St. 21 Front St W. **Hours:** 11:30 am-10 pm. Closed: 1/1, 12/25, 12/26 & Sun. **Reservations:** suggested. **Features:** casual dress; cocktails & lounge; a la carte. Local seafood & Mediterranean dishes, served in comfortable elegance. Sushi bar. Terrace dining in summer. 15% service charge. **Cards:** AE, DI, MC, VI

 (441/295-4207

HOG PENNY RESTAURANT & PUB
◆◆ *Ethnic* L $7-$18 D $9-$22

Location: Downtown just off Front St on Burnaby St. 5 Burnaby Hill HM12. **Hours:** 11:30 am-5 & 5:30-11 pm, 1/2-5/1 noon-3 & 5:30-10 pm. Closed: 12/25. **Reservations:** accepted. **Features:** casual dress; early bird specials; carryout; cocktails & lounge; entertainment; a la carte. Said to be Bermuda's oldest pub. Dark wood open beams. Cheerful, informal staff. English menu & local specialties well prepared. 15% service charge. **Cards:** AE, DI, DS, MC, VI.

(441/292-2534

LA TRATTORIA
◆◆ *Italian* L $6-$15 D $8-$23

Location: Adjacent to Washington Mall downtown on Washington Ln between Reid & Church sts. 22 Washington Ln HM11. **Hours:** 11:30 am-3:30 & 5:30-10:30 pm, Sun from 5:30 pm; 5 pm-10:30 pm, Fri-10:30 pm, off season. Closed: 1/1, 12/25. **Reservations:** accepted; large groups. **Features:** casual dress; children's menu; early bird specials; carryout; cocktails; a la carte. In a shopping alley; follow your nose to the garlic. Checkered tablecloths & a good selection of Italian dishes. Informal. 15% service charge. **Cards:** AE, MC, VI.

(441/295-1877

THE LOBSTER POT
◆◆ *Seafood* L $13-$37 D $20-$60

Location: Just off Front St on Bermudiana Rd, center of downtown Hamilton. 6 Bermudiana Rd HMO8. **Hours:** 11:30 am-3 & 6-11 pm, 1/1-4/1 noon-3 & 5:30-10 pm. Closed major holidays & Sun. **Reservations:** suggested. **Features:** casual dress; children's menu; carryout; cocktails & lounge; street parking; a la carte. Casual nautical ambiance. Wide variety of seafood specialties, lobster & landlubber selections. Convenient downtown location. **Cards:** AE, MC, VI.

(441/292-6898

MONTE CARLO RESTAURANT
◆◆◆ *Regional Italian* L $9-$16 D $10-$24

Location: Downtown behind courthouse. 9 Victoria St HMAX. **Hours:** noon-2:30 & 6:30-10 pm. Closed: Sun. **Reservations:** suggested. **Features:** casual dress; cocktails; a la carte. Warm, pleasant Mediterranean decor. Memorable south of France cuisine with an Italian influence. Cordial, attentive staff. **Cards:** AE, MC, VI.

(441/295-5453

PORTOFINO
◆◆ *Italian* L $9-$15 D $12-$25

Location: Corner Front St. 48 Bermudiana Rd HM01. **Hours:** 11:30 am-4 & 6-midnight, Sat from 6 pm, Sun 6 pm-11 pm. Closed: 1/1, 12/25, 12/26, 1st day of Cup Match & 12/31 for dinner. **Reservations:** accepted; for 3 or more. **Features:** casual dress; carryout; cocktails; a la carte. Lively, family-style Italian restaurant. Pasta, pizza & daily specials. **Cards:** AE, MC, VI.

(441/292-2375

THE RED CARPET
◆◆ *Continental* L $9-$19 D $18-$29

Location: Corner Burnaby Hill. 37 Reid St HM12. **Hours:** 11:30 am-3 & 5:30-10 pm. Closed: 1/1, 12/25, Sun & Good Fri. **Reservations:** suggested. **Features:** dressy casual; cocktails & lounge; street parking; a la carte. Downtown restaurant. Menu features Italian & Continental cuisine. **Cards:** AE, MC, VI.

(441/292-6195

RISTORANTE PRIMAVERA
◆◆◆ *Italian* L $13-$22 D $16-$38

Location: Just e of Hamilton Princess Hotel. 69 Pitts Bay Rd HM08. **Hours:** 11:45 am-2:30 & 6:30-10:30 pm, Sat & Sun from 6:30 pm. Closed: 1/1 & 12/25. **Reservations:** suggested. **Features:** dressy casual; cocktails; a la carte. Italian flavored decor. Well trained helpful staff. Very well prepared variety of Italian dishes. 15% service charge. **Cards:** AE, MC, VI.

(441/295-2167

ROSA'S CANTINA
◆◆ *Mexican* L $6-$14 D $9-$21

Location: Front St between King & Court sts. 121 Front St. **Hours:** noon-1 am. Closed: 12/25. **Reservations:** suggested. **Features:** casual dress; children's menu; health conscious menu items; carryout; cocktails; street parking; a la carte. Tex-Mex cuisine in casual, attractive Mexican decor. Balcony seating 15% service charge. **Cards:** AE, MC, VI.

(441/295-1912

TUSCANY RESTAURANT
◆◆◆ *Italian* L $9-$18 D $12-$25

Location: Bermuda House, alley entrance. 95 Front St. **Hours:** 11:45 am-2:30 & 6-10:30 pm, Sat from 6 pm. Closed: Sun 12/1-5/1. **Reservations:** suggested. **Features:** casual dress; cocktails; street parking; a la carte. On Front St across from cruise ship dock. Attractive dining room. Energetic staff. Very well prepared food. **Cards:** AE, MC, VI.

(441/292-4507

PAGET PARISH

LODGINGS

BARNSDALE GUEST APARTMENTS
◆◆ *Bed & Breakfast*

4/1-10/31	$125	XP $25-55
12/1-3/31 & 11/1-11/30	$90	XP $10-30

Location: Off Middle Rd. 2 Barnes Valley (PO Box DV 628, DEVONSHIRE). Fax: 441/236-4709. **Terms:** F4; Reserv deposit, 21 day notice; 10% service charge; 2 night min stay. **Facility:** 7 rooms. Attractive housekeeping & studio units. Pleasant garden setting. Meets AAA guest room security requirements. Extended stay discounts on request. 3 microwaves on request; 2 stories; exterior corridors. **All Rooms:** efficiencies, combo or shower baths. **Cards:** AE, MC, VI.

(441/236-0164

THE ELBOW BEACH BERMUDA, A RAFAEL RESORT
◆◆◆ *Hotel*

6/1-10/31	$285-550	XP $40
12/1-5/31 & 11/1-11/30	$165-340	XP $40

Location: At Elbow Beach. 60 South Shore Rd PG04 (PO Box HM 455, HAMILTON, HMBX). Fax: 441/236-8043. **Terms:** F18; Reserv deposit, 14 day notice; handling fee imposed; $15 service charge. **Facility:** 245 rooms. Elaborate guest facilities, handsome lobby & library bar. Attractively appointed rooms, pool cabanas & multi-unit 1-story beach houses. Majority of rooms with ocean view & balcony or patio. Hair dryer, iron & ironing board. 3 two-bedroom units. Service charge per person daily, varies with type of meal plan; 5 stories; interior/exterior corridors; putting green; beach, heated pool. Fee: 5 tennis courts (3 lighted). **Services:** giftshop. Fee: massage. **Recreation:** swimming, snorkeling & equipment. Fee: bicycles. **Cards:** AE, DI, MC, VI.

(441/236-3535

▲▲▲ FOURWAYS INN COTTAGE COLONY
◆◆◆◆ *Cottage*

4/1-10/31	$230-325	XP $40
12/1-3/31 & 11/1-11/30	$150-190	XP $40

Location: At Cobbs Hill Rd. 1 Middle Rd PGBX (PO Box PG 294, PAGET). Fax: 441/236-5528. **Terms:** F12; Reserv deposit, 21 day notice; handling fee imposed; 10% service charge; weekly/monthly rates; MAP avail, includes continental breakfast & dinner. **Facility:** 11 rooms. Luxurious rooms in secluded, quiet, refined cottage setting. 2 stories; exterior corridors; small heated pool. **Dining:** Afternoon tea; restaurant, see separate listing. **All Rooms:** efficiencies. **Cards:** AE, MC, VI. *(See color ad below)*

((441)236-6517

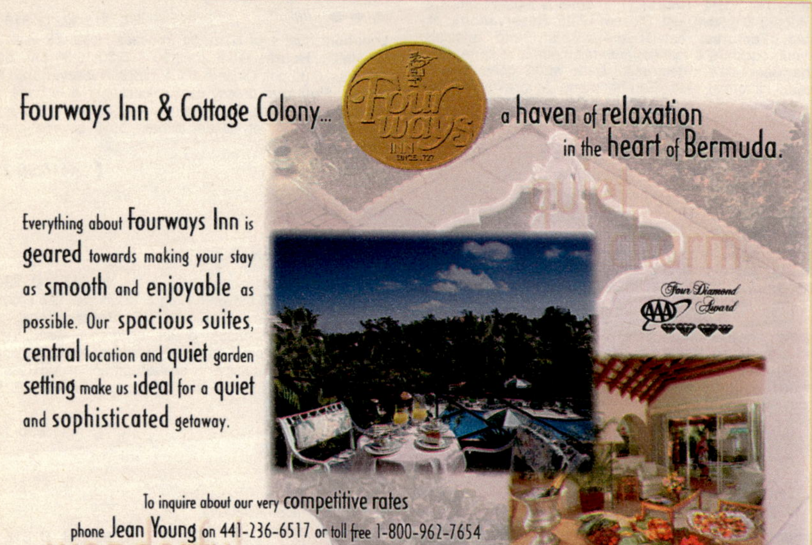

GRAPE BAY COTTAGES
◆◆◆ *Cottage*

4/1-11/15	$300	XP $20-35
12/1-3/31 & 11/16-11/30	$160	XP $10-20

Location: South Shore Rd 0.5 mi s on Grape Bay Dr, cottages at end of road on right. Grape Bay Dr PGBX (PO Box PG 137, PAGET). Fax: 441/236-1662. **Terms:** Reserv deposit, 21 day notice; handling fee imposed; 10% service charge. **Facility:** 2 rooms. 2 miles from downtown Hamilton. Secluded Bermuda cottages just above beach on Grape Bay. Simple, graceful decor. Ideal family or honeymoon location. Rates for up to 4 persons. $3000 per month Jan & Feb rate avail; 1 story; exterior corridors; oceanfront; beach. **Recreation:** swimming; hiking trails. **All Rooms:** kitchens. **Cards:** AE, MC, VI.

 (441/236-1194

GREENBANK & COTTAGES
◆◆ *Historic Cottage*

4/1-11/15	$95-140	XP $15-25
12/1-3/31 & 11/16-11/30	$75-105	XP $15-25

Location: On Salt Kettle Peninsula, off Harbour Rd. 17 Salt Kettle Rd PGBX (PO Box PG 201, PAGET). Fax: 441/236-2427. **Terms:** Reserv deposit, 21 day notice; 10% service charge; 2 night min stay. **Facility:** 11 rooms. Very pleasant, secluded location on peninsula overlooking Hamilton Harbour from the south. Guestrooms & cottages. Main house dates back to the late 18th-century. Cottages retain the feel of Old Bermuda. Sitting room with TV. Suites $210, $185, off season, up to 4 persons; 1 story; exterior corridors. **Recreation:** swimming. **All Rooms:** combo or shower baths. **Some Rooms:** 3 efficiencies, 6 kitchens. **Cards:** AE, MC, VI.

 (441/236-3615

AAA SAVE HARMONY CLUB
◆◆◆ *Hotel*

5/1-10/31	$550
11/1-11/30	$425
12/21-2/28 & 3/1-4/30	$415

Location: On South Shore Rd, 0.5 mi e of Elbow Beach, just w of jct of Middle Rd. 109 South Rd PG03 (PO Box PG 299, PGBX). Fax: 441/236-2624. **Terms:** Open 12/21-11/30; age restrictions may apply; reserv deposit, 7 day notice; package plans. **Facility:** 68 rooms. All-inclusive hotel. Rates include airport transfer, gratuities, motor scooter & taxes. Lovely exterior with Bermudian accents. Bright, pleasant rooms, all with hair dryer. 30 day advanced 25% discount, 30 day cancellation notice; 2 stories; interior/exterior corridors; putting green; sauna, whirlpool; 2 tennis courts. **Dining:** Dining room; 9:30 am-10, noon-3 & 6:30-8:30 pm; $65; cocktails; public by reservation only; afternoon tea. **Cards:** AE, CB, DI, MC, VI. **Special Amenities: Free breakfast and preferred room (subject to availability with advanced reservations).**

((441)236-3500

LOUGHLANDS GUEST HOUSE
◆◆ *Historic Bed & Breakfast*

3/15-11/14	$124	XP $60
12/1-3/14 & 11/15-11/30	$80	XP $40

Location: 0.3 mi e of Elbow Beach. 79 South Shore Rd PG03. **Terms:** Reserv deposit, 14 day notice; 10% service charge. **Facility:** 19 rooms. Stately mansion reflecting the Bermuda of yesteryear. Surrounded by nine acres of land-attractive landscaping. Traditional decor-modestly furnished. TV & refrigerator upon request. 2 stories; interior/exterior corridors; 1 tennis court. **All Rooms:** combo or shower baths.

(441/236-1253

SKY TOP COTTAGES
◆◆ *Cottage*

3/16-11/15	$100-130	XP $10-25
12/1-3/15 & 11/16-11/30	$80-100	XP $5-15

Location: 0.3 mi e of Elbow Beach. 65 South Shore Rd (PO Box PG 227, PGBX). Fax: 441/232-0446. **Terms:** Reserv deposit, 21 day notice; 10% service charge. **Facility:** 11 rooms. Hilltop setting with pretty gardens & delightful Bermudian landscapes. Light & airy studio apartments & cottages, some quaint rooms with iron & ironing board. Five minute walk to beach. 3% charge for credit card use; 2 stories; exterior corridors. **All Rooms:** combo or shower baths. **Some Rooms:** 10 kitchens. **Cards:** MC, VI.

(441/236-7984

AAA SAVE STONINGTON BEACH HOTEL
◆◆◆ *Hotel*

5/1-10/31	$326-370	XP $62-72
4/16-4/30	$276-312	XP $60-70
12/1-4/15 & 11/1-11/30	$178-212	XP $60-70

Location: Off South Shore Rd on Elbow Beach. 8 College Dr HMCX (PO Box HM 523, HAMILTON). Fax: 441/236-0371. **Terms:** Reserv deposit, 5 day notice; MAP avail; package plans. **Facility:** 64 rooms. Impressive, contemporary accommodations with scenic view of ocean & beach. All rooms with balcony or patio. Quality furnishings. Lovely public areas include cozy library. All rates include service charge; 2 stories; exterior corridors; beach, heated pool; 2 tennis courts. **Dining:** Dining room; 8 am-10, noon-2 & 7-8:15 pm; $53; cocktails; public by reservation only; afternoon tea. **Recreation:** swimming. Fee: motorbikes. **Cards:** AE, DI, MC, VI. **Special Amenities:** Free newspaper and free room upgrade (subject to availability with advanced reservations). *(See color ad below)*

((441)236-5416

AAA SAVE WHITE SANDS
◆◆ *Complex*

4/1-11/15	$235-295	XP $85
12/1-3/31 & 11/16-11/30	$164-214	XP $85

Location: 0.5 mi s of South Shore Rd. 55 White Sands Rd PGBX (PO Box PG 174). Fax: 441/236-2486. **Terms:** F6; Reserv deposit, 21 day notice; handling fee imposed; 10% service charge; BP avail; package plans; small pets only. **Facility:** 35 rooms. Overlooking Grape Bay & ocean. Hotel & cottage units avail. Good sized rooms, most with oceanview, many with balcony. 2 three-bedroom units, $510, $375 off season; 1 two-bedroom unit, $340, $250 off season; interior corridors; beach, heated pool. **Dining:** Restaurant; 8 am-9:45, noon-2:30 & 7-8:30 pm, hrs may vary, in winter; $15-$20; cocktails; afternoon tea. **Recreation:** swimming. Fee: mopeds. **Some Rooms:** 3 kitchens. **Cards:** AE, MC, VI. **Special Amenities:** Free local telephone calls and free newspaper.

((441)236-2023

RESTAURANTS

CAFE LIDO
◆◆◆ *Italian*   L $15-$17 D $25-$30

Location: Beachside; in The Elbow Beach Bermuda, A Rafael Resort. 60 South Shore Rd PG04. **Hours:** noon-3 & 6:30-10:30 pm, 11/15-3/31 noon-2:30 & 6:30-9 pm. Closed: 12/25-12/27. **Reservations:** suggested. **Features:** No A/C; dressy casual; cocktails; a la carte. Beachfront dining, creative colorful Mediterranean-influenced dishes. 15% service charge. **Cards:** AE, DI, MC, VI.

(441/236-9884

AAA FOURWAYS INN *Historical*
◆◆◆◆ *Continental*   L $15-$22 D $26-$42

Location: At Cobbs Hill Rd; in Fourways Inn Cottage Colony. 1 Middle Rd PGBX. **Hours:** noon-2:30 & 6:30-9:30 pm. **Reservations:** required. **Features:** formal attire; cocktails & lounge; entertainment; a la carte. Handsome restored Georgian style Bermuda manor house circa 1727. Gourmet cuisine & outstanding service. 15% service charge. **Cards:** AE, MC, VI. *(See color ad p 102)*

(441/236-6517

THE PARAQUET RESTAURANT
◆ *American*   **L** $4-$24   **D** $4-$24

Location: On South Rd, 0.5 mi e of Elbow Beach; in the Paraquet Guest Apartments. 68 South Shore Rd PGBX. **Hours:** 9:30 am-1:30 am. **Closed:** 2/1-2/28. **Reservations:** accepted. **Features:** casual dress; children's menu; carryout; a la carte. Very informal dining. Clean well-lighted dining room with formica tables. Counter service. Well-prepared meals; American & Bermudian cuisine.

✕   (441/236-5842

St. David's Parish

Restaurant

THE BLACK HORSE TAVERN
◆ *Seafood*   **L** $9-$18   **D** $9-$18

Location: Beside St. David's Post Office, overlooking Great Bay. Great Bay Rd DD02. **Hours:** 11 am-11 pm, Sun from noon, call ahead for summer hrs. Closed major holidays12/8-1/14 & Mon. **Reservations:** suggested; in season. **Features:** No A/C; casual dress; carryout; cocktails & lounge; a la carte. Casually comfortable, simple dining rooms serving quality seafood. Small summer terrace. Pretty setting overlooking bay. **Cards:** AE, MC, VI.

(441/293-9742

St. George's Parish

Lodgings

AUNT NEA'S INN AT HILLCREST
◆ *Historic Bed & Breakfast*

4/1-11/30	$120-225	XP $50
12/1-3/31	$105-210	XP $50

Location: 0.3 mi w from Kings Square, off Duke of York St. 1 Old Maids Ln & Nea's Alle y GE01 (PO Box GE 96, ST. GEORGE, MB, GEBX). Fax: 441/297-1908. **Terms:** Reserv deposit, 14 day notice; handling fee imposed; 10% service charge. **Facility:** 10 rooms. Restored early 18th-century guest house convenient to downtown St. George. Quiet location. Attractive grounds & nice view of harbor. Interior/exterior corridors; designated smoking area. **All Rooms:** combo or shower baths. **Cards:** AE, MC, VI.

(441/297-1630

THE ST. GEORGE'S CLUB
◆◆◆ *Resort*

12/20-1/4 & 3/29-10/25	$300-550
3/1-3/28 & 10/26-11/7	$250-400
12/1-12/19, 1/5-2/28 & 11/8-11/30	$165-200

Location: Just n of York St. 6 Rose Hill GEBX (PO Box GE 92, ST. GEORGE'S). Fax: 441/297-8003. **Terms:** Check-in 4 pm; reserv deposit, 21 day notice. **Facility:** 69 rooms. Modern well-equipped & attractively furnished cottage style units in time share colony with choice of harbour or golf course views. All rooms with patio or balcony. Convenience store. 41 two-bedroom units. All units for up to 4-6 persons. Service charge $6.40 per day per person; 1-2 stories; exterior corridors; heated pool; 3 tennis courts (2 lighted). **Services:** giftshop. **All Rooms:** kitchens. **Cards:** AE, DI, MC, VI.

(441/297-1200

Restaurants

THE CARRIAGE HOUSE
◆◆ *Continental*   **L** $8-$16   **D** $25-$35

Location: On Water St at Somers Wharf; just below police station. 22 Water St GEO5. **Hours:** 11:30 am-4:30 & 5:30-9:15 pm. Closed major holidays. **Reservations:** suggested. **Features:** casual dress; Sunday brunch; children's menu; early bird specials; carryout; cocktails & lounge; street parking; a la carte. Served in the Old World atmosphere of a restored 18th-century warehouse. 15% service charge. Very pleasant location in historic St George's, overlooking harbor; Outside dining. **Cards:** AE, DI, MC, VI.

(441/297-1730

THE WHITE HORSE TAVERN
◆◆ *American*   **L** $11-$17   **D** $12-$18

Location: King's Square; across from St George's Town Hall. 8 King's Square GE05. **Hours:** 8 am-5 & 6-10 pm. **Features:** No A/C; casual dress; children's menu; cocktails & lounge; street parking; a la carte. Old tavern on the harbor's edge in the center of St. George's. Informal good-natured service. American, English & Bermudian cuisine. Local fish specialties. Entertainment most evenings & Sun afternoons. **Cards:** MC, VI.

(441/297-1838

Sandys Parish

Restaurant

THE FROG & ONION PUB   *Historical*
◆◆ *Ethnic*   **L** $10-$17   **D** $12-$25

Location: Within the walls of the Royal Naval Dockyard. **Hours:** 11:30 am-1 am; 11:30 am-4 & 6-9:30 pm, 12/1-3/1. **Closed:** Mon in winter. **Reservations:** accepted. **Features:** casual dress; children's menu; carryout; cocktails & lounge; a la carte. Authentic English pub with fine display of nautical artifacts. Real pub fare, sausage & mash, burgers & sheperd's pie & the like. Very well prepared. 15% service charge. **Cards:** MC, VI.

✕   (441/234-2900

Smith's Parish

Lodgings

⬤⬤⬤ SAVE ANGEL'S GROTTO
◆◆ *Cottage*

4/1-11/15	$120-200	XP $30
12/1-3/31 & 11/16-11/30	$105-160	XP $10-20

Location: On Harrington Sound. 83 Harrington Sound Rd HS02 (PO Box HS81, HARRINGTON SOUND, HSBX). Fax: 441/293-4164. **Terms:** D12; Reserv deposit, 21 day notice; 10% service charge. **Facility:** 7 rooms. Apartments in traditional Bermuda house & cottages, on waters edge overlooking Harrington Sound. 1 two-bedroom unit. 1-2 stories; exterior corridors. **Recreation:** swimming, fishing, snorkeling; barbecue. **All Rooms:** kitchens. **Cards:** AE, MC, VI. **Special Amenities: Free local telephone calls and free room upgrade (subject to availability with advanced reservations).**

((441)293-1986

PALMETTO HOTEL & COTTAGES
◆ *Complex*

4/1-10/31	$170-210	XP $34
12/1-3/31 & 11/1-11/30	$134-178	XP $30

Location: In Flatts Village. 1 Harrington Sound Rd FLBX (PO Box FI-54). Fax: 441/293-8761. **Terms:** D12; Reserv deposit, 14 day notice. **Facility:** 42 rooms. Hotel & cottages with balcony or patio on Harrington Sound. 2 stories; interior/exterior corridors. **Recreation:** swimming, fishing. **All Rooms:** combo or shower baths. **Some Rooms:** kitchen, color TV. **Cards:** AE, MC, VI.

(441/293-2323

RESTAURANT

THE INLET RESTAURANT
◆◆◆ *Continental*   **L** $7-$16 **D** $17-$28

Location: In Flatts Village; in Palmetto Hotel & Cottages. 1 Harrington Sound Rd FL07. **Hours:** 8 am-10, noon-2:30 & 6:30-9:30 pm, Sun 8 am-11, noon-2:30 & 6:30-9:30 pm. **Reservations:** suggested. **Features:** casual dress; carryout; cocktails & lounge; a la carte. Pleasant dining room overlooking Harrington Sound. Friendly staff. Very well prepared local & International cuisine. Pub & patio dining avail. **Cards:** AE, MC, VI.

(441/293-2323

SOUTHAMPTON PARISH

LODGINGS

MUNRO BEACH COTTAGES
◆◆ *Cottage*

4/15-11/30	$186-236	XP $30
12/1-1/14	$140-185	XP $25
1/15-4/14	$110-160	XP $30

Location: 1 mi s of Middle Rd, at Port Royal Golf Club. 2 Port Royal Golf Course Rd SNBX (PO BOX SN 99, SOUTHAMPTON). Fax: 441/234-3528. **Terms:** Reserv deposit, 21 day notice, 2 nights; 6% service charge. **Facility:** 17 rooms. On 5 quiet & peaceful acres overlooking Whitney Bay. All cottages with barbecue. Groceries delivered for a small fee. Meets AAA guest room security requirements. Meets AAA guest room security requirements. 10 night savings program; 1 story; exterior corridors; oceanview; beach. **Recreation:** swimming, fishing. Fee: golf & tennis at Port Royal Golf Club, mopeds; can arrange start times. **All Rooms:** efficiencies. **Cards:** MC, VI. **Special Amenities: Free local telephone calls and free newspaper.**

((441)234-1175

POMPANO BEACH CLUB
◆◆◆ *Hotel*

5/1-11/14	$365-395	XP $30-50
4/1-4/30	$300-330	XP $30-50
12/1-3/31 & 11/15-11/30	$230-260	XP $30-50

Location: Off Middle Rd, 0.5 mi w via Pompano Beach Rd, adjacent to Port Royal Golf Club. 36 Pompano Beach Rd SB03. Fax: 441/234-1694. **Terms:** D11; Reserv deposit, 21 day notice; 10% service charge. **Facility:** 54 rooms. Fine location adjacent to Port Royal Golf Course on bluff overlooking ocean. Pleasant rooms, all with bathrobes, hair dryer, iron & ironing board. 8 coffeemakers on req; 2 stories; exterior corridors; oceanfront; beach, heated pool; 1 tennis court. **Recreation:** swimming, fishing, snorkeling equipment. Fee: snorkeling, windsurfing; bicycles. Rental: paddleboats. **Some Rooms:** 2 kitchens. **Cards:** AE, MC, VI.

(441/234-0222

THE REEFS
◆◆◆ *Complex*

4/18-11/6	$348-418	XP $30-78
4/1-4/17 & 11/7-11/30	$274-344	XP $24-64
12/1-3/31	$226-296	XP $66

Location: At Christian Bay. 56 South Shore Rd SN02. Fax: 441/238-8372. **Terms:** D14; Reserv deposit, 21 day notice; 10% service charge; monthly rates; BP avail; package plans; 5 night min stay, 4/18-11/6. **Facility:** 67 rooms. Distinctive cliffside setting overlooking South Shore beach. Rooms & cottages tastefully furnished. 1 three-bedroom unit, 4 two-bedroom units. Cottages, $340-$688; $228-$440 off season for up to 5 persons. Service charge in winter $16.50 daily; 2 stories; exterior corridors; oceanview; beach, heated pool; 2 tennis courts. **Dining:** Dining room, restaurant; 8-10 am, 12:30-3 & 7-8:45 pm, snack bar 11 am-4 pm summer only; cocktails; public by reservation only; afternoon tea. **Recreation:** swimming, snorkeling equipment; hiking trails. Fee: bicycles, motor bikes. **Some Rooms:** color TV. **Cards:** AE, MC, VI.

((441)238-0222

SONESTA BEACH RESORT
◆◆◆ *Resort*

5/1-8/31	$240-380	XP $10-30
4/1-4/30 & 9/1-11/15	$219-340	XP $30
12/1-3/31 & 11/16-11/30	$110-175	XP $30

Location: At Sinky Bay. South Shore Rd (PO Box HM 1070, HAMILTON). Fax: 441/238-8463. **Terms:** F16; Reserv deposit, 14 day notice; BP, MAP avail; package plans; small pets only. **Facility:** 407 rooms. Beautifully situated in cove setting. Pleasantly furnished rooms with balcony or patio, dehumidifier, hair dryer, iron & ironing board. Service charge varies according to meal plan; 4 stories; interior corridors; oceanview; beach, heated indoor pool, wading pool, saunas, whirlpools; playground. Fee: 6 tennis courts (2 lighted). **Dining:** 3 restaurants; 7 am-10 pm; $20-$30; cocktails; afternoon tea. **Services:** giftshop. Fee: massage. **Recreation:** swimming, charter fishing, shuffleboard, croquet. Fee: scuba diving & equipment, snorkeling, aerobic & step classes, cycles; bicycles, spa, motor bikes. Rental: snorkeling equipment. **All Rooms:** combo or shower baths. **Cards:** AE, DI, MC, VI.

((441)238-8122

SOUTHAMPTON PRINCESS HOTEL
◆◆◆◆ *Resort*

4/19-9/6	$320-465	XP $50
9/7-11/15	$275-425	XP $50
12/1-4/18 & 11/16-11/30	$160-210	XP $30

Location: Between Middle & South Shore rds. 101 South Shore Rd (PO Box HM 1379, HAMILTON). Fax: 441/238-8968. **Terms:** F16; Reserv deposit, 14 day notice; $6 service charge. **Facility:** 600 rooms. Impressive hilltop location with sweeping panoramic views of the Sound & ocean. Complete range of guest facilities. Service charge varies according to meal plan. $3 extra charge per day resort levy; 6 stories; interior corridors; putting green; beach, heated indoor pool. Fee: 18 holes golf; 11 tennis courts (3 lighted). **Services:** giftshop; area transportation. Fee: massage. **Recreation:** swimming; jogging. Fee: scuba diving. Rental: boats, paddleboats, snorkeling equipment; bicycles. **Cards:** AE, DI, JC, MC, VI.

(441/238-8000

WHALE BAY INN
◆◆ *Motel*

4/1-11/15	$120	XP $20
12/1-3/31 & 11/16-11/30	$90	XP $20

Location: 0.5 mi s of South Shore Rd. 34 Whaling Hill-,Whale Bay Rd SB03 (PO Box SN 544, SOUTHAMPTON, SNBX). Fax: 441/238-1224. **Terms:** D12; Reserv deposit, 21 day notice, 2 night dep req; handling fee imposed; 10% service charge. **Facility:** 5 rooms. Secluded, quiet, modern rooms overlooking 14th hole of Port Royal Golf Course. Pleasantly-furnished & decorated rooms. 1 story; exterior corridors. **All Rooms:** efficiencies.

(441/238-0469

RESTAURANTS

▲▲▲ THE HENRY VIII RESTAURANT AND PUB
◆◆◆ *Ethnic*   L $7-$19 D $22-$32

Location: On South Shore Rd. **Hours:** noon-2:30 & 6-10 pm, Sun noon-3 & 6-10 pm. Closed: 12/25, 12/26 for lunch & 1st day of Cup Match. **Reservations:** suggested. **Features:** casual dress; Sunday brunch; cocktails & lounge; entertainment; a la carte. Varied menu English Tudor pub. Entertainment in pub lounge. Terrace dining at lunch in season. 15% service charge. **Cards:** AE, DI, MC, VI.

(441/238-1977

LIGHTHOUSE TEA ROOM
◆◆ *Ethnic*   L $4-$10

Location: Gibbs Hill Lighthouse. 68 St Anne's Rd. **Hours:** 9 am-5 pm. Closed: 1/1-1/31. **Features:** No A/C; casual dress; children's menu; carryout. A great location from which to see the island. Light English fare with traditional English tea served anytime. Menu includes a wide variety of fine teas. **Cards:** AE, MC, VI.

☒

(441/238-8679

THE NEWPORT ROOM
◆◆◆◆ *French*   D $26-$35

Location: Between Middle & South Shore rds; in Southampton Princess Hotel. 101 S Shore Rd SNO2. **Hours:** Open 1/7-10/31; 6:30 pm-10 pm, 1/7-5/31; 7 pm-10:30 pm, 6/1-10/31. **Reservations:** required. **Features:** formal attire; cocktails; a la carte. Modern & classical cuisine served in luxurious dining room designed after the grand salon of an ocean yacht. Jacket & tie req. 15% service charge. **Cards:** AE, DI, JC, MC, VI.

☒

(441/238-8000

TIO PEPE
◆ *Italian*   L $8-$14 D $11-$25

Location: 0.5 mi e of Southampton Princess Hotel. 117 South Shore Rd HMFX. **Hours:** 11 am-10 pm; noon-10 pm 10/1-4/30. **Reservations:** suggested; in summer. **Features:** dressy casual; carryout; cocktails; a la carte. Basic home-style Italian cooking with some Spanish dishes; Lunch menu served to 5 pm. 15% service charge. **Cards:** AE, MC, VI.

☒

(441/238-1897

THE WATERLOT INN   *Historical*
◆◆◆◆ *Continental*   D $19-$38

Location: Between Middle & South Shore rds; in Southampton Princess Hotel. Middle Rd SN04. **Hours:** Open 12/1-12/31 & 4/1-11/30; 6:30 pm-9:30 pm. Closed: 1/1-3/31. **Reservations:** required. **Features:** semi-formal attire; cocktails & lounge; entertainment; a la carte. Restored 17th-century Bermuda house, on waterfront. Superb cuisine. Shuttle service from Southampton Princess Hotel. 15% service charge. Jacket req. **Cards:** AE, DI, JC, MC, VI.

(441/238-0510

LODGINGS

ASTWOOD COVE
◆◆ *Bed & Breakfast*

4/1-11/15	$120-150	XP $20-35
12/1-3/31 & 11/16-11/30	$80-94	XP $10-25

Location: 2 mi e of Horseshoe Bay. 49 South Shore Rd WK07. Fax: 441/236-1164. **Terms:** D16; Reserv deposit, 21 day notice; 10% service charge. **Facility:** 20 rooms. Studio & suite apartments with balcony or garden patio overlooking Astwood Natural Park. Short pleasant walk to ocean beaches. 2 stories; exterior corridors. **All Rooms:** efficiencies, shower baths.

((441)236-0984

MARLEY BEACH COTTAGES
◆◆ *Bed & Breakfast*

4/15-10/31	$180-260	XP $35
12/1-1/2, 3/15-4/14 & 11/1-11/30	$145-200	XP $28
1/3-3/14	$105-155	XP $22

Location: At Astwood Park. South Shore Rd PGBX (PO Box PG 278, PAGET). Fax: 441/236-1984. **Terms:** D2; Reserv deposit, 21 day notice; handling fee imposed; 10% service charge. **Facility:** 13 rooms. Private hilltop location with lovely view of Marley Beach. Spacious four units with fireplace. 1 story; exterior corridors; beach. **Recreation:** swimming. **Some Rooms:** 10 efficiencies, 3 kitchens. **Cards:** AE, MC, VI.

((441)236-1143

SURF SIDE BEACH CLUB
◆◆ *Cottage*

4/1-10/31	$185-215	XP $25
12/1-3/31 & 11/1-11/30	$115-145	XP $25

Location: At Cobbs Hill Rd. 90 South Shore Rd WKBX (PO Box WK 101, WARWICK). Fax: 441/236-9765. **Terms:** Reserv deposit, 14 day notice; 10% service charge. **Facility:** 37 rooms. Resort studios & cottages on hillside overlooking the ocean. Housekeeping accommodations, some efficiencies, some full kitchens. 2 two-bedroom apartment $325, 4/1-10/31; $220 off season; 2 stories; exterior corridors; oceanview; beach. **Recreation:** swimming, fishing, snorkeling. **Fee:** snorkeling equipment. **All Rooms:** combo or shower baths. **Some Rooms:** 10 efficiencies, 27 kitchens. **Cards:** AE, MC, VI.

(441/236-7100

RESTAURANT

PAW PAWS
◆◆ *Continental*   L $7-$15 D $15-$26

Location: Corner of Dunscombe Rd. 87 South Shore Rd WK08. **Hours:** 11 am-10 pm; in summer to midnight. Closed: 1/2-1/28 & Tues 12/1-3/15. **Reservations:** suggested. **Features:** casual dress; cocktails & lounge; a la carte. Full Continental menu & separate Bermuda speciality menu. Colorful tables, outside seating weather permitting. 15% service charge. **Cards:** MC, VI.

(441/236-7459

BONAIRE

Bonaire Tourism Corp.

SECOND LARGEST of the Netherlands Antilles, Bonaire is the least populated and developed of the "ABC" (Aruba, Bonaire and Curaçao) islands. From the thousands of pink flamingos to the raspberry coral reefs, Bonaire is enveloped in a pink hue. Not only is it surrounded by coral reefs, Bonaire *is* a reef, harboring an incredible variety of sea life. This, coupled with excellent underwater visibility, makes Bonaire one of the foremost diving and snorkeling spots in the world. Strict laws prohibiting spear fishing and the gathering of coral protect the delicate ecological balance of marine life in Bonaire's waters.

HISTORY, GOVERNMENT AND ECONOMY

When discovered by Amerigo Vespucci, sailing for Spain in 1499, Bonaire was the home of the Arawak Indians. Vespucci named the island after the Arawak word *boynare,* which means "low country." The Spaniards sent some of the natives to Spain and others to Hispaniola to work the copper mines; as a result, within 20 years no Arawak Indians were left on the island. Several caves around the island, particularly those at Boca Onima, bear Indian inscriptions that have never been deciphered.

In 1834 control passed to the Dutch, who realized that the abundant sunshine and scant rainfall created ideal conditions for the manufacture of salt through evaporation. It was the Netherlanders which first brought slaves to work the saltpans at the southern end of the island, an endeavor that thrived until abolition curtailed the labor supply and caused production to cease. The area, already agreeable to flamingos, became even more attractive, and the colorful, exotic birds moved into the deserted saltpans to build thousands of nests.

The Antilles International Salt Co. has revived the industry using an updated version of the old methods. Thanks to a sanctuary set aside from a portion of the old saltpans, the flamingos continue to exist in harmony with people. Bonaire's other industries are an oil storage terminal and rice packaging.

Autonomous within the Kingdom of the Netherlands, Bonaire is administered by an island council and has its own representative to the Crown. Though Dutch is the official language, Spanish, English and the colloquial tongue of Papiamento are still widely spoken.

SHOPPING

Shopping is not Bonaire's main attraction; even so, the island has good buys on jewelry, china, crystal, leather, linens and perfumes. Most of the shops in Kralendijk are on Breedestraat, J.A. Abraham Boulevard, Simon Bolivarstraat and Kerkweg. Such stores as Bonaire Craftsmen and Fundashon Arte Industria Bonairiano sell island handicrafts made of wood, shell, black coral, goatskin and sterling. Shopping opportunities also are available at Les Galeries, a mall in downtown Kralendijk.

The Divi Flamingo Beach Resort & Casino, Harbour Village Beach Resort, Plaza Resort Bonaire, Sand Dollar Condominium Resort and Sunset Beach Hotel all have shops that offer fashions, jewelry and perfumes. The Harbourside Mall in Kralendijk has several shops and restaurants. Store hours are Mon.-Sat. 8-noon and 2-6. Banking hours are Mon.-Fri. 8:30-4.

FOOD AND DRINK

Most of the best restaurants can be found in hotels or in Kralendijk. Menus vary from fresh seafood and steaks to Chinese, Indonesian and Continental cuisine. Waterfront restaurants specialize in conch, lobster, fresh fish, shrimp and, best of all, wonderful views of the sea, sailboats and sunsets. A number of restaurants serve such local specialties as goat stew, iguana, gumbo and cactus soup. Beer, wine and rum drinks complement meals. There is no lack of fresh drinking water since it is distilled from the sea.

SPORTS AND AMUSEMENTS

Most visitors come to Bonaire for outdoor recreation: Water sports and birdwatching head the list of popular activities. The island is home to thousands of tropical birds, including parrots, parakeets, pelicans, pearly-eyed thrashers, mangrove cuckoos and hummingbirds. The flamingo colonies are particularly colorful March through May, when the deep-pink parents raise their gray hatchlings. To photograph or observe these shy birds, approach them slowly and quietly. Do not disturb nest areas; they are off limits. The best places to birdwatch are at Goto Lake, Pekelmeer and Washington/Slagbaai National Park *(see Excursions and Sightseeing)*.

Diving is popular in Bonaire; the island and its reef are said to be among the top five dive destinations in the world. Of the more than 80 diving locations around the island, more than half are accessible from the shore. The best spots for diving are off the leeward side of the island. Klein Bonaire, an offshore uninhabited island, is an excellent location for underwater exploring. You can make arrangements for snorkeling, scuba diving, water skiing, sailing or deep-sea fishing for marlin, tuna or bonito at several hotels or at the various commercial establishments on the island. Guided snorkeling programs also are available.

Although diving is what Bonaire is primarily known for, the island also offers opportunities for windsurfing, sea kayaking, hiking, mountain biking and horseback riding, all of which provide alternative methods of exploring the island's natural beauty.

Nightlife in Bonaire is mainly centered at the island's hotels, many of which offer theme dinners and live entertainment. An evening outing might also consist of casino gambling, available at the Divi Flamingo Beach Resort and the Plaza Resort Bonaire. Another popular evening activity is attending the free slide shows presented weekly at the Bonaire Scuba Center, Captain Don's Habitat, the Divi Flamingo Beach Resort and the Sand Dollar Beach Club; more information is available at each establishment. Dancing and live music venues include Club Amistad, Go Bananas, Karel's and Fantasy Disco. *Bonaire Holiday,* available at hotel desks, lists island events, restaurants and entertainment.

EXCURSIONS AND SIGHTSEEING

A 13,500-acre (5,463-hectare) wildlife sanctuary, Washington/Slagbaai National Park covers most of the northwestern section, and nearly one-fifth of the island. The park protects many lizard and bird species that are unique to Bonaire. A map of the park is available at the gate; a $5 entrance fee per person is charged. Allow 4 hours for the 28-mile (45-km) driving tour, 2 hours for the 17-mile (28-km) tour. The rugged dirt roads should be attempted only in a four-wheel drive vehicle. The preserve is open daily 8-5; closed holidays. Last admission 1 hour, 30 minutes before closing.

THINGS TO KNOW

AREA: 112 square miles (290 sq km).

POPULATION: 14,500.

LANGUAGE: Dutch, Spanish, English and Papiamento.

CAPITAL: Kralendijk.

GOVERNMENT: Autonomous member of the Kingdom of the Netherlands.

TIME ZONE: Atlantic. Standard.

UNIT OF CURRENCY: Netherlands Antilles guilder, divided into 100 cents. $1 U.S.=approx. 1.79 guilders.

ELECTRICITY: 127 volts, 50 cycles AC; voltage varies with location.

CARS: U.S. license valid; drive on right.

IMMIGRATION REQUIREMENTS: Proof of U.S. citizenship (birth certificate with a raised seal or valid passport accompanied by a photo ID) and return or through ticket are required. Airport tax $10, interisland tax $5.50 per person over age 2.

FOR FURTHER INFORMATION:
Tourism Corporation Bonaire
10 Rockefeller Plaza, Suite 900
New York, NY 10020
(212) 956-5912 or (800) 266-2473
Bonaire Government Tourist Office
Kaya Simon Bolivar 12
Kralendijk, Bonaire, Netherlands Antilles
Phone (011) 599-7-8322

HOLIDAYS: Jan. 1; Carnival Rest Day, Feb.; Good Friday; Easter; Easter Monday; Rincón's Day and Queen's Birthday, Apr. 30; Labor Day, May 1; Ascension Day, May; Bonaire Day, Sept. 6; Dec. 25; Boxing Day, Dec. 26.

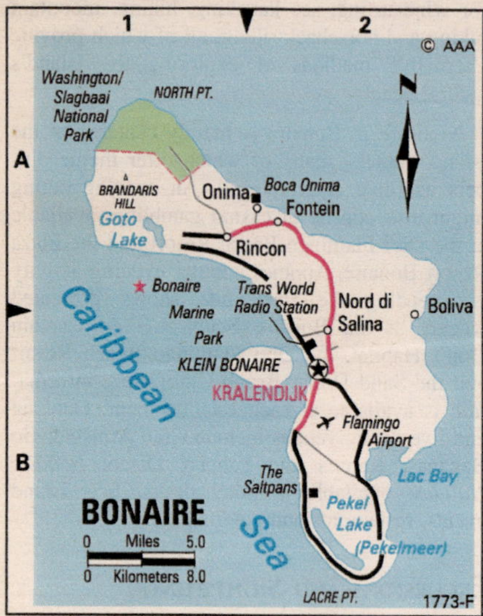

INDEX TO STARRED ATTRACTIONS

ATTRACTIONS OF EXCEPTIONAL
INTEREST AND QUALITY
Bonaire Marine Park - see Kralendijk

Full- or half-day sailing excursions and cocktail cruises are the perfect way to experience Bonaire's charms and climate; most resorts have information about charters. Air or sea excursions to the Venezuelan coast, 50 miles (80 km) south of Bonaire, also are available.

TRANSPORTATION

Flights are available several times weekly from Atlanta, Baltimore, Miami, Newark and Tampa. ALM Antillean Airlines and Air Aruba offer daily air connections. Bonaire also is a port of call for cruise ships.

You can tour Bonaire in a day on the island's excellent roads. Several car rental agencies serve the island. Minimokes (vehicles resembling small jeeps) and gurgels (Brazilian jeeps with canvas hoods) also are a good way to travel across Bonaire's desert interior. Bonaire Sightseeing offers bus tours of the island, as does Baranka Tours. Taxi rates are fixed, and you should check them before taking a cab.

> ## ATTRACTION ADMISSIONS
> Attraction admissions for this island are quoted in U.S. dollars.

POINTS OF INTEREST

KRALENDIJK (B-2) pop. 1,000

Kralendijk (Coral Dike) is the capital of Bonaire. The tropics and the Netherlands meet in this pink and orange town. Pelicans and flamingos can be seen at the salt flats and near the lagoons. Brilliantly plumed birds grace almost every tree; iguanas hide among the coral rocks. A fish market is open early in the morning on Bernhardweg, along the bay. For further information on Kralendijk contact the tourist office in the center of town.

BOCA ONIMA, near Fontein, is a grotto that has Indian drawings inscribed on its walls and ceiling.

★BONAIRE MARINE PARK, the coast and coral reefs around Bonaire and Klein Bonaire, offers a unique environment that can be explored by scuba diving and snorkeling. The park is controlled by certain restrictions and regulations that protect and allow best use of the island's coastline. Obtain a diving guide at dive operations or in local bookstores for a complete list of park guidelines. Guide service is available. Annual fee $10.

FONTEIN, with natural fresh water, tropical vegetation and fruit trees, is an oasis in an arid stretch of land.

GOTO LAKE is at the northern end of the island. Great numbers of colorful flamingos congregate here, at Bonaire's inland lake. The best time for viewing the flamingos is in the early morning.

LAC BAY, a landlocked bay shaded by an arc of dense mangrove trees, is ideal for picnicking, swimming, windsurfing and underwater exploring. It also is a popular spot for collecting driftwood.

PEKELMEER is the chief flamingo breeding ground. These birds skillfully construct nests of mud in which they hatch their young during March and April. The flamingos must be watched from a distance.

THE SALTPANS at Pekelmeer are a series of square ponds thickly salted by the sea. As the water evaporates, the beds turn various shades of pink, matching the flamingos, who choose to nest near the towering stacks of salt crystals. Three 30-foot obelisks used as navigational aids by the salt ships of the 1800s still stand, and primitive stone huts of the slaves who once worked the pans have been restored. On weekends the slaves walked almost the length of the island to their homes in Rincón, Bonaire's oldest village.

TRANS WORLD RADIO STATION is reputed to be the world's most powerful religious radio station. Its medium wave (AM) transmitter has an output of more than 500,000 watts and also is the most powerful privately owned transmitter in the Western Hemisphere. TWR also broadcasts on several shortwave frequencies. Tours are available. Phone (011) 599-7-8800

Lodgings & Restaurants

Kralendijk—1,000

Lodgings

CARIB INN
◆◆ *Motel*

12/15-4/12	$89-119	XP $10
12/1-12/14 & 4/13-11/30	$79-109	XP $10

Location: Center; (Post Office) 1.5 km s; from airport 2 km n. J A Abraham Blvd #46 (PO Box 68). Fax: 599/7-5295. **Terms:** Reserv deposit, no refund on deposits; handling fee imposed. **Facility:** 10 rooms. Quiet, well maintained waterfront lodging with full diving facilities. 1 two-bedroom unit, 1 three-bedroom unit. 3 bedroom house, $139-$149, rate for up to 4 persons; 2 stories; exterior corridors; oceanview; boat dock. **Services:** giftshop. **All Rooms:** shower baths. **Some Rooms:** 7 efficiencies, kitchen. **Cards:** AE, MC, VI.

(599/7-8819

SAND DOLLAR CONDOMINIUM RESORT
◆◆◆ *Apartment Complex*

12/16-4/14	$215-360
12/1-12/15 & 4/15-11/30	$180-310

Location: 2.5 km n from post office; just n of traffic circle. Kaya Gobernador N Debrot (PO Box 262). Fax: 599/7-8760. **Terms:** Reserv deposit, 21 day notice, in season, 14 day notice off season; 10% service charge. **Facility:** 72 rooms. Modern condominium studios & 1- to 3-bedroom units. 2 stories; exterior corridors; oceanview; beach access; 2 lighted tennis courts; boat dock. **Services:** giftshop. Fee: massage. **Recreation:** swimming, scuba diving, snorkeling. Fee: windsurfing. Rental: scuba & snorkeling equipment. **All Rooms:** kitchens. **Cards:** AE, DS, MC, VI.

(599/7-8738

Restaurants

CROCCANTINO
◆◆ *Italian* L $15-$25 D $15-$25

Location: Downtown on Kayi Grandi. Kaya Grandi 31. **Hours:** noon-2 pm & 6-10:30 pm; Sat & Sun 6 pm-10:30 pm. Closed: Sun. **Features:** casual dress; cocktails; street parking; a la carte. Modern decor; extensive Italian menu. Terrace & indoor dining. **Cards:** AE, MC, VI.

(599/7-5025

GREEN PARROT RESTAURANT
◆◆ *American* L $6-$10 D $8-$20

Location: 2.5 km n from post office, just n of traffic circle; in Sand Dollar Condominiums Resort. Kaya Gubernador N Debrot. **Hours:** 8 am-10 pm. **Reservations:** suggested. **Features:** No A/C; casual dress; cocktails; a la carte. Overlooking harbor & scuba diving training area. American & Regional cuisine. Informal, colorful. Feed the fish off the dock. **Cards:** AE, MC, VI.

(599/7-5454

RENDEZ VOUS RESTAURANT
◆◆ *Continental* L $3-$16 D $15-$25

Location: Downtown. Kaya L D Gerharts 3. **Hours:** noon-2 & 6-10:30 pm; Sat from 6 pm. Closed: Sun. **Reservations:** suggested. **Features:** casual dress; cocktails & lounge; street parking; a la carte. Terrace & indoor dining. Very well prepared Continental & Regional cuisine. Pleasant informal atmosphere. **Cards:** AE, MC, VI.

RICHARD'S
◆◆◆ *Steak and Seafood* D $13-$21

Location: 1.5 km s of center (Post Office) on the waterfront. J A Abraham Blvd 60. **Hours:** 6:30 pm-10:30 pm. Closed: Mon & 9/1-10/1. **Features:** No A/C; casual dress; carryout; cocktails & lounge; a la carte. Dining room open to the harbor. Very pleasant informal atmosphere. Regional seafood specialties & American cuisine. **Cards:** AE, MC, VI.

CAYMAN ISLANDS

Jon Simon / Bonaire Tourism Corp.

SURROUNDED BY sapphire waters and coral reefs, the Cayman Islands is an outdoor-lover's paradise. Neither a sleepy, secluded destination nor a luxury resort area, the Cayman Islands is the best of both worlds. Its reputation as one of the top diving spots in the Caribbean coupled with its proximity to Florida—the islands are about 480 miles (768 km) due south of Miami—also account for its increasing popularity. Of the three islands—Grand Cayman, Cayman Brac and Little Cayman—Grand Cayman, 22 miles (35 km) long and 8 miles (13 km) wide, is the largest and the best equipped to handle tourism. Most of the islands' inhabitants live on Grand Cayman near the capital city of George Town.

HISTORY, GOVERNMENT AND ECONOMY

The Cayman Islands were sighted in 1503 by Christopher Columbus while on his fourth and last voyage to the New World. It was Columbus who named them *Las Tortugas* for the large number of turtles in the waters. The present name comes from *caymanas,* a derivation of the Carib Indian name for the crocodile.

Although the islands were ceded to the British by the Treaty of Madrid in 1670, there was no serious attempt to settle them until the early 18th century, when a group from Jamaica moved in; they were recalled 3 years later over problems in protecting them from Spanish pirates. The earliest settlers, however, were believed to be from Oliver Cromwell's army, shipwrecked sailors and refugees fleeing religious persecution in Britain.

With the passing of the days of sail, the Cayman Islands lapsed into isolation until the 1950s, when air travel was introduced. Flights now serve all three islands, making them a readily accessible vacation spot.

Despite independence movements among its neighboring islands, the Cayman Islands are content with their status as a British crown colony. Formerly governed by Jamaica, the islands are now administered by a governor appointed by the queen.

The governor is president of the legislative assembly and chairman of the executive council. There are five electoral districts on Grand Cayman: George Town, West Bay, Bodden Town,

Northside and East End. Every 4 years elections are held to select 15 representatives from these districts, based on each area's population. These representatives form the legislative assembly, which is responsible for enacting laws.

The executive council consists of five elected ministers, while three members are appointed by the governor—the chief secretary, attorney general and financial secretary. Council ministers are responsible for the administration of the country, advising the governor on policy issues and instituting programs.

A big boost to the Cayman Islands is the lack of any direct taxes on income, property and inheritance. Grand Cayman ranks among the top banking and offshore financial centers in the world and has a reputation as a tax haven. This status is bolstered by a policy of allowing tax-free foreign investments and by the Confidential Relationships Law, which ensures the confidentiality of all foreign business transactions.

Though the biggest moneymakers are the banking, tourism and insurance industries, some Caymanians still depend upon the sea and soil for their livelihood. Relatively flat with no rivers, the Cayman Islands are covered by the tropical vegetation of mangroves, mangoes and palms. Trade is conducted mainly with Jamaica, the United States and Costa Rica.

Grand Cayman has one of the highest standards of living in the Caribbean. Visitors can explore the island without fear of being approached by street and beach vendors or beggars; the law prohibits such activity.

SHOPPING

Free-port shopping is plentiful on Cardinal Avenue in George Town. Cameras, projectors, radios, perfumes, watches, linens, china and British woolens are sold at reduced prices. Kirk Freeport Plaza contains The Coral Shop, La Parfumerie, Kirk Jewelers and the Waterford/Wedgwood Shop. Next door to the plaza is Coach Factory, which features leather goods. Treasure Cove, affiliated with Kirk Freeport, is on the opposite side of the street and consists of Coral Cove, Far Away Places, Gucci and La Parfumerie II.

Around the corner on Albert Panton Street, Kirk Gallery has such fine china as Royal Doulton and Rosenthal, Hummel figurines and Baccarat crystal. Next to the gallery is Kirk Leather, with products by Cartier, Pierre Balmain, Fendi and Yves Saint Laurent.

Anchorage Center Shopping Mall, accessible from pathways next to Coach Factory and between the shops on Harbour Drive, surrounds an open-air courtyard with a snack area. The mall contains Amazing China Turtle, with an array of island souvenirs, and City Duty Free, which has a large selection of Lenox china and crystal.

The English Shoppe, at the intersection of Cardinal Avenue and Harbour Drive, has jewelry and souvenirs among its merchandise. Caymania Freeport, with locations on Shedden Road and Fort Street, has a vast selection of perfumes and some jewelry. Easily recognized by its flying flags and attractive blue and white buildings, Elizabethan Square is situated on Shedden Road. This complex contains an American Express office and boutiques that offer children's clothing, leather goods, jewelry, sportswear and gift items.

The Seven Mile Beach area has several shopping plazas with a wide assortment of goods. These plazas, all on West Bay Road, include Coconut Place and The Falls Shopping Centre, both in close proximity to the Hyatt; Seven Mile Shops and Queen's Court, by the Treasure Island; and West Shore Plaza, not too far from the Radisson.

Island products make meaningful souvenirs: coral or conch-shell jewelry and sculpture, hammocks, and woven baskets. Antique gold and silver coins and coin jewelry are of high quality and a good value in the Caymans. Many shops in Grand Cayman and Cayman Brac offer local arts and crafts. For handicrafts with a unique touch, try Pure Art, with locations on South Church Street and at the Hyatt on West Bay Road. The products of the local artistic community can be seen at several galleries, including Kennedy/Cayman Fine Art in West Shore and Pure Art.

Shopping hours are generally Mon.-Sat. 9-5; some hotel shops are open on Sunday. Banking hours are Mon.-Thurs. 9-2:30, Fri. 9-1 and 2:30-4:30. Cayman dollars are available in denominations of $1, $5, $10, $25, $50 and $100.

FOOD AND DRINK

Although 90 percent of the islands' food is imported from Florida, noteworthy local dishes include turtle steak, conch, lobster and chowders. Locally grown vegetables and fruit—bananas, plantains, cassava and breadfruit—complement any meal.

Caymanians also enjoy their deep-fried or baked johnny cake, a doughy unseasoned concoction that resembles a heavy dough ball, and patties, pastry stuffed with beef, chicken or vegetables. "Bread Kind" refers to local vegetables such as yams, cassava, breadfruit and potatoes.

THINGS TO KNOW

AREA: 100 square miles (259 sq km).

POPULATION: 32,000.

LANGUAGE: English.

CAPITAL: George Town, Grand Cayman.

GOVERNMENT: British Crown Colony.

TIME ZONE: Eastern.

UNIT OF CURRENCY: Cayman dollar, divided into 100 cents. $1 U.S.=approx. .82 Cayman Island dollars. U.S. currency is widely accepted.

ELECTRICITY: 120 volts, 60 cycles AC.

CARS: Local permit ($5) required; drive on left.

IMMIGRATION REQUIREMENTS: Proof of U.S. citizenship (birth certificate, naturalization papers or passport), photo ID and return or through ticket are required. There is a 6-month limit on stay. Departure tax $10 US.

FOR FURTHER INFORMATION:
Cayman Islands Department of Tourism
420 Lexington Ave., Suite 2733
New York, NY 10170
(212) 682-5582
Cayman Islands Department of Tourism
The Pavilion, Cricket Square, Elgin Ave. P.O. Box 67
George Town, Grand Cayman, B.W.I.
(345) 949-0623

HOLIDAYS: Jan. 1; Ash Wednesday; Good Friday; Easter Monday; Discovery Day, May (3rd Mon.); Queen's Birthday (a designated Mon. in June); Constitution Day, July (1st Mon.); Monday after Remembrance Sunday, Nov.; Dec. 25; Boxing Day, Dec. 26.

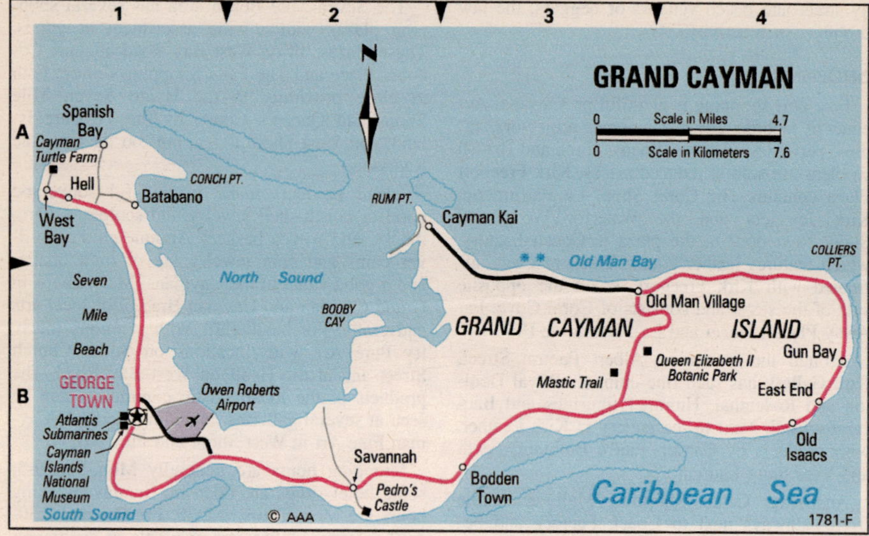

Pepperpot is a soup that contains callalu, a leafy, spinach-like vegetable, and potatoes seasoned with hot peppers and spices. Saltfish and *ackee,* a dish adopted from Jamaica, is another local favorite.

Restaurants featuring native fare include Pooh's in East End; the Crow's Nest, about 2 miles (3.2 km) south of George Town on South Sound Road; Liberty's in West Bay; and White Hall Bay and Champion House in George Town. There also are restaurants devoted to Chinese, Italian, German, Continental and Thai cuisine. Most dining establishments are in George Town, along Seven Mile Beach or in the hotels.

Desalination provides adequate drinking water in most areas of Grand Cayman. Pipelines leading from the reservoirs of the desalination plant have not yet been constructed in North Side and East End; water is safe in restaurants and hotels in these areas, but inquire otherwise. Pasteurized milk is imported from the United States.

Sports and Amusements

Vacationers come to the Cayman Islands to escape the pressures of the outside world; fishing and scuba diving are two means to this end. Rich catches of dolphin, blue marlin, wahoo and yellowfin tuna reward fishing enthusiasts. Little Cayman has bottom fishing outside the reef, bone fishing and fly fishing close to shore and tarpon fishing in a land-locked lake. Half- and full-day deep-sea charters are available. An international fishing tournament, Million Dollar Month, takes place throughout June. For entry information write P.O. Box 878, George Town, Grand Cayman, B.W.I.; phone (345) 949-7228.

Due to favorable currents and the proximity of deep open water to the shore, Northwest Point, Rum Point, Southwest Point, South Coast Drop Off and 12-Mile Bank are prime fishing destinations in Grand Cayman. Charter Boat Headquarters, (345) 945-4340, and Bayside Watersports, (345) 949-3200, serve as centralized booking agencies for charter boats in Grand Cayman; trips can be arranged for deep-sea, bottom, reef, bone and tarpon fishing. Marinas that are available to visiting yachtsmen include Cayman Islands Yacht Club and Harbour House, both in North Sound, and Morgan's Harbour Marina in West Bay.

Grand Cayman's trade winds coupled with water temperatures that average in the 80s provide excellent opportunities for windsurfing. Morritt's Tortuga Club Resort at East End boasts good winds and calm waters inside the reef area. Winds blow 15-25 knots (17-29 mph) in the winter and 10-20 knots (12-23 mph) in the summer; lessons and rentals are available from Cayman Windsurf at Morritt's Tortuga Club Resort and Mistral Sailboards Caribbean next to the Plantana condominiums on Seven Mile Beach. A windsurfing regatta is held at the Tortuga Club every January. With constant breezes blowing 6-12 knots (7-14 mph), Grand Cayman is a prime place to learn how to windsurf.

Parasailing is available on Grand Cayman; inquire at Aqua Delights at the Treasure Island Resort, or Red Sail Sports at the Hyatt or Westin for information on equipment rentals. A few operators offer water skiing. Sunfish, Hobie Cat and Jet Ski rentals are available at many hotels. Sailing regattas are scheduled by the local sailing club throughout the year, generally in conjunction with public holidays.

Landlubber activities range from cave exploring to sunbathing. Most of the caves that can be explored are on Cayman Brac. The only caves accessible on Grand Cayman are the Pirates' Caves in Bodden Town; the caves at East End and Pedro's Castle in Savannah are closed to the public.

Birdwatching opportunities abound on all three islands. The Grand Cayman and Cayman Brac parrots are found only in these islands, which also are home to more than 180 other resident and migratory species.

Seven Mile Beach, where 90 percent of the Caymans' resorts and water sports operations are found, lures swimmers and sun worshipers to the west coast of Grand Cayman. One of the longest unbroken white sand beaches in the Caribbean, Seven Mile Beach is actually about 5.5 miles (9 km) long. The beach received its name from the fact that it is 7 miles (11 km) from the northwest to the southwest point of Grand Cayman.

Colliers Point on the east end of the island also has a lovely beach. Old Man Bay and Cayman Kai, on the north coast of Grand Cayman, are secluded beaches with golden sands that are occasionally punctuated by exquisite beach houses. Smith Cove, on the south coast off South Church Street, is known for swimming and snorkeling rather than for a beach. Picnic tables are available, and shaded areas provide respite from the sun.

Rum Point, on the north central tip of the island, is a park area that overlooks the North Sound. Visitors can relax on the beach, swim or snorkel in the shallow waters and rest in hammocks shaded by *casaurina* trees, also known as Australian pines. Red Sail Sports operates a full-service water sports and dive facility; activities include diving, snorkeling, sailing, windsurfing and water skiing. A restaurant, snack bar, changing facilities and showers also are available. A ferry provides 40-minute trips from the Hyatt Regency Grand Cayman to Rum Point several times daily.

Hikers are attracted to the eastern tip of the island. Also popular with hikers is Cayman Brac, where a trek along the Bluff is rewarded with a view of the tropical wilderness where 150 species of resident and migratory birds can be spotted. A trail used primarily as a cow path leads to the caves that honeycomb the Bluff. Birdwatchers on Grand Cayman can obtain information at the Cayman Islands Bird Club's meetings held the last Tuesday of each month at the National Trust; phone (345) 949-0121.

Many hotels on Grand Cayman and Cayman Brac are equipped with tennis courts. Temporary health club memberships are offered by the Cayman World Gym, (345) 949-5132, on West Bay Road; The Fitness Connection, (345) 949-8485, just south of George Town on Glen Eden Road; and New Image Health Club, (345) 949-7016, on Smith Road in George Town.

Two types of golf can be played at the Jack Nicklaus designed Britannia Golf Course—regulation play on a nine-hole course and a Caymanian version on an 18-hole course. The Cayman course is played with a ball designed to travel half the distance of a regulation ball. Consisting of 103 acres (42 hectares), the Links at Safe-Haven is an 18-hole championship golf course off West Bay Road, 5 miles (8 km) north of George Town.

The Truman Bodden Sports Complex and Stadium in George Town features a variety of amateur and professional sporting events.

While water sports dominate the action in the Cayman Islands, most hotels offer some form of evening entertainment. Ports of Call, the bar at The Wharf restaurant at the south end of Seven Mile Beach, is known for its spectacular ocean view. Sharkey's Boca Bar Nightclub in the Falls Plaza on West Bay Road is a popular disco. Coconuts, a comedy club located in Legendz across from the Westin, is open Wednesday through Sunday.

The Cayman National Theatre Company presents a variety of events at the F.J. Harquail Cultural Center on West Bay Road from October to June, and the Cayman Drama Society stages productions at the Prospect Playhouse on Red Bay Road year-round. Top-name entertainers perform at the Lion's Centre on Crewe Road in the Red Bay area. Movies are shown regularly at the Cinema on West Bay Road.

Island festivities peak when the Cayman Islands honors their earliest settlers during Pirates Week in late October. Celebrations include colorful costumes, parades, treasure hunts and a lively re-enactment, when a group of Cayman residents costumed as rogues and wenches board a replica of a pirate ship and approach the harbor. The landing turns into a mock battle with those who ruled the sea lanes more than 200 years ago.

Other events include Batabano, a festival with costume parades and street dances held after Easter. In May, Cayman Brac hosts Bracchanal, a carnival that is much like Batabano, featuring dancing, costumes and Caymanian food. An open house and garden party at Government House and a parade are highlights of the Queen's Birthday celebration in mid-June.

Several publications provide information about local events, activities and points of interest. *The Caymanian Compass*, published Monday through Friday, is Grand Cayman's newspaper. *Key to Cayman*, a complimentary magazine distributed at hotels, contains a wide assortment of visitor information. *Horizon*, a free magazine published bimonthly by Cayman Airways, can be found at retail establishments and other points throughout Grand Cayman. *What's Hot* is a monthly feature magazine filled with an up-to-date listing of activities; it is available free of charge at many stores.

SCUBA DIVING

Scuba diving is the Cayman Islands' claim to fame: It is said that these islands are the most popular diving destination in the world. The Cayman Islands are actually the tips of three undersea mountains surrounded by vertical drop-offs that plunge thousands of fathoms to the bottom of the sea. The Cayman Trench drops to a depth of 23,000 feet.

The Cayman walls encircle the Cayman Islands. The drop-offs begin at 55-60 feet and provide spectacular underwater scenery. A barrier reef encircles Grand Cayman in the shallower depths preceding the walls. Visibility can range from 125 to 200 feet, and conditions for underwater photography are excellent. Surrounded by colorful corals and sponges, the wall at Bloody Bay on Little Cayman begins its drop-off at 18 feet, then plunges 1,200 feet.

Diving close to the shore often eliminates the need for boats. Sometimes only a mask, snorkel and fins are needed to explore shallow-water reefs. An even more intensive diving experience is available on live-aboard dive boats, which offer divers access to the best sites around the islands. A guided trip with a qualified dive master is recommended. Among the many reputable

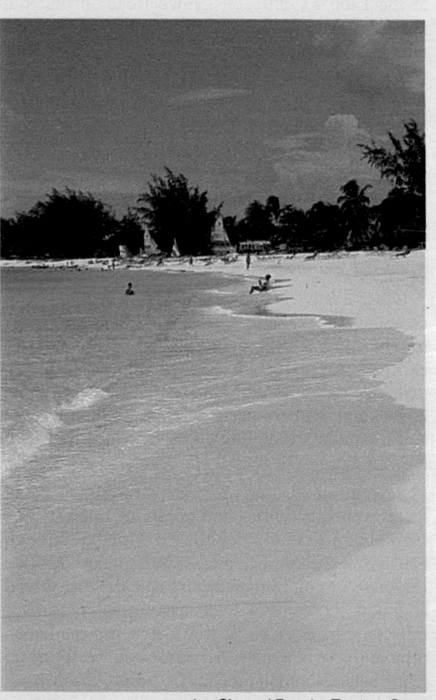

Jon Simon / Bonaire Tourism Corp.

dive operators are Bob Soto's, (345) 949-2022; Don Foster's Dive Cayman, (345) 945-5132; Quabbin Dive Center, (345) 949-5597; Quabo Dives, (345) 945-4769; and Red Sail Sports, (345) 945-5965.

All divers must possess a certification card from one of the international diving schools before any island dive shop will rent scuba gear. Most dive operations offer beginning divers a short "resort course" that provides enough familiarity with the equipment to allow them to take supervised, shallow diving trips. Harming or collecting coral or other marine life is illegal, as is spear fishing. A recompression chamber at George Town Hospital is staffed daily 24 hours; for emergencies phone 555.

The Cayman Islands have numerous recorded shipwrecks but divers are only able to see about a dozen. With more than 1,000 known diving locations it is impossible to list each one, but following are some of the most popular dive sites surrounding Grand Cayman.

The waters off the north side of the island include Eagle Ray Pass, an area of narrow canyons inhabited by eagle rays, barracudas, tarpons and sometimes sharks. For experienced divers only, Grand Canyon consists of giant canyons up to 150 feet wide that were formed by collapsed reefs. Hepp's Pipeline, with depths ranging from 20 to 60 feet, has two mini-walls that provide a home for stingrays and tropical fish. Divers can feed and pet friendly stingrays in 12 feet of water at Stingray City, considered one of the world's best shallow dive sites.

The west side of Grand Cayman also contains several renowned underwater sites. Aquarium, a shallow dive considered ideal for beginners, has tame parrotfish and angelfish that provide excellent photographic opportunities. Experienced divers will want to visit Big Tunnels, where two tunnels lead downward through a reef to open up on the Cayman Wall; one tunnel can be entered at 80 feet, while the other can be entered at 160 feet. At Bonnie's Arch, extraordinary marine life and spectacular arch formations can be viewed. Trinity Caves, a wall dive with dramatic caves and arches, features such sea life as sponges, black coral, sea turtles and eagle rays.

East coast spots favored by divers include Grouper Grotto, situated just before the 6,000 foot drop-off at the Cayman Trench. The Maze is a series of caverns, tunnels and archways that twist through an elaborate coral formation extending 500 feet along the East End Wall. Three Sisters is composed of three massive pinnacles of coral named Agnes, Bertha and Claire; each measures about 70 feet in diameter.

The south side of Grand Cayman also has many underwater wonders. Among them are Japanese Gardens, a series of narrow passages containing beautiful elkhorn coral formations and ropical fish, and Red Bay Gardens, known for striking elkhorn and antler coral, colorful caves and wide areas of sand.

Parrots Landing, a water sports park just south of George Town, offers easy access to some of the best shore diving on the island. The park contains barbecue grills, hammocks, picnic tables, sun decks and a pier. Diving gear can be rented, and dive boats leave the dock daily at 8 and 1.

Four popular dive sites are within 120 yards of Parrots Landing's shore. Devil's Grotto has numerous caverns and grottos as well as a long tunnel that leads to a room. Eden Rock, a good spot for inexperienced divers, consists of a coral cliff inhabited by tropical fish. Parrot's Reef, only 30 yards off the park's dock, contains the wreck of the *Anna Marie* and teems with parrotfish that swim among coral heads and sponges. About 150 yards from the dock, Polly's Perch is a wall dive that starts at 70 feet.

Many shipwrecks lie in the waters off the islands, such as the *Balboa*, a Norwegian freighter that sank off the George Town shore that in the 1932 hurricane. The *Cali* is a sunken cargo freighter near George Town harbor that houses such marine life as barracudas, parrotfish and lobsters.

Oro Verde, off the coast of Seven Mile Beach, is the wreckage of an old cargo vessel sunk purposely in 1980 for the enjoyment of underwater explorers. Off Cayman Brac in 1996, the Russian frigate *Capt. Keith Tibbeth* was sunk to form an artificial reef. The MV *Ridgefield*, which ran aground on the coral reef off Gun Bay, attracts divers and snorkelers. Other shipwrecks include the *Doc Polson* wreck, a barge off Grand Cayman's northwest corner, and the wreck of the *David Nicholson*, a vessel in 65 feet of water deliberately sunk offshore from the Sunset House Dive Resort.

Excursions and Sightseeing

A driving tour of Grand Cayman runs south from George Town along the South Sound coastal road that merges with the Bodden Town Road. Lined with tall Australian pines, the route travels through the historic outer districts, which were the heart of the island in the 17th and 18th centuries. Once a thriving settlement, Prospect was destroyed by a hurricane in 1846, leaving only a monument erected on the site of an 18th-century fort that was built to protect against Spanish pirates.

About 3 miles (4.8 km) east of Prospect in the Savannah area, Pedro St. James Castle is the oldest surviving structure in the Cayman Islands. Built in the 1780s as a private house by William Eden, the building served many purposes throughout the years before it was gutted by fire. The government now owns the landmark and is in the process of restoring it to its former state;

the restoration was expected to be completed by late 1997. The property affords a splendid view of the rugged south coast. At Otto Watler's Farm in Sanannah, visitors can purchase delicious dark brown honey. Also in Savannah, the Old Savannah Schoolhouse has been restored to reflect a typical 1950s Caymanian school.

Two cannons guard the entrance to Bodden Town, the first capital of the Cayman Islands, where you can explore Gun Square, the Slave Wall and the Pirates' Caves. It is believed that pirates once hid in the caves, an extensive maze of tunnels that eventually connects with underwater caves. Across the street is a cemetery where pirates are supposedly buried. Queen Victoria's Monument, erected by residents to commemorate the queen, is in the center of Bodden Town. Also along the way is caymanite, a multicolored rock found only in these islands.

The road traveling east out of Bodden Town is bordered on the left by a bird sanctuary, where such species as heron, snowy egret and black-necked stilt can be viewed at dawn and dusk. About a mile (1.6 km) before East End is the Blow Holes: As the incoming surf surges against the shore, water is forced through crevices in the coral rock, shooting more than 60 feet into the air to create a geyser effect.

Just northeast of the village of East End is Gun Bay, the scene of the "Wreck of the Ten Sails" in 1794. The two cannons in Bodden Town are from the wreck, and an anchor that protrudes from the water off East End's shore is believed to be from one of the ships. A monument and scenic overlook commemorating this maritime disaster was unveiled by Queen Elizabeth II in 1994. The coastal road continues through Old Man Village and ends at Rum Point.

You also can drive to the Cayman Turtle Farm on the rugged northwest coast and to the forbidding "Hell" coral formations near West Bay. The coral, which is more than 1.5 million years old, is colored by black algae and caymanite. Even though the coral limestone resembles charred ruins, folklore claims that the spot received its name in the 1930s when a visiting official from England fired at a bird near the formations, missed, and said "Oh hell." The Devil's Hangout is a souvenir shop where visitors may catch a glimpse of the devil. Tourists have made the post office of this tiny town popular by getting their postcards and letters canceled with the stamp of "Hell, Grand Cayman."

Sightseeing tour buses depart from hotels on Seven Mile Beach and head to George Town. The 2-hour tours include stops at Hell and the Cayman Turtle Farm, Tortuga Rum Company bakery and store, and a conch-shell house; the full-day tours also include stops at Cayman Kai and the Pirates' Caves. Cruises along Seven Mile Beach also are available. A free walking tour guidebook of the historical district of West Bay can be obtained from the National Trust Office off Eastern Avenue on Courts Road in George Town; phone (345) 949-0121.

Several boats offer afternoon and dinner cruises, and glass-bottom boat rides can be arranged at many resorts and water sports outlets. Picnicking, shelling, snorkeling and swimming are other popular activities.

A popular way to spend a day and to experience the Caymans is to participate in a North Sound Beach lunch/snorkeling trip. The all-day boat excursion features a native-style lunch prepared by the captain; diving for a conch to be used later as part of the meal; and three snorkeling stops, including Stingray City. These trips, available from more than 20 captains, can be booked through Bayside Watersports at Morgan's Harbour and the Falls Shopping Centre, (345) 949-3200; Charter Boat Headquarters in Coconut Place on West Bay Road, (345) 945-4340; and through Jackie's Watersports, (345) 945-5791. Half-day excursions without lunch also are offered.

Cayman Brac (brac means "bluff" in Gaelic) has a limestone bluff that runs the length of the island, rising to a height of 140 feet and plunging downward 6,000 feet into the sea. The top of the bluff is a popular hiking and bird-watching destination, especially the eastern part which contains the 180-acre (73-hectare) Parrot Reserve, a protected breeding area of the native Cayman Brac parrot. The 14-square-mile (36 sq-km) Brac, 89 miles (142 km) east of Grand Cayman, has excellent fishing, swimming, scuba-diving and exploring. There are many hidden caverns reputed to have once been the hideouts of pirates and their treasures. The Cayman Brac Museum, at Stake Bay on Cotton Tree Bay Road, includes artifacts pertaining to the island's seafaring history and illustrations of the islanders' daily lives many years ago; phone (345) 948-2390.

Little Cayman, 7 miles (11 km) northwest of Cayman Brac, is home to more than a hundred species of migratory fowl. Snorkeling, scuba diving and deep-sea fishing also are excellent on Little Cayman, which is just 12 square miles (31 sq km) in area. The diving at Bloody Bay Wall has been described as spectacular. The Booby Pond Nature Reserve on Little Cayman is home to one of the largest breeding colonies of Red-Footed Boobies in the Western Hemisphere. The smaller islands are less developed than Grand Cayman, but they provide a welcome change of pace and an opportunity to see the islands in a more natural form.

TRANSPORTATION

Cayman Airways, the national flag carrier, and Northwest and American airlines provide daily flights from Miami to Grand Cayman. USAir has flights from Charlotte and Baltimore. Cayman Airways also offers direct service from Houston, Atlanta, Orlando and Tampa to Grand Cayman and from Miami to Cayman Brac. Air Jamaica and Cayman Airways regularly fly between Grand Cayman and Montego Bay and Kingston, Jamaica. Grand Cayman also is a leading port of call for cruise ships, serving an average of 12-14 vessels per week.

Interisland service to Cayman Brac is provided by Cayman Airways. Island Air provides day trips to Cayman Brac and Little Cayman leaving from Grand Cayman. Flights from Grand Cayman to Little Cayman take approximately 40 minutes. Service from Grand Cayman to Cayman Brac is 18 minutes by jet, and 45 minutes by propeller plane. There is no jet service to Little Cayman.

It is best to rent a car if your accommodations are not in the Seven Mile Beach area. Major and local car rental agencies serve the island. Hertz, (345) 949-2280, offers discounts to AAA members. Driving permits are issued upon presentation of a valid driver's license and cost $5. Speed limits are 40 mph on West Bay Road in the Seven Mile Beach area and 25 mph in George Town; in other parts of the island, speed limits range from 25 to 50 mph. Driving is on the left side of the road.

Independent, privately-owned minibuses run between West Bay Road and George Town; buses stop at the side of the road by white circular bus stop signs. At Kirk Gallery on Albert Panton Street in George Town, visitors can catch the bus back to the resort area; bus stops also are on Shedden Road at the vacant lot across from the post office and along Harbour Drive. There is no set schedule posted as the frequency of the service is largely dependent on whether cruise ships are in port. Roughly, buses run about every half-hour between 7 a.m. and 10 or 11 p.m.

Taxis, motor scooters and bicycles are available on both Grand Cayman and Cayman Brac. Taxis, often driven by islanders versed in local folklore and history, can be chartered for island tours. Taxis do not have meters, as rates are fixed by the government. Visitors must be at least 17 to rent a scooter, and a scooter permit is required. The permit, which can be purchased for $5, does not entitle you to drive a car; if you plan to do both, two permits are necessary. Use caution when renting scooters or bicycles; although the island is relatively flat, traffic can be heavy in George Town and on portions of West Bay Road.

ATTRACTION ADMISSIONS

Attraction admissions for this island are quoted in U.S. dollars.

POINTS OF INTEREST

See map page 114.

GEORGE TOWN (B-1) pop. 13,000

Named for King George II of England, George Town is the capital of the Cayman Islands. It is a bustling city that serves as a center for shopping, banking, tourism and other businesses. The post office on Cardinal Avenue is a busy meeting place where locals exchange news; the hundreds of boxes on the outside of the building reflect the fact that there is no home or office mail delivery in Grand Cayman. Just 2 miles (3.2 km) from the airport, George Town is the gateway to Seven Mile Beach, which stretches north to West Bay.

Distinctive Caymanian architecture, with its ornate hand-carved trim and zinc roofs, adds a gingerbread character that can be seen in Pantonville, where three original houses have been restored. This area of the capital was named for the Panton family, who built, restored and still own these homes. In stark contrast is the modern Government Administration Building, known as "The Glass House," which contains the offices of the governor, the executive council ministers and their departments of government.

A tourist information booth is situated near the corner of Cardinal Avenue and Harbour Drive at the cruise ship north terminal kiosk; look for a circular booth in a fenced area. There also is a booth at Owen Roberts International Airport.

A pamphlet describing a self-guiding historic walking tour of central George Town is available at The National Trust tourist information bureaus and at the gift shop in the Cayman Islands National Museum. The tour focuses on 27 points of interest.

Some features of the tour include the Elmslie Memorial Church, built by Captain Rayal Bodden, a skilled shipbuilder whose signature timber roof framing is a structural highlight; the Peace Memorial, which once served as a town hall; the Clock Tower, built in honor of King George V; the public library, which has elaborate ceilings and houses an assortment of English novels; and an interesting collection of traditional and historic homes. Corita's Restaurant, a tour stop that was once the office of the country's first barrister, is a great place to sample such native dishes as conch and turtle stew.

A plaque on the corner of Fort Street and North Church Street commemorates the area where Fort George stood. Just a small portion of the wall remains. The coral-rock fort, which guarded the harbor's entrance, was constructed in the late 1700s to defend the island against the Spanish. Demolished in 1972 for a development project, the fort was last used as a watch post for German submarines during World War II. The Wholesome Bakery, just north of the intersection of Harbour Drive and Fort Street, serves rum cake, spicy beef patties and other Caymanian snacks.

When the legislature is not in session, the sergeant-at-arms is frequently available to provide tours through the Legislative Assembly Building on Fort Street. Visitors are permitted to observe the legislature in session from the upstairs gallery; appropriate dress is required.

***ATLANTIS* SUBMARINE** departs from S. Church St. at the George Town harbor. This 50-foot-long, 46-passenger submarine cruises along the Cayman Wall at a maximum depth of 120 feet, offering excellent views of the underwater world. A 15-minute ferry ride transports visitors between the dock and the submarine for the 1-hour tour.

Allow 1 hour, 30 minutes minimum. Twelve trips depart Mon.-Sat. beginning at 9 a.m. Fare $69; ages 4-12, $34.50. Under 4 are not permitted. Reservations are advised. AE, MC, VI. Phone (345) 949-7827 for information, or 949-7700 for reservations.

Atlantis Research Submersibles can accommodate two passengers and travel to a maximum depth of 1,000 feet. A large observation window affords passengers a view of deep-water undersea life. The submarines travel along the Cayman Wall to the wreck of the cargo ship *Kirkpride* that rests 800 feet below the surface.

Allow 1 hour, 30 minutes minimum. Mon.-Sat. 8-5. Fare $295. Under 7 are not permitted. AE, MC, VI. Phone (345) 949-8296 or (800) 253-0493.

CAYMAN ISLANDS NATIONAL MUSEUM, Harbour Dr. on the waterfront, houses changing exhibits of local and topical interest in what was once a jail, courthouse and government building. Features include an audiovisual presentation describing the Caymans' heritage, re-created habitats displaying indigenous flora and fauna and works of local artists. Allow 30 minutes minimum. Mon.-Fri. 9:30-5, Sat. 10-4; closed Good Friday and Dec. 25. Admission $5; senior citizens and ages 7-17, $2.50. Phone (345) 949-8368.

CAYMAN TURTLE FARM, 8 mi. (13 km) n. on the n.w. coast via Seven Mile Beach Rd. to West Bay following signs, is a research and breeding center for green sea turtles—the only place of its kind in the world. Green sea turtles were once the mainstay of the Cayman Islands' economy, but their numbers in the wild soon dwindled toward extinction. Five of the seven known species, including the endangered Ridley turtle from Mexico, are represented by some 15,000 turtles, which range in weight from a few ounces to 600 pounds.

The turtles from the farm, which was originally established to create a constant supply for export, are still used for local consumption and craftwork, though some of them are set free in hopes that their numbers will increase. The farm has self-guiding tours and a gallery with displays about the turtle. Visitors should be aware that any turtle products purchased are prohibited in the United States. Food is available.

Daily 9-5; closed Dec. 25. Admission $6; ages 6-12, $3. Phone (345) 949-3893.

North Side (B-3) pop. 900

MASTIC TRAIL, w. of Frank Sound Rd., is a 200-year-old footpath through a 2 million-year-old woodland area in the dense interior of the island. The National Trust offers hiking tours of the 2-mile trail where visitors can view native flora and fauna, including the endemic Grand Cayman parrot. The trail traverses rocks, swamps, high woods and farmland. The 2.5 hour hike is limited to 10 persons. Guided walks depart Mon.-Fri. at 8:30 and 3, Sat. at 8:30. Fee $30. Reservations are required. Not recommended for under age 6 or senior citizens. Comfortable study shoes and insect repellent are recommended. Phone (345) 949-1996.

QUEEN ELIZABETH II BOTANIC PARK, e. side of Frank Sound Rd., is a 65-acre park dedicated to preserving some of the islands native plants and animals. Along the loop trail, visitors can view some 200 labeled plants which represent 40 percent of the island's native flora. The restored Rankin Home features the Heritage Garden where a variety of traditional turn-of-the-20th-century blooming plants, vegetables and fruit trees are grown. The Iguana Habitat is home to 60 endangered Blue Iguanas. A visitors center offers changing displays. Food is available. Allow 1 hour, 30 minutes minimum. Daily 9-6:30. Admission $6.25; ages 6-12, $3.25. Phone (345) 947-9462.

LODGINGS & RESTAURANTS

CAYMAN BRAC

LODGINGS

BRAC REEF BEACH RESORT
◆◆   *Motor Inn*

12/19-4/19	$101	XP $10
12/1-12/18 & 4/20-11/30	$89	XP $10

Location: Just s of the airstrip. 2 mi from terminal on the West End. (PO Box 56, WEST END). Fax: 345/948-1207. **Terms:** F11; Reserv deposit, 30 day notice; 12% service charge. **Facility:** 40 rooms. Pleasant beachfront location. Excellent diving facilities. 2 stories; exterior corridors; oceanfront; beach; 1 lighted tennis court. **Services:** giftshop. **Recreation:** swimming, charter fishing, snorkeling; bicycles. Fee: fishing, scuba diving, scuba & snorkeling equipment. **Cards:** AE, DS, MC, VI.

(345/948-1323

DIVI TIARA BEACH RESORT
◆◆   *Motor Inn*

12/19-1/3	$140-200	XP $15-20
1/4-4/3	$125-195	XP $20
12/1-12/18 & 4/4-11/30	$95-140	XP $15

Location: On the ocean just s of airport, 2 mi by road from terminal; in West End. (PO Box 238). Fax: 345/948-1316. **Terms:** F16; Reserv deposit, 21 day notice, 7 day off season; 10% service charge. **Facility:** 71 rooms. Some with balcony or patio. Excellent recreational facilities. Meets AAA guest room security requirements. 2-3 stories, no elevator; exterior corridors; oceanfront; beach; 1 lighted tennis court. **Services:** giftshop. **Recreation:** swimming, paddleboats, snorkeling; bicycles. Fee: fishing. **All Rooms:** combo or shower baths. **Some Rooms:** 12 kitchens, color TV. **Cards:** AE, DS, MC, VI.

(345/948-1553

GEORGE TOWN (GRAND CAYMAN)

(See map page 114)

LODGINGS

CARIBBEAN CLUB
◆◆ *Cottage*

12/16-4/15	$325-440	XP $31
4/16-11/30	$210-315	XP $31
12/1-12/15	$200-305	XP $31

Location: 2.8 mi n of George Town; 3.8 mi from airport on 7 Mile Beach. (PO Box 30499, GRAND CAYMAN). Fax: 345/945-4443. **Terms:** Age restrictions may apply; reserv deposit, 60 day notice; 10% service charge. **Facility:** 18 rooms. 1- & 2-bedroom villas on oceanfront grounds; few oceanfront. 8 two-bedroom units for up to 4 persons; $310-$425, $190-$295 off season. Reservations advised; 1 story; exterior corridors; beach; 1 tennis court. **Recreation:** swimming. **All Rooms:** kitchens. **Cards:** AE, MC, VI.

(345/945-4099

GRAND CAYMAN MARRIOTT BEACH RESORT
◆◆◆◆ *Hotel*

12/20-1/3	$410-530	XP $20
1/22-4/17	$310-399	XP $20
12/1-12/19, 1/4-1/21, 4/18-8/28 &		
11/1-11/30	$210-310	XP $20
8/29-10/31	$195-240	XP $20

Location: 1.8 mi n of George Town; 2.8 mi from airport; on 7 Mile Beach. W Bay Rd (PO Box 30371 SMB, GRAND CAYMAN). Fax: 345/949-0288. **Terms:** F18; Reserv deposit, 11 day notice; $10 service charge. **Facility:** 309 rooms. Very attractive beachfront hotel with excellent recreational facilities. Meets AAA guest room security requirements. 1 & 2-bedroom suites, $900-$1300; $550-$900 off season; 5 stories; interior corridors; oceanfront; golf & tennis access; beach, whirlpool. **Dining:** Dining room, coffee shop; 7-11 am, 11:30-2:30 & 6-10 pm; $20-$32; cocktails; also, The Peninsula, see separate listing. **Services:** giftshop. Fee: massage. **Recreation:** swimming. Fee: scuba diving/snorkeling & equipment, windsurfing, parasailing, jet skis, scuba instruction, dive shop. **Cards:** AE, DI, MC, VI.

((345)949-0088

GRAND PAVILION, A GRAND HERITAGE HOTEL
◆◆◆ *Hotel*

1/4-4/8	$325-450	XP $50
12/1-1/3, 4/9-5/31 & 11/1-11/30	$235-410	
6/1-10/31	$165-285	

Location: 3 mi n of George Town across from 7 Mile Beach; 4 mi from airport. 7 Mile Beach (PO Box 30117 SMB, GRAND CAYMAN). Fax: 345/945-5353. **Terms:** Reserv deposit, 21 day notice; 10% service charge. **Facility:** 93 rooms. An attractive full service hotel with spacious guest rooms, upscale amenities, sparkling public areas. Meets AAA guest room security requirements. 1 three-bedroom unit, 4 two-bedroom units. 2 stories; interior corridors; 1 lighted tennis court. **Services:** giftshop. Fee: massage. **Recreation:** Fee: fishing, scuba diving/snorkeling & equipment, waterskiing. Rental: paddleboats. **Cards:** AE, DI, DS, MC, VI.

((345)945-5656

HYATT REGENCY GRAND CAYMAN
◆◆◆◆ *Resort Hotel*

12/20-1/3	$335-540	XP $45
1/4-4/12	$305-505	XP $45
12/1-12/19 & 11/1-11/30	$230-425	XP $45
4/13-10/31	$210-415	XP $45

Location: 2.5 mi n of George Town across from 7 Mile Beach in Britannia development; 3.5 mi from airport. 7 Mile Beach Rd (PO Box 1588 SMB, GRAND CAYMAN). Fax: 345/949-8528. **Terms:** Reserv deposit, 30 day notice; 10% service charge; BP, MAP avail. **Facility:** 308 rooms. On lush tropical grounds; elegant British Colonial design. Attractive rooms with small balcony or loggia terrace. Meets AAA guest room security requirements. 29 two-bedroom units, 12 three-bedroom units. 45 villas on golf course, 2-bedrooms $470-$700, 3-bedrooms $630-$950, 4 bedrooms $680-$1155; 5 stories; interior/exterior corridors; beach, whirlpools, full spa facilities; 4 lighted tennis courts. Fee: 18 holes golf. **Dining:** 4 restaurants; 7 am-10 pm; $9-$26; cocktails; also, Hemingway's Beach Club Restaurant, see separate listing. **Services:** giftshop. Fee: massage. **Recreation:** swimming. Fee: charter fishing, scuba diving/snorkeling & equipment, waterskiing, windsurfing, catamaran, cruise boat; ferry service to Rum Point. **Some Rooms:** 72 kitchens. **Cards:** AE, CB, DI, DS, JC, MC, VI.

((345)949-1234

PAN-CAYMAN HOUSE
◆◆◆ *Apartment Motel*

12/15-4/15	$320-410	XP $35
12/1-12/14 & 4/16-11/30	$190-270	XP $35

Location: 3 mi n of George Town; 4 mi from airport on 7 Mile Beach. West Bay Rd (PO Box 440, GRAND CAYMAN). Fax: 345/945-4011. **Terms:** Reserv deposit, 60 day notice; 6% service charge. **Facility:** 10 rooms. Quiet beachfront setting; rooms with balcony or patio. Barbecue. Meets AAA guest room security requirements. 8 two-bedroom units. 2 three-bedroom apartments, $340; $270 off season for up to 6 persons; exterior corridors; oceanfront; beach. **Recreation:** swimming. **All Rooms:** kitchens, shower baths. **Cards:** DS, MC, VI.

((345)945-4002

SLEEP INN
(AAA) (SAVE)
◆◆ **Motel**

12/23-1/3	$205	XP $15
1/4-4/8	$175-190	XP $15
12/1-12/22 & 4/9-11/30	$140	XP $10

Location: 1 mi n of George Town; 2 mi from airport, 7 Mile Beach area. West Bay Rd (PO Box 30111 SMB, GRAND CAYMAN). Fax: 345/945-6699. **Terms:** F12; Reserv deposit, 21 day notice, 7 day off season; 10% service charge. **Facility:** 115 rooms. Modern beachfront motel, poolside grill. Convenient to beach & George Town shopping. Meets AAA guest room security requirements. 2 stories; interior corridors; whirlpool. **Dining:** 6-10:30 am, 11-1 & 6-10:30 pm, in season (poolside). **Recreation:** beach access, dive-shop. **All Rooms:** combo or shower baths. **Cards:** AE, DI, DS, MC, VI. *(See color ad below)*

((345)949-9111

THE WESTIN CASUARINA RESORT
(AAA)
◆◆◆◆ **Resort Hotel**

12/20-1/3	$399-600	XP $25
1/4-4/17	$316-492	XP $25
4/18-8/28	$214-375	XP $25
12/1-12/19 & 8/29-11/30	$185-332	XP $25

Location: 3.2 ml w of George Town; 4.2 mi from airport on 7 Mile Beach. (PO Box 30620, 7 Mile Beach, GEORGE TOWN). Fax: 345/945-3804. **Terms:** F18; Reserv deposit, 15 day notice; package plans. **Facility:** 343 rooms. 2 two-bedroom units. 5 stories; interior corridors; oceanfront; golf access; beach, whirlpools; 2 lighted tennis courts. **Dining:** 3 restaurants; 7 am-11, 11:30-2:30 & 5:30-10:30 pm; Sun brunch 11:30 am-2:30 pm poolside dining; $25-$50. **Services:** giftshop. Fee: massage. **Recreation:** swimming, charter fishing; spa. Fee: fishing, sailboating, scuba diving/snorkeling & equipment, waterskiing, windsurfing. **Cards:** AE, MC, VI.

((345)945-3800

TREASURE ISLAND RESORT
◆◆◆ **Motor Inn**

12/23-1/3	$240-275	XP $30
1/4-4/4 & 1/4-4/4	$220-260	XP $30
12/1-12/22 & 4/5-11/30	$155-190	XP $30

Location: 1.5 mi n of George Town; 2.5 mi from airport on 7 Mile Beach. (PO Box 1817 George Town, GRAND CAYMAN). Fax: 345/949-8672. **Terms:** F17; 10% service charge. **Facility:** 278 rooms. Very attractive landscaped pool courtyards. Rooms with balcony or patio. Very good recreational facilities including a fine reef for snorkling. 5 stories; exterior corridors; beach; 1 tennis court. **Services:** giftshop. **Recreation:** swimming, snorkeling. Fee: scuba diving, scuba & snorkeling equipment; bicycles. **Cards:** AE, DI, MC, VI.

((345)949-7777

VILLAS OF THE GALLEON
(AAA)
◆◆◆ **Apartment Motel**

12/16-4/15	$320-555	XP $20-30
12/1-12/15 & 4/16-11/30	$235-405	XP $10-20

Location: 3 mi n from George Town; 4 mi from airport on 7 Mile Beach. (PO Box 1797, GRAND CAYMAN). Fax: 345/945-4705. **Terms:** F12; Reserv deposit, 21 day notice, in season; 7 days off season; 5% service charge. **Facility:** 60 rooms. Multi-sectional units with ocean view. Some with balcony or patio. 40 two-bedroom units. 3 stories, no elevator; exterior corridors; oceanfront; golf across street; beach. **Dining:** Restaurant nearby. **Recreation:** swimming. **All Rooms:** kitchens. **Cards:** AE, MC, VI.

((345)945-4433

RESTAURANTS

BELLA CAPRI
◆◆◆ **Italian**   L $8-$15   D $15-$27

Location: 3 mi n of George Town, 4 mi from airport; on 7 Mile Beach Rd, behind Fosters Food Fair. W Bay Rd. **Hours:** 11:45 am-2:30 & 5-10 pm, Sat & Sun 5:30 pm-10 pm. **Reservations:** suggested. **Features:** casual dress; children's menu; cocktails; a la carte. Pleasant dining in attractive surroundings. Also Caribbean cuisine. 15% service charge. **Cards:** AE, MC, VI.

(345/945-4755

CROW'S NEST RESTAURANT
◆◆ **American**   L $10-$16 D $20-$30

Location: 3 mi s of George Town on South Sound. **Hours:** 11:30 am-2 & 5:30-10 pm. Closed: Sun for lunch & 9/5-9/19. **Reservations:** suggested. **Features:** casual dress; carryout; cocktails; a la carte. Enclosed & patio dining overlooking beach & ocean. Simple, colorful decor, informal, friendly service. Excellent island cuisine & American standards. **Cards:** AE, MC, VI.

(345/949-9366

GRAND OLD HOUSE   *Historical*
◆◆◆ **Continental**   L $10-$16 D $18-$38

Location: 1.5 mi s of George Town. 648 S Church St. **Hours:** 11:45 am-2:30 & 6-10 pm, Sat & Sun from 6 pm. Closed: Sun 5/1-11/30. **Reservations:** suggested. **Features:** cocktails & lounge; a la carte. A former residence circa 1900 on the sea's edge. Dinner served on the veranda gazebo or inside dining rooms. 15% service charge. **Cards:** AE, MC, VI.

(345/949-9333

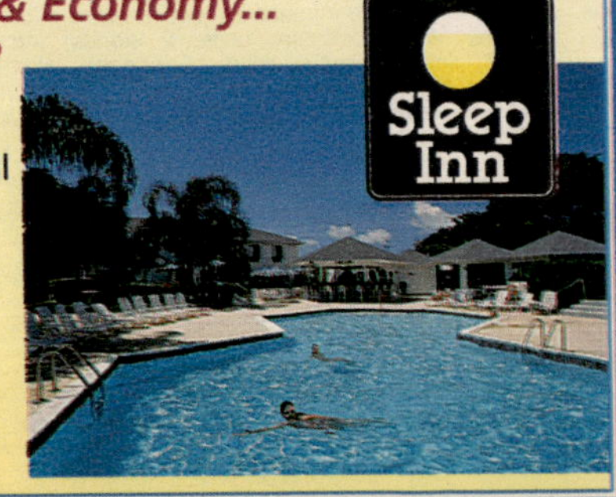

HEMINGWAY'S BEACH CLUB RESTAURANT
◆◆◆ *Continental*   **L** $10-$20 **D** $29-$45
Location: 2.5 mi n of George Town across from 7 Mile Beach in Britannia development, 3.5 mi from airport; in the Hyatt Regency Grand Cayman. 7 Mile Beach. **Hours:** 11:30 am-2:30 & 6-10 pm; grill menu avail 2:30 pm-6 pm. **Reservations:** suggested. **Features:** casual dress; cocktails; a la carte. Handsome tropical decor. Dining room overlooks the beach. Attentive staff. Very well prepared Regional & Continental cuisine. 15% service charge. **Cards:** AE, DI, DS, MC, VI.

☒   (345/945-1234

LANTANA'S
◆◆◆ *Continental*   **D** $18-$30
Location: 2.8 mi n of George Town, 3.8 mi from airport on 7 Mile Beach; in Caribbean Club. **Hours:** 5:30 pm-10 pm. **Reservations:** suggested; req in season. **Features:** casual dress; children's menu; cocktails & lounge; a la carte. Intimate dining. Island specialties. 15% service charge. **Cards:** AE, DS, MC, VI.

(345/945-5595

▲▲▲ LIBERTY'S RESTAURANT
◆ *Ethnic*   **L** $8-$20   **D** $8-$20
Location: 7 mi n to West Bay, 0.3 mi e on Church St to Reverend Blackman Rd, 0.3 mi n. **Hours:** 11:30 am-10 pm. Closed: 1/1 & 12/25. **Reservations:** accepted. **Features:** casual dress; carryout; cocktails; area transportation. A little off the beaten path, but well worth it! Authentic Caymanian cuisine, in generous portions. Seafood dinner buffet Wed, Fri & Sun evenings. **Cards:** AE, MC, VI.

☒   (345/949-3226

OTTMARS
◆◆◆ *Continental*   **D** $18-$36
Location: 3 mi n of George Town; across from 7 Mile Beach, 4 mi from airport; in Grand Pavilion, A Grand Heritage Hotel. 7 Mile Beach. **Hours:** 6 pm-11 pm. **Reservations:** suggested. **Features:** casual dress; children's menu; cocktails & lounge; a la carte. Elegant cuisine, romantic atmosphere. **Cards:** AE, DI, DS, MC, VI.

(345/945-5656

THE PENINSULA
◆◆◆ *Continental*   **L** $11-$21 **D** $20-$32
Location: 1.8 mi n of George Town; 2.8 mi from airport; on 7 Mile Beach; in Grand Cayman Marriott Beach Resort. **Hours:** 11:30 am-2:30 & 6-10 pm. **Reservations:** suggested; for dinner. **Features:** casual dress; children's menu; cocktails; a la carte. Choice of indoor or outdoor patio dining overlooking the ocean & a tropical fish pond. Creative menu selection. Relaxed yet elegant atmosphere. **Cards:** AE, MC, VI.

☒   (345/949-0088

RISTORANTE PAPPAGALLO
◆◆◆ *Northern Italian*   **D** $18-$36
Location: 7 mi n to West Bay 2.5 mi n via signs. Barkers West Bay. **Hours:** 6-10:30 pm. **Reservations:** suggested. **Features:** casual dress; cocktails; a la carte. Secluded tropical setting on edge of lagoon. Thatched roof dining rooms, featuring a large display of live parrots. Creative cuisine. 15% service charge. **Cards:** AE, MC, VI.

(345/949-3479

SMUGGLERS COVE CARIBBEAN CAFE & GRILL
◆◆◆ *Ethnic*   **D** $14-$30
Location: Waterfront, downtown Georgetown. **Hours:** 5:30 pm-10 pm. Closed: 12/25. **Reservations:** suggested; in season. **Features:** casual dress; carryout; cocktails & lounge; street parking; a la carte. Seaside dining. Relaxing attractive decor. Very well-prepared Caribbean cuisine with emphasis on seafood. Excellent staff. 15% service charge. **Cards:** AE, MC, VI.

(345/949-6003

THE WHARF RESTAURANT
◆◆◆ *Continental*   **L** $10-$17 **D** $20-$36
Location: 1 mi n. 7 Mile Beach. **Hours:** noon-2 & 6-10 pm, Sat & Sun 6 pm-10 pm. Closed: 4/16-11/30 for lunch. **Reservations:** suggested. **Features:** casual dress; children's menu; cocktails & lounge; a la carte. Waterfront location, attractive dining room, excellent island & Continental cuisine. Tarpon are fed off the dock every evening at 9 pm. **Cards:** AE, MC, VI.

☒   (345/949-2231

LITTLE CAYMAN

LODGING

LITTLE CAYMAN BEACH RESORT
◆◆ *Motor Inn*
12/20-4/17 $2808
12/1-12/19 & 4/18-11/30 $2552
Location: 0.5 mi e of airstrip. (Little Cayman BWI, Box 51). Fax: 345/948-1040. **Terms:** Reserv deposit, 30 day notice; handling fee imposed; 12% service charge. **Facility:** 42 rooms. Full dive facilities. Beach front property with modern rooms & pleasant surroundings. Rates include 3 dives per day. Non-diving rate avail; 2 stories; exterior corridors; oceanfront; beach; 1 lighted tennis court. Fee: boat dock. **Services:** giftshop. **Recreation:** swimming, charter fishing, snorkeling; bicycles. Fee: sailboating, scuba diving, scuba & snorkeling equipment, windsurfing. **All Rooms:** combo or shower baths. **Some Rooms:** 2 efficiencies. **Cards:** AE, MC, VI.

(345/948-1033

CURAÇAO

L ARGEST OF THE NETHERLANDS ANTILLES, Curaçao (kur-ah-SOW) lies 38 miles (61 km) off the coast of Venezuela. Small hills throughout the island offer a variety of scenery, but vegetation is sparse because of slight rainfall. Willemstad, the capital, is a bright mosaic of narrow streets lined with 18th-century Dutch-Caribbean houses topped with red tile roofs. Each house is painted a pastel shade, which lends a storybook Dutch charm.

HISTORY, GOVERNMENT AND ECONOMY

Curaçao shares much of its history with the other Dutch islands. Discovered in 1499 by Alonso de Ojeda, a lieutenant of Christopher Columbus, the island was named for the tribe of Caiquetios, an Arawak-speaking group which lived here. A more popular legend claims that Curaçao's name was derived from the Spanish word *curación*, meaning "cure," when several malarial sailors miraculously recovered after an extended visit to the island.

The initial Spanish colonizers were displaced early in the 17th century by Dutch settlers, who made the islands flourishing centers of trade. One of the first governors was Peter Stuyvesant, later governor of another island colony: New Amsterdam on Manhattan Island. The Netherlands Antilles changed hands several times in the early 19th century, but by 1815 the Dutch were here to stay.

Except for a brisk slave trade that ended in 1863, the 19th century was less than prosperous for Curaçao and its sister islands. Then the discovery in 1914 of oil in Venezuela made their position astride the trade routes important. Curaçao's economic mainstays today are banking, tourism and refinery facilities. It also has several large local industries, including a brewery that produces beer from distilled sea water; Senior & Co. Curaçao Liqueur; a battery manufacturer; the largest non-military drydock in the hemisphere; and cigarette, soap and paint factories.

Autonomous within the Kingdom of the Netherlands since 1954, the Netherlands Antilles are administered by a governor appointed by the Queen and a legislative and executive council for each island. One of the languages spoken on Curaçao is Papiamento, a colorful blend of Portuguese, Dutch, Spanish and English with African dialects.

SHOPPING

Because of the low import duty on most goods, Curaçao is an excellent shopping center; prices are often lower than in the products' countries of origin. Such international luxury goods

THINGS TO KNOW

AREA: 182 square miles (444 sq km).

POPULATION: 152,200.

LANGUAGE: Dutch, Papiamento, Spanish and English.

CAPITAL: Willemstad.

GOVERNMENT: Autonomous in the Kingdom of the Netherlands.

TIME ZONE: Atlantic.

UNIT OF CURRENCY: Netherlands Antilles guilder, divided into 100 cents. $1 U.S.=approx. 1.79 guilders.

ELECTRICITY: 110-130 volts, 50 cycles AC.

MINIMUM AGE FOR GAMBLING: 21.

CARS: U.S. license valid; drive on right.

IMMIGRATION REQUIREMENTS: Proof of U.S. citizenship (birth certificate accompanied by photo ID, naturalization papers or passport) and return or through ticket. Departure tax $5.65 interisland, otherwise $12.50.

FOR FURTHER INFORMATION:
Curaçao Tourist Board
475 Park Ave. S., Suite 2000
New York, NY 10016
(212) 683-7660 or (800) 328-7222
Curaçao Tourism Development Bureau
Pietermaai 19
P.O. Box 3266
Willemstad, Curaçao, Netherlands Antilles
Phone (599) 9-461-6000

HOLIDAYS: Jan. 1; Carnival Monday, Mon. before Ash Wednesday; Good Friday; Easter Monday; Queen's Birthday, Apr. 30; Labour Day, May 1; Ascension Day, 40th day after Easter eve; Flag Day, July 2; Dec. 25; Boxing Day, Dec. 26; Dec. 31.

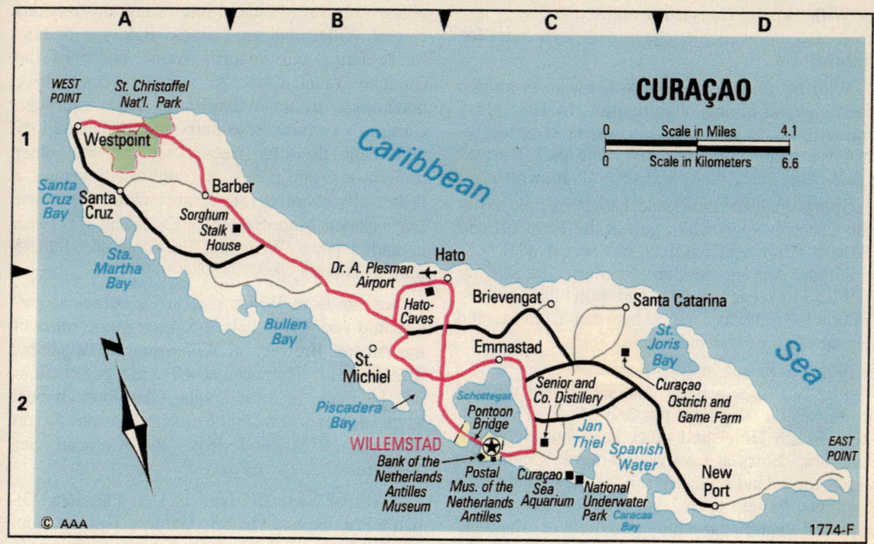

as Brazilian and Argentine leather goods, Portuguese embroidery and lace, Spanish shawls, Irish linen, French perfume, Oriental silk and ivory, Japanese and German cameras, Swiss watches, Italian jewelry, Delft porcelain and fine crystal can be found. Remember that products made from elephant ivory must be at least 100 years old to be allowed into the United States.

Curaçao's foremost shopping promenades are the Dr. Da Costa Gomezplein and the Heerenstraat in Willemstad. Designed for pedestrians, they are closed to traffic and their roadbeds have been raised to sidewalk level and covered with pink inlaid tiles.

Smart offerings combined with the excitement of a Middle Eastern bazaar are found on the Breedestraat and Madurostraat in Punda, the oldest section of Willemstad. Mini-malls on the outskirts of Willemstad worth visiting include Salinja Galleries and Bloempot Shopping Center.

Lining the canal leading to the Waaigat, a small basin, is the "Floating Market," a string of schooners from other islands, Venezuela and Colombia. Alive with color and buzzing with voices haggling over the prices of fresh fish, tropical fruit, vegetables and handicrafts, this seafaring market is a photographer's delight.

Shops in Curaçao are generally open Mon.-Sat. 8:30-noon and 2-6 and when ships are in port. Banking hours are Mon.-Fri. 8-3:30. The bank at the airport is open Mon.-Sat. 8 a.m.-8 p.m. and Sun. 9-4 for currency exchange.

FOOD AND DRINK

Like those on the other Dutch islands, restaurants on Curaçao set an international table, often combining Dutch, Spanish, American, Creole, Italian, Indonesian, French and Chinese cuisine on one board. Other specialties include *erwten soep*, a thick pea soup cooked with pork, ham and sausage, and *java honden portie*, an Indonesian dish of two fried eggs on a mountain of rice, ringed with steak, potatoes and vegetables. Seasonings include curry powder, soy sauce and pimiento paste.

Local specialties include *keshi yena*, a baked Edam cheese stuffed with meat or fish; *sopito*, a fish soup flavored with coconut; and *sopi juana*, otherwise known as iguana soup. Another local specialty is *rijsttafel* (rice table). This Dutch-Indonesian banquet consists of rice served with up to 20 side dishes. Local tap water distilled from the sea is so pure that minerals must be added for taste. Curaçao produces Curaçao Liqueur made from the *laraha*, a local variety of orange. Amstel Beer, the only beer made with distilled sea water, also is produced here.

SPORTS AND AMUSEMENTS

With 38 miles (61 km) of shoreline and 12.5 miles (20 km) of protected coral reef, recreation on Curaçao centers on the sea. The clear water draws swimmers, snorkelers, skiers, fishermen, sailors, windsurfers and scuba divers, and the secluded coves and beaches at Blauw Bay, Cas Abao, Santa Barbara, Santa Cruz, West Point, Jan Thiel, Knip Bay and the Curaçao Sea Aquarium are favorites for lounging. Game fishing for marlin, wahoo, kingfish and dolphin is best July through October. Fishing boats can be chartered for a half-day or a full day, and sailboats and speedboats can be rented by the hour. The Curaçao Yacht Club is in Spanish Water east of Willemstad. Windsurfing and scuba diving lessons also are available; check with your hotel for information.

With 68 diverse dive sites, Curaçao is known for its scuba diving opportunities. In 1983, 12.5 miles (20 km) of Curaçao's waters were designated a national marine park. The park features coral beds, steep walls and several shipwrecks.

Sports include tennis and basketball, played at the Curaçao Sport Club; golf at the Isla Golf and Squash Club; and baseball and soccer at S.D.K. Stadium, Antoine Maduro Stadium and smaller fields. Horseback riding and bowling also are available. Schooner races between Curaçao and Bonaire are occasionally held.

Written in the native Papiamento, Curaçao's *tumba* furnishes a lively and interesting musical comment on island politics and gossip. The Princess Beach Hotel and other large hotels present folkloric shows at least once a week. Centro Pro Arte, the island's theater for the performing arts, presents ballet, opera, symphonies and drama. Spirited visitors can enjoy gambling at island casinos or joining in the songs and dances at discos, clubs and Landhuis Brievengat. Among the casinos on the island are those at the Coral Cliff Resort and Beach Club, Princess Beach, Curaçao Casino Resort, Holiday Beach, Holland, Otrabanda, Plaza, Porto Paseo, San Marco, Sonesta Beach and Van der Valk Plaza hotels. *Island Activities,* available at hotel desks, lists weekly events and entertainment.

EXCURSIONS AND SIGHTSEEING

You can tour the island by car in about a day. The western tour along the main road from Piscadera Bay includes most of the island's beaches and plantation houses. Christoffel National Park, entered at Landhuis Savonet at the northwestern end of the island, is a 3,950-acre (1,600-hectare) wildlife preserve; it contains unusual rock formations, bat caves and white-tailed deer as well as Zorgvlied Plantation and Mount Christoffel, the highest point on the island. Well-marked roads traverse the park and ascend Mount Christoffel; an entrance fee is charged. Allow 2 hours minimum. The park is open Mon.-Sat. 8-4, Sun. 6-3; closed holidays. Admission is $15. Phone (599) 9-864-0363.

A shorter trip to Bullen Bay might include stops at the Flamingo Sanctuary and the fishing village of St. Michael. Interesting destinations east of Willemstad are Caracas Bay, site of Fort Beekenburg, and Spanish Water, home of the Curaçao Yacht Club. A popular 3-hour drive northwest from Willemstad heads through Curaçao's *cunucu,* or countryside, punctuated by wind-bent divi-divi trees, cactuses and other drought-resistant plants, en route to Brievengat, a beautifully restored 18th-century plantation house that is open Mon.-Sat. 9:15-12:15 and 3-6 (with extended hours Wed. and Fri.-Sat.) and Sun. 5 p.m.-2 a.m.

Not far from Willemstad are a botanical garden and zoo, open daily 9-5. Free group tours of the Amstel Brewery in Willemstad are available Tuesday and Thursday at 10 a.m.; reservations can be made at most hotels. Glass-bottom boat tours depart from the Curaçao Casino Resort daily at 10:30 and from the Curaçao Sea Aquarium.

North of Santa Barbara in Den Paradera, Dinah's Botanic and Historic Garden, a garden containing herbs and plants that have traditionally been used for the treatment of various ailments. A reconstructed settlement contains small huts with scenes depicting rural live. Tours are offered by appointment; phone (599) 9-767-5605.

TRANSPORTATION

Regular flights from Newark, New York, Atlanta, Tampa, Miami and Baltimore/Washington D.C. serve Curaçao's airport, which boasts the longest jet landing strip in the West Indies. ALM Antillean Airlines provides interisland service to Aruba, Bonaire, St. Maarten and other islands. Many ships call at Curaçao.

There are taxi stands at the airport, major hotels and in Willemstad; check the fixed fares before you ride. Car rentals are available from major U.S. companies and several local firms; a U.S. driver's license is acceptable. Hourly buses connect Willemstad with the airport.

ATTRACTION ADMISSIONS
Attraction admissions for this island are quoted in U.S. dollars.

POINTS OF INTEREST
See map page 125.

WILLEMSTAD (C-2) pop. 65,000

Often called "Little Amsterdam," Willemstad is capital of both Curaçao and the Netherlands Antilles. Its architecture is a tropical adaptation of the traditional Dutch style. The pastel colors characterizing government buildings and private homes alike are a legacy from a governor-general who complained in 1817 that the tropical sun's glare on the white-painted buildings caused his blinding headaches. To ease his discomfort, he decreed that thereafter only other colors would be used.

Curaçao's trademark, the swinging pontoon bridge called Queen Emma, spans Santa Anna Bay. Originally, pedestrians wearing shoes paid a toll of 2c to cross; the barefooted walked free. The toll was eventually eliminated after the wealthy routinely discarded their shoes before crossing. Today the bridge links the city's two sections—Punda and Otrobanda—along with the four-lane Queen Juliana Bridge, which arcs nearly 200 feet above the bay.

With its narrow streets and shopping promenade, Punda recalls old Holland. The Mini Zoo and Botanical Gardens contain island flora and small animals in a park with a playground. Architectural tours of the city include the classic colonial-style governor's mansion and Department of Finance building on Pietermaai, the Georgian-style Masonic Temple and the stately homes of the merchant princes in Scharloo.

Willemstad and Schottegat Harbor, the island's natural harbor, are designated as UNESCO's (United Nations Education, Scientific and Cultural Organization) World Heritage places. The World Heritage List consists of 552 world-wide places that offer a cultural and natural heritage that exhibits universal value.

BANK OF THE NETHERLANDS ANTILLES MUSEUM, 1 Breedsdtraat, houses a collection of Netherlands Antilles coins as well as a rotating exhibit of coins and bank notes from other countries. There also is a display of precious and semi-precious gemstones. Allow 30 minutes minimum. Mon.-Fri. 9-11:30 and 2-4:30. Free. Phone (599) 9-461-3600.

BETH HAIM JEWISH CEMETERY, n.w. of Willemstad at Schottegatweg West, was consecrated in 1659. It is perhaps the oldest Hebrew graveyard in the Western Hemisphere.

CENTRO PRO ARTE, Rykseenheid Blvd., is Curaçao's performing arts center. Theatrical productions and art exhibits are held regularly. Phone (599) 9-737-6111.

CURAÇAO MUSEUM, .5 mi. (.8 km) w. of the Queen Emma Bridge at Leeuwenhoek and Donder sts., is in an 1853 military hospital building which is a fine example of ornate Dutch architecture. The museum is furnished with antiques and contains Indian relics and an art gallery. Native plants grow in the surrounding gardens. Mon.-Fri. 9-noon and 2-5, Sat. 9-1, Sun. 10-4. Admission $2.65; under 14, $1.35. Phone 462-3873.

CURAÇAO OSTRICH AND GAME FARM has hotel pickups twice a day in season and once a day in the off-season. Visitors to this working/breeding ostrich farm can hold an egg or a day-old chick while they learn about the life cycle and lifestyle of this large, powerful, flightless bird. Allow 2 hours, 30 minutes minimum. Tues.-Sun. 8-5. Fee $15; ages 2-14, $7.50. Reservations at least 12 hours in advance are required. Phone (599) 9-560-1276.

CURAÇAO SEA AQUARIUM, 4 mi. (6 km) e. on Martin Luther King Blvd., displays more than 400 species of fish, crabs, lobsters, sea lions, sharks, stingrays, turtles, anemones, colorful sponges and coral, all natives of the reefs surrounding Curaçao. There also are scheduled feeding times. The Underwater Observatory is available for a close-up look at the underwater world. Animal Encounters has daily snorkel and dive tours with sharks, stingrays, turtles and lobsters. A popular beach is nearby.

Allow 1 hour minimum. Daily 8:30 a.m.-10 p.m. Animal Encounters dives daily at 9, 11, 1 and 3. Last snorkel at 3:30. Sea Aquarium admission (includes Underwater Observatory) $12.50, children $7. Animal Encounters $55 for divers, $30 for snorkelers. Beach admission $2.25. MC, VI. Phone (599) 9-461-6666.

FORT AMSTERDAM, adjoining the waterfront, was built in 1769 to protect the island from invaders. Formerly the living quarters of the directors of the West Indian Co., the fort now contains the official residence of the governor-general, the Ministry, Fort Church and government offices.

Fort Church, in the Fort Amsterdam compound, was built in 1769 and is the island's oldest Protestant church. Lodged in its southwest wall is a cannonball fired by the British in 1804. Mon.-Fri. 9-noon and 2-5. Phone (599) 9-461-1139.

FRANKLIN D. ROOSEVELT HOUSE, atop Ararat Hill, was constructed by the islanders in 1950 as a symbol of the friendship between the Netherlands and the United States during World War II.

HATO-CAVES, .5 mi. (1 km) n. of the Hato Airport, provides historical guided tours of more than 12 cave chambers, including Cathedral and Black Magic chambers. Allow 1 hour minimum. Tours depart daily on the hour 10-4. Admission $6.25; ages 4-12, $4.75. Phone (599) 9-868-0379.

MIKVÉ ISRAEL-EMANUEL SYNAGOGUE, at Hanchi Snoa and Columbus sts., was consecrated in 1732 and is the oldest active Jewish temple in continuous use in the Western Hemisphere. The sand-covered floor symbolizes the Israelites' wanderings in the desert before they reached the Promised Land. Services are held on Saturday and Jewish holidays. Open Mon.-Fri. 9-11:45 and 2:30-4:45. Free. Phone (599) 9-461-1067.

The Jewish Historical Museum, adjacent to the synagogue, is entered through the synagogue courtyard. Ritual objects dating from 1654 and a centuries-old ritual bath are displayed. Mon.-Fri. 9-11:45 and 2:30-4:45; closed Jewish and public holidays. Admission $2; ages 5-13, $1. Phone (599) 9-461-1067.

NATIONAL UNDERWATER PARK, covering an area from the Curaçao Sea Aquarium to the s.e. tip of the island, offers marked underwater trails and sunken ships for snorkelers and scuba divers to explore. The park features 14 signed dive sites.

PEDRO LUIS BRION STATUE, w. of the Queen Emma Bridge in Brionplein Square, commemorates a local hero who served under Simón Bolívar and pursued the hostile British in 1805.

POSTAL MUSEUM OF THE NETHERLANDS ANTILLES, Kaya Toni Prince, Punda, features a collection of stamps from the Netherlands Antilles and other countries as well as related artifacts, such as old post boxes and scales. The museum is housed in Punda's oldest building, which dates from 1693. Allow 30 minutes minimum. Mon.-Fri. 9-noon and 1:30-5, Sat. 10-3. Admission $2; ages 6-15, $1. Phone (599) 9-465-8010

SENIOR & CO. DISTILLERY, 3 mi. (5 km) e. on Schottegatweg Oost in the Chobolobo plantation house, makes Curaçao Liqueur. The orange-flavored product can be tasted and purchased. Self-guiding tours Mon.-Fri. 8-noon and 1-5 and when cruise ships are in port. Free. Phone (599) 9-461-3526.

SORGHUM STALK HOUSE, approximately 8 mi. (13 km) w. of the airport, at Dokterstuin 27, is typical of the dwellings in which most of the island's population lived in the mid-19th century. The two-room house, whose walls are made of loam and branches, and floor of loam, cow dung and caustic lime, and which is roofed with sorghum stalks, contains period artifacts. Food is available. Allow 30 minutes minimum. Tues.-Fri. 9-4, Sat.-Sun. 9-5. Admission $1.50; ages 10-18, 75c; ages 3-9, 50c. Phone (599) 9-864-2742.

WILLEMSTAD TROLLEY TRAIN TOUR departs from Fort Amsterdam near the Queen Emma Pontoon Bridge. This 1.25-hour tour goes through historic Willemstad past many sights, including the Floating Market, Scharloo, Bolo di Bruid (the "Wedding Cake House"), Mikve Israel Synagogue, Queen Wilhelmina Park, Waterfort Arches and Fort Amsterdam. The narration about the city's architecture and history is provided by friendly, knowledgeable residents. Schedule varies, depending upon cruise ship demand. Fare $16; ages 2-12, $12. Reservations are required. Phone (599) 9-462-8833.

LODGINGS & RESTAURANTS

CASABAO

LODGING

COMFORT SUITES CURACAO
Motel

7/1-8/31	$200	XP $20
12/1-12/14, 12/19-6/30 & 9/1-11/30	$188	XP $20
12/15-12/18	$160	XP $20

Too new to rate. **Location:** Follow signs to West Point, left at sign to Soto, Casabao on left. JFK Kennedy Blvd (PO Box 2133). Fax: 599/9465-2662. **Facility:** 40 rooms. Scheduled to open 12/15/98. **Cards:** AE, MC, VI. **Special Amenities: Free local telephone calls and free room upgrade (subject to availability with advanced reservations).** *(See color ad inside front cover)*

((599)9465-2620

WILLEMSTAD—65,000

LODGINGS

AVILA BEACH HOTEL
Country Inn

12/16-4/15	$108-225	XP $20
12/1-12/15 & 9/16-11/30	$105-195	XP $20
4/16-9/15	$100-185	XP $20

Location: 1 mi e of downtown; on waterfront. Penstraat 130 (PO Box 791). Fax: 599/9461-1493. **Terms:** F12; Reserv deposit, 21 day notice, 7 days; 12% service charge. **Facility:** 108 rooms. Charming inn on the waterfront. A former Governors Mansion, new section features modern decor & equipment; older section contains some basic rooms. 1 bedroom suites $260, $230-$240 off season; 2-3 stories; interior/exterior corridors; oceanfront; beach; 1 lighted tennis court. **Services:** giftshop; area transportation. **Recreation:** swimming. **All Rooms:** combo or shower baths. **Some Rooms:** 40 efficiencies, 7 kitchens. **Cards:** AE, DI, MC, VI.

(599/9461-4377

LIONS DIVE HOTEL & MARINA
Motor Inn

12/15-4/15	$150	XP $10
12/1-12/14 & 4/16-11/30	$130	XP $10

Location: Downtown; 3 km e, adjacent to the Curacao Seaquarium. Bapor Kibra. Fax: 599/9461-8200. **Terms:** F12; Reserv deposit, 7 day notice; 12% service charge. **Facility:** 72 rooms. Rustic Dutch Caribbean buildings of 2 & 3 floors. Rooms are pleasant & simply furnished. Free entrance to Seaquarium for guests; 2-3 stories, no elevator; exterior corridors; oceanview; beach; boat dock. **Services:** giftshop; area transportation. Fee: massage. **Recreation:** swimming, scuba diving, snorkeling. Fee: fishing. Rental: scuba & snorkeling equipment. **All Rooms:** shower baths. **Cards:** AE, DI, MC, VI.

(599/9461-8100

OTROBANDA HOTEL & CASINO
Motor Inn

12/16-4/15	$115	XP $15
12/1-12/15 & 4/16-11/30	$105	XP $10

Location: East bank of ship channel; at Otrabanda end of Queen Emma Pontoon Bridge. Breedestraat Otrobanda (PO Box 2092). Fax: 599/9462-7299. **Terms:** F12; Reserv deposit, 7 day notice; 12% service charge. **Facility:** 45 rooms. In the heart of the capital of Willemstad, on the west side. Interior corridors. **Services:** giftshop. **Cards:** AE, DI, DS, MC, VI.

(599/9462-7400

PRINCESS BEACH RESORT & CASINO
Resort Hotel

12/16-4/15	$210-285	XP $25
12/1-12/15 & 4/16-11/30	$140-205	XP $25

Location: Downtown; 4 km e, on waterfront; from airport 10 mi e. Dr Martin Luther King Blvd. Fax: 599/9736-4131. **Terms:** F18; Reserv deposit, 14 day notice, 7 in summer; 12% service charge; AP, CP, MAP avail. **Facility:** 341 rooms. Beachfront guest rooms; extensive recreation facilities. 2 two-bedroom units. Icon Hotel Mkt 305, 670, 4911. 9 whirlpool rms, extra charge; 2-5 stories; interior/exterior corridors; beach, wading pool. **Dining:** Dining room, restaurant; 6:30 am-11:30 pm; $15-$30; beachside grill. **Services:** giftshop; area transportation, to town. **Recreation:** swimming, scuba diving, snorkeling. Fee: charter fishing, fishing, dive shop. Rental: scuba & snorkeling equipment. **Cards:** AE, DI, DS, MC, VI.

((599)9736-7888

SONESTA BEACH RESORT & CASINO
Resort Hotel

12/23-1/2	$295-400	XP $40
1/3-4/12	$255-335	XP $40
12/1-12/22 & 4/13-11/30	$180-250	XP $40

Location: 5 km w on Piscadera Bay. Piscadera Bay (PO Box 6003). Fax: 599/9462-7502. **Terms:** F12; Reserv deposit, 21 day notice; 12% service charge; AP, BP, MAP avail. **Facility:** 248 rooms. A modern interpretation of traditional Dutch Colonial style architecture. Ample open-air lobby enhanced by numerous fountains. Adjacent to the International Trade Center. 8 whirlpool rms, extra charge; 3 stories; exterior corridors; oceanfront; beach, wading pool, whirlpools; 2 lighted tennis courts. **Dining:** 3 restaurants; 7 am-11 pm; $10-$30; cocktails; also, Portofino, Emerald Bar and Grille, see separate listing. **Services:** giftshop. Fee: massage. **Recreation:** swimming, scuba diving, snorkeling. Rental: scuba & snorkeling equipment. **Cards:** AE, MC, VI.

((599)9736-8800

RESTAURANTS

BELLE TERRACE
Continental   L $4-$35 D $15-$40

Location: 1 mi e of downtown on waterfront; in Avila Beach Hotel. **Hours:** noon-2:30 & 7-10 pm. **Reservations:** required. **Features:** No A/C; cocktails; a la carte. Very attractive open air dining room, overlooking beach. Elegant service. Local & international menu, Wed night Antillean theme; Sat barbecue. **Cards:** AE, DI, MC, VI.

(599/9461-4377

BISTRO LE CLOCHARD
◆◆◆ French
L $15-$30 D $20-$45

Location: Downtown; across the Queen Emma Pontoon Bridge in the Rif Fort at the entrance to ship channel. Rif Fort. **Hours:** noon-2 & 6:30-10:45 pm, Sat from 6:30 pm. Closed: 12/24, 12/31 & Sun. **Reservations:** suggested; for dinner. **Features:** cocktails & lounge; a la carte. Picturesque setting at mouth of ship channel. Elegant French/Swiss cuisine, fine service. Terrace open from 5 pm. **Cards:** AE, DI, DS, MC, VI.

(599/9462-5666

EMERALD BAR AND GRILLE
◆◆◆ Steakhouse
D $20-$35

Location: 5 km w on Piscadera Bay; in Sonesta Beach Resort & Casino. **Hours:** 6 pm-11 pm. Closed: Mon. **Reservations:** suggested. **Features:** casual dress; cocktails & lounge; entertainment; valet parking; a la carte. Traditional steakhouse menu in club-like setting. 12% service charge. **Cards:** AE, DI, DS, MC, VI.

(599/936-8800

LA PERGOLA   Historical
◆◆◆ Italian
L $10-$25 D $10-$25

Location: Downtown. Waterfront Arches 12. **Hours:** noon-10:30 pm, Sun from 6:30 pm. **Reservations:** suggested. **Features:** casual dress; cocktails & lounge; street parking; a la carte. Historic waterfront location within walls of old fort, fine ocean view. Very well prepared & served Italian dishes & fresh seafood. **Cards:** AE, DI, MC, VI.

(599/9461-3482

LAROUSSE RESTAURANT   Historical
◆◆◆ Ethnic
D $16-$25

Location: E of center. Penstraat 5. **Hours:** 6 pm-midnight. Closed: 9/1-9/15, 12/24, 12/31 & Mon. **Reservations:** suggested. **Features:** semi-formal attire; cocktails; a la carte. Charming 18th-century home; intimate European dining with French cuisine. **Cards:** AE, DI, MC, VI.

(599/9465-5418

PORTOFINO
◆◆◆ Northern Italian
D $20-$35

Location: 5 km w on Piscadera Bay; in Sonesta Beach Resort & Casino. **Hours:** 6 pm-11 pm, Sun brunch 11-2:30 pm $25. **Reservations:** suggested. **Features:** Sunday brunch; children's menu; cocktails; a la carte. Northern Italian cuisine including bruschetta portofino, pizza rustica & salmone alle erbe. Fine family ambiance. 12% service charge. **Cards:** AE, MC, VI.

(599/9736-8800

RODEO RANCH SALOON STEAKHOUSE
◆◆ Steakhouse
L $9-$25   D $9-$25

Location: At Curacao Seaquarium; 3.2 km s on Martin L King Blvd; exit Seaquarium. Bapor Kibra. **Hours:** 6 pm-11 pm, Sun noon-2 & 6-11 pm. Closed: 1/1 & 12/31. **Reservations:** suggested; on weekends. **Features:** casual dress; children's menu; salad bar; cocktails & lounge. Western ambiance; featuring US prime beef, barbecue chicken & seafood. **Cards:** AE, DI, MC, VI.

(599/9461-5157

DOMINICA

DEEP TROPICAL RAIN FORESTS, mountains and isolation have preserved the wild beauty of Dominica (Dohm-in-EE-kah), reminding visitors of an earlier, less commercial Caribbean. What the island lacks in nightlife, duty-free shops and white sand beaches, it makes up for with the natural splendor of its volcanic mountain ranges swathed in the rich green of towering trees, exotic ferns and flowers. Fed by the ample rainfall in the island's interior, numerous rivers wind through Dominica's primordial forest, which is home to such endangered species as the imperial and red-necked parrots.

HISTORY, GOVERNMENT AND ECONOMY

So named because Christopher Columbus discovered it on a Sunday, Dominica was a stronghold of the Carib Indians, who were the dominant indigenous group found on many of the Caribbean islands. Although the Carib population on many other islands was severely depleted, and in some instances wiped out, the Caribs on Dominica frustrated the efforts of the French and British to successfully colonize the island. In the 18th century the island became the scene of fierce battles between the French and the English for outright possession. It was not until the turn of the 20th century that the British, who had become Dominica's rulers in 1805, finally forced the Caribs onto a reservation.

Since gaining independence from Great Britain in 1978, Dominica has carefully nurtured its pristine resources. Rather than depending on high-rise resorts and glittering casinos for its economy, Dominica relies primarily on the export of produce. The island government also is encouraging tourism and light industry.

SHOPPING

Handcraft centers in the Old Market Plaza in Roseau and on the Carib Indian Territory offer handmade items, including finely woven baskets and Dominica's unique grass mats; also in the marketplace is the Dominica Museum, which is open Mon.-Fri. 9-4, Sat. 9-noon. There are several boutiques in Roseau and at some hotels throughout the island. Other buys include soaps made locally from fresh coconut oil, other toiletries, leather goods, cigars and cigarettes and cassette recordings of the traditional *jing-ping* folk music.

Duty-free shopping is available throughout Roseau. Whitchurch Ashburry Duty Free Shop, (767) 448-2181, is in the Garraway Hotel on Bay Front. Baroon International, LTD, (767) 449-2887, has outlets at 18 Kennedy Ave. and at the Prevo Cinemall on Old Street.

THINGS TO KNOW

AREA: 305 square miles (790 sq km).

POPULATION: 72,000.

LANGUAGE: English, but a French patois is widely spoken.

CAPITAL: Roseau.

GOVERNMENT: Independent republic.

TIME ZONE: Atlantic.

UNIT OF CURRENCY: Eastern Caribbean dollar. $1 U.S.=2.37 Eastern Caribbean dollars.

ELECTRICITY: 220-240 volts, 50 cycles AC.

CARS: Local permit (E.C. $30 for 1 month, E.C. $60 for 3 months) required; drive on left.

IMMIGRATION REQUIREMENTS: Proof of U.S. citizenship (birth certificate or naturalization papers with photo ID or passport) and return or through ticket are required. Departure tax is $12 US; under age 12 are exempt.

FOR FURTHER INFORMATION:
National Development Corporation
Dominica Tourist Office
10 E. 21st St., Suite 600
New York, NY 10010
(212) 475-7542
Division of Tourism
National Development Corporation
P.O. Box 293, Valley Road
Roseau, Dominica, W.I.
(767) 448-2045

HOLIDAYS: Jan. 1; Carnival, 2 days before Ash Wednesday; Good Friday; Easter Monday; May Day, May 1; Whit Monday, (8th Monday after Easter); August Monday, Aug. (1st Mon.); Independence Day, Nov. 3; Community Service Day, Nov. 4; Dec. 25; Boxing Day, Dec. 26.

Banking hours are Mon.-Thurs. 8-3, Fri. 8-5. Business hours are Mon.-Fri. 8-4, Sat. 8-1.

FOOD AND DRINK

The fine flesh of the *crapaud,* meaning "mountain chicken" but actually a frog, is a local delicacy available September through March. Other specialties include freshwater crayfish; *tee-tee-ree,* fried cakes made from tiny fish; *callaloo* soup, made from dasheen leaves and coconut cream; and *crabbacks,* the backs of black and red land crabs stuffed with highly seasoned crab meat. Nectar, syrups, jams and sherbets are available as well as locally made rums. Sea moss is a seaweed shake with milk and sugar or ginger beer.

SPORTS AND AMUSEMENTS

Dominica's many streams and rivers shaded by giant ferns attract both swimmers and canoeists. A few northern beaches offer swimming; Coconut Beach is the most appealing. About 25 miles (40 km) north of Roseau, it has silver volcanic sand and a mountain backdrop. Fishing on the island is good. Gamefishing Dominica, (767) 449-6638, and Rainbow Sportfishing, (767) 448-8650, provide boats and equipment for deep-sea fishing. Spectators can enjoy cricket, soccer, netball, tennis and basketball in season.

Scuba diving also is available and must be arranged through a local dive operator. Establishments include Anchorage Dive Center, (767) 448-2638; Castaways Dive and Watersports Center, (767) 449-6244; Dive Dominica, (767) 448-2188; East Carib Dive, (767) 449-6575; Nature Island Dive, (767) 449-8181; and Windward Islands Divers Ltd., (767) 445-5104.

The island has several spectacular dive sites, including the beautiful coral formations at Scott's Head. Across the bay at L'Abym, there is an incredible wall dive where divers swim through bubbling waters created by volcanic activity on the sea bed. The site is popularly known as "Champagne." On the north side of Cabrits National Park (*see place listing p. 133*), the marine park at Douglas Bay contains a snorkeling trail. There are wrecks at nearby Toucarie and Capucin.

Sea kayaking and mountain biking are two popular ways to discover Dominica. Nature Island Dive Center, on Soufriere Bay, offers hourly, half-day and full-day trips.

Dominica starts off the new year with Mas Domnik (Carnival), in late January and early February. The arts are celebrated during the Dominica Festival of Arts and National Exposition in mid July. Sports enthusiast can partake in the Dominica International Sports and Fishing Tournament in mid-May and Dive Fest in early July. The World Creole Music Festival is held in late October.

EXCURSIONS AND SIGHTSEEING

Dominica is famous for the exotic flora that grows wild around its river pools and rain forests. Morne Trois Pitons National Park, covering 17,000 acres (6,880 hectares), preserves much of this natural beauty in its primitive state. The park's nature trail offers one of the best showcases for viewing the various plants and flowers. The triple waterfalls at Trafalgar in Roseau Valley offer an ideal setting for a picnic within reach of wild orchids and tropical rain forests. Boiling Lake, giving evidence of underground volcanic activity, is said to be the largest lake of its kind in the world and the only one in the Western Hemisphere.

Dominica's Carib Indians distinguished themselves from other Caribbean tribes by fighting so fiercely that in 1748 both the English and French abandoned the island. Consequently, Carib descendants are among the island's inhabitants, and in 1903 the British set aside 3,700 acres (1,497 hectares) of land to establish the Carib Indian Territory on the east coast, where the Indians can practice their own culture and continue the craft of basket making. Trips to the territory can be arranged through your hotel or a local tour operator.

Whale-watching in Dominica is a popular activity with occasional sightings of sperm, pilot and melon-headed whales as well as bottlenose, Risso and spinner dolphins. Excursions can be arranged through Dominica Tours and Dive Dominica.

Roseau, Dominica's capital, occupies a picturesque setting on the banks of the Roseau River. Saturday mornings come alive with the bustle of the colorful market, whose cinnamon scent fills the air. The busy wharf area north of town caters to large freighters as well as the local wooden sloops. High stone walls surround the 1800s cathedral, St. Bernadette Chapel and the convent. The grass rugs that are in demand throughout the Caribbean are woven at Tropicrafts on Turkey Lane. Within walking distance are the Government House and a lush 44-acre (18-hectare) botanical garden.

A site pass is required for visiting selected tourist sites. Daily pass $5, weekly pass $10 or $2 per site. Passes can be obtained at such places as tour operators and attractions.

Transportation

International access into Dominica is facilitated via airports of neighboring Caribbean islands with connections to the island's two small airports: Canefield Airport, a short distance from Roseau, and Melville Hall Airport, on the northeastern tip of the island. Airlines servicing Dominica include Air Guadeloupe, American Eagle, Cardinal Airlines and LIAT. Major gateway connections to Dominica are from Antigua, Barbados, Guadeloupe, Martinique, Puerto Rico, St. Lucia, St. Maarten and St. Thomas.

Car rentals are available at the airports; taxis meet all flights. City and island sightseeing tours with a driver-guide are available. Two high-speed passenger ferries, the *L'Express Des Iles* and *Atlantica* connect Dominica with Guadeloupe and Martinique daily. Cruise ships call at the dock in the center of Roseau.

Attraction Admissions

Attraction admissions for this island are quoted in U.S. dollars.

Points of Interest

See map page 132.

Cabrits National Park (A-1)

On a forested, twin-peaked peninsula between Douglas and Prince Rupert's bays, Cabrits National Park contains the ruins of a military garrison used by British and French forces 1770-1854. Its centerpiece is Fort Shirley, which is surrounded by more than 50 major structures, including gun batteries, powder magazines, storehouses and barracks that housed up to 600 men.

Trails connecting the sites meander through thick tropical growth. Light clothing and comfortable shoes are recommended. Allow 4 hours minimum. Daily dawn-dusk. Free. Phone (767) 448-2731 or 448-2401.

Roseau (C-1) pop. 9,300

THE OLD MILL CULTURAL CENTRE AND LA VIE DOMNIK MUSEUM, .5 mi. (.8 km) s. of Canefield Airport, is in the boiling house of what was one of the largest sugar mills on the island. Exhibits chronicle the island's natural history and the cultural development of its inhabitants. The center and museum are closed for renovations and expected to open in late April 1998. Mon.-Fri. 9-1 and 2-4; closed holidays. Admission $2, children 85c. Phone (767) 449-1032.

Lodgings & Restaurants

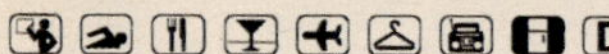

Roseau—9,300

Lodgings

FORT YOUNG HOTEL
◆◆ *Hotel*

12/14-4/14	$125-135	XP $20
12/1-12/13 & 4/15-11/30	$115-125	XP $20

Location: Across from Government House. Victoria St (PO Box 519). Fax: 767/448-5006. **Terms:** F12; Reserv deposit, 7 day notice; handling fee imposed; 10% service charge. **Facility:** 33 rooms. Restored 18th-century stone fort with rooms within the walls. Many rooms with balcony overlooking the bay. 1-2 stories; exterior corridors. **All Rooms:** combo or shower baths. **Cards:** AE, DS, MC, VI.

((767)448-5000

THE GARRAWAY HOTEL
◆◆◆ *Hotel*

12/1-4/30 & 11/1-11/30	$120	XP $25
5/1-10/31	$110	XP $25

Location: Just km e from Government Center on Bay Front. 1 Dame Eugenia Charles Blvd (PO Box 789). Fax: 767/449-8807. **Terms:** F12; Reserv deposit, 7 day notice; $10 service charge. **Facility:** 31 rooms. Modern hotel. Most rooms with view of the bay. 5 stories; interior corridors; street parking only. **Cards:** AE, DI, MC, VI.

(767/449-8800

PAPILLOTE WILDERNESS RETREAT
◆◆ *Motel*

12/1-8/31 & 10/14-11/30	$80	XP $15

Location: On Trafalgar Falls Rd, 6.5 mi ne. (PO Box 2287). Fax: 767/448-2285. **Terms:** D6; Open 12/1-8/31 & 10/14-11/30; reserv deposit, 21 day notice; handling fee imposed; 10% service charge. **Facility:** 8 rooms. Close to Trafalger Falls. Tropical garden landscaping. Modest rooms & furnishings, many with mountain view. Steep narrow road from Roseau. 2 two-bedroom units. Cottage 2-bedroom, 2-bath with kitchen, $175 for up to 6 persons; 2 stories; exterior corridors. **Services:** giftshop. **Recreation:** hiking trails. **All Rooms:** shower baths. **Some Rooms:** efficiency, color TV. **Cards:** AE, DS, MC, VI.

(767/448-2287

REIGATE HALL HOTEL
◆◆◆ *Country Inn*

2/1-3/31	$67-95	XP $150-160
12/1-1/31 & 10/1-11/30	$80	XP $120-150
4/1-9/30	$67	XP $110-135

Location: 1.3 mi w. Reigate Hall. Fax: 767/448-4034. **Terms:** D11; Reserv deposit, 14 day notice; handling fee imposed; 10% service charge. **Facility:** 17 rooms. Dramatic, mountainside setting. Balcony with view of Roseau & ocean. Steep, narrow road from Roseau. 2 whirlpool rms, extra charge; 1-2 stories; interior/exterior corridors; small pool; 1 lighted tennis court. **All Rooms:** combo or shower baths. **Cards:** AE, MC, VI.

(767/448-4031

DOMINICAN REPUBLIC

A RELAXED ATMOSPHERE is not just a promise in the Dominican Republic; it is a way of life. Old World charm lingers here in language, food, customs and thought. The emphasis placed on music, dance, history and art as well as the usual island activities of sunbathing and swimming make the Dominican Republic a popular Caribbean vacation destination.

Santo Domingo, capital and cultural center, preserves the Dominican Republic's rich history with its many churches, palaces, museums, forts, monuments and restored homes. Puerto Plata in the north and La Romana in the southeast are other major resort centers. Duarte Peak, at 10,417 feet (3,175 m), is the highest point in the Caribbean; just 50 miles (80 km) southwest, Lake Enriquillo, at 148 feet (54 m) below sea level, is the lowest point in addition to being one of the largest salt lakes in the Caribbean.

HISTORY, GOVERNMENT AND ECONOMY

The Dominican Republic occupies the eastern two-thirds of the island the Indians called *Quisqueya* and Christopher Columbus named Hispaniola; Haiti occupies the western third. When Columbus ran the *Santa María* aground on the northern coast on Dec. 25, 1492, he used the ship's salvaged lumber to build Fuerte de Navidad, or Fort Christmas. But about a year later, Columbus returned to discover the settlement destroyed and 38 of his men massacred.

Columbus then founded Isabela further east in the present-day Dominican Republic. The first European city in the New World, Isabela was to become Columbus' base of operations for the next 2 years. In 1496 Bartolomeo Columbus, Christopher's brother, founded New Isabela on the southern coast—where the Republic's capital of Santo Domingo thrives today. Because Columbus had left members of his family to colonize the island and returned to it after venturing throughout the Caribbean, the island is described as "the land Columbus loved best."

The only colony ever governed by its discoverer, Hispaniola was the base for excursions by many famous explorers, including Francisco Pizarro, Hernando Cortes, Hernando de Soto, Vasco de Balboa, Alonzo de Ojeda, Diego Velásquez and Juan Ponce de León. Considered the

THINGS TO KNOW

AREA: 18,816 square miles (48,733 sq km).

POPULATION: 7,200,000.

LANGUAGE: Spanish.

CAPITAL: Santo Domingo.

GOVERNMENT: Democratic Republic.

TIME ZONE: Atlantic.

UNIT OF CURRENCY: Peso, divided into 100 centavos, also called "chele." $1 U.S.=approx. 14.9 pesos. Keep all exchange receipts to reconvert to U.S. dollars. Only 30 percent of the original amount will be reconverted.

ELECTRICITY: 110 volts, 60 cycles AC.

CARS: U.S. license valid for 90 days; drive on right.

IMMIGRATION REQUIREMENTS: Proof of U.S. citizenship (birth certificate, naturalization papers or passport) and return or through ticket are required. Tourist card (available through air or sea carrier or upon arrival), $10, is good for 90 days and may be renewed twice. A $10 departure tax must be paid in U.S. dollars.

FOR FURTHER INFORMATION:
Dominican Republic Tourist Office
2355 Salzedo St., Suite 307
Coral Gables, FL 33134
(305) 444-4592
Ministry of Tourism, Government Offices
Bloque D, Ave. Mexico/30 de Marzo, Apartado 497
Santo Domingo, Dominican Republic
(809) 221-4660 or (800) 752-1151

HOLIDAYS: Jan. 1; Feast of the Epiphany, Jan. 6; Feast of Our Lady of High Grace, Jan. 21; Duarte's Day, Jan. 26; Independence Day, Feb. 27; Carnival, first Sun. after Feb. 27; Holy Thursday; Good Friday; Labor Day, May 1; Feast of Corpus Christi, June (1st Thurs.); Restoration Day, Aug. 16; Feast of Our Lady of Mercy, Sept. 24; Discovery Day, Oct. 12; Dec. 25.

oldest university in the Americas, the University of Santo Domingo was founded in 1538.

A base of political intrigue since its founding, the Dominican Republic has confronted many powers, including France, Spain, Haiti and the United States, in its struggle for independence. The French settled in western Hispaniola in 1697, and within 100 years the entire island had come under French rule. Spain regained the eastern two-thirds in 1809. The Dominican Republic declared its independence in 1821 to prevent invasion from Haiti. Shortly thereafter, however, troops from newly independent Haiti overran the Republic and held it for another 22 years.

Led by national hero Juan Pablo Duarte, the Republic gained its independence once again in 1844, but it was to be lost and gained yet one more time: Spain reannexed the territory in 1861 and held it until 1865, when fierce fighting led to the Republic's restoration.

Foreign parties were not the sole source of aggravation; the country has experienced a turbulent internal history as well. Political instability had become the rule by 1900, prompting U.S. troops to occupy the country 1916-24. Democracy was restored but short-lived: The dictator Rafael Trujillo came to power in 1930 and held it until his assassination in 1961. U.S. troops intervened again in 1965 following another civil uprising. Democracy was restored the following year, and the nation has enjoyed free elections since.

The present constitutional government provides legislative, executive and judicial branches. Dominicans in the national district and 29 provinces elect the president, senators and representatives every 4 years by direct vote.

The Dominican Republic has only recently started to promote tourism on a major scale, and agriculture continues to form the backbone of the economy. Sugar, cocoa, coffee, rice and tobacco cultivation flourish in this land of fertile valleys and foliage-clad mountains. A system of dams provides the power and water for irrigation. Also thriving in the island's tropical climate are more than 300 varieties of orchids. Agricultural income is supplemented by exports of large amounts of nickel and smaller quantities of bauxite and gold. Lush forests yield the cedar and mahogany that characterize many Dominican crafts.

SHOPPING

In Santo Domingo one shopping area extends along Calle El Conde from El Conde Gate eastward to the colonial section; the long thoroughfare is closed to vehicular traffic. There are less expensive shops nearby—along avenidas Duarte and Mella, near Columbus Park and along Mercedes. Plaza Central, at the intersection of avenidas 27th of February and Winston Churchill, and Plaza Naco on Avenida Tiradentes are popular shopping centers. Mercado Modelo, the public crafts market, is at the corner of avenidas Mella and Santome. Santo Domingo also offers several modern shopping malls.

Shopping opportunities in Puerto Plata can be found around Central Park, the Plaza Turisol and a popular crafts center near Playa Dorada. In Santiago shoppers go to Calle El Sol and the Mercado crafts market. Haggling is expected in the crafts markets but not at the commercial shops.

There are free-port zones at the Atarazana and the Centro de los Heroes in Santo Domingo, at Las Americas International Airport and at Puerto Plata International Airport. Duty-free purchases must be made in U.S. dollars and are delivered to your point of departure. Shopping hours are generally Mon.-Fri. 8:30-noon and 2:30-6, Sat. 8:30-noon. Banking hours are Mon.-Fri. 8-3.

One of the best buys is jewel-like amber—the Dominican Republic is one of the few spots in the Western Hemisphere where this fossilized resin is found. Larimar, a blue stone similar to turquoise, also is found in the Dominican Republic. Other good buys include embroidery, woven baskets, dolls, leather goods, art objects and handicrafts of local cedar and mahogany. Imported perfume and jewelry also are available.

Local handicrafts made of tortoise products, such as combs or jewelry, may not be imported into the United States under the Convention on International Trade in Endangered Species of Wild Fauna and Flora.

FOOD AND DRINK

The national dish, *sancocho,* is a hearty stew of vegetables and meats. The local staple is the plantain, served ripe or green in a variety of ways. Chicken dishes are popular and inexpensive; a favorite is fritters. Pork sausage, stewed goat and numerous seafood dishes also are traditional favorites. The locals are especially partial to a snack food of fried pork rinds, *chicharones.*

Numerous restaurants provide both East and West Indian specialties along with many Italian, French, Spanish and Chinese dishes. Mesón de la Cava (Restaurant in the Caves) on Avenida Mirador del Sur in Santo Domingo offers exotic dining and entertainment in a quaint "cave" more than 30 feet underground.

Other favorites in Santo Domingo include Cafe St. Michel on Avenida Lope de Vega, Guacara Taina on Avenida Mirador del Sur, Vesuvio I along Avenida George Washington near Alma Mater and Vesuvio II on Avenida Tiradentes. A 10-percent service charge is added to the bill in all restaurants and hotels; a tip of up to 10 percent more is customary for good service.

Dominican rum is the most popular drink, though imported brands claim a substantial following. Barcelo, Bermudez and Brugal are readily available. Dominican Republic beer rivals

DOMINICAN REPUBLIC
AND HAITI

INDEX TO STARRED ATTRACTIONS
ATTRACTIONS OF EXCEPTIONAL INTEREST AND QUALITY
Altos de Chavon - see La Romana
Lighthouse to Columbus - see Santo Domingo
Tomb of Christopher Columbus - see Santo Domingo

Scale in Miles
0   65.0
Scale in Kilometers
0   104.6

1778-F
© AAA

ATLANTIC   OCEAN
Caribbean   Sea

HAITI
DOMINICAN
REPUBLIC
ESPANIOLA

ATLANTIC
Golfe de la Gonâve
Caribbean

Voute í Englise
ÎLE DE LA TORTUE
Môle St.Nicholas
Port-de-Paix
Jean Rabel
Le Borgne
Baie de Henne
Limbé
Cap-Haitien
Milot
Trou du Nord
Fort Liberté
St. Raphael
Gonaives
Ennery
Rivière
Artibonite
St. Marc
Hinche
Montrouis
ÎLE DE LA GONÂVE
Anse á Galet
Pte á Raquette
L'Arcahaie
Cabaret
Desarmes
Mirebalais
Dame Marie
Jérémie
Anse-d'Hainault
Port à Piment
Coteaux
Port Salut
Pointe-a-Gravois
MASSIF DE LA HOTTE
ÎLE A VACHE
Les Cayes
Anse-à-Veau
Miragoane
Aquin
St. Louis du Sud
Mouillage Fouquet
Petit-Goâve
Grand Goâve
Léogâne
Kenscoff
Bainet
Jacmel
Marigot
PORT-AU-PRINCE
Petion-ville
Belle Anse
Jimani
Etang Saumâtre
Pedernales
Lago Enriquillo

Monte Cristi
Copey
Dajabón
Restauracion
Banica
Elias Pina
Lascahobas
El Cercado
Luperón
Puerto Plata
Sosúa
Rió San Juan
Mao
Villa Bisono
SANTIAGO
San J. de las Matas
Jánico
Moca
La Vega
San Francisco de Macoris
Castillo
Rincon
Jarabacoa
Contúi
Río
DOMINICAN REPUBLIC
Río Yaque del Norte
Las Matas
Constanza
San Juan
Bonao
Nagua
Sánchez
Samaná
Yuna
Bahiá Esconcesa
Bahiá de Samaná
Villa Rivas
Sabana De La Mar
Monte Plata
Bayaguana
Los Llanos
El Seibo
Pintado
El Macao
Hato Mayor
Higuey
Bávaro
Punta Cana
San Rafael de Yuma
Boca de Yuma
La Romana
Rió Chavon
ISLA SAONA
ISLA CATALINA
San Pedro de Macoris
SANTO DOMINGO
Boca Chica
Palenque
San Cristobal
Bani
Las Calderas
Azua
San Jose de Ocoa
Neiba
Rio Yaque del Sur
Barahona
Enriquillo
Oviedo
ISLA BEATA

121
151
150
100
100
300
109
300
220
214
213
200
200
209
209
208
102

German brands for robust flavor. Presidente is the local favorite, but Bohemia and Quisqueya also are popular.

If a milder form of refreshment is preferred, try a *batido,* or fruit shake. Dominican coffee is considered excellent, especially by those who like their coffee strong. Tap water is *not* considered safe to drink by visitors, even in the hotels. Water served in restaurants is generally safe, and bottled water is readily available.

SPORTS AND AMUSEMENTS

Though excellent swimming is available at several beaches, most of them are in out-of-the-way spots accessible only by car, taxi or bus. The Amber Coast, near Puerto Plata on the northern shore, and Boca Chica and La Romana on the southern shore have the best beaches with hotels within walking distance.

Marlin, wahoo, kingfish and barracuda are the desired catches of deep-sea anglers. Samaná on the northeast coast is noted for excellent bay and river fishing as well as hunting. Many important international fishing tournaments are held at Boca de Yuma, a sport-fishing center on the southeastern end of the island. Other prime fishing areas are Cumayasa, La Romana and Cabeza de Toro, east of the capital; Palmar de Ocoa and Barahona to the west; and Monte Cristi and Puerto Plata on the north coast.

Charter boats for sailing and yachting can be rented at most resorts by the hour or day. Opportunities for snorkeling and scuba diving are not as widespread as on other Caribbean isles; however, the reefs around Catalina Island, accessible by boat from La Romana, are popular for underwater exploring. Windsurfing, water skiing and other water sports can be arranged at the Puerto Plata resorts and at Casa de Campo near La Romana.

Facilities for such land sports as golf, tennis and horseback riding are excellent. Most hotels in Santo Domingo can provide guest passes to the Santo Domingo Country Club. Two 18-hole golf courses are available at Casa de Campo near La Romana. Puerto Plata has 18- and nine-hole courses at Playa Dorada. Tennis courts are found in the resort areas as well as in the city. Stables are in and around Santo Domingo, Puerto Plata and La Romana, where horseback riding proves to be a practical way to sightsee in the surrounding countryside.

Spectator sports in the Republic include horse racing, basketball, baseball, boxing and polo. A variety of competitions takes place at the Duarte Olympic Center at avenidas Maximo Gomez and 27 de Febrero in the center of Santo Domingo. Just northwest are the Hipodromo, the horse racing track, and Quisqueya Stadium, where baseball—the national sport—is played.

The Dominican Republic has lent more than its share of baseball talent to American teams.

Among the most notable players, past and present, are Juan Marichal; Jesus, Felipe and Matty Alou; Manny Mota; George Bell; Joaquin Andujar; Alejandro Peña; Pedro Guerrero; Pascual Perez; Rafael Ramirez; Tony Fernandez; Julio Franco; Juan Samuel; Mariano Duncan; Alfredo Griffin; Damaso Garcia; Jose Rijo; and Ramon Martinez. Though baseball is played year-round, the more acclaimed winter league plays October through January.

A country that gave the world a dance like the *merengue* is bound to have a lively nightlife. African, Spanish and Indian influences have been sifted, filtered and then combined in a swirl of *Criollo* activity and Latin good times. The nightclubs and casinos in Santo Domingo feature top-name entertainers; dance bands are featured at most restaurants and hotels. On weekend nights the clubs are bustling along the Malecón, a 12-mile (20-km) stretch of Avenida George Washington running west from the Ozama River.

The National Theater in Santo Domingo's Plaza de la Cultura *(see attraction listing p. 142)* regularly presents dramatic productions and orchestral performances. Plays also are staged at the Palace of Fine Arts (Palacio de Bellas Artes) and the Casa de Teatro in the capital. Four tourist publications—*Dominican Fiesta, Touring, The Santo Domingo News* and *The Puerto Plata News*—offer current information on entertainment and activities.

EXCURSIONS AND SIGHTSEEING

Major hotels and ground tour operators can arrange guided sightseeing tours. Tours away from the city visit coffee, sugar, banana, cocoa and pineapple plantations, rice paddies and tobacco farms. The drive along Duarte Highway, connecting Santo Domingo on the south coast to Puerto Plata on the north coast, affords a glimpse of the country's diverse interior. The highway cuts through the mountainous region of the island, an area noted for its coffee plantations. Popular stops along the way are La Vega, a typical island mountain town, and Santiago, where Bermudez Rum is made.

At Puerto Plata are opportunities to relax, swim or ride a cable car to the top of Mount Isabel de Torres. Along with a pastoral park and a massive statue of Christ the Redeemer, this peak offers a spectacular view of the countryside. East of town is Laguna Gri Gri, a national park near Río San Juan. Boats can be rented to explore the mangrove-lined lagoon and the island's north coast. About 50 miles (80 km) southeast of Río San Juan is the Samaná Peninsula, noted for its pristine white sand beaches and excellent sailing, diving and fishing opportunities.

West of Santo Domingo are San Cristobal, where the dictator Rafael Trujillo built a fabulous palace and college; Haina, the site of the island's largest sugar mill; Barahona, with its miles of unspoiled beaches; and Lake Enriquillo, one of the largest lakes in the Caribbean, complete with flamingos and crocodiles. Another worthwhile excursion is a 2-hour drive east from Santo Domingo to the acclaimed resort of La Romana. Here is Altos de Chavón (*see attraction listing p. 139*), a replica of a 16th-century Spanish village, with an artists' colony on a cliff overlooking the Chavón River.

TRANSPORTATION

American and Air Atlantic offer regular flights and packages to Puerto Plata and Santo Domingo from New York and Miami. American Airlines offers connections to Santo Domingo and Puerto Plata from San Juan, Puerto Rico. Flights from Miami to La Romana also are available from American Airlines. Flights from San Juan to La Romana are available from American Eagle.

The Dominican Republic has good highways, though the back roads are not as well maintained. The Duarte Highway bisects the country, connecting Santo Domingo with Santiago and Puerto Plata to the north. The Sanchez Highway stretches westward from Santo Domingo and the Mella Highway eastward. Rental cars are available. Unless otherwise posted, speed limits are 50 mph (80 km/h) on the highway, 35 mph (60 km/h) in suburban areas and 25 mph (40 km/h) in the city. A U.S. driver's license is valid in the Dominican Republic for 90 days.

Because Dominican law allows for detaining visitors who have become involved in accidents in which injuries are claimed, extreme caution is advised while driving. For some this possibility rules out driving altogether. Reasonable alternatives are available.

In the city most visitors prefer the convenience of taxis. There are four types. Regular taxis are government-regulated and rates are fixed; they are found at hotels and tourist spots. Radio taxis are dispatched and the rate is set over the phone. Public taxis, or *carros públicos*, are operated independently; they are available along established routes. Collective taxis, or *conchos*, also operate along major thoroughfares. Rates are fairly inexpensive. Regardless of the type of taxi used, the fare should be agreed upon before entering the vehicle.

Bus service is provided by Carib Tours and Metro Bus between cities and from Santo Domingo to the airport. Comfortable, inexpensive buses operate several times daily between Santo Domingo and Puerto Plata, a 4-hour ride. Schedules are printed in various tourist publications; reservations are advised.

Note: Rented vehicles cannot cross the border between the Dominican Republic and Haiti.

ATTRACTION ADMISSIONS

Attraction admissions for this island are quoted in U.S. dollars.

POINTS OF INTEREST

See map page 137.

BOCA CHICA BEACH (C-5)

About 20 miles (32 km) east of Santo Domingo, Boca Chica boasts a white sand beach and shallow, crystal-clear waters. The area has been a favorite vacation spot since being discovered by the Republic's elite in the late 1920s. Coral reefs provide a natural barrier, creating excellent conditions for water skiing, windsurfing, scuba diving and snorkeling. Modern accommodations are nearby.

LA ROMANA (C-6) pop. 120,000

A sugar town on the southeast coast, La Romana means "the scales"; the cane growers brought their crops here to be weighed and bought. Most of its residents work at the sugar mill, which offers tours by appointment. Recreation includes tennis, polo, horseback riding and golf at two 18-hole courses, all at the nearby 7,000-acre (2,832-hectare) resort of Casa de Campo. An all-day boat excursion to Catalina Island, with its small offshore reef and powdery beaches, can be arranged at the harbor near town.

A popular inland destination is Higüey, home of the Basilica of Altagracia. It is visited every January by lame and blind persons in search of a cure and is considered to be one of the island's finest examples of modern architecture. About 20 miles (32 km) west of La Romana is San Pedro de Macorís, the home of some of the country's— and America's—greatest baseball players.

★**ALTOS DE CHAVON,** high above the Chavón River, 8 mi. (13 km) e. via Casa de Campo, is a re-created 16th-century artisans' village designed to promote, exchange and showcase Dominican and international cultural activity. The Spanish influence can be seen along the cobblestone streets with their limestone buildings and wrought-iron balconies. Within these buildings are a craft center, three art galleries, a museum, ethnic restaurants and fine shops.

St. Stanislaus Church and a 5,000-seat open-air amphitheater dominate the self-contained community, which is host to many Dominican and international writers, painters, musicians and artisans.

The Amphitheater, built in the classic Greek tradition, presents Dominican and international performances all year. The theater was inaugurated by Frank Sinatra in 1978.

Chavón Art Galleries display monthly changing exhibits by Dominican and international painters, sculptors and photographers. Sun.-Thurs. 9-9, Fri.-Sat. 10-10.

The Crafts Center features artisans teaching traditional Dominican crafts, including pottery, basket making, silk-screen printing and weaving.

Regional Museum of Archeology interprets aboriginal evolution from the first pre-ceramic groups to the highly developed Taino Indians. The museum's fine collection of Taino art and artifacts was collected along the banks of the Chavón River. Daily 9-9.

St. Stanislaus Church was named after Poland's patron saint in honor of Pope John Paul II, who donated the saint's ashes to the community. The church is built entirely of hand-cut stone.

Puerto Plata (A-4)   pop. 60,000

Puerto Plata, meaning "silver port," was named so by Christopher Columbus in 1493 because of the silver mist that hovers around the nearby mountains at sunset. Soon after its founding by Columbus' brother Bartolomeo in 1496, Puerto Plata began to flourish as a trade center for the Spanish colonies. Increasing competition from newer ports, however, led to its demise, and by 1520 Puerto Plata had become overrun by smugglers. Illegal trade continued well into the 17th century, despite the crown's decree that the town be destroyed and abandoned. Legitimate trade resumed in the mid-1700s, but it is tourism that fuels the local economy today.

Puerto Plata's charm lies in its cobblestone streets, Victorian homes and leisurely pace of life. Horse-drawn carriages are available for city tours. Central Park attracts sightseers; a large gazebo adorns the site. Puerto Plata's Brugal Rum is considered to be among the world's finest; the distillery on Avenida Luis Ginebra offers tours Mon.-Fri. 9-noon and 2-5. The Amber Museum at calles Duarte and Villanueva features the country's "national gem." It is open Mon.-Fri. 9-6, Sat. 9-5; admission is charged.

Puerto Plata is the gateway to the 75 miles (120 km) of golden beach known as the Amber Coast. The many beaches along this beautiful strip include Sosúa, Long, Grande, Dorada and Cofresí. This glittering vista is best viewed from the top of Mount Isabel de Torres, which rises 2,565 feet above the sea. Cable cars climb the peak Thurs.-Tues. 8-5; long waits can be expected. The statue "Christ the Redeemer" and a botanical garden with walking paths crown the summit. Most of the major resorts are east of town along Playa Dorada.

Other interesting local attractions include Laguna Gri Gri, a national park near Río San Juan, and the town of Sosúa, a refugee colony of European Jews during World War II and the site of the island's largest dairy industry.

THE FORT OF SAN FELIPE dominates the waterfront as it has since 1520, when it was built to protect the country from English pirates and Carib Indians. The fort was used as a prison for political dissidents during the Trujillo regime. Guides conduct narrated tours. Thurs.-Tues. 9-noon and 2-5. Admission is charged; tipping is customary.

Santiago (B-4)   pop. 422,000

Santiago is the Dominican Republic's industrial center and second largest city. In addition to being the home of the world-famous *merengue* music, Santiago specializes in fine restaurants, robust Dominican coffee, fine handmade cigars and Bermudez Rum. In February and August this otherwise conservative city enjoys the merry-making of Carnival, when revelers don elaborate costumes and colorful horned masks.

Santiago actually had three beginnings. Bartolomeo Columbus founded Santiago de los Caballeros in 1495 after an inland settlement at La Vega was abandoned. The town was moved to present-day Jacagua a few years later, leveled by an earthquake in 1562, then rebuilt at its present site. The ruins at La Vega can still be seen. Just north at Santo Cerro, or Holy Hill, Christopher Columbus reputedly raised the first cross of Christianity in the New World. The hill affords a spectacular view of the valley below.

In Santiago's Duarte Park is the Catedral de Santiago Apostol. The Gothic and neoclassical cathedral was built 1868-95 and features a carved mahogany altar and stained-glass windows by Rincon Mora. Other points of interest are the Tobacco Museum, also in Duarte Park; the Museum of the City of Santiago, in the 19th-century town hall; and the Tomas Morel Museum of Folkloric Art, featuring a display of prize-winning Carnival masks. A good way to take in some of Santiago's historical and architectural sights is by horse-drawn carriage.

MONUMENT TO THE HEROES OF THE RESTORATION, s.e. section of the city, was constructed in the 1940s during the Trujillo era. Consisting of a two-story base topped by a 200-foot column and faced with native white marble, the monument offers an excellent view of the city. Murals by Spanish painter Vela Zanetti are displayed. Daily.

SANTO DOMINGO (C-5) pop. 1,700,000

Capital of the Dominican Republic, Santo Domingo was founded in 1496 by Bartolomeo Columbus. During the early 16th century, the city was the prize jewel of the Spanish colonies, enjoying great prosperity as the cultural center of the Caribbean and Spain's steppingstone to further explorations in the New World. It was during this period that many of the city's splendid cathedrals and palaces were built.

However, when Spain turned its interests toward the gold fields of Mexico, Santo Domingo faced a sudden decline in prestige and wealth. The final blow occurred in 1586 when Sir Francis Drake of England pillaged and burned the city, which survived only to suffer more attacks at the hands of the French and Haitians.

Many buildings and narrow streets reminiscent of the Old World have escaped the razing of expansive modernization projects. Ruins of city walls, ancient gates and crumbling fortresses in the colonial section are vivid reminders of the city's history. Most notable are the ruins of San Nicolas de Bari Hospital and the Monastery of San Francisco, first of their kind in the New World.

The Atarazana, a restored 16th-century marketplace, covers a city block across from the Alcázar de Colón. Art galleries, cafes and boutiques as well as faithful restoration work make this a most interesting section to visit. A departure from the area's pervasive antiquity is the Mercado Modelo, the modern crafts market at avenidas Mella and Santome. Across the Ozama River from the Alcázar are the ruins of the Chapel of the Rosary, the first shrine built in the Americas.

The western section of the city has benefited most from redevelopment. Of particular interest are the National Palace on Calle Moises Garcia and the Palace of Fine Arts (Palacio de Bellas Artes) at avenidas Independencia and Maximo Gomez. University City, site of the University of Santo Domingo, occupies several blocks west of Maximo Gomez. In the northwest section of the city are the Duarte Olympic Center, the Hipodromo and Quisqueya Stadium.

COLONIAL SANTO DOMINGO extends about 1 mi. (.6 km) w. from the bank of the Ozama River. It is bounded on the north by Av. Mella and on the south by the Caribbean Sea. Though Santo Domingo's history begins with the founding of New Isabela in 1496, it was not until 1502 when Gov. Nicolas de Ovando moved the settlement west of the Ozama that the city's development began. It is here that the New World's first fortress, cathedral, monastery, hospital, palaces and government offices were built.

At the heart of the colonial section is Columbus Park, where the bronze statue of Christopher Columbus stands. Two blocks east is the Ozama Fortress, within which stands the Tower of Homage. Built 1503-07, the tower is considered the oldest military construction in the New World. North along Calle de Las Damas is the National Pantheon, where the remains of some of the country's greatest heroes are enshrined.

Visitors to the colonial section are advised to wear comfortable shoes and light clothing, but not shorts. Those wearing shorts can be denied admission to some attractions. Caution should be exercised in this area, as visitors are often approached by locals begging for money.

Alcázar de Colón, n. end of Calle de Las Damas next to the Gate of San Diego, was the home of Columbus' son Diego and his descendants. Half fortress, half castle, the 22-room structure was built 1510-14 and has been restored. Furniture of period design, paintings and antiques donated by the University of Madrid add to the elegance of the interior. Guided tours in English and Spanish are available. Open Wed.-Mon. 9-5. Admission $1.50. Phone (809) 687-5361.

Casa del Cordon, 214 Calle Isabel la Católica, is where Diego Columbus lived while the Alcázar was under construction. Built in 1503 and spared by earthquakes, hurricanes and Sir Francis Drake, it is the oldest standing house in the Western Hemisphere. The structure now houses a bank and offices. Mon.-Fri. 8-4. Free.

Cathedral of Santo Domingo—Santa Maria la Menor, Arzobispo Meriño next to Columbus Park, was a 30-year undertaking completed in 1542. A fine example of Spanish Renaissance architecture with a vaulted Gothic interior, the limestone church was built from massive blocks. The high altar is splendidly carved. In 1586 Sir Frances Drake reputedly lived in the cathedral for 25 days.

Features include an emerald-encrusted crown belonging to Queen Isabella of Spain, a silver carillon by Cellini, a painting by Bartolomé Murillo and exquisite stained-glass windows crafted by Dominican artist Rincon Mora. Historical relics and art are contained in 15 small chapels. Guide service of the cathedral is available. Appropriate attire is required; persons in shorts are not admitted. Daily 9-4. Donations. Phone (809) 682-3848.

Duarte Museum, 308 Calle Isabel la Católica, is the 1813 birthplace of Juan Pablo Duarte, father of the Dominican Republic. The residence contains personal possessions and furniture of the patriot and the Duarte-Diez family, portraits of Duarte, paintings with historical themes and artifacts and documents of the independence period. Tues.-Sun. 8-noon and 2-4:30. Admission $1. Phone (809) 689-0326.

Museum of the Casas Reales, on Calle de Las Damas, is housed in an architecturally interesting and historically important complex that includes two palaces built in the early 16th century. Various facets of Spanish colonial life are depicted through artifacts, tapestries, maps and a re-created courtroom. Recovered treasures from sunken Spanish galleons and a large collection of arms and armor from the first through the 18th centuries also are displayed. Guided tours are available. Daily 9:30-5. Admission $1. Phone (809) 632-4202.

Museum of the Dominican Family, in the 16th-century Tostado House on Calle Padre Billini and Arzobispo Meriño, contains displays of household effects and furnishings that reflect styles throughout the Republic's history. The house's Gothic window is architecturally unique. Guided tours are available. Thurs.-Tues. 9-2:30. Admission $1.50. Phone (809) 682-4750.

San Francisco Monastery Ruins, on a hilltop n. of Av. Mercedes at Calle Hostos, are the remains of a Franciscan monastery said to be the first in the Americas. Construction began in 1514, but a series of natural disasters followed by Sir Francis Drake's 1586 rampage thwarted its completion. Free. Phone (809) 687-4722.

San Nicolas de Bari Ruins, Av. Mercedes, are the stone walls of the first hospital to be erected in the Americas. A wooden building that had housed the sick and injured since 1503 was replaced in 1530 by the stone structure; records contain accounts of facilities that included a number of wards, a chapel and a cemetery.

INDEPENDENCE PARK, w. end of Calle El Conde at avs. Bolivar and Independencia, contains two national icons. At the east end is El Conde Gate, one of the city's original entrance-ways and the site of the nation's 1844 proclamation of independence. To the west is the Altar of the Nation, a white marble mausoleum containing the remains of founding fathers Duarte, Sanchez and Mella. The images of both can be seen on the Dominican 20-peso bill. Daily dawn-dusk.

★LIGHTHOUSE TO COLUMBUS (El Faro a Colón), on the east side of the Ozama River, is a massive seven-story cross-shaped monument. The structure features 145 flood lamps that project a shining cross into the night sky. Displays in mahogany-trimmed rooms illustrate the discoveries of Christopher Columbus and how they changed the world.

Visitors also can see excellent scale models of the *Niña, Pinta* and *Santa María.* An entire hall is devoted to the construction of the monument which was dedicated in 1992, and includes photographs and drafts submitted by architects from throughout the world. Allow 1 hour minimum. Tues.-Sun. 10-5. Admission $1, children 50c. Phone (809) 591-1492, ext. 238.

★Tomb of Christopher Columbus, an ornate bronze box that is suspended above the ground, rests in the center of a three-story marble monu-ment guarded by the militia. The structure was erected after a series of transfers that carried the explorer's remains as far as Cuba.

Although some historians suggest Havana or Seville as the final resting place, strong evidence shows that the body was brought to Santo Domingo from Spain by his daughter-in-law. Hidden in the Cathedral of Santo Domingo during a British attack in 1541, the tomb was rediscovered several years later.

NATIONAL AQUARIUM, Av. de España, displays a variety of sea animals in tanks that reflect their natural habitats. A short film is presented. Food is available. Allow 30 minutes minimum. Tues.-Sun. 9:30-6; closed major holidays. Film presented on the hour Tues.-Thurs. and every 30 minutes Fri.-Sun. Admission $1. Phone (809) 592-1509.

NATIONAL BOTANICAL GARDENS, 400 acres (162 hectares) n.w. of downtown, displays exotic plants found in the area. Principal attractions are the Japanese Garden, the Great Ravine, the Floral Clock and the Orchid Pavilion. Horse-drawn carriages and a passenger train transport visitors through the park; rates vary. Tues.-Sat. 9-5. Admission $1, children 50c.

NATIONAL ZOOLOGICAL PARK, n. via Av. Tiradentes, preserves the natural environment of a wide variety of animals, which are allowed to roam freely. The park includes the African Plain, a children's zoo and one of the largest bird cages in the world. Five miles (8 km) of roads and walks traverse the park. Train tours also are available. Allow 2 hours minimum. Daily 8-6; closed Dec. 24-31. Admission 25c. Phone (809) 593-0107.

PARQUE LOS TRES OJOS DE AGUA (Park of the Three Eyes of Water) is s.e. via Las Americas Hwy. Three lagoons in 50-foot-deep caverns are accessible by limestone walkways; a fourth can be reached by water taxi. Stalactites, stalagmites and columns have created interesting formations. Several Tarzan movies have been filmed at the caverns. Swimming is not permitted. Guided tours are available. Open daily 8-5. Admission $1, children 50c. Phone (809) 591-1492, ext. 238.

PLAZA DE LA CULTURA, avs. Mexico and Maximo Gomez, represents the modern side of Santo Domingo. This cultural and educational center, distinguished by its progressive architecture, is set amid tropical gardens. All museums are open Tues.-Sun. 10-5. Free.

Modern Art Gallery contains a collection of contemporary paintings and sculpture by Dominican and foreign artists as well as changing displays by current artists. Tues.-Sun. 9-5. Admission $1. Phone (809) 685-2153.

Museum of the Dominican Man presents Dominican history and folklore from pre-Columbian times to the present. Exhibits include Indian artifacts excavated on the island and graphic displays charting migration in the Caribbean. Tues.-Sun. 9-5. Admission $1. Phone (809) 689-4672.

Museum of History and Geography is devoted to the political and military history of the nation. An extensive collection of photographs, documents, belongings of prominent national figures and other significant articles reconstruct decisive events in Dominican history. Tues.-Sun. 9-5. Free. Phone (809) 686-6668.

Museum of Natural History focuses on the natural characteristics and ecology of the island, from its creation to future developments. Of note is an extensive collection of mounted birds and fish. Tues.-Sun. 9-5.

National Library holds more than a million books and magazines. Its excellent research facilities require a good command of Spanish. Mon.-Fri. 8 a.m.-9 p.m., Sat. 8-noon. Free. Phone (809) 688-4086.

The National Theater, architect Teófilo Carbonell's imposing structure, offers ballets, operas, dramas and concerts by local and visiting artists. Changing exhibits and a permanent collection of artwork by Dominican artists are displayed in the third-floor exhibition rooms. Guided tours Mon.-Sat. 9-1. Free. Phone (809) 687-3191.

PRE-SPANISH ART HALL, Av. San Martín and Calle Lope de Vega, contains one of the finest collections of pre-Columbian Antillean art in the Caribbean. Daily 9-noon. Free.

LODGINGS & RESTAURANTS

BAVARO

LODGINGS

HOTEL CASINO BAVARO
◆◆◆ *Resort Hotel*

12/24-4/9	$100-135	XP $45-55
12/1-12/23 & 7/1-11/30	$70-90	XP $30-40
4/10-6/30	$57-70	XP $25-35

Location: 20 km n from Punta Cana Airport on Punta Cana Higuey Rd, in Bavaro Beach Resort Complex. (Apartado Postal N #1, HIGUEY). Fax: 809/686-5859. **Terms:** Reserv deposit. **Facility:** 234 rooms. Beautiful beachfront resort complex. Many rooms with oceanview. This is an "all inclusive" resort with elaborate recreatonal facilities. 3 stories; exterior corridors; 6 lighted tennis courts. Fee: 18 holes golf. **Services:** giftshop. Fee: massage. **Recreation:** paddleboats. Fee: fishing, sailboating, scuba diving/snorkeling & equipment, waterskiing, windsurfing; horseback riding. **Cards:** AE, DI, MC, VI.

(809/868-5797

HOTEL GOLF BAVARO
◆◆◆ *Resort Hotel*

12/24-4/9	$100-135	XP $45-55
12/1-12/23 & 7/1-11/30	$70-90	XP $30-40
4/10-6/30	$57-70	XP $25-35

Location: 20 km n from Punta Cana Airport, on Punta Cana Higuey Rd; in Bavara Beach Resort Complex. (Apartado Postal n #1, HIGUEY). Fax: 809/686-5859. **Terms:** Reserv deposit; 23% service charge. **Facility:** 126 rooms. Beautiful beachfront resort complex. Many rooms with ocean view. An "all-inclusive" resort with elaborate recreational facilities. 32 suites & 18 senior suites avail; 3 stories; exterior corridors; beachfront; 6 lighted tennis courts. Fee: 18 holes golf. **Services:** giftshop. Fee: massage. **Recreation:** paddleboats. Fee: fishing, sailboating, scuba diving/snorkeling & equipment, waterskiing, windsurfing; horseback riding. **Cards:** AE, DI, MC, VI.

(809/686-5797

HOTEL JARDIN BAVARO
◆◆◆ *Resort Hotel*

12/24-4/9	$100-135	XP $45-55
12/1-12/23 & 7/1-11/30	$70-90	XP $30-40
4/10-6/30	$57-70	XP $25-35

Location: 20 km n from Punta Cana Airport, n Punta Cana Higuey Rd; in Bavaro Beach Resort Complex. (Apartado Postal N #1, HIGUEY). Fax: 809/868-5859. **Terms:** Reserv deposit. **Facility:** 401 rooms. Beautiful beachfront resort complex. Many rooms with oceanview. This is an "all inclusive" resort with elaborate recreational facilities. 4 stories; exterior corridors; 6 lighted tennis courts. Fee: 18 holes golf. **Services:** giftshop. Fee: massage. **Recreation:** paddleboats. Fee: fishing, sailboating, scuba diving/snorkeling & equipment, waterskiing, windsurfing; horseback riding. **Cards:** AE, DI, MC, VI.

(809/686-5797

HOTEL PLAYA BAVARO
◆◆◆ *Resort Hotel*

12/24-4/9	$100-135	XP $45-55
12/1-12/23 & 7/1-11/30	$70-90	XP $30-40
4/10-6/30	$57-70	XP $25-35

Location: 20 km n from Punta Cana Airport on Punta Cana Higuey Rd, in Bavaro Beach Resort Complex. (PO Box 1, HIGUEY). Fax: 809/686-5859. **Terms:** Reserv deposit. **Facility:** 598 rooms. Beautiful beachfront resort complex with 4 like hotels. Many rooms with oceanview. This is an "all inclusive" resort with elaborate recreational facilities. 4 stories; exterior corridors; 6 lighted tennis courts. Fee: 18 holes golf. **Services:** giftshop. Fee: massage. **Recreation:** Fee: fishing, sailboating, scuba diving/snorkeling & equipment, waterskiing, windsurfing; horseback riding. Rental: paddleboats. **Cards:** AE, DI, MC, VI.

(809/686-5797

BOCA CHICA
(DOMINICAN REPUBLIC)

LODGING

HAMACA BEACH HOTEL & CASINO
◆◆ *Hotel*

4/1-11/30	$270-390	XP $80
12/1-3/31	$250-370	XP $80

Location: 8 km e of airport on Las Americos Ave; 32 km e from Santo Domingo on Las Americos Ave; Boca Chica. Ave Duarte, Boca Chica 2973. Fax: 809/523-6767. **Terms:** F3; Reserv deposit; handling fee imposed. **Facility:** 456 rooms. Located on white sand beachfront of Boca Chica. Some rooms with spectacular Caribbean sea view. 3 stories; interior corridors; beach; 4 lighted tennis courts; playground. **Services:** giftshop. Fee: massage. **Recreation:** swimming, charter fishing, paddleboats, sailboating, snorkeling & equipment, windsurfing; bicycles. Fee: fishing, scuba diving & equipment; horseback riding. Rental: boats. **Some Rooms:** 20 efficiencies. **Cards:** AE, DI, MC, VI.

(809/523-4611

LA ROMANA

LODGING

CASA DE CAMPO RESORT
◆◆◆ *Resort Complex*

12/21-1/4	$215-250	XP $50
1/5-4/12	$195-220	XP $35
12/1-12/20 & 4/13-11/30	$135-155	XP $35

Location: 5 mi se of city via signs, just off Rt 3. (PO Box 140). Fax: 809/523-8548. **Terms:** F12; Reserv deposit, 15 day notice, 12 in summer; handling fee imposed; 10% service charge. **Facility:** 450 rooms. 7,000 acre resort compound along Caribbean. Hotel rooms with balcony, 3- to 4-bedroom villas, with screen porch, some with private pool. 2,3 & 4 bedroom villas & luxury villas avail, for US reservations (800) 877-3643; 2 stories; exterior corridors; beach; playground. Fee: 36 holes golf, putting green; 13 tennis courts (10 lighted). **Services:** giftshop. Fee: massage. **Recreation:** swimming, snorkeling. Fee: charter fishing, fishing, sailboating, snorkeling equipment; horseback riding. **Some Rooms:** 150 kitchens. **Cards:** AE, MC, VI.

(809/523-3333

RESTAURANT

CASA DEL RIO
◆◆◆ *Continental*

D $25-$35

Location: 5 mi se of city via signs; in Casa de Campo Resort at altos de chav'on. **Hours:** 6 pm-11 pm. Closed: 7/1-8/31. **Reservations:** required. **Features:** semi-formal attire; children's menu; cocktails; area transportation. Overlooking the Chavon River. Elegant dining room, very well prepared Dominican & Continental cuisine. **Cards:** AE, MC, VI.

(809/523-3333

PUERTO PLATA—60,000

LODGINGS

HOTEL FLAMENCO BEACH
◆◆◆ *Resort Complex*

All Year $110 XP $15

Location: Playa Dorada Beach Complex. Playa Dorada Beach. Fax: 809/320-6319. **Terms:** Reserv deposit, 15 day notice; 10% service charge. **Facility:** 582 rooms. Attractive guest rooms with a Spanish decor. Extensive guest facilities. 3 stories, no elevator; exterior corridors; indoor pool; 2 tennis courts (Fee: 2 lighted). **Services:** giftshop. **Recreation:** scuba diving, snorkeling & equipment. Fee: sailboating, scuba equipment, windsurfing; horseback riding. **Cards:** AE, MC, VI.

(809/320-5084

PARADISE BEACH CLUB & CASINO
◆◆ *Resort Complex*

12/1-4/15	$280-320	XP $100-120
4/16-11/30	$130-170	XP $40-80

Location: Playa Dorada Beach Complex. Dorada Beach Complex (PO Box 337). Fax: 809/320-4858. **Facility:** 436 rooms. Ocean view with tropical setting. Meets AAA guest room security requirements. 3 stories, no elevator; exterior corridors; beach; 2 lighted tennis courts. **Services:** giftshop. Fee: massage. **Recreation:** swimming, sailboating, scuba diving/snorkeling & equipment, windsurfing; bicycles, horseback riding. **Some Rooms:** 72 efficiencies. **Cards:** AE, MC, VI.

(809/320-3663

RESTAURANT

VALENTINO'S RISTORANTE ITALIANO
◆◆ *Italian*

L $5-$15 D $5-$15

Location: In the Playa Dorado semi-circle, adjacent to Dorado Naco Hotel. Playa Dorado. **Hours:** 6 pm-11 pm. **Features:** No A/C; casual dress; children's menu; cocktails & lounge; entertainment. Pizza, veal, steak & chicken also served by capable & friendly staff in well lighted open air dining room or candle-lit patio. Casual atmosphere. **Cards:** AE, MC, VI.

(809/586-2019

PUNTA CANA

LODGING

PUNTA CANA BEACH RESORT
◆◆◆ *Resort Complex*

12/24-1/3	$240-280	XP $115-140
1/4-4/11	$160-190	XP $55-85
7/1-8/31	$140-174	XP $35-60
12/1-12/23, 4/12-6/30 & 9/1-11/30	$110-132	XP $37-66

Location: Punta Cana Airport; 7 km s on Hwy Higney Punta Cana to Resort. (PO Box 1083, SANTO DOMINGO). Fax: 809/687-8745. **Terms:** Reserv deposit, 3 day notice; $10 service charge. **Facility:** 400 rooms. Very attractive beachfront location. Pleasant rooms & very good quiet facilities. 3-4 stories; exterior corridors; beach; 4 lighted tennis courts; playground. **Services:** Fee: massage. **Recreation:** swimming, canoeing, charter fishing, paddleboats, sailboating, waterskiing, windsurfing. Fee: fishing, scuba diving/snorkeling & equipment; horseback riding. **Cards:** AE, DI, MC, VI.

(809/221-2262

RESTAURANT

"LA CANA"
◆◆◆ *Nouvelle Ethnic*   **D** $18-$20
Location: From Punta Cana Airport, 7 km s on Hwy Higuey; in the Punta Cana Beach Resort Complex. Hwy Higuey. **Hours:** 6:30 pm-10:30 pm. **Reservations:** suggested. **Features:** No A/C; casual dress; cocktails; entertainment; a la carte. "Nouvelle Caribbean" cuisine in elegantly informal specialty restaurant. Live piano music for romantic evenings. **Cards:** AE, DI, MC, VI.

(809/221-2262

SAMANA

LODGING

HOTEL GRAN BAHIA
◆◆◆ *Hotel*
All Year $200
Location: 10 km w on Samana Bay overlooking Cayo Lavantado. (Los Cacaos). Fax: 809/538-2764. **Terms:** Reserv deposit. **Facility:** 110 rooms. Elegant hotel at the entrance to Samana Bay. Natural setting, very pleasant rooms. 4-bedroom, 2 villas avail; rates on request; 5 stories; interior/exterior corridors; beach; 2 tennis courts. **Services:** giftshop. **Recreation:** swimming; hiking trails. **Cards:** AE, MC, VI.

(809/538-3111

SANTO DOMINGO

LODGINGS

HOTEL HISPANIOLA & CASINO
◆◆ *Hotel*
All Year $82   XP $36
Location: Corner of Ave Independencia & Ave Abraham Lincoln; 1 blk from Caribbean Sea. (PO Box 2112). Fax: 809/535-0876. **Terms:** F; Reserv deposit; handling fee imposed; 10% service charge. **Facility:** 165 rooms. Attractive Spanish style hotel most rooms with balcony. For reservations: (800) 887-3643 Premier Hotel Corp, 2600 SW 3rd Ave, Suite 600, Miami, Fl 33129; 5 stories; interior/exterior corridors. **Some Rooms:** 4 kitchens. **Cards:** AE, MC.

(809/221-1511

HOTEL SANTO DOMINGO
◆◆◆ *Hotel*
All Year $120-140   XP $23
Location: Corner of Ave Independencia & Ave Abraham Lincoln on the Malecon. (PO Box 2112). Fax: 809/535-4050. **Terms:** F12; Reserv deposit; handling fee imposed; 10% service charge. **Facility:** 215 rooms. Large, inviting rooms, some with balcony. Subdued sophisticated atmosphere in park-like setting, facing the Caribbean Sea. Meets AAA guest room security requirements. For reservations: Premier Hotel Corp, 2600 SW 3rd Ave, Suite 600, Miami, FL 33129; 4 stories; interior corridors; 3 tennis courts (Fee: 3 lighted). **Services:** Fee: massage. **Cards:** AE, MC.

(809/221-1511

HOTEL V CENTENARIO INTERCONTINENTAL SANTO DOMINGO
◆◆◆ *Hotel*
All Year $132-250   XP $15
Location: Facing the Caribbean Sea, on Maritime Dr. Ave George Washington 218. Fax: 809/221-2020. **Terms:** F12; Handling fee imposed; 10% service charge. **Facility:** 200 rooms. Attractive public areas, comfortable guest rooms, some rooms with balcony. Panoramic views. Meets AAA guest room security requirements. 16 stories; interior corridors; 1 lighted tennis court. **Services:** giftshop. **Cards:** AE, DI, MC, VI.

(809/221-0000

RENAISSANCE JARAGUA HOTEL & CASINO
◆◆◆ *Hotel*
All Year $140-220   XP $20
Location: On Maritime Dr. Ave George Washington 367. Fax: 809/686-0528. **Terms:** F12; 10% service charge. **Facility:** 300 rooms. Luxurious public areas convenient downtown location facing the Caribbean Sea. Handsome guest rooms. Full conference facilities. Meets AAA guest room security requirements. 10 stories; interior/exterior corridors. Fee: 4 lighted tennis courts. **Services:** giftshop. Fee: massage. **Cards:** AE, CB, DI, DS, MC, VI.

(809/221-2222

RESTAURANTS

MESON DE LA CAVA
◆◆◆ *Continental*   **L** $10-$20 **D** $15-$30
Location: Near the Se end of Paseode los Indios, on Ave Mirador Sur 1 km w from jct Ave Jimenez Nova & Ave Mirador Sur. Ave Mirador Sur. **Hours:** noon-4 & 6-2 am. Closed: 4/5 & 12/24 for dinner. **Reservations:** required. **Features:** casual dress; cocktails & lounge; entertainment. A charming restaurant built in a natural cavern 50 feet underground. **Cards:** AE, DI, MC, VI.

(809/533-2818

REINA DE ESPANA
◆◆◆ *Spanish*   **L** $10-$28 **D** $10-$28
Location: Corner Cervantes & Santiago; 3 blks n from Malacon & close to Renaissance Taraqua Hotel. Calle Cervantes 103. **Hours:** noon-midnight. **Reservations:** suggested; weekends. **Features:** casual dress; cocktails & lounge; a la carte. Spanish & Dominican cuisine served in a Medieval style villa. Attentive service. **Cards:** AE, MC, VI.

(809/685-2588

RESTAURANT CANTABRICO
◆◆◆ *Seafood*   **L** $10-$22 **D** $10-$22
Location: On Ave Independencia; adjacent to Cemetary & just w of Independence Park. Ave Independencia 54. **Hours:** noon-3 & 8-midnight. **Reservations:** suggested. **Features:** casual dress; cocktails & lounge; a la carte. Seafood & local Dominican specialties served in an attentive European atmosphere. **Cards:** AE, MC, VI.

(809/687-5101

RESTAURANT DON PEPE
◆◆◆ *Spanish*   **L** $10-$25 **D** $18-$35
Location: Corner Pasteur Ave & Santiago Esq St, 3 blks n from Malacon & close to V Centario Intercontinental Hotel. 41 Santiago Ave. **Hours:** 11:30 am-3 & 6-11 pm. **Features:** semi-formal attire; cocktails; valet parking; a la carte. Pleasant decor, formal service excellent Spanish cuisine. **Cards:** MC, VI.

(809/666-5481

TASCAMAR
◆◆◆ *Ethnic*   **D** $20-$30
Location: Facing the Caribbean Sea, on the Malacon Dr; in Hotel V Centenario Intercontinental Santo Domingo. Ave George Washington 218. **Hours:** 5 pm-midnight, Fri & Sat-1 am. Closed: Sun. **Features:** casual dress; cocktails & lounge; entertainment; fee for valet parking. Relaxing ambiance with cozy rustic sea decor. Spanish dishes with a Dominican touch. **Cards:** AE, DI, MC, VI.

(809/221-0000

VESUVIO
◆◆◆ *Italian*   **L** $13-$25 **D** $13-$25
Location: On Maritime Dr facing the Caribbean Sea. 521 George Washington Ave. **Hours:** 11 am-2 am. **Features:** casual dress; cocktails & lounge; a la carte. Since 1954. Extensive menu & wine list, native & International dishes. Italian specialties, professionally served in relaxing dining room or open air terrace. **Cards:** AE, DI, MC, VI.

(809/221-3333

GRENADA

POPULARLY KNOWN as "the spice isle," Grenada (Gre-NAY-da) has a moderate tropical climate that ensures the success of spice production. Bananas are the most plentiful crop, followed by an array of such spices as nutmeg, cocoa, mace, cloves, vanilla, cinnamon and ginger. The climate also lures travelers seeking an ideal Caribbean retreat. Its 133 square miles (344 sq km) of tropical landscape, encompassing volcanic mountains, lush valleys and pristine beaches, have distinguished it as one of the most beautiful of West Indian islands. Ninety miles (140 km) north of Trinidad, Grenada is the southernmost of the Windward Islands and offers a remoteness that is the essence of its appeal.

HISTORY, GOVERNMENT AND ECONOMY

Though Grenada was discovered by Christopher Columbus on his third voyage in 1498, the island was relatively neglected until 1650, when it was purchased by the governor of Martinique. The French began their colonization with a series of skirmishes that virtually exterminated the island's native Carib population. The survivors were pushed north to Le Morne des Sauteurs, where rather than surrender they jumped off the cliff to the jagged rocks below. Today the site of the Carib defeat is known as Carib's Leaper.

Once they were in complete control, the French introduced the cultivation of cocoa, coffee and cotton. During the wars between France and Great Britain, the island changed hands many times until it was finally ceded to Britain in 1783 by the Treaty of Paris. Slave labor and large plantation holdings brought prosperity to the island, which served as the headquarters of the British West Indies 1885-1958. After unsuccessful attempts to federate with other West Indian islands, Grenada assumed the status of an Associated State of Britain in 1967. The island became independent from the United Kingdom in 1974 and obtained dominion status within the Commonwealth.

Following a revolution in 1979, a People's Revolutionary Government replaced the parliament of Grenada. Revolutionary rumblings erupted into a coup against the presiding prime minister in October 1983, prompting U.S. and Eastern Caribbean military intervention. Political order in Grenada was re-established with an elected representative government.

SHOPPING

A Grenada spice basket, a handwoven pannier of palmleaf or straw filled with cinnamon, nutmeg, ginger, vanilla, cloves and other native spices, is an easy way to bring the aroma of Grenada back home. Straw and sisal items are

THINGS TO KNOW

AREA: 133 square miles (344 sq km).

POPULATION: 96,000.

LANGUAGE: English.

CAPITAL: St. George's.

GOVERNMENT: Independent. Member of the British Commonwealth of Nations.

TIME ZONE: Atlantic.

UNIT OF CURRENCY: Eastern Caribbean dollar. $1 U.S.=2.37 Eastern Caribbean dollars.

ELECTRICITY: 220 or 240 volts, 50 cycles AC.

CARS: Local license ($30 E.C.) required; drive on left.

IMMIGRATION REQUIREMENTS: Proof of U.S. citizenship (birth certificate or naturalization papers with photo ID or passport) and return or through ticket required. Departure tax $14 US.

FOR FURTHER INFORMATION:
Grenada Board of Tourism
800 Second Ave., Suite 4-K
New York, NY 10017
(212) 687-9554 or (800) 927-9554
Grenada Board of Tourism
The Carenage
St. George's, Grenada, West Indies
(473) 440-2279

HOLIDAYS: Jan. 1; Independence Day, Feb. 7; Carnival, late Feb.; Good Friday; Easter Monday; Labour Day, May 1; Whit Monday, May (8th Monday after Easter); Feast of Corpus Christi; Emancipation Day, Aug. (1st Mon.); Thanksgiving, Oct. 25; Dec. 25; Boxing Day, Dec. 26.

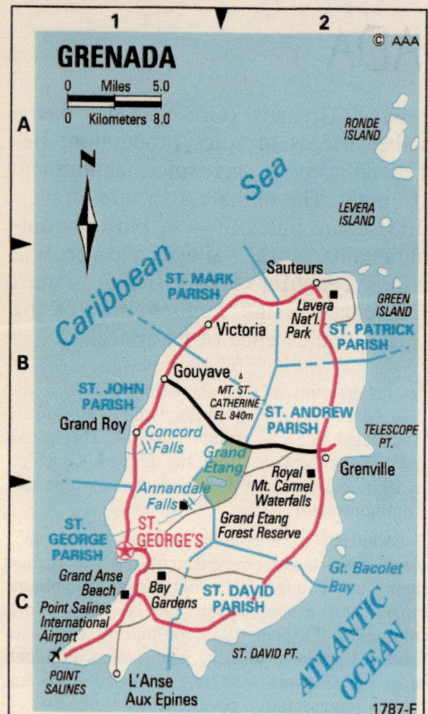

usually bargains, particularly at the Blind Handicraft Center and the Straw Mart in St. George's. Another good buy is wood carvings.

The Yellow Poui Art Gallery on Cross Street displays and sells paintings, sculpture and graphics by local artists. A shopping center in the hotel area in Grand Anse contains fine shops, especially ones that sell china, crystal and other luxury items. Shops are generally open Mon.-Fri. 8-11:45 and 1-3:45, Sat. 8-11:45. Banking hours are generally Mon.-Fri. 8-1 (also Fri. 1-5).

FOOD AND DRINK

An almost endless list of seafood and home-grown fresh fruit is available at most island hotels and restaurants. *Callaloo* soup, *crabbacks, lambi* (conch) dishes and avocado and nutmeg ice cream are local favorites. A liberal dose of Grenadian rum punch, made with lime juice, syrup, Angostura bitters, grated nutmeg and either Barbados or local rum, often helps encourage the visitor to experiment with the native cuisine. Gin and coconut water is another popular libation, as is the locally brewed Carib beer.

Traditional West Indian fare is served for lunch at Betty Mascoll's 1912 plantation home, Morne Fendue, in St. Patrick's on the northern tip of the island; reservations are required. Dinner favorites are Canboulay overlooking Grand Anse Beach, Mamma's in Belmont and The Red

Crab in L'Ance aux Epines; reservations are recommended.

SPORTS AND AMUSEMENTS

Since much of the island nation is mountainous, it is easy to understand why hiking is a popular activity. Although guides may be necessary for some excursions, opportunities exist for hikes to waterfalls, historic sites, scenic views and nature study. Sailing the island's clear waters is another available form of outdoor recreation. Grand Anse, a dazzling 2-mile (3.2-km) stretch of sand on southwestern Grenada, is considered one of the world's finest beaches. Grenada's dependencies of Carriacou, Petit Martinique and the Isle de Ronde also have scenic coves with white sand beaches.

Scuba diving has become a major sport and is good off Molinere Point and Point Salines. Experienced divers can reach the *Bianca C.*, a cruise ship that sank outside St. George's harbor in 1961; it is the largest shipwreck site in the Caribbean. Deep-sea vessels can be chartered for a half- or full-day. Arrangements for day sails and longer charters around Grenada and the Grenadines can be made at the marinas in St. George's and L'Ance aux Epines.

For an exotic Grenadian experience back on land, visit the 2,200-foot-high Grand Etang Lake, a huge lake-filled crater of an extinct volcano within a tropical bird sanctuary and forest reserve; local guides are available for hiking. Good resting spots include the Grand Etang Lake and the Visitor Centre. Annandale Falls, a mountain stream plunging 50 feet into an adjacent pool surrounded by flowers and plants, also provides an ideal setting for an afternoon off the beaten path. To the north of St. George's are the two Concord Falls. The first is accessible by road; the second by a hike through mountain terrain. La Sagesse Nature Center offers hiking trails, some 86 varieties of tropical birds, a banana plantation with guided tours and an extensive beach area.

Several area spice and cocoa plantations welcome visitors. Gouyave, a market town on the island's west coast, is a center of the nutmeg industry; its Dougaldston Estate plantation and spice station are open to the public. Grenville on the east coast also has a spice factory open for tours. Saturday in Grenville and St. George's is market day. Pastries, breads, fruits and vegetables and handmade baskets, bags and hats are among the items for sale. During the Rainbow City Festival in St. Andrews in early August, culture, music and exotic foods fill the streets.

Some hotels have tennis courts, and two tennis clubs are near St. George's. The Grenada Woodlands Golf Club has a nine-hole course. Cricket and soccer are the most popular spectator sports.

Because most visitors come to Grenada to soak up the sun, sail, snorkel or roam, the evenings tend to be much quieter than on some of the larger Caribbean islands. The hotels provide nightly entertainment in season, including dancing to popular music or calypso rhythms. When the sun finally sets, however, the majority of people are content to sit back, sip a rum punch and listen to a steel band.

EXCURSIONS AND SIGHTSEEING

Popular tours on Grenada include a 2.5-hour ridge tour past the 18th-century forts on Morne Jaloux Ridge above St. George's; the Bay Gardens *(see attraction listing p. 150)*; the fishing village of Woburn, where parts of "Island in the Sun" were filmed; a small rum factory at Woodlands; and the beaches at L' Anse aux Epines. A city tour of St. George's, which includes Market Square, the National Museum *(see attraction listing p. 150)* and surrounding 18th-century forts, also lasts about 2.5 hours.

A 3-hour mountain tour explores the island's tropical interior and passes spice, cocoa and banana plantations en route to Grand Etang National Park and Annandale Falls. A full-day tour departs St. George's and leads to Dougaldston Estate and the Nutmeg Processing Station at Gouyave before continuing by way of Victoria, Sauteurs, Levera Beach, Tivoli, Grenville and Grand Etang.

Full-day tours usually last 6 hours and visit most of the island's points of interest as well as some beaches; lunch is usually included. A special photographer's tour, conducted for a minimum of eight people, leads participants past 40 miles (64 km) of landscapes, ruins, villages, wildlife and native vegetation. If you wish to brave Grenada's narrow roads and hairpin turns yourself, road maps are available at the tourism office on the Carenage in St. George's. Most hotels provide information about guided tours.

Local hotels also will arrange all-day yacht cruises along the island's western and southern coasts. If your time on the island is short, you may want to take a cruise of St. George's harbor and the surrounding area aboard the *Rhum Runner.* Moonlight cruises also are available.

Another popular excursion is a visit to the remote island of Carriacou, 23 miles (37 km) northeast. Noted for some of the best beaches in the Caribbean, the island also is famous for its small boatyards where villagers build wooden schooners using hand tools and centuries-old techniques. Good times to visit are in February during Carnival, in early August when the Carriacou Regatta takes place and during Christmas.

TRANSPORTATION

BWIA International has direct flights from Miami and New York to the new Point Salines International Airport. American Airlines has daily flights from major United States gateways and from San Juan, Puerto Rico. There also are air connections to Grenada via Antigua, Barbados, Trinidad and St. Lucia as well as island-hopping service from St. Vincent. Many cruise lines also call at Grenada.

Taxis provide transportation between the airport and island hotels. Rental cars equipped for the island's left-hand driving are available in St. George's; a 2-day minimum rental is required. Driving conditions can be treacherous on some shoulderless, one-lane roads. Mopeds and minibuses provide alternative means of transportation. Buses regularly depart from the marketplace or the Esplanade in St. George's for all parts of the island. Inexpensive water taxis transport passengers across the harbor and to Grand Anse Beach.

The island of Carriacou can be reached by daily 15-minute flights and interisland ferries. Local boat service also reaches Grenada's satellite islands of Petit Martinique and Isle of Ronde. Several flights depart daily to and from Point Salines International Airport, and a daily flight arrives from Barbados. Boats depart twice a week from the Carenage.

ATTRACTION ADMISSIONS
Attraction admissions for this island are quoted in U.S. dollars.

POINTS OF INTEREST

LEVERA NATIONAL PARK (B-2)

This popular 450-acre scenic coastal park is on the northeast coast, in St. Patrick's Parish, and is visually dramatic. Levera pond and its mangroves are habitats for many species of waterfowl, including the scarlet ibis, hooded tanager and osprey. Levera Hill offers views of the park and the offshore islands. The vegetation of the upland area includes cactus and woody scrub, and provides shelter for iguanas and kites.

The park's shores are fringed with coconut palms and from May to September are hatcheries for sea turtles. Offshore, the sea grass beds shelter lobsters, while the coral reefs harbor colorful fish. The park has several beaches and a visitor center with changing and washroom facilities.

The park is open Mon.-Fri. 8-4, Sat.-Sun. 10-5. Admission is by donation. For more information phone (473) 442-1018.

St. George's (C-1) pop. 4,500

The streets of St. George's, the island's capital, wind in a medieval tangle up several steep hillsides. One hill is so steep that it divides St. George's, but a tunnel through the hill connects the two sections. These terraced ways, the red- and white-gabled houses and the lively Saturday morning market lend an Old World charm to the town, considered by many travelers to be among the most picturesque in the Caribbean.

Fishing boats and trade boats carrying fresh fruits and vegetables line St. George's inner harbor on Tuesday afternoons. Other activities along the harbor revolve around the tourist information office, the craft shops and the government buildings. A number of historic forts crown the nearby hilltops; the best restored of these is Fort George. Fort Frederick and Fort George both provide excellent views of the city from their scenic vantage points.

BAY GARDENS, 4 mi. (6.2 km) n.e. in St. Paul's, is a lush walk-through tropical garden landscaped with fish pools, fruit and spice trees and more than 3,000 species of plants and flowers in tropical bloom. Guides explain the growing and processing of spice plants. Daily 9-5; closed Jan. 1, Easter and Dec. 25. Admission $1. Phone (473) 440-5338.

GRENADA NATIONAL MUSEUM, on Young St., is housed in a former French army barracks and prison built in 1704. The museum traces the island's history with pictorial displays and artifacts from the Indian period, the colonial period, the 1979 revolution and the 1983 intervention. Mon.-Fri. 9-4:30, Sat. 10-1:30. Admission $1; under 18, 25c. Phone (473) 440-3725.

ROYAL MT. CARMEL WATERFALLS are in St. Andrew Parish, 16 mi. (26 km) from St. George's following signs. A guided 15-minute hike down a steep, wooded trail with handrails leads to the island's highest waterfall, Royal Mt. Carmel, set in lush tropical surroundings. While swimming is not permitted at Royal Mt. Carmel, it is permitted at the lower waterfall, which also offers a picnic area. Daily 9-5. Admission $1. Phone (473) 442-6493.

Lodgings & Restaurants

St. George's—4,500

Lodgings

BLUE HORIZONS COTTAGE HOTEL
◆◆   *Apartment Cottage*

| 12/16-4/15 | $160-180 | XP $50 |
| 12/1-12/15 & 4/16-11/30 | $110-120 | XP $35 |

Location: 5.5 mi s; 2 mi ne of airport. (PO Box 41). Fax: 473/444-2815. **Terms:** Reserv deposit, 28 day notice, 7 day in summer; 10% service charge. **Facility:** 32 rooms. Tropically landscaped, terraced, hillside setting. Rooms with balcony or terrace. Meets AAA guest room security requirements. 1-2 stories, no elevator; playground. **All Rooms:** efficiencies. **Cards:** AE, DI, DS, MC, VI.

((473)444-4316

CALABASH HOTEL
◆◆◆   *Cottage*

| 12/16-4/15 | $395-495 | XP $125-160 |
| 12/1-12/15 & 4/16-11/30 | $235-295 | XP $100-120 |

Location: In L'Anse aux Epines; 5 mi s of town; 3 mi ne of airport. (PO Box 382). Fax: 473/444-5050. **Terms:** Age restrictions may apply; reserv deposit, 14 day notice, 7 days off season; handling fee imposed; 10% service charge. **Facility:** 30 rooms. Duplex cottages & 2-story apartments on tropical grounds of secluded cove. 8 units with private pool; 1 story; exterior corridors; beach; 1 lighted tennis court. **Services:** giftshop. **Recreation:** swimming, paddleboats, sailboating, snorkeling & equipment, windsurfing. **Cards:** AE, MC, VI.

(473/444-4334

CINNAMON HILL
◆   *Apartment Motor Inn*

| 12/15-4/16 | $160-228 | XP $15-17 |
| 12/1-12/14 & 4/17-11/30 | $125-185 | XP $15-17 |

Location: 6 mi s; 2 mi ne of airport; in Grand Anse Beach area. (PO Box 292). Fax: 473/444-2874. **Terms:** F12; Reserv deposit, 21 day notice, 7 days in summer; 10% service charge. **Facility:** 20 rooms. Spanish-Mediterranean inspired complex, with spectacular views of Grand Anse Beach & town. Spacious suites with 2 bathrooms. Breakfast served in suites. Air conditioning in bedroom only. 6 two-bedroom units, $160-$228; $125-$185 off season, for up to 6 persons. 1-bedroom units for up to 6 persons; 1 story; exterior corridors. **Cards:** AE, DS, MC, VI.

(473/444-4302

FLAMBOYANT HOTEL & COTTAGES
◆   *Complex*

2/16-4/15	$295-375	XP $40
2/1-12/15 & 4/16-11/30	$150-265	XP $20

Location: On Grand Anse Beach, 6.5 mi s, 3 mi e of airport. (PO Box 214, ST. GEORGE'S). Fax: 473/444-1234. **Terms:** F18; Reserv deposit, 7 day notice, 14 day in winter; 10% service charge. **Facility:** 40 rooms. Casual & relaxing, cottages set on a breezy hillside. 2 two-bedroom units, $260-$340; $150-$215 off season; 2 stories; exterior corridors; oceanview; beach access. **Services:** giftshop. **Recreation:** swimming. **All Rooms:** combo or shower baths. **Some Rooms:** 23 efficiencies, color TV. **Cards:** AE, DI, DS, MC, VI. *(See ad below)*

((473)444-4247

HORSE SHOE BEACH HOTEL
◆   *Complex*

2/15-4/15	$150	XP $20
2/1-12/14 & 4/16-11/30	$115	XP $15

Location: In L'Ance aux Epines; 8 mi s of town; 4 mi ne of airport. (PO Box 174). Fax: 473/444-4844. **Terms:** F12; Reserv deposit, 21 day notice; 10% service charge. **Facility:** 22 rooms. Hilltop setting. Tropically landscaped grounds sloping down to beach. 12 cottages with shared kitchens, breakfast cooking only. 6 large modern rooms. 2 stories; exterior corridors; beach access. **Recreation:** swimming. **All Rooms:** combo or shower baths. **Cards:** AE, MC, VI.

(473/444-4244

RENAISSANCE GRENADA RESORT
◆◆◆   *Motor Inn*

2/15-1/3	$193-256	XP $25
1/4-4/15	$188-246	XP $25
4/16-11/30	$129-183	XP $25
2/1-12/14	$126-176	XP $25

Location: On Grand Anse Beach; 4 mi s of town; 2.5 mi ne of airport. (PO Box 441). Fax: 473/444-4800. **Terms:** F17; Reserv deposit, 14 day notice; 10% service charge. **Facility:** 186 rooms. Beachfront on extensive landscaped grounds. Very well furnished rooms with balcony or patio. Meets AAA guest room security requirements. 2 stories; exterior corridors; oceanview; beach; 2 lighted tennis courts. **Services:** giftshop. Fee: massage. **Recreation:** swimming, scuba diving, snorkeling & equipment. Fee: fishing, waterskiing, windsurfing. Rental: boats, scuba equipment. **Cards:** AE, DS, MC, VI.

(473/444-4371

REX GRENADIAN RESORT
◆◆◆   *Hotel*

12/24-1/3	$255-440	XP $45-135
12/1-12/23 & 1/4-4/22	$175-360	XP $65-135
4/23-11/30	$115-300	XP $45-110

Location: 1 mi n of airport; 6 mi s of town. Point Salines (PO Box 893). Fax: 473/444-1111. **Terms:** F12; 10% service charge. **Facility:** 212 rooms. Overlooking golden Tamarind Bay in the blue Caribbean. Tastefully modest to luxurious rooms. All rooms with balcony; some with garden or ocean view. All rooms with hairdryer, iron & ironing board. 3 stories, no elevator; exterior corridors; beach; 2 tennis courts (Fee: 2 lighted). **Services:** giftshop. Fee: massage, area transportation. **Recreation:** swimming, charter fishing, fishing, scuba diving, snorkeling & equipment, windsurfing; jogging. Fee: scuba equipment. Rental: paddleboats. **All Rooms:** combo or shower baths. **Some Rooms:** color TV. **Cards:** AE, DI, DS, MC, VI.

(473/444-3333

 **SPICE ISLAND BEACH RESORT**
◆◆◆   *Cottage*

12/15-4/15	$425-806
4/16-11/30	$339-618
12/1-12/14	$315-575

Location: On Grand Anse Beach; 5.5 mi s of town; 2 mi ne of airport. (PO Box 6). Fax: 473/444-4807. **Terms:** Age restrictions may apply; reserv deposit, 30 day notice, 14 day off season; 10% service charge; 7 night min stay, in season. **Facility:** 56 rooms. On 1600 feet of beachfront grounds. Attractively decorated rooms, with furnished balcony or terrace. 4 royal private suites have color cable television. 13 suites with private pool, $510-$565; $365-$405 off season; 32 whirlpool suites, $375-$425; $305-$425 off season; 4 royal priv pool suites $575-$750; 1-2 stories; exterior corridors; oceanview; beach; 1 lighted tennis court. **Dining:** Dining room; 7:30-10 am, 12:30-2:30 & 7-9:30 pm; $40-$45; cocktails; afternoon tea. **Services:** giftshop. **Recreation:** swimming, paddleboats, scuba diving, snorkeling & equipment, ocean kayaks & sunfish sailing; bicycles. Fee: fishing. Rental: scuba equipment. **All Rooms:** combo or shower baths. **Cards:** AE, DI, DS, MC, VI. **Special Amenities: Free newspaper.** *(See color ad below)*

((47)444-4423

CANBOULAY RESTAURANT
◆◆◆   *Ethnic*   D $35-$5

Location: 5.5 mi s; 2 mi ne of airport. **Hours:** 7 pm-9:3 pm. Closed major holidays & Sun. **Reservations:** su gested. **Features:** No A/C; children's menu; cocktails lounge; a la carte, also prix fixe. Open-air dining room on h overlooking town & sea. Island & International specialtie market fresh ingredients. Lite fare lunch menu. **Cards:** A MC, VI.

(473/444-440

LA BELLE CREOLE RESTAURANT
◆◆   *Continental*   D $35-$4

Location: 5.5 mi s, 2 mi ne of airport; in Blue Horizons Co tage Hotel. **Hours:** 7:30 am-10:30 & 7-9 pr **Reservations:** suggested. **Features:** No A/C; cocktails lounge. Open-air dining room; subtle, elegant atmospher Table d' hote menu with Continental & island recipes; ma ket fresh ingredient. A la carte offered off seaso **Cards:** AE, DI, DS, MC, VI.

(473/444-431

THE RED CRAB
◆◆   *Continental*   L $9-$15 D $15-$3

Location: 8 mi s; 4 mi ne of airport. L'Ance aux Epine **Hours:** 11 am-2 & 6-10:30 pm. Closed: 1/1, 12/25, 12/26 Sun. **Reservations:** suggested; for dinner. **Features:** N A/C; cocktails; a la carte. English pub atmosphere with te race. Very good selection of local seafood dishes & Interna tional specialties. Closed for lunch & dinner on maj holidays. **Cards:** AE, MC, VI.

(473/444-442

GUADELOUPE

K NOWN AS "the Emerald Isle," Guadeloupe lies midway between Puerto Rico and Venezuela. The "island" is really two smaller land masses joined by two bridges over a narrow channel called Rivière-Salée. Grande-Terre to the east typifies the French Antilles with rolling hills and sugarcane fields; Basse-Terre to the west is a rugged, mountainous is-

land dominated by the volcano of La Soufrière. Its hills and ravines are lush with hardwood forests, ferns, bamboo, bananas, hibiscus, bougainvillea and guava. One road follows the coast while another crosses the highlands, providing a spectacular drive.

Pointe-à-Pitre, Guadeloupe's commercial center on Grande Terre, and Basse-Terre, the capital, contrast busy port life with a French provincial atmosphere. This Gallic ambiance also is evident in Guadeloupe's island dependencies of Marie-Galante; La Désirade; St. Barthélemy; the islands of Les Saintes, where Norman-French speech and customs prevail; and St. Martin, where French and Dutch influences mingle.

HISTORY, GOVERNMENT AND ECONOMY

Called "the island of beautiful waters" by the Carib Indians, Guadeloupe was discovered by Christopher Columbus in 1493, on his second voyage. He named the island for the Spanish monastery of Santa Maria de Guadalupe de Estremadura, but Spain established no colonies due to fierce opposition from the Caribs. Guadeloupe and her sister island Martinique were settled by French colonists in 1635 and soon became important centers of sugar production.

Both islands were incorporated as departments of France in 1946 and elevated to regions in 1974, with each island holding representation in the French Parliament by two senators, four deputies and two members of the Economic Council. The local government consists of elected General and Regional Councils as well as a prefect, or governor; the island's inhabitants are French citizens.

SHOPPING

The French islands are excellent shopping centers, where perfumes and other luxury made-in-France products are sold at or below Paris, New York or St. Thomas prices. Rosébleu and A La Pensée on the Rue Frébault are among the most popular places to shop in Pointe-à-Pitre. Rues de Nozières and Schoelcher also have shops carrying French imports as well as madras cottons, watches, silver and china. Centre Saint-John Perse, on the harbor front, showcases many specialty shops, a hotel and several restaurants. The local outdoor market, Champs-Elysées, and the Place de la Victoire are worth visiting.

Most shops are open Mon.-Fri. 9-1 and 3-6, Sat. 9-1, and are closed holidays. Banking hours are Mon.-Fri. 8-noon and 2-4; summer hours are Mon.-Fri. 8-3. Stores can give up to 20-percent discounts on some luxury goods purchased with travelers checks or certain credit cards.

FOOD AND DRINK

Guadeloupe shares its cuisine with France. Delicacies like *escargots* are on the menus of many restaurants and can be savored with excellent French wines. Traditional Creole dishes available in most restaurants lend added zest to dining. *Colombo*, an Indian dish of curry-like seeds cooked with either beef, pork, chicken, mutton, conch or goat, is eaten with rice; stuffed crab and crayfish are prepared in a variety of ways; *callaloo* soup is made from greens and West Indian herbs; *court bouillon* combines a thick fish stew with rice; gumbos are eaten with rice and fried codfish; and yams are cooked in their skins and seasoned with butter and cheese. Gourmet menus list roasted wild goat, duckling and a salad of coconut and hearts of palm.

Meals taste best preceded by Punch Guadeloupéen called "Ti Punch," a delicious and quite potent rum potion. Rum is bottled locally, as is mineral water. Local milk and water are safe. At the airport and around the dock at Terre de Haut, one of the Saintes islands, barefoot children sell a delicious coconut pastry called *tourment d'amour.*

Guadeloupe boasts more than 200 restaurants, often modest in appearance but superior in cuisine. Served after noon, lunch is a big meal in Guadeloupe, as evidenced by the multicourse Creole lunches served at Chez Clara in Sainte Rose or Karacoli in Deshaies. Just outside of Gosier, La Creole-Chez Violetta also specializes in Creole cooking.

Interesting eateries can be found at the Port de Plaisance marina in Bas du Fort near Pointe-à-Pitre. Most hotels and restaurants include a 10- to 15-percent service charge in their prices. If not, this charge will be added to the final bill.

SPORTS AND AMUSEMENTS

Beaches of white, ochre and black volcanic sand offer almost unlimited opportunities for swimming, snorkeling, scuba diving, water skiing, windsurfing and other aquatic sports. Grande-Terre's southern coast boasts several good public beaches, including those at Sainte Anne, St. François and Gosier as well as tiny coves of white powdery sands only a hike away from the main beach road. Favorable trade winds called *les alizés* create conditions ideal for sailing, water skiing and windsurfing between Grande-Terre and the islet of Gosier, just off shore from Gosier.

Beginning scuba divers can enroll in several diving schools based at the Hotel Marissol and the Callinago Beach Hotel. Several water sport concessions are congregated on the beach at Gosier. Yacht chartering has become increasingly popular in recent years; arrangements can be made at Dufour Antilles, The Moorings, Stardus Marine, Star Voyages and Sunsail at Port de Plaisance in Bas du Fort; at Nautica in Gourbeyre or through any of the island's hotels.

Evasion Marine, a nautical school based at the marina at St. François, provides sailing and cruising lessons in 1-day, weekend, 2- and 3-week packages. Club Med and the Méridien St. François Hotel, among others, will arrange for boats for deep-sea fishing.

Riding, hiking, camping, mountain climbing, tennis and golf are some of the most popular recreational pursuits on land. The adventuresome wise to arm themselves with bug spray, might wish to camp or hike around the many waterfalls of Basse-Terre's Parc National; the tourism office at 5 Square de la Banque in Pointe-à-Pitre publishes *Walks and Hikes.* St. François boasts a championship golf course, and several of the larger hotels throughout the island have their own tennis courts. Cockfighting is in season from November through April, and horse racing takes place periodically at Baie-Mahault, Bellecourt and the St. Jacques Hippodrome at Anse Bertrand.

THINGS TO KNOW

AREA: 530 square miles (1,373 sq km).

POPULATION: 410,000.

LANGUAGE: French and Creole.

CAPITAL: Basse-Terre.

GOVERNMENT: Department and Region of France.

TIME ZONE: Atlantic.

UNIT OF CURRENCY: French franc, divided into 100 centimes. $1 U.S.=approx. 5.95 French francs.

ELECTRICITY: 220 volts, 50 cycles AC.

CARS: U.S. license valid; drive on right.

IMMIGRATION REQUIREMENTS: For stays under 3 months, proof of U.S. citizenship (passport, expired passport dating back not more than 5 years, birth certificate with raised seal accompanied by a government-authorized identification card or similar document with photo ID) and return or through ticket are required.

FOR FURTHER INFORMATION:

Guadeloupe Tourist Office
161 Washington Valley Rd.
Warren, NJ 07059-7121
(888) 448-2335

Guadeloupe Tourist Office
5 Square de la Banque
97181 Pointe-à-Pitre, Guadeloupe, F.W.I.
(590) 82-09-30

HOLIDAYS: Jan. 1; Mardi Gras; Easter Monday; Labor Day, May 1; Ascension Thursday; Slavery Abolition Day, May 27; Whit Monday, May (8th Monday after Easter); Bastille Day, July 14; Schoelcher Day, July 21; Feast of the Assumption, Aug. 15; All Saints Day, Nov. 1; Armistice Day, Nov. 11; Dec. 25.

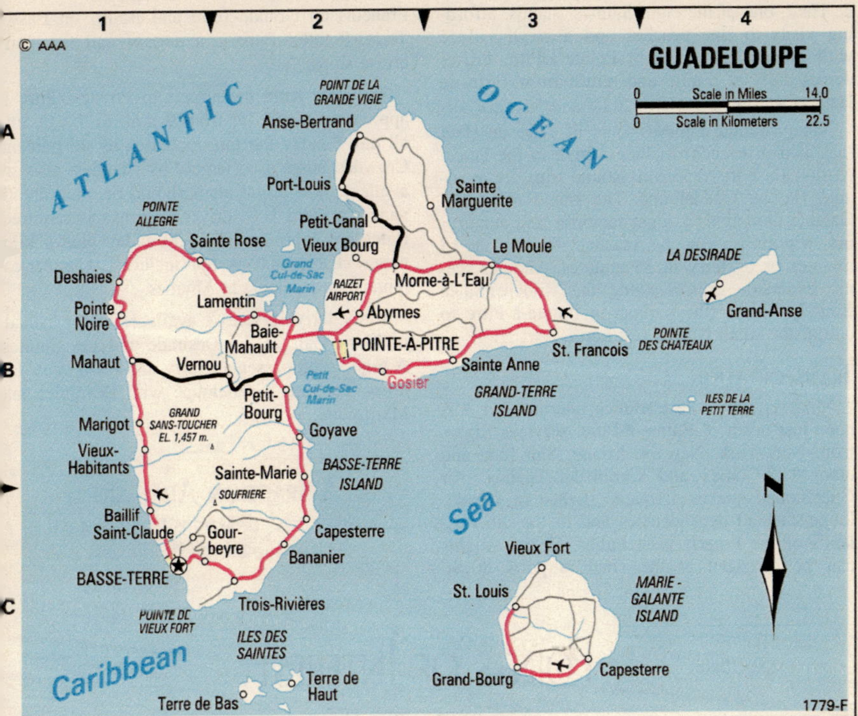

Although most island nightlife beats a hasty retreat at midnight, such clubs as Belle Epoque, Caraïbe Deux, Elysées Matignon, Shiva 1, TDZ, Victoria and Zenith provide some late action, as do the bars and clubs at the Auberge de la Vieille Tour, the Hamak, the Méridien St. François, the Novotel, the Marissol and the Salako hotels. Late-night dancing can be found at La Creole Beach Hotel, New Land in Gosier and La Chaîne in St. Félix. Traditional dances by the Ballet Folklorique of Guadeloupe are held frequently in Pointe-à-Pitre.

Several motion picture theaters show French and American films with French soundtracks. There is a casino in St. François and one in Gosier.

Guadeloupe has two seasonal festivals that captivate islanders and visitors alike. The first is the pre-Lenten carnival in February, which includes masked revelers and costumed dancers winding through the streets, parades with elaborate floats and street parties. The second, on a Saturday in early August, is called the *Fête des Cuisinières*, or the Women Cooks' Festival. The celebration begins with a religious service in the cathedral in Pointe-à-Pitre, followed by a 5-hour feast with much singing and dancing. Then there is a procession of women in Creole dress carrying exotic island specialties through the capital.

EXCURSIONS AND SIGHTSEEING

Guadeloupe's major road system encompasses about 1,200 miles (1,930 km). A 1-day tour of Grande-Terre might include a drive from Pointe-à-Pitre to Port-Louis and Anse Bertrand. After the spectacular cliffs at Pointe de la Vigie, the return trip leads through Le Moule, Pointe des Châteaux, Ste. Anne and Gosier. Another all-day excursion can be made by crossing the channel to Basse-Terre, following Route de la Traversée as it winds through the 73,240-acre (29,640-hectare) Parc National, then turning south along the coast to Basse-Terre and on to the archeological park at Trois-Rivières, and returning to Pointe-à-Pitre via the coast road.

Half-day excursions include a drive from Pointe-à-Pitre to the village of St. François, then east to Pointe des Châteaux, returning via Ste. Anne or Le Moule; and a drive along the Route de la Traversée through the national park to the white and golden beaches near Deshaies, returning through Sainte Rose. A detailed brochure on these drives is available from the tourist office in Pointe-à-Pitre.

Excursions to Guadeloupe's offshore islands of Les Saintes, Marie-Galante and La Désirade offer an alternative approach to sightseeing. Boat excursions leave Trois-Rivières Mon.-Sat. at 8 a.m. and 4 p.m. and Sun. at 7:30 a.m. for Terre de Haut, one of the eight Saintes islands, affording visits to fine beaches and a small village with quaint bistros. From Pointe-à-Pitre ferries depart daily at 8 a.m. and return from Terre de Haut at 4 p.m.

Ninety-minute minibus tours of Terre de Haut (narrated in French) include a visit to the island bastion Le Fort Napoléon. Round trips are available via Air Guadeloupe. The island of Marie-Galante, dotted with sugar factories and century-old windmills, can be reached by air in 15 minutes or by ferry in 35 minutes. Another scenic excursion cruises along the Rivière Salée from La Darse (the harbor) in Pointe-à-Pitre to one of the small islands just north.

TRANSPORTATION

Modern, new Pole Caraïbes International Airport, just north of Pointe-à-Pitre, services flights from New York, Newark, Miami, San Juan and other U.S. cities and Caribbean islands. Air Guadeloupe makes frequent flights to Guadeloupe's island dependencies and to the other islands of the French West Indies. Charter flights can be arranged at the small airports at St.

François on Grande-Terre and Baillif on Basse Terre. Pointe-à-Pitre is a port of call for many cruise ships.

Taxi fare from the airport to Pointe-à-Pitre i approximately $5.75; from 9 p.m. to 7 a.m. and all day Sunday the fare increases by 40 percent Crowded buses used largely by islanders also are available. Car rental plans should be made in advance; a valid U.S. driver's license is required Rates are approximately $50 a day plus a kilometer charge; gas is not included. Camper-car rentals are available at Abymes.

Daily ferry service is available to the island of Marie-Galante, La Désirade and Les Saintes A high-speed passenger ferry, the *Caribbean Express,* connects Guadeloupe with Dominica and Martinique.

ATTRACTION ADMISSIONS
Attraction admissions for this island
are quoted in U.S. dollars.

POINTS OF INTEREST
See map page 155.

BASSE-TERRE (C-1) pop. 15,000

Basse-Terre is the administrative capital of Guadeloupe. Known for its 17th-century cathedral, French provincial atmosphere and colorful port life, this charming city offers fine shops and open-air markets.

The city is at the base of 4,813-foot La Soufrière; Saint-Claude, above Basse-Terre, is the starting point for trips up the volcano. After driving through the East Indian village of Matouba, where such ancient rites as animal sacrifice are still practiced, another road runs through the Bains Jaunes rain forest to within a 20-minute climb of the summit. Beyond Basse-Terre to the east are the engraved rocks at Trois-Rivières, a string of fishing hamlets and Ste. Marie, where Christopher Columbus landed in 1493. Inland from Trois-Rivières are the well-known thermal baths at Ravine Chaude.

THE ARCHEOLOGICAL PARK OF ANCIENT ROCKS features sculpted and engraved rocks and relics left by Arawak Indians in a grotto deep in the forest of Trois-Rivières. Tours are available.

FORT LOUIS DELGRÈS, near the village of Gourbeyre, was built about 1650 by Charles Houel, the island governor appointed Marquis de Guadeloupe by Louis XIV. Guarding the approach to Basse-Terre, the fort served in several battles against the British.

SAINT-CLAUDE, at the base of La Soufrière, is noted for its coffee and banana plantations and stately homes.

ILES DES SAINTES (C-2)

The Saints Islands (Iles des Saintes) are a cluster of eight islands considered among the most beautiful in the Caribbean. Their isolation from the plantation system distinguishes them from sister islands and enables them to maintain a way of life in which fishing is still the main occupation and source of income.

Pain de Sucre (Sugar Loaf), a portion of Terre de Haut jutting into the sea, is named for its resemblance to a loaf of sugar. Terre de Haut can be reached by boat from Trois-Rivières or by daily ferry or flights from Pointe-à-Pitre. *Taxis de l'Ile,* or minibuses, provide transportation to the island's points of interest, including Le Fort Napoleon with its modern art gallery and cactus garden. There is a good view of Terre de Haut from the old stone watchtower on 1,014-foot Le Chameau, the island's highest point.

LE MOULE (B-3) pop. 11,900

Le Moule on Grande-Terre island has a beach that was once the battleground for Carib warriors and French and English soldiers. Le Moule also has an aquarium and two museums devoted to prominent West Indians.

EDGAR CLERC ARCHEOLOGICAL MUSEUM, 1.2 mi. (2 km) n. in Parc de la Rosette, has two rooms that house the permanent collection of archeological artifacts of the Carib and Arawak Indians. The building is surrounded by a tropical garden that overlooks the ocean. Mon.-Tues. and Thurs.-Fri. 9-12:30 and 2-5:30; Sat.-Sun. 9-12:30 and 2-6:30. Admission is charged. Phone (590) 23-57-57.

Petit-Bourg (B-2)

DOMAINE DE VALOMBREUSE, on Cabout St. s.w. of Pointe-à-Pitre on Basse-Terre island, is a 9-acre (3.6-hectare) tropical garden containing more than 450 varieties of plants and flowers. Also within the 20-acre (8-hectare) park is a bird sanctuary featuring some 300 species. Allow 1 hour minimum. Daily 9-5. Admission $8; under 12, $5. AE, MC, VI. Phone (590) 95-50-50.

Pointe-à-Pitre (B-2) pop. 100,000

Pointe-à-Pitre is the commercial capital of Guadeloupe and seat of the sub-prefecture of Grande-Terre. About 40 miles (64 km) northeast of Basse-Terre, Pointe-à-Pitre is reached by drawbridge from Basse-Terre Island. Colonial and modern buildings complement each other; white bungalows with red roofs are separated by tree-lined parks and a large market square. Place de la Victoire, punctuated by royal palms, shade trees and poincianas, is bordered by attractive wooden houses with balconies.

The limestone islet of Gosier, off the coast of the town of the same name, has a white coral beach. Farther east, swimming is delightful at Sainte Anne and Saint François as well as at Le Moule and Port-Louis. The coastline is particularly scenic between Le Moule beach and Pointe-des-Châteaux.

FORT FLEUR D'EPEE overlooks the bay with a view of The Saints Islands, Dominica and the mountains of Basse-Terre. Because of its strategic location, this 18th-century fort was the scene of fierce struggles between the French and English. Today preserved battlements, dungeons with underground passageways, some walls and a small chapel remain.

GUADELOUPE AQUARIUM, 6 mi. (1 km) w. of the marina in Bas du Fort, displays marine life

found in the waters around Guadeloupe. Allow 30 minutes minimum. Daily 9-7. Admission $7; ages 5-12, $4. Phone (590) 90-92-38.

MARIE-GALANTE is a pastoral island named for Columbus' ship *María Graciosa*. Transportation is available from Pointe-à-Pitre by air and ferry. Many of the women on this sugar island wear colorful *foulard* and *madras* costumes on traditional holidays.

SAINT FRANÇOIS, e. of Pointe-à-Pitre, is a fishing village noted for its square and buildings. A small airport at the nearby Hamak and Méridien St. François hotels offers charter flights to Guadeloupe's island dependencies.

SCHOELCHER MUSEUM, rue Peynier behind the market, is dedicated to abolitionist Victor Schoelcher, who is credited with ending slavery in the French West Indies in 1848. Housed in a 19th-century setting, the museum contains some of Schoelcher's personal belongings and traces the island's recent history. Mon.-Tues. and Thurs.-Fri. 8:30-11:30 and 2-5, Wed. and Sat. 8:30-12:30. Admission $2. Phone (590) 82-08-04.

LODGINGS & RESTAURANTS

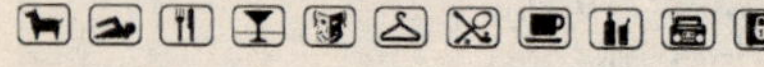

GOSIER (GAUDELOUPE)

LODGINGS

AUBERGE DE LA VIEILLE TOUR
◆◆◆   *Hotel*

12/23-4/24	$219-350	XP $35-70
12/1-12/22 & 4/25-11/30	$137-179	XP $35

Location: 6 km se of Pointe-A-Pitre. (Pointe-A Pitre, GOS-IER, 97190). Fax: 590/84-3343. **Terms:** F12; Reserv deposit, 7 day notice, in season; handling fee imposed. **Facility:** 180 rooms. Terraced grounds. Very attractive public area. Comfortable well appointed guest rooms. 1-3 stories; interior/exterior corridors; oceanfront; beach; 2 lighted tennis courts. **Recreation:** swimming, scuba diving, snorkeling. Fee: scuba & snorkeling equipment. **Cards:** AE, DI, MC, VI.

(590/84-2323

HOTEL RESIDENCE CANELLA BEACH
◆◆   *Hotel*

12/21-1/3 & 2/5-3/4	$160-291	XP $20-30
1/4-2/4 & 3/5-4/14	$160-282	XP $20-30
12/1-12/20 & 4/15-11/30	$98-199	XP $22-30

Location: On Pointe de la Verdure; 10 km se of Pointe-a-Pitre. (BP 73, GOSIER, 97190). Fax: 590/90-4444. **Terms:** F12; Reserv deposit, 14 day notice, 7 day off season. **Facility:** 146 rooms. Some rooms with oceanview. All units with balcony & kitchen. 3 stories; interior/exterior corridors; beach. **Services:** giftshop. **Recreation:** swimming, scuba diving, snorkeling & equipment. Fee: fishing, scuba equipment, waterskiing, windsurfing. Rental: canoes, paddleboats. **All Rooms:** efficiencies, combo or shower baths. **Cards:** AE, DI, MC, VI.

(590/90-4400

LA CREOLE BEACH HOTEL
◆◆   *Motor Inn*

12/20-1/5	$244-310	XP $59-99
1/6-4/26	$174-234	XP $47-56
12/1-12/19 & 4/27-11/30	$132-172	XP $45-54

Location: On Pointe de la Verdure; 10 km se from Pointe-a-Pitre; 3.5 km s of Hwy 4. (PO Box 61, GOSIER, 97190). Fax: 590/90-4666. **Terms:** F12; Reserv deposit, 3 day notice. **Facility:** 321 rooms. Beachfront vacation complex with some rooms facing garden. 27 two-bedroom units. 2-3 stories; interior/exterior corridors; beach. **Services:** giftshop. Fee: massage. **Recreation:** swimming, scuba diving, snorkeling. Fee: sailboating, scuba & snorkeling equipment, waterskiing, windsurfing. **All Rooms:** combo or shower baths. **Some Rooms:** 165 kitchens. **Cards:** AE, DI, MC, VI.

(590/90-4646

MARISSOL BAS-DU-FORT
◆◆   *Motor Inn*

12/22-1/5	$299	XP $65
2/5-2/26	$235	XP $35
12/1-12/21, 1/6-2/4 & 2/27-4/30	$225	XP $35
5/1-11/30	$160	XP $35

Location: In Bas du Fort; 6 km se of Pointe-a-Pitre, 1 km s of highway. (Bas du Fort, GOSIER). Fax: 590/90-8332. **Terms:** F16. **Facility:** 195 rooms. Landscaped beachfront grounds. Rooms & bungalows with balcony or patio. Rates for 12/22-1/2 includes a Christmas dinner & a New Year's Eve dinner; 1-3 stories; exterior corridors; beach; 1 lighted tennis court. **Services:** giftshop; massage. **Recreation:** swimming, scuba diving, snorkeling. Fee: scuba & snorkeling equipment, waterskiing, windsurfing. **Cards:** AE, MC, VI.

(590/90-8444

RESTAURANTS

LA VERANDA RESTAURANT
◆◆◆   *French*   **L** $20-$30 **D** $20-$30

Location: On Pointe de la Verdure, 10 km se of Pointe-a-Pitre; in Hotel Residence Canella Beach. 97190. **Hours:** 12:15 pm-2:30 & 7:15-10 pm. **Reservations:** suggested; in season. **Features:** casual dress; children's menu; health conscious menu; cocktails; a la carte. Relaxing ambiance with ocean view. Market-fresh cooking with Caribbean & Creole dishes. **Cards:** AE, DI, MC, VI.

(590/90-45-00

VILLA FLEUR D'EPEE
◆◆◆   *French*   **L** $15-$30 **D** $19-$40

Location: In Bas-du-Fort Section of Gosier. **Hours:** noon-2:30 & 7-10 pm. Closed: Sun; & Mon & Sat for lunch. **Reservations:** suggested. **Features:** No A/C; casual dress; cocktails; a la carte. Pretty hillside restaurant in historic location. Very well prepared French cuisine with a Caribbean accent. Seasonal menu changes. **Cards:** AE, MC, VI.

(590/90-86-59

JAMAICA

A MULTIRACIAL POPULATION and varied scenery are primary components of Jamaica's charm. Most Jamaicans are descendants of African slaves brought to the island between the 17th and 19th centuries, but Chinese, East Indians, Lebanese, Europeans and North Americans as well as nationals from neighboring republics, also have made

the island their home. This multiplicity, most evident in the port city of Kingston, reflects a special unity in the country's motto, "Out of many, one people."

Third largest of the Greater Antilles, Jamaica is 550 miles (880 km) south of Florida. About 146 miles (234 km) long and 51 miles (82 km) wide, the landscape is primarily one of contrasts, ranging from misty forest-clad mountains to bare scrubland and fields. The island's diverse terrain also is reflected in its beaches, which vary from fine coral sand in sheltered bays and inlets to black sand along the rugged coastline, where the mountains plunge straight into the sea. Montego Bay, Negril, Ocho Rios and Port Antonio are some of the most popular resort centers. Small towns and mountain villages might lack the comforts of the developed port cities but are rich in island lore and natural beauty. Blanketed with peach trees and strawberry fields, the summit of 7,402-foot Blue Mountain Peak provides a 90-mile (144-km) panorama on clear days.

HISTORY, GOVERNMENT AND ECONOMY

The Indians in Cuba had told Christopher Columbus of *Xaymaca*, the "land of wood and water." He attempted to land at St. Ann's Bay in May 1494, but was met by hostile Arawaks and had to remain offshore. After overcoming lighter resistance, he came ashore at Discovery Bay the next day, then landed at Montego Bay before moving on. Columbus made an inauspicious return in 1503; the last two ships of his fourth voyage were forced to run aground at St. Ann's Bay, and he and his crew were marooned there for more than a year. It wasn't until a small charter could be sent from Hispaniola that Columbus was able to return home, where he died 2 years later.

Diego Columbus, son of the explorer, returned to St. Ann's Bay in 1509 and founded Sevilla Nueva. The marshy site was soon abandoned, however, in favor of Santiago de la Vega (St. James of the Plain) at present-day Spanish Town. Having depleted the Arawak population through overwork and disease, the Spaniards turned to Africa for slaves and in 1517 imported the first of Jamaica's current majority race. The island was never fully developed as a Spanish colony, however, and in 1655 a British expedition literally walked into Spanish Town and took it over. The island was officially ceded to England in 1670 by the Treaty of Madrid.

Also during this time, West Indian buccaneers had made Port Royal their headquarters, giving the city a reputation as a bawdy mecca for the adventurous and the wicked. These were the days when Sir Henry Morgan rose to a commanding position among the privateers who dominated the Caribbean. His widespread successful adventures, however, overlapped the signing of peace with Spain, and he was recalled to England under arrest in 1672. When the Spanish again became a threat, he was knighted by Charles II and returned to Jamaica in 1674 as the deputy governor and the island's only honored pirate.

Kingston, the present capital, was built after an earthquake destroyed Port Royal on June 7,

1692. The flourishing slave trade and sugar and cotton plantations made Jamaica rich during the 18th century.

The cause of the slaves was supported by a group known as the Maroons, slaves freed by the Spanish to harass the English before the Spanish fled the island in 1660. Taking refuge in the hills of the Cockpit Country, these former slaves were joined by other fugitives. Together they successfully waged a guerrilla war against the English, and in 1738 the Maroons were granted self-rule and given title to their lands free of taxes. Descendants of the Maroons still live in this area; they are free of taxation and all government laws, except in the case of murder.

Although the slave trade was finally abolished in 1808, the oppression of this group did not improve. An uprising against the treatment of slaves took place in 1831; Baptist preacher Sam Sharpe led an islandwide revolt that forced the governor to declare martial law. So incensed were members of Britain's Parliament at the government's bloody crackdown, during which Sharpe and thousands more were executed, that abolition came shortly thereafter. Today Sam Sharpe is considered a national hero.

As a result of these frequent rebellions, slavery was abolished in 1834. Jamaica's newly freed population underwent years of economic and social hard times. As plantation life came to a gradual end, most workers took to the hills and practiced subsistence farming, a way of life that was to continue for generations. The 20th century, however, brought about sweeping reforms and a national identity. Marcus Garvey engendered racial pride, Alexander Bustamante organized a labor union and Norman Manley a political party. Increasingly, Jamaicans were making a place in the world.

The first civil governor of Jamaica was appointed in 1661, and the island was governed by a representative council until 1866, when a crown-colony government was established by act of Parliament. The island became independent within the British Commonwealth on August 6, 1962. A prime minister heads the government, which has its executive power vested in a cabinet; a governor general represents the British monarch. Legislative functions are assigned to a bicameral house. Sugar, bananas and coffee continue to fluctuate in prominence but are still the chief export crops. Since the 1960s bauxite and alumina exports and tourism have become the main earners of foreign exchange for the island.

SHOPPING

Jamaica was rich with the plunder of a continent in the days when Capt. Henry Morgan swaggered down the streets of Port Royal. Today the island is rich with merchandise from the four

THINGS TO KNOW

AREA: 4,411 square miles (11,424 sq km).

POPULATION: 2,500,000.

LANGUAGE: English and a local patois.

CAPITAL: Kingston.

GOVERNMENT: Independent. Member of the British Commonwealth of Nations.

TIME ZONE: Eastern.

UNIT OF CURRENCY: Jamaica dollar. $1 U.S.=approx. 36.0 Jamaica dollars. Though not consistently enforced, Jamaican law requires that Jamaican currency be used when paying for all goods and services. Credit cards may be used. Jamaican currency is available at airport and hotel exchange bureaus and commercial banks. Keep all exchange receipts; you must present them upon departure when you reconvert unspent Jamaican currency.

ELECTRICITY: 110-220 volts, 50 cycles AC—single and three phases; voltage varies with location.

CARS: U.S. license valid for 1 year, must be 21; drive on left.

IMMIGRATION REQUIREMENTS: Proof of U.S. residency (birth certificate, naturalization papers or passport) and return or through ticket are required when arriving directly from the United States. U.S. tourists must show a photo ID and funds to cover their stay. Tourist card is issued and required to be returned upon departure; tax, $500 Jamaican. There is a 6-month limit on stay for all visitors.

FOR FURTHER INFORMATION:

Jamaica Tourist Board
801 Second Ave., 20th Floor
New York, NY 10017
(212) 856-9727 or (800) 233-4582

Jamaica Tourist Board
2 St. Lucia Ave.
Kingston 5, Jamaica, West Indies
(876) 929-9200

Jamaica Tourist Board
Cornwall Beach
Montego Bay, Jamaica, West Indies
(876) 952-4425, 952-4428 or 952-2462

HOLIDAYS: Jan. 1; Ash Wednesday; Good Friday; Easter Monday; National Labour Day, May 23; Independence Day, Aug. (1st Mon.); National Hero's Day, Oct. (3rd Mon.); Dec. 25; Boxing Day, Dec. 26.

corners of the Earth. Free-port shops in Kingston, Montego Bay, Port Antonio, Negril and Ocho Rios have good buys on Swiss watches, cameras, French perfumes, British woolens and cashmeres, imported liquor, silverware, crystal, jewelry and bone china. Boutiques feature Jamaican resort clothes.

Island handicrafts include woodcarvings, inlaid boxes and trays, Jamaican dolls, straw hats, colorful baskets, pottery, shell articles and yard goods with vivid tropical prints. They are sold in specialty shops at the Kingston Crafts Market, north of the cruise ship pier in Kingston, and the Crafts Market at Harbour and Church streets in Montego Bay. Port Antonio has a straw market downtown, and the Ocho Rios Craft Park and the Olde Market are along Main Street in Ocho Rios.

East of Falmouth, the Caribatik factory produces regionally famous batik paintings and garments. Islanders often set up stalls along the roadside; you should be prepared to barter for good prices. The skill of Jamaican needlewomen has made the island's embroidered Irish linen dresses valued throughout the world. Paintings and sculptures by local artists make lasting souvenirs. A pound or so of Jamaica's excellent Blue Mountain Coffee also is a favorite take-home item.

Kingston's main shopping district is in the hotel district in New Kingston. A shopping arcade is on the grounds of Devon House, a 19th-century great house on Hope Road. There also are several shopping malls in the Kingston area. Mall shopping in Montego Bay is available at the City Centre Building on St. James Street. In Ocho Rios there are the Island Plaza, Little Pub Shopping Complex, Ocean Village Shopping Centre and the Taj Mahal—all on Main Street. Kingston shops are open Mon.-Sat. 9-5, but shops close at noon on Wed. in downtown Kingston and on Thurs. in New Kingston and Montego Bay. In Ocho Rios retail stores also are open Mon.-Sat. 9-5. Banking hours are Mon.-Thurs. 9-2, Fri. 9-4.

FOOD AND DRINK

The Jamaican national dish is *ackee* and saltfish, a dish made from imported salted cod and the fleshy lobes of the seeds of the ackee tree, cooked with onions, tomatoes and pepper in oil. Another staple is boiled rice and red beans called peas. On more exotic menus, gourmets will find goat cooked with Indian curry and served hot with boiled green bananas and rice, baked crab and pepperpot soup, a thick green "hot-pot" made of *callaloo,* Indian kale, salted pork, vegetables and pepper. West Indian lobster and red snapper dishes are abundant.

Another peppery-hot island specialty is jerk pork. This was a favorite dish of the Maroons, who roasted wild hog over a wood fire. The special flavoring is achieved through spices from a rich, peppery marinade and the type of wood used—the pimento (allspice) wood. Jerk pork and jerk chicken are available at roadside stands throughout the island.

Jamaica has a mouth-watering assortment of locally grown fruits and vegetables: mangoes, pawpaws, naseberries, sweetsops, soursops, ortaniques, otaheites, star apples, melons, rose apples, guinep, avocado pears, ugli fruit, tangerines, limes, pineapples, yams, green bananas, plantains, breadfruit, yampie, cocoa, cho-cho, pumpkins and beetroot. A delicious ice cream is made from coconut, pawpaw and soursop. Another favorite dessert is matrimony, a refreshing dish of oranges and the pulp of the star apple.

Rum is Jamaica's national drink. Consumed in an endless variety of concoctions, it can be mixed with ginger ale or coconut water, brewed with pimento berries to produce Pimento Dram Liqueur, aged with citrus peel, heated to a toddy or blended with coffee to produce Tia Maria Liqueur. Rumona is another rum liqueur. The island's most popular rum-based beverage is Planters Punch. Popular rum brands are Appleton, Myers's and Wray and Nephew's Whit Overproof.

Jamaica also brews a strong light beer called Red Stripe. Cooling nonalcoholic drinks include homemade ginger beer; sorrel, a Christmas favorite; and fruit punches made with pineapple, orange and tamarind juices and coconut water. Tap water is chlorinated and filtered.

Fine cuisine is offered at the Town House Restaurant in Montego Bay and the Blue Mountain Inn in Kingston. For seafood and local fare head for The Almond Tree, Moxon's or The Ruins in Ocho Rios; in Montego Bay try Marguerite's By-the-Sea, the family-oriented Pelican or the Wexford Grill. Montego Bay and Ocho Rios also have their share of Chinese, Italian, French and Continental restaurants. Tips average 15 to 20 percent.

SPORTS AND AMUSEMENTS

Swimming heads the list of sports and amusements in Jamaica. The most noted beaches with miles of white sand and crystal waters are on the north shore; Doctor's Cave Beach and Cornwall Beach at Montego Bay share an excellent strand. Negril Beach is a developing area on the western shore. Good beaches on the south shore include Alligator Pond and Bluefields near Savanna-La-Mar, and the black sand beaches in Kingston. Outside Kingston Harbour are the white sand beaches of Lime Cay and Maiden Cay. Mineral spas reputed to cure certain rheumatic ailments are in Bath, Kingston and Milk River.

Countless water sports opportunities await guests not content to merely lie on the beaches. The offshore islands and cays near Kingston, the coves around Ocho Rios, the offshore reefs at Montego Bay and the waters surrounding Port

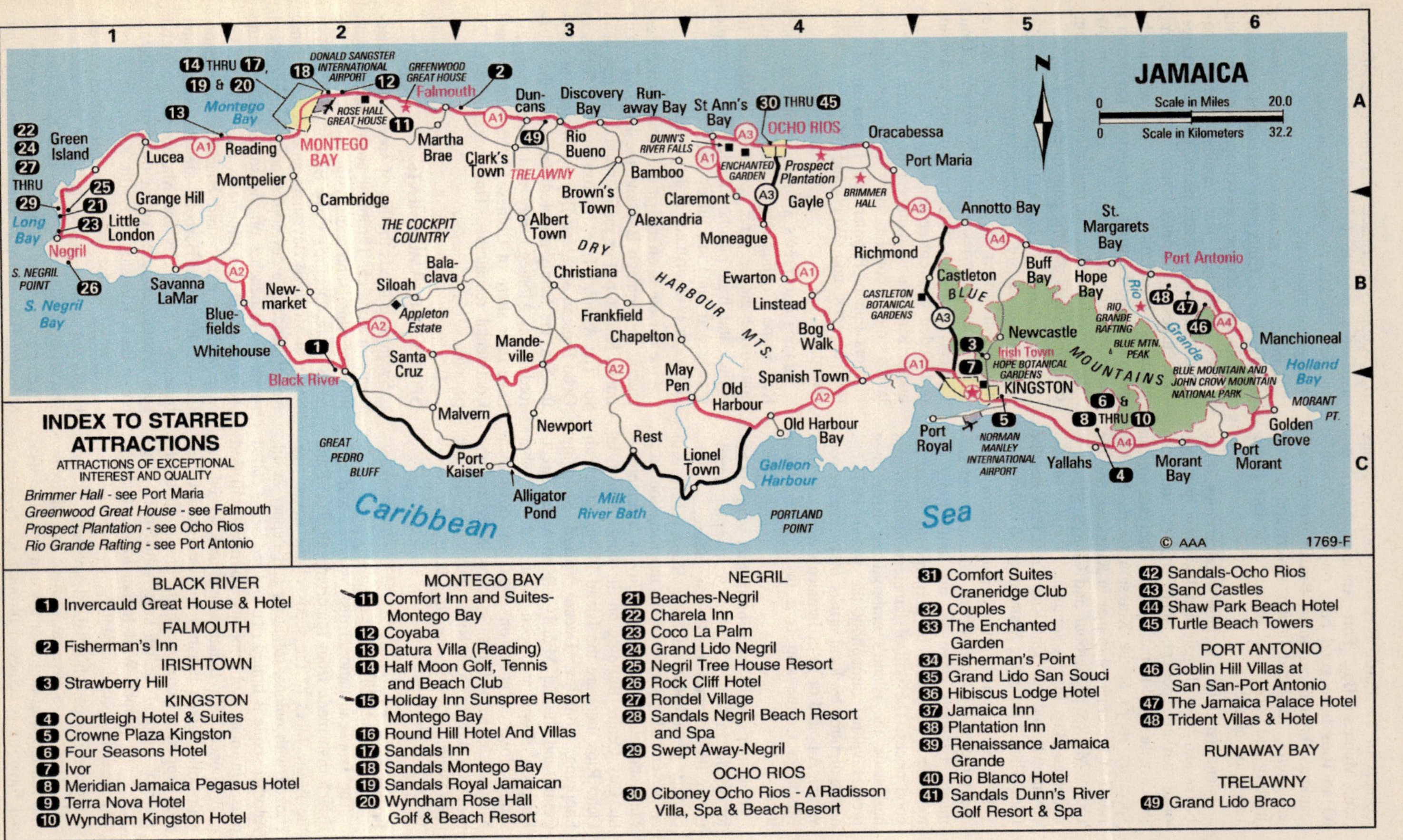

INDEX TO STARRED ATTRACTIONS

ATTRACTIONS OF EXCEPTIONAL INTEREST AND QUALITY

Brimmer Hall - see Port Maria
Greenwood Great House - see Falmouth
Prospect Plantation - see Ocho Rios
Rio Grande Rafting - see Port Antonio

BLACK RIVER
1 Invercauld Great House & Hotel

FALMOUTH
2 Fisherman's Inn

IRISHTOWN
3 Strawberry Hill

KINGSTON
4 Courtleigh Hotel & Suites
5 Crowne Plaza Kingston
6 Four Seasons Hotel
7 Ivor
8 Meridian Jamaica Pegasus Hotel
9 Terra Nova Hotel
10 Wyndham Kingston Hotel

MONTEGO BAY
11 Comfort Inn and Suites-Montego Bay
12 Coyaba
13 Datura Villa (Reading)
14 Half Moon Golf, Tennis and Beach Club
15 Holiday Inn Sunspree Resort Montego Bay
16 Round Hill Hotel And Villas
17 Sandals Inn
18 Sandals Montego Bay
19 Sandals Royal Jamaican
20 Wyndham Rose Hall Golf & Beach Resort

NEGRIL
21 Beaches-Negril
22 Charela Inn
23 Coco La Palm
24 Grand Lido Negril
25 Negril Tree House Resort
26 Rock Cliff Hotel
27 Rondel Village
28 Sandals Negril Beach Resort and Spa
29 Swept Away-Negril

OCHO RIOS
30 Ciboney Ocho Rios - A Radisson Villa, Spa & Beach Resort
31 Comfort Suites Craneridge Club
32 Couples
33 The Enchanted Garden
34 Fisherman's Point
35 Grand Lido San Souci
36 Hibiscus Lodge Hotel
37 Jamaica Inn
38 Plantation Inn
39 Renaissance Jamaica Grande
40 Rio Blanco Hotel
41 Sandals Dunn's River Golf Resort & Spa
42 Sandals-Ocho Rios
43 Sand Castles
44 Shaw Park Beach Hotel
45 Turtle Beach Towers

PORT ANTONIO
46 Goblin Hill Villas at San San-Port Antonio
47 The Jamaica Palace Hotel
48 Trident Villas & Hotel

RUNAWAY BAY

TRELAWNY
49 Grand Lido Braco

Antonio and Negril are good diving areas. Diving operators offer both guide services and courses for beginners.

Snorkel and scuba equipment, water skis, jet skis and small sailing craft can be rented from the larger resort hotels and at Turtle Beach in Ocho Rios. Arrangements for sailing can be made through the Morgan's Harbor Hotel in Kingston and the Montego Bay Yacht Club, where colorful regattas are held each winter. The Jamaica Tourist Board maintains a current list of charter companies.

Rafting is popular on the Rio Grande, Martha Brae and Great rivers *(see attraction listings under Port Antonio, Falmouth and Montego Bay, respectively)*. Less adventuresome visitors can discover the mysteries of the undersea world in a glass-bottom boat. The mountain streams offer good fishing for mullet; the sea yields marlin, dolphin, tarpon, barracuda, bonefish, snook, wahoo and small tuna.

Boats can be chartered for deep-sea fishing for half- or full-day trips at Kingston, Port Antonio, Ocho Rios, Montego Bay, Negril and Whitehouse. A fishing license is not required. Annual fishing tournaments include the Port Antonio International Spring Fishing Tournament in mid-March and the Montego Bay, Ocho Rios and Port Antonio marlin tournaments in early autumn.

You can attend horse racing Wednesday, Saturday and holidays at Caymanas Park, 6 miles (10 km) west of Kingston; pari-mutuel and quinella betting are permitted. Kingston has cricket matches on Saturday afternoons, January through April. Polo matches are held at Caymanas in Kingston, at Chukka Cove near Ocho Rios and at Drax Hall, also near Ocho Rios. Horseback riding is offered at Chukka Cove, the Double A Ranch near Montego Bay and at resort centers.

The island has 11 championship golf courses and tennis and squash courts open to hotel and villa guests. Among the major golf tournaments held are the Heinekin Golf Tournament in September, the Jamaica Open Pepsi Pro-Am in October and the Johnnie Walker World Championship of Golf in December.

Most hotels in Jamaica offer after-dinner entertainment, with many doubling as nightclubs and restaurants. Nightclubs and cabarets—The Club, Epiphany, Godfathers, Illusions, the Jonkanoo Lounge, Mingles and Mirage in Kingston, De Buss, Kaiser's Cafe and MXIII in Negril; Cave Disco, Disco Inferno and Sir Winston Reggae Club in Montego Bay; The Acropolis, The Little Pub, Maroon's, The Roof Club and Silk's in Ocho Rios; and Shadows and The Roof Club in Port Antonio—are available to suit almost every taste. Many clubs offer conventional orchestras; others echo with the distinctive rhythms of calypso and reggae bands. Floor shows are presented regularly in many of the larger clubs.

Jamaica's reggae sound, made world famous by Bob Marley, Peter Tosh and associates, is a prominent fixture in the lives of young Jamaicans. Shows featuring the nation's top performers take place regularly throughout the island. Three of the most popular are the Bob Marley Birthday Bash, held in early February near Ocho Rios; Reggae Sunsplash, a 5-night festival held in early August at Chukka Cove, on Jamaica's north coast east of Runaway Bay; and Reggae Sumfest also in August.

Visitors can enjoy the "Pantomime"—colorful social commentary—in winter at the Ward Theatre and The Little Theatre in Kingston. The National Dance Theatre Company also performs in Kingston. Films are shown in Kingston, Montego Bay, Ocho Rios, Port Antonio and Mandeville. For more information contact the Jamaica Tourist Board, which publishes two calendars of events during the year.

Evening canoe rides, available on the torchlit Great and White rivers, include dinner and a folkloric show on the riverbank. Walter Fletcher Beach at Montego Bay is the scene of colorful beach parties every Friday at 7 p.m. Gloucester Avenue in Montego Bay is blocked off every Monday night for the Mobay Nite Out street party. The Jamaica Tourist Board regularly schedules entertainment programs that include river rafting trips, dances, parties and barbecues, usually set in a secluded area near the major hotels. Inquire at your hotel for more information.

Excursions and Sightseeing

With more than 7,800 miles (12,480 km) of primary roads and 2,800 miles (4,480 km) of secondary roads linking every village and hamlet, Jamaica is popular for motor tours. Possible itineraries are numerous, the only limitation being the time you can spend.

Beginning and ending at Kingston, a driving tour around the island takes about 2 days. A condensed circle tour of the island out of Kingston might follow Rte. A3 to Ocho Rios and St. Ann's Bay on the north coast and return via A1 by way of Spanish Town, and include such sites as Castleton Botanical Gardens, restored plantations, Dunn's River Falls, Fern Gully, the Ewarton aluminum plant and the Cathedral of St. James.

South and west of Claremont via unimproved roads is the village of Nine Miles. Musician Bob Marley was born in Nine Miles in 1945 and interred there in 1981. The mausoleum grounds are open to the public; admission is charged.

Tour buses offering 3-hour tours of Kingston drive past the historic residences of the prime minister and governor general and through the campus of the University of the West Indies. They also include stops at the National Gallery of Jamaica, Hope Botanical Gardens and the Kingston Crafts Market.

The 3-hour Ocho Rios Tour takes in such area highlights as Prospect Estate, Dunn's River Falls, Shaw Park Gardens and Fern Gully. A 3-hour trip from Ocho Rios to Port Maria and Brimmer Hall Plantation also is available. Departing from Montego Bay, the 3- to 4-hour Great Houses Tour includes a complimentary drink at either Rose Hall *(see attraction listing p. 167)* or Greenwood Great House *(see attraction listing p. 164)*; reservations can be made through your hotel. Bus tours that include stops at YS Falls, the Black River and Appleton Estate provide lunch, drinks and hotel pickup; inquire at your hotel for information and reservations.

Scheduled morning and sunset cruises are available for tours of Montego Bay; snorkeling cruises also are available. Arrangements can be made through the tour desks at most hotels.

TRANSPORTATION

Easily accessible by air from several North American cities and Puerto Rico, Jamaica has international airports at Kingston and Montego Bay. Air service linking Kingston, Port Antonio, Ocho Rios, Negril and Montego Bay is available on Trans Jamaican Airlines or by charter. Ocho Rios and Montego Bay are ports of call for many cruise ships, which also call at Kingston and Port Antonio.

There are nearly 11,000 miles (17,600 km) of roadway in Jamaica. Since long-distance cab and limousine rides can be expensive, it is helpful to get an accommodations package that includes transportation between your hotel and the airport.

Two types of taxis operate on the island: those affiliated with the Jamaica Union of Travellers Association (JUTA) and those that are not. Non-affiliated taxis can be distinguished from private vehicles by their red license plate. Taxis are un-metered; maximum rates are merely suggested by the government, so it is always wise to determine the fare in advance.

Cars can be rented by the day or week; a U.S. driver's license is valid for 1 year. Driving on the left side of the road with the steering wheel on the right side of the vehicle complicates the navigation of the narrow, curving roads often found in the interior of the island; be prepared to relinquish your right-of-way. Though traffic is relatively light except in larger towns, roads are often frequented by domestic animals and people; allow 40 miles (62 km) to the hour. It might be wise to rent a car with a driver or hire a tour operator. Half- and full-day excursions are available from all the resort areas. Minibuses, inexpensive but usually very crowded, serve all areas of the island.

ATTRACTION ADMISSIONS
Attraction admissions for this island are quoted in U.S. dollars.

POINTS OF INTEREST
See map page 162.

DISCOVERY BAY (A-3) pop. 2,500

Christopher Columbus landed at Discovery Bay in 1494. Dedicated to this historic event is 2.75-acre (1-hectare) Columbus Park, 1.5 miles (2.4 km) west of Discovery Bay on Rte. A1. The park, on property owned by the Kaiser Bauxite Co., is open during daylight hours and provides a fine view of Discovery Bay. Interesting artifacts of early Jamaican life are present on the nicely landscaped grounds. Tours of the bauxite operations can be arranged, but requests should be made in advance; phone (876) 973-2221. Puerto Seco Beach also is worth visiting.

FALMOUTH (A-2) pop. 3,900

Falmouth is surrounded by sugar estates and cattle land. Once a leading port, the town has excellent examples of 19th-century Georgian architecture along with a faithful restoration of the early 19th-century courthouse destroyed by fire in 1926. Of special interest is the 1796 Falmouth Anglican Church on Rte. A1. Fresh fruit and vegetables are sold along Market Street.

★**GREENWOOD GREAT HOUSE,** 5 mi. (8 km) w. via Rte. A1, was built in 1790 by Richard Barrett, a relative of poet Elizabeth Barrett Browning. Having amassed considerable wealth from their sugar plantations, the Barretts presided over an estate that extended about 12 miles (19 km) along the coast from Little River to Falmouth. The great house is now an antiques museum with period furniture and decorations, family portraits, a rare collection of musical instruments and Wedgwood china made exclusively for the Barrett family.

Gardens adorn the property, which overlooks the ocean. A display of horse-drawn carriages and antique fire-fighting equipment also is on the grounds. Guided tours last about 30 minutes. Open daily 9-6. Admission $10; ages 5-12, $5. Phone (876) 953-1077.

MARTHA BRAE RAFTERS' VILLAGE, 3.5 mi. (5.6 km) s. on Market St., following signs, offers a relaxing trip down the Martha Brae River aboard a 30-foot bamboo raft. Food is available. Allow 1 hour, 30 minutes minimum. Raft trips are offered daily 8:30-4:30. Fare $40 per raft (accommodates two adults and one child under 12). Return transportation can be included in the fare upon request. Phone (876) 952-0889.

KINGSTON (C-5) pop. 661,600

Kingston was founded in 1692 when survivors of the Port Royal earthquake resettled around a piggery across the harbor. It became Jamaica's capital in 1872 and is today considered the island's cultural center. An earthquake and fire in 1907 destroyed most of the city, but it was immediately rebuilt. On a broad plain beneath the Blue Mountains, Kingston is built around a large harbor.

The new Kingston is even busier than the old; suburbs have grown up around residences of officials and wealthy merchants. The town and surrounding districts are well supplied with good hotels, and the wharfside crafts center is a shopper's mecca. North of downtown is 74-acre (30-hectare) National Heroes Park, where Jamaican leaders Alexander Bustamante, Norman Manley and Marcus Garvey are buried. West of the city, Caymanas Park offers horse racing on Wednesday, Saturday and holidays. The Jamaica Tourist Board office is at 2 St. Lucia Ave., Kingston 5.

Hellshire Beach, 14 miles (22 km) southwest of Kingston on the coast, has 200,000-year-old Two Sisters Cave with rare Arawak petroglyphs. Nearby is Fort Clarence Beach, a seaside recreational complex. Both beaches are popular with the locals on weekends.

BLUE MOUNTAIN PEAK, at 7,402 feet, is accessible by mule or on foot and is the island's highest peak. The 2-day trip offers thrilling views. Cuba is visible on a clear day.

BLUE MOUNTAINS AND JOHN CROW MOUNTAINS NATIONAL PARK is in eastern Jamaica spreading out across the parishes of St. Andrew, Portland, St. Thomas and St. Mary. The park consists of nearly 200,000 acres of land divided into three sections: Portland Gap, which includes Stony Hill and the Hills of St. Andrew; Hollywell and Annotto Bay; and Portland and Millbank which include the John Crow Mountains.

A pristine preserve offering mountain vistas, waterfalls, streams, lush rain forests and exotic flora and fauna, the park is the natural habitat for the Giant Swallowtail, the largest butterfly in the Americas with a 6-inch wingspan.

Numerous roads penetrate the park; however some roads can only be accessed by four-wheel drive vehicles. Footpaths branch off of the main roads, making hiking a popular way to explore the park. Guided tours are offered by various outfitters. Cabins are available for rent. For additional information contact the Jamaica Conservation and Development Trust, 95 Dumbarton Ave., Kingston 10; phone (876) 960-2848. Daily. Free. Phone (876) 977-8044.

BOB MARLEY MUSEUM, .5 mi. (.8 km) e. of jct. Waterloo and Hope rds. at 56 Hope Rd., is in the former home of Jamaican reggae singer Bob Marley. His life and career are recounted through his personal belongings, tour memorabilia and extensive information about his religion, politics and music. The guided tour also includes an herb garden and meditation area. Photography and tape recording are not permitted.

Allow 1 hour minimum. Mon.-Tues. and Thurs.-Fri. 9:30-5, Wed. and Sat. 12:30-6. Admission $2; under 13, $1; student (over age 12 with student ID) rates available. Phone (876) 927-9152.

CASTLETON BOTANICAL GARDENS, 15 acres 19 mi. (30 km) n., contains many species of tropical plants, including spice and fruit trees and a palm grove. Swimming is permitted in Wag Water River, which runs through the gardens. Daily 9-6. Free. Phone (876) 927-1257.

DEVON HOUSE, Hope and Waterloo rds., was commissioned in 1881 by George Stiebel, who is believed to have made his fortune in South American gold. The plantation-style mansion and its landscaped grounds are now maintained by the government as a showcase of Jamaican craftsmanship. Highlights include antiques, reproductions and other embellishments. Guided tours and food are available. Allow 30 minutes minimum. Tues.-Sat. 9:30-5. Admission $3; under 13, $1.50. Phone (876) 929-7029.

HOPE BOTANICAL GARDENS, 6 mi. (10 km) n. on Hope Rd., has more than 150 acres of flower beds, lawns and borders as well as a sunken garden. On the grounds are an orchid house, a lake, a zoo and a cactus garden. A 1758 stone aqueduct built on the old Hope sugar estate is still in use. Gardens daily 8-6; park daily 10-5:30; zoo daily 10-5. Free. Phone (876) 927-1257.

INSTITUTE OF JAMAICA, 14-16 East St., houses an outstanding West Indies reference library, a reading room, an art gallery and herbarium with more than 30,000 specimens. There also are maps and folklore exhibits, including the "shark papers," incriminating journals thrown overboard by a guilty sea captain and found years later in the belly of a shark. Mon.-Thurs. 9-5, Fri. 9-4; closed holidays. Free. Phone (876) 922-0620.

KING'S HOUSE, 5 mi. (8 km) n. off Hope Rd., is the official residence of the governor-general. The 175 acres of landscaped grounds include a large banyan tree with stiltlike roots. Mon.-Fri. 10-5. Free. Phone (876) 927-6424.

KINGSTON CRAFTS MARKET, 1 mi. (1.6 km) n. of Pier 1 at Port Royal St., is a large covered bazaar with gaily decorated booths displaying handicrafts and art objects. Straw items are popular purchases. Thurs.-Tues. 9-5, Wed. 9-noon. Phone (876) 922-5445.

KINGSTON PARISH CHURCH, at King St. and South Parade, was built in 1699 and reconstructed after the 1907 earthquake. The church contains monuments to prominent Jamaicans. Daily.

NATIONAL GALLERY OF JAMAICA, Orange St. and Ocean Blvd., exhibits the definitive collection of Jamaican art, tracing its development through different periods and movements. Works represent realism, symbolism, expressionism and surrealism as well as abstract and intuitive styles. The works of Edna Manley are featured prominently. Other artists represented include Carl Abrahams, Henry Daley, John Dunkley, Colin Garland, Albert Huie, Kapo and Namba Roy. Christopher Gonzales' statue of Bob Marley graces the foyer. Mon.-Thurs. 11-4:30, Fri. 11-4. Donations. Phone (876) 922-1561.

NEWCASTLE, 19 mi. (30 km) n. on Rte. B1, is a military camp for the Jamaican Defense Force. Nearly 4,000 feet above the sea on the southern slope of the Blue Mountains, Newcastle affords a magnificent view. The Old Stables serve as a starting point for a number of marked nature walks. Tours are available. Daily dawn-dusk. Free. Phone (876) 944-8114.

UNIVERSITY OF THE WEST INDIES, about 3 mi. (4.8 km) n. at Mona, features modern architecture and a collection of 18th-century artifacts. The 1799 chapel was moved from its original location on a sugar plantation and meticulously rebuilt. Original stone aqueducts are scattered throughout the campus. The university, established in 1948, is attended by students from all areas of the Caribbean. Visitors may drive through the grounds. Phone (876) 977-5941.

MANDEVILLE (B-3) pop. 34,500

A quiet elegance pervades the resort of Mandeville, 64 miles (102 km) west of Kingston in the 2,000-foot Manchester Mountains. Resembling a town in the English Midlands, Mandeville exudes back-country charm with its prim cottages and private gardens, town square and clock tower. The town's avid gardeners compete each May in the Manchester Flower Show, which draws visitors from all over the island.

Founded in 1814, Mandeville was named after the Earl of Mandeville, son of the Duke of Manchester—a governor of Jamaica. The town quickly became a retreat for wealthy Jamaican growers drawn by the peaceful setting and cool mountain breezes. Bauxite and alumina mining sustained the area economy beyond the 1940s. Mandeville is now at the heart of the island's citrus industry; the town market overflows with colorful fruits and flowers in season. Dominating Mandeville Square is the 1820 Georgian-style Mandeville Courthouse. Just south is the Parish Church, also built in 1820.

Golf, tennis and sightseeing by horseback or bicycle are enjoyable in the bracing mountain air. Golf and tennis can be played at the Manchester Club on Brumala Road, the Caribbean's first golf course. Golf Week, Jamaica's oldest tournament, is played on the club's nine-hole course in July. Tennis Week, purportedly the oldest tournament in the Caribbean, is played in August. A noteworthy attraction is nearby Marshall's Pen, an 18th-century great house on a 300-acre (12-hectare) cattle farm; extensive gardens, a bird sanctuary and hiking trails are on the property. House tours, horseback riding and native and village tours can be arranged; phone (876) 962-3725.

About 20 miles (32 km) west of Mandeville, Rte. A2 enters Bamboo Avenue, a grove of giant bamboo that creates a tropical canopy for about 3 miles (4.8 km). Paralleling the route southward is Black River. Once the center for crocodile hunting before the sport was prohibited, Black River is the largest navigable river in Jamaica and offers excellent freshwater fishing. Regular boat tours are available.

Only the most courageous sightseers will venture near the edge of Lover's Leap. On the coast about 40 miles (19 km) southwest of Mandeville, the sheer cliff stands about 1,700 feet over the sea. The cliff is the spot where two slaves once jumped to avoid separation; this romantic story is re-told daily by interpretive guides. A museum houses area artifacts. Mon.-Thurs. 9-6, Fri.-Sun. 9-7. Admission $3.

About 30 miles (48 km) southeast of town is Milk River Bath. The spring water is a constant 92 degrees Fahrenheit and is purportedly the most radioactive in the world. Bathers are limited to three 15-minute treatments per day. Daily 7 a.m.-9 p.m. Fee $2, children $1. Phone (876) 987-6544.

MONTEGO BAY (A-2) pop. 70,000

Montego Bay is an exciting, cosmopolitan resort with beautiful beaches and excellent accommodations. The shoreline is dotted with sparkling coves and luxury hotels offering the gamut of water sports. Such nearby great houses as Rose Hall *(see attraction listing p. 167)* and Greenwood *(see place listing p. 164)* are open to the public, and the ruins of the old British Fort Montego bears further witness to a rich history. On the northwest coast 119 miles (190 km) from Kingston, Montego Bay is accessible by plane, train or car. The municipal bus company serves the airport and the hotel strip.

MoBay, as the resort is known locally, was one of Jamaica's original settlements. Christopher Columbus called it *El Golfo de Buen Tiempo,* or "Fair Weather Gulf," back in 1494, but his successors were apparently not as impressed; the current name comes from the Spanish *manteca,* or lard, an early major export. Montego Bay later prospered as a sugar and banana port. Tourism was born in the late 19th century when Dr. Alexander McCatty began attracting wealthy North Americans to the "curative" waters off Doctor's Cave Beach.

At the center of town is busy Sam Sharpe Square, where the slave rebellion leader and hundreds more were hanged in 1832. The colonial government's harsh response to the uprising led England to abolish slavery 2 years later. A monument to Sharpe stands on the site. Northeast on Union Street is the Slave Ring, where slaves were bought, sold and traded.

The strand of MoBay's famous beaches begins just north of town at Walter Fletcher Beach. Further north are Doctor's Cave, Cornwall and Chatham beaches. All but Chatham Beach have changing facilities, food and a slight admission charge. More resorts and beaches extend eastward from the airport. South of town on a man-made peninsula is Freeport, a mostly industrial area that also is home to the Montego Bay Yacht Club and the Bob Marley Performing Centre.

The wild and forbidding Cockpit Country southeast of Montego Bay once harbored the Maroons, slaves who established their own villages after being freed by the Spanish. They were fierce warriors whose relentless guerrilla tactics were successful in frightening the British colonists into riding back-to-back on a single horse whenever they traveled through Maroon territory. Today their descendants welcome travelers to the historic "Land of Look Behind," though some may still warn, "Me no call you, you no come."

About 5 miles (8 km) southwest of Montego Bay on Rte. B8 near Anchovy is the Rocklands Feeding Station, where a wide variety of birds can be observed. Bird feedings take place daily at 3:30; admission is charged. Rafting on the Great River west of the city is offered daily 9-5, with a two-person maximum per raft; consult any tour operator or ask your hotel for information.

AN EVENING ON THE GREAT RIVER provides shuttle service from hotels to the departure site 10 mi. (16 km) w. on Rte. A1. Canoe rides up the torchlit Great River lead to a village where there is a native floor show of music and dancing. A Jamaican-style buffet dinner and open bar is available. Allow 4 hours minimum. Canoes depart Sun., Tues. and Thurs. at 7 p.m. Fare $55 (including shuttle transportation and dinner). Phone (876) 952-0527.

DOCTOR'S CAVE BEACH, off Gloucester Ave. in the hotel area, is one of the best beaches in the West Indies. At one time the property of Jamaican tourism pioneer Dr. Alexander McCatty, the beach now has changing rooms, a bar and a water sports desk. Daily dawn-dusk. Admission 70c.

ROSE HALL GREAT HOUSE, 7 mi. (11 km) e. of the airport on Rte. A1 following signs, is a restored 18th-century plantation mansion named after the original owner's wife. According to legend it is haunted by Annie Palmer, another former owner known as the White Witch of Rose Hall. She took in many slaves as lovers and was eventually murdered by them. Guided tours are available. Food is available.

Allow 30 minutes minimum. Daily 9-6. Candlelight tours are available Wed. 7-10 p.m. Admission $15; ages 6-12, $6. Candlelight tours $45. AE, MC, VI. Phone (876) 953-2323.

ST. JAMES PARISH CHURCH, Church and King sts., is a gray stone cruciform building dedicated in 1775. Almost destroyed by an earthquake in 1957, the church has been restored. It is considered to be one of the finest churches in Jamaica. Daily dawn-dusk.

NEGRIL (B-1) pop. 1,500

On Jamaica's western tip, Negril (ne-GRIL) is a 90-minute drive down the coast from Montego Bay. Two bays sheltered by coral reefs lie along a 7-mile (11 km) stretch of unbroken shoreline, creating excellent conditions for swimming, snorkeling, scuba diving, sailing, windsurfing, parasailing, water skiing and horseback riding. The longer and more popular beach is at Long Bay. To the north is the more private Bloody Bay—its name dates back to the whaling era. Swimsuits are optional wear at Bloody Bay.

Pirates knew Negril well during their time. The coastal setting was a favored hideaway of Jamaica's notorious "Calico Jack" Rackham. He was finally apprehended in 1720 while lounging at Bloody Bay with two female mates. Negril remained largely undiscovered, however, until the late 1960s when it became a haven for young escapists seeking freedom from the modern world. It remains an uncluttered destination; in order to preserve the beauty of the area, an ordinance

prohibits the building of any structure taller than the average palm tree.

Given its location at the island's westernmost point, Negril is famous for its spectacular sunsets. Popular vantage points are the numerous cafes at the rock cliffs along West End (also called Lighthouse) Road; Rick's Cafe is one of the most popular. At some cafes locals and visitors can be seen diving off the tall cliffs into the calm sea below. At the end of West End Road is the 100-foot Negril Point Lighthouse. Contact the lighthouse supervisor for permission to climb to the top; phone (876) 957-4875.

OCHO RIOS (A-4) pop. 7,800

Ocho Rios, or Ochee as the locals call it, is on the north shore about 55 miles (88 km) from Kingston. A ballooning tourist industry has reinforced the town's bauxite harvesting, manufacturing and mining industries. The town's antique charm is complemented by its fine hotels, beautiful scenery, good shopping, active nightlife and stable climate. All manner of water sports are available both within the bay and along the coast. Ocho Rios is a popular port of call for private yachts as well as cruise ships.

Some of the island's oldest communities are within a few miles of Ocho Rios. St. Ann's Bay, 7 miles (11 km) west via Rte. A3, is said to be the final resting place of Christopher Columbus' last ships. The ruins of Sevilla Nueva, Jamaica's first settlement, are 9 miles (14 km) west. Laid out by the Spanish in 1509, the site is currently the subject of archeological research.

Popular local tours include an excursion to Dunn's River Falls, a raft trip on the White River and a visit to Shaw Park Botanical Gardens, which has 34 acres (14 hectares) of tropical flora and a waterfall. The gardens are .75 miles (1.2 km) south on Rte. A3 then 1 mile (1.6 km) west, following signs; admission is charged. Ocho Rios' central location makes day trips to Kingston, Montego Bay and the interior manageable.

DUNN'S RIVER FALLS, 3 mi. (4.8 km) w. on Rte. A3, cascades 600 feet (183 meters) through tropical foliage. At one time the entire stretch of coastline was a series of rivers flowing from the mountains and suddenly gushing out of limestone rocks to form rows of cascades. The falls rush over layered tiers of smooth rock and flow directly to the beach.

A paved walkway parallels the falls, or visitors, assisted by guides, may climb to the top. Rubber-soled shoes with good traction are recommended; footholds have been carved in the most difficult places. Cameras should remain covered and secured when not in use. Official guides are available only inside the falls' gates. Swimming is permitted. Food is available.

Allow 1 hour, 30 minutes minimum. Open daily 9-5. Admission $6; under 12, $3; tipping customary for guided climb to the top. Rubber-soled shoes may be rented for $5. Phone (876) 974-2857.

ENCHANTED GARDEN, 1.2 mi. (2 km) s. of Rte. A1 jct. on Eden Bower Rd., encompasses 20 acres (8 hectares) of mountainside gardens with 14 waterfalls. Exotic birds inhabit a large walk-in aviary. Also featured is a seaquarium with tropical fish and numerous varieties of plants. Food is available. Allow 2 hours minimum. Guided tours are offered daily 9:30-4:30. Admission $20. Phone (876) 974-1400.

FERN GULLY, along Rte. A3, 1.5 mi. (2.4 km) s. of the Rte. A1 jct., is a tree-covered canyon with lush growths of ferns and tropical plants. The gorge descends for about 3 miles (4.8 km), following the course of a dry riverbed. Visitors should exercise caution, as the road is narrow and normally damp. Heavy rains can cause floods as well as mudslides and rockslides. There are a limited number of areas wide enough for vehicles to pull off the road.

HARMONY HALL, 4.5 mi. (7 km) e. on Rte. A3, is a restored 1886 Victorian structure that once was part of a pimento estate. The hall accommodates a small gallery that displays original paintings, prints, sculpture and tapestries by internationally known Jamaican artists. Food is available. Allow 30 minutes minimum. Daily 10-6. Free. Phone (876) 975-4222.

★**PROSPECT PLANTATION,** 3 mi. (4.8 km) e. on Rte. A3, following signs, offers a comprehensive jitney tour of a working 1,180-acre (478-hectare) plantation, including stops at the White River Gorge and Sir Harold's Viewpoint. Narrators provide the history and background of the various fruits grown on the plantation as well as information about native flora. Highlights of the tour include the Prospect College Chapel with its handmade furnishings and such demonstrations as coconut picking. Guided horseback rides are available on four different trails; reservations are required. Miniature golf and food are available.

Allow 1 hour, 30 minutes minimum. Tours depart Mon.-Sat. at 10:30, 2 and 3:30, Sun. at 11, 1:30 and 3. Miniature golf course open daily 9-5. Plantation $12, under 12 free. Miniature golf $5; under 12, $2.50. Horseback riding $20-$50, depending on duration. Phone (876) 974-2058.

RIO NUEVO BATTLE SITE is 6 mi. (10 km) e. on Rte. A3, following signs. On June 17, 1658, the British defeated Jamaican and Spanish forces at this site, giving Great Britain sovereignty over Jamaica until its independence in 1962. Daily dawn-dusk. Free.

PORT ANTONIO (B-5) pop. 16,000

About 60 miles (96 km) northeast of Kingston on the windward coast, Port Antonio was one of Jamaica's first tourist destinations. Its beautiful twin harbors at the foothills of the lush Blue

Mountains lured North America's elite in the early 20th century. Among the likes of William Randolph Hearst, Bette Davis, Ginger Rogers and J.P. Morgan was the irrepressible Errol Flynn, who made Port Antonio his home. Tours of a 2,500-acre (1,012-hectare) plantation on Flynn's property in the Priestman's River area are available by reservation; admission is charged; phone (876) 993-0667.

The two harbors, sheltered by Navy Island and Titchfield Peninsula, were largely responsible for the town's early success as a banana port. Since 1729 imposing Fort George has overlooked the harbors, once busy with lines of steamers waiting for their shipments of bananas. Today the docks no longer hum with the rhythm of banana loaders and the colorful refrain "come mister tallyman, tally me banana," but the charm of this port town has survived.

Of interest to sightseers and photographers are the port's ruins of Folly. Built in 1905 by a wealthy American engineer, this extravagant 60-room mansion lay vacant within 30 years, a victim of poor construction and neglect. Its crumbling walls and pillars are all that remain. The Folly Point Lighthouse stands at the end of the peninsula. Dominating the skyline on Bridge Street is the Romanesque Christ Church, built in 1840. Produce and crafts can be had at Musgrave Market on West Harbour east of the ferry dock.

Among the nearby scenic spots is Somerset Falls, about 10 miles (16 km) west, where the Daniels River plunges through a gorge in a series of cascades and pools; admission is charged. Most of the area's beaches extend east of town. Two of the most popular are San San and Boston, though Frenchman's Cove and Blue Lagoon also are frequented; admissions might be charged. Navy Island's beaches are accessible by regular water taxi service from West Harbour. Bathing suits are optional at the Cove on Navy Island.

NONSUCH CAVE AND ATHENRY GARDENS, 4.5 mi. (6.6 km) s.e. of town, following signs, are best reached by public transportation. Set on the 185-acre (75-hectare) lands of the old United Fruit Co., the well-labeled gardens boast several plant varieties, including bird of paradise, red ginger and royal poinciana. The Athenry Pavilion affords an excellent view of Port Antonio.

Nonsuch Cave, 55 feet (17 m) underground, is composed of nine chambers connected by lighted, paved walkways. Stalactites, stalagmites and other limestone formations create interesting works of nature. Tours and a complimentary drink offered daily 9-5. Admission $5. Phone (876) 993-3740.

★**RIO GRANDE RAFTING,** 5.5 mi. (9 km) w. on Rte. A4, offers a memorable 2.5-hour trip down the Rio Grande River on a 30-foot bamboo raft. Maximum capacity is two adults and one child under 12 per raft. Return transportation is avail-

able, or hired drivers will transport cars to the journey's end where they can be picked up by their owners. Food is available. Allow 2 hours, 30 minutes minimum. Daily 8:30-4:30; closed Good Friday and Dec. 25. Last trip begins 30 minutes before closing. Fare $45 per raft. MC, VI. Phone (876) 993-5778.

PORT MARIA (A-4) pop. 5,100

Port Maria was an important commercial center during the Spanish era, made possible in large part by its deep natural harbor. Of interest in town is St. Mary Parish Church, built in 1861. Northwest toward Oracabessa are several small, fine beaches, among them Pagee and Murdock's. At Galina is the Galina Point and Lighthouse.

On a mountain north of Port Maria is Firefly, the small retreat of Noel Coward, noted English playwright, actor and director. The house, 2.2 miles (3.6 km) north on Rte. A3, then 1 mile (1.6 km) west on Stuart Place track, contains the playwright's possessions; his grave is in the garden. Firefly is open Mon.-Sat. 8:30-4; admission is charged. Firefly was inspired by Coward's visit to nearby Goldeneye, the home of Ian Fleming, author of the James Bond novels. Goldeneye is not open to the public. Phone (876) 997-7201

★**BRIMMER HALL,** 5 mi. (8 km) s., following signs, offers jitney tours of a large plantation in operation. Guides identify and describe the crops and tropical flora encountered along the route. Food is available. Swimming is permitted. Tours daily at 11, 1:30 and 3:30. Admission $15; Additional fee for great-house tours. Phone (876) 994-2309.

PORT ROYAL (C-4) pop. 1,300

At the tip of a 10-mile (16 km) strip of land called the Palisadoes, Port Royal became the focus of British fortification efforts soon after their takeover in 1655. Construction of Fort Charles began in 1656, and within a few years there were five more forts manned by more than 2,500 soldiers. Port Royal also became headquarters for buccaneers and privateers who preyed on Spanish ships throughout the Caribbean. This era brought Port Royal great wealth and a reputation as one of the wickedest cities in the world.

Shortly before noon on June 7, 1692, as if by divine judgment, an earthquake and tidal wave destroyed 90 percent of city and claimed more than 2,000 lives; most of the city sank beneath the sea. Attempts were made to rebuild Port Royal, but a 1703 fire and numerous hurricanes thwarted all efforts and the site was eventually abandoned for Kingston across the harbor. Somewhere offshore are the remains of Sir Henry Morgan, who was buried in Port Royal in 1688.

Today this sleepy little fishing village belies its former self. An archeological museum housed in the Old Naval Hospital, built in 1819, preserves some of Port Royal's history; phone (876) 922-0620. Port Royal is reached by water taxi or bus from Kingston or by a 10-minute drive from Norman Manley International Airport. Boat trips can be arranged to visit the cays offshore from the Palisadoes. Lime Cay is the most popular.

FORT CHARLES, next to the Jamaican Coast Guard headquarters, was built beginning in 1656 and was one of few Port Royal structures to survive the 1692 disaster. The fort retains many of its old battlements. Horatio Nelson served as a naval lieutenant at Fort Charles in 1779. Fort open daily dawn-dusk. A maritime museum is open daily 10-4. Museum admission 25c. Phone (876) 967-8438

ST. PETER'S CHURCH is next to the Morgan's Harbour Hotel. Built in 1725 to replace Christ's Church, which slid into the sea in 1692, this church houses an 18th-century candelabrum, altar railings, an elaborate organ loft and monuments to a number of distinguished citizens. It also boasts a silver communion plate that was a gift from Sir Henry Morgan. Mon.-Sat. dawn-dusk. Services on Sun. Phone (876) 927-6579.

RUNAWAY BAY (A-3) pop. 500

Runaway Bay earned its name through its role in Jamaican history as an escape route for those in perilous predicaments. The last Spanish governor of Jamaica fled to Cuba in 1660, following the British invasion. Runaway slaves also took advantage of the bay's calm waters and strategic location to flee in small canoes. Later this strip of coastline was a sanctuary for Cuban refugees.

Today, as a developing resort area with hotels, nightclubs, tennis courts, golf courses and posh restaurants, Runaway Bay is still an escape, but for those running from the routine of everyday life. Chukka Cove Equestrian Centre, 5 miles (8 km) east on the former Llandovery Sugar Estate, offers riding and polo lessons and trail rides.

SILOAH (B-2) pop. 1,000

APPLETON ESTATE, 7 mi. (11 km) n. on Rte. A2 to Maggotty, then 3 mi. (4.8 km) e., has been producing sugar, molasses and rum since 1749. The distillery is set in a valley along the Black River. A guided tour provides a demonstration of various stages of the production process, including the extraction of the sugar from the raw cane. A tasting room is on the premises. Food is available. Allow 1 hour minimum. Mon.-Sat. 9-4. Admission $12; under 12, $6. MC, VI. Phone (876) 963-9215.

SPANISH TOWN (C-4) pop. 14,700

First known as Santiago de la Vega (St. James of the Plain), Spanish Town was founded by the Spaniards about 1534 after they abandoned their first city at Sevilla Nueva on the north coast. The British destroyed much of the original town in 1655, but remained to build new structures, many of them fine examples of Georgian architecture. Spanish Town served as capital of Jamaica until 1872, when the capital was moved to Kingston.

The ruins of 17th-century Colbeck Castle, reached by a slight detour off the road to Old Harbour, are worth visiting. The main facade is more than 100 feet (30 meters) high, and the

---

BOB MARLEY

Jamaica's distinctive reggae sound, instantly recognizable by its bouncy blend of percussion and bass with a slightly late rhythm guitar on the offbeat, found its way onto the world's popular music scene in the early 1970s. Desmond Dekker announced its arrival with his 1969 hit "The Israelites," and in 1972 Johnny Nash popularized the sound with "I Can See Clearly Now," as did Paul Simon with "Mother and Child Reunion." But it was Bob Marley and his group the Wailers, featuring Peter Tosh and Bunny Livingston, and later the back-up vocals of the I-Threes (Rita Marley, Marcia Griffiths and Judy Mowatt), who brought reggae the worldwide prominence it enjoys today.

As his European and American contemporaries did to rock 'n' roll, Bob Marley brought to reggae lyrics of pride and protest. He sang of black unity, in the tradition of national hero Marcus Garvey, and of the tenants of Rastafarianism, the uniquely Jamaican religion of which he was a devout member. Bob Marley and the Wailers released nine albums, as well as several compilations, outside of Jamaica. Among his more popular songs are "Get Up Stand Up," "Rastaman Vibration," "Jamming" and "Is This Love." Eric Clapton re-recorded Marley's song "I Shot the Sheriff" in 1974, bringing international acclaim to both Marley and the reggae sound.

Bob Marley died of cancer in 1981; he was just 36 years old. During his lifetime, many Jamaicans granted Marley the veneration usually accorded to their political and religious leaders. Shortly before his death, Marley was awarded the Order of Merit—Jamaica's third highest honor, and he is still spoken of in legendary terms. His birthday—February 6th—is recognized as Bob Marley Day.

our fortresslike towers are each 40 feet (12 meters) high with walls 3 feet (.9 meters) thick. The monumental construction hints that this castle was not only a residence but also a bastion against the fierce Maroons.

ARAWAK MUSEUM, 3 mi. (4.8 km) e. at White Marl on a 7-acre (2.8-hectare) Arawak settlement, has a small collection of Arawak Indian relics. Exhibits cover early migrations into the Western Hemisphere and the early history of Jamaica. Mon.-Thurs. 10-5, Fri. 10-4; closed Jan. 1, Good Friday, Easter and Dec. 25. Admission $3, children $1.50.

CATHEDRAL OF ST. JAMES, Barrett and Church Sts., was built by the Spanish about 1525 but destroyed and rebuilt by the British about 1660. The cathedral is the oldest in the former British colonies; it has served the Church of England for more than 300 years. Many English nobles and islanders are buried in the crypts beneath its floors. Daily dawn-dusk. Free.

JAMAICA ARCHIVES, on the town square, contains records dating from 1655. Mon.-Thurs. 9-4:30, Fri. 9-3:30.

JAMAICA FOLK MUSEUM AND OLD KING'S HOUSE is on the w. side of the town square. Rebuilt in 1802 following its destruction in 1761, only the Georgian facade remains of the house; the rest burned down in 1925. The house was once the official residence of colonial British governors. Early Jamaican relics are displayed in the coachhouse and stables. Mon.-Thurs. 10-5, Fri. 10-4; closed Jan. 1, Good Friday, Easter and Dec. 25. Admission is charged.

RODNEY MEMORIAL, on the n. side of the square, commemorates British admiral George Rodney and his 1782 victory over French forces off the shores of Dominica. His victory assured the safety of Jamaica and other British possessions in the Caribbean. The monument was moved to Kingston in 1872, but outraged Spanish Town citizens reclaimed it in 1889.

LODGINGS & RESTAURANTS

BLACK RIVER

LODGING

INVERCAULD GREAT HOUSE & HOTEL
◆ *Complex*

12/15-4/14	$61-92	XP $15
12/1-12/14 & 4/15-11/30	$50-80	XP $15

Location: Center on Rte A2. 66 High St (PO Box 12). Fax: 876/965-2751. **Terms:** F12; 10% service charge. **Facility:** 36 rooms. Simple decor. Older guest rooms in great house & modern villas. Overlooks south coast. Peaceful setting. 2 stories; exterior corridors; beachfront; 1 tennis court. **Services:** giftshop. **Recreation:** bicycles. **Cards:** AE, DS, JC, MC, VI.

(876/965-2750

FALMOUTH

LODGING

FISHERMAN'S INN
◆◆ *Motor Inn*

12/15-4/15	$100	XP $15
12/1-12/14 & 4/16-11/30	$90	XP $15

Location: 2 mi e on Rt A1. (PO Box 5). Fax: 876/954-4078. **Terms:** F8; Reserv deposit, 21 day notice; 10% service charge. **Facility:** 12 rooms. Pleasant modern small inn with well maintained rooms overlooking lagoon. Free boat transportation to secluded beach. 2 stories; interior/exterior corridors; oceanfront; beach access; boat dock. **Recreation:** swimming. Fee: charter fishing. **Cards:** AE, MC, VI.

(876/954-3427

FISHERMAN'S INN ON THE LUMINOUS LAGOON
◆◆ *Seafood*

Location: 2 mi e on Rt A1. **Hours:** 7-10:30 am, 11-1 & 6-10 pm. **Features:** casual dress; cocktails & lounge; a la carte. American & Jamaican cuisine served at poolside or inside dining room. Charming small inn with very pleasant service. Not fancy but worth visiting. 10% service charge & 15% government tax. **Cards:** AE, MC, VI.

(876/954-3427

TIME 'N' PLACE
◆ *Ethnic*   L $5-$18   D $5-$18

Location: 4 mi e on A1. **Hours:** 9 am-11 pm. **Features:** No A/C; casual dress; cocktails; a la carte. Real Jamaican food served in a palm thatched seaside bar or on the beach. Very casual & authentic island atmosphere & cuisine. **Cards:** MC, VI.

IRISH TOWN

LODGING

STRAWBERRY HILL
◆◆◆◆   *Cottage*

| 12/13-4/15 | $250-525 |
| 12/1-12/12 & 4/16-11/30 | $195-400 |

Location: N of Kingston on the Kingston Buff Bay Rd (B1), 6 mi s of Newcastle. (Irishtown PA St. Andrew Jamaica BWI). Fax: 876/944-8408. **Terms:** Reserv deposit, 14 day notice; handling fee imposed; $10 service charge. **Facility:** 14 rooms. Exquisite cottages & guest rooms, elegant rustic decor. Forest mountain setting 3100 feet above Kingston & the Caribbean. 2 two-bedroom units. 2 stories; exterior corridors; mountain view. **Services:** giftshop. Fee: massage. **Recreation:** hiking trails. **Some Rooms:** 4 efficiencies, 3 kitchens. **Cards:** AE, MC, VI.

(876/944-8400

KINGSTON—661,600

LODGINGS

COURTLEIGH HOTEL & SUITES
◆◆◆   *Hotel*

All Year $115-190   XP $10

Location: In center of New Kingdom. 85 Knutsford Blvd. Fax: 876/926-7744. **Terms:** $10 service charge. **Facility:** 118 rooms. 10 stories; interior corridors. **Some Rooms:** 20 kitchens. **Cards:** AE, MC, VI.

(876/929-9000

CROWNE PLAZA KINGSTON
◆◆◆   *Hotel*

All Year $159-295   XP $30

Location: 5 mi n in New Kingston. 17 mi from airport. (211A Constant Spring Rd). Fax: 876/925-5757. **Terms:** F19; Reserv deposit. **Facility:** 129 rooms. Very attractive public areas. Well furnished rooms. Nice location in Upper Kingston. Property meets AAA security requirements. 10 stories; interior corridors; 1 lighted tennis court. **Services:** giftshop. Fee: massage. **Some Rooms:** 6 efficiencies. **Cards:** AE, CB, DI, JC, MC, VI.

(876/925-7676

AAA SAVE FOUR SEASONS HOTEL
◆◆   *Hotel*

All Year $70-115   XP $15

Location: 14 mi from airport in New Kingston; off Half Way Tree Rd, on Ruthven Rd. 18 Ruthven Rd (PO Box 190). Fax: 876/929-5964. **Terms:** Reserv deposit, 3 day notice; $10 service charge; AP, BP, CP, MAP avail. **Facility:** 76 rooms. Quiet, refined hotel. Some large modern rooms, some with older decor. Nicely landscaped grounds. 2 stories; interior/exterior corridors. Fee: golf & tennis privileges at hotel nearby. **Dining:** Cocktails; dining room, see separate listing. **All Rooms:** combo or shower baths. **Cards:** AE, CB, DI, JC, MC, VI. **Special Amenities: Early check-in/late check-out and preferred room (subject to availability with advanced reservations).**

((876)929-7657

IVOR
◆◆   *Historic Country Inn*

All Year $115   XP $3

Location: 13 mi n of downtown Kingston from Papine tak Gordontown Rd to Skyline Dr; 6 mi nw via signs. Jacks Hi Rd (Jacks Hill Postal Agency). Fax: 876/702-0380 **Terms:** F4; Reserv deposit, 3 day notice; $12 servic charge. **Facility:** 3 rooms. Guest house & cottage circ 1870 in peaceful forested setting high above Kingston. Mag nificent view of city & harbor. Difficult drive, taxi recom mended. 1 two-bedroom unit. Closed 3 weeks i September; 1 story; interior/exterior corridors; mountain view. **Services:** area transportation. **Recreation:** hikin trails. **All Rooms:** shower baths. **Cards:** AE, MC, VI.

(876/702-027

MERIDIAN JAMAICA PEGASUS HOTEL
◆◆◆   *Hotel*

All Year $180   XP $3

Location: 3 mi n off Trafalgar Rd, in New Kingston o Knutsford Blvd,; 14 mi from airport. 81 Knutsford Blvd (PC Box 333, 5). Fax: 876/929-5855. **Terms:** F12; Reserv de posit; handling fee imposed; $9 service charge **Facility:** 325 rooms. Modern hotel in uptown business dis trict. Attractive public areas. All rooms with balcony, man with fine view of city & harbor. 3 two-bedroom units. 17 sto ries; interior corridors; mountain view; 2 lighted tenni courts; playground. **Services:** giftshop. **Recreation:** jog ging. **Cards:** AE, CB, DI, DS, MC, VI.

((876)926-3690

TERRA NOVA HOTEL
◆◆◆   *Hotel*

All Year $132   XP $2

Location: 14 mi from airport in New Kingston; off Hope R on Waterloo Rd. 17 Waterloo Rd. Fax: 876/929-4933 **Terms:** F12; Reserv deposit, 7 day notice. **Facility:** 3 rooms. Quiet, well-landscaped grounds. Attractive lobby & dining room. Very attractive well-maintained guest rooms. 2 stories; interior/exterior corridors. **Cards:** AE, DI, MC, VI.

((876)926-2211

AAA WYNDHAM KINGSTON HOTEL
◆◆◆   *Hotel*

All Year $185-210   XP $2

Location: 14 mi from airport on Knutsford Blvd betwee Trafalgar Rd & Oxford Rd in New Kingston. 77 Knutsfor Blvd (PO Box 112). Fax: 876/929-7439. **Terms:** F12; 10% service charge; monthly rates; CP avail. **Facility:** 30 rooms. Modern hotel in uptown business district. Fine public areas & attractive rooms. 18 stories; interior corridors; 2 lighted tennis courts; playground. **Dining:** 2 restaurants 6:30 am-11:30 pm; $10-$25; cocktails. **Services:** Fee: mas sage. **Cards:** AE, DI, MC, VI.

((876)926-5430

RESTAURANTS

BLUE MOUNTAIN INN
◆◆◆   *Continental*   D $25-$4C

Location: 9 mi ne on Rt B1, Gordon Town Rd. **Hours:** 7 pm, last seating at 9:30 pm. Closed major holidays & Sun **Reservations:** required. **Features:** No A/C; formal attire cocktails; a la carte. Fine dining in wooded mountain setting French service. 10% service charge. Taxi may be desirable due to location outside city. **Cards:** AE, MC, VI.

(876/927-1700

BULLSEYE STEAKHOUSE
◆ *Steakhouse*   L $8-$38   D $8-$38
Location: In New Kingston just n from Wyndham Kingston Hotel on Knutsford Blvd. 57 Knutsford Blvd. **Hours:** noon-10 pm, Fri & Sat-11 pm, Sun 4 pm-10 pm. **Features:** casual dress; children's menu; salad bar; beer & wine only; street parking; a la carte. Western style restaurant with good selection of steaks, seafood & salad bar. %15 tax. **Cards:** MC, VI.

(876/960-8609

DEVONSHIRE RESTAURANT
◆◆◆ *Continental*   L $8-$20   D $10-$33
Location: In New Kingston, jct Hope & Waterloo rds; on grounds of Devon House. 26 Hope Rd. **Hours:** noon-3 & 6-9:30 pm, Sat from 6 pm. Closed: Sun. **Reservations:** suggested. **Features:** No A/C; casual dress; cocktails & lounge; a la carte. Adjacent to historic Devon House. Gracious setting. Smart casual to formal dining. Excellent menu; orchard room features Thai cuisine. **Cards:** AE, MC, VI.

(876/929-7046

EL DORADO RESTAURANT
◆◆◆ *Continental*   L $14-$35   D $17-$35
Location: 14 mi from airport in New Kingston; off Hope Rd on Waterloo Rd; in Terra Nova Hotel. 17 Waterloo Rd. **Hours:** noon-3 & 7-10 pm. **Reservations:** suggested. **Features:** semi-formal attire; cocktails; a la carte. Fine dining in pleasant, restful setting; handsome dining room. Cordial well trained staff. 10% service charge & 12.5% government tax. **Cards:** AE, MC, VI.

(876/926-2211

FOUR SEASONS DINING ROOM
◆◆ *Continental*   L $5-$12   D $10-$22
Location: In New Kingston, off Half Way Tree Rd; in the Four Seasons Hotel. 18 Ruthven Rd. **Hours:** 7 am-10, noon-3 & 4-10 pm. **Reservations:** suggested. **Features:** casual dress; salad bar; cocktails & lounge; a la carte. Excellent Jamaican & Continental cuisine, German specialties. Veranda & inside dining. Pleasant, Old World atmosphere. 10% service charge 15% gratuity. **Cards:** AE, CB, DI, JC, MC, VI.

(876/926-7657

HEATHER'S
◆◆ *Continental*   L $6-$14   D $6-$14
Location: In New Kingston on Henning Rd off Oxford Rd, behind Wyndham & Pegasus Hotel. 9 Henning Rd 5. **Hours:** 10 am-11:30 pm. Closed: Sun. **Reservations:** suggested. **Features:** No A/C; casual dress; cocktails; a la carte. English & Indian specialties. Garden dining with covered seating. Pleasant, informal restaurant with friendly bar frequented by many American & other expatriates in Kingston. **Cards:** JC, MC, VI.

(876/926-2826

IVOR *Historical*
◆◆◆ *Continental*   L $8-$9   D $12-$18
Location: 15 mi n of downtown Kingston via Hope Rd; Gordantown Rd to Skyline Dr, 4 mi n via signs. Jacks Hill Rd. **Hours:** noon-2 & 7-9 pm. Closed: 12/24-12/28. **Reservations:** required. **Features:** No A/C; semi-formal attire; cocktails; a la carte. Magnificent view of Kingston from high in the forested mountains. Elegant food & gracious service. Difficult drive, taxi recommended. 10% GCT service charge. **Cards:** AE, MC, VI.

(876/977-0033

JADE GARDEN RESTAURANT
◆◆◆ *Chinese*   L $15-$30   D $15-$30
Location: In Sovereign Shopping Center, corner of Hope & Barbican rds. **Hours:** noon-10 pm. Closed major holidays. **Reservations:** suggested. **Features:** casual dress; carry-out; cocktails & lounge; a la carte. Elegant dining room. Extensive Chinese menu. On 2nd floor of shopping center. Smart casual attire. Government tax, $15. **Cards:** AE, JC, MC, VI.

(876/978-3476

MONTEGO BAY—70,000

LODGINGS

COMFORT INN AND SUITES
[FYI] *Apartment Motor Inn*

12/20-4/17	$138-330	XP $24
12/1-12/19 & 4/18-11/30	$96-282	XP $24

Under major renovation. **Location:** 10.5 mi e on A1; 8.5 mi e of airport. (PO Box 55). Fax: 876/953-3062. **Terms:** F16; Reserv deposit, 21 day notice, 14 day off season. **Facility:** 126 rooms. A mix of small studio & larger 1-& 2-bedroom apartments on the ocean. Attractive private beach. 2-bedroom units are for up to 4 persons. Rates are all-inclusive. Renovations scheduled for completion July, 1998; 3 stories, no elevator; interior/exterior corridors; oceanfront; beach; playground. Fee: 2 lighted tennis courts. **Services:** giftshop; area transportation. **Recreation:** swimming. Fee: horseback riding. **All Rooms:** efficiencies. **Cards:** AE, DI, MC, VI. *(See color ad inside front cover)*

(876/953-3250

AAA SAVE COYABA
◆◆◆◆ *Motor Inn*

12/16-4/15	$240-340	XP $30
12/1-12/15 & 4/16-11/30	$150-210	XP $30

Location: 6.3 mi e on Rt A1 4.2 mi e of airport. (Little River PO). Fax: 876/953-2244. **Terms:** F12; Reserv deposit, 14 day notice; BP, CP, MAP avail; package plans. **Facility:** 50 rooms. Very attractive public areas, beach pool. Handsome guest rooms. Responsive staff. All inclusive plans avail; 3 stories, no elevator; interior/exterior corridors; oceanfront; beach, whirlpool; 1 lighted tennis court; boat dock. Fee: golf, tennis instruction. **Dining:** 2 restaurants, cafeteria; 7 am-10 pm; $16-$23; cocktails. **Services:** giftshop. Fee: massage. **Recreation:** swimming, boating, paddleboats, sailboating, snorkeling & equipment, windsurfing, kayaks. Fee: scuba diving. **Cards:** AE, MC, VI. **Special Amenities:** Early check-in/late check-out and free room upgrade (subject to availability with advanced reservations).

((876)953-9150

DATURA VILLA (READING)
◆◆ *Country Inn*

12/15-4/15	$1400-3000
12/1-12/14 & 4/16-11/30	$1000-2400

Location: 3 mi w on A1, 0.3 mi s on Long Hill Rd, 0.3 mi w on private rd via signs. St James Parish, Longhill Rd (61 Irving Place, NEW YORK, NY, 10003). Fax: 876/952-1236. **Terms:** Reserv deposit, 60 day notice. **Facility:** 5 rooms. Country guest house on hillside overlooking Montego Bay. 9 acres of natural landscape. House comes fully staffed with cook/housekeeper, maids, laundress & gardner. Clean simple decor & furnishings. Rates for up to 4 persons. Housekeeper will purchase groceries but guests pay the bill. House can accommodate up to 10 persons. Reservations (212) 982-7678; 1 story; exterior corridors; oceanview; 1 tennis court. **All Rooms:** combo or shower baths.

(876/952-1236

HALF MOON GOLF, TENNIS AND BEACH CLUB
◆◆◆◆ *Resort Complex*

12/15-4/15	$330-1100	XP $80
12/1-12/14 & 4/16-11/30	$220-600	XP $50

Location: Oceanfront; 7.5 mi e on Rt A1; 5 mi e of airport. (PO Box 80). Fax: 876/953-2731. **Terms:** F12; Reserv deposit, 30 day notice, in winter; 14 day in summer; AP, BP, CP, MAP avail; package plans. **Facility:** 425 rooms. Beautifully landscaped grounds. Very inviting rooms with balcony or patio. Luxury cottages & villas fully staffed, 50 with private pools. Villas can be rented as multi or one bedroom units. 3 two-bedroom villas for up to 4 persons $800; off season $490. All inclusive plan avail; 1-2 stories; interior/exterior corridors; oceanfront; 18 holes golf, putting green, 18 hole putting green,; beach, wading pool, sauna, steamroom, whirlpool; 13 tennis courts (7 lighted), squash-4 courts,; playground. Fee: golf instruction; tennis instruction. **Dining:** Dining room, 5 restaurants; 7:30 am-6 & 7:30-9:30 pm; $30-$45; cocktails; open-air dining room & terrace, dancing; afternoon tea; also, Sugar Mill Restaurant, see separate listing. **Services:** giftshop. Fee: massage. **Recreation:** swimming; hiking trails, jogging, internationally certified croquet court. Fee: fishing, scuba diving/snorkeling & equipment, windsurfing; horseback riding, aerobic instruction. Rental: sailboats; bicycles. **Some Rooms:** 64 kitchens. **Cards:** AE, CB, DI, JC, MC, VI. *(See color ad below)*

((876)953-2211

HOLIDAY INN SUNSPREE RESORT MONTEGO BAY
◆◆◆ *Resort Motor Inn*

12/21-4/19	$326	XP $14
12/1-12/20 & 4/20-11/30	$175	XP $2

Location: 7 mi e on Rt A1; 4.7 mi e of airport. (PO Box 48 Rose Hall). Fax: 876/953-2840. **Terms:** F12; Reserv deposit, 3 day notice; handling fee imposed. **Facility:** 52 rooms. 4 interconnected buildings on ocean. Balcony or patio. Very good recreational facilities. 4 stories; interior/exterior corridors; oceanfront; beach; 4 lighted tennis courts playground. **Services:** giftshop. Fee: massage. **Recreation:** swimming, charter fishing, sailboating, snorkeling & equipment, windsurfing. Fee: fishing, scuba diving & equipment. **Cards:** AE, DI, MC, VI.

(876/953-248

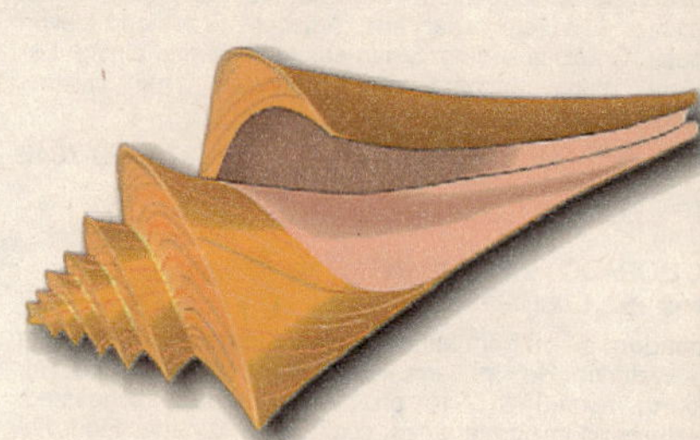

ROUND HILL HOTEL AND VILLAS
◆◆◆◆ *Resort Complex*

12/15-4/15	$390-780	XP $65
12/1-12/14 & 4/16-11/30	$220-480	XP $60

Location: 8.7 mi w on Rt A1; 10.7 mi w of airport. (PO Box 64). Fax: 876/956-7505. **Terms:** Reserv deposit, 30 day notice, 14 day in summer; weekly rates; AP, BP, CP, MAP avail; package plans; 10 night min stay, 12/22-1/2. **Facility:** 110 rooms. Secluded location. Spacious hillside grounds & gardens to the sea. Very attractive traditional guest rooms & elegant villas with maid & gardner; 29 villas with private pool. TV's & VCR's avail on request; 1-2 stories, no elevator; exterior corridors; oceanfront; beach; 5 tennis courts (2 lighted). **Dining:** Dining room; terrace; 7:30-10:30 am, 12:30-2:30 & 7:30-9:30 pm; $20-$50; cocktails. **Services:** giftshop; complimentary evening beverages, Tues; area transportation, to Montego Bay & golf. **Recreation:** swimming, snorkeling & equipment. Fee: charter fishing, scuba diving, waterskiing, windsurfing, glass-bottom boat; scuba instruction, padi certification. Rental: paddleboats, sailboats. **Some Rooms:** 27 kitchens. **Cards:** AE, CB, DI, JC, MC, VI.

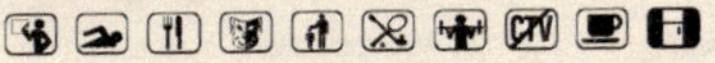

((876)956-7050

SANDALS INN
◆◆ *Resort Complex*

12/24-3/31	$2150-2405
4/1-11/30	$1995-2235
12/1-12/23	$1080-2225

Location: 2 mi w of Montego Bay International Airport. Kent Ave (PO Box 412). Fax: 876/952-6913. **Terms:** Age restrictions may apply; reserv deposit, 7 day notice; package plans; 3 night min stay. **Facility:** 52 rooms. Across the road from a small beach with tropical garden setting. Couples only. 3 stories, no elevator; interior corridors; oceanview; saunas, whirlpool; 1 lighted tennis court. **Dining:** 2 dining rooms; guest only; cocktails. **Services:** giftshop; complimentary evening beverages. **Recreation:** swimming, canoeing, fishing, sailboating, scuba diving, snorkeling, waterskiing, windsurfing, hobie cats. **Cards:** AE, MC, VI.

((876)952-4140

SANDALS MONTEGO BAY
◆◆ *Resort Complex*

12/1-12/23 & 4/2-11/30	$2270-2825
12/24-4/1	$2350-3200

Location: 5 mi e of airport, 0.5 mi w on Kent Ave via signs. (PO Box 100). Fax: 876/952-0816. **Terms:** Age restrictions may apply; reserv deposit, 21 day notice; 3 night min stay. **Facility:** 244 rooms. Couples only resort. Excellent recreational facilities. Guest rooms & cottages. Room decor ranges from good to excellent. 3 stories; interior/exterior corridors; oceanfront; putting green; beach, whirlpools; racquetball court, 4 lighted tennis courts. **Dining:** 4 dining rooms; guests only; day or evening passes for vistors; cocktails. **Services:** giftshop; complimentary evening beverages. Fee: massage. **Recreation:** swimming, boating, fishing, paddleboats, sailboating, scuba diving/snorkeling & equipment, waterskiing, windsurfing; sports court. **Cards:** AE, MC, VI.

((876)952-5510

SANDALS ROYAL JAMAICAN
◆◆◆ *Resort Complex*

12/24-4/1	$2770-3800
12/1-12/23 & 4/2-11/30	$2660-3690

Location: 5.5 mi e on Rt A1; 4 mi e of airport. (PO Box 167). Fax: 876/953-2788. **Terms:** Age restrictions may apply; reserv deposit, 21 day notice, 14 days off season; 3 night min stay, off season. **Facility:** 190 rooms. Tropical garden setting. Rates include taxes & gratuities. 2-3 stories; interior/exterior corridors; oceanfront; golf privileges; beach, saunas, whirlpools; 3 tennis courts (2 lighted). **Dining:** 4 restaurants; 7:30-10 am, 12:30-2 & 6:30-3 am, guest only; health conscious menu; cocktails; patio dining; afternoon tea. **Services:** giftshop; complimentary evening beverages. **Recreation:** swimming, canoeing, scuba diving/snorkeling & equipment, waterskiing, windsurfing. Fee: charter fishing, fishing, kayaks, glass-bottom boat. Rental: paddleboats, sailboats. **Cards:** AE, MC, VI.

((876)953-2231

WYNDHAM ROSE HALL GOLF & BEACH RESORT
◆◆◆ *Resort Hotel*

1/3-4/4	$154-169	XP $23
12/1-12/19 & 4/5-11/30	$113-128	XP $23

Location: 10 mi e on Rt A1; 8 mi e of airport. (PO Box 999, ROSE HALL). Fax: 876/953-2617. **Terms:** F12; Open 12/1-12/19 & 1/3-11/30; 10% service charge. **Facility:** 488 rooms. Attractive setting, beautifully landscaped grounds. Pretty tropical decor in guest rooms. Excellent beach facilities. 7 stories; interior corridors; oceanfront; beach; 6 lighted tennis courts; playground. Fee: 18 holes golf. **Services:** giftshop. Fee: massage. **Recreation:** swimming, sailboating, cnorkeling, windsurfing; jogging. Fee: charter fishing, scuba diving. **Cards:** AE, DI, MC, VI.

((876)953-2650

RESTAURANTS

AMBROSIA RESTAURANT
◆◆◆ *Continental*   D $15-$30

Location: 10 mi e on Rt A1; 8 mi e of airport; in Wyndham Rose Hall Golf & Beach Resort. **Hours:** 6:30 pm-10 pm. Closed: Wed. **Reservations:** suggested. **Features:** No A/C; casual dress; cocktails & lounge; valet parking. Beautiful setting overlooking golf course & ocean. Mediterranean & regional cuisine. **Cards:** AE, CB, DI, DS, JC, MC, VI.

(876/953-2650

THE GEORGIAN HOUSE   *Historical*
◆◆ *Continental*   L $5-$7   D $24-$33

Location: Center; just ne of Sam Sharpe Sq, corner of Orange & Union sts. 2 Orange St. **Hours:** 11 am-3 & 6-11 pm. **Reservations:** suggested. **Features:** casual dress; cocktails; area transportation. 18th-century home housing restaurant & art gallery. Very attractive dining room. Hours may vary off season. **Cards:** AE, DI, MC, VI.

(876/952-0632

JULIA'S RESTAURANT
◆◆◆ *Italian*   D $35-$45

Location: 3 mi sw. Steep climb up Boque Hill Rd off Route A1. **Hours:** 5 pm-10:30 pm. **Reservations:** required. **Features:** No A/C; casual dress; cocktails & lounge; valet parking; area transportation. 800 ft above Montego Bay-very steep switch backroad. Taxi recommended. 15% tax & 10% svc chg. **Cards:** AE, MC, VI.

(809/952-1772

LYCHEE GARDEN
◆◆ *Chinese*   **L** $5-$18   **D** $9-$25
Location: Downtown s of Sam Sharp Square East St off Union St. 18 East St. **Hours:** 11:30 am-10 pm, Sat & Sun from 5 pm. **Reservations:** suggested. **Features:** casual dress; carryout; cocktails & lounge; area transportation; a la carte. Downtown restaurant. Simple decor, extensive menu. **Cards:** AE, MC, VI.

(876/952-9428

MARGUERITE'S
◆◆◆ *Seafood*   **D** $15-$30
Location: 0.7 mi n; 2 mi s of airport just s of Doctor's Cave Beach. Gloucester Ave. **Hours:** 6 pm-10:30 pm. **Reservations:** suggested. **Features:** No A/C; casual dress; cocktails & lounge; street parking; area transportation; a la carte. Overlooking bay; beautiful sunsets. Pub style lunches in adjacent Margaritaville sports bar. 10% service charge & 15% government tax. **Cards:** AE, MC, VI.

(876/952-4777

SUGAR MILL RESTAURANT
◆◆◆ *Continental*   **L** $9-$19   **D** $15-$35
Location: 1.4 mi e, 5 mi e of Airport on Rt A1, 1 mi e of main entrance; in the Half Moon Resort. **Hours:** noon-3 & 7-10 pm. **Reservations:** required. **Features:** semi-formal attire; cocktails & lounge; entertainment; a la carte. Innovative menu offers wide variety of European & Caribbean dishes. Fine setting overlooking golf course & the sea. 10% service charge & 15% government tax. **Cards:** AE, MC, VI.

(876/953-2314

NEGRIL—1,500

LODGINGS

BEACHES-NEGRIL
◆◆◆ *Resort Hotel*
12/19-3/20	$3470-4620	XP $875
12/1-12/18 & 3/21-11/30	$3320-4270	XP $875

Location: 2 mi e from center on Route A1. Norman Manley Blvd (PO Box 12). Fax: 809/957-9269. **Terms:** D16; Reserv deposit. **Facility:** 205 rooms. All inclusive family resort with excellenct & most attractive dining & recreational facilities. Handsome grounds & great beach. One child only; adult only restaurant. Rates are all inclusive. US office 4950 SW 72nd Ave 2nd floor, Miami, FL 33155 (800-726-3257); 3 stories, no elevator; exterior corridors; oceanfront; miniature golf; beach; 2 lighted tennis courts; playground. **Recreation:** swimming, paddleboats, scuba diving/snorkeling & equipment; bicycles. **Cards:** AE, DI, MC, VI.

(809/957-9270

◆ CHARELA INN
◆◆◆ *Motor Inn*
12/15-4/30	$154-187	XP $25-40
12/1-12/14 & 5/1-11/30	$105-124	XP $25

Location: 1.5 mi e on Rt A1. (PO Box 33). Fax: 876/957-4414. **Terms:** F9; Reserv deposit, 21 day notice, 14 day in summer; handling fee imposed; 10% service charge; MAP avail. **Facility:** 49 rooms. Beachfront lodging; attractive guest rooms & very pleasant restaurant. Library & TV room. 2 two-bedroom units. 3 night min stay 5/1-12/14, 5 night 12/15-4/15; 2 stories; exterior corridors; oceanfront; beach. **Dining:** Restaurant; $11-$32; cocktails; entertainment Thurs & Sat evenings; restaurant, see separate listing. **Services:** giftshop; complimentary evening beverages. **Recreation:** swimming, sailboating, windsurfing, 3 hour boat cruise on Tue, kayaks. **All Rooms:** combo or shower baths. **Some Rooms:** whirlpools. **Cards:** MC, VI. **Special Amenities: Early check-in/late check-out and free newspaper.**

((876)957-4648

COCO LA PALM
◆◆◆ *Hotel*
12/15-4/14	$160-190	XP $15
12/1-12/14 & 4/15-11/30	$130-150	XP $15

Location: 1.5 mi e from center on Rt A1. Norman Manley Blvd. Fax: 876/957-3460. **Terms:** F12; Check-in 4 pm; reserv deposit, 14 day notice; 10% service charge. **Facility:** 42 rooms. Oceanfront hotel on beautiful beach. Modern well equipped guest rooms & public facilities. 2 stories; exterior corridors; beach. **Recreation:** swimming. **All Rooms:** shower baths. **Cards:** AE, DI, DS, MC, VI.

((876)957-4227

◆ GRAND LIDO NEGRIL
◆◆◆◆ *Resort Motor Inn*
12/20-3/27	$5060
12/1-12/19, 3/28-6/12 & 10/17-11/30	$4360
6/13-10/16	$4140

Location: 5 mi e on Rt A1. (PO Box 88). Fax: 876/957-5517. **Terms:** Age restrictions may apply; handling fee imposed; 3 night min stay. **Facility:** 210 rooms. Handsome all-inclusive resort. On "7 Mile Beach" at Bloody Bay. Rates include all taxes & gratuities. Meets AAA guest room security requirements. 2 stories; interior/exterior corridors; oceanfront; beach, whirlpools; 4 tennis courts (2 lighted). Fee: sauna, steam room. **Dining:** Dining room, 3 restaurants; 24 hours; cocktails. **Services:** giftshop; complimentary evening beverages; area transportation, to Montego Bay. Fee: massage. **Recreation:** swimming, sailboating, scuba diving/snorkeling & equipment, waterskiing, windsurfing, kayaks, glass-bottom boat; bicycles, aerobic instruction. **Some Rooms:** whirlpools. **Cards:** AE, DI, MC, VI. **Special Amenities: Early check-in/late check-out and free breakfast.** *(See color ad p 180)*

((876)957-5010

◆ NEGRIL TREE HOUSE RESORT
◆◆ *Motor Inn*
12/16-4/15	$115-145	XP $15
12/1-12/15 & 4/16-11/30	$85-115	XP $15

Location: 2.5 mi n on A1. Norman Manley Blvd (PO Box 29). Fax: 876/957-4386. **Terms:** F12; Reserv deposit, 14 day notice; handling fee imposed; 10% service charge. **Facility:** 67 rooms. Beachfront lodging with casual, lively atmosphere. Twin bed rooms can be converted into kings. 1 two-bedroom unit. 2 stories; exterior corridors; oceanfront; beach, whirlpool. **Dining:** Restaurant; 7 am-midnight; to 11 pm in summer; $12-$22; cocktails. **Recreation:** swimming, full water sports. **All Rooms:** combo or shower baths. **Some Rooms:** 18 efficiencies. **Cards:** AE, MC, VI. **Special Amenities: Early check-in/late check-out and free room upgrade (subject to availability with advanced reservations).**

((876)957-4287

ROCK CLIFF HOTEL
◆ *Motor Inn*
12/15-4/30	$115-140	XP $30
12/1-12/14 & 5/1-11/30	$80-90	XP $20

Location: 2 mi w on Lighthouse Rd. West End Rd (PO Box 67). Fax: 876/957-4108. **Terms:** F12; Reserv deposit, 14 day notice; handling fee imposed; 10% service charge. **Facility:** 33 rooms. Pleasant, simply furnished guest rooms, most with excellent oceanviews. Attractive setting on cliffs; wonderful sunsets. 2 two-bedroom unit with kitchen, $290, $190 off season for up to 6 persons; 2 stories; exterior corridors; oceanfront. **Services:** giftshop; area transportation. **Recreation:** swimming. Fee: scuba diving. Rental: scuba equipment. **Cards:** AE, MC, VI.

(876/957-4331

AAA RONDEL VILLAGE
◆◆◆ *Complex*

12/15-4/16	$100-200	XP $25-30
12/1-12/14 & 4/17-11/30	$70-145	XP $20-25

Location: 1 mi e on Rt A1. (PO Box 96). Fax: 876/957-4915. **Terms:** F10; Reserv deposit, 31 day notice, 22 day in summer; 10% service charge; BP, MAP avail. **Facility:** 16 rooms. Attractive beachfront, garden villas & guest rooms on well-landscaped grounds. Some gardenview guest rooms across road from beach. 4 two-bedroom units. High rate for 2-bedroom villa for up to 4 persons (capacity 6); 1-2 stories; exterior corridors; oceanfront; beach, whirlpool. **Dining:** Restaurant; 7:30 am-10:45 & 6:30-9:30 pm; Cafe 2 pm-9 pm; Snack Bar 10:30 am-6 pm; $5-$15; cocktails; beach bar. **Recreation:** swimming, full water sports avail. **Some Rooms:** 8 kitchens, whirlpools. **Cards:** AE, JC, MC, VI.

((876)957-4413

AAA SANDALS NEGRIL BEACH RESORT AND SPA
◆◆◆ *Resort Motor Inn*

12/23-3/31	$3220-3920
12/1-12/22 & 4/1-11/30	$3030-3680

Location: 4.5 mi e on Rt A1. (PO Box 12). Fax: 876/957-5338. **Terms:** Age restrictions may apply; reserv deposit, 21 day notice; handling fee imposed; 3 night min stay. **Facility:** 223 rooms. On "7 Mile Beach". Attractively landscaped grounds. Rates include all taxes & gratuities, excluding departure tax. 2-3 stories, no elevator; interior/exterior corridors; oceanfront; beach, saunas, steamrooms, whirlpools; racquetball court, 4 lighted tennis courts. Fee: spa facilities. **Dining:** 4 restaurants; 7:30-10 am, 12:30-2 & 6-10 pm, guests only. Breakfast, 8-11 am; snack grille 10 am-6 pm & 11 pm-3 am; cocktails. **Services:** giftshop, complimentary evening beverages. Fee: massage. **Recreation:** swimming, canoeing, paddleboats, sailboating, scuba diving/snorkeling & equipment, windsurfing, kayaks, glass-bottom boats; sports court. Fee: charter fishing. **Cards:** AE, MC, VI.

((876)957-5216

AAA SWEPT AWAY-NEGRIL
◆◆◆ *Resort Complex*

12/24-3/31	$3332-4200
12/1-12/23	$2912-3640
4/1-11/30	$3150-3990

Location: 5 mi e on Rt A1. (PO Box 77). Fax: 876/957-4060. **Terms:** Age restrictions may apply; reserv deposit, 21 day notice; 3 night min stay. **Facility:** 134 rooms. Very attractive beach villas. Elaborate sports complex. All inclusive rates couples only age 18 & over. 2 stories; exterior corridors; oceanfront; beach, sauna, steamrooms, whirlpool; racquetball courts, 10 lighted tennis courts, tennis instruction, squash courts, 5 clay tennis courts, 5 hard surface. **Dining:** Dining room, 2 restaurants; 7:30-10:30 am, 12:30-2:30 & 7:30-10 pm; $12-$30; also, Feathers, see separate listing. **Services:** giftshop. Fee: massage. **Recreation:** swimming, charter fishing, sailboating, scuba diving, snorkeling, waterskiing, sunfishing; bicycles, jogging, sports court. Fee: fishing; horseback riding, beauty salon, spa. **All Rooms:** shower baths. **Cards:** AE, DI, MC, VI.

((876)957-4061

Restaurants

AAA CHARELA INN RESTAURANT
◆◆◆ *French*

L $11-$25   D $11-$30

Location: 1.5 mi e on Rt A1; in Charela Inn. **Hours:** 7:30 am-10 pm. **Reservations:** suggested; in winter. **Features:** No A/C; casual dress; cocktails & lounge. Terrace & indoor dining by the sea. Very pleasant atmosphere, well-prepared food. Regional specialties. 12.5% service charge added. **Cards:** MC, VI.

(876/957-4648

COSMO'S SEAFOOD RESTAURANT
◆ *Seafood*

L $6-$30   D $6-$30

Location: 2 mi e on Rt A1. **Hours:** 11:30 am-5 pm & 6:30-10 pm; bar opens at 9 am. Closed: 4/2 & 12/25. **Features:** No A/C; casual dress; cocktails & lounge; a la carte. Authentic well-prepared native cuisine in grass-roofed beachside setting. Unpretentious; very informal service. 15% tax & 10% service charge. **Cards:** MC, VI.

(876/957-4784

FEATHERS
◆◆◆ *Continental*

D $15-$30

Location: 5 mi e on Rt A1; in Swept Away-Negril. **Hours:** 7 pm-11 pm. Closed: Mon. **Reservations:** suggested. **Features:** No A/C; health conscious menu; cocktails & lounge; entertainment. Pleasant dining room features excellent diet conscious menu. Smart casual attire appropriate for dinner. 15% GCT & 10% service charge added for guests not staying at hotel. **Cards:** AE, DI, MC, VI.

(876/957-4062

LIFEBOAT RESTAURANT
◆◆ *Seafood*

L $4-$20   D $12-$23

Location: 2 mi w on West End Rd (Lighthouse Rd); in Mariner's Inn. **Hours:** 7:30 am-11 pm. **Features:** No A/C; casual dress; cocktails & lounge; a la carte. Informal dining on cliffside terrace overlooking the ocean. Very well prepared seafood. 10% service charge added. **Cards:** MC, VI.

(876/957-0393

RICK'S CAFE
◆ *Seafood*

L $11-$30   D $11-$30

Location: 3 mi w on Lighthouse Rd. **Hours:** 2 pm-10 pm. **Features:** No A/C; casual dress; cocktails & lounge. Popular spot on a rocky cliff. Locals & visitors can be seen diving into clear grotto waters. Features fresh seafood. Very informal. Happy hour 8 pm-10 pm. 22.5% GCT/service charge.

(876/957-4335

OCHO RIOS—7,800

LODGINGS

CIBONEY OCHO RIOS-A RADISSON VILLA, SPA & BEACH RESORT
◆◆◆◆ *Resort Complex*

12/21-1/3	$3416-5846
2/1-4/4	$3066-5496
12/1-12/20, 1/4-1/31 & 4/5-11/30	$2716-5146

Location: 1 mi e on Rt 3A. Main St (PO Box 728). Fax: 876/974-5838. **Terms:** Age restrictions may apply; reserv deposit, 14 day notice; handling fee imposed; daily rates; package plans; 3 night min stay. **Facility:** 289 rooms. Fine secluded setting; beautiful grounds. Elegant villas & modern, attractive hotel rooms. Superb facilities. 33 two-bedroom units. Rates are all inclusive. 3 bedroom villa rates for up to 6 persons; 2 stories; interior/exterior corridors; oceanview; golf privileges; beach, saunas, whirlpools; 6 lighted tennis courts, tennis instruction. **Dining:** 4 dining rooms, 2 cafeterias; 7 am-10 pm, guests only; snack bar open to 2 am; cocktails. **Services:** giftshop. Fee: massage. **Recreation:** swimming, scuba diving & equipment, windsurfing, kayak, glass-bottom boat; squash court. **Some Rooms:** 224 kitchens, whirlpools. **Cards:** AE, DI, MC, VI. **Special Amenities: Early check-in/late check-out and preferred room (subject to availability with advanced reservations).** *(See color ad p 179)*

((876)974-1027

COMFORT SUITES-OCHO RIOS
◆◆◆ *Motel*

12/16-4/15 & 7/1-7/31	$165	XP $20
8/1-8/31	$150	XP $20
12/1-12/15, 4/16-6/30 & 9/1-11/30	$130	XP $20

Location: 0.3 mi w of downtown on DaCosta Dr up steep hill via signs. 17 DaCosta Dr. Fax: 876/974-8070. **Terms:** F12; Reserv deposit; $10 service charge; AP, MAP avail; package plans; pets. **Facility:** 79 rooms. Attractive modern one & two bedroom suites on hillside overlooking Ocho Rios Harbor, excellent landscaping. 24 two-bedroom units. 6 one bedroom units without kitchen avail. Kitchen utensils avail; 3 stories; exterior corridors; whirlpool; 2 lighted tennis courts. **Dining:** Restaurant; 7:30 am-10 pm; $10-$20; cocktails. **Services:** giftshop; area transportation, shuttle to beach. Fee: massage. **Some Rooms:** 73 kitchens, whirlpools. **Cards:** AE, MC, VI. *(See color ad inside front cover)*

((876)974-8050

COUPLES
◆◆◆ *Resort Hotel*

12/21-3/28	$3120-4250
12/1-12/20 & 3/29-11/30	$2850-3860

Location: 5 mi e on Rt A3. (PO Box 330, ST. ANN). Fax: 876/975-4439. **Terms:** Age restrictions may apply; reserv deposit, 22 day notice; handling fee imposed; 3 night min stay. **Facility:** 212 rooms. Fine beachfront setting, very attractive rooms & facilities. A few small rooms. Some with balcony. Rates include taxes & gratuities. Off shore island with pool, whirlpool & bar. 3-5 stories; interior corridors; oceanfront; 18 holes golf; beach; 5 tennis courts (3 lighted). **Services:** giftshop; area transportation. Fee: massage. **Recreation:** swimming, sailboating, snorkeling, waterskiing, windsurfing; bicycles, horseback riding. Fee: fishing. **All Rooms:** combo or shower baths. **Cards:** AE, MC, VI.

(876/975-4271

THE ENCHANTED GARDEN
◆◆◆ *Resort Complex*

12/23-4/15	$300-430
12/1-12/22 & 4/16-11/30	$250-380

Location: From jct A3 just w on Da Costa Rd to Eden Bower Rd s up steep hill via signs. (PO Box 284). Fax: 876/974-5823. **Terms:** Age restrictions may apply; reserv deposit, 21 day notice; 3 night min stay. **Facility:** 113 rooms. Very attractive guest rooms set in 20 acre nature preserve overlooking Ocho Rios. 14 waterfalls, aviary & seaquarium. Some steep walkways. 40 plunge pools with 1-bedroom units; 3 stories, no elevator; interior/exterior corridors; oceanview; beach access; 2 lighted tennis courts. Fee: 18 holes golf. **Services:** giftshop. Fee: massage. **Recreation:** swimming. Rental: boats. **All Rooms:** combo or shower baths. **Cards:** AE, DI, MC, VI.

(876/974-1400

FISHERMAN'S POINT
◆◆ *Condo Motor Inn*

12/16-4/15	$120-130	XP $50
12/1-12/15 & 4/16-11/30	$100-110	XP $30

Location: Center on Turtle Beach; adjacent to cruise ship terminal. (PO Box 747). Fax: 876/974-2894. **Terms:** F12; Reserv deposit, 14 day notice; handling fee imposed. **Facility:** 55 rooms. Very attractive setting. Apartment decor varies. All units good size. 6 two-bedroom units. 3-bed units $180-$255 12/16-4/15; $120-$165 4/16-11/30; 3-4 stories, no elevator; interior/exterior corridors; oceanfront; beach; 2 lighted tennis courts; playground. **Recreation:** swimming. **All Rooms:** kitchens, combo or shower baths. **Cards:** AE, MC, VI.

((876)974-5317

GRAND LIDO SAN SOUCI
◆◆◆◆ *Resort Hotel*

12/16-4/15	$610-940	
12/1-12/15 & 4/16-11/30	$590-720	XP $70

Location: 3 mi e on Rt A3. (PO Box 103). Fax: 876/994-1544. **Terms:** Age restrictions may apply; reserv deposit, 7 day notice; handling fee imposed; weekly rates; package plans; 3 night min stay. **Facility:** 146 rooms. Fine beachfront lodging with excellent recreational facilities, well decorated guest rooms & a responsive staff. An all inclusive resort. 82 units with extra shower. 2-3 stories, no elevator; exterior corridors; oceanfront; golf privileges; beach, sauna, whirlpools; 2 lighted tennis courts. **Dining:** 3 restaurants, cafeteria; 7:30 am-9:30 pm, dress code casual elegance, beach grill & terrace dining 2 nights a week; health conscious menu; cocktails; afternoon tea. **Services:** giftshop; massage. **Recreation:** swimming, sailboating, scuba diving, snorkeling, waterskiing, windsurfing, glass bottom boats, water tricycles; bicycles, aerobic instruction, extensive spa facilities, includes mineral baths, yoga. **Some Rooms:** 3 kitchens, whirlpools. **Cards:** AE, DI, MC, VI. **Special Amenities: Early check-in/late check-out and free breakfast.** *(See color ad p 180)*

((876)994-1206

HIBISCUS LODGE HOTEL
◆◆ *Motor Inn*

12/15-4/30	$87-96	XP $37
12/1-12/14 & 5/1-11/30	$77-87	XP $30

Location: 0.5 mi e on Rt A3. (PO Box 52). Fax: 876/974-1874. **Terms:** F8; Reserv deposit, 14 day notice; $10 service charge. **Facility:** 26 rooms. Charming & immaculate island style guestrooms simply decorated. Very attractive grounds overlooking the sea. 2 stories; exterior corridors; oceanfront; whirlpool; 1 lighted tennis court. **Dining:** Restaurant; 7:30 am-10, noon-2:30 & 6-10 pm; $9-$30; also, The Almond Tree Restaurant, see separate listing. **Recreation:** swimming. **All Rooms:** combo or shower baths. **Cards:** AE, CB, DI, JC, MC, VI. **Special Amenities: Free breakfast and free room upgrade (subject to availability with advanced reservations).**

((876)974-2676

WELCOME TO THE REAL JAMAICA.™

Real privacy. Real luxury. Really great food.
At Ciboney, the Caribbean's Premier AAA Four-Diamond all-inclusive beach resort.

Travel agents call your favorite tour operator or 800-777-7800. Consumers call your AAA travel agent or 800-333-3333.

PASS IT ON!

If others you know are planning a trip, tell them about the world's largest travel agency: **AAA.**

Find yourself on a sunset cruise, in a mineral spa or putting for birdie on a championship golf course. Find yourself in paradise at one of SuperClubs' three magnificent Grand Lido Resorts.

Lost and found for the soul.

Grand Lido Negril and Grand Lido Sans Souci are both recipients of the AAA 4-Diamond Award. The triple crown will soon be complete with our newest resort, Grand Lido Braco.

At Grand Lido Resorts, you'll discover a Super-Inclusive world of sumptuous cuisine, gracious service and infinite possibilities. Even free weddings. All for one upfront price and tipping is never permitted.

If this sounds like what you're looking for, you've found yourself in the right place.

Call your travel agent or SuperClubs at 1-800-GO-SUPER/Ext. 7182. Contact us on the Internet at: www.superclubs.com

Grand Lido
RESORTS
Negril · Sans Souci · Braco

JAMAICA INN
◆◆◆◆   *Motor Inn*

12/16-3/15	$525-1200
3/16-4/15	$450-1100
12/1-12/15 & 4/16-11/30	$275-555

Location: Oceanfront; 1.7 mi e on Rt A3, just n off road to Shaw Park. (PO Box 1). Fax: 876/974-2449. **Terms:** Age restrictions may apply; reserv deposit, 14 day notice; $10 service charge. **Facility:** 45 rooms. Charming & tranquil setting. Gracefully furnished guest rooms with balcony & patio all overlooking the ocean. Excellent service. Private beach. Refined ambiance recalls Jamaica of Old. Jackets preferred in winter months in dining room; tax included in rates; 2 stories; exterior corridors; beach. **Recreation:** swimming, sailboating, snorkeling & equipment. **Cards:** AE, MC, VI.

((876)974-2514

PLANTATION INN
◆◆◆   *Motor Inn*

12/15-3/14	$215-785	XP $44
12/1-12/14	$130-455	XP $44
3/15-11/30	$130-310	XP $44

Location: 1.5 mi e on Rt A3. (PO Box 2). Fax: 876/974-5912. **Terms:** F12; Reserv deposit, 14 day notice, 7 day off season. **Facility:** 80 rooms. On bluff overlooking sea. Refined atmosphere. Pleasant rooms with balcony & sea view. 2 two-bedroom units, 2 three-bedroom units. 2 stories; exterior corridors; oceanfront; beach; 2 tennis courts (1 lighted). **Services:** giftshop. Fee: massage. **Recreation:** swimming, sailboating, snorkeling & equipment, windsurfing. Fee: scuba diving & equipment. **Some Rooms:** 2 kitchens. **Cards:** AE, DI, MC, VI.

(876/974-5601

RENAISSANCE JAMAICA GRANDE
◆◆◆   *Resort Complex*

12/1-12/31	$260-280	XP $35
1/1-4/13	$225-245	XP $30
4/14-11/30	$165-185	XP $35

Location: Center, on beach off Main St. (PO Box 100). Fax: 876/974-5378. **Terms:** F12; Reserv deposit, 3 day notice; handling fee imposed; 10% service charge. **Facility:** 720 rooms. Excellent resort property. All inclusive rate plan avail; 14 stories; interior corridors; oceanfront; beach; 2 lighted tennis courts. **Services:** giftshop. Fee: massage. **Recreation:** swimming. Fee: fishing, scuba diving, waterskiing, windsurfing. Rental: sailboats. **Cards:** AE, CB, DI, MC, VI.

(876/974-2201

RIO BLANCO HOTEL
◆◆   *Apartment Motor Inn*

12/15-4/13	$79-159	XP $15
12/1-12/14 & 4/14-11/30	$69-129	XP $10

Location: 2 mi e on A3; just e of Rio Blanco Bridge. (PO Box 252). Fax: 876/994-1049. **Terms:** F12; Reserv deposit, 7 day notice, 14 off season; handling fee imposed; 10% service charge. **Facility:** 60 rooms. Modern attractive 1-bedroom & studio apartments in quiet location across highway from beach. Well-landscaped grounds. 2-bedroom unit $160, $125 off season for up to 4 persons; 3 stories, no elevator; exterior corridors; 1 tennis court. **Some Rooms:** 30 efficiencies, 30 kitchens, color TV. **Cards:** AE, MC, VI.

(876/994-1880

(AAA) SANDALS DUNN'S RIVER GOLF RESORT & SPA
◆◆◆   *Resort Hotel*

12/24-4/1	$2920-3870
12/1-12/23 & 4/2-11/30	$2395-3420

Location: 4.5 mi w on Rt A3. (PO Box 51). Fax: 876/972-1611. **Terms:** Age restrictions may apply; reserv deposit. **Facility:** 256 rooms. Beautiful grounds, excellent facilities. Very attractive rooms. All inclusive; rates include tax & gratuities. 2-6 stories; interior/exterior corridors; oceanfront; pitch & putt; beach, saunas, whirlpools, hot tubs; 4 tennis courts (2 lighted). **Dining:** 4 restaurants, cafeteria; 1 open air & terrace, guests only; 6:30 am-9:30 pm; cocktails. **Services:** giftshop; complimentary evening beverages; area transportation, to Dunns River/Ocho Rios. Fee: massage. **Recreation:** swimming, sailboating, scuba diving, snorkeling, waterskiing, windsurfing, glass-bottom boat rides. Fee: fishing. **Cards:** AE, MC, VI.

((876)972-1610

(AAA) SANDALS OCHO RIOS RESORT AND GOLF CLUB
◆◆◆   *Resort Hotel*

12/24-4/1	$2465-2960
12/1-12/23 & 4/2-11/30	$2215-2710

Location: 1 mi e on Rt A3. Main St (PO Box 771). Fax: 876/974-5700. **Terms:** Age restrictions may apply; reserv deposit, 30 day notice; handling fee imposed. **Facility:** 237 rooms. Oceanfront setting with tropical gardens. Rates include taxes & gratuities. 5 stories; interior corridors; 18 holes golf; beach, saunas, whirlpools; 2 lighted tennis courts. **Dining:** 4 restaurants; 7:30-10 am, 12:30-2 & 6-9:30 pm, public by reservation, dancing; $35; cocktails. **Services:** giftshop; complimentary evening beverages; massage; area transportation, to Montego Bay. **Recreation:** swimming, canoeing, paddleboats, sailboating, scuba diving, snorkeling, kayaks, glass bottom boat. Fee: charter fishing. **Cards:** AE, JC, MC, VI.

((876)974-5691

LAST-MINUTE DEPARTURE CHECK:

DRIVER'S LICENSE

TRAVELERS CHECKS

CAR REGISTRATION & INSURANCE CARD

AAA MEMBERSHIP CARD

CREDIT CARDS

FILM AND CAMERA

SAND CASTLES
◆◆   *Apartment Motor Inn*

12/16-4/20	$120-284	XP $30-35
12/1-12/15 & 4/21-11/30	$85-219	XP $30

Location: Center, adjacent to Turtle Beach. Main St. Fax: 876/974-2247. **Terms:** F12; Reserv deposit, 7 day notice; handling fee imposed. **Facility:** 153 rooms. Attractive apartments adjoining Turtle Beach. Pleasant courtyards. Some 3-story penthouse units, some units with ocean view. 12 two-bedroom units. 8 two-bedroom penthouse apartments $284; $219 off season for up to 4 persons; 2-3 stories, no elevator; interior/exterior corridors; beach. **Services:** giftshop. **Recreation:** swimming. **All Rooms:** combo or shower baths. **Some Rooms:** 89 efficiencies, 64 kitchens. **Cards:** AE, MC, VI.

(876/974-2255

SHAW PARK BEACH HOTEL
◆◆   *Motor Inn*

12/15-4/25	$174-190	XP $26
12/1-12/14 & 4/26-11/30	$137-155	XP $28

Location: 1.7 mi e on Rt A3 following signs. (PO Box 17). Fax: 876/974-0782. **Terms:** F12; Reserv deposit, 14 day notice, 7 in summer; handling fee imposed; 10% service charge. **Facility:** 118 rooms. Pleasant rooms that vary in size with balcony or patio & ocean view. 12 two-bedroom deluxe units $277-$431, off season $162-$267 for 2-4 persons; 2 stories; interior/exterior corridors; oceanfront; beach; 2 lighted tennis courts; playground. **Services:** giftshop. Fee: massage. **Recreation:** swimming. Fee: fishing, sailboating, scuba diving & equipment, snorkeling, windsurfing. **All Rooms:** combo or shower baths. **Some Rooms:** 12 kitchens, color TV. **Cards:** AE, DI, MC, VI.

(876/974-2552

TURTLE BEACH TOWERS
◆   *Condo Hotel*

12/16-4/21	$125-198	XP $10-12
12/1-12/15 & 4/22-11/30	$94-132	XP $10

Location: Center, near cruise ship passenger terminal. (PO Box 73). Fax: 876/974-5014. **Terms:** F12; Reserv deposit, 7 day notice; 10% service charge. **Facility:** 110 rooms. 4 multi-story condo buildings. Pleasant setting. 29 two-bedroom units, 3 three-bedroom units. For US reservations: (212) 251-1800; 12 stories; interior corridors; beach view; beach; 2 lighted tennis courts. **Recreation:** swimming. **All Rooms:** kitchens. **Some Rooms:** color TV. **Cards:** AE, MC, VI.

(876/974-2801

RESTAURANTS

THE ALMOND TREE RESTAURANT
◆◆◆   *Continental*   L $7-$12   D $15-$32

Location: 0.5 mi e on Rt A3; in Hibiscus Lodge Hotel. **Hours:** 7:30 am-10, noon-2:30 & 6-10 pm. **Reservations:** suggested. **Features:** No A/C; casual dress; cocktails & lounge; a la carte. Beautiful setting. Terrace dining overlooking Caribbean Sea. Cuisine features both European & Island specialties. Very attractive bar with sing seats. 10% charge, 13% Government tax. **Cards:** AE, CB, DI, MC, VI.

(876/974-2813

DRAGONS
◆◆◆   *Chinese*   D $10-$13

Location: Center of Ocho Rios on the beach; in Renaissance Jamaica Grande. **Hours:** 6 pm-11 pm. Closed: Mon & Tues. **Reservations:** suggested. **Features:** casual dress; cocktails & lounge; a la carte. Cantonese & Szechuan cuisine; pleasant atmosphere off south tower lobby of this large oceanfront resort. 10% service charge & 12.5% government tax. **Cards:** AE, CB, DI, DS, MC, VI.

(876/974-2200

EVITA'S   *Historical*
◆◆◆   *Italian*   L $7-$18   D $10-$22

Location: From jct Rt A1 & Eden Bower Rd, just s up steep hill. Eden Bower Rd. **Hours:** 11 am-11 pm. **Reservations:** suggested. **Features:** No A/C; casual dress; children's menu; cocktails & lounge; a la carte. Charming converted 1860 gingerbread house on hillside overlooking town & bay. Very well prepared Italian cuisine & island specialties. Fresh homemade pasta. 10% service charge & 15% government tax. Outside verandah & fans. **Cards:** AE, MC, VI.

(876/974-2333

JAMAICA INN DINING ROOM
◆◆◆   *Continental*   L $7-$22   D $15-$40

Location: Oceanfront 1.7 mi e on A 3, just n of rd to Shaw Park. **Hours:** 8-10 am, 1-2:30 & 7:30-9 pm. **Reservations:** suggested. **Features:** No A/C; semi-formal attire; cocktails; entertainment; valet parking; a la carte. Very romantic terrace dining overlooking the sea. Formal service, excellent cuisine. 10% service charge. **Cards:** AE, MC, VI.

(876/974-2514

THE RUINS RESTAURANT & GARDENS
◆◆   *Chinese*   L $6-$22   D $6-$22

Location: On DaCosta 0.2 mi jct a-3 convenient to downtown & cruise ship dock. Da Costa Dr. **Hours:** noon-2:30 & 6-9:30 pm, Sun 6 pm-9:30 pm. **Reservations:** suggested; in season. **Features:** No A/C; casual dress; cocktails & lounge; a la carte. Dining area set against large natural waterfall backdrop. American cuisine avail. **Cards:** AE, DI, MC, VI.

(876/974-2442

PORT ANTONIO—16,000

LODGINGS

GOBLIN HILL VILLAS AT SAN SAN-PORT ANTONIO
◆◆◆   *Resort Complex*

12/15-4/14	$1730-2140	XP $105-175
12/1-12/14 & 4/15-11/30	$1445-1795	XP $105-175

Location: 6 mi e on Rt A4. (PO Box 26). Fax: 876/925-6248. **Terms:** Reserv deposit, 30 day notice. **Facility:** 28 rooms. Ideal for families. Beautiful, secluded location in Blue Mountain Foothills overlooking San San Bay. Full-time housekeeper prepares meals & launders clothes. 16 two-bedroom units. 1-bedroom units for up to 3 persons; 2-bedroom units for up to 6 persons. Weekly rates include car if desired; 2 stories; exterior corridors; oceanview; beach access; 2 lighted tennis courts. **Services:** area transportation. **All Rooms:** kitchens. **Cards:** AE, MC, VI.

(876/993-7443

THE JAMAICA PALACE HOTEL
◆◆◆ *Resort Hotel*

12/15-4/14	$230-400
12/1-12/14 & 4/15-11/30	$210-355

Location: 3.3 mi e on Rt A4. (PO Box 277). Fax: 876/993-7759. **Terms:** Reserv deposit, 30 day notice. **Facility:** 80 rooms. Palatial estate nestled in wooded hillside location overlooking Turtle Crawl Bay. Accommodations vary in size. Gracious appointments. Rental TV's; 2 stories; exterior corridors; oceanview; beach access. **Services:** giftshop; area transportation. Fee: massage. **Cards:** AE, JC, MC, VI.

(876/993-7720

TRIDENT VILLAS & HOTEL
◆◆◆◆ *Resort Complex*

12/16-4/15	$385-800	XP $100
12/1-12/15 & 4/16-11/30	$220-500	XP $150

Location: 2.3 mi e on Rt A4. (PO Box 119). Fax: 876/993-2960. **Terms:** Reserv deposit, 21 day notice; 10% service charge. **Facility:** 26 rooms. Secluded, beautifully manicured grounds along coral coastline. Very attractive rooms & villas with balcony or terrace, offering spacious accommodations. Gracious staff. 1 two-bedroom unit, 1 three-bedroom unit. For reservations: (201) 902-7878; 1-2 stories; exterior corridors; oceanfront; beach; 2 tennis courts. **Services:** giftshop. **Recreation:** swimming, sailboating; hiking trails. Fee: horseback riding. **Cards:** AE, MC, VI. *(See color ad below)*

(876/993-2602

RESTAURANT

POSEIDON RESTAURANT AND LOUNGE
◆◆◆ *Continental*   L $4-$10 D $10-$18

Location: At Fern Hill Club Hotel. **Hours:** 7 am-11 pm. **Features:** No A/C; casual dress; cocktails. Beautiful setting overlooking Port Antonio Harbor & Blue Mountains. 10% service charge. **Cards:** AE, MC, VI.

(876/993-7374

READING

RESTAURANT

NORMA AT THE WHARF HOUSE
◆◆◆ *French*   D $25-$32

Location: 5 mi w of Montego Bay on A1. **Hours:** 6:30 pm-9:30 pm. Closed: Mon & 6/1-9/1. **Reservations:** required. **Features:** No A/C; casual dress; cocktails; a la carte. Converted 18th century sugar warehouse. Nouvelle French/Caribbean cuisine. **Cards:** MC, VI.

(876/979-2745

TRELAWNY

LODGING

GRAND LIDO BRACO
◆◆◆ *Resort Motor Inn*

12/1-1/10	$450-560
2/7-4/10	$430-540
1/11-2/6 & 4/11-11/30	$380-480

Location: On Rt A-1 midway between Montego Bay & Ocho Rios; 1 mi w of Rio Bueno Village. (Rio Bueno PO). Fax: 876/954-0020. **Terms:** Age restrictions may apply; reserv deposit, 60 day notice; 3 night min stay. **Facility:** 232 rooms. Elegant seaside all inclusive lodging. Ambiance recreates Jamaican village including shops, craft vendors, an open market & excellent beach facilities. US reservations: International lifestyles; no elevator; exterior corridors; oceanfront; putting green; beach; 3 lighted tennis courts. **Services:** giftshop. Fee: massage. **Recreation:** swimming, sailboating, snorkeling & equipment, windsurfing, bicycles, jogging. Fee: fishing; horseback riding. Rental: boats. **Cards:** AE, JC, MC, VI.

(876/954-0000

MARTINIQUE

ONE OF THE LARGEST islands in the Lesser Antilles, Martinique is 50 miles (80 km) long and 22 miles (35 km) wide. The mountainous island has two main peaks: volcanic Mont Pelée in the north and Les Pitons du Carbet in the central section.

It is easy to see why the Carib Indians once designated Martinique as the Isle of Flowers—bougainvillea, hibiscus, anthuriums, bamboo and wild orchids deck the woodlands; forests with many varieties of flowering trees rim the hills. Plantation fields with crops containing bananas, pineapples, sugarcane and coffee can be found throughout this fertile island. Martinique's tropical visage is scarred only by the ruins of St. Pierre, the result of an eruption of Mont Pelée in 1902.

HISTORY, GOVERNMENT AND ECONOMY

Christopher Columbus sighted Martinique in 1493 but did not land until his fourth voyage in 1502, when he named the island after St. Martin of Tours. Arawak and Carib Indians called the island *Madinina,* the "island of flowers." Because of opposition from the Indians, no settlement took place until 1635, when the French made the island a center for sugar production. France and Britain battled for the island throughout the 17th and 18th centuries until France gained permanent control in 1814.

Like Guadeloupe, Martinique is a department and region of France, represented in the French Parliament by two senators and four deputies. The island is administered by elected general and regional councils as well as by a prefect, or governor. The seat of government is Fort-de-France.

SHOPPING

Martinique offers enough goods and bargains to suit the needs of most shoppers. French perfumes, china, linens, jewelry, crystal and other luxury imports are sold at or below prices in Paris, New York or St. Thomas. The main shopping district is in Fort-de-France along rues Antoine Siger, Victor Hugo and Schoelcher, where shops sell madras cottons, watches, silver and crystal at low prices.

Roger Albert's "free-port" store specializes in French perfume, leather goods, sportswear and crystal, and Cadet-Daniel in crystal and silver. It is not truly a "free port," but instead offers a 20 percent discount on purchases paid for with travelers checks or charged to a credit card.

At the Caribbean Arts Center on the seafront, artisans sell their tapestries, Creole dolls, straw baskets, ceramics, handmade jewelry and souvenirs. As on many other Caribbean isles, rum is a popular purchase; 16 varieties are available on the island.

Shops are open Mon.-Fri. 8:30-6, Sat. 9-noon, and are closed holidays. Banking hours are Mon.-Fri. 7:30-noon and 2:30-4. Stores can give up to 20-percent discounts on some luxury goods purchased with travelers checks or certain credit cards.

FOOD AND DRINK

Martinique's cuisine is a mix of classic French and Creole. Local specialties include *colombo,* an Indian dish of currylike seeds cooked with either beef, pork, chicken, mutton, conch or goat and eaten with rice; *boudin,* a spicy local blood sausage; and *callaloo,* a soup made from greens and West Indian herbs. Typical Creole seafood dishes might include such exotic ingredients as *oursins,* sea urchins; *lambi,* conch; and *langouste,* local rock lobster or crayfish. Local beverages include potent rum punch, bottled rum, beer and mineral water. Water and milk are safe to drink.

More than 350 restaurants in Martinique have elevated Creole and French cooking to its highest level of artistic perfection. Chez Mally Edjam, a little restaurant on the north coast at Basse-Pointe, serves fine Creole lunches. A favorite among islanders and tourists for its Creole specialties is Colibri in Morne-des-Esses. Known for its seafood, Les Filets Bleus is on Ste. Anne's southern beach. Le Foulard, in Schoelcher just north of Fort-de-France, prepares very good meals. An excellent Fort-de-France restaurant is La Mouina, situated on the outskirts of town. Most hotels and restaurants include a 10- to 15-percent service charge in their prices or add it to the final bill.

Sports and Amusements

Beaches of white, ochre and black volcanic sand offer unlimited opportunities for swimming, skin diving, scuba diving, water skiing and other aquatic sports. Among the island's most popular beaches are Diamant Beach, about 21 miles (34 km) from Fort-de-France on the southwest coast, and the sandy strand at Salines near Ste. Anne. Scuba diving services, including courses for beginners, are available to guests at hotels in the Pointe du Bout resort area and elsewhere.

The Pointe du Bout area also is a popular spot for sailing; most hotels rent various types of sailing craft. Large boats can be chartered through Caraibes Evasion, Soleil et Voile, Star Voyages Antilles and Tropic Yachting, all at the Pointe du Bout Marina, and through several other charter companies around the island. Memberships of most U.S. yacht clubs are honored at the two yacht clubs in Fort-de-France. Most of the larger hotels and the marina at Fort-de-France charter boats for deep-sea fishing.

Other recreational pursuits include horseback riding, hiking, mountain climbing, tennis and golf. An alternative to the resort environment, camping is permitted at Anse-à-l'Ane, Diamant, Le Marin, Macabou, Ste. Anne and Ste. Luce on Martinique's southern coast and at Grand Rivière in the north. Horseback rides through the country and canefields are conducted through several private clubs and ranches.

A fine 18-hole par-71 golf course is at Trois-Ilets near the Pointe du Bout marina-hotel area. Besides the hotel tennis courts, the tennis clubs in Fort-de-France and Vieux Moulin, as well as the Golf Country Club, offer temporary memberships to visiting players. Spectator sports include soccer matches, held every Sunday at the stadium in Fort-de-France.

An annual event that captures the island's mystery and charm is Carnival, a celebration for Vaval, the legendary king of the Carnival. Preparations last for 5 weeks, ending on Ash Wednesday. The streets of Fort-de-France are jammed with participants masked and costumed in black, white and red to depict *les diablesses*. They perform the *beguine,* a twisting, uninhibited dance that to the Martiniquais is a way of life. On Ash Wednesday the parade of rhythmic dancing and singing is a wake for Vaval and leads to the waterfront where his funeral pyre is built. When dusk falls *les diablesses* dance in a frenzy of

THINGS TO KNOW

AREA: 425 square miles (1,101 sq km).

POPULATION: 392,000.

LANGUAGE: French and Creole.

CAPITAL: Fort-de-France.

GOVERNMENT: Department and Region of France.

TIME ZONE: Atlantic.

UNIT OF CURRENCY: French franc divided into 100 centimes. $1 U.S.=approx. 5.95 French francs.

ELECTRICITY: 220 volts, 50 cycles AC.

CARS: U.S. license valid; drive on right.

IMMIGRATION REQUIREMENTS: For stays under 3 months, adults and children are required to have proof of U.S. citizenship (passport, an expired passport dating back no more than 5 years, birth certificate with raised seal accompanied by a government-authorized identification card or similar document with photo) and a return or through ticket.

FOR FURTHER INFORMATION:
Martinique Promotion Bureau
444 Madison Ave.
New York, NY 10022
(800) 391-4909
Martinique Tourist Office
Boulevard Alfassa
97206 Fort-de-France,
Martinique, F.W.I.
Phone (596) 63-79-60

HOLIDAYS: Jan. 1; Mardi Gras; Easter Monday; Labor Day, May 1; Slavery Abolition Day, May 22; Ascension Thursday; Whit Monday, May (8th Monday after Easter); Bastille Day, July 14; Feast of the Assumption, Aug. 15; All Saints Day, Nov. 1; Armistice Day, Nov. 11; Dec. 25.

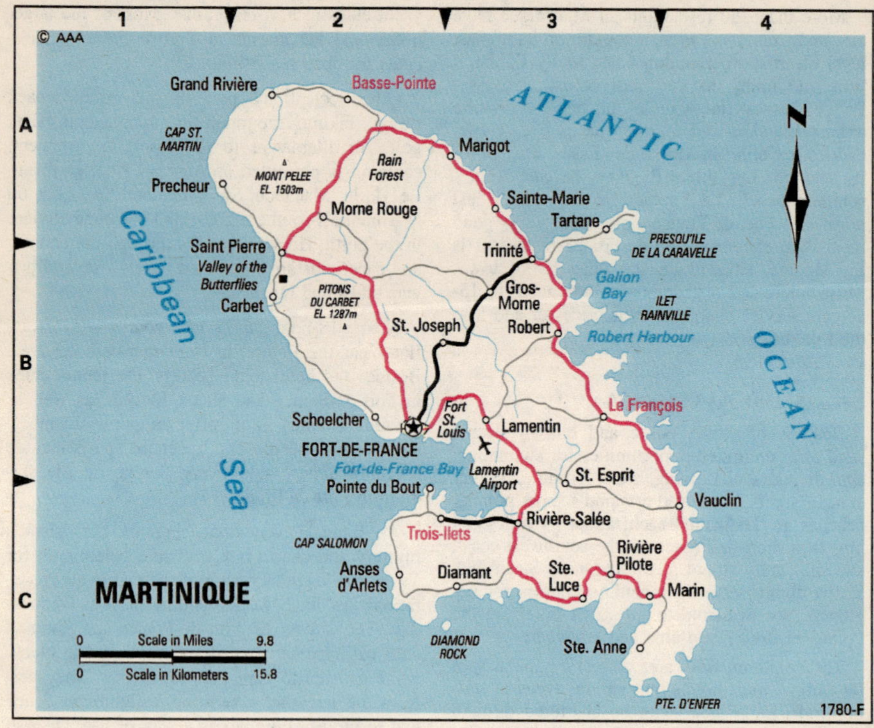

shadows and flickering flames until Vaval's effigy is burned and Carnival is over for another year.

There is dancing and entertainment at Manikou Nights, L'Alibi, Manhattan, Le Negresco, Xnakis Club and the New Hippo Club as well as at several major hotels, such as La Batelière. There is a casino at the Méridien Trois Ilets Hotel, and the Casino de la Batelière Plazza is near La Batelière Hotel. Theater life in Fort-de-France revolves around the Théâtre Municipal, where the spotlight falls each February on a visiting Parisian opera company and dramatic troupe. Dance exhibitions performed by the Grands Ballets de la Martinique are frequently held at the major hotels. Several theaters show French and American films with French soundtracks.

Excursions and Sightseeing

Good roads, including many four-lane highways, afford pleasant excursions. These include a 5-hour drive to the old capital of St. Pierre, where the historical museum can be visited, and on to Grand Rivière, returning through quaint fishing villages on the eastern coast. A 4-hour trip from Fort-de-France to the southern half of the island includes stops at Trois-Ilets, birthplace of Empress Josephine; Pointe du Bout, which offers a fine view of the capital across the bay; and Anses d'Arlets, a small fishing village. Diamant

Beach affords a view of Diamond Rock, a giant offshore monolith. Return is through Rivière-Salée.

A half-day drive can be made from Fort-de-France along the island's west coast to St. Pierre, returning the same route. A 5-hour excursion to Ste. Anne might include a stop for a swim at Ste. Anne Beach or nearby Plage des Salines; return via St. Esprit and Ducos.

Fascinating views of the underwater world are offered on glass-bottom boats and 1-hour aquascope excursions.

Transportation

There are flights from Montreal, Toronto, New York, Newark, Miami and San Juan; connecting flights are available from other U.S. cities. Air Martinique provides interisland flights to St. Lucia, St. Vincent, Dominica, Barbados, St. Martin and Antigua; information about schedules is available at Martinique's Lamentin Airport. More than two dozen cruise lines include Fort-de-France on their itinerary.

Taxi fare from the airport to Fort-de-France is about $15; fares are 40 percent higher between 8 p.m. and 6 a.m. Rental cars are available at the airport, Fort-de-France and Pointe du Bout; camper-car rentals can be arranged at Anse Mitan.

Collective taxis, private cars or minibuses that serve as jitney buses, will take up to eight passengers to many standard destinations. The name of the final destination is marked on the car. These "group" taxis stop running at 6 p.m. Collective taxi fare from Fort-de-France to Lamentin Airport is about $1.60, to Ste. Anne $4, to Trois Ilets (Pointe du Bout) $2.50, and to St. Pierre $2.20. Crowded buses, used primarily by islanders, also serve sections of Martinique.

A ferry links Fort-de-France with Pointe du Bout and Fort-de-France with Anse Mitan, Anse-à-l'Ane and Grande Anse d'Arlet. A high-speed passenger ferry, the *Caribbean Express,* connects Martinique with Dominica and Guadeloupe.

ATTRACTION ADMISSIONS

Attraction admissions for this island are quoted in U.S. dollars.

POINTS OF INTEREST

CARBET (B-2) pop. 3,000

VALLEY OF THE BUTTERFLIES (Vallée des Papillons), 20 mi. (32 km) n. on Hwy. 10, is a butterfly garden cultivated amidst the ruins of Habitation Anse Latouche, one of the island's earliest 17th-century plantations. The plantation was destroyed by the eruption of Mont Pelée in 1902. A greenhouse on the property also houses many species of butterflies. The best time for observation is 10-3. Food is available. Allow 30 minutes minimum. Daily 9:30-4:15. Admission $7; under 12, $5. Phone (596) 78-19-19.

FORT-DE-FRANCE (B-2) pop. 100,000

Capital of the "island of flowers," Fort-de-France is stepped like an amphitheater around the celebrated Place de la Savane. This lovely park contains a marble statue of the Empress Josephine, who was born across the bay near Trois-Ilets. Fort St. Louis dominates the harbor promontory. The Schoelcher Library across from La Savane and the yacht basin are of interest. The Sacré-Coeur de Balata basilica and the Balata Garden (Jardin de Balata) are in the suburbs north of Fort-de-France.

CATHEDRAL CHURCH OF FORT-DE-FRANCE (Cathédrale Saint-Louis) has Byzantine decor and stained-glass windows. Daily dawn-dusk. Free. Phone (596) 73-59-78.

COURT OF JUSTICE BUILDING, corner of rue Schoelcher and rue Moreau de Jonnes, features a statue of Victor Schoelcher, the man responsible for freeing the slaves in the French West Indies in 1848. Mon.-Fri. 7:30-1 and 3-6. Free. Phone (596) 59-72-01.

DEPARTMENTAL MUSEUM OF MARTINIQUE (Musée Départemental de la Martinique), 9 rue de la Liberté, houses relics from prehistoric Arawak Indian excavations and has exhibits about contemporary everyday life. Mon.-Fri. 9-1 and 2-5, Sat. 9-noon. Admission $3; ages 3-12, $2. Phone (596) 71-57-05.

STATUE OF PIERRE BELAIN D'ESNAMBUC, in Place de la Savane facing Fort-de-France Bay, commemorates the man who founded the French colony here in 1635, the first European colony established on the island.

LE FRANÇOIS (B-3)

CLEMENT DISTILLERY (Distillerie Clément), at the L'Acajou Estate 1.2 mi. (2 km) w. toward Le St-Esprit, is one of the finest rum distilleries on the island. Visitors can tour the distillery and estate, and free tastings are offered. The 18th-century home of the company's founder evokes plantation life. Tropical gardens are on the grounds. Allow 1 hour minimum. Daily 9-6. Admission $6.50. Phone (596) 54-62-07.

St. Pierre (A-2) pop. 5,000

Sometimes called the Pompeii of the New World, St. Pierre is 20 miles (32 km) northwest of Fort-de-France. Amid this active tropical town are the ruins of the old St. Pierre, which was destroyed by the eruption of Mont Pelée in 1902. St. Pierre was never buried under lava, which bypassed the town on its run to the sea some miles north, but the capital and its population of 30,000 were destroyed within 3 minutes by the exploding volcano's intense heat and gas. There was one survivor, a prisoner who was protected by the thick walls of his cell. Walls and foundations are all that remain of the magnificent theater that was once the heart of the "Paris of the West Indies."

Near Carbet on the scenic coastal route between Fort-de-France and St. Pierre, painter Paul Gauguin made his home in 1887. The Carbet Gauguin Museum (admission charged) is open 10-5:30; phone (596) 78-22-66. Another point of interest along this route is La Vallée des Papillons, the Valley of the Butterflies, where multitudes of these flighty beings swirl around their human observers; phone (596) 78-19-19.

FRANCK A. PERRET VOLCANOLOGICAL MUSEUM (Franck A. Perret Musée Volcanologique), on rue Victor Hugo in the center of town, exhibits items salvaged after the eruption of Mont Pelée along with photographs of the ruins. Photography is not permitted. Allow 30 minutes minimum. Wed.-Mon. 9-5. Admission $10. Phone (596) 78-15-16.

MONT PELÉE, now dormant, erupted on May 8, 1902, annihilating all but one of St. Pierre's 30,000 inhabitants—a man imprisoned in the basement of the jail. Cars can be driven to within an hour's walk of the summit. Cars, drivers and guides are available at Morne Rouge, a popular vacation spot for Martiniquais.

Trois-Ilets (C-2) pop. 4,500

Across the bay from Fort-de-France, Trois-Ilets is near the birthplace of Marie Josephe Rose Tascher de la Pagerie, the Creole beauty who later reigned as Napoleon's Empress Josephine. La Pagerie, her partially restored home, and the church where she was christened can be visited (*see attraction listing*). The town also contains La Maison de la Canne, a museum featuring exhibits about the sugar industry; phone (596) 68-32-04.

LA PAGERIE MUSEUM (Musée de la Pagerie), in the old kitchen quarters of Empress Josephine's family home, contains mementos of the Empress and of the Napoleonic period. A few of Napoleon's love letters are displayed. A tropical garden is on the grounds of the sugar plantation. Tues.-Fri. 9-5, Sat.-Sun. 9-1 and 2:30-5. Admission $4; under 12, $1. Phone (596) 68-34-55.

Lodgings & Restaurants

Basse-Pointe (Martinque)

Lodging

HOTEL PLANTATION DE LEYRITZ
◆◆ *Historic Cottage*

12/1-12/20 & 4/21-11/30	$110	XP $28
12/21-1/3	$210	XP $28
1/4-4/20	$170	XP $28

Location: 2 km w of jct Rt N1 & D21; following signs. Basse-Pointe 97218 (97218 Basse-Pointe, BASSE-POINTE). Fax: 059/678-244. **Terms:** F11; Reserv deposit, 21 day notice, 7 day off season; handling fee imposed. **Facility:** 66 rooms. Picturesque 18th-century sugar plantation on spacious grounds. Modest to more upscale cottages & rooms decorated in traditonal Creole style. 1-2 stories; interior/exterior corridors; 1 lighted tennis court. **Services:** giftshop. **Recreation:** hiking trails. **All Rooms:** combo or shower baths. **Cards:** AE, MC, VI.

☎ 059/678-5392

Restaurant

LEYRITZ PLANTATION RESTAURANT *Historical*
◆◆ *Ethnic*   L $20-$35 D $20-$50
Location: 2 km w of jct Rt N1 & D21; following signs; in Hotel Plantation De Leyritz. Basse-Point. **Hours:** 7:30 am-10, noon-2:30 & 7:30-9:15 pm. **Reservations:** suggested. **Features:** No A/C; casual dress; children's menu; cocktails & lounge; a la carte. Creole specialties served in former sugar plantation ruins. A local historic attraction. **Cards:** AE, MC, VI.

☎ 059/678-5392

Le Francois (Martinque)

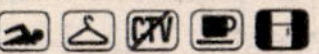

Lodging

FREGATE BLEUE INN
◆◆◆ *Bed & Breakfast*

12/20-4/30	$200	XP $20
12/1-12/19 & 5/1-11/30	$120	XP $20

Location: 5 km s on RN 6. Pass Francois on Rd N6 then towards either Vauclin or Marin, following signs. Pass Francois 97240 (97240 Le Francois, LE FRANCOIS). Fax: 059/654-7878. **Terms:** F12; Reserv deposit, 21 day notice, 7 day off season; handling fee imposed. **Facility:** 7 rooms. Hilltop inn with view of the Atlantic coastline in the distance. Tastefully decorated rooms with Creole antiques. Some rooms with balcony. For US reservations: (212)477-1600; 1-2 stories; interior/exterior corridors. **All Rooms:** efficiencies, combo or shower baths. **Cards:** AE, MC, VI.

(059/654-5466

Trois-Ilets (Martinique)

Lodgings

HOTEL SOFITEL BAKOUA
◆◆◆ *Hotel*

12/22-1/7	$252-308	XP $51-100
1/8-3/31	$230-280	XP $51
12/1-12/21 & 4/1-11/30	$145-160	

Location: On La Pointe du Bout, Pointe Du Bout, TROIS-ILETS, 97229). Fax: 059/066 0041. **Terms:** Reserv deposit, 30 day notice; handling fee imposed. **Facility:** 139 rooms. Beachfront property, with view of Fort-de-France across bay. Landscaped grounds. 3 stories, no elevator; exterior corridors; oceanfront; beach; 2 lighted tennis courts. **Services:** giftshop. Fee: area transportation. **Recreation:** swimming, paddleboats, scuba diving. Fee: fishing, scuba equipment, waterskiing, windsurfing. **Cards:** AE, DI, MC, VI.

(059/666-0202

LE MERIDIEN MARTINIQUE
◆◆ *Hotel*

12/15-4/15	$220-265	XP $65-110
12/1-12/14 & 4/16-11/30	$162	XP $65

Location: On La Pointe du Bout. Trois-Ilets (BP 894, 97425 Fort-De-France, TROIS-ILETS). Fax: 059/666-0074. **Terms:** F12; Reserv deposit, 30 day notice, 20 days off season; handling fee imposed. **Facility:** 295 rooms. Beachfront property, close to lthe casing, marina & tourist shops. Some units with French balcony & view of the Fort-de-France Bay. 7 stories; interior corridors; beach. Fee: 2 lighted tennis courts. **Services:** giftshop. Fee: area transportation. **Recreation:** swimming, paddleboats, scuba diving, snorkeling, windsurfing. Fee: waterskiing. Rental: scuba equipment. **Cards:** AE, CB, DI, DS, MC, VI.

(059/666-0600

NOVOTEL CAROLIA CARAYOU
◆◆ *Hotel*

12/23-4/15	$190	XP $39-45
12/1-12/22 & 4/16-11/30	$147	XP $55

Location: On La Pointe du Bout. Pointe Du Bout (Pointe Du Bout 97229 Trois-Ilets, TROIS-ILETS). Fax: 059/666-0057. **Terms:** F16; Reserv deposit, 14 day notice, 7 day off season; handling fee imposed. **Facility:** 200 rooms. Beachfront property, close to the marina & tourist shops. Patio or balcony. For US reservations: (212)575-2228; 1-2 stories; exterior corridors; beach; 1 lighted tennis court. **Services:** giftshop. Fee: area transportation. **Recreation:** swimming, scuba diving, snorkeling, windsurfing. Fee: scuba & snorkeling equipment, waterskiing. **All Rooms:** shower baths. **Cards:** AE, CB, DI, MC, VI.

(059/666-0404

PUERTO RICO

A VERDANT INTRO-DUCTION awaits the visitor to the U.S. Commonwealth of Puerto Rico, which boasts 600 miles (965 km) of palm-fringed coastline and a luxuriant interior of montane thicket, palm, dwarf and rain forests. The 110-mile-long (177-km), 35-mile-wide (56-km) island is a progressive blend of old and new. Nowhere is this more evident than in San Juan, with its centuries-old Spanish fortresses and glamorous resort hotels. Out on the island, as the Puerto Ricans refer to the remainder of the country, the changes are less dramatic but no less important.

Puerto Rico has made great strides economically and today enjoys one of the highest standard of living in the Caribbean. The island is a major banking and business center, and San Juan is the Caribbean's primary air and cruise hub. Complementing this progress, the Commonwealth, with the Institute of Puerto Rican Culture, has fostered an atmosphere in which writers, painters, sculptors, musicians and actors flourish, and has taken steps to preserve the island's crafts, folklore, dances, music and architecture.

HISTORY, GOVERNMENT AND ECONOMY

Originally named *Borínquen* (Island of the Brave Lord) by the Taíno Indians, Puerto Rico was discovered by Christopher Columbus in 1493 during his second voyage to the New World. He landed on the northwestern part of the island and named the island San Juan Bautista. The island derived its present name, however, from the exclamation *"Qué puerto rico!"* (What a rich port!), said to have been made by Juan Ponce de León upon entering the bay. He established the first settlement at Caparra in 1508 and in 1510 he was appointed the island's first governor by Spain's King Ferdinand. The capital was transferred to its present site and named San Juan Bautista de Puerto Rico in 1521, the year of de León's death.

The Spanish used the island to protect their ships from pirates and attacks by other countries. This strategic area of land was attacked unsuccessfully by Sir Francis Drake, occupied by English forces in 1598, burned and plundered by the Dutch in 1625 and subjected to other sieges until a last attempt by the British in 1797.

Puerto Rico remained a loyal Spanish colony until 1897, when Luis Muñoz Rivera obtained the Charter of Autonomy, which gave the island dominion status. However, before the charter could go into effect, Spain became engaged in the Spanish-American War. In 1898 Puerto Rico became part of the United States by the terms of the Treaty of Paris. The Foraker Act of 1900 enabled the island to establish a civil government under the direction of a U.S.-appointed governor; in 1917 the Jones Act made the Puerto Rican people citizens of the United States and provided for the creation of a local senate.

The first native-born governor was Jesús T. Piñero, appointed by President Harry S. Truman in 1946. The following year Truman signed an act giving Puerto Rico the authority to choose its chief executive by popular vote. Luis Muñoz Marín, the first elected governor, held the office until 1965, when he was succeeded by Roberto Sánchez Vilella. A Congressional resolution signed by President Truman in 1952 elevated Puerto Rico to the status of a free commonwealth associated with the United States.

SHOPPING

The best buys to look for in Puerto Rico are traditional island crafts. Calle Fortaleza in Old

San Juan, a 20-minute bus or 10-minute taxi ride from the Condado section of resort hotels, is the center of a large and varied collection of shops selling both crafts and imports—Thai silks, Spanish furniture and antiques, jewelry and items from the Philippines, India, Mexico and Europe. The tourist information center at La Casita at Pier 1 and the Institute of Puerto Rican Culture in the Ballajá Sector have lists of the numerous craft shops where artisans ply their trade in front of visitors.

Local artisans can be seen at La Casita at Pier 1 every Saturday and Sunday from noon to 8. On Calle Marina in Old San Juan, opposite Pier 3, is the Plazoleta del Puerto—a delightful collection of shops specializing in traditional crafts. Some of the most notable island crafts include mundillo or bobbin lace; *santos,* or hand-carved religious figurines; *cuatros,* hand-made 10-string guitars; devil's masks made from coconut husks or papier mache; hand-embroidered linens, blouses and dresses; Spanish-style jewelry of copper, gold and silver filigree; hand-painted scarves and clothing; handbags; hammocks; baskets; ceramics; musical instruments; original artwork; and items made of mahogany. Cigars and rum made in Puerto Rico also are popular buys.

Old San Juan has a reputation as an art center, harboring many galleries that sell paintings and sculpture by Puerto Rican artists. The Plaza Las Americas in San Juan and the Plaza del Caribe Shopping Center in Ponce offer a full range of local and continental products. For last-minute purchases, San Juan's airport also has shopping counters which are open daily, with varied hours based on airline schedules.

In addition to usual holidays, many shops and restaurants are closed on Good Friday. While banking hours are Mon.-Fri. 9-2:30, some banks also are open Sat. 10-noon. Though some plants and fruits may be brought to the United States, it is best to check with the USDA Plant Protection and Quarantine Department in San Juan before departure; phone (787) 766-5206.

FOOD AND DRINK

Fruits, vegetables, poultry and fish, prepared with a strong Spanish and island accent, are found in abundance. Roast pork, lobster dishes and seafood platters are specialties in many restaurants. Fruit is often combined with main dishes for a tropical flavor. Buffets featuring American, French, Italian, Chinese and native fare are popular at several hotels.

Some of the delightful Puerto Rican dishes include *arroz con pollo,* rice with chicken; *pasteles,* a local variation of the tamale made of ground plantain with meat, olives, raisins and chickpeas wrapped in plantain leaves and boiled; *lechón asado,* or barbecued pig; *pastelillos,* thin dough filled with meat or cheese and deep fried; *tostones,* green plantains fried in deep fat; *jueyes,* fresh land crabs, shelled and boiled; *paella,* rice with saffron, chicken and seafood; and *asopao,* rice with chicken or shrimp, cooked with wine sauce and often garnished with peas, pimientos, asparagus and hard-boiled eggs. Tap water is safe to drink and milk is pasteurized. A tip of 15 percent, with more for special service, is customary.

SPORTS AND AMUSEMENTS

The Caribbean, with its clear, warm water, is ideal for both scuba diving and snorkeling. Coral reefs and cays in many areas provide natural harbors for an array of beautiful and exotic sea life—coral, sea horses, starfish and tropical fish.

One of the best diving spots is off the northeastern coast of Puerto Rico around a small

---

THINGS TO KNOW

AREA: 3,435 square miles (8,897 sq km).

POPULATION: 3,692,000.

LANGUAGE: Spanish and English.

CAPITAL: San Juan.

GOVERNMENT: Commonwealth associated with the United States.

TIME ZONE: Atlantic.

UNIT OF CURRENCY: U.S. dollar.

ELECTRICITY: 110 volts, 60 cycles AC.

MINIMUM AGE FOR GAMBLING: 21.

CARS: U.S. license valid for 120 days; drive on right.

IMMIGRATION REQUIREMENTS: There are no immigration requirements for U.S. citizens.

FOR FURTHER INFORMATION:
Puerto Rico Tourism Co.
575 Fifth Ave., 23rd Floor
New York, NY 10017
(212) 599-6262 or (800) 223-6530
Tourism Information Center
Luis Muñoz Marín International Airport
Isla Verde, Puerto Rico
(787) 791-1014

HOLIDAYS: In addition to U.S. holidays: Three Kings Day, Jan. 6; Hostos' Birthday, Jan 10; Palm Sunday; Good Friday; Easter; Emancipation Day, Mar. 22; De Diego Day, Apr. 18; Muñoz Rivera's Birthday, July 18; Constitution Day, July 25; Barbosa's Birthday, July 27; Discovery of Puerto Rico, Nov. 19.

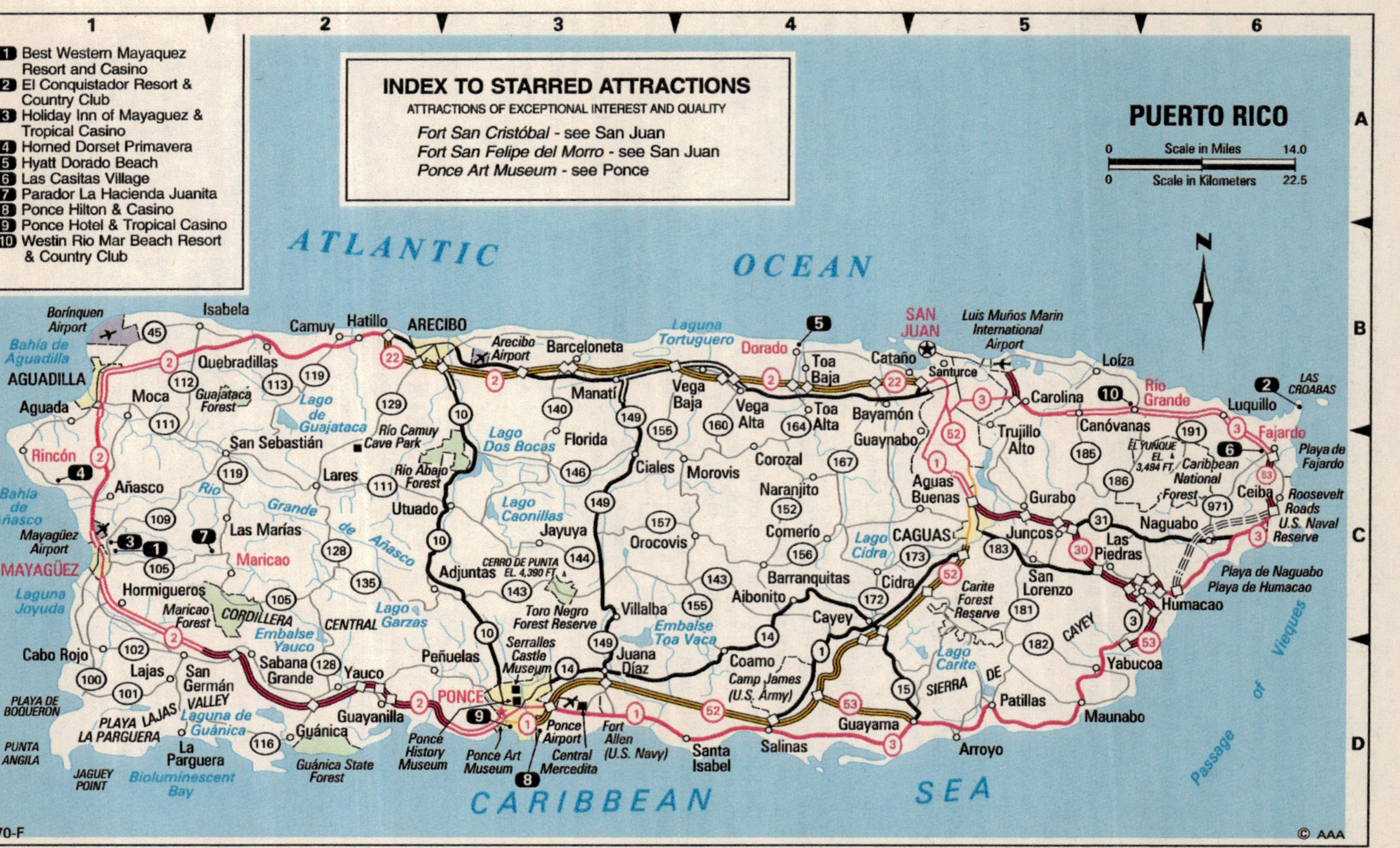
INDEX TO STARRED ATTRACTIONS
ATTRACTIONS OF EXCEPTIONAL INTEREST AND QUALITY
Fort San Cristóbal - see San Juan
Fort San Felipe del Morro - see San Juan
Ponce Art Museum - see Ponce
1 Best Western Mayaquez Resort and Casino
2 El Conquistador Resort & Country Club
3 Holiday Inn of Mayaguez & Tropical Casino
4 Horned Dorset Primavera
5 Hyatt Dorado Beach
6 Las Casitas Village
7 Parador La Hacienda Juanita
8 Ponce Hilton & Casino
9 Ponce Hotel & Tropical Casino
10 Westin Rio Mar Beach Resort & Country Club
PUERTO RICO
Scale in Miles
Scale in Kilometers
N
ATLANTIC OCEAN
CARIBBEAN SEA
Passage of Vieques
AGUADILLA
MAYAGÜEZ
SAN JUAN
CAGUAS
PONCE
ARECIBO
Dorado
Rio Grande
Fajardo
Rincón
Maricao
Borinquen Airport
Bahía de Aguadilla
Bahía de Añasco
Mayaguez Airport
Laguna Joyuda
PLAYA DE BOQUERON
PUNTA ANGILA
JAGUEY POINT
PLAYA LAS CROABAS
Playa de Fajardo
U.S. Naval Reserve
Roosevelt Roads
Ceiba
Luquillo
Naguabo
Humacao
Playa de Naguabo
Playa de Humacao
Yabucoa
Maunabo
Arroyo
Patillas
Guayama
Salinas
Santa Isabel
Fort Allen (U.S. Navy)
Central Mercedita
Ponce Airport
Ponce Art Museum
Ponce History Museum
Serralles Castle Museum
Guayanilla
Peñuelas
Guánica
Guánica State Forest
Laguna de Guánica
La Parguera
Bioluminescent Bay
PLAYA DE LA PARGUERA
Lajas
Cabo Rojo
San Germán
Hormigueros
Sabana Grande
Yauco
Embalse Yauco
Las Marias
Maricao Forest
CORDILLERA
LAGUNA VALLEY
CENTRAL GARZAS
Lago de Guánica
Adjuntas
CERRO DE PUNTA EL 4,390 FT.
Toro Negro Forest Reserve
Lago Caonillas
Jayuya
Utuado
Lares
Rio Camuy Cave Park
Rio Abajo Forest
Lago Dos Bocas
Florida
Manati
Barceloneta
Hatillo
Camuy
Quebradillas
Isabela
Moca
Añasco
Aguada
Guajataca Forest
Lago de Guajataca
San Sebastián
Ciales
Orocovis
Morovis
Corozal
Naranjito
Comerio
Barranquitas
Aibonito
Coamo
Camp James (U.S. Army)
Juana Diaz
Villalba
Embalse Toa Vaca
Lago Garzas
Vega Baja
Vega Alta
Toa Alta
Toa Baja
Bayamón
Cataño
Guaynabo
Aguas Buenas
Cidra
Lago Cidra
Cayey
SIERRA DE CAYEY
Carite Forest Reserve
Lago Carite
Cidra
San Lorenzo
Gurabo
Juncos
Las Piedras
Canóvanas
Carolina
Trujillo Alto
Santurce
Luis Muñoz Marin International Airport
Loiza
EL YUNQUE EL 3,494 FT.
Caribbean National Forest
ATLANTIC OCEAN
CARIBBEAN SEA
© AAA
1770-F

chain of islands. Visibility is exceptionally good in these waters, which range in depth from about 15 to 60 feet. The southwestern coast near La Parguera and the waters surrounding the eastern islands of Vieques and Culebra, dotted with many reefs, also are excellent spots for diving.

Diving or snorkeling excursions from either the beach or a charter boat can be arranged for an hour, a day or longer; beginners might want to stay along the beach where there is a sheltered cove. There are courses for both beginning and advanced snorkelers and divers. The longer and more expensive advanced courses usually feature night dives or search and recovery expeditions. Major hotels and resorts have information about lessons and packages.

With 272 miles of coastline, the island is ringed with good beaches with public facilities, called *balnearios,* which offer lockers, showers and parking for a nominal fee. They are open Tues.-Sun. 8-6 and are closed election days, Good Friday and the Tuesday following Monday holidays. Luquillo Beach, east of San Juan near El Yunque, is one of the most beautiful and popular beaches. Surfing conditions are excellent along the north and west coast. Rincón, on the west coast of the island facing the Mona passage, is very popular with winter surfers; the town has many surf shops.

Steady trade winds provide excellent opportunities for boating and sailing, particularly in San Juan Bay and the waters off Fajardo and La Parguera, which are well protected by coral reefs. Boats and equipment for sailing or deep-sea fishing can be rented from charter operators and marinas in San Juan, Mayaguez, Fajardo, Humacao and other towns. Game fish abound in Puerto Rico's waters, where more than 30 world records have been set, and include marlin, sailfish, mackerel, dolphin fish and wahoo. Snook, grouper, snapper, tarpon and amberjack teem along the southern coast. For more information contact the Department of Natural Resources at (787) 722-5938.

The International Billfish Tournament is held in late August and early September; other fishing tournaments take place throughout August and September.

Puerto Rico offers golfers 16 courses to play. Landscaped championship golf courses are at Club Río Mar in Río Grande, two each are at the Hyatt Cerromar Beach and Hyatt Dorado Beach hotels in Dorado, El Conquistador Resort & Country Club in Fajardo, Palmas del Mar in Humacao and Punta Borinquen in Aguadilla. Other golf courses on the island include the Bahia Beach Plantation and the Berwind Country Club in Río Grande, Ramey Golf Club in Aguadilla and the Dorado del Mar in Dorado.

Tennis courts are available at San Juan Central Park, which has 17, and at many of the hotels in the Condado and Isla Verde areas of San Juan. Hotels out on the island with more than 10 tennis courts are Hyatt Cerromar Beach and Hyatt Dorado Beach in Dorado, El Conquistador Resort & Country Club in Fajardo and Palmas del Mar in Humacao. Horseback riding stables can be found at Palmas del Mar in Humacao and at Hacienda Carabali.

Spectator sports in Puerto Rico cover a wide range of interests reflecting both Spanish and American cultures. One of the local favorites is basketball; Puerto Ricans eagerly await the beginning of the basketball season in May. Second only to basketball in popularity is baseball, whose season runs from October through February; the game is played at the Hiram Bithorn Stadium in San Juan. Another popular and exciting sport is horse racing; races with pari-mutuel and daily double betting take place at the El Nuevo Comandante Racetrack Wednesday, Friday, Sunday and holidays at 2:30. Paso Fino horse shows, featuring Puerto Rico's own smooth-gaited breed, take place regularly around the island.

Note: Policies concerning admittance of children to pari-mutuel betting facilities vary. Phone for information.

Activities in Puerto Rico do not end at sundown. Supper clubs feature elaborate floor shows, dining and dancing. The Performing Arts Center in San Juan regularly presents internationally acclaimed musicians, opera and ballet stars in its three theaters. One of the oldest municipal theaters in the Western Hemisphere, Old San Juan's restored Tapia Theater offers performances every weekend. Another historic cultural center in Old San Juan is the Ateneo Puertoriqueno, which produces all kinds of cultural events throughout the year.

The Puerto Rico Symphony Orchestra gives performances at the University of Puerto Rico in October and November. Elegant government-regulated casinos are found in most of the large hotels. Various hotels offer a weekly rendition of the Le Lo Lai Festival, sponsored by the Puerto Rico Tourism Co. This colorful extravaganza of Puerto Rican folksongs and dances showcases the European and Afro-Antillean heritage of the island; phone (787) 723-3135 weekdays, or (787) 791-1014 weekends.

In June is the Pablo Casals Festival, which commemorates the famous Spanish cellist. During these first 2 weeks in June, internationally acclaimed artists perform in San Juan at the Performing Arts Center. San Juan Bautista Day is celebrated on June 25 with public parties, bonfires on the beaches, street dances and concerts. Constitution Day on July 25 marks the anniversary of the island's commonwealth status; parades, fireworks and regattas are held throughout the island.

A copy of *Qué Pasa* (What's Happening) is available at hotel desks and at the Puerto Rico

Tourism Co.'s information centers. This quarterly, 96-page booklet lists events, scenic tours, points of interest, restaurants, nightclubs, shops and visitor information for San Juan and places out on the island.

EXCURSIONS AND SIGHTSEEING

With about 3,000 miles (4,800 km) of good roads, Puerto Rico is popular for motor excursions. Though San Juan receives the majority of attention, it is a good idea to venture out on the island to get a true picture of Puerto Rico. For detailed information about guided driving tours, consult the Puerto Rico Tourism Co.'s information centers at the International Airport in Isla Verde, La Casita near Pier 1 in Old San Juan and the PRTC Headquarters at the La Princesa Building, also in Old San Juan. Self-guiding driving and walking tours are detailed in *Qué Pasa*, the official guide to Puerto Rico.

Many interesting sites are only a short distance from San Juan—famous resorts, craft villages, forests, beaches and scenic areas. For example, a half-day tour from San Juan to the El Yunque Recreation Area in the Caribbean National Forest *(see place listing p. 195)* might include a drive through the villages of Río Grande and Lóiza, a scenic town where intricate masks are carved out of coconut shells by descendants of the town's original black plantation slaves.

Another half-day trip from San Juan is a visit to Las Cabezas de San Juan, a beautiful, ecologically diverse area operated by the Conservation Trust of Puerto Rico. Known locally as El Faro (the lighthouse), the reserve is home to indigenous and endangered species and features each of Puerto Rico's unique ecosystems. Reservations are required; phone (787) 722-5882 Mon.-Fri., or (787) 860-2560 on weekends.

A full day should be allotted for a round-trip drive from San Juan to Arecibo *(see place listing p. 195)*, including stops at Vega Baja, Manati, the grounds of the Arecibo Observatory and, near Lares, the Río Camuy Cave Park and the world's third largest underground river. Part of the drive follows a scenic coastal road, Rte. 681.

A drive through coffee country from Manati to Ponce *(see place listing p. 196)* on rtes. 140 and 10, then to San Juan via Rte. 1, might include stops at rock formations and at Central Mercedita near Ponce, where sugar is refined. For a taste of the resort life, visit El Conquistador on the east coast or Palmas del Mar on the southeastern shore. Other renowned resort hotels, the Hyatt Cerromar Beach and Hyatt Dorado Beach, are about 30 miles (48 km) west of San Juan.

Longer excursions out on the island are usually worth the extra effort. A 3-day tour from San Juan to Ponce might include overnight stops in Mayagüez *(see place listing p. 196)* and La Parguera, then passing through San Germán *(see place listing p. 197)* and Ponce. Evening boat trips from La Parguera in Cabo Rojo cruise Bioluminescent Bay *(see attraction listing p. 196)*, where the water is illuminated by miniscule marine life known as dinoflagellates, which produce a glowing chemical light when disturbed on moonless nights.

An interesting attraction in the southwestern area is the Guánica State Forest, a scrub and cactus landscape that was the site of the American landing in 1898. It was here that a population of the supposedly extinct Puerto Rican whippoorwills was discovered in 1961. For the hardy traveler, a 4-day tour beginning and ending in San Juan and reaching Ponce via Barranquitas can include extensive sightseeing along the highway winding through the Cordillera Central, Puerto Rico's mountain range.

Guided tours provide insight into some of the island's more popular attractions. A 3-hour guided tour of San Juan includes visits to Fort San Felipe del Morro (El Morro Castle), Fort San Cristóbal, San José Church, San Juan Gate, Capilla del Cristo, (Christ Chapel), La Princesa and its paseos, the Capitol Building and the University of Puerto Rico. The 4-hour El Yunque Rain Forest Tour explores the rain forest's waterfalls, observation tower and tropical plants; a full-day tour that includes swimming at Luquillo Beach also is available.

Boat and airplane charters to Mona Island, about 40 miles (64 km) west of Puerto Rico and inhabited by a variety of wildlife, are available on the west coast; for information phone the Department of Natural Resources at (787) 724-8774. The islands of Vieques and Culebra off the east coast are reached by plane from San Juan or ferry service from Fajardo.

TRANSPORTATION

Puerto Rico is accessible by air from most mainland cities in a matter of hours. There also is air service between San Juan and Mayagüez, Ponce or Fajardo. American Airlines provides daily non-stop service from Miami to Ponce. Several U.S. carriers operate out of San Juan's Luis Muñoz Marín International Airport and reach most major U.S. cities. Many of the flights continue to other Caribbean islands. Rafael Hernandez Airport in Aguadilla and Eugenio Maria de Hostos Airport in Mayagüez serve the west coast of the island.

Having long been a popular port of call, Puerto Rico is one of the largest home-based cruise ship ports in the world.

Transportation in San Juan includes metered taxicabs at the airport, hotels and other locations throughout the city; taxis can be rented by the hour. Taxis are the fastest way to get to San Juan from the airport. Flat fares from the airport to Isla Verde, to Condado and to Old San Juan are $8, $12 and $16 respectively; there is a 50c per piece of luggage charge. The fare from the piers to Old San Juan or Puerto de Tierra is $6, to Condado is $10, to Isla Verde is $16.

The bus system also operates throughout the metropolitan area. Stops are designated by a red post or a metal standard bearing the word *Parada*; fare 50c. *Públicos,* public cars that follow established routes between all towns on the island, run during daylight hours. Marked by the letters P or PD following the numbers on their license plate, *públicos* can usually be hailed from the main plaza of a town. *Públicos* are the least expensive transportation available, but prospective riders must wait until the car is full.

Rental cars also are available, as are chauffeur-driven cars. A valid U.S. driver's license is good in Puerto Rico for up to 120 days. Speed limits are posted in miles per hour and are strictly enforced.

Ferry service provides interesting and inexpensive interisland links. Crossing the bay every 30 minutes, a ferry connects Old San Juan with the municipality of Cataño; fares are very inexpensive. Passenger and car ferry service also regularly follows the triangular route linking Fajardo on the east end of the island with the islands of Vieques and Culebra.

POINTS OF INTEREST

See maps on pages 192 and 198.

AGUADILLA (B-1) pop. 59,300

LAS CASCADAS AQUATIC PARK, Rte. 2 at Km 126.5, is a 16-acre (6-hectare) water park surrounded by cascading waterfalls. The site affords a spectacular view of Aguadilla Bay. Food is available. Daily 10-5, early Apr.-early Sept. Admission $12.95; over 55, $10.95; under 12, $8.95; family rate available. AE, MC, VI. Phone (787) 891-4090.

ARECIBO (B-2) pop. 93,400

The Arecibo Observatory, at the end of Hwy. 625, operates the world's largest and most sensitive radio/radar telescope. The telescope consists of a huge bowl-shaped reflector 1,000 feet in diameter and a receiving structure suspended 450 feet above the reflector. It is used by scientists from around the world to study deep-space objects and natural radio emissions, the planets and Earth's atmosphere. A 1-hour self-guiding audiotape tour is available Tues.-Fri. at 2 in either English or Spanish. The grounds are open Sun. 1-4:30. Phone (787) 878-2612.

RIO CAMUY CAVE PARK, 12 mi. (19 km) s. off Hwy. 129, is a 300-acre park whose massive cave network encompasses one of the largest underground river systems in the world. Following an introductory slide presentation, trams transport visitors to the mouth of one of the caves, where guided walking tours begin. The park also contains nature trails, a picnic area, playground and visitor center. It is recommended that visitors arrive early, as the park fills up quickly. Food is available.

Park open Tues.-Sun. 8-4. One-hour tours depart periodically. Last tour begins 30 minutes before closing. Admission $10; ages 2-12, $7. Phone (787) 898-3100.

CARIBBEAN NATIONAL FOREST (C-6)

Elevations in the forest range from 1,000 ft. to 3,533 ft. at El Yunque. Refer to AAA maps for additional elevation information.

The Caribbean National Forest occupies 27,890 acres (11,287 hectares) 25 miles (40 km) east of San Juan in the Luquillo Mountains. Referred to locally as El Yunque, the name of a 3,533-foot (1,077-m) peak in the forest, the area also is called the Luquillo Experimental Forest. Proclaimed a forest reserve by Theodore Roosevelt in 1903, the Caribbean National Forest is the only tropical U.S. national forest; it is administered by the U.S. Department of Agriculture Forest Service.

The annual rainfall is extremely heavy, and at the high elevations it exceeds 200 inches. Moisture drips from massive trees, dense plants, ferns and moss. Hundreds of streams course down the mountainsides, creating countless falls and pools. The rain forest is the recipient of about 50 billion gallons of rain a year.

Moist, misty and generally cool, the forest supports a dense system of vegetation. Largest are the towering hardwoods, their crowns hung with vines; many trunks or limbs support a fringe of air plants, a large number containing blossoms. Beneath these giants are smaller trees and shrubs that shade flowers, herbs, mosses and tree ferns growing as high as 30 feet.

The montane thicket covering valleys and slopes above 2,000 feet is generally composed of trees and a ground cover of ferns, vines and begonias. Extensive stands of sierra palms grow on steep slopes at higher elevations and along streams. The dwarf forest, its trees about 12 feet high, is found on the highest slopes. In all, the forest harbors more than 240 species of trees, four forest types and dozens of waterfalls. More than 50 of these species of trees are found only in Puerto Rico.

Such resplendent birds as tanagers, woodpeckers, cuckoos, euphonia and the Puerto Rican tody inhabit the forest. The birds usually remain hidden, but their calls and whistles are heard frequently. The Puerto Rican parrot, an extremely rare and endangered species, also inhabits the rain forest and is found only in this part of the island. *Coquíes,* tiny inch-long tree frogs, fill the forest with their high-pitched notes, which resemble the singing of their own name.

The El Portal Tropical Forest Center, a visitor and environmental education center, is at the entrance to the forest at the junction of Hwys. 191 and 988. Featuring information about the natural features and importance of El Yunque and tropical forests in general, the center offers interactive exhibits and a film. The center is open daily 9-5. Admission is charged.

The Yokahú Observation Tower, in the El Yunque Recreation Area, offers a magnificent view of the forest and the northeast coast of Puerto Rico. El Yunque Recreation Area is reached by Rte. 191. The Sierra Palm Visitor Center at Km 11.6 offers cultural and ecological exhibits and is open daily 9-5. Picnic areas and some well-maintained trails are at Km 12. Several trails lead to scenic waterfalls; the longer trails climb the summits of El Yunque or El Toro. In all, the forest contains 30 miles (48 km) of soft and paved trails.

Three other forest roads, rtes. 186, 966 and 988, skirt the western, northern and eastern boundaries, offering views of the coast. Luquillo Beach, reached by Rte. 3, is popular, especially on weekends.

For more information contact the Forest Supervisor, Caribbean National Forest, P.O. Box 490, Palmer, Puerto Rico 00721. Phone (787) 888-1880.

LAJAS (D-1) pop. 23,300

BIOLUMINESCENT BAY, 5 mi. (8 km) s. near the fishing village of La Parguera, is the more famous of Puerto Rico's two bioluminescent bays. Microorganisms in the bay cause the water to shimmer and glow when disturbed. Evening boat trips depart from the Villa Parguera pier. Other cruises to Vieques Island's Mosquito Bay can be arranged through Casa del Frances. Evening boat trips depart nightly at 7:30. Fare $12, children $8. Phone (787) 899-5784 for La Parguera information or (787) 744-3751 for Mosquito Bay information.

MAYAGUEZ (C-1) pop. 100,400

On the west coast, Mayagüez is an important commercial port for sugar, coffee and fruit as well as one of the world's largest tuna-packing centers. It also is distinguished as the center of the island's needlework industry and as the home of the College of Agriculture and Engineering of the University of Puerto Rico. An elegant plaza dominates the center of the city, which was almost destroyed by an earthquake in 1918.

High in the central mountain range near Mayagüez, Maricao Forest Reserve has a stone observation tower that provides fine views of the west and south coasts. Hawks and many other birds reside here all year along with the 25,000 fish raised yearly at the Maricao Fish Hatchery. Mayagüez is about 95 miles (152 km) from San Juan; half-hour flights depart frequently.

MAYAGUEZ ZOO, 1 mi. (1.6 km) n. off Rte. 108, following signs, displays tropical plants and animals in their natural settings. More than 340 animal species, including Bengal tigers and Andean condors, have been collected from tropical climates around the world. All birds, mammals and reptiles are identified in English and Spanish. Wed.-Sun. 9-4. Admission $3; ages 13-18, $2; under 12, $1. Phone (787) 834-8110.

TROPICAL AGRICULTURE RESEARCH STATION, on Rte. 65 between rtes. 2 and 108, is the tropical research center of the U.S. Department of Agriculture. Since its establishment in 1901, the station has fostered the development of more than 2,000 tropical plant species from around the world. A well-marked self-guiding tour covers most of the important areas. Because of frequent afternoon rains, morning tours are best. Mon.-Fri. 7-4; closed holidays. Free. Phone (787) 831-3435.

PONCE (D-3) pop. 187,700

An important commercial port on the south coast, Ponce is the center of the island's sugar, rum and coffee industries and has some of the largest textile mills in the Caribbean. In its center are two tree-shaded plazas bordering the graceful Cathedral of Our Lady of Guadalupe. Behind the cathedral is the Parque de Bombas, one of the oldest volunteer firehouses on American soil. It is painted in bold red and black stripes, and the trucks are painted a bright red. Now a museum, the building is one of the most photographed features of the island.

The Alhambra residential section has more than 125 Spanish-style estates. And throughout the city some 400 buildings have been restored, particularly on Isabel and Reina streets. A steep hill called *El Vigía* (The Watchman) was once a lookout post. A visitor information center is located in the Fox Delicias Mall, facing the plaza.

Scenic Toro Negro Forest, 17 miles (27 km) northeast of Ponce via rtes. 10 and 143, contains bamboo-fringed Guineo Reservoir and the island's tallest peak, Cerro de Punta, as well as picnic and swimming facilities. It is open daily 8-5; the pool is closed Mondays.

★**PONCE ART MUSEUM,** Avenue Las Americas opposite Catholic University, displays important paintings and sculpture from Europe and the Americas, including local and Latin American works, from the 13th through the 20th centuries. Highlights from the permanent collection include works by such artists as Eugène Delacroix, Lord Frederick Leighton, Bartolomé Esteban Murillo, José Ribera, Auguste Rodin, Peter Paul Rubens, Anthony Van Dyck and Diego Velázquez. Traveling exhibits also are presented.

The 1959 house, which was converted to a museum in 1978, was designed by Edward Durell Stone and now houses two gardens, an amphitheater and a library. Allow 1 hour, 30 minutes minimum. Daily 10-5; closed Jan. 1, Jan. 6, Good Friday and Dec. 25. Admission $4; under 12, $2. Phone (787) 848-0505.

PONCE HISTORY MUSEUM, on the town square at Isabel and Mayor sts., is housed in two neoclassical buildings. Ten exhibition halls contain displays depicting the city's ecology, economy, architecture, government and elements of daily life. Guided tours are available. Mon. and Wed.-Fri. 10-5, Sat.-Sun. 10-6. Admission $3; over 64, $1.50; under 13, $1. Phone (787) 844-7071.

SERRALLES CASTLE MUSEUM is at 17 El Vigía. Guided tours of this Spanish Revival home, built in the 1930s, provide insights into the lifestyle of its owner, a wealthy sugar and rum merchant. Scenic city and coastal views are offered from an upstairs terrace. Food is available. Tues.-Thurs. 9:30-4:30, Fri.-Sun. 10-5. Admission $3; over 61, $2; ages 3-15, $1.50. Phone (787) 259-1774.

TIBES INDIAN CEREMONIAL CENTER, on Rte. 503, Km 2.7, features seven pre-Taino ballcourts as well as the oldest burial ground yet uncovered in the Antilles. Excavations begun in 1975 have revealed 187 human skeletons believed to have belonged to an aboriginal Indian population called the Igneris. The center includes a re-created Indian village, a museum with permanent and temporary exhibits and a shop. Wed.-Sun. 9-4; closed Jan. 1, Good Friday and Dec. 25. Admission $2; ages 5-12, $1. Phone (787) 840-2255.

CASINOS

• Holiday Inn of Ponce Casino, on Hwy. 2 (at Km 221.2 sector El Tuque). Daily noon-4 a.m. Phone (787) 844-1200.

SAN GERMAN (D-1) pop. 35,000

Established on the south coast in 1512, San Germán was moved inland in 1570 to its present location midway between Mayagüez and Ponce. The Inter-American University of Puerto Rico, founded in 1912, is here.

ART MUSEUM AND LIBRARY (Museo de Arte y Casa de Estudio), 7 Esperanza St., displays collections of religious art and objects, including antique altar pieces and vestments worn by Puerto Rico's first cardinal. Taino artifacts and temporary exhibits by local artists also are displayed. Wed.-Sun. 10-3; closed major holidays. Free. Phone (787) 892-8870.

PORTA COELI CHURCH, Ramas and Dr. Veve sts., overlooking one of San Germán's two plazas, was built in 1606 and is the oldest church under the American flag to remain intact. Restored as a museum, the church has wooden statues, paintings, ornaments and liturgical objects from Puerto Rico's historic churches; images carved by 16th-century *santeros* (saint makers); Spanish mosaics of Biblical scenes; and paintings by the 18th-century artist José Campeche. Tues.-Sun. 9-noon and 1-4; closed holidays. Free. Phone (787) 892-5845.

SAN JUAN (B-5) pop. 437,700

One of the oldest capital cities in the Western Hemisphere, San Juan is the principal city of the Commonwealth of Puerto Rico. Enveloped within the metropolitan core are the inner districts of Hato Rey, Río Piedras and Santurce, all bonded to San Juan by the public transportation system. The sprawling urban area also encompasses the municipalities of Bayamón, Carolina,

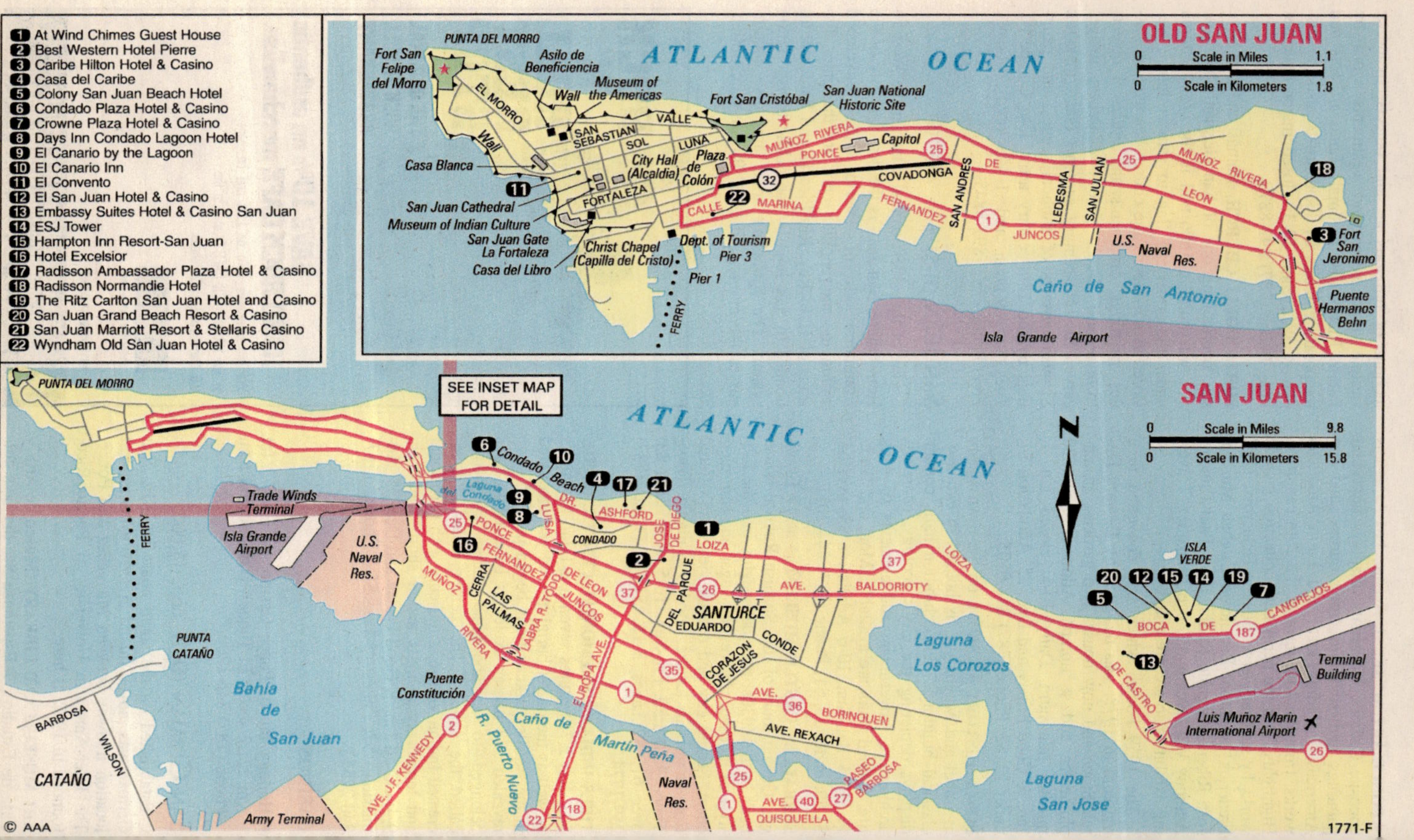

1 At Wind Chimes Guest House
2 Best Western Hotel Pierre
3 Caribe Hilton Hotel & Casino
4 Casa del Caribe
5 Colony San Juan Beach Hotel
6 Condado Plaza Hotel & Casino
7 Crowne Plaza Hotel & Casino
8 Days Inn Condado Lagoon Hotel
9 El Canario by the Lagoon
10 El Canario Inn
11 El Convento
12 El San Juan Hotel & Casino
13 Embassy Suites Hotel & Casino San Juan
14 ESJ Tower
15 Hampton Inn Resort-San Juan
16 Hotel Excelsior
17 Radisson Ambassador Plaza Hotel & Casino
18 Radisson Normandie Hotel
19 The Ritz Carlton San Juan Hotel and Casino
20 San Juan Grand Beach Resort & Casino
21 San Juan Marriott Resort & Stellaris Casino
22 Wyndham Old San Juan Hotel & Casino
OLD SAN JUAN
Scale in Miles
Scale in Kilometers
ATLANTIC OCEAN
PUNTA DEL MORRO
Fort San Felipe del Morro
Asilo de Beneficiencia
EL MORRO
Wall
Museum of the Americas
San Juan National Historic Site
Fort San Cristóbal
VALLE
SAN SEBASTIAN
SOL
LUNA
Casa Blanca
City Hall (Alcaldia)
Plaza de Colón
FORTALEZA
San Juan Cathedral
Museum of Indian Culture
San Juan Gate
La Fortaleza
Casa del Libro
Christ Chapel (Capilla del Cristo)
Dept. of Tourism
Pier 3
Pier 1
FERRY
CALLE MARINA
MUÑOZ RIVERA
PONCE
Capitol
COVADONGA
FERNANDEZ
JUNCOS
SAN ANDRES
DE
LEDESMA
SAN JULIAN
MUÑOZ RIVERA
LEON
U.S. Naval Res.
Caño de San Antonio
Isla Grande Airport
Fort San Jeronimo
Puente Hermanos Behn
SAN JUAN
Scale in Miles
Scale in Kilometers
ATLANTIC OCEAN
PUNTA DEL MORRO
Trade Winds Terminal
Isla Grande Airport
U.S. Naval Res.
FERRY
PUNTA CATAÑO
Bahía de San Juan
BARBOSA
WILSON
CATAÑO
Army Terminal
Puente Constitución
AVE. J.F. KENNEDY
R. Puerto Nuevo
Caño de
Martín Peña
Naval Res.
EUROPA AVE.
LABRA R. TODD
MUÑOZ RIVERA
CERRA
LAS PALMAS
PONCE
FERNANDEZ JUNCOS
DE LEON
LUISA
DR.
ASHFORD
CONDADO
Condado Beach
Laguna del Condado
SEE INSET MAP FOR DETAIL
JOSE DE DIEGO
DEL PARQUE
SANTURCE
EDUARDO
CORAZON DE JESUS
CONDE
LOIZA
BALDORIOTY
AVE.
AVE. REXACH
BORINQUEN
PASEO BARBOSA
QUISQUELLA
AVE.
Laguna Los Corozos
ISLA VERDE
BOCA
DE
CANGREJOS
DE CASTRO
187
Terminal Building
Luis Muñoz Marin International Airport
Laguna San Jose
© AAA
1771-F

Cataño, Guaynabo and San Juan. The Aqua Express, a daily ferry service, connects Old San Juan at Pier 2 with Cataño and Hato Rey; fare 50c.

Luxury hotels lining Avenida Ashford distinguish the Condado Beach section, known as the Gold Coast. Attractive shops, dining spots, supper clubs, casinos and beachfronts dotted with umbrellas, palm trees and Spanish residences grace this popular resort area.

On Avenida Ponce de León is Puerto Rico's Archives and General Library, one of the last buildings to be erected by the Spanish. Built in 1877, it has functioned as a prison, a cigar factory and a rum plant. Red-tiled floors, stained-glass windows, chandeliers and a chapel make this building interesting. Bayamón Central Park, west of San Juan on Rte. 2, offers train rides Sat.-Sun. 9-5.

BACARDI PLANT, 2.5 mi. (4 km) w. of Cataño at Km. 2.6 on SR 888, across the straits from Fort San Felipe del Morro (El Morro Castle), is the world's largest rum factory. A ferry connects Old San Juan port and the dock at Cataño, where you can take a taxi to the plant. Displays and samples are offered. One-hour tours depart every 20 minutes Mon.-Sat. 9-10:30 and noon-4, mid-Jan. to mid-Dec. Free. Phone (787) 788-1500.

BOTANICAL GARDEN (Jardín Botánico) is at jct. SR 847 and Hwy. 1 in Río Piedras. This 75-acre (30-hectare) garden, part of the University of Puerto Rico, features native and tropical flora, including aquatic and herb gardens and areas devoted to heliconia, bamboo, orchids and palms. Guided 60- to 90-minute tours are available. Open daily 9-4:30. Free. Phone (787) 763-4408.

THE CAPITOL (El Capitolio), on Avenue Ponce de León, is built of Georgia marble in the Renaissance style. Flanked by the commonwealth's legislative offices, the building has a rotunda with an illuminated coat of arms at the apex. A pamphlet available on the second floor explains the symbolism of the rotunda's mosaics. Mon.-Fri. 8:30-5. Free. Phone (787) 721-6040, ext. 2458.

FORT SAN JERONIMO, behind the Caribe Hilton Hotel, was built 1791-96. An interesting contrast to the modern hotel, the fort houses a museum of Spanish military history, armor and weapons. Wed.-Sun. 9:30-noon and 1-4:30. Free.

UNIVERSITY OF PUERTO RICO, on Avenue Ponce de León in Río Piedras, a residential suburb of San Juan, has an enrollment of more than 42,000 students. A museum exhibits paintings by José Campeche and Francisco Oller as well as archeological displays. Museum open Mon.-Fri. 9-4:30 (also Thurs. 4:30-9), Sat. 9-3. Phone (787) 764-0000.

Ponce de León Museum, 10 mi. (16 km) s. at Km. 6.6 on Hwy. 2 in Villa Caparra, overlooks the foundation of the explorer's home. The museum contains items found during excavations in the area and exhibits about the early colonial period. Daily 9-4. Admission $3; over 64, $1.50; under 13, $1. Phone (787) 844-7071.

CASINOS

● San Juan Marriott Casino, Hwy. 26 to Ashford Ave. E. exit, then 1.5 mi. (2 km) to 1309 Ashford Ave. Daily noon-4 a.m. Phone (787) 722-7200.

OLD SAN JUAN

Settled in 1521, the seven-square-block area of *Viejo* San Juan remains partially enclosed by walls which once were believed necessary to protect San Juan Harbor. Spain continued this construction for 244 years. By the 19th century the military stronghold, protected by the fortresses of San Felipe del Morro and San Cristóbal, had developed into a quaint residential and commercial community. Restored to its former grandeur, the old city exudes the atmosphere of colonial Spain with its pastel-colored houses, filigreed balconies, hidden plazas and narrow streets.

Paved with *adoquines,* bluish glazed bricks used for ballast in Spanish galleons, some streets in the old quarter are so narrow that the walls on both sides can be touched with outstretched arms. Other charming remnants of early times are the street staircases that scaled this hilly section. Halfway between the cathedral and San Juan Gate on Callejón de las Monjas and one block above it are two of these survivors. A prime example of colonial opulence is *La Fortaleza,* one of the oldest executive mansions still in use in the Western Hemisphere.

A series of bridges link the islet with the resort areas of Condado and Isla Verde as well as the residential communities of Santurce and the suburbs of Hato Rey and Río Piedras. The Plaza de Colón, where Old San Juan begins, is dominated by a statue of Christopher Columbus erected in 1893 to commemorate the 400th anniversary of his discovery of Puerto Rico. Today the plaza adjoins the main shopping district on Calle Fortaleza; city buses make frequent stops here. Narrow streets and slow-moving traffic make walking the most practical way to explore the old city.

Appropriately found where the cruise ships dock at Pier 1, the Museum of the Sea exhibits ships models, antique maritime instruments and other nautical equipment; it is open when cruise ships are in port. A visitor information center is at La Casita near Pier 1. La Princesa, on Paseo de la Princesa, is the headquarters of the Puerto Rico Tourism Co. The restored building, which was a jail 1837-1976, also houses an art gallery with changing exhibits; phone (787) 721-2401 or 721-2416.

ASILO DE BENEFICENCIA, off El Morro, was constructed in the 1840s to house the indigent. The grounds are accented with gardens and courtyards. Inside features include archeological items, rocks, tools, masks from Latin cultural backgrounds and copper geometric figures. Temporary exhibits also are presented. Allow 1 hour minimum. Mon.-Fri. 8-5; closed major holidays. Free. Phone (787) 723-3720.

CASA BLANCA, Calle San Sebastián, crowns the seawall in the harbor. The fortified white mansion was erected in 1523 for Juan Ponce de León, but the conquistador died before its completion. His family lived here for 250 years, until the Spanish government acquired it for a military headquarters. The mansion is furnished with 16th and 17th century antiques.

Allow 30 minutes minimum. Tues.-Sun. 9-noon and 1-4:30; closed Jan. 1 and Good Friday. Guided tours are available Mon.-Fri. by appointment. Admission $2; over 59 and ages 6-12, $1. Guided tour $1; over 59 and ages 6-12, 50c. Phone (787) 724-4102.

CASA DEL LIBRO (House of Books), 255 Calle Cristo, is a restored and furnished 18th-century house, which has a specialized library of 4,000 books that includes many pre-16th-century and rare editions. The emphasis of the museum is upon book arts and the book as an art form. Tues.-Sat. 11-4:30. Free. Phone (787) 723-0354.

CHRIST CHAPEL (Capilla del Cristo), on Calle Cristo, only has room for some 30 worshipers. The church is built on the spot where a horse and rider leaped over the 70-foot bluff in 1753; legend says that both survived. The chapel contains an altar made of silver and gold as well as antique ornaments and paintings. Open Tues.-Wed. 10:30-3:30. Free. Phone (787) 723-1895.

CITY HALL (Alcaldía) fronts the Plaza de Armas. The facade of this 1789 building is said to have been inspired by the city hall in Madrid, Spain. It contains a small museum chronicling San Juan's history. An information center is near the Calle San Francisco entrance. Mon.-Fri. 8-4, Sat. 9-5. Phone (787) 724-7171.

FINE ARTS MUSEUM, Calle Cristo, displays sculpture and paintings dating from the 15th century. Restoration is in progress.

LA FORTALEZA, the governor's palace, is at the foot of Calle Fortaleza. The oldest executive mansion in the Western Hemisphere still in use, it has been the residence of 180 governors and the seat of Puerto Rico's government for more than 4 centuries. Special attractions include wrought-iron gates, terraced gardens, a mahogany staircase, marble floors, a mosaic-studded chapel and the room once used by the Puerto Rican treasury for storing gold. Free guided tours in English are available. Open Mon.-Fri. 9-4. Guided tours in English begin at the Calle Fortaleza entrance at 10, 11, 1, 2 and 3. Phone (787) 721-7000, ext. 2211, or 2358.

MUSEUM OF INDIAN CULTURE (Museo del Indio), 109 Calle San José, displays pottery, stone tools and other artifacts belonging to several Indian cultures that inhabited Puerto Rico and neighboring islands in the pre-Columbian era. Tues.-Sat. 9-noon and 1-4:30. Free. Phone (787) 721-2864.

MUSEUM OF THE AMERICAS is on the second floor of the historic Cuartel de Ballaja, off El Morro. The museum presents permanent and temporary exhibits with a concentration on the artwork of the Americas. Displays include archeological artifacts, sculpture, Amazon Indian photographs and objects, folk art, a peasant's house and a replica of a country chapel. Free 40-minute guided tours are available by reservation. Allow 1 hour, 30 minutes minimum. Tues.-Fri. 10-4, Sat.-Sun. 11-5; closed major holidays. Free. Phone (787) 724-5052.

PLAZA DE SAN JOSE is bounded by calles San Sebastian, Cristo and San José. Several historic structures and museums are here as well as a statue of Juan Ponce de León fashioned from bronze cannons captured from the British in 1797.

Casa de los Contrafuertes, or Buttress House, is considered one of the oldest private residences in the old city. The second floor of the heavily buttressed early 18th-century structure contains the Latin American Graphic Arts Museum, which exhibits small religious figures carved from wood, some of which are more than 200 years old. Below is the Pharmacy Museum. Wed.-Sun. 9-4:30. Phone (787) 753-1797.

Dominican Convent, 98 Norzagaray, was formerly the headquarters of the Institute of Puerto Rican Culture. From 1898 to 1966 the 16th-century Spanish colonial convent housed the Antilles Command of the U.S. Army. Cultural activities are regularly presented in the interior patio, which is surrounded by arcaded galleries. A small museum also is here. The convent is open Mon.-Sat. 9-5. The museum is open Wed.-Sun. 9-noon and 1-4:30. Phone (787) 721-6866.

Pablo Casals Museum contains memorabilia, manuscripts and photographs of the famous Spanish cellist who lived in Puerto Rico for nearly 20 years. Videotapes of Festival Casals concerts can be viewed upon request. Tues.-Sat. 9:30-5:30. Admission $1, children 50c. Phone (787) 723-9185

San José Church is reputedly the second oldest church in the Western Hemisphere. Dominican friars began construction on this original chapel for the Dominican monastery in 1532. Its interior features vaulted Gothic ceilings, a collection of religious paintings and frescoes, Ponce de León's family coat of arms and a figure of Christ on the cross that might date back to the mid-16th century. Mon.-Wed. and Fri. 7-3, Sat. 8-1, Sun. mass at noon. Phone (787) 725-7501.

San Juan Museum of Art and History, at Calle Norzagaray, displays Puerto Rican art in its east and west galleries. Concerts and other cultural events take place in the museum's interior patio. Audiovisual shows trace the history of San Juan. Mon.-Fri. 8-noon and 1-4. Phone (787) 724-1875.

SAN JUAN CATHEDRAL, Calle Cristo, is a rare example of Gothic architecture. Built in the 1540 and damaged repeatedly by the elements, the present structure is the result of several restorations. Featured are a circular staircase, vaulted ceilings, 16th-century chalices, the relic of San Pio and a Renaissance Madonna. The marble tomb of Juan Ponce de León rests near the transept. Daily 8:30-4, Mon.-Fri. mass at 12:15, Sat. mass at 7:30 p.m., Sun. mass at 9 and 11 a.m. Phone (787) 722-0861.

SAN JUAN NATIONAL HISTORIC SITE contains the fortifications built by the Spanish to protect San Juan and the treasure-laden fleets that sailed past the city en route to Spain. El Cañuelo, on Isla de Cabras at the entrance to San Juan Harbor, was built about 1610 as a wooden structure, destroyed by the Dutch in 1625 and rebuilt in stone in the 1660s. The tiny fort is undergoing restoration. Comfortable walking shoes are recommended. Daily 8-6. Free.

★**Fort San Cristóbal** stands on a hill at the e. edge of Old San Juan n. of Ave. Muñoz Rivera. A complex of six outworks and one fort built 1634-1783, the fort's powerful artillery repelled British forces attacking from the east in 1797. The first shot of the Spanish-American War in Puerto Rico was fired from the fort in 1898. Gunrooms, barracks and officers quarters surround the main building's courtyard. The various units are connected to the main structure by tunnels and dry moats.

★**Fort San Felipe del Morro** (El Morro Castle), covering about 200 acres on the northwest tip of Old San Juan, is the most strategic of San Juan's defense systems. Its defenders repelled attacks by the British, Dutch and French over the course of 300 years. Six levels of impressive batteries rising 140 feet out of the sea afford a beautiful harbor view. A network of ramps and stairways connects the ramparts.

Construction began in 1539 with a simple tower designed to guard the channel to the harbor. Most of the massive earthworks and fortifications were built between 1589 and the 1650s, and the fort was completed by 1787. The fort contains a museum with examples of 16th- and 17th-century armor and weapons, a chapel and audiovisual exhibits. Allow 1 hour minimum.

San Juan Gate (Puerta de San Juan), at the foot of Caleta de San Juan, is the most impressive and last remaining of three gates of the old city wall. The 1639 gate stands more than 16 feet tall.

Utuado (C-2) pop. 35,000

Utuado, in the Cordillera Central, is a departure point for trips to Río Abajo State Forest, reached via Rte. 10 to Rte. 621. Teak and mahogany trees cover the oddly shaped karst hills of the 5,730-acre (2,319-hectare) forest, which contains a recreation area and offers exploring possibilities in dozens of mountain caves and ruined sugar mills. Nearby off Rte. 10 is manmade Dos Bocas Lake, a long, winding hydroelectric reservoir. One- or 2-hour launch trips on the lake, including stops at several mountain villages, depart the wharf Mon.-Sat. at 6:30, 8:30, 10, 11, 1, 2, 4 and 5; Sun. on the hour 8-2 and 4-5. Phone (787) 879-1838.

The Caguana Indian Ceremonial Ball Park, 7.5 miles (12 km) west of Utuado on Rte. 111, was constructed by Taino Indians for recreation and worship more than 700 years ago. The restored park is open daily 8:30-4:30. Phone (787) 894-7325.

LODGINGS & RESTAURANTS

CABO ROJO

RESTAURANT

TINO'S RESTAURANT
◆◆ *American*   **L** $6-$23   **D** $6-$23
Location: In Joyuda's Beach; Hwy 2 or 52 to Cabo Rojo; Rd 100 to Joyuda exit (Rd 102), Km 13.6. Rd 102, KM 13.6 00623-9719. **Hours:** 11 am-10 pm. **Features:** casual dress; carryout; cocktails & lounge. Casual family atmosphere. Puerto Rican seafood specialty Mofongo Relleno con Mariscos. **Cards:** AE, MC, VI.

☎ 787/851-2976

DORADO

LODGING

HYATT DORADO BEACH
◆◆◆◆ *Resort Hotel*

12/20-3/31	$400-515	XP $45
4/1-5/31 & 10/1-11/30	$250-300	XP $45
12/1-12/19	$240-290	XP $45
6/1-9/30	$180-240	XP $45

Location: In Dorado Beach; from San Juan Hwy 22 to Dorado exit; km 12.8 w on Rd 693. Hwy 693 00646. Fax: 787/796-2022. **Terms:** F18; Reserv deposit, 30 day notice; 10 night min stay, 12/22-12/30. **Facility:** 298 rooms. On 1000 acres of tropical landscaped grounds. Elegant resort atmosphere. Rooms in 2- & 3-story clusters. Balcony or patio. 1-3 stories; exterior corridors; oceanfront; beach, wading pool, sauna. Fee: 36 holes golf, golf equipment & instruction; 7 tennis courts (2 lighted), tennis equipment & instruction. **Dining:** 3 dining rooms; 7 am-9:30 pm; casino Wed-Sun; $20-$30; cocktails; public by reservation only; also, Su Casa, see separate listing. **Services:** giftshop. Fee: massage, area transportation. **Recreation:** swimming. Fee: charter fishing, water sports. Rental: bicycles. **All Rooms:** combo or shower baths. **Cards:** AE, CB, DI, DS, JC, MC, VI.

☎ (787)796-1234

RESTAURANT

SU CASA
◆◆◆ *Ethnic*   **D** $25-$38
Location: In Dorado Beach; from San Juan Hwy 22 to Dorado exit; km 12.8 w on Rd 693; in Hyatt Dorado Beach. Dorado Beach 00646. **Hours:** 6:30 pm-11 pm. **Reservations:** required. **Features:** No A/C; casual dress; cocktails; entertainment; a la carte. In original plantation house overlooking ocean. Some balcony tables. **Cards:** AE, DI, MC, VI.

☎ 787/796-1234

FAJARDO

LODGINGS

EL CONQUISTADOR RESORT & COUNTRY CLUB
◆◆◆◆ *Resort Complex*

12/1-4/30	$315-495	XP $40
5/1-11/30	$185-390	XP $40

Location: 31 mi ne of San Juan International Airport; Hwy 3 to Fajardo exit, 0.5 mi w, then follow signs. 1000 El Conquistador Ave 00738. Fax: 787/860-3200. **Terms:** F12; Reserv deposit; AP, BP, CP, MAP avail. **Facility:** 751 rooms. Situated atop a 300 ft cliff on the northeast coast of Puerto Rico. Spectacular site, boasts incomparable views of both the Atlantic Ocean & the Turquoise Caribbean Sea. A warm Spanish decor. 5 stories; interior/exterior corridors; beach, indoor pool, wading pool, whirlpools; 7 tennis courts (4 lighted). Fee: parking; 18 holes golf; marina. **Dining:** Dining room, 5 restaurants, coffee shop; disco; casino; $15-$45; cocktails. **Services:** giftshop. Fee: massage, area transportation. **Recreation:** swimming, charter fishing, fishing, scuba diving, snorkeling; water taxi to Palomino Island. Fee: sailboating, scuba & snorkeling equipment, waterskiing, windsurfing; horseback riding. Rental: boats, paddleboats. **Some Rooms:** whirlpools. **Cards:** AE, CB, DI, DS, JC, MC, VI. *(See color ad back cover)*

☎ (787)863-1000

LAS CASITAS VILLAGE
◆◆◆◆◆ *Resort Hotel*

12/23-4/16	$970-2290
12/1-12/22, 4/17-6/30 & 9/16-11/30	$725-1700
7/1-9/15	$525-1565

Location: 31 mi ne of San Juan International Airport; Hwy 3 to Fajardo exit, 0.5 mi w, then follow signs. 1000 El Conquistador Ave 00738. Fax: 787/860-3200. **Terms:** Reserv deposit, 7 day notice; handling fee imposed; EP, MAP avail. **Facility:** 133 rooms. Most elegant villas atop a 300 ft cliff on the Northeast coast of Puerto Rico. Spectacular site boasts incomparable views of both the Atlantic Ocean & the turquoise Caribbean Sea. Exemplary service. Meets AAA guest room security requirements. 47 two-bedroom units, 27 three-bedroom units. 2-3 stories; exterior corridors; beach, whirlpool; 7 tennis courts (4 lighted). Fee: parking; 18 holes golf; marina. **Dining:** 24 hours, disco, casino; cocktails. **Services:** giftshop. Fee: massage, area transportation. **Recreation:** swimming, charter fishing, fishing, scuba diving, snorkeling, water taxi to Palomino Island; horseback riding. Fee: sailboating, scuba & snorkeling equipment, waterskiing, windsurfing. Rental: boats, paddleboats. **All Rooms:** kitchens. **Some Rooms:** whirlpools. **Cards:** AE, CB, DI, DS, JC, MC, VI. *(See color ad below)*

（ (787)863-6855

RESTAURANT

ISABELE'S GRILL
◆◆◆◆ *American* 　　　　D $40-$60

Location: 31 mi ne of San Juan International Airport; Hwy 3 to Fajardo exit; 0.5 mi w, follow signs. Located inside El Conquistador Resort Complex. **Hours:** 6 pm-midnight, Sun brunch 11 am-3 pm, 11/24-6/5. **Reservations:** required. **Features:** casual dress; cocktails & lounge; fee for parking & valet parking. Smoke free premises. **Cards:** AE, CB, DI, DS, JC, MC, VI.

（ 787/863-1000

LODGING

PARADOR LA HACIENDA JUANITA
◆◆ *Historic Country Inn*

All Year	$72	XP $12

Location: 30 mi se from Mayaguez Airport; Hwy 2, 14 mi towards San German; on 119, 10 mi to km 16, turn right on 3 mi to 105 km 23.5. Road 105, Km 23.5 (PO Box 777, 00606). Fax: 787/838-2551. **Terms:** F12; Reserv deposit, 3 day notice; handling fee imposed. **Facility:** 21 rooms. Winding roads leads to this country inn, high up in the cool tropical mountains. A restored 1836 wooden-cement structure of a coffee plantation. Rustic accommodations, delightful surroundings. 2 stories; exterior corridors; mountain view; 1 tennis court. **Services:** giftshop. **Some Rooms:** color TV. **Cards:** AE, MC, VI.

（ 787/838-2550

LODGINGS

BEST WESTERN MAYAQUEZ RESORT AND CASINO
◆◆◆ *Hotel*

All Year	$145-170	XP $25

Location: 3.2 km n via Hwy 2, 0.4 km e via Hwy 102. Rt 104 (PO Box 3781, 00681). Fax: 787/265-3020. **Terms:** F12; Reserv deposit, 3 day notice; package plans. **Facility:** 140 rooms. Attractive hillside hotel in garden setting. Meets AAA guest room security requirements. Executive floor, $10 extra charge; 5 stories; interior corridors; wading pool, whirlpool; 3 lighted tennis courts, tennis instruction; playground. Fee: parking. **Dining:** Restaurant; 6:30 am-11 pm; $14-$24; cocktails; also, El Castillo, see separate listing. **Cards:** AE, DI, DS, MC, VI.

（ (787)832-3030

HOLIDAY INN OF MAYAGUEZ & TROPICAL CASINO
◆◆ *Motor Inn*

All Year	$131-141	XP $10

Location: Hwy 2, km 149.9 n of downtown; 0.5 mi from Mayaquez Airport. 2701 Hwy 2 00680. Fax: 787/833-1300. **Terms:** F18; Reserv deposit, 3 day notice. **Facility:** 152 rooms. Landscaped pool courtyard. Meets AAA guest room security requirements. Interior corridors. **Services:** giftshop. **Cards:** AE, DI, DS, MC, VI.

（ 787/833-1100

RESTAURANT

EL CASTILLO
◆◆◆ *Continental*   **D** $13-$30
Location: 3.2 km n via Hwy 2, 0.4 km e via Hwy 102; in Best Western Mayaquez Resort and Casino. **Hours:** 7 am-11 pm. **Reservations:** suggested. **Features:** semi-formal attire; cocktails & lounge; fee for parking; valet parking; a la carte. Attractive dining room overlooking pool very well prepared continental & Caribbean cuisine. **Cards:** AE, DI, DS, MC, VI.

(787/832-3030

PONCE—187,700

LODGINGS

PONCE HILTON & CASINO
◆◆◆ *Resort Hotel*

All Year $200-220   XP $40
Location: Hwy 52 follow Ponce exit 1 km to Hwy 2, then w 1.2 km to Hwy 14, then s 2 km, follow signs. Santiago de Los Caballero Ave 00731 (PO Box 7419, 00732). Fax: 787/259-7674. **Terms:** F16; Reserv deposit, 3 day notice. **Facility:** 152 rooms. Lush tropical landscaping. All rooms have private balcony. 13 whirlpool rms, extra charge; 4 stories; exterior corridors; oceanview; putting green; beach; playground. Fee: parking; 4 lighted tennis courts. **Services:** giftshop. Fee: massage. **Recreation:** swimming, scuba diving, snorkeling & equipment. Fee: charter fishing, fishing, scuba equipment; bicycles. Rental: boats. **Cards:** AE, DI, DS, MC, VI.

(787/259-7676

PONCE HOTEL & TROPICAL CASINO
◆◆ *Motor Inn*

All Year $100-170   XP $15
Location: Hwy 2 on km 221.2; sector El Tuque, w of downtown. Hwy 2, El Tuque 00731 (3315 Ponce Bypass). Fax: 787/841-8085. **Terms:** F17; Reserv deposit. **Facility:** 119 rooms. On hillside overlooking Caribbean. Some rooms with balcony. Casino. 5 stories; interior corridors; oceanview. **Services:** giftshop. **Cards:** AE, DI, MC, VI.

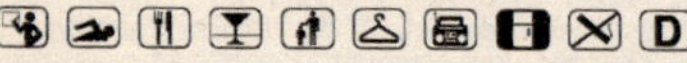

(787/844-1200

RESTAURANTS

LA MONSERRATE SEA PORT
◆◆ *Seafood*   **L** $13-$29 **D** $13-$29
Location: From Hwy 52 to Hwy 2, on km 218.6 (ocean side), sector Las Cucharas. Hwy 2 km 218.6. **Hours:** 11 am-10 pm. Closed major holidays, 12/24 & 12/31. **Features:** No A/C; casual dress; cocktails & lounge; a la carte. Relaxing, with the breeze of the ocean. Seafood dishes & salads. Oceanfront terrace & dining room. **Cards:** AE, DI, DS, MC, VI.

(787/841-2740

MARKS AT THE MELIA
◆◆◆ *Continental*
                                 L $14-$20 **D** $19-$30
Location: In Melia Hotel facing the Parone de Bombas (Old Fire Station) in the Plaza. **Hours:** noon-3 & 6-11 pm, Sun from noon. Closed: Mon & Tues. **Reservations:** required. **Features:** semi-formal attire; Sunday brunch; cocktails & lounge; a la carte. **Cards:** AE, MC, VI.

(787/284-6275

RINCON

LODGING

HORNED DORSET PRIMAVERA
◆◆◆◆ *Country Inn*

12/15-4/15 $380-800   XP $50
12/1-12/14, 4/16-4/30 & 5/1-11/30 $280-650   XP $50
Location: Rincon e on Rt 115 to Rt 429, 1 mi s to distance marker km 3.0. Rt 429 km 3.0 00677 (Apartado 1132). Fax: 787/823-5580. **Terms:** Age restrictions may apply; check-in 4 pm; reserv deposit, 45 day notice, 15 days, off season; 7 night min stay, 12/15-1/15. **Facility:** 31 rooms. Secluded, very private Spanish Colonial estate on The Mona Straits. Handsome rooms, several with private plunge pools. Separate villa. Elegant dining. 2 stories; exterior corridors; oceanview; beach. **Services:** Fee: massage. **Recreation:** swimming. **All Rooms:** combo or shower baths. **Cards:** AE, MC, VI.

(787/823-4030

RESTAURANT

HORNED DONSET PRIMAVERA DINING ROOM
◆◆◆◆ *French*   **D** $56-$88
Location: From Rincon e on route 115 to route 429, 1 mi s to distance marker km 3.0. Apartado 1132 00677. **Hours:** 7 pm-10 pm. **Reservations:** required. **Features:** No A/C; semi-formal attire; cocktails. Elegant, formal dining room, Spanish design. Highly creative French cuisine & excellent service. Tasting menu avail. **Cards:** AE, MC, VI.

(787/823-4030

RIO GRANDE

LODGING

(AAA) (SAVE) **WESTIN RIO MAR BEACH RESORT & COUNTRY CLUB**
◆◆◆◆ *Resort Hotel*

12/20-4/19 $400-600   XP $40
12/1-12/19, 4/20-5/31 & 10/1-11/30 $245-420   XP $40
6/1-9/30 $205-375   XP $40
Location: 19 mi e of San Juan Airport, from jct Rt 3 & Rt 968, 0.8 mi n on Rt 968. 6000 Rio Mar Blvd 00745. Fax: 787/888-6204. **Terms:** F17; Reserv deposit, 3 day notice; $7 service charge; AP, MAP avail; package plans; pets, by reservation only. **Facility:** 600 rooms. Handsome, very well equipped resort with extensive beach, tennis & golf facilities. Guest rooms are attractive & hotel facilities are excellent. Meets AAA security requirements. 7 stories; interior corridors; oceanfront; putting green; beach, wading pool, sauna; 13 tennis courts (2 lighted). Fee: parking; 36 holes golf. **Dining:** Dining room, 6 restaurants; 6 am-1 am; $9-$25. **Services:** giftshop. Fee: massage, area transportation. **Recreation:** swimming, kayaks, parasailing; jogging, driving range instructions avail. Fee: scuba diving/snorkeling & equipment, windsurfing; bicycles. Rental: boats. **All Rooms:** combo or shower baths. **Cards:** AE, CB, DI, DS, JC, MC, VI. *(See color ad p 209)*

((787)888-6203

SAN JUAN—437,700

(See map page 192)

LODGINGS

AT WIND CHIMES GUEST HOUSE
◆◆ *Historic Bed & Breakfast*

12/15-4/30	$85-105	XP $15
12/1-12/14 & 5/1-11/30	$75-95	XP $15

Location: In Condado area; corner McCleary Ave & Taft St; 1 blk from beach. 53 Taft St 00911. Fax: 787/726-5321. **Terms:** F12; Reserv deposit, 10 day notice. **Facility:** 14 rooms. Originally built in 1920's. Antiques & Spanish furnishings. Hand painted pictures & handmade soft goods. Some small rooms. Meets AAA guest room security requirements. Extended stay rates, off season; 2 stories; interior/exterior corridors; street parking only. **All Rooms:** shower or tub baths. **Some Rooms:** 6 efficiencies. **Cards:** AE, DS, MC, VI.

((787)727-4153

BEST WESTERN HOTEL PIERRE
◆◆◆ *Motor Inn*

12/15-4/30	$136-156	XP $10
12/1-12/14 & 5/1-11/30	$119-129	XP $10

Location: Hwy 26 to de Diego, 0.3 mi n on de Diego Ave. 105 de Diego Ave 00914. Fax: 787/721-3118. **Terms:** F12; Handling fee imposed. **Facility:** 184 rooms. Elegantly casual. Good location between Condado & business district. Meets AAA guest room security requirements. 8 stories; interior corridors. **All Rooms:** combo or shower baths. **Some Rooms:** efficiency. **Cards:** AE, CB, DI, DS, MC, VI.

(787/721-1200

AAA SAVE CARIBE HILTON
◆◆◆ *Hotel*

12/22-4/30	$330	XP $35
12/1-12/21 & 5/1-11/30	$239	XP $27

Location: Between New & Old San Juan; off Munoz Rivera. San Geronimo Grounds 00902-1872 (PO Box 9021872). Fax: 787/724-6992. **Terms:** F16; Reserv deposit, 3 day notice; handling fee imposed; AP, BP, CP, MAP avail. **Facility:** 672 rooms. All with balcony. Breathtaking gardens & comfortable guest rooms. Meets AAA guest room security requirements. 20 stories; interior/exterior corridors; oceanfront; beach, wading pool, sauna, whirlpool. Fee: parking; racquetball court, 6 lighted tennis courts, squash-1 court. **Dining:** 5 restaurants; 24 hours; $14-$28; cocktails; casino. **Services:** giftshop. **Recreation:** swimming. Rental: scuba & snorkeling equipment. **All Rooms:** combo or shower baths. **Cards:** AE, CB, DI, DS, MC, VI. **Special Amenities: Free newspaper.**

((787)721-0303

AAA SAVE CASA DEL CARIBE
◆ *Bed & Breakfast*

12/15-4/30	$85-105	XP $15
12/1-12/14 & 5/1-11/30	$75-95	XP $10

Location: On Calle Caribe, just off Ashford Ave in Condado section. Calle Caribe 57 00907. Fax: 787/723-2575. **Terms:** F12; Reserv deposit, 10 day notice; 3 night min stay, in season; pets, by reservation only. **Facility:** 9 rooms. Simple decor, excellent location in heart of Condado area. 1 story; interior/exterior corridors; designated smoking area. **All Rooms:** combo or shower baths. **Some Rooms:** kitchen. **Cards:** AE, DS, MC, VI. **Special Amenities: Free breakfast and free local telephone calls.**

((787)722-7139

COLONY SAN JUAN BEACH HOTEL
◆◆◆ *Hotel*

12/1-4/14	$175-450	XP $20
4/15-11/30	$139-335	XP $20

Location: From junction with Isla Verde Ave just n on Tartak St, 1.2 km w of airport. #2 Jose M Tartak St 00979. Fax: 787/253-0220. **Terms:** F12; Reserv deposit, 14 day notice; handling fee imposed. **Facility:** 83 rooms. Handsome guest rooms many facing the ocean very pretty section of beach directly in front of hotel. 10 stories; interior corridors; oceanfront; beach. **Recreation:** swimming. **All Rooms:** combo or shower baths. **Cards:** AE, CB, DI, DS, MC, VI.

(787/253-0100

AAA CONDADO PLAZA HOTEL & CASINO
◆◆◆◆ *Hotel*

12/1-4/30	$245-360	XP $25
5/1-11/30	$185-315	XP $25

Location: At w end of Ashford Ave. 999 Ashford Ave 00907. Fax: 787/721-4613. **Terms:** F12; Reserv deposit, 3 day notice; handling fee imposed; 7% service charge; MAP avail. **Facility:** 570 rooms. Twin mid-rise towers. Oceanfront & lagoon-side with balcony. Extensive facilities. 10 stories; interior corridors; oceanview; golf privileges; beach, wading pool, whirlpools, saltwater pool. Fee: 2 lighted tennis courts. **Dining:** 5 restaurants, coffee shop; 24 hours, casino; $9-$40; cocktails. **Services:** giftshop. Fee: massage. **Recreation:** swimming. Fee: charter fishing, water sports. **Some Rooms:** 70 efficiencies, whirlpools. **Cards:** AE, DI, DS, MC, VI. *(See color ad back cover)*

((787)721-1000

CROWNE PLAZA HOTEL & CASINO
◆◆◆ *Hotel*

12/15-4/15	$199-233	XP $20
12/1-12/14 & 4/16-11/30	$152-188	XP $10

Location: 1 km n of San Juan International Airport; in Isla Verde. Hwy 187, Km 1.5 00913 (PO Box 38079, Airport Station). Fax: 787/253-0079. **Terms:** F19; Reserv deposit, 3 day notice. **Facility:** 250 rooms. Balcony & ocean views from all rooms. Meets AAA guest room security requirements. 12 stories; interior corridors; oceanfront; beach, indoor/outdoor pool. Fee: parking. **Services:** giftshop. **Recreation:** swimming. **Cards:** AE, CB, DI, DS, JC, MC, VI.

(787/253-2929

DAYS INN CONDADO LAGOON HOTEL
◆◆ *Motel*

12/15-4/14	$109-119	XP $20
12/1-12/14 & 4/15-11/30	$79-89	XP $10

Location: In Condado close to convention center & overlooking Condado Lagoon. 6 Clemenceau St 00907. Fax: 787/724-4356. **Terms:** F11; Reserv deposit, 5 day notice; 5% service charge. **Facility:** 50 rooms. Pleasant recently renovated lodging close to convention center & Condado beach. Meets AAA guest room security requirements. 7 stories; interior corridors. **Cards:** AE, DI, DS, MC, VI.

(787/721-0170

⊕ SAVE EL CANARIO BY THE LAGOON
◆ **Motel**

12/15-4/30	$105-115	XP $10
12/1-12/14 & 5/1-11/30	$80-90	XP $10

Location: In Condado; just s of Ashford at Joffrey. 4 Calle Clemenceau 00907. Fax: 787/723-8590. **Terms:** F12; Reserv deposit, 4 day notice. **Facility:** 40 rooms. In residential surroundings. Some with balcony. Meets AAA guest room security requirements. 4 stories; interior corridors. **Dining:** Restaurant nearby. **All Rooms:** shower baths. **Cards:** AE, CB, DI, DS, MC, VI. **Special Amenities:** Free breakfast and free newspaper. (See color ad below)

((787)722-5058

⊕ SAVE EL CANARIO INN
◆ ◆ **Bed & Breakfast**

12/15-4/30	$99	XP $10
12/1-12/14 & 5/1-11/30	$75	XP $10

Location: In Condado. 1317 Ashford Ave 00907. Fax: 787/722-0391. **Terms:** F12; Reserv deposit, 4 day notice; $3 service charge. **Facility:** 25 rooms. Pink stucco villa with cheerful decor & tiled floors. Small tropical garden. 3 stories, no elevator; interior corridors; whirlpool. **Dining:** Restaurant nearby. **All Rooms:** combo or shower baths. **Cards:** AE, DI, DS, MC, VI. **Special Amenities:** Free breakfast and free newspaper.

((787)722-3861

⊕ SAVE EL CONVENTO
◆ ◆ ◆ ◆ **Historic Hotel**

12/20-4/15	$315-375	XP $25
12/1-12/19 & 4/16-11/30	$220-280	XP $25

Location: Center of Old San Juan across from San Juan Cathedral on Calle Cristo. 100 Cristo 00901. Fax: 787/721-2877. **Terms:** F13; Package plans. **Facility:** 59 rooms. Built in 1651 as the first Carmelite Convent in the New World. Now an elegant, small hotel with unique guest rooms & personalized service. 5 stories; interior corridors; outdoor plunge pool. **Dining:** Cafeteria; Continental breakfast for house guests 6:30-10:30 am. **Recreation:** small casino. **All Rooms:** combo or shower baths. **Some Rooms:** whirlpools. **Cards:** AE, DI, DS, MC, VI. **Special Amenities:** Free breakfast and free newspaper. (See color ad below)

((787)723-9020

EL SAN JUAN HOTEL & CASINO
◆◆◆◆   *Resort Hotel*

12/1-4/30	$345-525	XP $40
5/1-11/30	$260-440	XP $40

Location: 2 km nw of airport; in Isla Verde. 6063 Isla Verde Ave 00902-2872 (PO Box 9022872). Fax: 787/253-0178. **Terms:** F12; Reserv deposit, 3 day notice; MAP avail. **Facility:** 389 rooms. Elegant marble & wood-panelled lobby & public areas. Excellent & extensive facilities. 10 whirlpool rms, extra charge; 10 stories; interior corridors; oceanfront; golf privileges; beach, wading pool, saunas, whirlpools; 3 lighted tennis courts. Fee: parking. **Dining:** 6 restaurants; 24 hrs; $12-$30; cocktails; also, Back Street Hong Kong, see separate listing. **Services:** giftshop. Fee: massage. **Recreation:** swimming, scuba diving, snorkeling; tour deck. Fee: charter fishing, scuba & snorkeling equipment, water-skiing, windsurfing. Rental: boats. **Cards:** AE, CB, DI, DS, JC, MC, VI. A Preferred Hotel. *(See color ad back cover)*

((787)791-1000

EMBASSY SUITES HOTEL & CASINO SAN JUAN
◆◆◆   *Motel*

12/20-4/15	$295	XP $25
12/1-12/19 & 4/16-11/30	$175	XP $15

Location: Jct with Isla Verde Ave, just s on Tartak. 0.5 mi w of airport at Tartak exit of Rt 187. (8000 Tartak St, Isla Verde, 00979). Fax: 787/791-0555. **Terms:** F17; Check-in 4 pm; reserv deposit, 3 day notice. **Facility:** 300 rooms. Modern sitting room, bedroom suites convenient to Isla Verde Beach airport & downtown San Juan. 8 stories; interior corridors. Fee: parking. **Services:** giftshop. **Cards:** AE, CB, DI, DS, MC, VI.

(787/791-0505

ESJ TOWERS
◆◆   *Apartment Hotel*

12/25-4/18	$225	XP $35
12/1-12/24 & 4/19-11/30	$170-175	XP $35

Location: In Isla Verde; 2 km nw of airport. 6165 Avenida de Isla Verde 00979-5765 (ESJ Ste 2200, Carolina). Fax: 787/791-5888. **Terms:** F12. **Facility:** 273 rooms. Some with balcony. Studio units in hi-rise apartment building. Meets AAA guest room security requirements. 20 two-bedroom units, 10 three-bedroom units. 17 stories; interior corridors; beach; playground. **Services:** giftshop. **Recreation:** swimming. **Cards:** AE, CB, DI, DS, JC, MC, VI.

(787/791-5151

HAMPTON INN RESORT-SAN JUAN
◆◆◆   *Motel*

12/22-1/3 & 2/1-2/28	$154-174	
12/1-12/21, 1/4-1/31 & 3/1-11/30	$129-149	

Location: 2 km nw of airport in Isla Verde area. On Isla Verde Ave, close to intersection with Hwy 187. 6530 Isla Verde Ave 00979. Fax: 787/791-8757. **Facility:** 200 rooms. Modern, attractive lodging close to airport & Isla Verde beaches. 5 stories; interior corridors. **Cards:** AE, DI, DS, MC, VI.

(787/791-8777

HOTEL EXCELSIOR
◆◆   *Hotel*

12/16-4/20	$136-149	XP $15
4/21-11/30	$114-127	XP $15
12/1-12/15	$112-125	XP $15

Location: In Miramar section of downtown San Juan; corner Ponce de Leon (SR 25) & Cuevillas. 801 Ponce de Leon 00907. Fax: 787/723-0068. **Terms:** F10; Reserv deposit; handling fee imposed. **Facility:** 140 rooms. Overlooking Condado Lagoon. Large rooms. Very complete guest services. Meets AAA guest room security requirements. 11 stories; interior corridors. **Services:** area transportation. **Some Rooms:** 60 efficiencies. **Cards:** AE, DI, DS, MC, VI.

(787/721-7400

RADISSON AMBASSADOR PLAZA
HOTEL & CASINO
◆◆◆   *Hotel*

1/7-4/16	$245-385	XP $30
12/1-1/6 & 4/16-11/30	$230-325	XP $20

Location: In Condado. 1369 Ashford Ave 00007. Fax: 787/723-6151. **Terms:** D18; AP, BP, CP, MAP avail. **Facility:** 233 rooms. Walking distance to beach. Elegantly informal. All-suite tower. 20 whirlpool rms, extra charge. Microwave avail upon request; 8 stories; interior corridors; whirlpool, rooftop pool. **Dining:** 3 restaurants; 6:30 am-12:30 am; $10-$30; cocktails. **Services:** giftshop. **Recreation:** beauty salon, casino. **Cards:** AE, CB, DI, DS, JC, MC, VI. **Special Amenities:** Early check-in/late check-out and free newspaper.

((787)721-7300

AAA SAVE RADISSON NORMANDIE HOTEL
◆◆◆ *Hotel*

| 12/1-4/12 | $220-250 | XP $30 |
| 4/13-11/30 | $175-205 | XP $30 |

Location: Between New & Old San Juan; off Munoz Rivera, corner of Rosales adjacent to San Geronimo Fortress. Ave Munoz Rivera 00902 (Call Box 50059). Fax: 787/729-3083. **Terms:** F16; Reserv deposit; EP, MAP avail; package plans. **Facility:** 180 rooms. Art deco architecture inspired by ocean liner S.S. Normandie. Most units with sun room. Meets AAA guest room security requirements. 8 stories; interior corridors; oceanview; beach access. Fee: parking. **Dining:** Dining room, restaurant; 6 am-11 pm; $8-$18; cocktails. **Services:** giftshop. **Recreation:** swimming; beauty salon. **Cards:** AE, CB, DI, DS, JC, MC, VI. **Special Amenities: Early check-in/late check-out and free newspaper.** *(See ad below)*

((787)729-2929

AAA THE RITZ CARLTON SAN JUAN HOTEL AND CASINO
◆◆◆◆ *Resort Hotel*

| 1/1-4/30 | $435-635 | XP $35 |
| 12/1-12/31 & 5/1-11/30 | $335-535 | XP $35 |

Location: 1 km n of San Juan International Airport on Isla Verde Ave (SR 187). 6961 SR 187 00979. Fax: 787/253-0700. **Terms:** F18; Reserv deposit; package plans. **Facility:** 414 rooms. Exquisite service by professionally trained staff eager to please & meet guests' needs. 10 stories; interior corridors; oceanfront; beach, saunas, steamrooms, whirlpools, full service spa; 2 lighted tennis courts. Fee: parking. **Dining:** 24 hrs; $25-$40; afternoon tea; restaurants nearby. **Services:** giftshop. Fee: massage, area transportation. **Recreation:** swimming, charter fishing, full array of watersport equiptment; casino. Fee: windsurfing. Rental: paddleboats. **All Rooms:** combo or shower baths. **Cards:** AE, DI, DS, MC, VI.

((787)253-1700

AAA SAVE SAN JUAN GRAND BEACH RESORT & CASINO
◆◆◆ *Hotel*

| 12/18-4/19 | $325-675 | XP $35 |
| 12/1-12/17 & 4/20-11/30 | $235-545 | XP $35 |

Location: 1.5 km nw of airport on Isla Verde Ave. 187 Isla Verde Ave 00914 (PO Box 6676, 00914-6676). Fax: 787/791-7540. **Terms:** F16; Check-in 4 pm; AP, MAP avail. **Facility:** 401 rooms. Excellent conference facilties. Very attractive guest rooms & public areas. 16 stories; interior/exterior corridors; oceanfront; 1 holes golf; beach; 1 tennis court. Fee: parking. **Dining:** 5 restaurants; 24 hrs; $15-$30. **Services:** giftshop. Fee: massage. **Recreation:** swimming, all water sports may be arranged; full spa. **Some Rooms:** whirlpools. **Cards:** AE, DI, DS, MC, VI. **Special Amenities: Free room upgrade and preferred room (each subject to availability with advanced reservations).**

((787)791-5000

SAN JUAN MARRIOTT RESORT & STELLARIS CASINO
◆◆◆◆ *Resort Hotel*

| 12/1-4/30 | $380 | XP $25 |
| 5/1-11/30 | $270 | XP $25 |

Location: In Condado area; on Ashford Ave corner of Calle Caribe. 1309 Ashford Ave 00907. Fax: 787/722-6800. **Terms:** F18; Check-in 4 pm. **Facility:** 525 rooms. Modern, very attractive hotel. Excellent facilities & staff. Meets AAA guest room security requirements. 21 stories; interior corridors; oceanfront; beach; 2 lighted tennis courts. Fee: parking. **Services:** giftshop. Fee: massage. **Recreation:** swimming. Rental: boats. **Cards:** AE, CB, DI, DS, JC, MC, VI.

(787/722-7000

WYNDHAM OLD SAN JUAN HOTEL & CASINO

◆◆◆ *Hotel*

12/1-4/30 & 11/23-11/30	$170	XP $15
5/1-11/22	$125	XP $15

Location: Adjacent to the cruise ship terminal, in Old San Juan. 100 Brumbaugh St 00901-2620. Fax: 787/721-1111. **Terms:** F18. **Facility:** 240 rooms. Overlooks cruise ship terminal & Old San Juan. Modern, attractive rooms & public facilities. Casino. Meets AAA security requirements. Max occupancy 3 adults or 2 adults & 2 children per room; 9 stories; interior corridors. **Services:** giftshop. **Cards:** AE, CB, DI, DS, JC, MC, VI.

((787)721-5100

RESTAURANTS

AMADEUS

◆◆ *American*   L $15-$22 **D** $15-$22

Location: In Old San Juan across from Plaza San Jose, just off Calle Cristo on San Sebastian. San Sebastian 106 00901. **Hours:** noon-midnight. Closed: Mon. **Features:** casual dress; cocktails & lounge; street parking; a la carte. Informal dining in the heart of Old San Juan. Well prepared Regional & American cuisine. **Cards:** AE, MC, VI.

(787/722-8635

AUGUSTO'S

◆◆◆◆ *Continental*   L $15-$30 **D** $18-$35

Location: In Miramar section of downtown San Juan; corner of Ponce de Leon (SR 25) & Cuevillas; in Hotel Excelsior. 801 Ponce de Leon Ave 00907. **Hours:** noon-3 & 7-9:30 pm, Sat 7 pm-9:30 pm. Closed: Sun & Mon. **Reservations:** required. **Features:** casual dress; cocktails & lounge; entertainment; valet parking; a la carte. Classical Austrian lunch haute cuisine without the heavy sauces. Smoking permitted in lounge only. **Cards:** AE, MC, VI.

(787/725-7700

BACK STREET HONG KONG

◆◆◆ *Chinese*   D $17-$33

Location: 2 km nw of airport in Isle Verde; in El San Juan Hotel & Casino. Avenida de Isla Verde 00902. **Hours:** 6 pm-midnight, Sun from 1 pm. **Reservations:** suggested. **Features:** semi-formal attire; cocktails; fee for parking & valet parking; a la carte. Elaborate architectural dining room removed from Seattle World's Fair. Attentive service. **Cards:** AE, MC, VI.

(787/791-1000

COBIA

◆◆◆ *Seafood*   D $11-$25

Location: In Condado area; on Mezzanine level of Condado Plaza Hotel & Casino. 999 Ashford Ave 00907. **Hours:** 5 pm-midnight. **Reservations:** accepted. **Features:** casual dress; cocktails & lounge; fee for parking & valet parking; a la carte. Informal seafood restaurant. Large variety of fresh fish, creative preparation & presentation. Very pleasant service. **Cards:** AE, DI, MC, VI.

(787/721-1000

DON PEPES RESTAURANT
◆◆◆ *Spanish*   L $20-$30 D $20-$30
Location: In Condado; just s of Magdallena Ave. 65 Luisa St 00907. **Hours:** noon-3:30 & 7-11:30 pm, Sat 7 pm-midnight, Sun noon-11 pm. Closed: 12/24. **Reservations:** suggested. **Features:** semi-formal attire; cocktails; valet parking; a la carte. Wide variety of menu items, including many Spanish dishes. Owner/chef. **Cards:** AE, DI, DS, MC, VI.

✕   (787/723-1082

LA PICCOLA FONTANA
◆◆◆◆ *Northern Italian*   D $20-$40
Location: 2 km nw of airport in Isla Verde; in El San Juan Hotel. Avenida de Isla Verde 00902. **Hours:** 6 pm-midnight. **Reservations:** required. **Features:** semi-formal attire; cocktails; fee for parking & valet parking; a la carte. Elegant Italian dining. Extensive northern Italian menu. Professional, courteous responsive service. **Cards:** AE, CB, DI, DS, JC, MC, VI.

                               (787/791-1000

METROPOL
◆◆ *Cuban*   L $6-$25   D $6-$25
Location: Hwy 26 to de Diego Ave exit 0.3 mi n on de Diego Ave, adjacent to Best Western Hotel Pierre. 105 de Diego 00914. **Hours:** 11:30 am-10:30 pm. **Features:** casual dress; cocktails & lounge. Pleasant decor. Very well prepared Cuban & other Carribbean cuisine. Cordial service. **Cards:** AE, DI, DS, MC, VI.

                               (787/268-3075

METROPOL RESTAURANT
◆◆ *Cuban*   L $6-$25   D $6-$25
Location: 2 km nw of airport, just w of jct with route 187 on Isla Verde Ave. Boca Cangrejos Rd 00914. **Hours:** 11:30 am-11 pm. **Features:** casual dress; cocktails & lounge. Casual dining atmosphere & very attentive service. Wide variety of menu items. **Cards:** AE, DI, DS, MC, VI.

                               (787/791-5585

PIKAYO
◆◆◆ *Caribbean*   D $22-$42
Location: Condado area in Tanama Princess Hotel on Joffre St, just off Ashford Ave across from convention center. 1 Joffre St 00907. **Hours:** 6 pm-10:30 pm. Closed: Sun. **Reservations:** required. **Features:** casual dress; cocktails; valet parking; a la carte, also prix fixe. Fusion of Puerto Rican, French & Californian cuisine. Excellent, imaginative menu. Attractive dining room. Attentive service. **Cards:** AE, DI, MC, VI.

✕   (787/721-6194

RAMIRO'S RESTAURANT
◆◆◆◆ *Ethnic*   L $20-$40 D $25-$50
Location: In Condado; just s of Ashford Ave & close to convention center. 1106 Magdalena Ave 00907. **Hours:** noon-3 & 6:30-10:30 pm, Sat 6 pm-11 pm, Sun noon-3:30 & 6-10 pm. **Reservations:** suggested. **Features:** semi-formal attire; cocktails; valet parking; a la carte. International creative cuisine with a French & Spanish touch. Chef/owner. Elegant service. **Cards:** AE, DI, MC, VI.

✕   (787/721-9049

RESTAURANT AJILI-MOJILI
◆◆◆ *Ethnic*   L $11-$20 D $11-$20
Location: In Condado across from convention center. 1052 Ashford Ave 00907. **Hours:** noon-3 & 6-10 pm, Sat 6 pm-11 pm, Sun 5 pm-10 pm. Closed: 12/25. **Reservations:** suggested. **Features:** casual dress; cocktails; valet parking. Puerto Rican cuisine in cheerful neighborhood restaurant. **Cards:** AE, MC, VI.

                               (787/725-9195

RESTAURANT UNO
◆ *Argentine*   L $11-$22 D $11-$20
Location: In Condado; just s of Ashford Ave, jct Magdalena & Condado aves. 56 Condado Ave 00907. **Hours:** 11:30 am-midnight, Fri & Sat-2:30 am. **Features:** casual dress; cocktails. Variety of interesting dishes featuring Argentinean cuisine. Casual, cafe style dining. **Cards:** AE, DI, DS, MC, VI.

                               (787/721-5572

RISTORANTE II PERUGINO
◆◆◆ *Italian*   D $16-$31
Location: In Old San Juan just above San Juan Cathedral. 105 Calle Cristo 00901. **Hours:** 6:30 pm-11 pm. Closed: 7/1-7/31. **Reservations:** required. **Features:** semi-formal attire; cocktails; fee for valet parking; a la carte. Small, simpatico, high ceiling courtyard restaurant. Imaginative fresh-market cooking, classical music. Owner/chef. **Cards:** AE, MC, VI.

                               (787/722-5481

RISTORANTE TUSCANY
◆◆◆◆ *Northern Italian*   D $14-$26
Location: In Condado area; on Ashford Ave corner of Calle Caribe; in San Juan Marriott Resort & Stellaris Casino. 1309 Ashford Ave 00907. **Hours:** 6 pm-11 pm. **Reservations:** suggested. **Features:** semi-formal attire; cocktails; entertainment; fee for valet parking; a la carte. Elegant food & service, graceful atmosphere. **Cards:** AE, CB, DI, DS, JC, MC, VI.

✕   (787/722-7000

St. Barthélemy

AFFECTIONATELY CALLED St. Barts, St. Barthélemy (St. Barte-le-MEE) lies 125 miles (200 km) northwest of Guadeloupe at the northern end of the Leeward Islands. St. Barts' residents are probably the least "Caribbean" of the islands' people. Because the island's rocky, arid soil never supported slave plantations and due to an unlikely 100-year owner-

ship by Sweden, most residents are fair-skinned. Remnants of the Swedish ownership remain, most notably in the name of the capital, Gustavia. A trip around the tiny island, however, reveals scenes reminiscent of 17th-century France, a legacy of the island's original settlers maintained by today's reserved and self-sufficient residents. A quiet island with more than a dozen white sand beaches, St. Barts also has rocky hillsides and lush green valleys.

History, Government and Economy

Discovered by Christopher Columbus in 1493 and named for his brother Bartolomeo, St. Barts was first settled by French colonists from nearby St. Kitts in 1648. The settlement failed, however, and in 1651 the French sold the island to the Knights of Malta. Five years later it was raided by the fierce Caribs, then abandoned until 1673 when it was again settled by the French, but from Normandy and Brittany.

This colony succeeded, in large part because French buccaneers brought to the island vast quantities of plunder from Spanish galleons. One such pirate, Monbars the Exterminator, reputedly maintained his headquarters on St. Barts, and his treasure is said to be hidden among the coves and buried in the island sands.

Except for a brief British takeover in 1758, St. Barts remained in French hands until 1784 when it was ceded to Sweden in exchange for trading rights in Gothenburg, Sweden. The Swedes declared St. Barts a neutral and free port, and made fortunes in trade for many years. Following a protracted economic decline, the Swedish people voted to sell the island back to France. France agreed to repurchase the island and maintained its free-port status. St. Barts is a dependency of Guadeloupe, which is a department and region of France.

The people of St. Barts are industrious, spiritual and soft-mannered. Some work in the emerging tourist trade, but these private people return quietly to their homes at the end of the day. Lacking significant agricultural and industrial opportunities, the men have taken to the sea and are considered superb sailors and fishermen. Many of the women spend their days weaving straw hats, baskets and similar items to sell to tourists. Tropical fruits are produced, and some lead and zinc deposits are mined on the island.

Shopping

St. Barts is a duty-free port; therefore, perfumes, cosmetics, china, crystal, watches, imported jewelry, resort wear, liquor and tobacco sell at fair prices. Some selections are limited, but there are enough bargains to warrant setting aside time for shopping, particularly for "name" merchandise. Besides duty-free items, there is delicately woven reed work unique to St. Barts as well as straw goods, handcrafted sandals, bonnets, seashells, pottery and island artwork.

Downtown Gustavia has about three dozen boutiques and duty-free shops, among them shops specializing in brightly colored, hand-painted and hand-blocked tropical fashions. Le 4Ti Marché is an open-air market devoted to local arts and crafts; it is open in the morning Monday through Saturday. A number of chic boutiques also can be found at La Villa Créole in St. Jean and La Savane Commercial Center opposite the airport.

Most shops are open daily 8-noon and 2-4; however they close at noon Wed. and Sat. Banking hours are Mon.-Fri. 8-noon and 2-3:30; a bank at Les Galeries du Commerce in St. Jean is open Tues.-Sat. until 5. Banks are closed on holidays and afternoons preceding holidays. U.S. dollars are accepted everywhere, and prices are often quoted in dollars. Credit cards are usually accepted.

FOOD AND DRINK

Dining on St. Barts can be a memorable experience. Renowned chefs from France frequently visit the island to teach classes, and young chefs who have trained in some of France's greatest restaurants enjoy plying their trade on St. Barts. Combining local fruits and spices with classical French traditions, they have made the island a Caribbean showcase of French cuisine.

Most restaurants are small, but each is different either in food, setting or atmosphere. Some are beach cafes featuring fresh lobster and charcoal-grilled steaks; some specialize in seafood; and some, particularly in the finer hotels, present traditional French cuisine.

In Gustavia some of the restaurants are housed in quaint little buildings dating back to the Swedes and early French settlers. La Rotisserie is a deluxe French deli offering picnic fare and afternoon gourmet treats. Other popular daytime eateries include Cheeseburger in Paradise, next to Le Select; L'Escale Pizzeria; and Taste Unlimited. Most hotels and restaurants include a 10- to 15-percent service charge in their prices. If not, this charge will be added to the bill. Reservations are always a good idea. Some restaurants might be closed in September and October for refurbishing or due to their owners' vacations.

St. Barts offers the usual Caribbean fare in the way of beer and potent rum punch. The wine connoisseur, however, will appreciate a visit to La Cave in Marigot. This shop houses some 300,000 bottles of some of France's best vintages kept under strictly controlled conditions.

SPORTS AND AMUSEMENTS

For many the attraction to St. Barts is its quiet, leisurely pace. There are no casinos, large resorts or organized activities and few nightclubs. You won't find a single golf course on the island, though there is a driving range, and only a few tennis courts. Instead the emphasis is on sand and surf. Opportunities abound for swimming, yachting and sailing, windsurfing, deep-sea fishing, scuba diving and snorkeling.

The gleaming white sand beaches are all public and free; most are never crowded, and complete privacy is often readily available. The beaches of Grand Cul de Sac, on the northeast shore, and St. Jean are both in the vicinity of hotels, restaurants and water sports outlets. Flamands, to the northwest of St. Jean, is a classic stretch of white sand fringed with palm trees. Favored by island families on Sundays, the secluded beaches at Marigot and Lorient on the north shore are otherwise quiet.

In the south, Gouverneur offers complete privacy; Saline, just to the east, is more popular. Shell Beach, so named because it is covered with seashells, can be reached on foot from Gustavia.

THINGS TO KNOW

AREA: 8 square miles (21 sq km).

POPULATION: 5,000.

LANGUAGE: French and English.

CAPITAL: Gustavia.

GOVERNMENT: Dependency of the French Overseas Department of Guadeloupe.

TIME ZONE: Atlantic.

UNIT OF CURRENCY: French franc, divided into 100 centimes. $1 U.S.=approx. 5.9 French francs.

ELECTRICITY: 220 volts, 50 cycles AC.

CARS: U.S. license valid; drive on right.

IMMIGRATION REQUIREMENTS: For stays under 3 months, proof of U.S. citizenship (passport, expired passport dating back not more than 5 years, birth certificate with raised seal accompanied by a government-authorized identification card or similar document with photo) and return or through ticket are required. Departure tax 10 francs to St. Martin or Guadeloupe, otherwise 15 francs.

FOR FURTHER INFORMATION:
French West Indies Tourist Board
444 Madison Ave.
New York, NY 10022
(202) 659-7779

Office du Tourisme
Quai du Général de Gaulle,
BP 113
Gustavia 97098 Cedex
St. Barthélemy F.W.I.
Phone (011) 590-27-87-27

HOLIDAYS: Jan. 1; Mardi Gras; Mi-Carême (Mid-Lent); Easter Monday; Labor Day, May 1; Ascension Thursday; Whit Monday; Slavery Abolition Day, May 27; Bastille Day, July 14; Schoelcher Day, July 21; Assumption Day and St. Barts/Pitea Day, Aug. 15; Festival of St. Barthélemy, Aug. 24; All Saints Day, Nov. 1; Armistice Day, Nov. 11; Dec. 25.

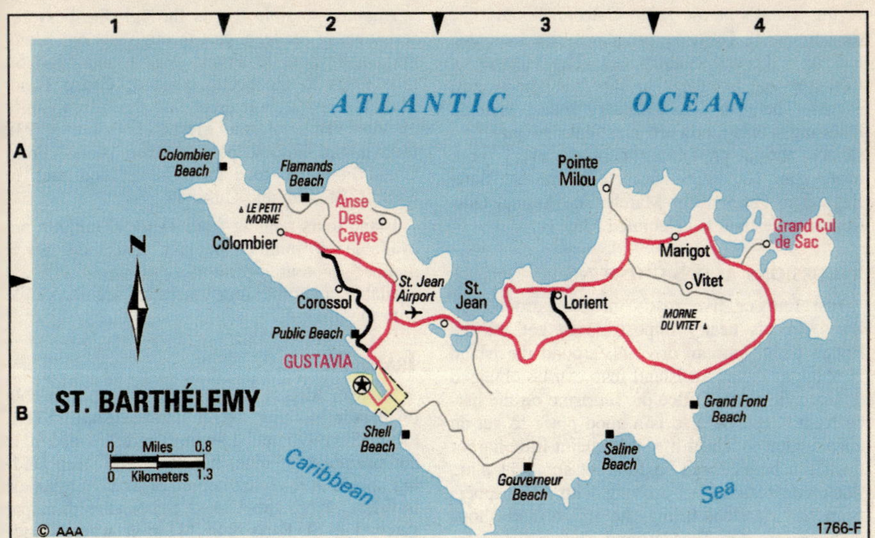

Public Beach is near the commercial pier on the other side of town. The least accessible is Colombier in the northwest. It can be reached by boat from Gustavia or by car to the village of Colombier, then a 20-minute hike down a scenic path. Although sunbathing *au naturel* is prohibited, topless sunbathing is common.

Lying about midway between the major yachting centers of Antigua and Virgin Gorda, St. Barts is naturally a popular yachting destination. Gustavia's harbor has docking facilities for about 40 yachts, and there also are anchorages at nearby Public, Corossol and Colombier. Loulou's Marine in Gustavia carries yachting supplies and accessories, and their bulletin board is one source of local yachting information. Sailing information also is available from the Office du Tourisme on the harborfront in Gustavia. A full-day round-trip sail from Gustavia to Ile Fourchue, an uninhabited island, and Colombier is available. Other charter trips also can be arranged.

Windsurfing is perhaps the most popular sport on the island; the colorful, billowing sails are a common offshore sight. Rentals and lessons are available at outlets in St. Jean, Grand Cul de Sac, Marigot and Flamands. Sailing enthusiasts can rent Sunfish and Hobie Cats in St. Jean and Grand Cul de Sac. St. Barth Wind School in St. Jean and Mistral School in Grand Cul de Sac offer specialized instruction.

The waters around St. Barts abound in tazard, wahoo, dolphin, bonito, barracuda and marlin. Deep-sea fishing expeditions can be arranged through Boat Charter Agency and Yacht Charter Agency; other possibilities are posted on bulletin boards near the Paul et Virginie Boutique, the

Banque Nationale de Paris (BNP) and Loulou's Marine in Gustavia.

Licensed, accredited divemasters at La Marine Service in Gustavia conduct dive schools and have all the necessary gear available. Two scuba clubs can be found on the beach at St. Jean. Snorkeling is good in many areas off the beaches and islets; the waters off Gouverneur, St. Jean and Grand Cul de Sac are usually the calmest. Most hotels rent snorkels, masks and fins, but they can be in limited supply. Gear is sold in Gustavia and St. Jean. An alternative to diving is a trip in the *Atlantis*. This craft offers a 1-hour undersea panorama; phone (590) 27-81-00.

The landlubber might enjoy horseback riding on St. Barts. Ranch des Flamands offers 2-hour rides along Flamands Bay or into St. Jean. Instruction is provided for beginning riders; for information and reservations phone (590) 27-80-72.

Although limited, nightlife on St. Barts is not totally lacking. Sailors and young locals gather at Le Select or across the street at the Bar de l'Oubli in Gustavia. The lounges at the upscale Carl Gustaf Hotel and the Mandala Restaurant, both overlooking the harbor, are popular with visiting yachtsmen. During the winter season, live jazz is on the menu at some spots. Dancing is limited, but some possibilities are Le Bain de Minuit in St. Jean and Le Petit Club in Gustavia. *St. Barth Magazine* and *Le Journal de St. Barth* contain information about current entertainment. Published regularly during the winter season, they are distributed free all over the island.

The year's most important event is the annual Festival of St. Barthélemy, celebrated on the weekends before and after August 24—feast day of the island's patron saint. Colorful booths line the streets of Gustavia, giving it the look and feel of a French country fair. The villages of Corossol and Lorient also schedule late-August events. There is a mid-January music festival, featuring world-renowned classical and jazz musicians and a pre-Lenten carnival every year. More than 100 boats compete in the St. Barts Regatta in February or March. The Annual Gastronomic Festival is celebrated May 1-10.

Excursions and Sightseeing

Just four or five roads meander around St. Barts, so it's nearly impossible to get off the beaten path; you can drive all around the island in about an hour. An island map can be obtained in Gustavia at the Office du Tourisme on the harborfront. Gustavia also is a good place to get an introduction to island life; this quaint little harbor town can be explored on foot. At about 11 a.m., sleek catamarans start arriving with day trippers from St. Maarten, filling the streets and shops with visitors. On Tuesday and Thursday visitors can mingle with the locals at a small public market on rue Duquesne.

Northwest of Gustavia is the fishing village of Corossol. Except for being barefoot or in sandals, the older women could be seen bustling about any little village in Brittany or Normandy. Their modest, long-sleeved dresses are vestiges of their French provincial origins, as are their shoulder-length bonnets called *quichenottes* or "kiss-me-nots." These bonnets still offer protection from the sun but once also thwarted the unwanted advances of suitors. Even while peddling their straw products to tourists these women are camera shy and do not like to be photographed. Similar scenes can be found in the nearby village of Colombier.

Also in Corossol is the Inter-Oceans Museum, housing an extensive collection of seashells and unique items from the marine world; phone (590) 27-62-97. From Colombier you can continue north to the secluded beach of Flamands where an easy hike takes you to the top of Le Petit Morne. The view is of the uninhabited offshore islands to the north and Pointe Milou to the east.

Another possible trip is through the busy resort town of St. Jean, east through Lorient, along the north shore to Pointe Milou and Marigot, then south to the rocky coast of Grand Fond. Then it's just a short drive into the hilly vicinity of Vitet. The volcanic Morne du Vitet, at 938 feet, is the highest peak on the island. From Grand Fond the road turns inland and back to Lorient, St. Jean and Gustavia.

Island tours ranging from 45 to 90 minutes are available by minibus or taxi, and there are a number of tour operators. Full-day tours are available, and other tour itineraries are negotiable with the drivers.

Transportation

St. Jean Airport has a short landing strip able to handle nothing larger than 20-seat STOL (Short Take-Off and Landing) aircraft, and it is not equipped for night landings. The steep landing approach tests the nerves of even veteran air travelers. From the United States, the principal gateway to St. Barts is St. Maarten, where Windward Island Airways and Air St. Barthélemy fly in from Juliana Airport. Air St. Barthélemy and Air Guadeloupe also fly from Esperance Airport on the French side in St. Martin. These flights take about 15 minutes.

Other flights are available from San Juan, St. Thomas, Guadeloupe and Dominica. It is 30 minutes from San Juan to St. Thomas, where Virgin Air has connecting flights to St. Barts, a 45-minute trip. Air Guadeloupe also flies from Guadeloupe in about an hour and from Martinique and Dominica in about 2 hours. Most carriers offer several flights daily; Air Guadeloupe flies from Dominica about five times a week. St. Barts also is a port of call for some cruise ships.

Taxis are available at the airport; the minimum fare is about $5, and the fare to most hotels is less than $10. Fares increase by 50 percent Mon.-Sat. from 8 p.m. to 6 a.m. and all day Sun. and holidays. Rates are fixed, but it is always a good idea to agree upon the fare in advance. There are just two taxi stands on St. Barts: at the airport and along rue de la République in Gustavia. For other taxi service phone (590) 27-66-31.

Several major and local car rental agencies operate from the airport. Rates are about $60 per day and include unlimited mileage, collision damage insurance and free delivery and pickup; rates are discounted in the summer. Most agencies require a 3-day minimum rental, and most take major credit cards. A U.S. driver's license is valid. Gurgels and minimokes, or other jeeplike vehicles, make the most sense for traveling the island's narrow, hilly roads. Most have manual transmissions, however, so you will probably need to know how to operate a stick shift.

Car rental plans can sometimes be made in advance through your hotel. Several hotels have their own fleet of cars, and because their parking space can be limited they might request you book your car through them. Motorbikes also are available for rent at about $25 per day with a $100 deposit; a valid driver's license is required. Though the law is not always enforced, helmets are required on the island when operating two-wheeled vehicles, including bicycles.

Several catamarans depart Philipsburg, St. Maarten, every morning except Sunday. These are 1-day round-trip excursions, but the skippers will take one-way passengers on a space-available basis for about $30. The ferry *St. Barth Express* departs Gustavia for Philipsburg and Marigot Mon., Wed. and Fri. at 8 and returns at 5.

ATTRACTION ADMISSIONS

Attraction admissions for this island are quoted in U.S. dollars.

POINTS OF INTEREST

See map page 213.

GUSTAVIA (B-2)

St. Barts' harbor town and capital, Gustavia was called Carenage by the French for the shelter it provided to damaged ships. The present name dates back to 1784, which marked the beginning of the island's Swedish era. The Anglican Episcopal Church on the harborfront was built in 1855.

Three forts built in the mid- to late 17th century protected the harbor. The sites of Fort Karl, overlooking Shell Beach south of town, and Fort Gustave, at the base of the lighthouse to the north, reward hikers with idyllic panoramas. Fort Oscar, at the tip of Gustavia Peninsula, houses the Ministry of Armed Forces and is closed to the public.

MUNICIPAL MUSEUM OF ST. BARTHÉLEMY, n. end of rue Schoelcher on the peninsula, contains a variety of exhibits pertaining to the island's history and natural environment. Finely woven baskets, hats and other items are of special interest. Allow 30 minutes minimum. Mon.-Fri. 8:30-11:30 and 3-5:30; closed holidays. Admission $2; under 12 free. Phone (590) 27-89-07.

LODGINGS & RESTAURANTS

ANSE DES CAYES (ST. BARTHELEMY)

LODGING

HOTEL MANAPANY COTTAGES
◆◆◆ *Cottage*

12/21-1/5	$725-785
1/6-4/12	$455-520
12/1-12/20 & 9/1-11/30	$255-405
4/13-8/31	$300-325

Location: 2 km w of airport. (BP 114, ANSE DES CAYES, 97133). Fax: 590/27-75-28. **Terms:** Reserv deposit, 7 day notice, 60 days 12/21 to 1/5; 10 night min stay, 12/24-1/7. **Facility:** 46 rooms. Good to very good cottages, some beachfront. 20 two-bedroom cottages, $1240-$1380 for 4 persons in season; 1 story; exterior corridors; beach; 1 lighted tennis court. **Services:** giftshop. **Recreation:** swimming, scuba diving, snorkeling. Rental: scuba & snorkeling equipment. **All Rooms:** combo or shower baths. **Cards:** AE, DI, MC, VI.

(590/27-66-55

RESTAURANT

OUANALAO
◆◆ *Continental*   L $12-$20 D $25-$40
Location: 2 km w of airport; in Hotel Manapany Cottages. Anse des Cayes 97133. **Hours:** noon-3 & 7-10 pm. **Reservations:** suggested. **Features:** No A/C; casual dress; Sunday brunch; cocktails & lounge; a la carte. French, Italian & Caribbean cuisine. Pleasant decor & cordial service. **Cards:** AE, DI, MC, VI.

(590/27-66-55

GRAND CUL-DE-SAC (ST. BARTHELEMY)

LODGING

SERENE BEACH HOTEL
◆◆◆   *Hotel*

12/21-1/4 & 2/1-2/28	$320	XP $70
12/1-12/20, 1/5-1/31, 3/1-8/25 & 10/25-11/30	$200	

Location: 8 km e from Gustavia Town Harbor; 6 km from airport. (BP 19, GRAND CUL-DE-SAC, 97095CEDEX). Fax: 590/27-7547. **Terms:** Open 12/1-8/25 & 10/25-11/30; reserv deposit, 30 day notice, 15 days in season; handling fee imposed; weekly/monthly rates; small pets only. **Facility:** 41 rooms. All ground floor rooms with private patio amid tropical gardens. 9 cottages $280, $180 off season; for 2 persons; extra person $25; 1 story; exterior corridors; beachfront; beach. **Dining:** Restaurant; 7 am-10, noon-2:30 & 7:15-11 pm; $25-$40; cocktails. **Services:** giftshop. **Recreation:** swimming, snorkeling & equipment, watersports. Fee: scuba diving & equipment, windsurfing; bicycles. Rental: canoes. **All Rooms:** shower baths. **Cards:** AE, DI, MC, VI.

((590)27-6480

GUSTAVIA

RESTAURANT

L'ESCALE
◆◆   *Italian*

L $15-$30 D $15-$30

Location: Downtown on the waterfront. Rue Jeanne d'Arc 97133. **Hours:** 11 am-11 pm. **Reservations:** suggested. **Features:** No A/C; casual dress; cocktails & lounge; entertainment; street parking; a la carte. Upbeat eatery on the waterfront. Open air. Wide range of pasta plus woodburning pizza, fresh local seafood & fish entrees. **Cards:** MC, VI.

(590/27-81-06

GUSTAVIA (ST. BARTHELEMY)

LODGINGS

CARL GUSTAF HOTEL
◆◆◆   *Suite Hotel*

12/20-1/7	$1270
1/8-4/14	$1050
12/1-12/19, 4/15-5/31 & 10/16-11/30	$690
6/1-10/15	$520

Location: 0.5 km s towards Mt Lurin. Rue des Normands 97099 (BP 700, GUSTAVIA). Fax: 590/27-8237. **Terms:** Reserv deposit; handling fee imposed. **Facility:** 14 rooms. Very attractive individual suites with patio & private pool, overlooking harbor. 7 two-bedroom units, $1250; off season $520 for up to 4 persons; 1 story; exterior corridors; beach access. **Services:** giftshop. Fee: massage. **Recreation:** Fee: boating. **All Rooms:** efficiencies, shower baths. **Cards:** AE, MC, VI.

(590/27-8283

HOTEL FILAO BEACH
◆◆◆   *Cottage*

12/19-1/3	$400-636	XP $60
1/4-3/31	$327-581	XP $60
12/1-12/18 & 10/16-11/30	$218-400	XP $60
4/1-8/31	$181-363	XP $60

Location: 1 km e of airport. (PO Box 667, CEDEX). Fax: 590/27-6224. **Terms:** Open 12/1-8/31 & 10/16-11/30; reserv deposit, 60 day notice. **Facility:** 30 rooms. On Baie St. Jean. White sand beach. Landscaped tropical grounds, private screened patios. 1 story; exterior corridors; beach. **Recreation:** swimming, scuba diving. Fee: snorkeling, windsurfing. Rental: scuba & snorkeling equipment. **Cards:** AE, DI, MC, VI.

(590/27-6484

RESTAURANT

CARL GUSTAF HOTEL DINING ROOM
◆◆◆◆   *French*

L $15-$32 D $25-$55

Location: 0.5 Km s towards Mt Lurin; in Carl Gustaf Hotel. Rue des Normands 97099. **Hours:** noon-2 & 7-10 pm. **Reservations:** suggested. **Features:** No A/C; semi-formal attire; cocktails & lounge; a la carte. Elegant open terrace dining room overlooking port. Innovative market cuisine. Wine cave to include 160 references. **Cards:** AE, MC, VI.

(590/27-82-83

St. Eustatius and Saba

See map page 220.

QUIET AND TINY, with an area of merely 11.8 square miles (31 sq km), St. Eustatius (also called Statia) consists of two dormant volcanoes linked by a central plain. While the northern volcano has been eroded to a cluster of hills, the southern one, known as the Quill, rises precipitously to nearly 2,000 feet. Climatic conditions vary strikingly for such a small island: The Atlantic side has strong winds and low vegetation; the Caribbean side is calm with tall palms and breadfruit and banana trees. Even smaller is Saba, only 5 square miles and located just north of Statia. Along with St. Maarten, Statia and Saba form the Windward Islands of the Dutch Caribbean.

History, Government and Economy

Christopher Columbus first sighted St. Eustatius on his second voyage in 1493. Never settled by Spain, the island was first colonized by France in 1629, then by Holland in 1636. Like Saba and St. Maarten, St. Eustatius changed hands many times before Dutch possession finally became permanent in 1816.

During its early years St. Eustatius developed into a prosperous center for the slave trade and mercantile exchange of the eastern Caribbean, earning the nickname "The Golden Rock." It also was a vital depot for supplies shipped from Europe to the American Revolutionaries. In 1776 St. Eustatius became the first foreign government to officially recognize the United States by firing a salute from Fort Oranje to the American brig *Andrew Doria.* But the Dutch settlers' pro-American sympathies ultimately led to the sacking of St. Eustatius by the British in 1781, an event that marked the end of the tiny island's prosperity.

Shopping

Saba's local specialities are Saba lace, including handcrafted blouses, handkerchiefs and linens, and Saba Spice, an aromatic blend of 150 proof cask rum, brown sugar, fennel seed, cinnamon, nutmeg and cloves.

Food and Drink

Spiny lobster in garlic sauce, whelk stew, bread baked in stone ovens and various shrimp and goat dishes are popular on St. Eustatius. Local restaurants serve such specialties as iguana, tripe and bullfoot soup and curried vegetables.

Sports and Amusements

Reef and wreck diving is popular in St. Eustatius. Several vendors offer PADI certification,

---

THINGS TO KNOW

AREA: St. Eustatius: 11.8 square miles (28 sq km); Saba: 5 square miles (1.9 sq km).

POPULATION: 3,200.

LANGUAGE: Dutch, English and Papiamento.

CAPITAL: Oranjestad, St. Eustatius; The Bottom, Saba.

GOVERNMENT: Netherlands Antilles autonomous within the Kingdom of the Netherlands.

TIME ZONE: Atlantic.

UNIT OF CURRENCY: Netherlands Antilles guilder, divided into 100 cents. $1 U.S.=approx. 1.79 guilders.

ELECTRICITY: 110 volts, 60 cycles AC.

CARS: U.S. license valid; drive on right.

IMMIGRATION REQUIREMENTS: Proof of U.S. citizenship (birth certificate, naturalization papers or passport) and return or through ticket.

FOR FURTHER INFORMATION:

St. Eustatius and Saba Tourist Office
P.O. Box 6322
Boca Raton, FL 33427
(561) 394-8580 or (800) 722-2394

St. Eustatius and Saba Tourist Bureau
Oranjestad, St. Eustatius Netherlands Antilles
(011) 599-382433

HOLIDAYS: Jan. 1; Good Friday; Easter, Easter Monday; Coronation Day, Apr. 30; Labor Day, May 1; Ascension Thursday, May (2nd Thurs.); Emancipation Day, July 1; Carnival, late July; Antillean Day, Oct. 21; Statia/America Day, Nov. 16; Dec. 25; Boxing Day, Dec. 26.

dive packages and equipment rental, including Dive Statia, 011-599-3-82435; Golden Rock Dive Center, 011-599-3-82964 or (800) 311-6658; and Scubaqua, 011-599-3-82160. In Saba, Sea Saba Dive Center offers various dive packages; phone 011-599-4-62246.

The Statia Marine Park offers some 30 sites where divers can view coral reefs, drop-offs and canyons as well as historical wrecks. Sites range from Fallows Bay to the White Wall area and from Jenkins Bay to North Point and Oranjebaai. No boat anchoring is permitted in the park. Fee $3 per dive.

The Saba Marine Park, which encircles the entire island, has marked dive sites and snorkel trails. Surrounded by waters with a visibility up to 200 feet, Saba is ideal for divers.

Excursions and Sightseeing

Sightseeing is concentrated near Fort Oranje in Oranjestad, the capital of St. Eustatius. The fort, built in 1629 by the French, was enlarged in 1636. Maps for walking tours past many 17th-, 18th- and 19th-century buildings are available at the St. Eustatius Tourist Bureau. Three Widows' Corner near the fort features an 18th-century townhouse and a 19th-century Victorian home in a charming tropical courtyard. The town also contains a few shops and inns, the governor's mansion, the Dutch Reformed Church, the ruins of the Honen Dalim Synagogue, a library and a local history museum. The museum contains exhibits from the pre-Columbian and colonial periods.

The tourist office has information about tours, cruises, swimming, snorkeling and scuba diving.

Guides lead hikes to the top of the Quill, whose crater contains a lush tropical rain forest.

Day trips from St. Eustatius to Saba are possible. The smallest of the Netherlands Antilles and possibly the only island in the Caribbean without a beach, Saba is a tiny volcanic island draped with lush vegetation. The rocky shoreline of the island contains tidepools home to numerous sealife.

A rainforest exists some 3,000 feet above sea level; a constant cloud of moisture surrounds the rainforest. Various trails lead hikers into the rainforest where 15 species of wild orchids live along with such other tropical foliage as ferns, giant elephant ears and banana and mango trees. Here 1,064 steps chiseled from vertical rock connect the village of Windwardside with The Bottom, the island's capital. These steps were the island's only thoroughfare until a twisting road was built by hand in the 1940s. At 1,900 feet, Windwardside offers a superb view of the Caribbean.

The Saba Museum is housed in an 1840s sea captain's cottage; contact the tourist bureau for more information. Descend by jeep to The Bottom, 1,000 feet below, and head for the Saba Artisans' Foundation for locally designed fashions.

Transportation

St. Eustatius' Franklin Delano Roosevelt Airport has daily flights to St. Maarten via Windward Islands Airways as well as flights to Saba and St. Kitts. Windjammer cruises call here twice monthly. Car rental information can be obtained at the tourist office in Oranjestad.

St. Kitts and Nevis

SEPARATED BY A MERE 2 miles (3.2 km), St. Kitts and Nevis (NEEV-is) constitute one of the world's tiniest nations. Their beauty and charm, however, are not proportional to their size. Dominated by 3,792-foot (1,156-m) Mount Liamuiga (LEE-a-moo-EE-ga), mountainous St. Kitts contains some of the islands' finest beaches. Nevis embraces a single peak rising from the sea to a cloud-shrouded height of 3,232 feet (985 m). Beaches of coral sand are found along its shores. Missing from St. Kitts and Nevis is the profusion of towering resorts found on many of the bigger, more developed islands, as by law no building can be taller than the palm trees. Its visitors can still enjoy the rustic atmosphere and slow-paced "island time" that some say makes for real relaxation.

History, Government and Economy

When Christopher Columbus discovered the two sister islands in 1493, the cloud-encircled volcanic peak of the smaller island inspired him to call it *Las Nieves*, meaning "the snows;" over the years the island's name has evolved into simply Nevis. The explorer named the larger island St. Christopher, but the British adopted the diminution St. Kitts after Sir Thomas Warner established a settlement, the first English colony in the West Indies, at Old Road Town in 1623. The next year the French also established a colony, and the Anglo-French rivalry for control of the islands was to last for the next 160 years.

After changing hands several times, the islands fell under British rule in 1783 through the Treaty of Versailles. Evidence of their turbulent history remains in the battlegrounds and ruined forts on St. Kitts. Today inhabitants pursue the more peaceful activities of accommodating tourists and growing sugarcane, sea island cotton and other products.

The two islands became an Associated British State in 1967. On Sept. 19, 1983, the British Union Jack was replaced by the green, red, yellow and black flag of the newly independent nation of St. Kitts and Nevis. The governmental structure includes a prime minister, governor-general and legislature for St. Kitts and an Island Assembly with a premier and deputy governor-general for Nevis.

Shopping

Shopping activity on the islands centers on Basseterre, the capital of St. Kitts. Clusters of modern shops surrounding the "Circus," the town's main square at Fort Street and Liverpool Row, provide local crafts, souvenirs and some duty-free imports. Two blocks east near the ferry

THINGS TO KNOW

AREA: St. Kitts: 68 square miles (176 sq km); Nevis: 36 square miles (93 sq km).

POPULATION: 46,000.

LANGUAGE: English.

CAPITAL: Basseterre, St. Kitts; Charlestown, Nevis.

GOVERNMENT: Independent. Member of the British Commonwealth of Nations.

TIME ZONE: Atlantic.

UNIT OF CURRENCY: Eastern Caribbean dollar. $1 U.S.=2.37 Eastern Caribbean dollars.

ELECTRICITY: 220 volts, 60 cycles AC.

MINIMUM AGE FOR GAMBLING: 21.

CARS: Local license required; drive on left.

IMMIGRATION REQUIREMENTS: Proof of U.S. citizenship (birth certificate, naturalization papers or passport) and return or through ticket are required. Departure tax $10 US.

FOR FURTHER INFORMATION:
St. Kitts and Nevis Tourism Office
414 E. 75th St.
New York, NY 10021
(212) 535-1234 or (800) 582-6208
St. Kitts and Nevis Tourism Office
St. Kitts and Nevis Department of Tourism
Pelican Mall, Bay Road
Basseterre, St. Kitts
(869) 465-4040

HOLIDAYS: Jan. 1; Good Friday; Easter Monday; Labour Day, May (1st Mon.); Whit Monday, May (8th Monday after Easter); Queen's Birthday, June (2nd Sat.); August Monday, Aug. (1st Mon.); Independence Day, Sept. 19; Dec. 25; Boxing Day, Dec. 26.

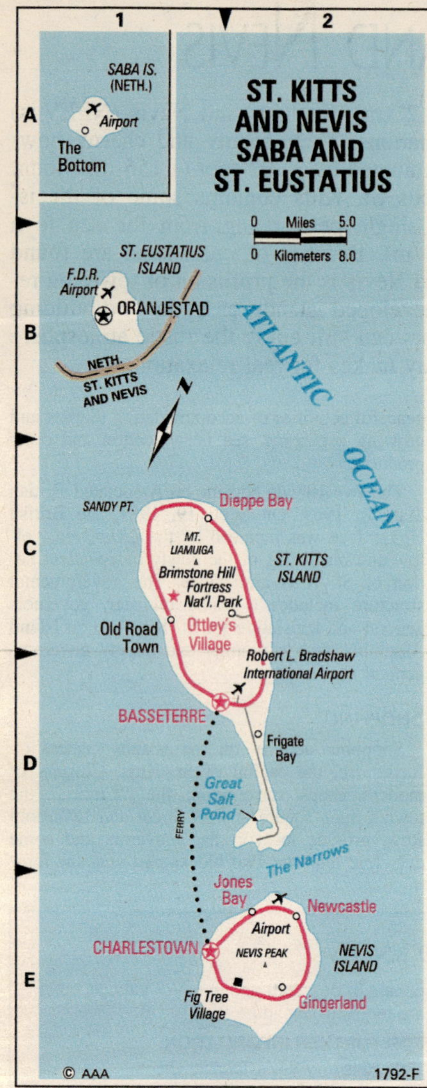

INDEX TO
STARRED ATTRACTIONS

ATTRACTIONS OF EXCEPTIONAL INTEREST AND QUALITY
Brimstone Hill Fortress National Park - see place listing

dock the Pelican Mall offers 26 duty-free shops in a pleasant indoor setting of traditional Kittitian facades and pastel colors.

A favorite take-home item is a hand-painted tropical fashion from Caribelle Batik. They can be purchased in Basseterre and Charlestown, Nevis, but visitors to their factory at Romney Manor west of Old Road Town also can witness the batik process. Stamp collectors will appreci-

ate visits to the St. Kitts Philatelic Bureau in Basseterre and the Nevis Philatelic Bureau in Charlestown.

Store hours are generally Mon.-Wed. and Fri.-Sat. 8-noon and 1-4, Thurs. 8-noon. Banking hours are Mon.-Fri. 8-3 (also Fri. 3-5).

FOOD AND DRINK

The cuisine of St. Kitts and Nevis is highlighted with exotic Caribbean and continental flavors. Beef, chicken, pork and seafood all are complemented by homegrown fruit and vegetables. Such favorite native dishes as Creole red bean soup, conch chowder, goat water (a soup) and boiled saltfish stew are served in several local restaurants. Conch fritters and saltfish balls make good appetizers.

St. Kitts' own Carib Beer is a good complement to a hearty West Indian meal. Two other local products—Ting, a grapefruit-based soft drink, and CSR (Cane Spirit Rothschild), distilled from fresh cane juice—make a fine blend.

SPORTS AND AMUSEMENTS

Besides those along Frigate Bay, good beaches are found along the south coast, at Dieppe Bay and along the southeast peninsula. The 18-hole Frigate Bay golf course lies on the narrowest portion of the island, between the Caribbean Sea and the Atlantic Ocean. Evening entertainment is provided by many of the area hotels. Jack Tar Village-Royal St. Kitts Resort features the only fully operational gaming casino.

The waters between St. Kitts and Nevis are the final resting place for more than 390 ships sunk 1492-1825, yet only some one dozen sites have been identified. Experienced divers can explore many of the sites. Arrangements for dive trips can be made through most hotels. For a fee local fishermen will take you deep-sea fishing. A favorite spot for experienced divers is "The Caves," a series of coral grottoes on Nevis' west coast.

Water sports at Turtle Beach on the southeast peninsula include scuba diving, snorkeling, windsurfing and sailing. PADI certification courses, full- and half-day charters and underwater camera and videocamera rentals also are available. Free transportation is provided for guests of the Ocean Terrace Inn.

Most hotels on Nevis have tennis courts and will make arrangements for guests to go deep-sea fishing and horseback riding. The Four Seasons Resort has an 18-hole golf course that winds up the slope of Mount Nevis. Hiking to the top of Mount Nevis adds to the recreational activities available on the island. Nevis also offers isolated beaches and unspoiled, uncluttered countryside.

Special events on the islands start with National Carnival in late December. Highlights of the 10-day event include a beauty and talent pageant, calypso contests, parades and musical entertainment. The St. Kitts and Nevis Triathlon, in mid-May, starts with a 2.5-mile ocean swim from Nevis to St. Kitts and is followed by a 45-mile mountain bicycle race and a 14-mile run.

Excursions and Sightseeing

Excursions on St. Kitts can be breathtaking—both aesthetically and physically. Climbing Mount Liamuiga is an all-day affair; the crater, 1,192 feet (363 m) below the peak, is the usual stopping point. Hikers can explore the tropical forest, which abounds with deer, monkeys, fruits and flowers, while enjoying a coastal view of the sea. The monkeys, left behind by the French who kept them as pets, now outnumber the human population by a ratio of more than 2.5-to-1.

Other sites worth investigating are Brimstone Hill Fortress, positioned 800 feet (244 m) atop a rock cliff; the Carib Indian petroglyphs at Wingfield Estate and West Farm; Bloody Point near Challengers village, the site of a Carib Indian massacre in 1626; and Caribelle Batik, housed at Romney Manor, a 17th-century great house set above Old Road Town. In a churchyard at Middle Island is the tomb of Sir Thomas Warner, the British founder of St. Kitts.

Eco-Tours offers various walking tours of Nevis. The Eco-Ramble covers the uninhabited east coast and included the 18th-century New River and Coconut Walk Estates. The Mountravers Hike visits Montravers House, the Nevisian version of a Mayan ruin. The Historic Charlestown tour begins at the Museum of Nevis History and highlights the town's history. Phone (869) 469-2091 for information and reservations.

Fun-loving seafarers will enjoy an all-day cruise aboard the catamaran *Spirit of St. Kitts*.

The day includes a beach barbecue and snorkeling. For information and reservations phone (869) 465-7474. Mariners Pub, in Nevis, offers daily cruises aboard a glass-bottom catamaran; phone (869) 469-1993.

St. Kitts' scenic southeast peninsula is accessible via the Dr. Kennedy A. Simmonds Highway, a modern roadway completed in 1990. The 6-mile (10-km) highway leads from Frigate Bay east of Basseterre to Major's Bay, just 2 miles (3.2 km) from Nevis. The peninsula's mountainous terrain affords spectacular views of the Great Salt Pond, the sea and offshore islands.

Transportation

Air connections to St. Kitts' Robert L. Bradshaw International Airport are available from Puerto Rico, the U.S. Virgin Islands, Antigua and St. Maarten. A local driver's license is required to drive on the islands and can be obtained for $30 E.C. at the airport or the Police Traffic Department in Basseterre. Taxis are readily available. Port Zante in St. Kitts is a leading port of call for cruise ships.

Nevis is accessible from St. Kitts via a brief flight or regular 45-minute ferry trips aboard the *Caribe Queen*. A taxi tour around St. Kitts takes about 4 hours. Minimokes are a fun way to get around.

Attraction Admissions

Attraction admissions for this island are quoted in U.S. dollars.

Points of Interest

See map page 220.

Nevis

Nevis is a volcanic island surrounded by coral reefs. Forested slopes rise from palm-lined beaches to the island's cloud-shrouded summit. Relatively untouched by tourism, Nevis attracts those in search of a quiet escape. Except for the Four Seasons Resort, lodging consists mostly of small family-run businesses—cottages and a few sugar plantations converted to inns, many of which are nestled among the foothills of Nevis Peak.

As on many of the Caribbean isles, the use of slave labor at sugar plantations on Nevis created a wealthy upper class. During the 19th century the islands, including Nevis, quickly became the haunt of the elite of British society, who frequented the island's mineral baths and hot springs at the Bath Hotel, considered one of the most ambitious structures built in the West Indies in 1778.

Jamestown, the former capital that fell prey to an earthquake and tidal wave in 1680, can still be visited by snorkelers and scuba divers.

Among the historic figures associated with Nevis is Alexander Hamilton, the American author and statesman, who was born here in 1757. When he was a captain, Horatio Nelson courted and married Fanny Nisbet in Nevis. Montpelier Plantation was the site of their 1787 marriage, in which the future King William IV of England acted as best man. Their vows were recorded at St. John's Church in Fig Tree Village.

CHARLESTOWN (E-1)

During the Spanish Inquisition many Jews fled South America to the Caribbean to escape persecution. The Jewish community on Nevis can be traced to the 1650s with a tombstone in the Jewish cemetery dated 1658. Visitors to Charlestown can view an archeological dig taking place at an old stone building in partial ruin. The site, adjacent to the government administration building is believed to be one of the Caribbean's oldest synagogues.

THE HORATIO NELSON MUSEUM, .5 mi. (.8 km) s. behind the Bath Hotel, displays a large collection of memorabilia associated with Adm. Horatio Nelson, a frequent visitor to Nevis. Allow 30 minutes minimum. Mon.-Fri. 9-4, Sat. 10-noon; closed holidays. Admission $2; under 12, $1. Phone (869) 469-0408.

MUSEUM OF NEVIS HISTORY AT THE BIRTHPLACE OF ALEXANDER HAMILTON, .2 mi. (.4 km) n., is housed in a reconstruction of Alexander Hamilton's birthplace. A series of small exhibits relates to both Hamilton and the history of Nevis. Of interest is a bronze plaque commemorating the visit made by a group of 144 Englishmen in 1607 who landed on the island, spent 6 days and went on to found Jamestown, Virginia, the first permanent English settlement. Mon.-Fri. 8-4, Sat. 10-noon; closed holidays. Free. Phone (869) 469-5786.

ST. KITTS

St. Kitts is being developed to handle tourism on a larger scale. Though a long way from the opulent, self-contained resorts of the Bahamas, Bermuda and Puerto Rico, gambling casinos, tennis courts, golf courses and condominium complexes are gradually changing the face of the island. Frigate Bay, which is lined with some of the island's best beaches, has been the target of most of the commercial development. If you prefer simple island charm, St. Kitts still has many secluded beaches and personal, family-style inns to choose from.

BASSETERRE (D-2) pop. 18,500

Bordering a harbor on the island's southern end, Basseterre is the principal city and capital of St. Kitts. The town has preserved many early examples of West Indian and Georgian architecture;

a good example of the former is the Treasury building on the waterfront. But the architectural legacy of British colonialism can best be seen in Independence Square, originally the slave market. This park of manicured lawns and shade trees includes the Catholic church and several 18th-century homes. Another landmark is the ornate Victorian clock tower in the "Circus," the town's main square.

GREG'S SAFARIS, with pick-up service at local hotels, offers several half- and full-day guided tours. The half-day Plantation Tour takes in some of the island's restored coffee and sugar plantations. The half-day Rainforest Tour features a nature walk through a lush rain forest. The physically challenging full-day Volcano Tour involves a 1,200-foot (366-m) hike to the rim of Mount Liamuiga. Tours are available daily. Volcano tours $50, Plantation and Rainforest tours $35-$40. Phone (869) 465-4121.

★BRIMSTONE HILL FORTRESS NATIONAL PARK (C-1)

Nine miles (14 km) west of Basseterre on a hill 800 feet (244 m) above the sea, this massive British fortress was built by slaves over a 100-year period beginning in the late 1600s. Once known as "The Gibraltar of the West Indies," Brimstone Hill was so intimidating that ship captains often changed course rather than come within range of its powerful guns. The British believed the fort to be impregnable, but the French proved them quite wrong in 1782. Despite the French victory, the British regained the fort a year later through the Treaty of Versailles.

Today visitors can explore the fortress and enjoy the panoramic view that inspired Her Majesty, Queen Elizabeth II, to declare this site a national monument in 1985. Exhibits chronicle the history of the fortress and the struggle between the British and French for control of the islands during the 1700s. Allow 1 hour minimum. Daily 9:30-5:30; closed Good Friday and Dec. 25. Admission $2; under 14, $1. Phone (869) 465-2609 or 466-7784.

OTTLEY'S (C-2)

LODGE GREAT HOUSE GARDENS, at the Lodge Estate, contains anthuriums, ginger, heliconia, orchids and more than 40 varieties of hibiscus. Tea is served at 4 p.m. Open Mon.-Fri. 10-4. Admission $2, children free. Phone (869) 465-7233.

LODGINGS & RESTAURANTS

NEVIS

CHARLESTOWN

LODGING

AAA FOUR SEASONS RESORT NEVIS
◆◆◆◆◆ *Resort Hotel*

12/19-4/3	$625-685	XP $55
12/1-12/18, 4/4-5/29 & 10/31-11/30	$425-485	XP $55
5/30-10/30	$275-335	XP $55

Location: Pinney's Beach; transportation via van & water launch from St. Kitts regional airport. (PO Box 565). Fax: 869/469-1112. **Terms:** F17; Reserv deposit; 10% service charge; AP, MAP avail; package plans. **Facility:** 196 rooms. Former coconut plantation. Elegant, luxurious rooms with view of tropical beach or golf course. Golf course on slopes of Mt. Nevis. Meets AAA guest room security requirements. 3 two-bedroom units, 2 three-bedroom units. 2-5 bedroom villas with private pool, $650-$4000; $300-$2700 off season; 2 stories; exterior corridors; putting green; beach, heated pool, wading pool, saunas, whirlpool; playground. Fee: 18 holes golf; 10 tennis courts (3 lighted), clay & hard surface tennis courts. **Dining:** Dining room, 3 restaurants; 7 am-10 pm; $19-$42; cocktails; dining room, see separate listing. **Services:** giftshop. Fee: massage, area transportation. **Recreation:** swimming, sailboating, scuba diving, snorkeling, windsurfing; hiking trails, lap lanes, driving range, sea kayaks, waterbikes, billiards. Fee: charter fishing, scuba & snorkeling equipment, waterskiing. Rental: boats. **Some Rooms:** 5 kitchens. **Cards:** AE, JC, MC, VI.

((869)469-1111

RESTAURANT

FOUR SEASONS DINING ROOM
◆◆◆◆ *Continental*   **D** $25-$43

Location: Pinney's Beach; transportation via van & water launch from St. Kitts Regional airport; in Four Seasons Resort Nevis. **Hours:** 6:30 pm-10 pm. **Reservations:** suggested. **Features:** No A/C; semi-formal attire; children's menu; health conscious menu; cocktails & lounge; a la carte. Innovative mix of New American & Caribbean cuisine in stately dining room overlooking ocean. Elegantly casual ambiance. **Cards:** AE, CB, DI, JC, MC, VI.

(869/469-1111

GINGERLAND

LODGINGS

GOLDEN ROCK HOTEL PLANTATION INN
◆◆ *Cottage*

12/20-4/15	$200	XP $80
12/1-12/19 & 4/16-11/30	$130	XP $45

Location: 5.5 mi e of Charlestown. (PO Box 493, CHARLESTOWN). Fax: 869/469-2113. **Terms:** D12; Reserv deposit, 21 day notice, 14 in summer; 10% service charge. **Facility:** 14 rooms. Cottages on hillside overlooking ocean & panoramic views. Restored stone sugar plantation among picturesque ruins & tropical gardens. Warm hospitality. 1 two-bedroom unit. 2 bedroom, 1815 Sugar Mill. Suite $165-$235; 2 stories; exterior corridors; 1 tennis court. **Services:** area transportation. **Recreation:** snorkeling equipment; hiking trails. **All Rooms:** shower baths. **Cards:** AE, MC, VI.

(869/469-3346

OLD MANOR ESTATE & HOTEL
◆◆ *Historic Country Inn*

12/1-12/14 & 4/15-11/30	$160-185	XP $35
12/15-4/14	$125-150	XP $35

Location: 4.5 mi e of Charlestown. (PO Box 70). Fax: 869/469-3388. **Terms:** F12; Age restrictions may apply; reserv deposit, 14 day notice; handling fee imposed; 10% service charge. **Facility:** 13 rooms. Reconstructed 18th-Century sugar plantation, landscaped grounds. Spacious rooms & suites. 1 two-bedroom unit. 2 stories; exterior corridors. **Services:** area transportation. **All Rooms:** combo or shower baths. **Cards:** AE, MC, VI.

(869/469-3445

RESTAURANT

GOLDEN ROCK DINING ROOM *Country Inn*
◆◆ *Ethnic*
                         L $5-$18   **D** $35

Location: 5.5 mi e of Charlestown; in Golden Rock Hotel Plantation Inn. **Hours:** 8 am-10, noon-2:30 & seating at 7:30-8 pm. **Reservations:** suggested. **Features:** No A/C; children's menu; cocktails & lounge. Lobster, fish & local produce. Picturesque stone terrace courtyard of 1815 plantation. 12/15-5/30 buffet Sat night with live entertainment; $35 adults, $17.50 children, & 10% service charge. **Cards:** AE, MC, VI.

(869/469-3346

JONES BAY

RESTAURANT

MISS JUNE'S CUISINE *Country Inn*
◆◆◆ *Ethnic*

Location: 4 mi nw of Charlestown. PO Box 75. **Hours:** Mon, Wed & Fri; one seating, cocktails begin at 7:30 pm. Closed major holidays. **Reservations:** required. **Features:** No A/C; casual dress; cocktails; prix fixe, buffet. Trinidadian hostess/chef welcomes guests in to her home in a dinner party atmosphere. A unique event. Buffet offering Asian & West Indian specialties. Price inclusive of service, tax & all beverages. **Cards:** MC, VI.

(869/469-5330

NEWCASTLE

LODGINGS

AAA **SAVE** **THE MOUNT NEVIS HOTEL & BEACH CLUB**
◆ ◆ ◆   *Hotel*

12/15-4/15	$190-270	XP $35
12/1-12/14 & 4/16-11/30	$130-190	XP $35

Location: 1 mi e of airport. Shaws Rd (PO Box 494, CHARLESTOWN). Fax: 869/469-9375. **Terms:** F12; Reserv deposit, 28 day notice, 14 days off season; 10% service charge; MAP avail. **Facility:** 32 rooms. Spectacular views of the mountains, ocean & tropical vegetation. Modern rooms, studio or 1-bedroom apartments. All units with balcony or patio. 2 bedroom suite with kitchen $460-$285, $320-$340 off season; 2 stories; exterior corridors; oceanview; beach access. **Dining:** 2 restaurants; 8 am-10 pm, Sun-2:30 pm; $25-$30; cocktails; restaurant, see separate listing. **Services:** area transportation, to beach club. **Recreation:** swimming, fishing, scuba diving, snorkeling, boat excursions. Fee: scuba & snorkeling equipment, water-skiing. Rental: boats. **All Rooms:** shower baths. **Some Rooms:** 16 kitchens. **Cards:** AE, MC, VI. **Special Amenities:** Free local telephone calls and free room upgrade (subject to availability with advanced reservations).

((869)469-9373

NISBET PLANTATION BEACH CLUB
◆ ◆ ◆ ◆   *Cottage*

12/21-4/14	$425-525	XP $20-105
11/1-11/30	$285-355	XP $15-70
12/1-12/20 & 4/15-10/31	$255-325	XP $15-70

Location: 1 mi e of airport. St. James Parish. Fax: 869/469-9864. **Terms:** Reserv deposit, 28 day notice, 14 in summer; 10% service charge. **Facility:** 38 rooms. Elegant cottages on grounds of former coconut plantation. White sand beach. Rates include breakfast & dinner daily, afternoon tea, postage, laundry, watersports & tennis; 2 stories; exterior corridors; oceanview; beach; 1 tennis court. **Services:** giftshop. **Recreation:** swimming, snorkeling equipment. **All Rooms:** combo or shower baths. **Cards:** AE, DI, DS, MC, VI.

(869/469-9325

RESTAURANTS

THE MOUNT NEVIS RESTAURANT
◆ ◆ ◆   *Continental*
L $3-$15   D $25-$30

Location: 1 mi e of airport; in The Mount Nevis Hotel & Beach Club. Shaws Rd. **Hours:** 8 am-10, noon-2:30 & 6:30-10 pm, Sun 8 am-3 pm. **Reservations:** suggested. **Features:** No A/C; casual dress; children's menu; cocktails & lounge; a la carte. Relaxing with nature. Spectacular views with mountains, ocean & tropical surroundings. Open terrace dining. Homemade pasta served daily. **Cards:** AE, MC, VI.

(869/469-9373

NISBET PLANTATION DINING ROOM   *Country Inn*
◆ ◆ ◆   *Continental*

Location: 1 mi e of airport. St. James Parish. **Hours:** 7:30 pm-8:30 pm seating. **Reservations:** required. **Features:** cocktails; prix fixe. Elegant candlelight dining in historic plantation home. Continental specialties with island influences. Casual beachfront barbecue with band Thursday nights. **Cards:** AE, DI, DS, MC, VI.

(869/469-9325

ST. KITTS

BASSETERRE—18,500

LODGINGS

COCONUT BEACH CLUB
◆ ◆   *Motor Inn*

12/16-4/15	$265
12/1-12/15 & 4/16-11/30	$125

Location: Frigate Bay; 3 mi se of Golden Rock Int'l Airport. (PO Box 1198). Fax: 869/466-7085. **Terms:** 10% service charge. **Facility:** 60 rooms. Modern suites on Caribbean sea & short walk to Atlantic beaches & public golf course. Some with upper floor balcony offers sweeping views of the area. 14 two-bedroom units. 2 stories; exterior corridors; oceanview; beach. **Recreation:** swimming. **All Rooms:** combo or shower baths. **Some Rooms:** 31 efficiencies, color TV. **Cards:** AE, MC, VI.

(869/465-8597

Pink, black and white sand beaches — the Caribbean has them all. But it isn't sand that counts, it's safety. Before you go in, be sure that lovely beach doesn't border water that conceals a dangerous undertow.

OCEAN TERRACE INN
◆◆   *Motor Inn*

2/15-4/14	$93-194	XP $35
2/1-12/14 & 4/15-11/30	$81-140	XP $25

Location: At w end of Basseterre, jct Wigley Ave. (PO Box 5). Fax: 869/465-1057. **Terms:** F12; 10% service charge. **Facility:** 72 rooms. Terraced gardens in genteel suburb overlooking harbor. Warm, welcoming staff. 8 one-bedroom apartments, $140-$194; 6 two-bedroom apartments, $208-$194 for up to 6 persons; 3 stories; exterior corridors; street parking only; beach access; 1 tennis court. **Services:** gift-shop; area transportation. **Recreation:** swimming, charter fishing, scuba diving, snorkeling & equipment. Fee: scuba equipment. **Cards:** AE, DI, DS, MC, VI.

(869/465-2754

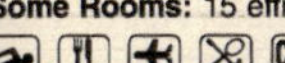

DIEPPE BAY

LODGING

THE GOLDEN LEMON INN AND VILLAS
◆◆◆◆   *Historic Country Inn*

2/16-4/15	$465	XP $100
2/1-12/15 & 4/16-11/30	$390	

Location: At n end of island; 16 mi from airport & Basse-terre. Dieppe Bay. Fax: 869/465-4019. **Terms:** Age restric-tions may apply; reserv deposit, 21 day notice, 14 off season; handling fee imposed; 10% service charge. **Facility:** 28 rooms. Renovated 17th-century stone manor & contemporary villas. Black sand beach, long verandas. Many villas with private pool. For US reservations: (800) 633-7411. 11 two bedroom villas $865 for 4 persons; off-season $700; 2 stories; interior/exterior corridors; 1 tennis court. **Services:** Fee: area transportation. **Recreation:** swimming, snorkeling equipment; horseback riding. **All Rooms:** combo or shower baths. **Some Rooms:** 15 efficiencies. **Cards:** AE, MC, VI.

((869)465-7260

OTTLEY'S VILLAGE

LODGING

OTTLEY'S PLANTATION INN
◆◆◆◆   *Historic Country Inn*

12/15-4/16	$295-435	XP $95
12/1-12/14 & 4/17-11/30	$220-335	XP $75

Location: 6 mi nw of Basseterre. (PO Box 345, BASSE-TERRE). Fax: 869/465-4760. **Terms:** Age restrictions may apply; reserv deposit, 30 day notice; handling fee imposed; 10% service charge; MAP avail; package plans, 5 or 7 days. **Facility:** 17 rooms. Elegantly restored 18th-century planta-tion on 35 acres of terraced lawns nestled between Mt Lia-muiga overlooking the Caribbean Sea. Elegant rooms. 1 two-bedroom unit. 2 stories; exterior corridors. **Dining:** Din-ing room; cocktails; also, The Royal Palm Restaurant, see separate listing. **Services:** area transportation, beach/town. **Recreation:** rain forest nature trail. **Some Rooms:** whirl-pools. **Cards:** AE, DS, MC, VI. *(See color ad below)*

((869)465-7234

RESTAURANT

THE ROYAL PALM RESTAURANT
◆◆◆   *Continental*

Location: 6 mi nw of Basseterre; at Ottley's Plantation Inn. **Hours:** 8 am-10 & noon 3 pm, dinner seating 8 pm. Sunday brunch 11 am-2 pm. **Reservations:** required; for dinner. **Features:** No A/C; casual dress; cocktails, prix fixe. Grace-ful setting amid stone ruins & gardens. Fine cuisine, excel-lent preparation & presentation. Pleasant service. **Cards:** AE, DS, MC, VI. *(See color ad below)*

(869/465-7239

St. Lucia

LUSH GREENERY, endless banana plantations, wooded mountains and fertile valleys are just some of the elements that harmonize to make St. Lucia (St LOO-sha) a "picture postcard" island. This tropical paradise, which is 27 miles (43 km) long and 14 miles (22 km) wide, contains 19,000 acres (7,689 hectares) of rain forest. Quaint fishing villages and enticing beaches provide a backdrop that complements the diverse landscape of the interior. Gros and Petit Pitons, regal twin peaks separated by a picturesque bay, are prominent landmarks.

History, Government and Economy

The first settlers were the peace-loving Arawak Indians, who probably came to St. Lucia to escape the warlike Caribs. However, the Arawak presence did not endure—the Caribs eventually followed and succeeded in driving them off the island by A.D. 800.

Although it has not been established whether Christopher Columbus or Juan de la Cosa discovered St. Lucia, the first European to settle on the island was pirate Francois de Clerc. In 1550, de Clerc attacked passing Spanish ships from his base on Pigeon Island.

The English attempted to settle the island in 1605 and 1639, but the fierce Caribs thwarted their efforts on both occasions. In 1650 the French finally established the first permanent settlement; a treaty with the Caribs was signed in 1660. About this time, a bitter dispute originated in which each country claimed ownership of the territory.

A 150-year-long struggle for control ensued, as St. Lucia changed hands between the feuding French and British 14 times. The island was ultimately ceded to the British in 1814 and became one of the Windward Islands in 1838.

Sugar plantations flourished from the mid-1700s to the mid-1800s. With African slaves providing free labor, the industry thrived. Once slavery was abolished in 1834, a labor shortage ensued that contributed to the industry's decline. Such epidemics as smallpox and cholera also impeded prosperity during the remainder of the 19th century. The economy improved in the early 20th century, as a greater emphasis was placed on the cultivation of bananas and cocoa. Although the sugar industry briefly resurged, production eventually ceased in the 1960s.

As a provision of the West Indies Act of 1967, St. Lucia became entirely self-governing in internal affairs. The United Kingdom retained authority in regard to defense and external matters. On Feb. 22, 1979, the island obtained full independence. That same year, St. Lucia became a member of the British Commonwealth of Nations.

THINGS TO KNOW

AREA: 238 square miles (616 sq km).

POPULATION: 145,000.

LANGUAGE: English and Kweyol.

CAPITAL: Castries.

GOVERNMENT: Independent. Member of the British Commonwealth of Nations.

TIME ZONE: Atlantic.

UNIT OF CURRENCY: Eastern Caribbean dollar. $1 U.S.=2.37 Eastern Caribbean dollars.

ELECTRICITY: 220 volts, 50 cycles AC.

CARS: Temporary license valid for 3 months; must be 18. Drive on left.

IMMIGRATION REQUIREMENTS: Proof of U.S. citizenship (birth certificate with photo identification or passport) and return or through ticket are required. Departure tax $11 US.

FOR FURTHER INFORMATION:
St. Lucia Tourist Board
800 Second Ave., 4th Floor
New York, NY 10017
(212) 867-2950 or (800) 456-3984
St. Lucia Tourist Board
Pointe Seraphine
Castries, St. Lucia, West Indies
(758) 452-4094

HOLIDAYS: Jan. 1-2; Carnival, Feb.; Independence Day, Feb. 22; Good Friday; Easter Monday; Labour Day, first Mon. in May; Whit Monday, May (8th Monday after Easter); Feast of Corpus Christi, June; Emancipation Day, Aug.; Thanksgiving, Oct.; St. Lucia Day, Dec. 13; Dec. 25; Boxing Day, Dec. 26.

The country remains a stable parliamentary democracy, with a governor-general designated by Queen Elizabeth II. Agriculture and tourism are economic mainstays; bananas, the island's chief crop and export, account for about 80 percent of total economic revenue.

SHOPPING

Local goods available on St. Lucia include batik fabrics, perfumes, straw works, unglazed pottery, and handicrafts produced from wood, shell and black coral. The island is particularly known for its cane furniture and batik designs.

These items can be obtained at the Pointe Seraphine Duty Free Shopping Craft Vendors Complex near Castries. Some popular stores at Pointe Seraphine are Columbian Emeralds International, with a dazzling selection of gemstone jewelry; Little Switzerland, featuring Hummel and Lladró figurines, Waterford and Baccarat crystal, and such fine china as Royal Doulton, Wedgwood and Villeroy & Boch; The Bagshaws, a small boutique with hand-painted Caribbean fashions in original designs; Images, a perfumery with a variety of elegant fragrances; and Benetton, with an impressive array of international apparel.

Several shops and restaurants can be found at the Rodney Bay Marina, near Gros Islet at the north end of the island. While browsing in boutiques offering beachwear, local crafts, electronics and island souvenirs, visitors can enjoy splendid views of the bay and of gleaming yachts docked in the marina.

Downtown Castries also provides shopping opportunities such as those at the Castries Market Arcade. Artsibit Gallery, at Brazil and Mongiraud streets, displays works of Caribbean artists. Shoppers can choose from an assortment of pottery, sculpture, paintings and hand-painted T-shirts. J.Q. Charles, St. Lucia's largest department store, is at the intersection of Bridge Street and William Peter Boulevard. The Sea Island Cotton Shop on Bridge Street presents island fashions designed to keep visitors cool in the harsh Caribbean sun.

William Peter Boulevard, lined with souvenir shops and banks, is the city's center of shopping activity. Y. De Lima's merchandise consists of Pentax and Vivitar cameras, Bulova and Casio watches, French perfume and gold jewelry. A multitude of street vendors make their home on the boulevard as well as on many other streets in the downtown area. Gablewoods, a small shopping complex just north of Castries off the Castries-Gros Islet Highway, contains a drug store, a bank, a supermarket, a food court and several small boutiques that offer bathing suits, resortwear, artwork and souvenirs.

Eudovic Art Studio is on the southern side of Castries off the road that snakes up the slopes of Morne Fortune. Woodcarvings fashioned from

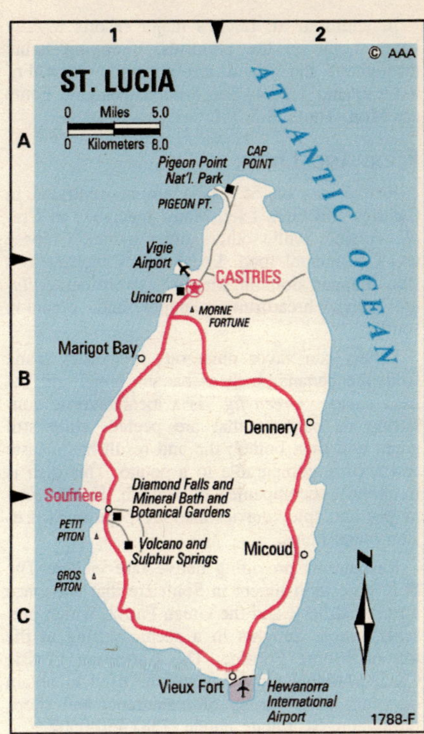

mahogany, teak and cedar are exhibited in a small gallery; works are available for purchase at the adjacent shop. Visitors can observe artisans performing wood finishing in the workshop area.

Also on Morne Fortune is Caribelle Batik, situated in Howelton House on Old Victoria Road. Clothing enhanced by unique colors and patterns is available for purchase, and the dye-resistant method incorporated by the batik process is demonstrated by workers as they create freehand designs. On the terrace at the rear of the facility, shoppers can sip a refreshing drink and relish the view of Castries. Caribelle Batik also has a small store on Bridge Street.

Another Morne Fortune landmark is Bagshaw Studios, which features clothing, place mats, tablecloths, wall hangings and other fabrics hand painted with cheery island motifs. Workers create brightly colored designs from a stenciled pattern during the silk-screening process, which can be observed in the print shop. Caribbean Perfumes, also on the Morne, creates exotic fragrances from herbs and tropical flowers found throughout St. Lucia.

Choiseul, a small coastal village in the southwest portion of the island, is the site of the Choiseul Art and Craft Center. Artists produce traditional Carib Indian crafts, including clay pottery and hand-woven baskets constructed from straw and wicker.

In addition, St. Lucia's major resorts usually have shops on the premises. Shopping hours throughout the island are generally Mon.-Fri. 8-12:30 and 1:30-4, Sat. 8-noon. Banking hours are Mon.-Thurs. 8-3, Fri. 8-5.

FOOD AND DRINK

Restaurants on St. Lucia are concentrated in Castries and Gros Islet. Many specialize in Creole cuisine, while others offer Italian, Chinese and Continental food. Local dishes include lobster, snapper, dolphin, kingfish, swordfish, *callaloo* soup, breadfruit, plantain and pumpkin souffle.

Diners can savor numerous specialties made from the banana, such as banana bread and banana salad. *"Green fig"* is a local favorite consisting of bananas that are peeled while still green and then boiled; the end result has a taste and texture comparable to a potato. This dish is frequently accompanied by saltfish. Hearty *pepperpot* and spicy curries also are popular St. Lucian menu items.

Restaurants providing native fare include The Still, an establishment in Soufrière that was once a rum distillery, and the Green Parrot, which presents Creole delights in a scenic setting at the top of Morne Fortune. The Caribbean Classic Card, available for a fee, can be used to obtain discounts at a variety of restaurants and shops throughout St. Lucia; phone (758) 450-0507.

SPORTS AND AMUSEMENTS

Aquatic pastimes—water skiing, snorkeling and boating among them—are popular recreational pursuits on St. Lucia. Conditions for windsurfing are good at Reduit Beach on the northwest coast and at Vieux Fort at the island's southern tip; The St. Lucian and The Royal St. Lucian hotels on Reduit Beach rent equipment to the public. The St. Lucian also offers parasailing.

Day or sunset cruises operate out of Castries Harbour; longer excursions to Martinique or south to St. Vincent and the Grenadines also are available. Sailing enthusiasts can charter boats with or without a crew at Marigot Bay, Rodney Bay Marina and Vigie Marina. Deep-sea fishing charters are provided by Mako Watersports, (758) 452-0412, and Captain Mike's, (758) 452-7044. The main catches are barracuda, blue marlin, kingfish, tuna, swordfish and wahoo.

Because of St. Lucia's volcanic origins, black sand is found on some beaches. The most popular beaches in St. Lucia are on the north and west coasts; the turbulent waters of the Atlantic coast are not recommended for swimming. Anse Chastanet, just north of Soufriére, is named for the hotel that graces its shores. The beach area, accented by a hilly panorama, is flanked by a restaurant and dive shop. Farther north, the quaint fishing village of Anse La Raye boasts a picturesque beach with a wealth of graceful palms. Nearby, Marigot Bay is a charming tropical cove peppered with colorful yachts. Visitors can just relax and sip a refreshing drink in the shade, or take a swim in the cove's tranquil waters.

Although the beige-sand beach at La Toc Bay south of Castries, is a great place to soak up the sun and enjoy the view, swimming is not advised due to occasional strong currents. Choc Bay north of Castries in the vicinity of several major resorts, has calm waters ideal for swimming. Reduit Beach, the northwest coast's premier water sports center, offers such activities as water skiing, windsurfing, sailing and snorkeling. Individuals primarily interested in relaxation will appreciate the abundance of beige sand and shady palms.

Sun worshipers will revel in the fine selection of secluded white-sand beaches at Pigeon Point; the area is connected to the island by a manmade causeway. Conditions are excellent for swimming, and a nearby restaurant provides refreshment. At the extreme southern tip of the island, Vieux Fort consists of miles of white-sand beaches against a backdrop of coconut palms. From this expanse of land, the contrast between the deep blue Caribbean waters and the murky hues of the Atlantic is apparent. All of St. Lucia's beaches, even those fronted by resorts, are open to the public. The island also possesses several isolated stretches of beach accessible only by boat.

Scuba St. Lucia, at the Anse Chastanet Hotel in Soufrière, offers diving courses geared toward certification as well as daytime and evening diving expeditions; phone (758) 459-7000. Buddie's Scuba, (758) 452-5288, and Dive Fair Helen (758) 451-7716, are situated on the Vigie Peninsula near Castries. Dolphin Divers is at Rodney Bay Marina, (758) 452-9485, and at the Moorings at Marigot Bay, (758) 451-4357.

Because of St. Lucia's volcanic origins, divers can experience a spectacular sampling of steep underwater drop-offs and unspoiled marine life. The waters off the west coast provide the best opportunities for diving, with most of the sites concentrated between Marigot Bay and Choiseul. *Lesleen M.,* a 165-foot vessel south of Marigot Bay that was deliberately sunk in the 1980s, has several compartments that can be explored. For the less adventurous, *Volga* is an easy 20-foot wreck dive near Castries.

Anse Chastanet Reef contains a colorful display of coral and a 150-foot-deep wall; this reef also is home to a large school of squid. Keyhole Pinnacles is another popular dive site just south of Anse Chastanet. Four pinnacles, accentuated by fascinating coral formations and a variety of marine life, rise from the bottom of the sea to within 10 or 15 feet of the surface. Piton Wall, a site that features a vibrant assortment of coral nd sponges, begins at about 30 feet and plunges o a depth of 1,300 feet.

Horseback riding, an excellent way to tour St. ucia, can be arranged through Trim's Riding entre at Cas-en-Bas in Gros Islet; phone (758) 50-8273. Nine-hole golf courses are scenically ituated at Cap Estate, (758) 450-8523, and San- als resort, (758) 452-3081, ext. 6054. Tennis is layed at several hotels and at the St. Lucia Rac- uet Club. Legacies of the island's English heri- age are the popular spectator sports of soccer nd cricket. Cricket matches can be observed on unday near the Choc Bay War Memorial in the orthwestern portion of the island.

Several of the major resorts have exercise cen- ers; non-guests can usually participate for a fee. he St. Lucia Racquet Club, at the Club St. Lu- ia, has a gym that offers fitness classes and veight-training machines; phone (758) 450-0551. t the Le Sport resort, fitness buffs can work out sing machines and free weights; phone (758) 50-8551. Sandals, (758) 452-3081, contains a tate-of-the-art exercise facility. The latest equip- nent can be found at Gonard Laborde's Gym on lospital Road; phone (758) 452-2788.

Many villages in St. Lucia host Friday night treet parties, known locally as "jump-ups." The nost popular of these is held in Gros Islet, a mall fishing town in northern St. Lucia. Locals nd tourists alike enjoy the carnival atmosphere, vhere the pulsating beat of reggae and soca mu- ic permeates the air. Food vendors stationed on he sidewalk grill spicy Caribbean delights as nerrymakers dance to the latest soca tunes. Many hotels arrange round-trip bus transporta- ion to the Gros Islet "jump-up."

Island nightlife centers on the hotels, where teel bands perform folk music, calypso and reg- ae. The island also plays host to a number of ultural events. Masquerade bands take to the treets during the annual Carnival celebration eld 2 days before Ash Wednesday; a multitude f activities take place in the days preceding this vent.

In mid-May the Jazz Festival occurs at various ites throughout St. Lucia. This 4-day event ighlights local, Caribbean and international per- ormers. In late June, fishermen decorate their essels in celebration of St. Peter's Day. The fes- ivals of La Rose and La Marguerite occur on Aug. 30 and Oct. 17, and St. Lucia's Day on Dec. 13. International Creole day is in October.

EXCURSIONS AND SIGHTSEEING

Those exploring St. Lucia's interior will be re- varded with views of the island's lush greenery. Drivers will often encounter roosters and other arm animals during their travels and may have o stop and wait patiently while a stray cow or oat wanders slowly across the road.

It is not unusual to see a native diligently valking with a huge display of bananas perched precariously on his or her head. Sightseers will be overwhelmed by the seemingly endless maze of banana plants, sometimes wrapped in peculiar plastic bags which serve as protection against in- sects. Colorful rum shops, often ramshackle in appearance, serve as neighborhood meeting spots where locals exchange the latest news.

Pigeon Point off the northwestern coast is named for Admiral Rodney's carrier pigeons, which were once housed at the ruined fort. Joined to the main island by a causeway, the area is now a national park which contains Arawak remnants, lookouts, gun batteries and barracks set amid tropical plantlife *(see Castries p. 230)*. Union Agricultural Station, also in the northern portion of the island, is the headquarters of the Forestry Division. The station has a minizoo with animals native to St. Lucia, a medicinal herb garden and a nature trail; phone (758) 450-3212.

Marigot Bay, a popular yacht harbor with an inviting beach, is a half-hour coastal drive south of Castries. Nearby, at the colorful fishing village of Anse la Raye, fishermen continue to craft their vessels out of logs. Also south of Castries is Soufrière, which can be reached by a long but scenic drive or by boat, which also provides an oceangoing view of *Les Pitons*. Soufrière's vol- cano acts as a safety valve; it releases small amounts of pressure, forestalling a major vol- canic eruption. Boat excursions include a stop during which passengers take a bus tour to the volcano as well as to the nearby sulphur springs *(see Soufrière p. 231)*.

From Soufrière the road toward Fond St. Jacques penetrates the island's rain forest, which can be seen by organized tour. Hikers may spot the Amazon versicolor parrot and are rewarded with views such as orchids and anthuriums grow- ing wild, and agoutis and manicous playing. The rain forest also can be toured by arranging a guide through the Forestry Division; phone (758) 450-2231. Visitors are cautioned to dress appro- priately, as the forest can be extremely muddy in areas.

Excursions also can be made to two of the is- land's giant banana plantations: Marquis Estate in the northern part of the island and Errard Es- tate in the Dennery area. The Marquis tour pro- vides a trip down the unspoiled Marquis River. Practical footwear and clothing are advised, as grounds are often muddy. The rise and fall of St. Lucia's once-thriving sugar industry is the sub- ject of an organized tour at Invergoil Estate; a re- stored sugar mill is on the grounds. Excursions to the lighthouse at Moule a Chique Peninsula also are available.

Dramatic views of St. Lucia's rugged terrain and lush rain forest are possible by helicopter. Flights glide past such sites as the inspiring twin Pitons and the 18th-century fortifications on Morne Fortune. Narrated tours are offered by

Eastern Caribbean Helicopters, (758) 453-6953, and St. Lucia Helicopters, (758) 453-6950.

TRANSPORTATION

Flights from New York, Miami and San Juan arrive at Hewanorra International Airport on the island's southern tip. Vigie Airport, just outside of Castries, services on-island charters and inter-island flights to and from Barbados, Trinidad, Antigua, San Juan and several other islands; flights also arrive from Miami and New York aboard BWIA. Most resorts in the northern end of the island furnish complimentary transportation to guests flying into Hewanorra; the trip usually takes about an hour.

While there is no organized public bus system in St. Lucia, the minibuses do run frequently between Castries and such points as Vigie, Gros Islet and Vieux Fort. Although there is no set schedule, buses stop at designated sites approximately every 30 minutes. Service between Castries and some outlying villages may be limited to once a day. Several companies provide taxi service. Fares are fixed, and drivers also are trained as tour guides. Cars can be rented; a temporary license, which costs $12 US and is valid for months, is required. Hertz, with outlets at both airports and Rodney Bay Marina, offers discounts to AAA members; phone (758) 452-0679.

POINTS OF INTEREST

See map page 227.

CASTRIES (B-2) pop. 57,400

Castries, St. Lucia's capital, is a bustling harbor town surrounded by rolling hills. Only a few historic landmarks stand; since its founding by the French in the 18th century, Castries has been destroyed by fire four times.

The town's colorful downtown market on Jeremie Street has been in existence since 1895; it is open Monday through Saturday 6-6. Saturday is the best time to visit the market, which is renowned for its lush tropical fruits, fresh vegetables, exotic spices, wicker furniture, wood carvings and handicrafts. Boutiques in town sell European perfumes, jewelry, clothes and fabric. Some shops sell handmade cane furniture and batik clothing, for which the island is noted.

Bordered by Peynier, Laborie and Micoud streets, the 1890s Cathedral of the Immaculate Conception reveals impressive murals by St. Lucian artist Dunstan St. Omer. Derek Walcott Square, next to the cathedral, is named for the island's Nobel prize-winning poet. The square contains a 400-year-old Saman tree and a monument to the St. Lucians who died in World Wars I and II. An antique map collection focusing on St. Lucia and the Caribbean Sea can be found at the National Library on Bourbon Street.

Morne Fortune, or "hill of good fortune," is on the southern side of Castries. The 845-foot-high hill offers a striking view of Castries Harbour, Vigie Peninsula and the northern portion of the island. The road winds past Government House, a Victorian-style residence occupied by the governor-general. At the top of the Morne are the remains of Fort Charlotte, which changed hands between British and French forces during the 18th and 19th centuries. A monument marks the site of a battle fought in 1796. Many of the structures have been restored to house the University of the West Indies.

PIGEON POINT NATIONAL PARK, 7 mi. (11 km) n., is connected to the mainland by a man-made causeway. At the park's western end are the crumbling barracks, magazines and ramparts of Fort Rodney, built in the late 1700s and named for British Adm. George Rodney. From the fort's excellent vantage points, Rodney monitored the French fleet in Martinique.

The park's 40 acres (16 hectares) are enhanced by tropical flowers and gazebos. A hike to the top of the fort will reward visitors with a spectacular view that accentuates the contrast between the lush landscape of the Caribbean side of St. Lucia and the rugged terrain of the east coast. Daily 8:30-6. Admission (includes Pigeon Point Museum) $4. Phone (758) 450-8167.

Pigeon Point Museum, near the park entrance, features displays devoted to the historical significance of the park's stone-and-brick military ruins. Visitors can interact with the exhibits by listening to narratives through headphones and participating in other hands-on exercises. Mon.-Sat. 9-5. Phone (758) 452-5005.

UNICORN, docked at Vigie Cove, is a 140-foot replica of a 19th-century brig. The impressive vessel, with its billowing white sails, appeared as the slave ship in the television series "Roots." Passengers depart for a land excursion at Castries. On the return boat trip, visitors can take a swim at Anse Cochon. Farther north, *Unicorn* docks briefly at picturesque Marigot Bay, a tropical setting that has appeared in such films as "Dr. Doolittle."

Trips depart Tues.-Fri. at 9 and return at 4. Fare $70; under 11, $35. Fare includes lunch and beverages. Phone (758) 452-8232.

SOUFRIERE (C-1) pop. 8,500

Established by the French in 1746, the quaint west coast village of Soufrière is actually a low-lying volcanic crater. The town derived its name from the bubbling pits of sulphur at the nearby Volcano and Sulphur Springs (*see attraction listing*). Once the flourishing French capital, Soufrière is now a sleepy fishing village characterized by traces of French Colonial architecture and black sand beaches.

Soufrière is perhaps most renowned as the home of the towering twin Pitons, volcanic peaks that spring forth majestically from the ocean to a height of more than a half-mile (.8 km). Gros Piton (2,619 ft./798 m) can be climbed by experienced hikers; Petit Piton (2,438 ft./743 m) is not considered safe to climb. Anse des Pitons, a picturesque bay, separates the Pitons.

The town's marketplace, especially active on Saturday, can be recognized by its charming gingerbread trim. Situated near the waterfront on Bay Street, the market offers fresh fruits and vegetables, spices and island crafts. For additional information, phone the Soufrière branch of the St. Lucia Tourist Board at (758) 459-7419.

DIAMOND FALLS AND MINERAL BATHS AND BOTANICAL GARDENS is about 1.5 mi. (2.4 km) s.e. King Louis XVI of France had bathhouses built for his troops at this site just prior to the French Revolution. Visitors can bathe in the mineral-rich pools. The exotic tropical garden is filled with colorful flora and fauna. A path that winds through landscaped grounds leads to a magnificent waterfall; the unique coloration of the rocks is due to mineral deposits left by the streaming water. Daily 10-5. Admission $3; under 13, $1.25. Bathing charge $2.75. Phone (758) 459-7565.

VOLCANO AND SULPHUR SPRINGS (La Soufrière), 2 mi. (3.2 km) s.e., is a 7-acre (2.8-hectare) crater that has been dormant since 1780. It is often referred to as the world's only "drive-in" volcano, since a road leads directly there. A path winds around a portion of the crater past bubbling pools that spew grayish mud reputed to have therapeutic qualities. Smoldering hot springs produce steaming bursts of sulphurous gases said to relieve respiratory ailments. Open daily 8-4:30. Admission $1.25. Fee includes guide service.

LODGINGS & RESTAURANTS

CASTRIES

LODGINGS

CANDYO INN
◆◆ *Country Inn*

| 12/16-4/15 | $80-95 | XP $15 |
| 12/1-12/15 & 4/16-11/30 | $65-80 | XP $15 |

Location: On Rodney Bay; 6.5 mi n of George FS Airport. (PO Box 386). Fax: 758/452-0774. **Terms:** F12; Reserv deposit, 21 day notice; handling fee imposed; 10% service charge. **Facility:** 12 rooms. Charming & cozy pink Spanish style inn. Interior corridors; beach access, small pool. **All Rooms:** combo or shower baths. **Some Rooms:** 8 kitchens. **Cards:** AE, MC, VI.

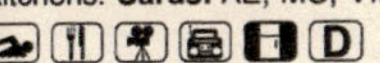

(758/452-0712

CARIBBEES HOTEL
◆◆ *Motor Inn*

| 12/1-4/15 | $90 | XP $20 |
| 4/16-11/30 | $70 | XP $20 |

Location: 3 mi n of Vigie Airport on Chaussee Rd. 34 mi n of Hewannora International Airport. PO Box 1720, La Pansee Rd. Fax: 758/453-1999. **Terms:** F12; Reserv deposit, 3 day notice; handling fee imposed; 10% service charge. **Facility:** 55 rooms. Situated off narrow road atop steep hill. Most rooms offer a spectacular view of the sea. Meets AAA guest room security requirements. 1-4 stories, no elevator; exterior corridors; oceanview. **Services:** giftshop; area transportation. **All Rooms:** combo or shower baths. **Cards:** AE, DS, MC, VI.

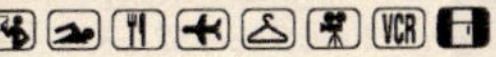

(758/452-4767

THE GREEN PARROT INN
◆ *Historic Country Inn*

| 12/16-4/15 | $110 | XP $50 |
| 12/1-12/15 & 4/16-11/30 | $90 | XP $40 |

Location: 3 mi s; on the Morne. The Morne Rd (PO Box 648). Fax: 758/453-2272. **Terms:** F11; Reserv deposit, 7 day notice; handling fee imposed; 10% service charge; CP, MAP avail; package plans. **Facility:** 55 rooms. Attractive hillside setting overlooking the city of Castries & the Caribbean Sea. 4 stories, no elevator; interior corridors; oceanview. **Dining:** 2 restaurants; $20-$35; cocktails. **Services:** giftshop. **Recreation:** hiking trails. **Some Rooms:** 4 kitchens. **Cards:** AE, DS, MC, VI.

((758)452-3399

THE ISLANDER HOTEL
◆ *Motor Inn*

| 12/15-4/14 | $120-130 | XP $20-25 |
| 12/1-12/14 & 4/15-11/30 | $85-90 | XP $20-25 |

Location: 6.5 mi n of George FS Charles Airport. Rodney Bay (PO Box 907, 0000). Fax: 758/452-0958. **Terms:** F12; Reserv deposit, 3 day notice; handling fee imposed; 10% service charge. **Facility:** 62 rooms. Family ambiance. All rooms with balcony on ground level with garden views. 2 two-bedroom units. 1 story; exterior corridors; beach access. **Services:** giftshop. **All Rooms:** combo or shower baths. **Some Rooms:** 20 efficiencies, 2 kitchens. **Cards:** AE, DI, DS, MC, VI.

(758/452-8757

REX PAPILLON
◆◆ *Resort Motor Inn*

All Year $300-377   XP $60
Location: 7 mi n of George FS Charles Airport on Reduit Beach; 41 mi n of Hewannora International Airport. (PO Box 512). Fax: 758/452-9332. **Terms:** D12; Reserv deposit, 21 day notice; handling fee imposed; 10% service charge. **Facility:** 140 rooms. All-inclusive resort. 2-3 stories, no elevator; exterior corridors; beach. Fee: 2 lighted tennis courts. **Recreation:** swimming, charter fishing, sailboating, scuba diving, snorkeling & equipment, windsurfing. Fee: scuba equipment, waterskiing. **All Rooms:** combo or shower baths. **Some Rooms:** color TV. **Cards:** AE, DI, MC, VI.

(758/452-0984

▲▲▲ SAVE REX ST. LUCIAN
◆◆ *Resort Motor Inn*

12/1-4/15 & 11/1-11/30 $175   XP $45
4/16-10/31 $140   XP $45
Location: 7 mi n of George FS Charles Airport on Reduit Beach; 41 mi n of Hewannora International Airport. (PO Box 512). Fax: 758/452-8331. **Terms:** D12; Reserv deposit, 14 day notice; 10% service charge; BP, MAP avail. **Facility:** 120 rooms. Beachfront resort on extensive grounds. Rooms with balcony or patio. 3 stories; exterior corridors; beach; 2 tennis courts (Fee: 2 lighted). **Dining:** 2 restaurants; 7:30 am-10 pm; $11-$30; cocktails. **Services:** giftshop. **Recreation:** swimming, sailboating, snorkeling, sunfishing. Fee: scuba diving, waterskiing, parasailing, windsurfing & instruction. Rental: scuba & snorkeling equipment. **Cards:** AE, DI, MC, VI. **Special Amenities: Free room upgrade and preferred room (each subject to availability with advanced reservations).** *(See color ad below)*

((758)452-8351

▲▲▲ SANDALS HALCYON ST. LUCIA
◆◆◆ *Resort Hotel*

All Year $3320-4460
Location: 1 km of George Charles International Aiport; 55 km n of Hewanorra International Airport. Chak Bay (PO Box GM 910). Fax: 758/451-8435. **Terms:** Age restrictions may apply; reserv deposit, 42 day notice; package plans; 3 night min stay. **Facility:** 170 rooms. 2 stories; exterior corridors; beach, sauna, steamrooms, whirlpools, beach accessories including kayak; 2 lighted tennis courts. Fee: 1 holes golf. **Dining:** Dining room, 2 restaurants; 7 am-3:30 am. **Services:** giftshop. Fee: area transportation. **Recreation:** swimming, paddleboats, sailboating, scuba diving, snorkeling, windsurfing. **Cards:** AE, DS, MC, VI.

((758)453-0222

▲▲▲ SANDALS ST. LUCIA GOLF RESORT AND SPA
◆◆◆ *Resort Complex*

12/22-3/31 $3800-7200
12/1-12/21 & 4/1-11/30 $3640-6980
Location: 3 mi s of George FS Charles Airport; 32 mi n of Hewannora International Airport. (PO Box 399). Fax: 758/452-1012. **Terms:** Age restrictions may apply; reserv deposit, 21 day notice; handling fee imposed; package plans; 3 night min stay. **Facility:** 273 rooms. Landscaped grounds on bluff overlooking beach. 30 suites with small private pool. 4-7 stories; interior/exterior corridors; 9 holes golf; beach; 5 lighted tennis courts. **Dining:** 5 restaurants; public by reservation only. **Services:** giftshop. Fee: massage. **Recreation:** swimming, paddleboats, sailboating, scuba diving/snorkeling & equipment, waterskiing, windsurfing. Fee: water skiing instructions, windsurfing instructions, scuba certification course. **Cards:** AE, DI, DS, MC, VI.

((758)452-308

WINDJAMMER LANDING-VILLA BEACH RESORT
◆◆◆ *Resort Complex*

1/5-2/13 & 2/22-4/18 $240-700   XP $45
12/18-1/4 & 2/14-2/21 $385-690   XP $45
12/1-12/17 & 4/19-11/30 $160-595   XP $45
Location: From George FS Charles Airport, 5 mi n, 1 mi w via signs; Labrelotte Bay. (PO Box 1504). Fax: 758/452-9454. **Terms:** Reserv deposit, 30 day notice; 10% service charge. **Facility:** 112 rooms. Very attractive hillside villas overlooking Labrelotte Bay. Secluded location; excellent guest facilities. 25 two-bedroom units, 27 three-bedroom units. 1-bedroom villas with/without private pool $240-$350 for 2 persons; 2-bedroom $340-$485 for 4 persons; 3-bedroom $425-$560 for up to 6 persons; 2 stories; exterior corridors; oceanview; beach; 2 lighted tennis courts. **Services:** giftshop. Fee: massage. **Recreation:** swimming, snorkeling & equipment, waterskiing, windsurfing. Fee: scuba diving. Rental: scuba equipment. **All Rooms:** combo or shower baths. **Cards:** AE, MC, VI.

(758/452-0913

WYNDHAM MORGAN BAY RESORT
◆◆◆ *Hotel*

| 1/3-4/10 | $353-405 | XP $176-203 |
| 12/1-12/19 & 4/11-11/30 | $285-330 | XP $143-165 |

Location: From George FS Charles Airport, 3 mi n. (PO Box 2167, GROS ISLET). Fax: 758/450-1050. **Terms:** D18; Open 12/1-12/19 & 1/3-11/30; $10 service charge. **Facility:** 238 rooms. Family ambiance. Simple & elegant by the sea with a European touch. 3 stories, no elevator; exterior corridors; oceanview; putting green; beach; 4 tennis courts (2 lighted); playground. **Services:** giftshop. Fee: massage, area transportation. **Recreation:** swimming, charter fishing, fishing, paddleboats, sailboating, snorkeling, scuba & snorkeling equipment, waterskiing, windsurfing. Fee: scuba diving; horseback riding. **Cards:** AE, DI, MC, VI.

(758)450-2511

RESTAURANTS

CAPONE'S
◆◆ *Italian*   D $12-$26

Location: 6 mi n from George FS Charles Airport. 19 Brazil St. **Hours:** 7 pm-midnight; adjacent pizza parlor from 11 am. Closed major holidays & Mon. **Reservations:** suggested; in season. **Features:** casual dress; cocktails; a la carte. Art deco setting, speak-easy atmosphere. Well-prepared cuisine. **Cards:** AE, MC, VI.

758/452-0284

THE GREEN PARROT RESTAURANT
◆◆ *Regional Caribbean*   L $10-$25 D $20-$35

Location: 3 mi s; on The Morne. Old Morne Rd. **Hours:** 7 am-midnight. **Reservations:** required; for dinner. **Features:** No A/C; casual dress; cocktails & lounge; a la carte. Local & Continental dishes, served in attractive dining room overlooking city & harbor; magnificent view. **Cards:** AE, DS, MC, VI.

758/452-3399

LODGINGS

ANSE CHASTANET
◆◆◆ *Country Inn*

12/20-4/15	$385-630	XP $80-150
12/1-12/19, 4/16-5/31 & 11/1-11/30	$205-420	XP $35-105
6/1-10/31	$166-380	XP $35-85

Location: 1.3 mi n of Soufriere; 30 mi s of Castries via West Coast Rd; 20 mi n of Hewanorra Intl Airport. (PO Box 7000). Fax: 758/459-7700. **Terms:** Age restrictions may apply; reserv deposit, 21 day notice, 14 days off season; 10% service charge. **Facility:** 49 rooms. On steep hillside overlooking sea & pitons. Separate cottage units, secluded & rustic, also spacious rooms on beach. Rough access road. Special wedding facilities avail; 2 stories; exterior corridors; oceanview; beach; 1 tennis court. **Services:** giftshop. Fee: massage. **Recreation:** swimming, charter fishing, sailboating, snorkeling & equipment, windsurfing; hiking trails. Fee: scuba diving & equipment. **All Rooms:** shower baths. **Cards:** AE, DI, DS, MC, VI.

758/459-7000

LADERA RESORT
◆◆◆ *Resort*

12/18-1/6	$460	XP $25
1/7-3/31	$410	XP $25
12/1-12/17 & 4/1-11/30	$245	XP $15

Location: 2 mi s. (PO Box 225). Fax: 758/459-5156. **Terms:** Age restrictions may apply; reserv deposit, 3 day notice, in season. **Facility:** 24 rooms. Unique resort of villas without a fourth wall while retaining total privacy. Spectacular views of ocean & pitons. 6 two-bedroom units, 3 three-bedroom units. 1 story; exterior corridors; beach access. **Services:** giftshop. **Recreation:** snorkeling. **All Rooms:** shower baths. **Cards:** AE, DI, MC, VI.

758/459-7323

St. Martin/St. Maarten

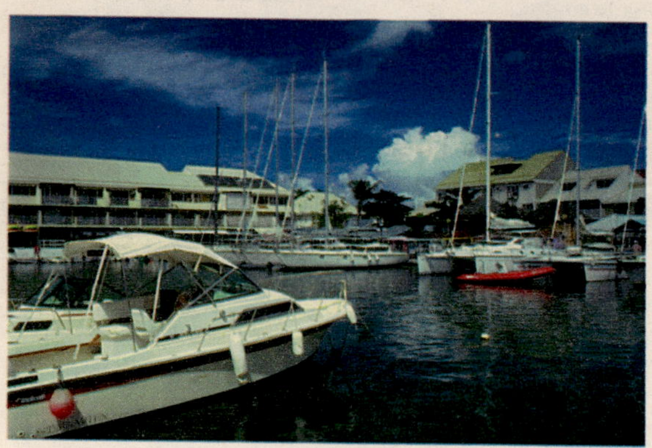

SHARED BETWEEN FRANCE and the Netherlands, St. Martin/St. Maarten is the smallest territory in the world governed by two sovereign states. St. Maarten is smaller but somewhat more developed than St. Martin, its French counterpart. Until a few years ago the island was a largely undiscovered hideaway; today modern tourist accommodations are plentiful. Philipsburg, the capital of St. Maarten, is on a sandbar between Great Bay and Great Salt Pond. Marigot, the quintessentially French capital of St. Martin, is known for its fine shopping and as a haven for yachts, as are Oyster Pond and Great Bay in St. Maarten.

History, Government and Economy

The Arawaks were the first to inhabit the island in pre-Columbian times. The Caribs, who eventually replaced their peace-loving predecessors, called the island *Soualiga*, meaning "land of salt," due to its numerous salt ponds. When Christopher Columbus discovered the island during his second voyage in 1493, he named it after St. Martin of Tours.

Spanish colonization didn't come until about 1640; until then they battled with the Dutch and French for the island's coveted anchorages and valuable salt ponds. In 1634 a Spanish battery went up at Pointe Blanche, southeast of present-day Philipsburg, and on the peninsula where the ruins of Fort Amsterdam can now be found, and the island was defended successfully until the Spanish finally abandoned it in 1648. The island was then settled by French and Dutch prisoners and their countrymen from nearby St. Kitts and St. Eustatius.

The two remaining contestants decided to divide the island, and local legend holds that they defined the border through a walking contest. A Frenchman and a Dutchman started in the same spot, walked around the island in opposite directions and drew the boundary line where they met. In reality, though, the 1648 Treaty of Concordia granted France the greater portion of the island because its navy could offer greater protection. Though claims to the territory remained in some dispute for another 170 years, the settlers' idea of harmonious coexistence has lasted.

In 1948 the islanders, who by this time considered themselves one people, erected a monument commemorating their 300 years as neighbors.

The salt ponds remained important economically through the 19th century. Sugar cane and tobacco, however, brought only brief prosperity; slaves were imported to work the plantations in the late 1700s, but following abolition in 1848 most of the plantations fell to ruin. A devastating hurricane followed by an earthquake in 1819 foreshadowed the island's economic decline. It was not until 1939 when the island declared itself a free port that the economy began to turn around. An airport was built in the late 1950s, and the tourism industry was born.

Dutch St. Maarten became part of the Netherlands Antilles in 1845. French St. Martin has been a dependency of the French overseas department of Guadeloupe since 1946.

Shopping

The two capitals of Philipsburg and Marigot are a treasureland for shoppers. Duty-free luxury imports include Dutch and French silver, crystal, Delftware, cameras, French perfume, china, fashions, jewelry, Italian leather and electronics. Inexpensive souvenirs are available among such plentiful island wares as hand-drawn and embroidered linens, ceramics, woodcarvings, straw goods, original paintings, St. Martin music and books, cane furniture and *pareu,* a length of fabric that is twisted and turned depending on how it is worn.

The island's shopping mecca is Philipsburg's Frontstreet, where more than 100 shops line the mile-long (1.6 km-long) thoroughfare. Hidden behind Frontstreet are numerous shops along Backstreet and Cannegieter Street—all connected by *steegjes,* or alleyways. Island handicrafts are for sale along the pier and in nearby Wathey Square. Other shopping opportunities are available west of town in the Simpson Bay and Maho Bay areas.

In Marigot the shops center on Port la Royale on the marina and across the street along rue Général de Gaulle and rue de la Liberté. Rue de la République, the road leading to the ferry pier, also has several fine shops. Boutiques in Marigot specialize in European designer fashions and tropical clothing. Wednesday and Saturday mornings Market Square on the harbor bustles with the activity of locals selling fresh food and handicrafts.

Shopping hours on the Dutch side are generally Mon.-Sat. 8-noon and 2-6, and on the French side Mon.-Sat. 9-12:30 and 3-7. Banking hours in Philipsburg are Mon.-Fri. 8:30-3. In Marigot banking hours are Mon.-Fri. 8:30-1:30.

FOOD AND DRINK

Few experienced travelers would disagree that St. Martin/St. Maarten offers some of the best dining in the Caribbean. The dual nationality of the island adds a dimension of culinary variety, and there are more than 150 fine restaurants to choose from. French and West Indian menus predominate, though Italian and American also are popular.

As expected of a former French colony, St. Martin is especially renowned for its cuisine, both in its classic version and its Creole cousin. Northeast of Marigot is the tiny village of Grand Case, considered the island's gourmet capital; some of the island's best French and West Indian restaurants can be found here. In Marigot there are several Gallic restaurants as well as those offering other cuisines. Marigot also features several French-style sidewalk cafes.

The restaurants in Philipsburg and elsewhere in St. Maarten offer greater variety. In addition to French, the finest in West Indian, Italian, American, Mexican, Thai, sushi, Argentinean, Indonesian and even Chinese cuisines can be found.

THINGS TO KNOW

AREA: 37 square miles (96 sq km).

POPULATION: 60,000.

LANGUAGE: St. Martin: French, Dutch, English and Creole. **St. Maarten:** English, Dutch, Spanish, French and Papiamento.

CAPITAL: Marigot, St. Martin; Philipsburg, St. Maarten.

GOVERNMENT: St. Martin: Dependency of the French Overseas Department of Guadeloupe. **St. Maarten:** Netherlands Antilles autonomous in the Kingdom of the Netherlands.

TIME ZONE: Atlantic.

UNIT OF CURRENCY: St. Martin: French franc, divided into 100 centimes; $1 U.S.=approx. 5.9 francs. **St. Maarten:** Netherlands Antilles guilder divided into 100 cents; $1 U.S.=approx. 1.79 guilders.

ELECTRICITY: St. Martin: 220 volts, 60 cycles AC. **St. Maarten:** 110 volts, 60 cycles AC.

MINIMUM AGE FOR GAMBLING: 18.

CARS: U.S. license valid; drive on right.

IMMIGRATION REQUIREMENTS: St. Martin: For stays under 3 months, proof of U.S. citizenship (passport, expired passport dating back not more than 5 years, birth certificate with raised seal accompanied by a government-authorized identification card or similar document with photo) and return or through ticket; departure tax 20 francs. **St. Maarten:** Proof of U.S. citizenship (valid passport, expired passport dating back not more than 5 years, or birth certificate with raised seal accompanied by a government-authorized identification or similar document with photo) and return or through ticket; departure tax $20.

FOR FURTHER INFORMATION:
St. Martin Tourist Office
10 E. 21st St.
New York, NY 10010
(212) 529-9069
St. Martin Tourist Office
Harborfront
Marigot, St. Martin
(590) 87-57-21
St. Maarten Tourist Bureau
Imperial Building, 2nd Floor Walter Nisbeth Rd., #23
Philipsburg, St. Maarten
5995-22-337
(800) 786-2278

HOLIDAYS: St. Martin: Jan. 1; Mardi Gras; Easter Monday; Queen's Birthday, April 30; Labor Day, May 1; Ascension Thursday; Whit Monday; Bastille Day, July 14; Schoelcher Day, July 21; Feast of the Assumption, Aug. 15; All Saints Day, Nov. 1; Concordia Day, Nov. 11; Armistice Day; Dec. 25; Boxing Day, Dec 26. **St. Maarten:** Jan. 1; Good Friday; Easter Monday; Queen's Birthday, Apr. 30; Labor Day, May 1; Ascension Thursday; St. Maarten's Day, Nov. 11; Dec. 25; Boxing Day, Dec. 26.

Restaurants add a 10- to 15-percent service charge to the bill.

St. Maarten's own Guavaberry Island Folk Liqueur makes a good take-home item. Six bittersweet flavors are available and can be sampled at a tasting house at the east end of Frontstreet in Philipsburg. The island's tap water is purified; bottled water also is widely available.

Sports and Amusements

Most daytime activities on the island are water oriented and take place on white sand beaches and in secluded coves. The island is fringed with some three dozen beaches. Great Bay and Little Bay beaches are the most accessible from Philipsburg. To the west are Simpson Bay Beach, replete with water sports outlets; tiny but popular Maho Beach, at the end of the airport runway; Mullet Bay Beach, with convenient facilities; and secluded Cupecoy Beach, lined with sandstone cliffs and caves. Scenic Dawn Beach on the east coast also is good for snorkeling.

On the French side west of Simpson Bay Lagoon are unspoiled Long Bay Beach and intimate Rouge Beach. Mile-long (1.6 km) Grand Case Beach on the northwest shore has calm, clear waters. Orient Beach on the northeast shore is the island's most popular. Topless bathing is common on the French side; bathing *au naturel* is possible at Orient and other designated beaches.

Such water sports concessions as scuba diving, snorkeling, windsurfing, parasailing, water skiing and jet skiing are concentrated around Grand Case Beach, Anse Marcel and Orient Beach in St. Martin and Great Bay, Little Bay and Simpson Bay in St. Maarten. Ocean Explorers at Simpson Bay offers the Sea Walk, in which participants don specially made bell helmets for a walk on the sea floor; swimming is not required.

The island's coral reefs teem with marine life, and its waters allow for visibility of up to 200 feet. Experienced divers have many interesting diving spots to choose from, including the Alleys, bound by cliffs and ledges; Green Key; Flat Island; and Hen and Chick, small islands with beautiful elkhorn coral reefs. Outside Great Bay is the 1801 wreck of the British warship HMS *Proselyte*.

Several firms offer scuba diving lessons lasting about 3 hours. Picnic sails and snorkeling trips to such nearby deserted islands as Tintamarre (Flat Island) and Pinel or Prickly Pear islands also are available. Arrangements for diving and snorkeling trips and lessons can be made through all the island's marinas and major hotels. Deep-sea fishing charters can be arranged at Bobby's Marina and Great Bay Marina in Philipsburg,

Port la Royale in Marigot and Port Lonvilliers in Anse Marcel. Dolphin, kingfish, sailfish, blue marlin and wahoo are the main catches.

But those seeking land-based activities need not feel so out of the swim of things. Horseback riding is available at Crazy Acres Riding Center in Cole Bay, St. Maarten, and Caid and Isa in Anse Marcel, St. Martin; guided excursions are available. Tennis courts can be found at most hotels and resorts, and many are lighted. Le Privilège, a sports and spa complex in Anse Marcel, has six lighted courts as well as exercise equipment, squash courts and a pool. An 18-hole golf course is available on the Dutch side at Mullet Bay Resort.

The island is definitely not lacking in nighttime diversions. Evening entertainment takes place primarily at nine hotel casinos, all on the Dutch side, and the resorts, where carnival shows and Caribbean music are on tap. St. Maarten's club scene centers on the Maho area, where Cheri's Cafe and Club Amnesia attract youthful revelers. Another popular night spot is Salsa at the Atlantis Casino. In St. Martin there is L'Atmosphère at Port la Royale in Marigot and Le Privilège in Anse Marcel.

In late February or early March, St. Maarten hosts a regatta that includes yacht races and soirees. A popular event is Carnival, held around Shrove Tuesday and Ash Wednesday in St. Martin and during the last two weeks in April in St. Maarten.

EXCURSIONS AND SIGHTSEEING

The island is easily toured by car, but caution should be exercised—many side roads are rough and narrow, and wandering livestock are common, especially on the French side. Steep roads should not be attempted following rains. The border between the Dutch and French sides can be traversed freely. Road maps are available at the airport, car rental agencies located at the airport and the tourist offices in Philipsburg and Marigot.

On a peninsula between Great Bay and Little Bay is Fort Amsterdam, built by the Dutch in 1631 but occupied by the Spanish 1633-48. Peter Stuyvesant, eventual governor of America's New Netherland colony, lost his right leg here while battling the Spanish in 1644. The unimproved site is accessible via the Divi Little Bay Beach Resort. Due north atop Fort Hill are the ruins of

Fort William, which dates to 1801. A steep hike to the top rewards the adventurous with a spectacular panorama; driving is not recommended.

Another excellent vantage point is the roadside lookout a few miles west on Cole Bay Hill. Several neighboring islands can be seen, including on a clear day St. Kitts and Nevis—about 45 miles (72 km) southeast. Union Road, the route north from Cole Bay Hill, is the quickest way to Marigot; at the halfway point stands the Border Monument, erected in 1948 to commemorate the islanders' 300 years as neighbors. A longer but worthwhile route proceeds west past the airport and through the island's lowlands, circling Simpson Bay Lagoon. En route are some of the island's finest resorts.

An interesting stop is La Belle Creole, on a peninsula west of Nettle Bay. The dream of Claude Philippe, former maître d' at New York's Waldorf Astoria, this copy of a Mediterranean village was under construction on and off for more than 25 years; a deluxe resort now occupies the site. La Belle Creole sustained damage from Hurricane Luis in September 1995; a reopening date has not been announced.

From Philipsburg the especially scenic east coast of St. Maarten is accessible via Sucker Garden Road. The first turnoff leads to Guana Bay Point and the second to Dawn Beach and Oyster Pond. Both routes are steep and meandering, but the vistas to be enjoyed are worth the effort. Most noticeable among the numerous offshore landmarks is the French island of St. Barthélemy, about 14 miles (23 km) offshore. Picturesque Oyster Pond, reminiscent of the French Riviera, is a favorite anchorage of Caribbean boaters.

North of Oyster Pond is the rural area of Orléans, seemingly untouched by time and tourism, and the large Etang aux Poissons, or Fish Lake. Further north along the coast are popular Orient Beach and several smaller, more secluded spots. Off the eastern shore of rural French Cul de Sac is uninhabited Pinel Island, a favorite day-sail destination where water sports and facilities are available. To the west is Anse Marcel; the resort Le Meridien L'Habitation was the site of a summit meeting between United States President George Bush and French President François Mitterand in December 1989.

From French Cul de Sac the road turns westward through Grand Case. This charming former

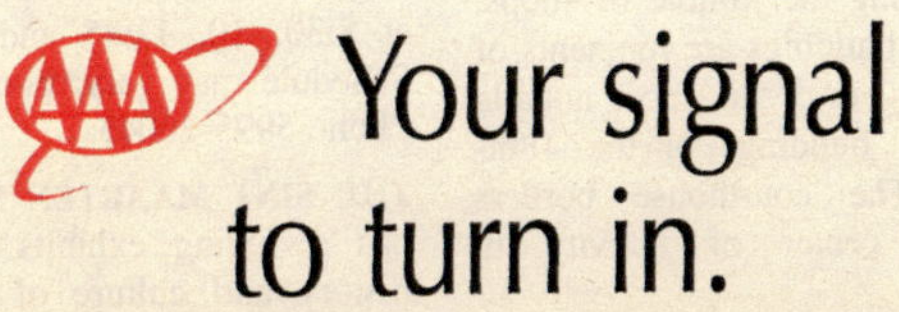

fishing village has earned its reputation as the island's gourmet capital. The Creole-style structures along the main road house some of the island's best restaurants. And at numerous roadside food stands, or *lolos,* barbecued lobster, chicken and ribs and such Caribbean specialties as plantains and johnnycakes are sold.

The road south passes Paradise Peak; at 1,391 feet it is the highest point on the island. On clear days the view encompasses both capitals and the island's patchwork of blue and green. The road to the inland village of Colombier, south of Paradise Peak, is lined on the north by lush tropical flora and on the south by rolling green hills decorated with long, meandering stone walls.

Glass-bottom boat trips, picnic sails and luncheon, sunset and moonlight yacht cruises are available out of the marinas at Philipsburg, Simpson Bay, Cole Bay, Marigot, Anse Marcel and Oyster Pond. Day trips to nearby Anguilla, St. Barthélemy, Saba, St. Eustatius and St. Kitts and Nevis also can be arranged. The 36-passenger submarine SS *Odyssey* departs Simpson Bay several times daily to explore the island's coral reefs and the 1801 wreck of the HMS *Proselyte;* for information and reservations phone 5995-52642.

Transportation

Princess Juliana International Airport has direct flights from San Juan, Miami, Dallas/Fort Worth and New York. ALM Antillean Airlines offers daily service from Curaçao; LIAT from Antigua, Montserrat, St. Croix, St. Kitts, St. Thomas and Tortola; and Windward Islands Airways from Anguilla, St. Eustatius and Saba. Air Guadeloupe has daily flights from Guadeloupe, Air St. Barthélemy from St. Barthélemy and Air Martinique from Martinique. In addition to Juliana Airport, Air Guadeloupe and Air St. Barthélemy fly into Esperance Airport, a small domestic airstrip in Grand Case. Philipsburg is a port of call for many cruise ships. Smaller ships dock at Marigot.

By law, automobiles rented from companies with outlets at Princess Juliana Airport cannot be picked up at the airport; courtesy shuttles transport visitors to the rental car lots. Automobiles rented from outlets not near the airport are delivered free to hotels, and many hotels have car rental offices on the premises. Most cars have automatic transmissions and air conditioning. Motor scooters also are available; caution is advised due to rough roads and steep hills. Major credit cards are accepted.

Taxis are abundant on both the Dutch and French sides. Taxi rates are regulated, but it is always wise to agree on the fare in advance. Rates increase by 25 percent from 10 p.m. to midnight and by 50 percent from midnight to 6 a.m. Each additional passenger over two is an extra $2. The rates from Princess Juliana Airport are posted at the taxi stand outside. Tipping is customary. The two capitals of Philipsburg and Marigot are connected by inexpensive public buses that operate from 6 a.m. to 10 p.m.

The islands of Anguilla, St. Barthélemy, Saba and St. Eustatius are accessible by any one of several boats operating out of Philipsburg in St. Maarten. Several ferries to Anguilla operate out of Marigot in St. Martin.

Attraction Admissions
Attraction admissions for this island are quoted in U.S. dollars.

Points of Interest
See map page 236.

St. Maarten

Philipsburg (C-3) pop. 32,000

Philipsburg is the busy Dutch capital. Its three main thoroughfares are usually crammed with shoppers browsing through stores stocked with duty-free luxuries. Among the jumble of shops, restaurants and modern buildings are remnants of an earlier Philipsburg. One of the most notable of the town's historic buildings is the 18th-century courthouse. The courthouse borders Wathey Square, the center of activity in Philipsburg.

ST. MAARTEN'S 12 METRE CHALLENGE, departing from Bobby's Marina downtown on Frontstreet, allows passengers to compete in yacht races while sailing on actual America's Cup contenders. Each passenger has the choice of helping man the boat or just sitting back and relaxing. Prior sailing experience is not necessary. Allow 2 hours minimum. Departures daily at 8:30, 10, 11:45 and 1:30; closed Dec. 25. Schedule may vary; phone ahead. Fare $60. VI. Phone 5995-20045.

THE SINT MAARTEN MUSEUM, 7 Frontstreet, has revolving exhibits depicting primarily the history and culture of the island. Among the items displayed are Indian artifacts, old maps and photos and artifacts from the island's forts and plantations. An 18th-century Chinese porcelain dinner service is featured. The museum's collections are housed on the second floor of a restored 19th-century townhouse. Mon.-Fri. 10-4, Sat. 10-1. Donations. Phone 5995-23379

WHITE OCTOPUS **CATAMARAN,** departing Bobby's Marina, is a sleek 75-foot craft with upper and lower decks. Passage is provided to St. Barthélemy and back; free drinks and snacks are offered. Allow 1 hour, 30 minutes each way. Departures Mon.-Tues. and Thurs.-Sat. at 9; departs Capt. Oliver's Marina at Oyster Pond Wed. at 9. Returns at 5. Fare $55; under 12, $30. Reservations are suggested. AE, MC, VI. Phone 5995-24096.

St. Martin

Marigot (B-3) pop. 15,000

The quaint harbor town of Marigot (MAR-ego) is thoroughly French. The traditional architecture of wrought-iron balconies and fretwork trim can be seen along its busy streets and residential roads, and a stroll among the shops and sidewalk cafes of Port la Royale can transport visitors to the French Riviera. The restored ruins of 18th-century Fort St. Louis overlook Marigot's harbor, providing an excellent view; the fort can be reached on foot via the steps behind the Sous-Préfecture off rue de L'Hôpital.

Adding to the quaintness, a tree-lined promenade borders the water's edge where there is a series of pleasure boat slips. At the far end of the boulevard is the town marketplace.

ARCHAEOLOGICAL MUSEUM, at Sandy Ground just outside the city center on the waterfront, presents "On the Trail of the Arawaks," a permanent collection of pre-Columbian pottery and artifacts depicting the cultures of the island's first inhabitants. Early island photographs also are displayed. Mon.-Sat. 9-1 and 3-7. Admission $5; under 12, $3. Phone (590) 29-22-84.

Lodgings & Restaurants

French Cul-De-Sac (St. Martin)

Lodging

HOTEL MONT VERNON
◆◆◆ *Resort Hotel*

12/20-1/3	$275-435	XP $60
1/4-3/29	$245-405	XP $60
12/1-12/19 & 3/30-11/30	$145-280	XP $60

Location: Ne of island; 18 km from Juliana Airport & 3 km from Grand Case Airport. Baie Orientale 97150 (B.P. 1174-Baie Orientale, FRENCH CUL-DE-SAC). Fax: 590/87-3727. **Terms:** Reserv deposit, 7 day notice, 3 days off season. **Facility:** 370 rooms. On sloping hillside overlooking Orient Bay. Large rooms with balcony, with ocean or garden view. 1-3 stories, no elevator; exterior corridors; beach. Fee: 2 lighted tennis courts. **Services:** giftshop. Fee: area transportation. **Recreation:** swimming, scuba diving/snorkeling & equipment. **All Rooms:** comb, shower or tub baths. **Cards:** AE, MC, VI.

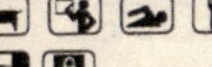

(590/87-6200

Grand Case (St. Martin)

Lodgings

ESMERALDA RESORT
◆◆◆ *Resort Hotel*

12/19-1/2 & 2/2-2/22	$350-800	XP $50
1/3-2/1 & 2/23-4/11	$275-750	XP $50
12/1-12/18 & 4/12-11/30	$180-400	XP $25

Location: 3 km se of Grand Case Airport, in Orient Bay. Baie Orientale 97071 (BP 5141, MARIGOT). Fax: 590/87-3518. **Terms:** F12; Reserv deposit, 30 day notice; handling fee imposed. **Facility:** 78 rooms. Luxurious, fully-equipped 1- to 4-bedroom cottages all with private terraces scattered on hillside overlooking Orient Bay. 1 story; exterior corridors; oceanview; beach; 2 lighted tennis courts. **Services:** giftshop. **Recreation:** swimming, charter fishing, scuba diving, snorkeling & equipment. Fee: fishing, scuba equipment, waterskiing, windsurfing. **Some Rooms:** 45 efficiencies, color TV. **Cards:** AE, MC, VI.

(590/87-3636

AAA **SAVE** **HOTEL PAVILLON BEACH**
◆◆   *Motel*

12/15-4/14	$260	XP $40
12/1-12/14 & 4/15-11/30	$170	XP $20

Location: W end of Grand Case Village. (BP 5133, GRAND CASE, 97070). Fax: 509/87-7104. **Terms:** F5; Reserv deposit, 30 day notice, 14 day off season; handling fee imposed; pets. **Facility:** 17 rooms. Modern rooms with large balcony on Grand Case Bay. Limited parking. 1-2 stories; interior/exterior corridors; oceanfront; beach. **Dining:** Restaurant nearby. **Recreation:** swimming. **All Rooms:** efficiencies, shower baths. **Cards:** AE, MC, VI. **Special Amenities: Free room upgrade (subject to availability with advanced reservations).** *(See color ad below)*

(590)87-9646

RESTAURANTS

L'AUBERGE GOURMANDE
◆◆◆   *French*   **D** $17-$25

Location: Center. 89 Blvd de Grand Case 97150. **Hours:** 6 pm-10 pm. **Closed:** Wed. **Reservations:** required. **Features:** casual dress; cocktails; street parking; a la carte. Small candlelit dining room with classic French cuisine in historic creole home. Excellent homemade dessert & ice cream. **Cards:** AE, MC, VI.

590/87-73-37

LE FISH POT
◆◆◆   *Seafood*   **D** $15-$30

Location: In Grand Case Village. 97150. **Hours:** 6:30 pm-10 pm. **Reservations:** required. **Features:** No A/C; casual dress; cocktails & lounge; street parking; a la carte. Classical French cuisine with tropical influence. Elegant, open-air waterfront dining by candlelight. **Cards:** AE, MC, VI.

590/87-50-88

LE TASTEVIN
◆◆◆   *French*   **L** $6-$19 **D** $20-$31

Location: Center. 86 Blvd de Grand Case 97150. **Hours:** noon-2:15 & 6-10:30 pm. **Reservations:** suggested. **Features:** No A/C; casual dress; cocktails; street parking; a la carte. Open balcony dining room on bay. Lobster, seafood, moderately-priced lunch specials. Nouvelle presentation. Relaxed, country-tropical charm. 15% service charge. **Cards:** AE, MC, VI.

590/87-55-45

LITTLE BAY (ST. MAARTEN)

LODGING

BELAIR BEACH HOTEL
◆◆   *Apartment Motel*

12/20-1/2 & 1/31-2/27	$355-409	XP $45
1/3-1/30 & 2/28-4/10	$255-299	XP $45
12/1-12/19 & 4/11-11/30	$209-249	XP $35

Location: 5 km w of Philisburg; 7.2 km e of airport, 5 km se on Welgelen Rd. (PO Box 940, LITTLE BAY) Fax: 599/5-25295. **Terms:** F18; Reserv deposit, 21 day notice; handling fee imposed; 15% service charge. **Facility:** 67 rooms. Well equipped, 2-bedroom, 2-bath apartments al overlooking beach; patio or balcony. For US reservations (203)847-6377; 4 stories; exterior corridors; oceanview beach; 1 tennis court. **Recreation:** swimming. **Fee:** scuba diving, snorkeling, waterskiing, windsurfing. **Cards:** AE, DI, MC, VI.

599/5-23362

MAHO BAY (ST. MAARTEN)

LODGING

MAHO BEACH HOTEL & CASINO
◆◆◆   *Resort Hotel*

12/21-4/4	$225-840	XP $40-50
12/1-12/20, 4/5-5/31, 7/1-8/31 & 11/1-11/30	$175-600	XP $40-50
6/1-6/30 & 9/1-10/31	$155-540	XP $40-50

Location: 0.6 km w of airport. Maho Bay. Fax: 599/55-3180. **Terms:** Reserv deposit, 21 day notice; 15% service charge. **Facility:** 604 rooms. Large sleek rooms. All with balcony, some oceanfront rooms. White sand beach. Bustling resort with a lot of shopping & activities to offer. 3 two-bedroom units. For US reservations: (212)969-9220; 4-9 stories; interior corridors. **Fee:** parking; 4 lighted tennis courts. **Services:** giftshop. **Fee:** massage. **Recreation:** fishing, snorkeling. **Fee:** charter fishing, snorkeling equipment. **Cards:** AE, DI, MC, VI.

599/55-2115

MARIGOT (ST. MARTIN)

LODGINGS

ANSE MARGOT HOTEL
◆◆   *Hotel*

12/26-1/3	$209-322
1/4-4/1	$178-274
12/1-12/25 & 4/2-11/30	$150-249

Location: 4 km w of Margot center, 7 km from Juliana Airport. Baie Nettle 97150. Fax: 590/87-9213. **Terms:** Reserv deposit, 15 day notice, 7 days off season. **Facility:** 96 rooms. Clusters of buildings on landscaped tropical grounds on Simpson Lagoon. Some compact rooms but with a simple charm. 35 loft suites, $209-$322; $211-$299 off season; 2-3 stories; exterior corridors; beach access; boat dock. **Services:** giftshop. **Recreation:** swimming, scuba diving. Fee: waterskiing, windsurfing. Rental: sailboats, scuba equipment. **Cards:** AE, DI, DS, MC, VI.

(590/87-9201

HOTEL LA SAMANNA
◆◆◆   *Resort Hotel*

12/13-4/19	$600-1050	XP $75
12/1-12/12, 4/20-5/31 & 11/1-11/30	$450-750	XP $75
6/1-9/1	$350-750	XP $75

Location: 8 km w on Long Bay; 2.5 km e of Julianna Airport. (BP 4077, MARIGOT, 97064). Fax: 590/87-8786. **Terms:** F12; Open 12/1-9/1 & 11/1-11/30; reserv deposit, 21 day notice, 28 days in season. **Facility:** 82 rooms. Individual Mediterranean-style cottages on landscaped grounds beside outstanding white sand beach. Luxury level services. A preferred hotel. 32 two-bedroom cottages, $1650-$2200 for 4 persons. 6 three-bedroom cottages, $2200-$3150 for up to 6 persons. Coffeemakers & CD player rentals on request; 2 stories; exterior corridors; oceanview; beach; 3 tennis courts (1 lighted). **Services:** giftshop. Fee: massage. **Recreation:** swimming, snorkeling, waterskiing, windsurfing. Fee: snorkeling equipment. **Some Rooms:** 7 kitchens. **Cards:** AE, DI, DS, MC, VI.

(590/87-6400

LE FLAMBOYANT HOTEL & RESORT
◆◆◆   *Resort Hotel*

12/19-1/3	$240-280	XP $56
1/4-4/10	$200-240	XP $56
12/1-12/18 & 4/11-11/30	$150-190	XP $56

Location: In Nettle Bay, 3 km w from center. Rt des Terres Basses. Fax: 590/87-9957. **Terms:** F12; Reserv deposit, 14 day notice; handling fee imposed. **Facility:** 271 rooms. On Simpson Bay Lagoon. Large rooms with spacious kitchen, on balcony. Landscaped grounds. Some rooms with lagoon views. 11 two-bedroom units. 2-bedroom duplex suite, $430; $315-$395 off season; 1 bedroom suite $215-$310; 1-3 stories, no elevator; exterior corridors; beach access; boat dock; playground. Fee: 1 lighted tennis court. **Services:** giftshop. Fee: area transportation. **Recreation:** swimming, paddleboats, scuba diving, snorkeling, windsurfing. Fee: snorkeling equipment. Rental: boats, scuba equipment. **Some Rooms:** 200 kitchens. **Cards:** AE, DI, MC, VI.

((590)87-6000

RESTAURANTS

LA VIE EN ROSE
◆◆   *French*   L $9-$26   D $22-$30

Location: Center; corner rue de la Republique & Blvd de France. rue de la Republique 97150. **Hours:** 11:30 am-2:30 & 6:30-10 pm. **Reservations:** required; for dinner. **Features:** No A/C; casual dress; cocktails & lounge; street parking; a la carte. Balcony overlooking harbour market. Light breakfast & lunch served downstairs in casual cafe-bistro. Romantic, classical French cuisine at dinner. **Cards:** AE, MC, VI.

(590/87-54-42

MARIO'S BISTRO
◆◆◆   *French*   D $15-$25

Location: Just e of Sandy Ground Bridge, 1 km w of town center. Mornerond. **Hours:** 6:30 pm-10:30 pm. Closed: 12/24 & Sun. **Reservations:** suggested. **Features:** No A/C; casual dress; cocktails. Outstanding contemporary French cuisine with global & regional influences. Bright, colorful open air dining room overlooking the water. **Cards:** MC, VI.

(590/87-0636

OYSTER POND (ST. MAARTEN)

LODGING

OYSTER BAY BEACH RESORT
◆◆◆ *Hotel*

12/20-3/31	$170-600	XP $40
12/1-12/19 & 4/1-11/30	$120-400	XP $40

Location: 9 km ne of airport. (PO Box 239, OYSTER POND). Fax: 599/5-36695. **Terms:** F12; Reserv deposit, 21 day notice; 15% service charge. **Facility:** 40 rooms. Charming tropical inn on slip of land between marina & the ocean. Spectacular views from private balcony or porch of marina, courtyard, or ocean. 2 stories; exterior corridors; beach. **Recreation:** swimming. Fee: charter fishing. **All Rooms:** combo or shower baths. **Some Rooms:** 20 efficiencies. **Cards:** AE, MC, VI.

(599/5-36040

RESTAURANT

OYSTER BAY BEACH RESORT RESTAURANT
◆◆◆ *French*   L $12-$20 D $15-$30

Location: 9 km ne of airport; in Oyster Bay Beach Resort. **Hours:** 8 am-9 pm. **Reservations:** suggested. **Features:** No A/C; casual dress; cocktails & lounge; a la carte. Eclectic mix of Caribbean & French dishes served in open air tiled dining room overlooking the sea. Fresh lobster, herbed fish & renowned souffles. Fresh market cuisine. Elegant & romantic. 15% service charge. **Cards:** AE, DI, MC, VI.

(599/5-22206

OYSTER POND (ST. MARTIN)

LODGING

HOTEL CAPTAIN OLIVER
◆◆ *Country Inn*

12/22-1/4	$170-265
12/1-12/21, 1/5-3/16 & 10/3-11/30	$73-140
3/17-10/2	$50-98

Location: On e side of island; 12 km from airport. BP 645 97150. Fax: 590/87-4084. **Terms:** Reserv deposit, 7 day notice, 14 days 12/22-1/4. **Facility:** 50 rooms. On Oyster Pond. Relaxed, family atmosphere. All rooms with balcony. Ocean or marina views avail. Bright, airy rooms with lofty ceilings. 1 story; exterior corridors; marina. **Services:** giftshop; area transportation. **Recreation:** charter fishing, scuba diving, snorkeling. Fee: fishing, scuba & snorkeling equipment. **All Rooms:** efficiencies. **Cards:** AE, MC, VI.

(590/87-4026

RESTAURANT

CAPTAIN OLIVER'S
◆◆ *Seafood*   L $7-$23 D $15-$23

Location: On e side of island; 12 km from airport; in Hotel Captain Oliver's. **Hours:** 7 am-midnight. **Reservations:** suggested. **Features:** No A/C; casual dress; cocktails; entertainment; a la carte. Open-air deck overlooking Oyster Pond & marina. Fresh seafood with French & Creole influence. Also barbecue grill. **Cards:** AE, MC, VI.

(590/87-4026

PHILIPSBURG (ST. MAARTEN)

LODGING

HOLLAND HOUSE BEACH HOTEL
◆◆ *Hotel*

12/16-4/15	$155-200	XP $15
12/1-12/15 & 4/16-11/30	$99-139	XP $15

Location: Centre. 35 Front St (PO Box 393, PHILIPSBURG). Fax: 599/5-24673. **Terms:** F12; Reserv deposit, 14 day notice; handling fee imposed; 15% service charge. **Facility:** 54 rooms. Busy downtown location. All rooms with balcony. Many with ocean view. 4 stories; interior corridors; street parking only; beach. **Services:** giftshop. **Recreation:** swimming. Fee: charter fishing, scuba diving, snorkeling. **Some Rooms:** 46 efficiencies. **Cards:** AE, DI, DS, MC, VI.

(599/5-22572

RESTAURANTS

RISTORANTE DA LIVIO
◆◆◆ *Italian*   D $18-$31

Location: Center. 159 Front St. **Hours:** noon-2 & 6-10 pm, Sat from 6 pm. Closed: Sun. **Reservations:** suggested. **Features:** No A/C; casual dress; cocktails & lounge; a la carte. Some waterfront terrace tables. Classical music & candlelight. Limited parking. 15% service charge. **Cards:** AE, MC, VI.

(599/5-22690

▲▲▲ THE WAYANG DOLL
◆◆◆ *Ethnic*   D $22-$27

Location: Center. 167 Front St. **Hours:** 6:45 pm-10 pm. Closed: Sun & 9/15-10/15. **Reservations:** suggested; in season. **Features:** No A/C; casual dress; cocktails; street parking. Indonesian Rijsttafel, offering tastings of many authentic dishes. Authentic decor & taped Japanese Gamalan music. Open-air dining room overlooking the bay. 15% service charge. **Cards:** AE, MC, VI.

(599/5-22687

St. Vincent and The Grenadines

See map page 245.

THE BAREFOOT LIFE of a traditional West Indian island is readily available on St. Vincent, 18 miles (29 km) long and 11 miles (18 km) wide. Relatively unknown to tourists until recently, St. Vincent is one of the most picturesque of the Windwards, with quaint fishing villages, coconut and arrowroot

plantations and palm-fringed coves of black volcanic sand. St. Vincent and its string of Grenadine islands, which reach south to Grenada, offer some of the best sailing, swimming, diving and snorkeling in the Caribbean. Complementing these pleasures are the small comfortable inns that provide much of the guest accommodations on St. Vincent and its sun-swept satellite islands, which include Bequia, Mustique, Canouan, Petit St. Vincent, Mayreau, Palm, Union and Young islands.

History, Government and Economy

Generations before Christopher Columbus arrived in the area in 1498, fierce Carib Indians from the South American mainland had annihilated St. Vincent's original population of gentle Arawaks. St. Vincent was left relatively undisturbed until the 18th century when, despite the hostility of the Caribs, the French, Dutch and British began to vie for settlement. Near the close of the 18th century the Caribs were deported to the Bay of Honduras. By the Treaty of Paris in 1763, France ceded the island to Britain but recaptured it in 1779. Britain gained final possession in 1783 by the Treaty of Versailles. Independence from Britain was finally granted in 1979.

That same year La Soufrière, the 4,048-foot volcano in the north, erupted, spewing ash that filtered all the way to Barbados, 95 miles (152 km) west. While necessitating the evacuation of Carib descendants living on the volcano's slopes, the eruption posed no threat to the capital of Kingstown, 30 miles (48 km) south.

Sharing the characteristics of the other Windward Islands, St. Vincent relies on tourism and agriculture as its main sources of income. Cut flowers have become St. Vincent's newest export. Green mountains and productive valleys cover the island. The rural Mesopotamia Valley, also called Marriaqua Valley, is the focus of much agricultural activity. Besides breadfruit, introduced from Tahiti by Captain Bligh of "Mutiny on the Bounty" fame, bananas, coconuts and arrowroot constitute the principal crops.

Shopping

Kingstown's main street has several interesting shops, a few selling clothing with island motifs. Sea island cotton with screened designs is available at Batik Caribe. The St. Vincent Craftsmen Shop, just up from the banana boat loading dock, is filled with a large variety of macrame items, jewelry and straw handicrafts, some made on the spot. A cluster of shops is tucked in the courtyard of the Cobblestone Hotel, inland from the main waterfront road. Shopping hours are generally Mon.-Fri. 8-noon and 1-4, Sat. 8-noon, though some stores are open Mon.-Fri. 8-4. Banking hours are Mon.-Fri. 8-1 (also Fri. 2-5). Some banks are open Mon.-Fri. 8-3.

Food and Drink

Traditional West Indian cuisine—local fish, island produce and thick soups—as well as international flavors are available at hotels. Grand View Hotel at Villa Point, 10 minutes southeast of Kingstown, offers a typical island meal. Other hotel restaurants worth investigating are in the Cobblestone and the Heron. Hotel kitchens often use the bountiful produce from the native market at the far end of the main street.

Sports and Amusements

The beaches at Villa Bay, Indian Bay and in the Grenadines are excellent for swimming, sunning, snorkeling and scuba diving. Sailing, boating, fishing and diving equipment can be rented for either half- or full-days.

Tennis courts are available; the Kingstown Tennis Club offers its facilities to non-members. Spectator sports include cricket, netball and soccer.

The Emerald Isle Casino, 30 miles (48 km) outside of Kingstown in Penniston Valley, is a popular nightspot for gambling, dancing and socializing.

Excursions and Sightseeing

A hike to La Soufrière involves a full day and requires good physical conditioning. The trip to the still-active volcano begins by car along the coast and crosses the famed Rabacca dry river, then proceeds on foot through the Bamboo Forest and straight up the 4,048-foot summit for an unparalleled view. The Vermont Nature Trail and Trinity Falls also provide scenic outlooks. Another all-day excursion for the adventurous leaves Chateaubelair by boat for the spectacular Falls of Baleine.

Day trips also can be made on island schooners and motorized mailboats to Bequia and other islands of the Grenadines. Bequia, Union Island and Canouan are accessible by plane. Bequia airport is 4 miles (6.4 km) south of Port Elizabeth and can accommodate small capacity propeller aircraft. Port Elizabeth's harbor area has colorful shops along the waterfront as well as lodgings, restaurants and water sports facilities. The production of hand-carved wooden sailboats is a prosperous industry on Bequia.

If you have less time you can take a half-day drive through the Mesopotamia Valley, which includes hillsides covered with banana and arrowroot crops and the craggy windward shore. On the leeward shore the quaint fishing village of Layou boasts the Carib Stones, huge sacrificial altars with carved heads and petroglyphs from pre-Columbian, Arawak and Carib Indians. Farther north lies the traditional fishing village of Barrouallie, which has remained unchanged for centuries. Close to Kingstown, Dorsetshire Hill and Mount Saint Andrew offer pleasant climbs.

The capital city of Kingstown is an enjoyable place to explore, with its mixture of English and French architectural styles, exemplified by 19th-century houses and such historic buildings as Wesleyan Hall and St. George's Cathedral. St. Mary's Cathedral is an architectural wonder incorporating a variety of styles; it has Roman arches, Gothic spires and a myriad of balconies, turrets, battlements and courtyards.

Also of interest are Kingstown's 20-acre (8-hectare) Botanical Gardens. Founded in 1765, they are the oldest in the Western Hemisphere. The gardens are home to Captain Bligh's breadfruit tree, grown from the original plant, and other unusual trees, including the Cannon Ball and the Sealing Wax Palm. Also at the gardens is an archeology museum.

THINGS TO KNOW

AREA: 133 square miles (344 sq km).

POPULATION: 106,500.

LANGUAGE: English.

CAPITAL: Kingstown.

GOVERNMENT: Independent. Member of the British Commonwealth of Nations.

TIME ZONE: Atlantic.

UNIT OF CURRENCY: Eastern Caribbean dollar. $1 U.S.=2.37 Eastern Caribbean dollars.

ELECTRICITY: 220 volts, 50 cycles AC.

MINIMUM AGE FOR GAMBLING: 18.

CARS: Local temporary license or international driver's license required; drive on left.

IMMIGRATION REQUIREMENTS: Proof of U.S. citizenship (birth certificate, driver's license, naturalization papers or passport), a photo ID and return or through ticket are required. Departure tax about $8 US.

FOR FURTHER INFORMATION:
St. Vincent and The Grenadines
801 Second Ave., 21st Floor
New York, NY 10017
(212) 687-4490 or (800) 729-1726
St. Vincent and The Grenadines
Government Administrative Building
Bay Street
P.O. Box 834
Kingstown, St. Vincent, W.I.
(784) 457-1502

HOLIDAYS: Jan. 1; St. Vincent and the Grenadines Day, Jan. 22; Good Friday; Easter Monday; Labour Day, May (1st Mon.); Whit Monday, May (8th Monday after Easter); Caricom Day, July (2nd Mon.); Carnival, July (2nd Tues.); August Monday, Aug. (1st Mon.); Independence Day, Oct. 27 (or Mon., Oct. 28, if holiday falls on a Sun.); Dec. 25; Boxing Day, Dec. 26.

Nearby Fort Charlotte, built in 1806, has dungeons and mounted guns. Paintings that trace the island's history are in the old officers' quarters. Perched 600 feet (183 m) above the city, it affords a magnificent view of the harbor and of the Grenadines. The dockside market comes alive on Saturday mornings when vendors and fishermen gather to sell their goods; the weekly loading of the banana boats enhances this vibrant scene. The St. Vincent Craftsmen Government Handicraft Centre on the airport road has projects all around the island, developing the skills of St. Vincent's native artists.

TRANSPORTATION

Air connections are via Antigua, Barbados, Grenada, Martinique, St. Lucia, San Juan, Puerto Rico, and Trinidad. Public buses operate in Kingstown and throughout St. Vincent; rental cars are available with or without driver. Of the 600 miles (960 km) of roads on the island, about 400 miles (640 km) are paved. The many small islands that constitute the Grenadines are accessible via small boats or planes. A large ferry, the MV *Baracuda* makes three-weekly runs, and the MV *Admiral* makes daily trips between St. Vincent and Bequia.

These islands possess a natural, unspolled beauty that is fading from some of the more commercially developed Caribbean islands. A few of the Grenadines are owned exclusively by one resort or hotel; reservations for these secluded accommodations are often required a year in advance.

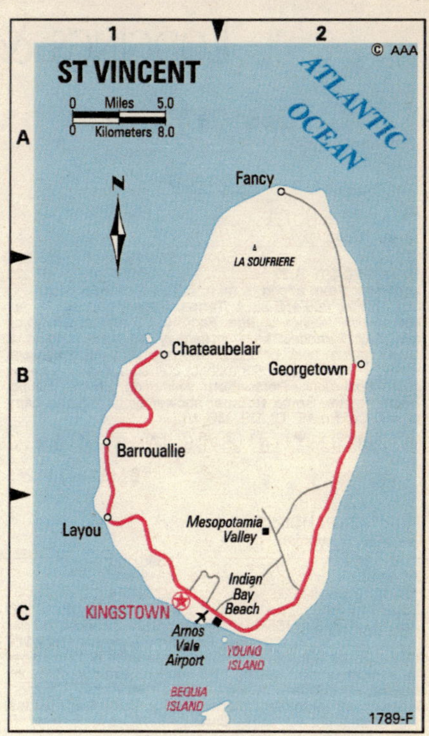

LODGINGS & RESTAURANTS

BEQUIA ISLAND

LODGINGS

FRANGIPANI HOTEL
◆◆   *Complex*

12/15-4/14	$55-150	XP $25
12/1-12/14 & 4/15-11/30	$40-120	XP $25

Location: From airport, 4 mi n; 0.3 mi s of town dock. (PO Box 1). Fax: 809/458-3824. **Terms:** Reserv deposit, 21 day notice; 10% service charge. **Facility:** 15 rooms. On Admiralty Bay. 7 modest units in century old main building. 8 newer garden units behind on sloping hill. Limited services 9/1-9/30. 2 stories; interior/exterior corridors; beach; 1 tennis court; boat dock. **Recreation:** swimming, charter fishing. Rental: boats. **Some Rooms:** shower baths, shared bathrooms. **Cards:** AE, DI, DS, MC, VI.

((809)458-3255

PLANTATION HOUSE
◆◆◆   *Complex*

12/20-1/6	$396-448
1/7-4/14	$353-400
12/1-12/19 & 4/15-11/30	$226-283

Location: From airport, 4 mi n; 1.5 mi s of town dock. (PO Box 16). Fax: 809/458-3612. **Terms:** Reserv deposit, 30 day notice; 10% service charge. **Facility:** 27 rooms. On Admiralty Bay. 10 tastefully decorated lodge units & 17 cottages in tropical garden setting. 1-2 stories; exterior corridors; beach; 1 lighted tennis court. **Services:** giftshop. **Recreation:** swimming, charter fishing, snorkeling; bicycles. **All Rooms:** shower baths. **Cards:** AE, MC, VI.

((809)458-3425

KINGSTOWN

LODGINGS

GRAND VIEW BEACH HOTEL
◆◆   *Motor Inn*

12/15-4/14	$210-270	XP $60
12/1-12/14 & 4/15-11/30	$130-190	XP $45

Location: From airport 1 mi s, 0.3 mi on side road via sign. (PO Box 173, VILLA POINT). Fax: 809/457-4174. **Terms:** D12; Reserv deposit, 21 day notice; 10% service charge. **Facility:** 19 rooms. A restored plantation house overlooking the ocean. 1-2 stories; interior/exterior corridors; beach access; 1 lighted tennis court. **Services:** Fee: massage. **All Rooms:** combo or shower baths. **Cards:** AE, DI, MC, VI.

((809)458-4811

THE LAGOON MARINA & HOTEL
◆   *Motor Inn*

12/16-4/15	$95-100	XP $10
12/1-12/15 & 4/16-11/30	$75-90	XP $10

Location: 4.5 mi s; 2.5 mi s of airport. (Box 133, BLUE LAGOON). Fax: 809/458-4308. **Terms:** F10; Reserv deposit, 14 day notice; 10% service charge. **Facility:** 19 rooms. Overlooking yacht harbor. All rooms with balcony. 2 stories; exterior corridors; beach. Fee: marina. **Recreation:** swimming, charter fishing. **Some Rooms:** color TV. **Cards:** AE, MC, VI.

(809/458-4308

SUNSET SHORES BEACH HOTEL
◆◆   *Motor Inn*

12/16-4/15	$140	XP $25
12/1-12/15 & 4/16-11/30	$115	XP $25

Location: 4 mi s; 1.5 mi s of airport. (PO Box 849, VILLA). Fax: 809/457-4800. **Terms:** Reserv deposit, 14 day notice; 10% service charge. **Facility:** 32 rooms. Relaxed elegance by the beach. Tropical garden landscaping. Rooms with balcony or patio. 2 stories; exterior corridors; beach. **Recreation:** swimming, snorkeling & equipment, windsurfing. **Cards:** AE, DS, MC, VI.

(809/458-4411

VILLA LODGE HOTEL
◆◆   *Motor Inn*

12/15-4/14	$115-270	XP $10-15
12/1-12/14 & 4/15-11/30	$130-190	XP $10-15

Location: 3 mi s; from airport, 1 mi s off the Windward Hwy. (Box 1191, INDIAN BAY). Fax: 809/457-4468. **Terms:** F12; Reserv deposit, 14 day notice; 10% service charge. **Facility:** 10 rooms. Overlooking Indian Bay. All rooms with balcony. 2 stories; interior/exterior corridors. **All Rooms:** combo or shower baths. **Cards:** AE, DS, MC, VI.

(809/458-4641

RESTAURANTS

BASIL'S BAR & RESTAURANT
◆   *Caribbean*   L $10-$14 D $14-$21

Location: Downtown at Cobblestone Inn. Upper Bay St. **Hours:** 8 am-10 pm. Closed major holidays & Sun, except Carnival. **Reservations:** suggested. **Features:** casual dress; cocktails & lounge; minimum charge-$15; street parking; a la carte. Rustic decor. Regional dishes. **Cards:** AE, DS, MC, VI.

(809/457-2713

THE FRENCH RESTAURANT
◆◆ *French*   **L** $8-$10 **D** $18-$28
Location: 1.5 mi s of airport; at Young Island Ferry Landing. **Hours:** noon-2 & 7-9:30 pm. Closed: Sun, 9/1-10/15 & 12/24-12/25. **Reservations:** suggested; in season. **Features:** No A/C; casual dress; cocktails & lounge; a la carte. Open air dining with view of Young Island. Chef/owner. **Cards:** AE, DS, MC, VI.

(784/458-4972

LIME N PUB
◆◆ *Caribbean*   **L** $15-$20 **D** $20-$40
Location: 1.5 mi s of airport, adjacent to Young Island Ferry Landing. **Hours:** 10 am-midnight. Closed: 12/25. **Reservations:** suggested. **Features:** No A/C; casual dress; cocktails & lounge; a la carte. Dining on water's edge with view of Young Island. Continental & West Indian dishes. **Cards:** AE, MC, VI.

(809/458-4227

PALM ISLAND

LODGING

PALM ISLAND BEACH CLUB
◆◆◆ *Resort Cottage*

12/1-1/9 & 2/1-4/14	$415	XP $150
1/10-1/31	$350	XP $140
4/15-11/30	$325	XP $135

Location: 1 mi e of Union Island, accessed via private boat launch, Palm Island. Fax: 809/458-8804. **Terms:** D12; Reserv deposit, 30 day notice; handling fee imposed; 10% service charge. **Facility:** 24 rooms. A cabana-village resort on secluded tropical island with beautiful white sand beach. Cottages with private indoor/outdoor showers. For reservations: Carib Com, Inc 1-800-999-7256; 1 story; exterior corridors; oceanfront; no parking; beach; 1 tennis court; boat dock. **Services:** giftshop. **Recreation:** swimming, charter fishing, fishing, snorkeling & equipment, windsurfing; jogging. **All Rooms:** shower baths. **Cards:** AE, DS, MC, VI.

(809/458-8824

YOUNG ISLAND

LODGING

YOUNG ISLAND RESORT
◆◆◆ *Resort Cottage*

12/20-2/28	$450-675	XP $100
3/1-4/11	$370-620	XP $100
12/1-12/19 & 4/12-11/30	$325-530	XP $100

Location: On Young Island, just off the coast of St Vincent; 1.5 mi s of airport to ferry landing. (PO Box 211, KINGSTOWN). Fax: 784/457-4567. **Terms:** D12; Reserv deposit, 30 day notice, 14 day off season; 10% service charge. **Facility:** 30 rooms. A cabana-village resort on tropical island with lush foliage. Beach level to high hillside cottages with spectacular views. Cottages with private indoor/outdoor shower. 1 story; exterior corridors; beach; 1 lighted tennis court; boat dock. **Services:** giftshop; area transportation. **Recreation:** swimming, charter fishing, sailboating, snorkeling, windsurfing. Rental: scuba equipment. **All Rooms:** shower baths. **Cards:** AE, MC, VI.

((784)458-4826

RESTAURANT

YOUNG ISLAND RESORT RESTAURANT
◆◆◆ *Caribbean*   **D** $35-$40
Location: Just off the coast of St Vincent; 1.5 mi s of airport to ferry landing; in Young Island Resort. **Hours:** 7:30 pm-9:30 pm. **Reservations:** required; non-hotel guest. **Features:** No A/C; casual dress; cocktails & lounge; prix fixe. 2-minute ferry ride from Villa Beach. Beautiful setting; fine West Indian & Continental cuisine. Weekly barbecue. Menu changes daily. **Cards:** AE, MC, VI.

(784/458-4826

TRINIDAD AND TOBAGO

TRINIDAD IS THE southernmost island of the West Indies. It was once an extension of the northern coast of Venezuela, but the lowlands were washed away by the Orinoco River centuries ago; at the closest point only 7 miles (11 km) of sea separate Trinidad and Venezuela. Port of Spain, the capital, is one of the Caribbean's most cosmopolitan cities. People from China, Britain, India, France, Holland, Portugal, Spain and many other countries make their home here along with descendants of the Arawak and Carib Indians and African slaves. The architecture is as varied, with ornate mansions, Spanish patios and tiled roofs, French grillwork, cathedrals, mosques and temples.

Initially called Asunción, Tobago's present name is said to be derived from the Spanish word for tobacco. It is said that Tobago was the island on which both the Swiss Family Robinson and Daniel Defoe's Robinson Crusoe were shipwrecked. Today's visitors will find wide, white beaches and small contemporary hotels. Many Trinidadians leave the hustle and bustle of their island to vacation on subdued Tobago, some 20 miles (32 km) away.

HISTORY, GOVERNMENT AND ECONOMY

Trinidad was originally inhabited by several Amerindian tribes, including the Caribs, who called the island *Iere,* meaning "land of the hummingbird." However, Christopher Columbus' imagination was stirred by three mountain peaks when he sighted land in 1498, and he called the island La Trinidad for the Holy Trinity. He claimed it for Spain, but a permanent settlement, San José de Oruña, was not established until 1592.

The 1600s saw raids by the Dutch and French, but the Spanish retained control. Crop failures kept the island poor until 1783, when a Spanish proclamation offered land grants to immigrants willing to develop agriculture and commerce. In 1797, attracted by the resulting prosperity, the British sent an expedition that gained control of

THINGS TO KNOW

AREA: Trinidad: 1,864 square miles (4,828 sq km); Tobago: 116 square miles (300 sq km).

POPULATION: 1,300,000.

LANGUAGE: English.

CAPITAL: Port of Spain, Trinidad.

GOVERNMENT: Republic within the British Commonwealth.

TIME ZONE: Atlantic.

UNIT OF CURRENCY: Trinidad and Tobago dollar. $1 U.S.=approx. 6.22 Trinidad and Tobago dollars.

ELECTRICITY: 110-220 volts, 60 cycles AC; voltage varies with location.

CARS: U.S. license valid for 3 months; drive on left.

IMMIGRATION REQUIREMENTS: Return or through ticket and passport are required. Departure tax $13.50 US.

FOR FURTHER INFORMATION:
Sales, Marketing and Reservations Tourism Services (SMARTS)
7000 Blvd. East
Guttenberg, NJ 07093
(201) 662-3403
Tourism & Industrial Development Company of Trinidad and Tobago Ltd.
10-14 Phillips St. P.O. Box 222
Port of Spain, Trinidad, W.I.
(868) 623-1932 or (888) 595-4868
Tobago Division of Tourism
N.I.B. Mall
Scarborough, Tobago, W.I.
(868) 639-2125 or 639-4636

HOLIDAYS: Jan. 1; Spiritual Baptist Liberation Shouters Day, Mar. 30; Good Friday; Easter Monday; Eid-ul-Fitr (Moslem Holy Day), April or May; Indian Arrival Day, May 30; Labour Day, June 19; Whit Monday, May (8th Monday after Easter); Feast of Corpus Christi; Emancipation Day, Aug. 1; Independence Day, Aug. 31; Republic Day, Sept. 24; Divali (Hindu Festival of Lights), late Oct.; Dec. 25; Boxing Day, Dec. 26.

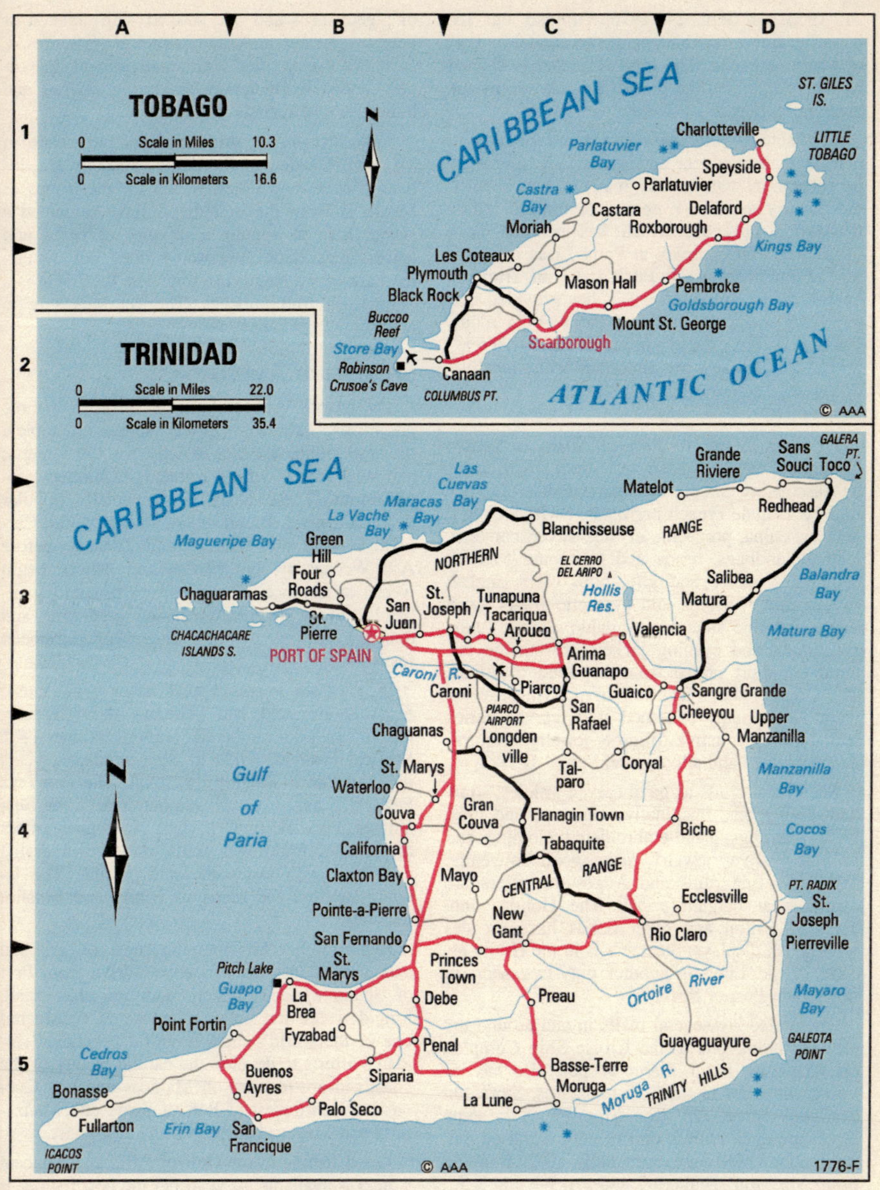

the island. Trinidad was formally ceded to Great Britain by the Treaty of Amiens in 1802.

Inhabited by Caribs when first sighted by Columbus, Tobago was subsequently coveted as a strategic position by every major power operating in the Caribbean. As a result the island changed hands more than any other in the West Indies; during the 17th and 18th centuries it was taken and retaken by France, Britain, Holland and Spain. In accordance with an agreement in 1749, Tobago was left unmolested for 13 years, but the struggle began anew when the reprieve ran out. The island finally came under the British Crown in 1814, becoming a crown colony in 1876.

In 1888 Trinidad and Tobago were united politically. The richest and second largest country of the British West Indies, the islands acquired independence within the commonwealth on Aug.

31, 1962. On Sept. 24, 1976, Trinidad and Tobago became a republic, with the capital at Port of Spain, Trinidad. The prime minister is elected by the people, and the president is chosen by the electoral college.

The islands' principal exports are petroleum, petroleum byproducts and sugar. The discovery of substantial natural gas reserves has enabled the country to embark upon a revitalized industrialization program, which has resulted in a large industrial complex at Point Lisas off Trinidad's southwest coast. Pitch Lake on Trinidad, an enormous asphalt reservoir, has provided material for surfacing many of the world's roads. Cocoa, coffee, citrus products and—increasingly—tourism also are important economically.

SHOPPING

Frederick Street in Port of Spain is known throughout the Caribbean and South America for its fascinating shops and merchandise. Luxury imports include French perfumes, Swiss watches, jewelry, china, porcelain, crystal, silver, cameras, leather handbags, beads and petitpoint. Modern department stores and gift shops offer English tweeds and worsteds and synthetic fibers. Irish linens and fine silks are available; dresses, suits and sports and evening jackets are custom tailored on short notice from imported materials. The Oriental shops feature ivory carvings, brassware, saris, richly patterned silks, carved curios and furniture, native filigree jewelry, embroidered slippers and silk apparel.

Such local crafts as hand-carved articles, straw and sisal goods, imaginative ceramics and tiles, vivid paintings, hand-embroidered clothing and gold and silver jewelry make good souvenirs. Trinidad's fine rums and Angostura bitters are available at bargain prices. The Holiday Inn, Trinidad Hilton and other hotels have arcades with lavish displays; Stecher's is in the Hilton arcade. Y. de Lima is another duty-free shop in downtown Port of Spain.

There also are several malls in and around the city, including one at the Cruise Ship Complex on Wrightson Road. Piarco Airport also has inviting shops for last-minute purchases. Stores on Frederick Street are open Mon.-Fri. 8-4; some stores are open until 5, on Fri. until 6 and on Sat. until noon. Malls are open daily 10-7. Banking hours are Mon.-Thurs. 9-2 and Fri. 9-1 and 3-5.

FOOD AND DRINK

The food on Trinidad is as cosmopolitan as the island; British, American, Continental, Creole, Chinese and Indian dishes are available. Popular dishes include *sancoche* and *callaloo,* excellent thick soups; stuffed cascadura, a freshwater fish; crabmeat served in the shell; the island's famous small oysters; and *roti,* an East Indian dish consisting of curried meat or vegetables stuffed into a rolled, soft, flour shell. *Pelau* is a combination of pigeon peas and rice cooked with chicken or beef in coconut milk and pumpkin. *Pastelles,* a cornmeal pastry filled with meats, raisins and capers, rolled in fig leaves or aluminium foil and boiled, is a Christmas speciality.

Angostura bitters originated and are made in Trinidad. Created in the early 1800s by Dr. Johann Siegert as a digestive aid for the troops of Simon Bolivar, the ingredients have remained a secret. Said to contain a mixture of herbs and spices, the recipe supposedly does not contain the bark of the Angostura tree. The local rum is a favorite in fruit punches. The water is safe to drink.

SPORTS AND AMUSEMENTS

The islands' African heritage surfaces in three art forms: calypso, satirical songs on topical themes; limbo, a dance strictly for the athletic; and steel bands, with instruments fashioned from oil drums. These bands are especially popular during Carnival. Based in Trinidad's capital, Carnival is held the Monday and Tuesday before Ash Wednesday, but parties and dances begin weeks in advance. Costumes, calypso and steelband contests and the crowning of a king and queen make this the best known of Caribbean festivals.

In alternate years, 3-week steel band music festivals are held late February through early March: In odd-numbered years it is the T&T Musical Festival, while in even-numbered years it is the Pan is Beautiful Festival. The Pan Jazz Festival is held every November. Yearly, the Best Village Folk Festival in late November offers displays of traditional skills, dance and drama combined with tastes of local cuisine. The islands also are the scene of Hindu and Muslim festivals.

Beautiful beaches line the coast of Trinidad and none is less than an hour's drive from Port of Spain. Maracas Beach, with its white sand, limpid water and coconut palms, is considered one of the world's most beautiful beaches. Trinidad's efforts to develop the natural beauty of the coastland are focused on Maracas and Las Cuevas bays northwest of Port of Spain and Manzanilla and Mayaro beaches on the east coast.

Good fishing in the Gulf of Paria and adjacent waters is available all year, but the best fishing is from June through September. Boats, guides and equipment are available for hire. Yachting is best from May through November; the Trinidad Yacht Club will arrange sailing parties.

Inland activities on Trinidad include golf, hunting and some lively spectator sports. Eighteen-hole golf is played at St. Andrew's (Moka) Golf Club and Pointe-a-Pierre Golf Course. Large hotels usually have facilities catering to tennis buffs. Hunting season in Trinidad runs October through February.

Horse racing takes place at two tracks: the Union Park in San Fernando in spring and fall and at Easter, and the Santa Rosa Racing Track in Arima during late May, July and August. For spectators and players alike Trinidad offers such popular sports as cricket, January through April; field hockey, January through June; and soccer, which generally runs July through December.

The calypso singers, steel bands and Port of Spain's long history as a sailor's town have earned the island a reputation for its own raucous, gaudy, exciting brand of nightlife. Clubs throughout town vibrate with the beat of Trinidadian dance and music, and stay open until the wee hours of the morning. Hotels also have entertainment, but it is geared toward those with more conservative tastes.

Recreation on Tobago centers on the sea. The island's many inlets, bays, shoals and reefs are excellent for fishing with line or spear; boats, guides and equipment are available for hire. Scuba diving and snorkeling are excellent at Buccoo Reef, and there is bathing at the Nylon Pool, 2 miles (3.2 km) out in the Caribbean. For landlubbers, Mount Irvine Golf Course has an 18-hole course.

EXCURSIONS AND SIGHTSEEING

Most sightseeing excursions can be arranged at hotels.

Lovely drives around Port of Spain enable visitors to relish the island's tropical beauty. Lady Chancellor Road affords a panorama of the city, the Gulf of Paria and San Fernando Hill. Lady Young Road also offers fine views of the city and the hills. Excellent views of the countryside, Venezuela and the sea are available from the Shrine of Our Lady of Fatima in Laventille and from Fort George, both a short distance from Port of Spain.

The North Coast Road to Las Cuevas Bay is spectacular; most of it is between 500 and 1,500 feet above sea level and overlooks La Vache and Balata bays. This 34-mile (54-km) round trip from Port of Spain is the most popular shore excursion with Caribbean cruise passengers, as it highlights Trinidad's great scenic variety. Also high in Trinidad's northern mountain range at 1,200 feet is the Asa Wright Nature Center. Tours can be arranged out of Port of Spain to the center, which has a former estate house and day- and week-long nature programs.

The northwest coast road to Carenage and Chaguaramas also is particularly scenic. This area includes the islands of Monos and Gaspar Grande (described by the locals as "down the islands"), the latter containing an interesting group of caves on its southern end. The Gasparee Caves are entered by a long winding staircase to the bottom, where stalactites and stalagmites can be seen. A nature trail on Gaspar Grande leads to mounted guns left from World War II and offers a panoramic view of the sea and surrounding islands.

The driving tour from Port of Spain to the Maraval Valley passes through the San Juan citrus orchards and the Santa Cruz Valley, where planters' houses of French and Spanish colonial days and the great samaan trees still stand. Maracas Bay and Maracas Beach climax the drive from Port of Spain along the Saddle Road.

On the southern end of the island is Pitch Lake, which has supplied asphalt to pave streets all over the world for decades. From Port of Spain the trip to Pitch Lake travels along the Uriah Butler Highway through Chaguanas, noted for its East Indian jewelry; Pointe-à-Pierre, the site of a large oil refinery and the Wildfowl Trust; and San Fernando. Circle tours of Trinidad, lasting 7 hours, travel past the Gulf of Paria, across the central plains, through Pointe-à-Pierre and San Fernando, continue past sugarcane and coconut plantations to Mayaro Beach and return via Manzanilla Beach. Lunch and swimming are included.

Trips by boat and automobile into the Caroni Bird Sanctuary, returning via an East Indian village, last about 4 hours. The sanctuary is the nest for thousands of scarlet ibises; visitors can witness their spectacular early evening flight from around 5 until sundown. A 5-hour cruise in Port of Spain Bay also is available.

An excursion on Tobago might include a tour of Old Fort King George, the Botanical Gardens and the shopping district in Scarborough, combined with a drive past coconut plantations and beaches to Store Bay and Plymouth. A cruise to the Coral Gardens and the Natural Aquarium at

Buccoo Reef provides an opportunity for snorkeling and swimming. Both of these excursions take about a half day.

A pleasant full-day drive on Tobago follows Windward Road along the Atlantic coast from Scarborough to Charlotteville. Visitors can take a pleasant detour off Windward Road, traveling northwest from Roxborough to Parlatuvier. The well-maintained, two-lane Roxborough-Parlatuvier Road climbs across the spine of the island, passing through forest and cultivated land. As the road descends to Parlatuvier, it provides a fine view of the Caribbean side of the island.

Boats depart from Speyside to Little Tobago, where guides conduct walks through a 450-acre (182-hectare) bird sanctuary. This is the only place in the world other than New Guinea where the gold-plumed greater birds of paradise exist in a natural habitat.

Transportation

Daily direct flights to Trinidad leave New York and Miami; other flights from New York and Miami stop at San Juan, Barbados and other intermediate islands. There is regular and frequent air service between Trinidad and the other Caribbean islands and nearby Venezuela. Trinidad also is a port of call for some cruise lines. Cars can be rented by the day or week; driving is on the left. Trinidad's 4,600 miles (7,360 km) of asphalted highways are among the best in the Caribbean. City and island sightseeing tours with a driver-guide are available in Port of Spain. Taxis are abundant.

Twenty-minute flights between Trinidad and Tobago are available several times a day. The MV *Panorama* and the MV *Tobago,* automobile passenger ferries with dining rooms and bars, make the 5.5-hour trip between the two islands; phone (868) 625-4906. Cars can be rented on Tobago, which has about 220 miles (352 km) of good roads. Public buses traverse the island several times daily and charge very reasonable rates.

Attraction Admissions

Attraction admissions for this island are quoted in U.S. dollars.

Points of Interest

See map page 249.

Tobago

Scarborough (C-2) pop. 17,000

Scarborough, the main city and administrative center of Tobago, is on Rockley Bay on the island's southern shore. Its native market is most active on Wednesday and Saturday. The Coral Gardens on Buccoo Reef is a popular spot for both snorkelers and divers.

The ruins of Old Fort King George overlook the city at its highest point. Built 1784-87, the fort originally was named Fort Castries by the French. When the British took over, they renamed the fort after their king. Within the fort is The Tobago Museum where exhibits include prehistoric Amerindian artifacts, historical maps and documents and local history displays. The Rockery Vale sugar estate, parcelled out in the late 1800s, now is home to the 17-acre Botanic Gardens and the Welbeck House.

Crusoe's Cave, 10 miles (16 km) west of Scarborough is named for Daniel Defoe's fictional Robinson Crusoe and is a subterranean cave that traverses Crown Point and Store Bay. The ruins of Fort James are nearby at Plymouth; a powder magazine on the grounds has been restored.

Trinidad

Port of Spain (B-3) pop. 57,400

Busy markets, exotic houses of worship and modern buildings give Port of Spain a cosmopolitan atmosphere. The city has been the capital of Trinidad since 1757 and the capital of both Trinidad and Tobago since they were united in 1889. From the hills north of the city, the coast of Venezuela can be seen across the Gulf of Paria.

BLACK VIRGIN, 30 mi. (48 km) s., is an impressive statue in the church of Notre Dame de Montserrat at Tortuga. Open daily 6-6. Donations. Phone (868) 636-0769.

CARONI SWAMP BIRD SANCTUARY, 7 mi. (11 km) s. on the Uriah Butler Hwy., is a large refuge. The brilliant scarlet ibis and several other species can be viewed in late afternoon; binoculars are helpful. Tour operators offer afternoon 2.5-hour round trips; inquire at your hotel desk. Extended trips and morning trips are available by request. Departures daily at 4; closed Dec. 25. Fare $10; children $5; under 7 free. Reservations are recommended. Phone (868) 645-1305.

THE CATHEDRAL OF THE HOLY TRINITY(Anglican), facing Woodford Sq. and entered from

Queen St., was built 1816-18. The altar and choir stalls are particularly noteworthy. Open daily 6 a.m.-6 p.m. Free. Phone (868) 623-7271.

CATHOLIC CATHEDRAL at Independence Sq., was begun in 1816 and consecrated in 1851. Daily 5:30-noon and 3:30-6:30. Free. Phone (868) 623-5232.

NATIONAL MUSEUM AND ART GALLERY, s.w. corner of Queen's Park Savannah at 117 Frederick St., is guarded by Spanish cannons that date from 1797 and an anchor that Columbus lost in Trinidad. The museum has displays about natural history, industry, geology and archeology. Of special note are elaborate costumes worn during Carnival Week celebrations as well as a display of folk art and crafts, paintings and sculpture. Allow 1 hour minimum. Tues.-Sat. 10-6. Free. Phone (868) 623-5941.

QUEEN'S PARK SAVANNAH, in the center of the fashionable residential district, covers nearly 200 grassland acres (81 hectares). The Stollmeyer House in the eastern section was built in 1904 as a copy of Balmoral Castle in Scotland; other excellent examples of Grand Colonial Architecture surround the park. Cricket, football and rugby events are held here. The Emperor Valley Zoo and the Botanic Gardens, laid out in 1820, face the northern side of the park; Memorial Square and the National Museum are on the park's east side. Daily 24 hours. Free.

RED HOUSE, on Woodford Sq., is a handsome building containing the House of Representatives and other governmental offices. Visitors are free to enter and walk around. Daily 8-4. Free. Phone (868) 623-2450.

ROYAL BOTANIC GARDENS, adjoining the president's house, contain about 70 acres (28 hectares) of tropical plants and trees, including lotus lilies, monkey pods and puzzles and Ceylon willows. Evening band concerts occasionally take place. Guided tours are available. Open daily 7-6. Free.

San Fernando (B-4)   pop. 30,100

San Fernando, Trinidad's second largest city, is built on a hill on the Gulf of Paria. Sugar estates and factories are nearby; oilfields lie to the southeast.

PITCH LAKE, s.w. at La Brea, covers 100 barren acres (40 hectares). The hard surface will bear traffic. About 165,000 tons of asphalt are excavated yearly. Local legend attributes the origin of this lake to the Great Spirit, anguished by the Chayma Indians' sacrifice of the sacred hummingbird. In retribution, the Great Spirit caused the earth to swallow up the guilty, leaving the lake as a reminder.

Lodgings & Restaurants

Tobago

Scarborough

Lodgings

BLUE HORIZON RESORT (SCARBOROUGH)
◆◆ *Motel*

12/16-4/15	$75-90	XP $12-25
12/1-12/15 & 4/16-11/30	$50-60	XP $12

Location: 6 mi nw of town; jct Shirvan & Buccoo rds, 0.5 mi on Jacamar Dr, follow sign. Jacamar Dr (MT Irvin Station). Fax: 868/639-0433. **Terms:** F12; Reserv deposit, 10 day notice; 10% service charge. **Facility:** 14 rooms. Set on a hill overlooking Mt. Irvine Golf Course & bay. 4 two-bedroom units. 1 story; exterior corridors. **Services:** area transportation. **All Rooms:** efficiencies, combo or shower baths. **Cards:** AE, MC, VI.

(868/639-0432

KARIWAK VILLAGE
◆◆ *Motor Inn*

12/15-4/14	$120
12/1-12/14 & 4/15-11/30	$75

Location: On Crown Point, just outside airport. Crown Point (PO Box 27). Fax: 868/639-8441. **Terms:** Reserv deposit, 7 day notice; 10% service charge. **Facility:** 24 rooms. Secluded setting; attractive lodging & facilities; very well maintained. 1 story; exterior corridors. **Services:** area transportation. **All Rooms:** shower baths. **Cards:** AE, DI, MC, VI.

(868/639-8442

LE GRAND COURLAN RESORT & SPA
◆◆◆ *Resort Hotel*

12/21-4/15	$250-295	XP $50
12/1-12/20 & 4/16-11/30	$200-225	XP $50

Location: 9 mi sw of town, 8 mi ne of airport; on w coast. Black Rock (PO Box 25). Fax: 868/639-9292. **Terms:** D12; Reserv deposit, 14 day notice, 7 day off season; 10% service charge. **Facility:** 78 rooms. Coastal hillside setting overlooking the sea. Spacious & attractively decorated guest rooms. Extensive spa facilities in relaxing atmosphere. Meets AAA guest room security requirements. 18 whirlpool suites $425-$475; $375 off season; 3 stories; exterior corridors; beach; 2 lighted tennis courts. **Services:** giftshop. Fee: massage. **Recreation:** swimming, boating, sailboating, scuba diving, snorkeling equipment, windsurfing. Fee: snorkeling, scuba equipment; bicycles. **Cards:** AE, DI, MC, VI.

(868/639-9667

MOUNT IRVINE BAY HOTEL & GOLF CLUB
◆◆◆ *Resort Hotel*

12/17-4/15	$235-390	XP $25
12/1-12/16 & 4/16-11/30	$165-320	XP $25

Location: 7 mi sw of town, 7 mi ne of airport, on w coast in Mt Irvine Area. (PO Box 222). Fax: 868/639-8800. **Terms:** D12; Reserv deposit, 7 day notice; 10% service charge. **Facility:** 105 rooms. Overlooking beach & Mt. Irvine Bay. Some duplex cottages; all units with balcony or patio. For reservations: Utell International; 119 W 57th St, New York, NY 10019; 2 stories; exterior corridors; oceanview; beach access. Fee: 18 holes golf; 2 lighted tennis courts. **Services:** giftshop. Fee: massage. **Recreation:** swimming, scuba diving, snorkeling. Fee: fishing. Rental: sailboats, scuba & snorkeling equipment. **Cards:** DI, MC, VI.

(868/639-8871

PALM TREE VILLAGE
◆◆ *Motor Inn*

12/15-4/14	$120-240	XP $33-60
12/1-12/14 & 4/15-11/30	$75-175	XP $33-60

Location: 5 mi n of Crown Point Airport on Milford Rd; from Scarborough, 3 mi s on Rockley Bay off Milford Rd. (PO Box 327). Fax: 868/639-4180. **Terms:** F12; Reserv deposit, 14 day notice; 5% service charge. **Facility:** 38 rooms. Motel rooms & duplex villas on beach. Attractive facilities. 18 two-bedroom units. Rates for up to 4 persons in villas; 1 story; exterior corridors; oceanview; beach; 1 tennis court. **Services:** area transportation. **Recreation:** swimming, scuba diving, snorkeling. Fee: windsurfing; horseback riding. Rental: scuba & snorkeling equipment. **All Rooms:** shower baths. **Some Rooms:** 18 kitchens. **Cards:** AE, MC, VI.

(868/639-4347

RESTAURANTS

DILLON'S SEAFOOD RESTAURANT
◆ *Seafood*   D $12-$27

Location: 0.3 mi e of Crown Point Airport. Milford Rd. **Hours:** 6 pm-midnight; 10% service charge. Closed: 12/25, 6/1-6/30 & Mon. **Reservations:** suggested. **Features:** casual dress; cocktails & lounge; entertainment. Plain exterior, attractive dining room. Excellent selection of fresh seafood. Attentive service. **Cards:** MC, VI.

(868/639-8765

KARIWAK VILLAGE RESTAURANT
◆◆ *English*   L $10-$15 D $18-$20

Location: On Crown Point, just outside airport; in Kariwak Village Hotel. **Hours:** 7:30 am-9:30 pm; 10% service charge, also 15% VAT. **Reservations:** suggested. **Features:** No A/C; casual dress; children's menu; cocktails & lounge. Very well prepared & presented West Indian cuisine. Attractive island decor. Accent on fresh herbs, grown on premises. **Cards:** AE, DI, MC, VI.

(868/639-8442

ROUSELLE'S RESTAURANT
◆◆ *Continental*   D $20-$30

Location: 0.3 mi e on Old Windward Rd. Old Windward Rd Bacolet. **Hours:** 6:30 pm-11 pm. Closed: Sun. **Reservations:** suggested. **Features:** No A/C; casual dress; cocktails & lounge; street parking. Small attractive seaside restaurant. Very well prepared island & Continental cuisines. **Cards:** MC, VI.

(868/639-4738

TRINIDAD

PORT OF SPAIN—57,400

LODGINGS

ALICIA'S HOUSE
◆ *Bed & Breakfast*

All Year	$50-58

Location: Off Lady Young & Cirrcular Rd to Coblentz Gardens. (7 Coblentz Gardens). Fax: 868/623-8560. **Terms:** Reserv deposit; 10% service charge. **Facility:** 17 rooms. Very nice hillside location, in quaint guest house setting. 3 stories; interior/exterior corridors; street parking only. **All Rooms:** combo or shower baths. **Cards:** AE, MC, VI.

(868/623-2802

KAPOK HOTEL
◆◆ *Hotel*

All Year	$89-143	XP $13

Location: Just n of jct Circular & Maraval rds; n end of Queen's Park Savannah. 16-18 Cotton Hill St Clair. Fax: 868/622-9677. **Terms:** F12; Reserv deposit, 3 day notice. **Facility:** 71 rooms. Pleasant location convenient to all downtown activities. Simple well-maintained decor. 15 efficiencies, $130-$143 for up to 2 persons; 8 stories; interior corridors. **Services:** giftshop. **All Rooms:** combo or shower baths. **Some Rooms:** 15 efficiencies. **Cards:** AE, DI, MC, VI.

(868/622-6441

TRINIDAD HILTON & CONFERENCE CENTER
◆◆◆ *Hotel*

12/1-2/7 & 2/13-11/30	$180-225	XP $50
2/8-2/12	$215-285	XP $50

Location: On Belmont Hill off Lady Young & Circular Rd overlooking Queen's Park Savannah. (PO Box 442). Fax: 868/624-4485. **Terms:** F; Reserv deposit; 10% service charge. **Facility:** 394 rooms. Superior hillside location, all rooms with private balcony. $1.95 energy surcharge; 6-12 stories; interior corridors; 2 lighted tennis courts. **Services:** giftshop. Fee: massage. **Some Rooms:** 9 efficiencies. **Cards:** AE, DI, MC, VI.

(868/624-3211

TURKS AND CAICOS ISLANDS

THE TINY ISLANDS of Turks and Caicos (KAY-kos) lie southeast of the Bahamas and north of the Dominican Republic and Haiti. The Turks and Caicos are comprised of eight major islands and some 40 smaller cays, most of which remain uninhabited. Grand Turk and Salt Cay are in the Turks, and North, Middle (also known as Grand), South, East and West Caicos and Providenciales (also known as Provo) are in the Caicos. The two groups are separated by the Turks Island Passage. Of the Atlantic group, these beautiful islands resemble those found farther south, with dazzling white or gold sand and sparkling waters. Most of the resorts are on Provo and Grand Turk; more intimate accommodations are available on the other islands. The islands' business, banking and government center is Cockburn Town on Grand Turk.

HISTORY, GOVERNMENT AND ECONOMY

The Turks and Caicos might have been among the islands mentioned in Christopher Columbus' 1492 diary, but there is no official record of discovery until Juan Ponce de León arrived in 1512. The native inhabitants were the Arawak Indians, whose population was almost destroyed by the French and Spanish. The British finally took control of the islands under the Treaty of Madrid, and during the American Revolution they were the territory of Loyalists and pirates. At the end of the war the Loyalists and settlers from Bermuda began producing salt and set up cotton and sisal plantations, ventures that eventually supported the islands for many years. Tourism is now the mainstay of the economy. The Turks are named for the Turk's Head Cactus, while Caicos is a derivation of *cayos*, the Spanish word for "small island."

SHOPPING, FOOD AND DRINK

Compared with some other islands, shopping and dining opportunities are limited. Shoppers commonly purchase stamps and coins and souvenirs crafted from straw or seashells. Liquor and tobacco are available at duty-free prices. Local restaurants serve such seafood delicacies as conch stew, spiny lobster, grouper, turtle and wahoo. Other restaurants serve French, Italian, Chinese, German and Mexican dishes. Some of the islands' fruit and rum libations are popular aperitifs.

SPORTS AND AMUSEMENTS

The focal point for recreation in the Turks and Caicos is the nearly 230 miles (368 km) of beaches. North Caicos and Provo each claim a 12-mile (19-km) stretch of sand; North Caicos also boasts a 5-mile (6.4-km) strand at Sandy Point. Swimming, snorkeling and scuba diving

---

THINGS TO KNOW

AREA: 193 square miles (500 sq km).

POPULATION: 14,000.

LANGUAGE: English.

CAPITAL: Grand Turk.

GOVERNMENT: British Crown Colony.

TIME ZONE: Eastern. DST.

UNIT OF CURRENCY: U.S. dollar.

ELECTRICITY: 110 volts, 60 cycles AC.

MINIMUM AGE FOR GAMBLING: 18.

CARS: U.S. license valid; drive on left.

IMMIGRATION REQUIREMENTS: Proof of citizenship (birth certificate, naturalization papers or passport) and a photo ID are required. A return or through ticket also is required. Departure tax $15.

FOR FURTHER INFORMATION:
Turks and Caicos Tourist Board
Pond Street P.O. Box 128
Grand Turk, Turks and Caicos Islands
(649) 946-2321
(800) 241-0824

HOLIDAYS: Jan. 1; Commonwealth Day, Mar. 9; Good Friday; Easter Monday; Queen's Birthday, June (2nd weekend); Emancipation Day, Aug. 1; Columbus Day, Oct. 13; International Human Rights Day, Oct. 26; Dec. 25; Boxing Day, Dec. 26.

are understandably popular activities at most resorts. The scuba diving is said to be among the best in the world, especially off Provo and Grand Turk. Of particular interest is The Wall off Provo. Dive operators based at resorts on Grand Turk, North and South Caicos, Provo and Salt Cay provide rentals for scuba diving as well as the services of a divemaster.

The annual migration of the humpback whale takes place in the winter. These eastern Atlantic whales travel through the Turks Island passage to the Mouchoir and Silver banks to the south; they mate and give birth to their young in these waters. The whales can be observed from the shore south of Grand Turk and Salt Cay, and whale-watching charters also can be arranged.

Fishing is a favorite pastime throughout the islands; the Caicos are noted for bonefishing. Pine Cay has a freshwater lake, and South, Middle and North Caicos, Pine Cay and Provo offer guides who can predict where the best catch will be. Deep-sea fishing can be arranged at North Caicos, Provo, Grand Turk and South Caicos. Boat rentals for sailing are available at Provo, Pine Cay, South Caicos and at most hotels.

Tennis courts are available to guests of hotels on North Caicos, Pine Cay and Provo. The Provo Golf Club offers an 18-hole championship course. Hotels offer information about sightseeing. Some interesting sites include old churches, the 19th-century Bermudian Great White House (open by appointment) on Salt Cay, caves on Middle Caicos, the herd of wild horses roaming outside an 1820 house called Highlands on South Caicos, and ruins of the salt industry. Hotels also offer some nightlife in the way of after-dinner dancing and pubs. The Turquoise Reef Resort on Providenciales has a casino.

Boats from many towns participate in the annual regatta at South Caicos in May. Carnival is celebrated in September with the coronation of the queen and the parade in which each island is represented.

TRANSPORTATION

Provo can be reached regularly by air from Miami. Grand Turk can be reached via Provo, while South Caicos can be reached from Nassau weekly. Island-hopping flights stop at Grand Turk, South Caicos, North Caicos, Salt Cay and Provo. Arrangements also can be made for flights to the Bahamas and the Dominican Republic. Bicycles, mopeds and cars can be rented on Grand Turk and Provo. Chartering a boat is an excellent way to see a wide variety of islands while you enjoy the sun and sea.

POINTS OF INTEREST

See map on pages 10 and 11.

GRAND TURK

TURKS & CAICOS NATIONAL MUSEUM is in Guinep Lodge in the center of Cockburn Town. The building, a Bermudian style mid-1800s house constructed of native stone, houses artifacts from the Molasses Reef shipwreck, said to be the oldest European wreck discovered in the Western Hemisphere. Several exhibits portray the culture and natural history of the islands. A 5-minute film is presented.

Artifacts from what is said to be the oldest Lucayan Indian site in the Bahamian archipelago, dating to 750 A.D., also are displayed. Guided tours are available. Allow 1 hour minimum. Mon.-Fri. 9-4 (also Wed. 4-6), Sat. 9-1; closed major holidays. Admission $5; students 50c. Phone (649) 946-2160.

PROVIDENCIALES

Larger in size than Bermuda, Provo has become the islands' tourism center. Not a single wheeled vehicle was in use on the island until 1965; it now has miles of good roads and a variety of fine accommodations and restaurants.

CAICOS CONCH FARM, n.e. tip of the island at Leeward Going Through, is a 5-acre (2-hectare) working conch farm. The facilities include a hatchery, greenhouse and nursery housed under a geodesic dome. Audiovisual presentations, slide shows and lectures educate visitors about the farm's operation, the islands' marine environment and dolphin behavior. Allow 30 minutes minimum. Mon.-Sat. 9-5. Admission $6. Phone (649) 946-5849.

LODGINGS & RESTAURANTS

GRAND TURK

LODGINGS

SALT RAKER INN
◆◆ *Country Inn*

All Year	$85-150	XP $20

Location: W side of Island in Cockburn Town; 2 mi from airport. Duke St (PO Box 1). Fax: 649/946-2817. **Terms:** F12; Reserv deposit, 28 day notice. **Facility:** 13 rooms. Well-maintained property across from ocean & a small beach. Pleasant setting. Varied room size & decor. Dec-Mar 10% service charge; 2 stories; exterior corridors; oceanview; beach. **Recreation:** swimming, charter fishing, snorkeling. Fee: scuba diving, snorkeling equipment; bicycles. **All Rooms:** shower baths. **Cards:** AE, DS, MC, VI.

(649/946-2260

TURKS HEAD INN
◆◆ *Historic Country Inn*

All Year	$90-110	XP $20

Location: W side of island, in Cockburn Town; 2 mi from airport. (PO Box 58). Fax: 649/946-1716. **Terms:** Reserv deposit, 7 day notice. **Facility:** 7 rooms. Pretty Caribbean house circa 1840, walled garden & beach across the lane. Former home of American Consul. 2 stories; interior/exterior corridors; oceanview; beach. **Recreation:** swimming. **All Rooms:** shower baths. **Cards:** AE, MC, VI.

(649/946-2466

RESTAURANTS

JAN & DAVE'S CONCH CAFE AT WATERS EDGE
◆ *Seafood*

	L $5-$10	D $12-$19

Location: W side of island in Cockburn Town; 3 mi from airport. Duke St. **Hours:** noon-10 pm. Closed: 9/1-9/30. **Reservations:** accepted. **Features:** No A/C; casual dress; cocktails & lounge; street parking; a la carte. Very good local cuisine. Casual dining on the beach; great spot for sunset. **Cards:** AE, MC, VI.

(649/946-1680

SECRET GARDEN RESTAURANT
◆◆ *Seafood*

	L $6-$10	D $13-$24

Location: W side of Island in Cockburn Town; 2 mi from airport; in Salt Raker Inn. Duke St. **Hours:** 7 am-9 pm. **Reservations:** required. **Features:** No A/C; casual dress; cocktails & lounge; a la carte. Casual decor, friendly service. Very well prepared local & Continental cuisine. 8% meal tax. **Cards:** AE, DS, MC, VI.

(649/946-2260

NORTH CAICOS

LODGING

OCEAN BEACH HOTEL CONDOMINIUMS
◆◆ *Apartment Motor Inn*

All Year	$110-195	XP $40

Location: N coast of island; 6 mi from airport. Whitby (B.W.I). Fax: 649/946-7386. **Terms:** F12; Reserv deposit, 30 day notice. **Facility:** 8 rooms. Secluded location with fine beachs. Modern apartment style units. Transportation arranged when making reservations. By reservation only 6/1-11/1. 2 two-bedroom units. For US & Canada reservations: (905) 336-2876; Fax (905) 336-9851, RR 3 Campbellville, Ontario Canada L0P 1B0; 2 stories; exterior corridors; oceanfront; beach. **Recreation:** swimming, charter fishing, scuba equipment. Fee: snorkeling; bicycles. **All Rooms:** combo or shower baths. **Some Rooms:** 6 kitchens. **Cards:** AE, MC, VI.

(649/946-7113

PROVIDENCIALES

LODGINGS

BEACHES TURKS & CAICOS RESORT & SPA
◆◆◆ *Resort Hotel*

12/21-1/5	$235-295	XP $50-100
1/6-4/7	$210-270	XP $50-100
12/1-12/20 & 4/8-11/30	$140-180	XP $50-100

Location: From airport; 7 mi e on n coast. Lower Bight Rd (PO Box 186). Fax: 649/946-8001. **Terms:** Age restrictions may apply; reserv deposit; 10% service charge; 3 night min stay. **Facility:** 224 rooms. Extensive facilities. Elegantly equipped rooms & villa suites in lushly tropical gardens. Meets AAA guest room security requirements. 12 two-bedroom units. Rates are based on double occupancy; all inclusive of meals, beverage & activities. Honor bar & 25 whirlpool rms, extra charge; 3 stories; interior/exterior corridors; oceanfront; beach; 2 lighted tennis courts; playground. Fee: 18 holes golf. **Services:** giftshop. Fee: massage. **Recreation:** swimming, boating, charter fishing, paddleboats, scuba diving/snorkeling & equipment, windsurfing; bicycles. **Some Rooms:** 13 kitchens. **Cards:** AE, MC, VI.

(649/946-8000

AAA **SAVE** **COMFORT SUITES-PORTS OF CALL**
FYI *Motel*

12/20-4/19	$165-185	XP $20
12/1-12/19 & 4/20-11/30	$135-145	XP $20

Too new to rate. **Location:** On n coast at Grace Bay, 8 mi from airport. Grace Bay Rd. Fax: 649/946-5444. **Terms:** F17; Reserv deposit, 14 day notice; 10% service charge; package plans. **Facility:** 98 rooms. 3 stories; interior/exterior corridors. **Dining:** Restaurant nearby. **Cards:** AE, DS, MC, VI. *(See color ad inside front cover)*

((649)946-8888

LE DECK HOTEL & BEACH CLUB
◆◆   *Motor Inn*

12/21-1/5	$160-185	XP $25
1/6-4/20	$145-170	XP $25
12/1-12/20 & 4/21-11/30	$110-135	XP $25

Location: N coast at Grace Bay; 7.5 mi e of airport. (Box 144 Grace Bay). Fax: 649/946-5770. **Terms:** F12; Reserv deposit, 14 day notice; 10% service charge; 7 night min stay, 12/21-1/5. **Facility:** 25 rooms. Pleasant guest rooms & most facing landscaped courtyard. Fine beachfront location. 2 two-bedroom units. 2 junior suites avail for up to 4 persons; 1-bedroom unit with full kitchen & living room; 2 stories; exterior corridors; beach. **Recreation:** swimming, charter fishing. **All Rooms:** shower baths. **Some Rooms:** kitchen. **Cards:** AE, MC, VI.

(649/946-5547

OCEAN CLUB
◆◆◆   *Resort Complex*

12/20-4/30	$215-865	XP $55
5/1-6/30	$185-599	XP $55
12/1-12/19 & 11/1-11/30	$175-575	XP $55
7/1-10/31	$165-525	XP $55

Location: N coast at Grace Bay 9.5 mi e of airport. (PO Box 240, BWI). Fax: 649/946-5845. **Terms:** Reserv deposit, 21 day notice; $10 service charge; package plans; 7 night min stay, in season. **Facility:** 96 rooms. Variety of modern studio, 1 & 2 bedroom condominium sytle units. 16 two-bedroom units. 3 stories, no elevator; exterior corridors; beach; 1 lighted tennis court. Fee: adjacent golf course. **Dining:** Restaurant; poolside dining 6:30 am-5 pm; dining room 5 pm-9:30 pm; $16-$32; cocktails. **Services:** giftshop. **Recreation:** swimming, charter fishing, fishing. Fee: sailboating, scuba diving/snorkeling & equipment, windsurfing; bicycles. Rental: paddleboats. **All Rooms:** efficiencies. **Cards:** AE, DS, MC, VI.

((649)946-5880

TURQUOISE REEF RESORT & CASINO
◆◆◆   *Hotel*

12/21-1/3	$220-295	XP $30
2/1-2/28	$195-265	XP $30
1/4-1/31 & 3/1-4/5	$190-260	XP $30
12/1-12/20 & 4/6-11/30	$125-180	XP $30

Location: N coast at Grace Bay; 8 mi e from airport. Leeward Hwy (Box 205, Grace Bay). Fax: 649/946-5522. **Terms:** Reserv deposit, 14 day notice, in season; 7 days in summer; 10% service charge; MAP avail; package plans. **Facility:** 228 rooms. Overlooking 12 miles of white sand beach. Island style rooms each with balcony or patio, in 10 interconnected buildings. 3 stories; exterior corridors; oceanfront; beach, whirlpool; 2 lighted tennis courts. Fee: 18 hole PGA golf course nearby. **Dining:** 2 restaurants; 7 am-10, noon-3 & 6-11 pm; $8-$15; cocktails; also, Portofino, see separate listing. **Services:** giftshop. **Recreation:** swimming. Fee: scuba diving/snorkeling & equipment, windsurfing; scooter rental. Rental: boats. **Cards:** AE, DS, MC, VI.

((649)946-5555

BELLA LUNA RISTORANTE
◆◆◆   *Italian*   D $14-$30

Location: On n coast at Grace Bay 8 mi e of airport. Grace Bay Rd. **Hours:** 6:30 pm-9:30 pm. Closed: Mon & 9/1-9/30. **Reservations:** suggested. **Features:** cocktails; a la carte. Open air terrace & indoor dining, featuring colorful wall & ceiling murals. Creative menu selection with extensive fresh pasta & seafood offerings. **Cards:** AE, MC, VI.

(649/946-5214

CAICOS CAFE
◆◆   *Seafood*   L $9-$24 D $15-$26

Location: N coast at Grace Bay area; 8 mi e of airport. Governor's Rd. **Hours:** noon-3, 6-10 pm. Closed: Sun lunch. **Reservations:** suggested. **Features:** No A/C; casual dress; cocktails; a la carte. Menu offers grilled fresh seafood & meat, Caribbean & French influences. Open air dining, island art work. **Cards:** AE, MC, VI.

(649/946-5278

COCO BISTRO
◆◆◆   *Ethnic*   D $15-$25

Location: N coast at Grace Bay; 8.5 mi e of airport. Grace Bay Rd. **Hours:** 6 pm-9:30 pm. Closed: 6/15-10/15. **Features:** casual dress; cocktails & lounge; a la carte. Excellent Mediterranean & Island cuisine. Seating in colorful dining room decorated with original local art or on romantic patio in the midst of the island's only palm grove. Friendly service. **Cards:** AE, MC, VI.

(649/946-5369

LE JARDIN
◆◆   *Continental*   L $6-$14 D $15-$26

Location: N coast at Grace Bay; 7.5 mi e of airport, in Le Deck Hotel. **Hours:** 7 am-3 & 6:30-10 pm. **Reservations:** accepted. **Features:** No A/C; casual dress; children's menu; cocktails & lounge; a la carte. Pleasant patio & dining overlooking beach & ocean. French & Caribbean cuisine. Specializing in fresh seafood. **Cards:** AE, MC, VI.

(649/946-5547

PORTOFINO
◆◆◆   *Italian*   D $15-$31

Location: N coast at Grace Bay; 8 mi e from airport, in Turquoise Reef Resort & Casino. **Hours:** 6:30 pm-10 pm. Closed: Mon & Tues. **Reservations:** suggested. **Features:** casual dress; cocktails & lounge; a la carte. Attractive dining room overlooking beach & ocean. Very well prepared regional & Italian cuisine, pleasant service. **Cards:** AE, DS, MC, VI.

(649/946-5555

Virgin Islands, British

I SLANDS TINGED with the warm colors of a Paul Gauguin painting and white sand beaches cooled by refreshing breezes characterize the Virgin Islands. About 60 miles (96 km) east of Puerto Rico, the archipelago lies directly in the path of the trade winds and enjoys a pleasant climate with moderate rainfall and maximum sunlight. The principal

British islands are Tortola, Virgin Gorda, Anegada and Jost Van Dyke; except for the flat coral island of Anegada, both the U.S. and British Virgins are volcanic in origin.

Though not as developed as their U.S. sisters, the British Virgin Islands have a distinctive appeal. Tortola has the capital, Road Town, with its serene harbor and rugged 1,780-foot (543-m) Mount Sage. Virgin Gorda has an untamed natural beauty, and uninhabited Norman Island is reputed to be the "Treasure Island" of Robert Louis Stevenson fame. Some of the smaller, secluded islands are privately owned and offer the ultimate in escapist vacations.

History, Government and Economy

The British Virgin Islands saw their first Europeans when Christopher Columbus arrived in 1493. Except for some copper on Virgin Gorda, the Spanish found little of interest on the islands and eventually lost them to the British in 1628. However, it was the Dutch who settled Tortola and initiated the lucrative sugar trade, which sparked the envy of other countries. Yet, despite battles between the French, Spanish, Dutch, Danes and various pirates, Britain regained the islands in 1666 and has held them ever since. Today the islands constitute a territory, administered by a queen-appointed governor and a locally elected government headed by a Chief Minister. While livestock raising is still important, offshore banking and tourism and its related industries dominate the islands' economy.

Shopping

Most of the retail shops in the islands are found along Main Street in Road Town or along the harbor in Virgin Gorda. Because there is no duty on British imports, bargains can be found on some English china, fabrics and foods. Among other bargains are rum, whiskey and gin as well as intricate straw goods, island crafts, jewelry and fabric designs. One popular shopping area in Road Town is Main Street, which has shops offering souvenirs, spices, jewelry and china. Such native spices as Tortola's rum pepper sauce or BVI Caribbean seasoning are found at the gourmet shop in the Tropic Isle Shopping Center at the Village Cay Marina and at the airport.

Local stamps are unique in that they are the only stamps in the British Commonwealth sold in a denomination of U.S. currency, official tender in the British Virgins. Stamps are available in Road Town or at the small post office at West End on Tortola. Credit cards and travelers cheques are accepted at most hotels and restaurants.

Food and Drink

Except for seafood, mutton, beef or home-grown vegetables and fruit, all food is imported. Tortola and Virgin Gorda have the largest selection of restaurants. On other inhabited islands a small hotel or inn is often the only establishment. Hotels usually serve three meals a day and have wine lists as well as a wide assortment of liquors and fruit drinks. Island cuisine is characterized by fish or seafood dishes, the most popular being fungi and fish. Fungi is made of corn meal and mixed with onions, sweet peppers and okras, then boiled into cakes and served with boiled fish and green vegetables.

Sports and Amusements

The islands' most popular activity and biggest drawing card is sailing. Their reputation as a mecca for yachting enthusiasts, though long known by advocates of the sport, has been discovered by amateur sailors and tourists. As a result hundreds of yachts are available for charter. The more than 40 islands and cays are ripe for exploring.

Many half- or full-day cruises include a picnic lunch or dinner, snorkeling, swimming or tours of such sites as Virgin Gorda's Baths—gigantic boulders forming a labyrinth of grottoes and beaches. The best equipped marinas are on Tortola, Virgin Gorda and Peter Island. You should make reservations for longer sailing excursions during the peak season, December through February *(see Planning Your Trip, Charter Tips).*

Deep-sea fishing is another popular activity in the British Virgin Islands, where record catches of blue marlin, tuna and wahoo have been made. Special competitions take place June through November.

The clarity of the waters off these islands creates superb scuba and snorkeling conditions. Especially notable is the wreck of the RMS *Rhone* located off Salt Island; this wreck is ranked as one of the top-rated sites by several diving publications. Expert guides are available, and arrangements can be made through any of the islands'

many dive shops or hotels. Caribbean Images and Rainbow Visions in Tortola rent cameras and offer courses on underwater photography.

The variety of birds, including pink flamingos, inhabiting the flat island of Anegada also make a visit worthwhile. Some 154 species of birds are found throughout the British Virgin Islands. Tennis courts can be found at hotels on Virgin Gorda, Tortola and Peter Island.

The appeal of the British Virgin Islands is tranquility, which means few dance clubs and no high-rises, jets or mammoth cruise ships. Evening diversions, therefore, are minimal. Moonlight cruises, listening to a steel band or dancing to after-dinner music at one of the hotels constitute most of the organized activities. Festival, held in Tortola the first week in August, in Virgin Gorda during Easter weekend, is popular with visitors and residents alike. It includes parades, dances, food fairs, beauty contests and band competitions.

The Welcome, the bimonthly tourist news magazine available free throughout the islands, provides up-to-date information. The British Virgin Islands Tourist Board maintains an office in Road Town and at the yacht harbor in Virgin Gorda.

Transportation

Tortola can be reached by plane from St. Thomas, St. Maarten, St. Croix, Antigua, St. Kitts or San Juan via Air Sunshine, American Eagle or LIAT. Virgin Gorda has frequent connections with St. Thomas and San Juan. Frequent

THINGS TO KNOW

AREA: 59 square miles (153 sq km).

POPULATION: 18,700.

LANGUAGE: English.

CAPITAL: Road Town, Tortola.

GOVERNMENT: Dependent Territory of the United Kingdom.

TIME ZONE: Atlantic.

UNIT OF CURRENCY: U.S. dollar.

ELECTRICITY: 110-120 volts, 60 cycles AC; voltage varies with location.

CARS: Local permit ($10) valid for 90 days; drive on left.

IMMIGRATION REQUIREMENTS: Proof of U.S. citizenship (passport or birth certificate) and a photo ID for stays under 6 months and return or through ticket are required. Departure tax $10 by air, $5 by sea.

FOR FURTHER INFORMATION:
British Virgin Islands Tourist Board

370 Lexington Ave., Suite 1605
New York, NY 10017
(212) 696-0400 or (800) 835-8530
British Virgin Islands Tourist Board
3390 Peachtree Rd., N.E.
Suite 1000, Lenox Towers
Atlanta, GA 30326
(404) 240-8018
British Virgin Islands Tourist Board
2nd Floor, AKARA Building
Wickham's Cay 1
Road Town, Tortola, British Virgin Islands
(284) 494-3134

HOLIDAYS: Jan. 1; Commonwealth Day, Mar. (2nd Mon.); Good Friday; Easter Monday; Whit Monday, May (8th Monday after Easter); Sovereign's Birthday, second Saturday in June; Territory Day, July 1; Festival Monday, Tuesday and Wednesday, Aug. (1st Mon., Tues. and Wed.); St. Ursula's Day, Oct. 21; Heir to the Throne's Birthday, Nov. 14; Dec. 25; Boxing Day, Dec. 26.

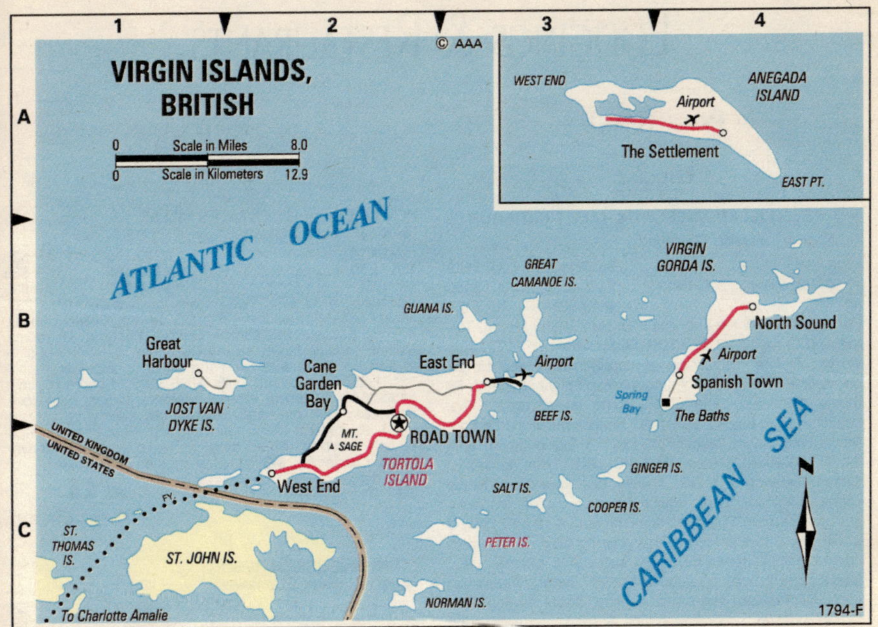

interisland flights link Tortola with Anegada. Charter flights are available through Fly BVI and Gorda Aero Services.

While inland transportation is fairly limited, taxis are available on Tortola and Virgin Gorda, and some offer tours of the island. Rental cars can be hired on Tortola, Virgin Gorda and Anegada, and with limited availability on Jost Van Dyke; a local driver's license good for 90 days is required and can be obtained at car rental agencies or the traffic licensing office.

A ferry service operates daily between Charlotte Amalie, St. Thomas in the U.S. Virgin Islands, and West End, Tortola, and takes approximately 45 minutes; a 90-minute ferry runs to Road Town, Tortola. Phone (284) 495-4617 for fares and schedules. Within the British Virgin Islands, ferry service operates daily from Road Town, Tortola, to Virgin Gorda, Jost Van Dyke and Peter Island. Phone Jost Van Dyke Ferry, (284) 494-2997; Peter Island Ferry, (284) 494-2561; Smith's Ferry, (284) 495-4495; or Speedy's Fantasy (284) 495-5240. North Sound Express operates a ferry between Beef Island and North Sound, Virgin Gorda; phone (284) 495-2271. Virgin Gorda Ferry Service runs from Beef Island to The Valley, Virgin Gorda; phone (284) 495-5240. Some of the more remote islands can only be reached by sailboat or motorboat out of Tortola and Virgin Gorda.

POINTS OF INTEREST

TORTOLA

Its name meaning "turtledove" in Spanish, 24-square-mile (62-sq-km) Tortola is the largest of the British Virgin Islands. It rests in the shadow of 1,780-foot Mount Sage, where traces of a primeval rain forest can still be found. Settled first by the Dutch and then the English in 1666, Tortola was granted its charter in 1773.

Road Town is the largest village and the seat of government. Fishing, scuba diving, snorkeling, sailing, swimming, windsurfing and burro or horseback riding are popular diversions.

VIRGIN GORDA

Expanses of unspoiled beaches characterize Virgin Gorda (The Fat Virgin). Ten miles (16 km) long and 2 miles (3.2 km) wide, the island is the third largest of the British group and commands the Anegada Passage. Settled by the English in the late 1600s, Virgin Gorda was developed into agricultural estates. With the abolition of slavery in 1834, the population—once more than 8,000—dwindled to about 3,000.

Excursions on Virgin Gorda include trips to serene Spring Bay, Valley Trunk Bay, North Sound, the boulder-strewn labyrinth of grottoes and beaches known as the Baths, and Coppermine Point, site of the Spanish mines.

LODGINGS & RESTAURANTS

PETER ISLAND

LODGING

PETER ISLAND RESORT & YACHT HARBOUR
◆◆◆◆ *Resort Complex*

12/19-4/11	$615-1125	XP $150
12/1-12/18, 4/12-4/30 & 11/16-11/30	$490-925	XP $150
5/1-11/15	$410-825	XP $150

Location: Taxi & ferry service from Beef Island Airport, Tortola. (PO Box 211, TORTOLA). Fax: 284/495-2500. **Terms:** F; Age restrictions may apply; reserv deposit, 30 day notice; 10% service charge; package plans. **Facility:** 58 rooms. Secluded 1800 acre, private island resort. Five beautiful palm-fringed beaches. Beachfront & harborfront rooms with private balcony or patio. 1 four-bedroom unit, $4200; $2020 off season. TV & VCR avail upon request; 2 stories; exterior corridors; beach, sea kayaks; 4 tennis courts (2 lighted), tennis equipment; marina. Fee: tennis instruction. **Dining:** Dining room, restaurant; 8-10 am, 12:30-3 & 7-9 pm; $25-$38; cocktails; public by reservation; dress code for dining room, Sat night buffet $50; afternoon tea. **Services:** giftshop; area transportation, Tortola. Fee: massage. **Recreation:** swimming, boating, charter fishing, fishing, sailboating, snorkeling, scuba & snorkeling equipment, windsurfing; bicycles, hiking trails, sports court, nightly movie, sightseeing & shopping excursions to neighboring islands. Fee: scuba diving, daysailing. **Some Rooms:** 3 kitchens, color TV. **Cards:** AE, MC, VI. A Preferred Hotel.

((284)495-2000

TORTOLA

LODGINGS

FORT RECOVERY ESTATES VILLAS
◆◆◆ *Suite Motel*

12/21-4/14	$210-240	XP $35
12/1-12/20, 4/15-5/31 & 11/1-11/30	$140-165	XP $35
6/1-10/31	$135-150	XP $35

Location: 8 mi w of Road Town, on s shore. (Box 239, ROAD TOWN). Fax: 284/495-4036. **Terms:** Reserv deposit, 90 day notice; 10% service charge. **Facility:** 17 rooms. Quaint, seaside facility on the Caribbean Sea. Variety of 1- to 4-bedroom villas. 2 two-bedroom units. 2-bedroom units $215-$350; 3-bedroom units $395-$585; 4-bedroom units $450-$640; 2 stories; exterior corridors; beach; boat dock. **Services:** Fee: massage. **Recreation:** swimming, snorkeling & equipment; hiking trails, jogging. Fee: boating, windsurfing; bicycles. **All Rooms:** kitchens, combo or shower baths. **Cards:** AE, MC, VI. *(See color ad below)*

(284/495-4354

LONG BAY BEACH RESORT
◆◆◆ *Resort Complex*

12/19-4/17	$190-290	XP $30
12/1-12/18, 4/18-5/31 & 11/1-11/30	$140-210	XP $30
6/1-10/31	$110-180	XP $30

Location: 11 mi nw of Road Town; on n coast. (PO Box 433). Fax: 284/495-4677. **Terms:** F12; Reserv deposit, 30 day notice; 10% service charge. **Facility:** 115 rooms. A mix of deluxe beachfront & hillside standard units. Secluded facility overlooking the Atlantic Ocean. For US reservations: (914) 833-3300; 2-3 stories; exterior corridors; beach; 3 tennis courts (2 lighted). **Services:** giftshop. **Recreation:** swimming, snorkeling. Fee: snorkeling equipment. **All Rooms:** combo or shower baths. **Some Rooms:** 37 kitchens. **Cards:** AE, DS, MC, VI.

(284/495-4252

SUGAR MILL HOTEL
◆◆◆   *Resort Complex*

12/21-4/14	$195-280	XP $15
12/1-12/20, 4/15-7/30 & 11/1-11/30	$165-215	XP $15
10/1-10/31	$155-195	XP $15

Location: 11 mi nw of Road Town; on n coast at Apple Bay. (PO Box 425, ROAD TOWN). Fax: 284/495-4696. **Terms:** F11; Open 12/1-7/30 & 10/1-11/30; age restrictions may apply; reserv deposit, 30 day notice; 10% service charge; 3 night min stay, in season. **Facility:** 21 rooms. Secluded hillside location overlooking the Atlantic Ocean. Rooms range in size from compact standard units with austere appointments to more spacious multi-room suites. 1 two-bedroom unit. Villa's, $150-$350; 2 stories; no elevator; exterior corridors; beach, small pool. **Recreation:** swimming, snorkeling. **All Rooms:** combo or shower baths. **Some Rooms:** 19 efficiencies, color TV. **Cards:** AE, MC, VI.

🏊 🍴 📺 ✕ VCR ▢ ▤ D   ((284)495-4355

🔺 AAA 🟦 SAVE TAMARIND CLUB HOTEL
◆◆   *Country Inn*

12/15-4/15	$150-185	XP $10
12/1-12/14 & 4/16-11/30	$90-110	XP $10

Location: 3 mi w of airport on N West in the East End section of the Island above Josiah's Bay. Josiah's Bay Rd (PO Box 509 East End). Fax: 284/495-2858. **Terms:** F18; Reserv deposit, 30 day notice; $10 service charge. **Facility:** 9 rooms. Secluded Spanish style inn with fine food, attractive rooms & hospitable staff. One mi from beach. 3 two-bedroom units. Exterior corridors. Restaurant, see separate listing. **All Rooms:** shower baths. **Cards:** MC, VI. **Special Amenities: Early check-in/late check-out and free room upgrade (subject to availability with advanced reservations).** *(See color ad below)*

📶 🏊 🍴 📺 🏋 PV 📠 ▤ D   ((284)495-2477

TREASURE ISLE HOTEL
◆◆   *Motor Inn*

12/20-4/14	$170-230	XP $15
4/15-6/30	$130-190	XP $15
12/1-12/19 & 7/1-11/30	$95-125	XP $15

Location: 0.5 mi e of Road Town. Pasea Estate (PO Box 68, ROAD TOWN). Fax: 284/494-2507. **Terms:** F11; Reserv deposit, 14 day notice; 10% service charge. **Facility:** 43 rooms. Across from marina on hillside. Mostly typical motel units with a Caribbean appeal. All rooms look over the harbor. Many with twin beds. 2 stories; exterior corridors; 1 tennis court. **Services:** area transportation. Fee: massage. **Recreation:** Fee: sailboating. **All Rooms:** shower baths. **Cards:** AE, DS, MC, VI.

🏊 🍴 📺 ✕ ▤ ▢ 📠 ▤   (284/494-2501

<u>RESTAURANTS</u>

CAPRICCIO DI MARE
◆   *Italian*   L $6-$13   D $6-$13

Location: In Road Town on Waterfront Dr, across from ferry docks. Abbot Bldg, Waterfront Dr. **Hours:** 8 am-9 pm. Closed: 12/25. **Features:** No A/C; casual dress; children's menu; carryout; cocktails; street parking; a la carte. Casual open-air setting offering gourmet pizza, pasta, large salad & panini sandwiches.

(284/494-5369

GARDEN RESTAURANT
◆◆◆   *Continental*   D $18-$22

Location: 11 mi nw of Road Town on n coast; in Long Bay Beach Resort. **Hours:** 6:30 pm-9:30 pm. **Reservations:** suggested. **Features:** No A/C; dressy casual; cocktails & lounge. Excellent seafood. West Indian cuisine specialties in terraced dining room. **Cards:** AE, DS, MC, VI.

(284/495-4252

THE JOLLY ROGER INN
◆◆   *American*   L $6-$21   D $6-$21

Location: In West End; just n of Public Ferry Dock. **Hours:** 8 am-10 pm; in season to 11 pm. **Features:** No A/C; casual dress; Sunday brunch; carryout; cocktails; entertainment; a la carte. Casual daily menu offers seafood, signature pizza, & burgers. Nightly creative Caribbean Fusion specials. Barbecue Fri & Sat. Waterfront deck. **Cards:** AE, MC, VI.

(204/495-4559

SUGAR MILL RESTAURANT
◆◆◆   *Continental*   D $18-$26

Location: 11 mi nw of Road Town on n coast at Apple Bay; in Sugar Mill Hotel. **Hours:** Open 12/1-7/31 & 10/1-11/30; seatings 7 pm-8:30 pm. **Reservations:** suggested. **Features:** No A/C; cocktails & lounge; prix fixe. Intimate dining in rustic setting. 4-course dinner reflects local & international influences. Although the service has a formal edge the atmosphere remains casual. 10% service charge. **Cards:** AE, MC, VI.

(284/495-4355

TAMARIND CLUB RESTAURANT
◆◆◆   *Continental*   L $6-$12   D $14-$21

Location: 3 mi w of airport on N West in the East End section of the Island above Josiah's Bay. Josiah's Bay Rd. **Hours:** 7:30 am-9:30, noon-3 & 7-9:30 pm. **Reservations:** accepted. **Features:** No A/C; casual dress; Sunday brunch; cocktails & lounge; a la carte. Outstanding European/Caribbean cuisine. Very pleasant setting & friendly service. 15% service charge. Fri & Sat additional Indian dishes. **Cards:** MC, VI.

(284/495-2477

VIRGIN ISLANDS, U.S.

TAKEN TOGETHER, all three U.S. Virgin Islands—St. Thomas, St. Croix and St. John—create the ideal West Indies vacation package. Charlotte Amalie (a-MAL-ya), capital of the islands, typifies the Caribbean town with its delightful shops and patios, winding streets and Old World, Continental flavor. Its picturesque harbor is among the busiest cruise ports in the Caribbean. Varied nightlife and a resort atmosphere make St. Thomas the liveliest of the U.S. Virgins. The largest of the islands, St. Croix is dotted with the ruins of plantation greathouses and secluded beaches. St. Croix also offers shopping and amusement opportunities, but at a slower, less hectic pace. For those seeking peace, quiet and natural beauty, St. John is the archetype of the remote and undeveloped Caribbean isle. The beautiful Virgin Islands National Park covers about two-thirds of the island.

HISTORY, GOVERNMENT AND ECONOMY

Christopher Columbus discovered the Virgin Islands during his second voyage in 1493. His fleet of 17 ships first anchored off the north coast of Santa Cruz, or St. Croix as the French would later call it, then sailed off to the chain of smaller islands on their northern horizon. Columbus named the chain in honor of the 11,000 virgins who in legend were martyred with St. Ursula in a battle with a pagan ruler in the third century.

The English and French attempted to colonize St. Croix as early as 1625; the Dutch and Spanish made later appearances. After changing hands several times, St. Croix was ceded to the Knights of Malta in 1653, then sold to the French. The Danish West India & Guinea Co., permanently chartered in 1671, established Denmark's first settlement in the West Indies on St. Thomas under Gov. Georg Jorgen Iversen. St. John was acquired in 1684, St. Croix in 1733.

Denmark ruled these islands for nearly 250 years, with the exception of two brief periods of British administration in the early 19th century. The Danish West Indies became the U.S. Virgin Islands in 1917, when Denmark sold them to the United States. The American government, which desired a naval base in the Caribbean and proximity to the Panama Canal, purchased the islands

for $25 million. Many of Charlotte Amalie's thoroughfares still bear Danish names.

Today the U.S. Virgin Islands are an unincorporated territory of the United States, and its people are American citizens. The islands were administered by a governor appointed by the president until 1970, when the first gubernatorial election was held.

Tourism to the U.S. Virgin Islands began to boom in the 1960s partly because of the closing of Cuba to tourists from the United States. The number of visitors quickly escalated from about 100,000 per year to more than a million. At the same time tourism was rising, the islands' population tripled. Other islanders were attracted by the relative economic security.

Hurricanes Marilyn and Luis left their calling cards as they passed through the U.S. Virgin Islands in September 1995, with St. Thomas receiving the most damage from the storms. The islands quickly recovered, and all hotels, shops and attractions on St. Croix and St. John are once again open.

SHOPPING

Among the bargains in the U.S. Virgin Islands are imported liqueurs and local rums. In some instances, considerable savings are possible on Royal Copenhagen, Limoges, Wedgwood, Bing and Grondahl china; Baccarat, Waterford, Lalique, Daum and Val St. Lambert crystal; Swiss watches; island wearing apparel; jewelry and precious gems; English doeskin products; cashmere sweaters from Scotland; and designer fashions from Europe. Silver bracelets, earrings, cuff links, table settings, fine perfumes and Danish silver also can be found. Handicrafts include basketry, hats, handbags, dolls and embroideries.

Hundreds of tiny shops crowd the narrow streets of Charlotte Amalie; at its center is Royal Dane Mall. Havensight Mall, at the cruise ship dock, has about 60 shops and restaurants. Atop St. Peter Mountain in the center of St. Thomas, Mountain Top offers a spectacular view of the north coast in addition to shopping opportunities. Also in St. Thomas, Tillett Gardens was once a Dutch farm and now is a marketplace for local arts and crafts. In St. Croix, King Street in Christiansted is lined with shops and arcades, as is Frederiksted's waterfront; King's Alley Walk offers 17 stores, three restaurants and hotel suites. Shopping on St. John centers around Mongoose Junction and Wharfside Village in Cruz Bay, which feature specialty shops, restaurants and water sports outlets.

Shopping hours are Mon.-Sat. 9-5; Havensight Mall is open daily 8-6. Banking hours are Mon.-Thurs. 9-2:30 and Fri. 9-2 and 3:30-5.

FOOD AND DRINK

Restaurants serve native Creole and Danish dishes as well as French, Mexican, Polynesian, Oriental and Middle Eastern cuisine, but the specialties are usually American, with steaks and seafood popular. Many hotels have individual specialties.

The Virgin Islands' tropical climate produces an abundance of exotic culinary favorites, including papayas, mangoes, avocados, sapodillas and a particularly sweet pineapple. Leaves of wild herbs and plants, combined with meat, fish, okra and other native ingredients, make the most truly native of all dishes, a thick island soup called *kallaloo*. Cornmeal and okra are combined to make *fungi* (FOON-gee), a common side dish.

Ripe soursop is used as a fruit and in ice cream; it also is made into a refreshing non-alcoholic drink, as is tamarind. Desserts include tarts made with pineapple, coconut, guava and guavaberry. Drinking water, obtained by the desalinization of seawater or from rainwater cisterns, is safe in hotels and restaurants. Tipping customs are the same as in the United States.

SPORTS AND AMUSEMENTS

All of the Virgin Islands are havens of lovely beaches and pools, providing excellent scuba diving and snorkeling. Buck Island Reef, 6 miles (10 km) northeast of Christiansted, St. Croix, is a national monument and the only underwater U.S. national park. Underwater signs and arrows guide snorkelers through the coral reefs and identify the multitude of colorful fish and plant life that inhabit the area. There also is an underwater trail off the north shore of St. John at Trunk Bay. Though St. Thomas does not offer underwater parks or trails, Coki Point Beach and various shipwrecks are excellent spots for snorkeling.

Beginning divers enjoy investigating the more than 300 reefs around the islands; the experienced usually head for spots in the Windward Passage northwest of St. John. In a protected

THINGS TO KNOW

AREA: 133 square miles (344 sq km).

POPULATION: 101,800.

LANGUAGE: English.

CAPITAL: Charlotte Amalie, St. Thomas.

GOVERNMENT: U.S. territory.

TIME ZONE: Atlantic.

UNIT OF CURRENCY: U.S. dollar.

ELECTRICITY: 110-120 volts, 60 cycles AC.

CARS: U.S. license valid; drive on left.

IMMIGRATION REQUIREMENTS: Proof of U.S. citizenship (birth certificate, naturalization papers or passport) is required to enter the Virgin Islands and to return to the United States.

FOR FURTHER INFORMATION:

U.S. Virgin Islands Department of Tourism
1270 Avenue of the Americas
New York, NY 10020
(212) 332-2222 or (800) 372-8784
U.S. Virgin Islands Department of Tourism
1 Tolbod Gade
Charlotte Amalie, St. Thomas
(340) 774-8784 or (800) 372-8784
U.S. Virgin Islands Department of Tourism
41 AB Queen Cross St.
Christiansted, St. Croix
(340) 773-0495

HOLIDAYS: In addition to U.S. holidays: Three Kings Day, Jan. 6; Transfer Day, Mar. 31; Holy Thursday; Good Friday; Easter Monday; Carnival, late Apr.; Organic Act Day, June (3rd Mon.); Danish West Indies Emancipation Day, July 3; Supplication Day, July (4th Mon.); Columbus/Puerto Rico Friendship Day, Oct. (2nd Mon.); Local Thanksgiving, Oct. (3rd Mon.); Liberty Day, Nov. 1; Dec. 26.

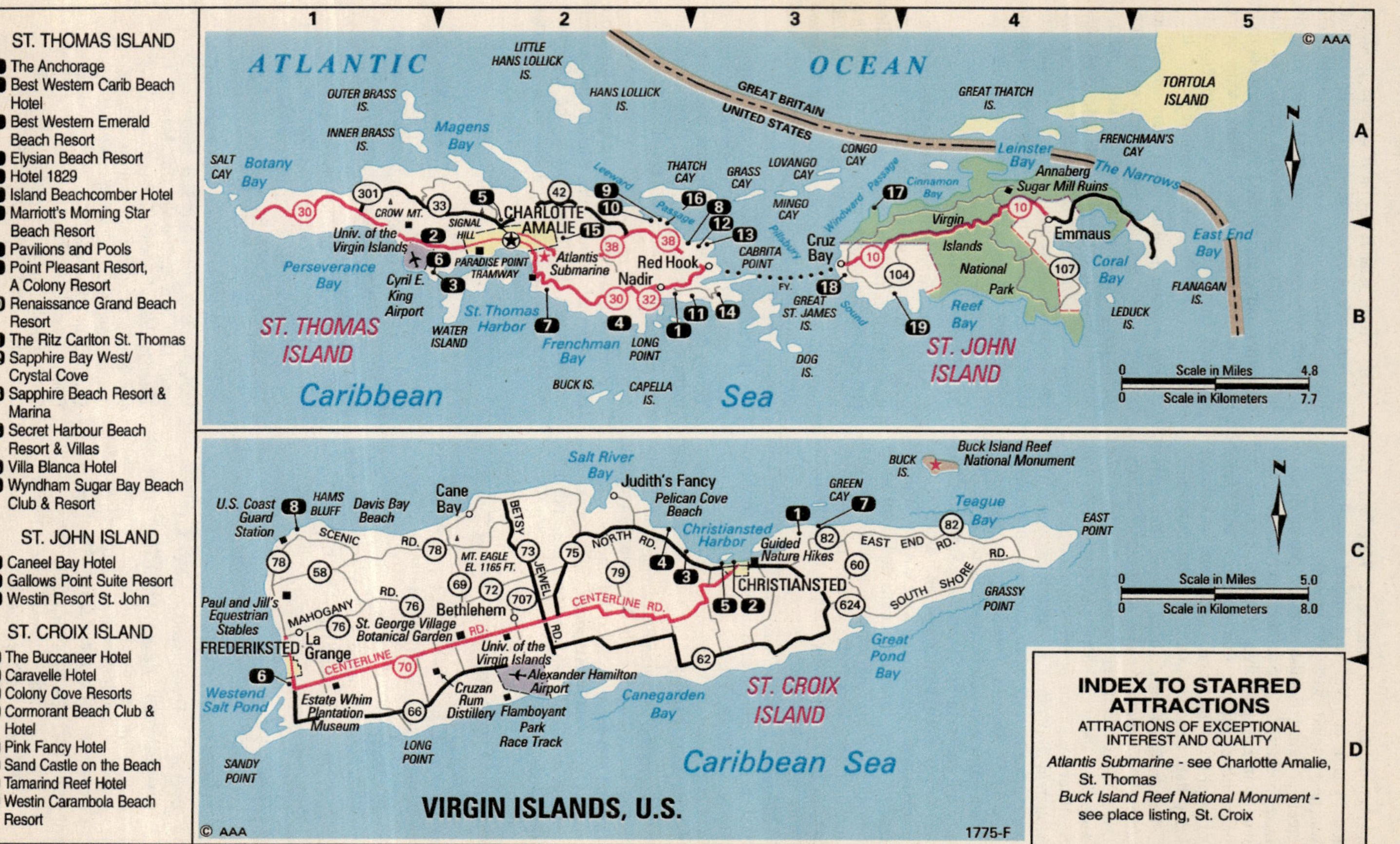

VIRGIN ISLANDS, U.S.
ST. THOMAS ISLAND
ST. JOHN ISLAND
ST. CROIX ISLAND
ATLANTIC OCEAN
Caribbean Sea
TORTOLA ISLAND
GREAT BRITAIN
UNITED STATES
East End Bay
FRENCHMAN'S CAY
GREAT THATCH IS.
The Narrows
Leinster Bay
Annaberg Sugar Mill Ruins
Emmaus
Coral Bay
LEDUCK IS.
FLANAGAN IS.
Virgin Islands National Park
Reef Bay
Cinnamon Bay
CONGO CAY
LOVANGO CAY
MINGO CAY
GRASS CAY
CABRITA POINT
Windward Passage
Pillsbury Sound
Cruz Bay
GREAT ST. JAMES IS.
DOG IS.
THATCH CAY
HANS LOLLICK IS.
LITTLE HANS LOLLICK IS.
OUTER BRASS IS.
INNER BRASS IS.
SALT CAY
Botany Bay
Magens Bay
Perseverance Bay
CROW MT.
SIGNAL HILL
CHARLOTTE AMALIE
PARADISE POINT TRAMWAY
Cyril E. King Airport
Univ. of the Virgin Islands
WATER ISLAND
St. Thomas Harbor
Red Hook
Nadir
Atlantis Submarine
Frenchman Bay
LONG POINT
BUCK IS.
CAPELLA IS.
Leeward Passage
Caribbean Sea
Scale in Miles 4.8
Scale in Kilometers 7.7
Scale in Miles 5.0
Scale in Kilometers 8.0
EAST POINT
Teague Bay
GRASSY POINT
SOUTH SHORE RD.
Great Pond Bay
GREEN CAY
BUCK IS.
Buck Island Reef National Monument
EAST END
CHRISTIANSTED
Christiansted Harbor
Guided Nature Hikes
Pelican Cove Beach
Judith's Fancy
Salt River Bay
Canegarden Bay
Alexander Hamilton Airport
Cruzan Rum Distillery
Flamboyant Park
Race Track
ST. CROIX ISLAND
NORTH SHORE RD.
CENTERLINE RD.
Cane Bay
Davis Bay Beach
HAMS BLUFF
SCENIC RD.
MAHOGANY RD.
La Grange
St. George Village Botanical Garden
Bethlehem
Univ. of the Virgin Islands
MT. EAGLE EL. 1165 FT.
JEWEL
BETSY
Estate Whim Plantation Museum
FREDERIKSTED
Westend Salt Pond
SANDY POINT
LONG POINT
U.S. Coast Guard Station
Paul and Jill's Equestrian Stables
CENTERLINE RD.
© AAA
1775-F

INDEX TO STARRED ATTRACTIONS
ATTRACTIONS OF EXCEPTIONAL INTEREST AND QUALITY
Atlantis Submarine - see Charlotte Amalie, St. Thomas
Buck Island Reef National Monument - see place listing, St. Croix

ST. THOMAS ISLAND
1 The Anchorage
2 Best Western Carib Beach Hotel
3 Best Western Emerald Beach Resort
4 Elysian Beach Resort
5 Hotel 1829
6 Island Beachcomber Hotel
7 Marriott's Morning Star Beach Resort
8 Pavilions and Pools
9 Point Pleasant Resort, A Colony Resort
10 Renaissance Grand Beach Resort
11 The Ritz Carlton St. Thomas
12 Sapphire Bay West/ Crystal Cove
13 Sapphire Beach Resort & Marina
14 Secret Harbour Beach Resort & Villas
15 Villa Blanca Hotel
16 Wyndham Sugar Bay Beach Club & Resort

ST. JOHN ISLAND
17 Caneel Bay Hotel
18 Gallows Point Suite Resort
19 Westin Resort St. John

ST. CROIX ISLAND
1 The Buccaneer Hotel
2 Caravelle Hotel
3 Colony Cove Resorts
4 Cormorant Beach Club & Hotel
5 Pink Fancy Hotel
6 Sand Castle on the Beach
7 Tamarind Reef Hotel
8 Westin Carambola Beach Resort

cove near Buck Island off the south shore of St. Thomas is the 190-foot World War I cargo vessel *Cartenser Sr.* On St. Thomas, dive shops operating through major hotels offer equipment rental, diving excursions and lessons; there are independent shops as well. The National Park Service offers identical services at Cinnamon Bay in St. John. Dive shops in St. Croix are located near dive sites in Cane Bay, Christiansted, Frederiksted and Salt River.

For swimming and sunbathing, Magens Bay on the north coast of St. Thomas is considered one of the top 10 beaches in the world, as is Trunk Bay on St. John. On St. Croix, some of the out-of-the-way inns and hotels have superb beaches and plenty of privacy. For sailors, and landlubbers with binoculars, there is the Rolex Regatta on Easter weekend.

Deep-sea fishing is popular. The most important gamefish are blue marlin, sailfish, dolphin, kingfish, tuna and wahoo. The Atlantic Blue Marlin Tournament is held in mid-August. Fishing boats are available for charter on all three islands. Sailboats and yachts also can be chartered on all three islands; private cruises are available around the Virgin Islands to Puerto Rico.

For those who prefer land-based pastimes, St. Croix has an 18-hole championship golf course at the Westin Carambola Beach Resort, an 18-hole course at The Buccaneer and a 9-hole course at the Reef Hotel. St. Thomas also sports an 18-hole championship course at the Mahogany Run Golf Course. You can play tennis at hotels and on public courts. St. Croix has many magnificent trails for horseback riding. Horse races are held on holidays at Clinton Phipps Race Track on St. Thomas and Flamboyant Park on St. Croix. Softball and baseball are played during the season on both St. Thomas and St. Croix, and some locals gather for cricket matches on Sunday.

Though sea, sun and sand are the islands' main attractions, there are enough evening pastimes to keep the spirit alive well after sunset. Dinner dancing, jazz, calypso music, limbo dancing and native acts are featured in many hotels and nightclubs. There are dance clubs on all three islands and movie theaters on St. Croix and St. Thomas.

Island Center, a cultural complex on Peppertree Hill on St. Croix, presents plays, musicals and other performances by well-known artists from the United States and neighboring islands. Similar fare is offered at the Reichhold Center for the Arts, an amphitheater on St. Thomas. In keeping with its more sedate climate, St. John offers a fish fry at Cruz Bay every Friday from 6 p.m. to midnight. Check with *St. Thomas This Week* and *St. Croix This Week* magazines to find out what's happening and where.

EXCURSIONS AND SIGHTSEEING

Island tours are most easily arranged through your hotel activities desk. A 2-hour tour of St. Thomas stops at Drake's Seat and Mountain Top. Trips to the island's eastern end visit beach clubs and fishing centers. Sunset and harbor cruises are available from Charlotte Amalie.

A scenic trip to Magens Bay for swimming also departs from Charlotte Amalie; sailboats and beach equipment can be rented. A 2-hour tour to the island's western end passes a World War II submarine base, the University of the Virgin Islands and Brewer's Bay on the way to Crown Mountain. The return trip includes a stop at the old sugar mill at Estate Contant; admission is included. Safari bus tours of the island are often less expensive than taxi tours.

Perhaps the best of the many excellent scenic vantage points in Charlotte Amalie is Paradise Point atop Flag Hill. Southeast of Havensight Mall via a steep roadway, the site is especially popular at sunset. Paradise Point Tramway *(see attraction listing p. 271)* transports visitors to the hilltop. West of the harbor along Crown Bay is the fishing village of Frenchtown, where the descendants of settlers from St. Barts continue to live off the sea.

Popular excursions on St. Croix include 3-hour glass-bottom boat or catamaran trips to Buck Island Reef National Monument *(see place listing p. 268)* for snorkeling; refreshments are included. Beach barbecues are available with some all-day sails. Arrangements can be made at local dive shops in Christiansted Harbor. Full- and half-day tours of local highlights are available, including the rain forest and Salt River, where Columbus landed. In February and March the St. Croix Landmarks Society conducts house tours that include restored sugar mills, greathouses and elegant mansions.

You can hire one of several safari guides for exploring St. John. A popular day excursion tours the Virgin Islands National Park *(see place listing p. 269)*, visits the Annaberg Sugar Mill ruins and includes lunch and swimming at Trunk Bay. For those more interested in aquatic sports, boat trips to St. John are available that include 2 hours in Francis Bay for swimming and snorkeling.

TRANSPORTATION

Direct jet service is available from the U.S. mainland via several airlines. Commuter airlines fly between Puerto Rico, St. Thomas and St. Croix. Many cruise ships call at Charlotte Amalie and Frederiksted.

The Vitran bus service on St. Croix, St. John and St. Thomas is mainly for local traffic. Taxi service on St. Thomas and on St. Croix is good, and you also can rent cars on both islands. Taxi rates are set in advance and apply per passenger. It is always wise to agree on the fare in advance. Parking is usually very scarce in Charlotte Amalie; a public lot east of Fort Christian costs 50c per hour. Taxi service is available on St. John as well, and jeeps can be rented by the day or week. A U.S. driver's license is valid.

Daily ferry service to Cruz Bay, St. John, is available from Red Hook, a 20-minute trip, and Charlotte Amalie, a 45-minute trip, on St. Thomas. Daily ferry service also links both Charlotte Amalie and St. John with the British Virgin Islands of Tortola and Virgin Gorda; proof of citizenship is required.

POINTS OF INTEREST

See map page 266.

ST. CROIX

Old Danish towns rising above the Caribbean characterize lovely St. Croix (pop. 60,000). Santa Cruz, as it was known by Christopher Columbus, rivaled Barbados as the leading sugar producer in the West Indies; great plantation houses recall these days of wealth on the 82-square-mile (212-sq-km) island. Modern St. Croix, the easternmost point in the United States, is the agricultural and industrial center of the U.S. Virgin Islands as well as a major tourist destination.

Self-guiding tours: The U.S. Virgin Islands Department of Tourism provides a walking tour brochure covering Christiansted and Frederiksted.

★ BUCK ISLAND REEF NATIONAL MONUMENT (C-4)

Two miles (3.2 km) off the northeast coast of St. Croix, Buck Island offers snorkeling, swimming, picnicking and exploring. The foremost attraction of the national monument, the only underwater park in the U.S. national park system, is the fine barrier reef offshore. Of the 880 acres (356 hectares) in the park, only 143 (58 hectares) are land. Underwater trails offer excellent opportunities for snorkeling; markers identify the reef's fauna and flora. Full- and half-day trips to Buck Island can be arranged through several companies on St. Croix; snorkeling equipment and instruction are available. Admission free. Full-day trip $55. Phone (340) 773-1460.

CHRISTIANSTED (C-3) pop. 2,600

Christiansted has preserved the 18th-century buildings of its Danish settlers. Solid stone buildings in pastel colors with bright red tile roofs line the cobblestone sidewalks, adding a touch of European charm. The town's symmetry, with streets running at right angles to the waterfront, makes it popular for walking tours. The shopping area centers on King and Company streets, next to Christiansted National Historic Site.

CHRISTIANSTED NATIONAL HISTORIC SITE covers three city blocks along the waterfront and town square. It includes such landmarks of the Danish colonial period as 1749 Fort Christiansvaern, the best preserved of the five remaining Danish forts in the Virgin Islands; the Old Scalehouse; the Old Danish Customs House; the Danish West India & Guinea Co. Warehouse; and the Government House, once capitol of the Danish West Indies.

The Steeple Building, St. Croix's first Lutheran church, houses a museum with Arawak and Carib Indian relics. A self-guiding tour starts at Fort Christiansvaern, where brochures can be obtained from the National Park Service headquarters. Be careful when walking on the area's uneven sidewalks and stairs. Mon.-Fri. 8-4:30, Sat.-Sun. 9-4. Admission $2. Phone (340) 773-1460.

GUIDED NATURE HIKES are offered by the St. Croix Environmental Association. Various hikes are offered; options include those that feature the rain forest, beaches, mangroves, and human as well as natural history. Most hikes are moderate in their level of difficulty. All hikes begin at the hike location; transportation to the site is not provided. For further information contact SEA, Suite 3, Arawak Building, Gallows Bay, Christiansted, VI 00820.

Allow 2 hours minimum. Hours vary; phone for schedule. Fee $20; under 10, $12. Reservations are recommended. Phone (340) 773-1989.

FREDERIKSTED (D-1) pop. 1,100

The emancipation of slaves was proclaimed on July 3, 1848, at Fort Frederik on the waterfront at the northern edge of Frederiksted. Destroyed by a fire in 1878, Frederiksted was restored during the Victorian era, as reflected in the town's architecture.

Modern Frederiksted operates at a slower pace than Christiansted, except when cruise ships dock in Frederiksted's deepwater port. Visitor information is available at the entry to the pier. Fort Frederik houses art and cultural exhibits, including a police museum which details the history of the town.

Of historical interest are the palatial ruins of Judith's Fancy, the former residence of the governor of the Knights of Malta. Set on an estate of several hundred acres, it has a view of the site where Christopher Columbus anchored at Salt River in 1493. Due to the greeting he received from the Carib Indians, Columbus named it the Cape of the Arrows.

CRUZAN RUM DISTILLERY, on West Airport Rd., offers tours and rum tastings at its Diamond Estate. Mon.-Fri. 9-4. Admission $3, children $1.

ESTATE WHIM PLANTATION MUSEUM, 1.5 mi. (2.4 km) e. on Centerline Rd., is a restored three-room plantation house furnished with antiques, china, paintings and silver. A museum in the cookhouse contains sugar- and rum-making equipment, household and military articles and reproductions of old engravings. A restored stone sugar mill with large grinding mechanisms typical of those used in the late 18th century also is on the grounds. Guided tours are available. Mon.-Sat. 10-3. Admission $5, children $1. Admission $5; under 13, $1. Phone (340) 772-0598.

PAUL AND JILL'S EQUESTRIAN STABLES, at Sprat Hall, 1.5 mi. (2.4 km) n. via rtes. 63 and 58, offers 2-hour guided horseback rides through a rain forest, to hidden Danish ruins and across seaside hilltops. Moonlight rides also are available. Riding lessons are provided. Allow 2 hours minimum. Rides Mon.-Sat. Nature tour fee $50. Reservations are required. Weight limit for men is 200 lbs., for women 180 lbs. Phone (340) 772-2880 or 772-2627.

ST. GEORGE VILLAGE BOTANICAL GARDEN is 4 mi. (6.2 km) e. on Centerline Rd. This 17-acre (7-hectare) tropical garden surrounds the ruins of a 19th-century workers' village. Tropical poinsettias are flamboyant in July, and hibiscus unfold all year. Daily 7-3. Admission $3; under 12, $1. Phone (340) 692-2874.

ST. JOHN

St. John (pop. 3,500) owes its reputation as a quiet, largely undeveloped haven to the generosity of Laurance Rockefeller. His love of the island's beauty moved Rockefeller in the 1950s to purchase as much of St. John as he could lay his money on, then to donate most of it to the United States for the creation of a national park, ensuring that "this thing of beauty will be a joy forever." Rockefeller saw his wish fulfilled in 1956 with the dedication of Virgin Islands National Park.

Smaller than Manhattan Island, 19-square-mile (49-sq-km) St. John is scalloped by lovely bays rimmed with white sand beaches of pristine beauty. The most famous is Trunk Bay, where the National Park Service maintains an underwater snorkel trail. Bordeaux Mountain, at 1,277 feet, dominates the island's rugged topography, and the lush forests conceal ruins of forts and plantation houses and traces of the Arawak and Carib Indians, the island's pre-Columbian inhabitants. Small museums at Cruz Bay exhibit relics of these peoples; their cryptic petroglyphs can be seen on rocks at Reef Bay, along Reef Bay Trail and other places.

The subdued atmosphere of Cruz Bay, the island's main town, conceals a history as a bustling center for the cotton, sugar and rum trade in the days when plantations thrived on St. John. A slave revolt occurred in 1733; the rebels held St. John for 6 months against the Danes and the British before the French finally overran them. Prosperous plantation farming continued through the mid-1830s and limited production continued until 1916, lasting through the emancipation of slaves in 1848.

Accommodations on St. John range from rustic to rich. Platform campsites front the beach at Cinnamon and Maho bays, while Caneel Bay, the world-renowned luxury resort developed by Laurance Rockefeller, occupies the site of an 18th-century sugar estate.

VIRGIN ISLANDS NATIONAL PARK

Virgin Islands National Park encompasses about one half of St. John and Hassel Island as well as 5,650 acres (2,287 hectares) of offshore waters. Swimming, snorkeling and boating are popular; equipment can be rented. Hiking trails lead to scenic overlooks and into deep valleys such as Reef Bay. Ruins of Danish sugar plantations can be seen; the ruins of Annaberg Sugar Mill are among the most preserved and accessible.

Park programs range from guided hiking and snorkeling trips to illustrated evening programs at the campground amphitheater. Two-hour guided safari bus tours depart daily from the public ferry dock.

Park waters are popular cruising grounds for boaters. To protect the coral reefs and seagrass beds, moorings have been installed in many areas. Boaters are encouraged to contact the park for information related to safe boating.

The Virgin Islands National Park visitor center, in Cruz Bay north of the ferry dock, has information and exhibits relating to the park. It is open daily 8-4:30; phone (340) 776-6201. Park admission is free. Annaberg Ruins and Trunk Bay $4.

Cruz Bay is the site where visitors can board the *Coral Explorer*, a semi-submarine that allows passengers to view underwater life as it cruises along a shallow reef; phone (340) 775-1555 for information and reservations.

Accommodations consist of cottages, tents and tent sites at the campground at Cinnamon Bay, 4 miles (6.2 km) northeast of Cruz Bay. Camping and water sports equipment can be rented, and supplies are available. Reservations must be made well in advance. Contact Cinnamon Bay Campground, P.O. Box 720, Cruz Bay, St. John, U.S. Virgin Islands 00831; phone (340) 776-6330 or (800) 539-9998.

At Maho Bay, 6 miles (9 km) northeast of Cruz Bay, canvas cottages are connected by wooden walkways that meander through the thickly wooded hillside. Camping supplies and water sports equipment are available. Reservations also must be made well in advance. Contact Maho Bay Camp, Cruz Bay, St. John, U.S. Virgin Islands 00830; phone (340) 776-6240 or (800) 392-9004.

For further information about the park write the Park Superintendent, Virgin Islands National Park, 6010 Estate Nazareth, St. Thomas, U.S. Virgin Islands 00802-3406; phone (340) 775-6238.

St. Thomas

Settled by Danes in 1672, St. Thomas (pop. 48,200) covers 32 square miles (83 sq km) of hilly terrain about 40 miles (64 km) east of Puerto Rico. Crown Mountain, at 1,550 feet, and Signal Hill, at 1,505 feet, are the highest points. From the road that cuts through the mountain range, both sides of the island can be seen. Near the top of the range is Drake's Seat, from which Sir Francis Drake is supposed to have charted the course of the channel now bearing his name. From this point there is a fine view of Magens Bay, many islands and the Atlantic Ocean.

In the days of piracy, St. Thomas was a favorite hideout for Captain Kidd, Bluebeard and Blackbeard. The towers from which buccaneers are said to have searched the sea for potential victims are now hotels.

St. Thomas' checkered past has left the landscape dotted with contrasting architectural styles. Pastel houses line narrow cobblestone streets and alleys, where the doors reflect the Dutch heritage and the red tile roofs, the Danish. The elaborate iron grillwork was left by the French, and the patios lend a Spanish accent.

Tourism is the chief means of livelihood on St. Thomas. Tennis, golf, boating, swimming and fishing are available; spear fishing and snorkeling are excellent near the coral reefs around the island. Magens Bay on the north coast has a beautiful heart-shaped sand beach.

Charlotte Amalie (B-2) pop. 19,300

The only town on St. Thomas, Charlotte Amalie (a-MAL-ya) is the territorial capital of the U.S. Virgin Islands. This town, climbing up the steep sides of Mafolie Mountain, Frenchman's Hill and Solberg, once served as the home port for such unsavory characters as Captain Kidd, Bluebeard and Blackbeard. Sir Francis Drake employed the port's favorable location to descend upon the gold-laden galleons that sailed through the Anegada Passage en route to Spain.

Under the Danish colonial government the port accommodated one of the world's biggest slave trade operations, routing slaves from Africa to other areas in the Caribbean and on the mainland. From Emancipation Garden, the city's central square, slaves heard the proclamation giving them freedom in 1848.

Valdemar Hill Drive offers a panoramic view of Charlotte Amalie and its deepwater harbor, usually busy with several major cruise ships, container ships, island sloops and yachts. The 17th-century warehouses now house shops and restaurants that accommodate the tourist trade. Distinctive among the city's old buildings is the governor's office, the Government House, furnished with antiques and paintings by native impressionist Camille Pissarro.

At the base of the nearby "Ninety-Nine Steps," one of the few remaining stair-streets that once helped residents traverse the hilly town, is Government Hill, a wealthy residential community of the 18th century. Crown House, a national historic landmark, is a fine example of how wealthy Danish planters lived during the sugar heyday.

Historically significant churches include the Dutch Reformed Church, one of the first outside New York's Dutch colony; and the Frederick Lutheran Church, where silver equipment more than 2 centuries old is still in use. The Jewish Synagogue is the second oldest in the Western Hemisphere and still has sand on its floor to symbolize the Jews' flight from Egypt through the desert.

★*ATLANTIS* **SUBMARINE** departs from the West Indian Co. dock in Building VI of Havensight Mall for a 1-hour underwater voyage of the reef surrounding Buck Island, at a maximum depth of 90 feet. Colorful sponge gardens, exotic fish and unusual coral formations are among the sights. A 30-minute ferry ride transports visitors between the dock and the submarine.

Allow 2 hours minimum. Trips depart Tues.-Sat. 9-2 (also Fri. 2-3), Sun. 11-2. Fare $72; ages 13-17, $36; ages 4-12, $27. Children under 36 inches tall are not permitted. Reservations are advised. AE, MC, VI. Phone (340) 776-0288 for information, or 776-5650 for reservations.

CORAL WORLD, 7.5 mi. (12 km) n.e. at 6450 Coki Point, is a 4.5-acre marine park. Highlights include an underwater observatory where visitors can view the activity of a coral reef through 24 glass windows in a three-story tower standing 100 feet offshore. The mid-level deck of the tower features the 50,000-gallon Predator Tank, where large ocean dwellers, including sharks, moray eels and stingrays, roam. The top level offers changing exhibits as well as great island views.

The Caribbean Reef Encounter is an 80,000-gallon tank that re-creates the island's natural environment. Circular glass walls allow visitors to view the reef ecosystem. The Marine Gardens Aquarium has 21 aquariums that house fluorescent coral and natural seascapes.

Mangrove Lagoon shows the stages of development on a mangrove ecosystem, including viewing windows on each end of the 70-foot-long exhibit where visitors can see the underwater animals living among the mangrove roots. Four saltwater pools feature baby sharks, stingrays, turtles and a touch pool.

The park also includes two amphitheaters, interpretive displays and daily feedings and dives. Visitors also can swim, snorkel or dive next door at Coki Beach. Food is available.

Allow 1 hour minimum. Open daily 9-5:30. Guided tours of the park Mon., Thurs. and Sat.-Sun. at 3. Park admission $16; ages 3-12, $8. AE, DI, DS, MC, VI. Phone (340) 775-1555.

FORT CHRISTIAN, on the waterfront near Emancipation Garden Park, is a red masonry structure that once housed the entire St. Thomas colony. Built by the Danes in 1672, it has been reconstructed several times. Several cells display a collection of Arawak and Carib artifacts and items relating to the early Danish settlers. Mon.-Fri. 9-5; closed holidays. Free. Parking 50c per hour. Phone (340) 776-4566.

NEW HERRNHUT, about 2.5 mi. (4 km) e. of town, is a church built by Moravian missionaries in 1738.

PARADISE POINT TRAMWAY is across from Havensight Mall and the cruise ship dock. Gondolas transport passengers 700 feet up a mountainside to Paradise Point. The 3.5-minute ride offers views of the harbor and Charlotte Amalie. Daily 8:30-5. Fare $10; under 14, $5. Phone (340) 774-9809.

ROYAL DANE MALL, off Main St., is a group of shops housed in former warehouses for trading goods and rum. The stores are open Mon.-Sat. 9-5, Sun. 9-1 (depending upon cruise ship schedule).

LODGINGS & RESTAURANTS

ST. CROIX

LODGINGS

THE BUCCANEER HOTEL
◆◆◆ *Resort Hotel*

12/20-4/1	$220-575	XP $45
12/1-12/19 & 4/2-11/30	$175-355	XP $45

Location: On SR 82; 2.5 mi e of Christensted. (PO Box 25200, 00824-5200). Fax: 340/778-8215. **Terms:** F12; Reserv deposit, 14 day notice, winter, 7 day summer. **Facility:** 140 rooms. Sprawling 250 acre golf resort overlooking Caribbean. Built on ruins of old sugar plantation. Variety of rooms, some beachfront; balcony, terrace or patio. Friendly, attentive service. Meets AAA guest room security requirements. 5 whirlpool rms, extra charge; 1-2 stories; interior/exterior corridors; beach; boat dock. Fee: 8 tennis courts (2 lighted). **Services:** giftshop. Fee: massage, area transportation. **Recreation:** swimming, charter fishing, snorkeling & equipment; hiking trails, jogging. Fee: sailboating, scuba diving & equipment, windsurfing. Rental: boats. **Cards:** AE, CB, DI, DS, MC, VI.

(340/773-2100

AAA SAVE CARAVELLE HOTEL
◆◆◆ *Hotel*

12/15-4/14	$134-144	XP $22
4/15-11/30	$104-114	XP $20
12/1-12/14	$102-112	XP $22

Location: In Christiansted. 44A Queen Cross St 00820. Fax: 340/778-7004. **Terms:** Reserv deposit, 7 day notice; $10 service charge; package plans. **Facility:** 44 rooms. Located quietly on the water's edge in Historic Christiansted. Comfortable guest rooms, most with harbour view. Meets AAA guest room security requirements. 3 stories, no elevator; exterior corridors. **Dining:** Restaurant; 7 am-11 pm; $17-$21; cocktails. **Services:** giftshop. **Recreation:** scuba instruction. Fee: scuba diving. Rental: scuba equipment. **All Rooms:** shower baths. **Cards:** AE, DI, DS, MC, VI. **Special Amenities: Free room upgrade and preferred room (each subject to availability with advanced reservations).**

((340)773-0687

AAA SAVE COLONY COVE RESORTS
◆◆◆ *Condo Motel*

12/20-4/14	$195-220	XP $20
12/1-12/19 & 4/15-11/30	$135-160	XP $20

Location: 2 mi w of Christiansted. From Hwy 75 & the 5 corners, follow Golden Rock Rd 0.3 mi. 3221 Golden Rock 00820-4339. Fax: 340/773-5397. **Terms:** F6; Reserv deposit, 21 day notice; handling fee imposed. **Facility:** 60 rooms. Spacious 2-bedroom units on tropically landscaped grounds. All with private balcony. Most have view of the ocean, pool & gardens. Eco-center & herbal gardens. Meets AAA guest room security requirements. Rates for up to 5 persons. A/C in bedroom areas only. 10% optional service charge; 3 stories, no elevator; exterior corridors; beach; 1 lighted tennis court. **Dining:** Restaurant nearby. **Services:** Fee: area transportation. **Recreation:** swimming. Fee: scuba diving, snorkeling, kayaks. Rental: scuba & snorkeling equipment. **All Rooms:** kitchens. **Cards:** AE, MC, VI. **Special Amenities: Early check-in/late check-out and preferred room (subject to availability with advanced reservations).** *(See color ad below)*

((340)773-1965

CORMORANT BEACH CLUB & HOTEL
◆◆◆ *Motor Inn*

12/21-4/14	$180-230	XP $35
12/1-12/20 & 4/15-11/30	$130-160	XP $35

Location: 2.5 mi nw of Christiansted via SR 83 & 75, 0.5 mi ne following signs. 4126 La Grande Princesse 00820. Fax: 340/778-9218. **Terms:** F12, Reserv deposit, 30 day notice, 7 days 4/15-12/20. **Facility:** 52 rooms. Very attractive large rooms with balcony or patio on long stretch of beach. 48 condominiums with full kitchen & guest laundry. 7 two-bedroom units, 7 three-bedroom units. 2 & 3-bedroom condo units $325-$475; $225-$365 off season; 3 stories, no elevator; oceanfront; beach; 2 tennis courts. **Recreation:** swimming. Fee: scuba diving/snorkeling & equipment. **Cards:** AE, CB, DI, DS, MC, VI.

(340/778-8920

(AAA) (SAVE) PINK FANCY HOTEL
◆◆ Historic Bed & Breakfast

12/15-4/15	$120	XP $15
12/1-12/14 & 4/16-11/30	$90	XP $15

Location: In Christiansted. 27 Prince St 00820. Fax: 340/773-6448. **Terms:** F12; Reserv deposit, 21 day notice, 7 days off season; weekly rates; package plans. **Facility:** 13 rooms. Complex dating from 1780 Danish townhouse. On National Register of Historic Places. Convenient to recreational & shopping facilities. Meets AAA guest room security requirements. 1-2 stories; exterior corridors; street parking only. **Dining:** Restaurant nearby. **Services:** complimentary evening beverages. **All Rooms:** efficiencies. **Cards:** AE, CB, DI, DS, MC, VI. **Special Amenities:** Early check-in/late check-out and preferred room (subject to availability with advanced reservations).

((340)773-8460

SAND CASTLE ON THE BEACH
◆ Apartment Motel

12/20-4/17	$115-305	XP $40
12/1-12/19, 4/18-6/15 & 11/1-11/30	$75-225	XP $30
6/16-10/31	$65-180	XP $20

Location: 0.5 mi s of Frederiksted, on the beach. 127 Smithfield 00840. Fax: 340/772-1757. **Terms:** Age restrictions may apply; reserv deposit, 60 day notice, 30 day, off season. **Facility:** 20 rooms. Compact, pleasant 1-bedroom apartments & studios. Most with patio or balcony, many with beach view, some upgraded suites with very attractive decor. Meets AAA guest room security requirements. Energy surcharge, 10% daily; 2 stories; exterior corridors; beachfront; beach. **Recreation:** swimming. **All Rooms:** combo or shower baths. **Some Rooms:** 6 efficiencies, 10 kitchens. **Cards:** AE, DS, MC, VI.

(340/772-1205

(AAA) (SAVE) TAMARIND REEF HOTEL
◆◆◆ Motor Inn

12/18-1/4	$175-200	XP $25
12/1-12/17 & 1/5-4/30	$160-180	
5/1-11/30	$145-160	

Location: 3 mi e of Christiansted on East End Rd (SR 82). 5000 Southgate 00820. Fax: 340/773-3989. **Terms:** Reserv deposit, 21 day notice; $10 service charge; package plans. **Facility:** 46 rooms. Spacious guest rooms in tropical colors. All rooms with either landscaped patio or balcony overlooking the sea with views of Green Cay. Peaceful locations. Meets AAA guest room security requirements. Exterior corridors; oceanfront; beach; 4 lighted tennis courts; marina. **Dining:** 2 restaurants; 7 am-10 & noon-10 pm; $17-$25; cocktails. **Services:** giftshop. **Recreation:** swimming, canoeing, charter fishing, snorkeling & equipment; croquet. Fee: scuba diving & equipment, windsurfing. **All Rooms:** shower baths. **Some Rooms:** 19 efficiencies. **Cards:** AE, MC, VI. **Special Amenities:** Early check-in/late check-out and free local telephone calls.

((340)773-4455

WESTIN CARAMBOLA BEACH RESORT
◆◆◆ Resort Hotel

12/17-4/12	$275-370	XP $15
12/1-12/16 & 4/13-11/30	$185-270	XP $15

Location: Midway between Christensted & Frederiksted on Northshore Dr, 8.3 mi from airport. Estate Davis Bay 00851-3031 (PO Box 3031, KINGSHILL, 00851). Fax: 340/778-1682. **Terms:** F18; Reserv deposit, 15 day notice; 10% service charge. **Facility:** 151 rooms. Elegantly furnished large guest rooms, many with ocean view from porch or balcony. Secluded spot, nestled between cliff & the sea. Meets AAA guest room security requirements. 2 stories; exterior corridors; beach; 4 tennis courts (2 lighted). **Services:** giftshop; area transportation. **Recreation:** swimming, snorkeling. Fee: scuba diving, scuba & snorkeling equipment. **All Rooms:** shower baths. **Cards:** AE, CB, DI, DS, MC, VI.

(340/778-3800

RESTAURANTS

CORMORANT BEACH CLUB RESTAURANT
◆◆ Continental   D $17-$26

Location: 2.5 mi nw of Christiansted via SR 83 & 75, 0.5 mi ne following signs; in Cormorant Beach Club. 4126 La Grande Princesse 00820. **Hours:** 6:30 pm-9:30 pm. **Reservations:** suggested. **Features:** No A/C; casual dress; cocktails & lounge; a la carte. Well-prepared entrees served in beautiful beachfront setting. Menu blends Regional & Continental cuisine. **Cards:** AE, DI, MC, VI.

(340/778-8920

KENDRICKS
◆◆◆ Continental   D $15-$26

Location: In Christiansted; at jct of Company & King Cross sts. King Cross St 00820. **Hours:** 6 pm-9:30 pm. Closed: 12/25. **Reservations:** suggested. **Features:** No A/C; dressy casual; health conscious menu items; carryout; cocktails & lounge; street parking. Charming, courtyard setting. Varied selection of creatively prepared traditional dishes & pasta. Family owned & operated. Daily fresh seafood specials. **Cards:** AE, MC, VI.

(340/773-9199

TIVOLI GARDENS
◆◆ American   L $7-$16   D $11-$25

Location: In Christiansted; upstairs corner of Queen Cross & Strand sts. 39 Strand St 00820. **Hours:** 11:15 am-2:30 & 6-9:30 pm, Sat & Sun from 6 pm. **Reservations:** suggested; in season. **Features:** No A/C; casual dress; health conscious menu items; carryout; cocktails & lounge; entertainment; street parking. Varied menu served in an open air setting, some tables with water view. **Cards:** AE, MC, VI.

(340/773-6782

THE TOP HAT
◆◆◆ Continental   D $20-$27

Location: In Christiansted. 52 Company St 00820. **Hours:** 6 pm-9:30 pm. Closed: Sun & 5/1-7/31. **Reservations:** suggested. **Features:** casual dress; cocktails & lounge; street parking; a la carte. Upstairs in converted townhouse. Scandinavian specialties. Same owner/chef since 1970. Light fare in lounge. Extensive wine list. All entrees include salad/antipasto bar. **Cards:** AE, DI, DS, MC, VI.

(340/773-2346

TUTTO BENE CAFE
◆◆ Italian   L $6-$12   D $13-$20

Location: In Christiansted. 2 Company St 00820. **Hours:** 11:30 am-2:30 & 6-10 pm, Sat & Sun from 6 pm. **Features:** casual dress; carryout; cocktails; street parking; a la carte. Menu changes daily. Homemade classical Italian cuisine in streetside bistro setting. Interesting pasta & gourmet pizza selection. **Cards:** AE, DS, MC, VI.

(340/773-5229

St. John

Lodgings

CANEEL BAY HOTEL
◆◆◆◆ *Resort Complex*

12/20-3/31	$350-750	XP $50
12/1-12/19, 4/1-4/30 & 11/16-11/30	$300-550	XP $50
5/1-11/15	$250-450	XP $50

Location: On Caneel Bay, reached by ferry from Charlotte Amalie Waterfront. Rt 20, North Shore Dr 00831 (PO Box 720, CRUZ BAY). Fax: 340/693-8280. **Terms:** F16; Age restrictions may apply; reserv deposit, 28 day notice; $10 service charge. **Facility:** 166 rooms. Beautiful resort complex on 170 acres of landscaped grounds of former sugar plantation. Attractive, well furnished units near or along 7 beaches. Deluxe cottages. Secluded, quiet setting. Some cellular phone avail for rental; 1-2 stories; exterior corridors; beach; 11 tennis courts; boat dock; playground. **Services:** giftshop. Fee: massage. **Recreation:** swimming, boating, sailboating, snorkeling & equipment, windsurfing; hiking trails. Fee: charter fishing, scuba diving. Rental: scuba equipment. **All Rooms:** combo or shower baths. **Cards:** AE, CB, DI, MC, VI.

(340/776-6111

GALLOWS POINT SUITE RESORT
◆◆◆ *Condo Complex*

12/15-3/31	$275-365	XP $35
12/1-12/14, 4/1-5/31 & 11/1-11/30	$195-275	XP $35
6/1-10/31	$145-195	XP $35

Location: 0.3 mi s of ferry dock. Gallows Point Rd 00831 (PO Box 58, 00831-0058). Fax: 340/776-6520. **Terms:** Age restrictions may apply; reserv deposit, 30 day notice; handling fee imposed; package plans. **Facility:** 50 rooms. Spacious 1-bedroom & bi-level loft units. All have harbour or oceanview. Meets AAA guest room security requirements. Rates for up to 2 persons; 2 stories; exterior corridors. **Dining:** Dining room; also, Ellington's, see separate listing. **Services:** giftshop; area transportation, to ferry dock. **Recreation:** snorkeling. **All Rooms:** kitchens, shower baths. **Some Rooms:** color TV. **Cards:** AE, DI, MC, VI. *(See color ad below)*

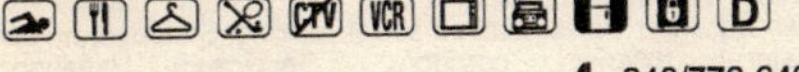

(340/776-6434

WESTIN RESORT ST. JOHN
◆◆◆ *Resort Complex*

1/3-4/10	$320-850	XP $50
12/19-1/2	$450-625	XP $45
12/1-12/18 & 4/11-11/30	$245-600	XP $50

Location: 2 mi se of Cruz Bay on hwy. Great Crux Bay 00831 (PO Box 8310). Fax: 340/779-4985. **Terms:** F12; Reserv deposit, 15 day notice. **Facility:** 331 rooms. 34 acres tropically landscaped grounds. Contemporary accomodations. Many rooms with balcony or patio. 7 one & two-bedroom suites with whirlpool. 3 bedroom suites with kitchens & private pool. Meets AAA guest room security requirements. 30 two-bedroom units, 24 three-bedroom units. 10 three-bedroom units with private pool; 2-3 stories, no elevator; exterior corridors; beach; 6 lighted tennis courts; boat dock. **Services:** giftshop. Fee: massage. **Recreation:** swimming, charter fishing, snorkeling, scuba & snorkeling equipment, windsurfing; jogging. Fee: scuba diving. **All Rooms:** combo or shower baths. **Some Rooms:** 96 kitchens. **Cards:** AE, CB, DI, DS, MC, VI.

(340/693-8000

Restaurants

ASOLARE
◆◆◆ *Regional Specialty*   D $20-$36

Location: Just n of Cruz Bay. Northshore Rd. **Hours:** 5:30 pm-9 pm. **Reservations:** suggested. **Features:** No A/C; casual dress; cocktails; a la carte. Open-air terrace of old stone home high above Cruz Bay, sweeping views & breathtaking sunsets. Menu imaginative, blends Asian & tropical influences utilizing fresh ingredients. House special is the famous chocolate pyramid. **Cards:** AE, MC, VI.

(340/779-4747

ELLINGTON'S
◆◆◆ *Continental*   D $13-$38

Location: 0.3 mi s of ferry dock; in Gallows Point Suite Resort. Gallows Point Rd 70831. **Hours:** 5:30 pm-10 pm. Closed: Wed 7/1-10/1. **Reservations:** suggested. **Features:** No A/C; casual dress; children's menu; cocktails. Seafood, steak, pasta all served in open air setting. Overlooking Cruz Bay Harbour with gorgeous views of St Thomas & sunsets. **Cards:** AE, MC, VI.

(340/693-8490

GALLOWS POINT SUITE RESORT
St. John, USVI 00831

Nestled on a tropical peninsula all suites are waterfront with full kitchens, dining and living areas, balconies and beautiful views. Freshwater pool, sundecks and acclaimed snorkeling. 5 minutes walk to Cruz Bay.

Call 1-800-323-7229

ST. THOMAS

LODGINGS

THE ANCHORAGE
◆◆◆ *Condo Motel*

12/15-4/14	$320-420	XP $20
12/1-12/14 & 4/15-11/30	$215-315	XP $20

Location: 3 mi e on SR 38 to jct 32, 3.5 mi to jct SR 322 then 2 mi se. 6222 Estate Nazareth 00802 (PO Box 8529, 00801). Fax: 340/775-5901. **Terms:** F12; Reserv deposit, 30 day notice; $10 service charge; 3 night min stay. **Facility:** 11 rooms. Individual decorated units in a residential community. Some with loft bedrooms. All rooms with balcony or patio, most with ocean view. 9 two-bedroom units, 2 three-bedroom units. Rates for up to 4 persons; 3 stories, no elevator; exterior corridors; beach; 2 lighted tennis courts. **Recreation:** swimming. **All Rooms:** kitchens. **Cards:** AE, MC, VI. *(See color ad below)*

 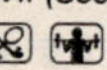  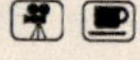  

(340/775-2600

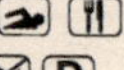 **BEST WESTERN CARIB BEACH HOTEL**
◆◆ *Motor Inn*

12/15-4/14	$125-155	
4/15-11/30	$92-132	
12/1-12/14	$89-129	XP $15

Location: 1 blk from airport terminal. (70-C Lindbergh Bay, 00802). Fax: 340/777-4131. **Terms:** F; Reserv deposit, 3 day notice; 5% service charge; package plans. **Facility:** 65 rooms. All rooms with balcony or patio. Meets AAA guest room security requirements. 2 stories; interior/exterior corridors; oceanview; beach. **Dining:** Restaurant; 7 am-10:30 & 6-10 pm; $10-$16; cocktails. **Services:** area transportation, shuttle to town & beach. **Recreation:** swimming, charter fishing. **All Rooms:** combo or shower baths. **Cards:** AE, CB, DI, DS, MC, VI. **Special Amenities:** Free room upgrade and preferred room (each subject to availability with advanced reservations).

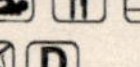  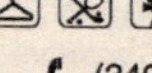

((340)774-2525

BEST WESTERN EMERALD BEACH RESORT
◆◆◆ *Resort Motor Inn*

12/15-4/14	$199-249	XP $25
12/1-12/14 & 4/15-11/30	$145-185	XP $25

Location: 2.5 mi w of Charlotte Amalie, on Lindbergh Bay; 1 mi from airport. (8070 Lindbergh Bay, 00802). Fax: 340/776-3426. **Terms:** F12; Reserv deposit, 7 day notice; 8% service charge; package plans. **Facility:** 90 rooms. Modern tastefully appointed guestrooms. All rooms with balcony & ocean view. Rock waterfall at pool. Meets AAA guest room security requirements. 3 stories, no elevator; exterior corridors; beach. **Dining:** Dining room; 6:45-10:30 am, 11:30-2:30 & 6-10 pm; $8-$25; cocktails; pool/beach bar 11:30-8 pm. **Services:** area transportation, shuttle to town. **Recreation:** swimming, scuba & snorkeling equipment. Fee: scuba diving, snorkeling, windsurfing, sea kayaks, beach floats. Rental: sailboats. **Cards:** AE, CB, DI, DS, MC, VI. **Special Amenities:** Free room upgrade and preferred room (each subject to availability with advanced reservations).

((340)777-8800

ELYSIAN BEACH RESORT
◆◆◆ *Resort Complex*

12/21-4/15	$225-630	XP $25
12/1-12/20 & 4/16-11/30	$175-445	XP $25

Location: 3 mi e of Charlotte-Amalie on SR 38 to jct SR 32, 3.5 mi to jct SR 3222, then 2 mi se. (6800 Estate Nazareth, 00802). Fax: 340/776-0910. **Terms:** D12; Reserv deposit, 21 day notice, 7 days off season. **Facility:** 170 rooms. Luxury resort in a magnificent setting; offers variety of fine dining. Terraced on hillside overlooking beach. 1, 2 & 3 loft bedroom units avail, ideal for families. Meets AAA guest room security requirements. 3-4 stories, no elevator; exterior corridors; beach; 1 tennis court. **Services:** giftshop; area transportation. Fee: massage. **Recreation:** swimming, snorkeling, scuba equipment, windsurfing. Fee: sailboating, scuba diving. **Some Rooms:** 56 kitchens. **Cards:** AE, DI, DS, MC, VI.

(340/775-1000

HOTEL 1829
◆◆ *Historic Country Inn*

12/20-4/30	$90-235	XP $20
12/1-12/19 & 5/1-11/30	$70-170	XP $15

Location: In Charlotte Amalie on Government Hill. Government Hill (PO Box 1567, 00804). Fax: 340/776-4313. **Terms:** Age restrictions may apply; reserv deposit, 21 day notice, 7 day in summer. **Facility:** 15 rooms. Charming 19th century landmark building. Some rooms offer magnificent town & harbor views. Limited street parking; 5 stories, no elevator; exterior corridors. **Services:** giftshop. **All Rooms:** shower baths. **Cards:** AE, DS, MC, VI.

(340/776-1829

ISLAND BEACHCOMBER HOTEL
◆◆ *Motor Inn*

| 12/20-3/31 | $130-145 | XP $20 |
| 12/1-12/19 & 4/1-11/30 | $100-115 | XP $20 |

Location: 2.5 mi w of Charlotte Amalie; on airport access road, 1 mi from airport. Airport Rd (PO Box 302579, 00803). **Fax:** 340/774-5615. **Terms:** Reserv deposit, 7 day notice; handling fee imposed; 10% service charge. **Facility:** 47 rooms. On Lindbergh Bay. Motel-type units with patio, many along beach. 1-2 stories; exterior corridors; beach. **Services:** giftshop; area transportation. **Recreation:** swimming. **All Rooms:** shower baths. **Cards:** AE, CB, DI, DS, MC, VI. *(See color ad below)*

((340)774-5250

MARRIOTT'S MORNING STAR BEACH RESORT
◆◆◆ *Resort Motor Inn*

12/19-4/10	$350-450	XP $40
12/1-12/18, 4/11-6/12 & 10/17-11/30	$280-360	XP $40
6/13-10/16	$210-270	XP $40

Location: 1 mi e of Charlotte Amalie on Frenchman's Bay Rd. 5 Estate Bakkeroe 00801 (PO Box 7100). **Fax:** 340/776-3054. **Terms:** F18; Reserv deposit, 7 day notice; handling fee imposed. **Facility:** 96 rooms. Bright yellow buildings clustered between the beach & cliffs. Garden or sea view, patio or balcony. Meets AAA guest room security requirements. 2-3 stories, no elevator; exterior corridors; beach. **Fee:** 2 lighted tennis courts. **Services:** giftshop. **Recreation:** swimming, charter fishing. **Fee:** scuba diving/snorkeling & equipment. **Cards:** AE, CB, DI, DS, JC, MC, VI.

((340)776-8500

PAVILIONS AND POOLS
◆◆ *Cottage*

| 12/21-3/31 | $250-275 | XP $25 |
| 12/1-12/20 & 4/1-11/30 | $180-195 | XP $25 |

Location: On Smith Bay Rd (SR 38), 7 3/10 mi e of Charlotte Amalie on ne coast. 6400 Estate Smith Bay 00802. **Fax:** 340/775-6110. **Terms:** F12; Reserv deposit, 21 day notice, in winter, 10 day in summer. **Facility:** 25 rooms. Unique colony of villas, each with private patio, swimming pool & kitchen offering lots of privacy. 1 story; exterior corridors. **Recreation:** snorkeling equipment. **All Rooms:** kitchens, shower baths. **Cards:** AE, MC, VI.

((340)775-6110

POINT PLEASANT RESORT, A COLONY RESORT

◆◆◆ *Apartment Motor Inn*

12/21-4/11	$290	XP $25
4/12-11/30	$195	XP $25
12/1-12/20	$185	XP $25

Location: SR 38, 8 mi e of Charlotte Amalie, on n coast. 6600 Estate Smith Bay #4 00802. Fax: 340/776-5694. **Terms:** F21; Reserv deposit, 14 day notice; handling fee imposed; MAP avail; package plans. **Facility:** 95 rooms. Natural hillside setting with superb views of Water Bay & Pillsbury Sound. Nicely furnished studios, also 1- & 2-bedroom suites; all with balcony or patio. Meets AAA guest room security requirements. 4 two-bedroom units. Four 2-bedroom units, $335-$495; 3-6 stories, no elevator; exterior corridors; small beach; 1 lighted tennis court. **Dining:** Restaurant; 6 pm-10 pm, poolside grill 7:30 am-8:30 pm; $18-$32; cocktails. **Services:** giftshop. Fee: massage. **Recreation:** swimming, sailboating, snorkeling, windsurfing; guest cars, 4 hours daily limit; gas & insurance not included. **All Rooms:** kitchens, combo or shower baths. **Cards:** AE, DI, DS, MC, VI. **Special Amenities: Free local telephone calls and free room upgrade (subject to availability with advanced reservations).** *(See color ad p 277)*

((340)775-7200

RENAISSANCE GRAND BEACH RESORT

◆◆◆◆ *Resort Hotel*

12/1-3/31	$295-355
4/1-5/30	$225-285
5/31-11/30	$155-215

Location: On SR 38; 7 mi e of Charlotte Amalie on n coast. Smith Bay Rd 00801 (PO Box 8267). Fax: 340/775-2185. **Terms:** Reserv deposit, 21 day notice, 3 day in season. **Facility:** 290 rooms. Many rooms with balcony or patio. On good stretch of beach. Meets AAA guest room security requirements. Twelve 2-bedroom suites bi-level, $750-$875. 36 whirlpool rms, extra charge; 2-3 stories, no elevator; exterior corridors; beach; 6 lighted tennis courts; boat dock. **Services:** giftshop. Fee: massage, area transportation. **Recreation:** swimming, snorkeling & equipment, windsurfing; jogging. Fee: boating, charter fishing, scuba diving & equipment. **Cards:** AE, CB, DI, DS, JC, MC, VI. *(See color ad below)*

(340/775-1510

THE RITZ CARLTON ST THOMAS

◆◆◆◆ *Resort Hotel*

12/19-4/30 & 10/1-11/30	$425-525	XP $30
12/1-12/18	$300-395	
5/1-9/30	$225-275	XP $35

Location: 3 mi e on SR 38 to jct SR 32, 3.5 mi to jct SR 322, 2 mi se. 6900 Great Bay 00802. Fax: 340/775-4444. **Terms:** F18; Reserv deposit, 30 day notice. **Facility:** 152 rooms. Spanish Mediterrenean style resort on sloping grounds overlooking small coved beach & neighboring islands. Elegantly equipped guest rooms & suites. 3 stories, no elevator; exterior corridors; beach; tennis instruction. Fee: 3 lighted tennis courts. **Dining:** Dining room, 2 restaurants; 6 am-10 pm; $13-$38; cocktails; also, The Ritz Carlton Dining Room, see separate listing. **Services:** giftshop. Fee: massage. **Recreation:** swimming, scuba & snorkeling equipment; Catamaran cruises, beauty salon, full spa services. Fee: canoeing, sailboating, scuba diving, snorkeling, windsurfing; in-room video games. Rental: paddleboats. **Cards:** AE, CB, DI, DS, MC, VI.

(340/775-3333

SAPPHIRE BAY WEST/CRYSTAL COVE

◆◆ *Apartment Motel*

12/20-4/15	$165-310	XP $20
12/1-12/19 & 4/16-11/30	$130-255	XP $20

Location: SR 38, 7.5 mi e of Charlotte Amalie. 6345 Smith Bay 00802 (PO Box 9395, 00801). Fax: 340/779-6109. **Terms:** F12; Reserv deposit, 30 day notice; 3 night min stay. **Facility:** 27 rooms. Peaceful location, set back from beach. Spacious units. Barbecue grill avail for guest use. 4 two-bedroom units. 2 stories; exterior corridors; beach; 2 lighted tennis courts. **Recreation:** swimming; sports court. **All Rooms:** kitchens. **Cards:** AE, MC, VI. *(See color ad p 276)*

(340/775-0111

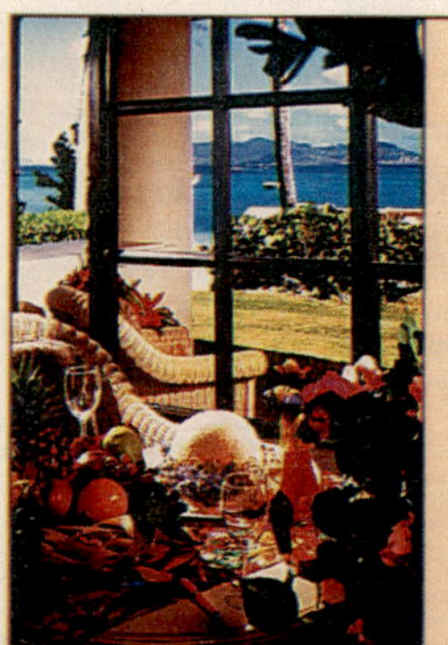

SAPPHIRE BEACH RESORT & MARINA
◆◆◆ *Resort Complex*

12/20-4/11	$295-440	XP $40
12/1-12/19 & 4/12-11/30	$225-325	XP $40

Location: SR 38, 8.5 mi e of Charlotte Amalie. Rt 6, Smith Bay (PO Box 8088, 00801). Fax: 340/775-4024. **Terms:** F12; Reserv deposit, 14 day notice; MAP avail; package plans. **Facility:** 171 rooms. Contemporary suites & villas on long beach. Fully furnished kitchens. All rooms with private balcony or patio & view of Sapphire Beach or marina. Meets AAA guest room security requirements. 3 stories, no elevator; exterior corridors; beach, wading pool; 4 tennis courts; playground. Fee: marina. **Dining:** 2 restaurants; 7:30-10:30 am, 11:30-2:30 & 6-10:30 pm; $11-$22; cocktails. **Services:** giftshop. Fee: massage. **Recreation:** swimming, sailboating, snorkeling & equipment, windsurfing, sunfish sailboats,; beach volleyball. Fee: scuba diving & equipment, dive shop, kayaks, scuba & windsurfing instructions. **Cards:** AE, MC, VI. **Special Amenities: Free room upgrade and preferred room (each subject to availability with advanced reservations).**

((340)775-6100

SECRET HARBOUR BEACH RESORT & VILLAS
◆◆◆ *Complex*

12/20-4/12	$210-495	XP $35
12/1-12/19 & 4/13-11/30	$129-299	XP $35

Location: 6 mi se off SR 322 on Estate Nazareth Bay; on se coast. 6280 Estate Nazareth 00802. Fax: 340/775-1501. **Terms:** F13; Reserv deposit, 14 day notice, 7 days in summer; weekly/monthly rates; package plans. **Facility:** 84 rooms. Spacious studio & 1- to 2-bedroom apartments with private balcony or patio. Hillside & beachfront units, private coved beach. Lovely ocean views. Meets AAA guest room security requirements. 16 two-bedroom units. 3 stories, no elevator; exterior corridors; beachfront; beach; 4 tennis courts; boat dock. **Dining:** Restaurant; 8 am-3 & 6-10:30 pm; $18-$24; cocktails. **Services:** giftshop. Fee: area transportation, Red Hook & town. **Recreation:** swimming, charter fishing, fishing. Fee: scuba diving/snorkeling & equipment, windsurfing, parasailing. Rental: sailboats. **All Rooms:** kitchens. **Cards:** AE, MC, VI. **Special Amenities: Free local telephone calls and preferred room (subject to availability with advanced reservations).**
(See color ad below)

((340)775-6550

VILLA BLANCA HOTEL
◆◆ *Motel*

12/15-4/30	$115-135	XP $15
12/1-12/14 & 5/1-11/30	$75-95	XP $15

Location: 1.5 mi e on SR 38. 4 Raphune Hill 00801 (PO Box 7505). Fax: 340/779-2661. **Terms:** F5; Reserv deposit, 21 day notice, 14 days off season. **Facility:** 14 rooms. All rooms have balcony & great views of Charlotte Amalie Harbor from their hillside setting. Relaxed, guest oriented, homey atmosphere. Owners home open to guests. Meets AAA guest room security requirements. Exterior corridors. **All Rooms:** shower baths. **Some Rooms:** 11 efficiencies, 3 kitchens. **Cards:** AE, CB, DI, DS, MC, VI.

(340/776-0749

WYNDHAM SUGAR BAY BEACH CLUB & RESORT
◆◆◆ *Resort Hotel*

1/3-4/4	$375-435	XP $188-218
12/1-12/19 & 4/5-11/30	$270-330	XP $135-165

Location: On SR 38, 8.5 mi e of Charlotte Amalie. 6500 Smith Bay Rd 00802. Fax: 340/777-7200. **Terms:** D18; Open 12/1-12/19 & 1/3-11/30; $10 service charge. **Facility:** 300 rooms. Buildings terraced down hillside, all rooms with patio overlooking Smith Bay or St John. Meets AAA guest room security requirements. Rates are all-inclusive; 3-4 stories; exterior corridors; beach; 5 lighted tennis courts. **Services:** giftshop. Fee: massage. **Recreation:** swimming, charter fishing, fishing. Fee: sailboating, scuba diving, scuba & snorkeling equipment, windsurfing. **Cards:** AE, DI, MC, VI.

(340/777-7100

RESTAURANTS

THE AGAVE' TERRACE
◆◆◆ *Continental*   D $18-$36

Location: SR 38, 8 mi e of Charlotte Amalie on n coast; in Point Pleasant Resort. 6600 Estate Smith Bay 00802. **Hours:** 6 pm-10 pm. **Reservations:** suggested. **Features:** No A/C; dressy casual; children's menu; health conscious menu items; carryout; cocktails & lounge. Open-air dining room on cliffside setting with breathtaking views of the sea & neighboring islands. Offering unique preparations of the freshest local seafood & lobster. Live Steel Band Tues & Thurs. **Cards:** AE, MC, VI.

(340/775-4142

CRAIG AND SALLY
◆◆◆ *Continental*   L $9-$13 D $15-$30
Location: SR 30 in Frenchtown area. 22 Honduras.
Hours: Wed-Fri 11:30 am-3 pm; Wed-Sun 5:30 pm-10 pm.
Closed: Mon & Tues. **Reservations:** suggested.
Features: dressy casual; cocktails; a la carte. "Passionate"
cuisine with an Italian vein, imaginative combination of the
fresh ingredients. Extensive wine list, romantic interior.
Cards: AE, MC, VI.

☒   (340/777-9949

EUNICE'S TERRACE
◆ *East Caribbean*   L $5-$13 D $9-$30
Location: SR 38 7 mi e of Charlotte Amalie on n coast.
6076 Estate Smith Bay 00802. **Hours:** 10 am-5 & 6-10 pm,
Sun 5 pm-10 pm. **Reservations:** suggested. **Features:** No
A/C; casual dress; children's menu; carryout; cocktails; en-
tertainment. Open-air second floor setting offering authentic
West Indian cuisine including fried & broiled fresh fish,
conch, lobster, fried plantains & fungi. **Cards:** AE, DS, MC,
VI.

(340/775-3975

HERVE RESTAURANT & WINE BAR
◆◆◆ *French*   L $7-$18 D $19-$32
Location: On Government Hill. Government Hill.
Hours: 11:30 am-3 pm; 6 pm-10 pm nightly.
Reservations: suggested. **Features:** casual dress; cock-
tails & lounge; street parking; a la carte. Excellent French-
American cuisine with a Caribbean flair in a terrace of
historic building with panoramic views of town & harbor. Ex-
tensive wine list. **Cards:** AE, MC, VI.

☒   (340/777-9703

HOOK, LINE, & SINKER
◆◆ *American*   L $6-$11 D $8-$19
Location: SR 30 at Frenchtown Yacht Harbor. 2 Honduras.
Hours: 7 am-11 pm, Sun 10 am-3 pm. **Features:** No A/C;
casual dress; Sunday brunch; cocktails; a la carte. Crisp
open-air wood dining room overlooking the yacht harbor &
with views of town in distances. Casual setting offering fresh
seafood, pasta, & beef. **Cards:** AE, MC, VI.

(340/776-9708

RAFFLES
◆◆ *Continental*   D $14-$23
Location: Just off SR 32; 1 mi w of Red Hook, 0.5 mi s on
Compass Point Marina following signs. 6300 Estate Froy-
denhoj #17 00802. **Hours:** 5:30 pm-10:30 pm. Closed: Mon.
Reservations: suggested. **Features:** No A/C; casual dress;
cocktails & lounge. Relaxed dining room with some outdoor
seating. Specialties include many interesting fresh seafood
preparations, marinated duck & steak. **Cards:** AE, MC, VI.

(340/775-6004

THE RITZ CARLTON DINING ROOM
◆◆◆◆ *Continental*   D $25-$38
Location: 3 mi e on SR 38 to jct SR 32, 3.5 mi to jct SR
322, 2 mi se; in The Ritz Carlton St Thomas. 6900 Great
Bay 00802. **Hours:** 6:30 pm-10 pm. Closed: Mon.
Reservations: required. **Features:** dressy casual; Sunday
brunch; cocktails; entertainment; valet parking; a la carte.
Elegant dining room with views of neighboring islands. Car-
ibbean inspired Continental cuisine. Extensive wine list.
Cards: AE, CB, DI, DS, MC, VI.

☒   (340/775-3333

ROMANO'S
◆◆◆ *Italian*   D $16-$28
Location: On Coral World Rd, just n of jct SR 38, in Smith
Bay. 6697 Smith Bay 00802. **Hours:** 6 pm-10:30 pm.
Closed: Sun, 8/15-9/30 & 12/23-12/26. **Reservations:** sug-
gested. **Features:** dressy casual; children's menu; cocktails;
a la carte. Cozy dining room decorated with original art &
Dali prints. Pasta, seafood, & veals. Nightly specials.
Cards: AE, MC, VI.

(340/775-0045

VICTOR'S NEW HIDE OUT
◆◆ *Caribbean*   L $7-$27 D $12-$27
Location: SR 30, following signs; between airport & center
of Charlotte Amalie, overlooking submarine base. 103 Sub
Base 00803. **Hours:** 11:30 am-3:30 & 5:30-10 pm, Sun from
5:30 pm. **Reservations:** suggested. **Features:** No A/C; ca-
sual dress; cocktails & lounge. Panoramic view of Crown
Bay Harbor. Large, airy dining room. Well-prepared native
Caribbean dishes & seafood. **Cards:** AE, MC, VI.

(340/776-9379

OTHER PORTS OF CALL

VENEZUELA

Sir Walter Raleigh, searching for El Dorado, found in Venezuela "a lively prospect." Its promise fulfilled, this country is now the third largest producer of oil in the world and enjoys the highest standard of living in South America. These advantages, coupled with the beauty of its 750-mile (1,200-km) coastline, naturally make Venezuela a favorite stopover for cruise ships. Popular ports of call include Litoral, a Latin American Riviera; Caracas, the political and entertainment capital; trading centers such as Valencia and Maracaibo; and the "pearl island" of Margarita.

CARACAS pop. 5,000,000

The capital and leading tourist attraction of Venezuela, Caracas is a modern city with reminders of the Spanish colonial period. The ancient Plaza Bolívar, shaded by trees and paved with intricate mosaics, was named for Simón Bolívar, the statesman and liberator of Venezuela, Bolivia, Colombia, Ecuador and Peru, born here in 1783.

Similarly titled but in striking contrast is the Simón Bolívar Center in the heart of new Caracas; here are twin-towered skyscrapers, modern office buildings and shopping arcades. Also of interest are the Capitol, National Pantheon and the fine parks and museums. Providing a scenic backdrop is Mount Avila; the summit, accessible by cable car, provides a memorable view.

BIRTHPLACE OF THE LIBERATOR (Casa Natal del Libertador), near Plaza Bolívar, is a reconstruction of the house where Simón Bolívar was born and raised. The residence, decorated by Venezuelan artist Tito Salas, contains mementos of Bolívar's life and military campaigns. Free.

Bolívar Museum (Museo Bolivariano), adjoining the liberator's birthplace, houses relics of the conquest, colonial and independence periods. Free.

CAPITOL (El Capitolio), Avenue Universidad, contains an historical art gallery, a mural of the battle of Carabobo and a bronze urn containing the 1811 Declaration of Independence. Free.

CATHEDRAL, on Plaza Bolívar, is a massive 16th-century church with a lovely Spanish facade. Inside are paintings by Bartolomé Murillo, Peter Paul Rubens and the Venezuelan artist Arturo Michelena.

CITY HALL (Concejo Municipal), on Plaza Bolívar, features paintings by native artist Emilio Boggio and contains the Museum of the Creole Way of Life, with displays of miniature figures dressed in Venezuelan costumes, all handmade by Raúl Santana. Free.

MUSEUM OF COLONIAL ART (Museo de Arte Colonial), on the Avenue Panteón, is an attractive 18th-century red-tiled building with colonial furniture, paintings and tapestries. Free.

MUSEUM OF CONTEMPORARY ART (Museo de Arte Contemporáneo), in Central Park, exhibits modern artwork by 20th-century national and international artists. Free.

MUSEUM OF FINE ART (Museo de Bellas Artes), Plaza Morelos in Los Caobos Park, contains paintings by 19th-century and modern artists, including El Greco. Particularly noteworthy is a fine collection of ceramics and china. Free.

MUSEUM OF NATURAL SCIENCE (Museo de Ciencias Naturales), Plaza Morelos in Los Caobos Park, contains displays of plants and animals unique to Venezuela. Free.

NATIONAL PANTHEON (Panteón Nacional) has the tomb of Bolívar and other revolutionary heroes.

PARK OF THE EAST (Parque del Este), at the eastern end of the valley, has a lake, miniature train, zoo, aviary and exotic plants. Admission is charged.

SAN FRANCISCO CHURCH, where Bolívar was given his title of the Liberator in 1813, is the city's oldest church. The 16th-century building is noted for its spacious naves and handsomely carved altars.

UNIVERSITY CITY (Ciudad Universitaria), is the site of Central University, noted for its modern architecture. The complex provides facilities for more than 40,000 students and has a 174-acre (70-hectare) garden with murals and sculptures for visitors.

CUMANA pop. 212,400

Founded in 1520, Cumana (then known as New Toledo) was among the first Spanish settlements in the Americas. The fort ruins and old churches are part of that period's legacy.

Water sports facilities include boats for water skiing, fishing cruisers and paddle boats. Cumana can be reached by sea or by a 15-minute flight from Margarita Island.

ISLA DE MARGARITA (MARGARITA ISLAND) pop. 200,000

Isla de Margarita is reached by sea from Puerto La Cruz and Cumana or by air from Caracas, Valencia and Cumana. Discovered by Christopher Columbus in 1498 during his third voyage, the island has been a pearl fishery since its colonial days; it remains the Caribbean's most important source of pearls. The best time to visit is September and October when the pearl fleets operate. Skin divers enjoy the waters of the innumerable lagoons and coves. Tax-free shopping in Porlamar also is popular.

LA ASUNCION, a living museum, is a small town in a setting of flowers and trees. Many historic buildings and fortresses date from the rule of the Spanish, who founded it in 1524. Its cathedral contains a life-size statue of the Virgin Mary clad in a robe of pearls.

MARACAIBO pop. 1,249,700

Maracaibo, Venezuela's second city, is the center of the nation's oil wealth thanks to rich deposits of petroleum under Lake Maracaibo. Founded in 1576, it became an inland trade center in 1688 and a world oil center by 1914. Local industries, such as shipbuilding and the production of leather goods, beer, chocolate and coffee, provide the city with its major exports.

Non-industrial features of Maracaibo include a glimpse of two unusual Indian tribes, the Guajiros and the Motilones. The former have elaborate costumes and live in stilt-raised houses in Sinamaica Lagoon. The Motilones, formerly hostile to non-Indians, reside at Machiques, south of Maracaibo. Also of interest is the lively Maracaibo Market on the downtown dock. Thousands enjoy the 4-day Carnival in March.

MARACAY pop. 600,000

About 68 miles (110 km) west of Caracas on the Trans-Andean Highway, Maracay is an industrial city and center of a rich coffee and sugar region. It is perhaps best known for the fabulous remnants of the Juan Vincent Gómez rule. Gómez, head of the Venezuelan government from 1908 until his death in 1935, chose the city as the site of his unofficial capital and residence. Twelve miles (20 km) from Maracay is Henry Pittier National Park, famous for its flora and fauna. Great beaches can be found in Choroní and Cata.

LAKE VALENCIA, outside the city, is the second largest lake in Venezuela. The island-dotted lake is especially fine for boating.

LAS DELICIAS, Gómez' country estate 6 mi. (10 km) from downtown Maracay, resembles a feudal domain. It has been converted into a public park and zoo.

MAESTRANZA BULLRING, a replica of the one in Seville, Spain, features some of the world's finest matadors.

VALENCIA pop. 1,300,600

Founded in 1555, Valencia lies in a warm, fertile valley in northern Venezuela, about 80 miles (130 km) west of Caracas at the western end of Lake Valencia. Of special architectural interest are the capitol, 18th-century cathedral and Cellis House. Puerto Cabello, the closest port to Valencia, is about 30 miles (48 km) to the north.

CARABOBO MONUMENT (Monumento de Carabobo), one of the great battlefields in the War of Independence, is where Bolívar and his forces routed the Spanish army in 1821, ending Spanish resistance in Venezuela. A monument and the Avenue of Heroes commemorate Bolívar's victory.

AAA TOURS FOR ONLY $15.00

Embark on a journey of learning and adventure, open the door to history, culture, geography, sightseeing opportunities and more with AAA TRAVEL VIDEOS.

AAA introduces videos of North America's most popular vacation areas including:

New England	Pacific Northwest	North Central
Florida	Mid Atlantic	Alaska & Yukon Territory
California	Southeast	Quebec & the Atlantic Provinces
Southwest	Hawaii	Ontario
Western Great Lakes	Gulf Coast	Alberta•British Columbia•
Eastern Great Lakes	Appalachian Trail	Manitoba•Saskatchewan
New York & New Jersey	Great Plains	Colorado
New York City	Washington, D.C.	National Parks/South & East
San Francisco & Wine Country	Los Angeles/S. California	National Parks/North & West
Mexico Yucatan	Windward Islands	Puerto Rico
Mexico Baja	Lake Powell	Bermuda
Mexico Central	Antigua•Barbuda	British Virgin Islands
U.S. Virgin Islands	Bahamas	Jamaica

HERE'S HOW TO ORDER

To order, call 1-800-875-5000 today. Have your membership card and MasterCard or VISA ready. Or, send your name, address, membership number, video selections and check or money order (plus $3.75 for shipping and handling) to:

AAA Travel Video

695 South Colorado Blvd. • Suite 270 • Denver, CO 80222

LANGUAGE TIPS

GENERAL EXPRESSIONS

DUTCH

Please ....Alstublieft
Thank you .... Dank u zeer
Excuse me...............................Neemt u mij niet kwalijk
Yes.. Ja
No.. Neen
Good morning ....Goedendag
Good evening.................................Goedenavond
Good-bye ....Tot ziens
Do you speak English? ....Spreekt u Engels?
I do not understand ....Ik begrijp niet
Please repeat...........................Zegt u het nog eens
Sir...Mijnheer
Madam...Mevrouw
Miss .... Juffrouw

FRENCH

Please ....S'il vous plait
Thank you .... Merci
Excuse me................................Excusez-moi
Yes... Oui
No.. Non
Good morning .... Bonjour

Good evening...............................Bonsoir
Good-bye ....Au revoir
Do you speak English? ....Parlez-vous anglais?
I do not understand .... Je ne comprends pas
Please repeat........................... Repetez, s'il vous plait
Sir... Monsieur
Madam...Madame
Miss .... Mademoiselle

SPANISH

Please .... Por favor
Thank you .... Gracias
Excuse me................................Disculpeme usted
Yes..Si
No..No
Good morning .... Buenos dias
Good evening...........................Buenas noches
Good-bye .... Hasta la vista
Do you speak English? ....¿Habla usted ingles?
I do not understand ....No entiendo
Please repeat........................... Repita, por favor
Sir..Senor
Madam.. Senora
Miss .... Senorita

ON THE ROAD

ENGLISH

1. Please show me the road to____.
2. I want to go to____.
3. Are we far from____?
4. Where are we?
5. May I park here?
6. Go straight ahead.
7. To the right.
8. To the left.
9. How far is
   a. a garage?
   b. a gas station?
   c. a doctor?
   d. a police station?
   e. a telephone?
   f. a post office?
   g. a hotel?
   h. a restaurant?

DUTCH

1. Wilt u mij de weg naar____ wijzen.
2. Ik wil naar____.
3. Zijn we ver van____?
4. Waar zijn we?
5. Mag ik hier stoppen?
6. Rijdt u rechtdoor?
7. Rechts.
8. Links.
9. Hoe ver hier vandaan is
   a. een garage?
   b. een benzinestation?
   c. een doktor?
   d. een politie-bureau?
   e. een telefooncel?
   f. een postkantoor?
   g. een hotel?
   h. een restaurant?

FRENCH

1. Veuillez m'indiquer la route a____.
2. Je desire aller a____
3. Sommes-nous loins de____?
4. Ou sommes nous?
5. Puis-je m'arreter ici?
6. Roulez tout droit.
7. A droit
8. A gauche
9. A quelle distance se trouve
   a. un garage?
   b. un poste a essence?
   c. un medecin?
   d. un poste de police?
   e. une cabine?
   f. la poste?
   g. un hotel?
   h. un restaurant?

SPANISH

1. Sirvase indicarme el camino para____.
2. Quiero ir a____?
3. ¿Estamos lejos de____?
4. ¿Donde estamos?
5. ¿Puedo detenerme aqui?
6. Siga el camino recto.
7. A la derecha
8. A la izquierda
9. ¿A que distancia esta
   a. un garage?
   b. una estacion de gasolina?
   c. un medico?
   d. una comisaria de policia?
   e. una cabina?
   f. la oficina de correos?
   g. un hotel?
   h. un restaurant?

At The Restaurant

Dutch

Water	Water
Coffee	Koffie
Tea	Thee
Milk	Melk
Beer	Bier
Wine	Wijn
Cider	Appelwijn
Lemonade	Citroenlimonade
Hors d'oeuvres	Hors d'oeuvres
Bread	Brood
Soup	Soep
Eggs	Eiren
Fish	Vis
Lobster	Kreeftesla
Meat	Vlees
Beef	Rundvlees
Beefsteak	Biefstuk
Pork	Varkenvlees
Ham	Ham
Mutton	Schapevlees
Venison	Wild
Veal	Kalfvlees
Chicken	Kip
Rice	Rijst
Potatoes	Aardappelen
Vegetables	Groenten
Salad	Salade
Tomatoes	Tomaten
Cabbage	Kool
Green peas	Doperwten
Green beans	Princesseboontjes
Cauliflower	Bloemkool
Mushrooms	Champignons
Cheese	Kaas
Fruit	Fruit
Pastries	Gebak
Ice cream	Ijs
Cookies	Beschult
Orange	Sinaasappel
Apple	Appel
Banana	Banaan
Grapes	Druiven
Pear	Peer
Cherries	Kersen
Strawberries	Aardbeien
Sugar	Suiker
Cream	Room
Salt	Zout
Pepper	Peper
Oil	Olie
Vinegar	Azijn
Mustard	Mosterd
Garlic	Knoflook
Butter	Boter
Jam	Jam
Knife	Mes
Fork	Vork
Spoon	Lepel
Bottle	Fles
Glass	Glas
Cup	Kopje
Plate	Bord
Napkin	Servet
Rare	Half rauw
Medium	Gaar
Well done	Gebakken
Warm	Warm
Iced, cold	Gekoeld
Give me the menu	Geeft u mij het menu
I should like	Ik sou willen.
How much is the meal?	Hoeveel kost de maaltijd?
Is service included?	Is de bediening inbegrepen?
The bill, please.	De rekening, alstublift.
Breakfast	Ontbijt
Lunch	Lunch
Dinner	Diner

French

Water	Eau
Coffee	Cafe
Tea	The
Milk	Lait
Beer	Biere
Wine	Vin
Cider	Cidre
Lemonade	Citronnade
Hors d'oeuvres	Hors d'oeuvres
Bread	Pain
Soup	Soupe
Egg	Oeuf
Omelette	Omelette
Fish	Poisson
Lobster	Homard
Shrimp	Crevette
Oyster	Huitre
Clam	Moule
Meat	Viande
Beef	Boeuf
Beefsteak	Bifteck
Pork	Porc
Ham	Jambon
Mutton	Mouton
Lamb	Agneau
Veal	Veau
Chicken	Poulet
Rice	Riz
Potatoes	Pommes de terre
Vegetables	Legumes
Salad	Salade
Tomatoes	Tomates
Lettuce	Laitue
Green peas	Petits pois
Beans	Haricots
Asparagus	Asperges
Carrots	Carottes
Mushrooms	Champignons
Cheeses	Fromages
Fruits	Fruits
Pastries	Patisseries
Ice cream	Glace
Cookies	Biscuits
Orange	Orange
Apple	Pomme
Banana	Banane
Strawberries	Fraises
Sugar	Sucre
Cream	Creme
Salt	Sel
Pepper	Poivre
Butter	Beurre
Oil	Huile
Vinegar	Vinaigre
Mustard	Moutarde
Gravy, sauce	Sauce
Garlic	Ail
Jam	Confiture
Knife	Couteau
Fork	Fourchette
Spoon	Cuiller
Bottle	Bouteille
Glass	Verre
Cup	Tasse
Plate	Assiette
Napkin	Serviette

Roasted .... Roti
Fried... Frit
Rare .... Saignant
Medium.. A point
Well done .... Cuit
Warm...Chaud
Iced..Glace
Show me the menu. .... Montrez-moi le menu.
I should like.. Je voudrais.
What is the price of the meal?.....Quel est le prix du repas?
Is service included?................... Le service est-il compris?
The bill, please. ....L'addition, s'il vous plait.
Breakfast... Petit dejeuner
Lunch ....Dejeuner
Dinner...Diner

SPANISH

Water...Agua
Coffee.. Cafe
Tea.. Te
Milk .... Leche
Beer ....Cerveza
Wine..Vino
Cider ....Sidra
Lemonade .... Limonada
Hors d'oeuvres ....Entremesas
Bread .... Pan
Soup ....Sopa
Eggs.. Huevos
Omelette .... Tortilla
Fish...Pescado
Lobster .... Langosta
Shrimp, prawn .... Langostino
Oyster.. Ostra
Clam..Almeja
Meat..Carne
Beef .... Vaca
Beefsteak..Bistec
Pork ....Cerdo
Ham ....Jamon
Mutton .... Cordero
Lamb...Cordero
Veal.. Ternera
Chicken.. Pollo
Rice..Arroz
Potatoes... Patatas
Vegetables...Legumbres
Salad.. Ensalada
Tomatoes .... Tomates

Lettuce..., Lechuga
Peas..Guisantes
Beans .... Habichuelas
Asparagus ....Esparrago
Carrots...Zanahorias
Mushrooms.. Hongos
Cheese..Queso
Fruits .... Frutas
Pastries...Pasteleria
Ice cream ....Helados
Cookies.. Bizcochos
Orange .... Naranja
Apple.. Manzana
Banana .... Banana
Strawberries...Fresas
Sugar .... Azucar
Cream...Crema
Salt .... Sal
Pepper...Pimienta
Butter .... Mantequilla
Oil... Aceite
Vinegar .... Vinagre
Mustard...Mostaza
Sauce, gravy.. Salsa
Garlic... Ajo
Jelly.. Jalea
Knife...Cuchillo
Fork..Tenedor
Spoon... Cuchara
Bottle...Botella
Glass .... Vaso
Cup .... Taza
Plate..Plato
Napkin .... Servilleta
Roasted .... Assado
Fried..Frito
Rare ....Poco pasado
Medium.. A punto
Well done ....Bien pasado
Warm...Caliente
Frozen .... Helado
Show me the menu. .... Muestreme el menu.
I should like.. Yo quiero.
How much is the meal?............ Cuanto cuesta el cubierto?
Is service included?.................... Esta incluido el servicio?
The bill, please. ....La cuenta, por favor.
Breakfast... Desayuno
Lunch ....Almuerzo
Dinner...Comida

INDEX TO TOWNS AND AREAS

Aguadilla, Puerto Rico 195
Andros Island, Bahamas 61
Anguilla 33
Anse Des Cayes, St. Barthélemy 215
Antigua and Barbuda 36
Arecibo, Puerto Rico 195
Aruba 46
Bahamas 57
Barbados 77
Basse-Pointe, Martinique 188
Basse-Terre, Guadeloupe 156
Basseterre, St. Kitts 224
Basseterre, St. Kitts and Nevis 222
Bathsheba, Barbados 83
Bavaro, Dominican Republic 143
Bequia Island, St. Vincent and The Grenadines 246
Bermuda 91
Bimini Islands, Bahamas 62
Black River, Jamaica 171
Boca Chica, Dominican Republic 144
Boca Chica Beach, Dominican Republic 139
Bonaire 108
Bridgetown, Barbados 83, 87
Brimstone Hill Fortress National Park,
St. Kitts and Nevis 222
Buck Island Reef National Monument,
U.S. Virgin Islands 268
Cabo Rojo, Puerto Rico 202
Cabrits National Park, Dominica 133
Caracas, Venezuela 280
Carbet, Martinique 187
Caribbean National Forest, Puerto Rico 195
Casabao, Curaçao 129
Castries, St. Lucia 230, 231
Cayman Brac, Cayman Islands 120
Cayman Islands 112
Chalky Mount, Barbados 86
Charlestown, Nevis 223
Charlestown, St. Kitts and Nevis 222
Charlotte Amalie, U.S. Virgin Islands 270
Christiansted, U.S. Virgin Islands 268
Cumana, Venezuela 280
Curaçao 124
Devonshire Parish, Bermuda 95, 99
Dickenson Bay, Antigua 43
Dieppe Bay, St. Kitts 225
Discovery Bay, Jamaica 164
Dominica 131
Dominican Republic 135
Dorado, Puerto Rico 202
Dunmore Town, Bahamas 67
Eleuthera Island, Bahamas 62
English Harbour, Antigua 41, 43
Fajardo, Puerto Rico 202
Falmouth, Jamaica 164, 171

Fort-De-France, Martinique 187
Frederiksted, U.S. Virgin Islands 269
Freeport, Bahamas 62, 68
French Cul-De-Sac, St. Martin/St. Maarten 239
George Town, Cayman Islands 119, 121
George Town, Bahamas 69
Gingerland, Nevis 223
Gosier, Guadeloupe 158
Grand Bahama Island, Bahamas 62
Grand Case, St. Martin/St. Maarten 239
Grand Cul-De-Sac, St. Barthélemy 216
Grand Turk, Turks and Caicos Islands 256, 257
Great Abaco Island, Bahamas 63
Great Exuma Island, Bahamas 63
Green Turtle Cay, Bahamas 70
Grenada 147
Guadeloupe 153
Gunthorpes, Antigua 41
Gustavia, St. Barthélemy 215, 216
Hamilton, Bermuda 99, 100
Hamilton (City), Bermuda 96
Hamilton Parish, Bermuda 95, 99
Harbour Island, Bahamas 63, 71
Hope Town, Bahamas 71
Iles Des Saintes, Guadeloupe 156
Irish Town, Jamaica 172
Isla De Margarita, Venezuela 281
Jamaica 159
Jones Bay, Nevis 223
Kingston, Jamaica 165, 172
Kingstown, St. Vincent and The Grenadines 246
Kralendijk, Bonaire 110, 111
La Romana, Dominican Republic 139, 144
Lajas, Puerto Rico 196
Le François, Martinique 187, 189
Le Moule, Guadeloupe 156
Levera National Park, Grenada 149
Little Bay, St. Martin/St. Maarten 240
Little Cayman, Cayman Islands 123
Long Island, Bahamas 64
Lucaya, Bahamas 62
Maho Bay, St. Martin/St. Maarten 240
Mamora Bay, Antigua 44
Mandeville, Jamaica 166
Maracaibo, Venezuela 281
Maracay, Venezuela 281
Maricao, Puerto Rico 203
Marigot, St. Martin/St. Maarten 239, 241
Marsh Harbour, Bahamas 72
Martinique 184
Mayaguez, Puerto Rico 196, 203
Meads Bay, Anguilla 35
Montego Bay, Jamaica 166, 173
Nassau, Bahamas 65, 72, 73
Negril, Jamaica 167, 176

New Providence Island, Bahamas 64
Newcastle, Nevis 224
North Caicos, Turks and Caicos Islands 257
North Side, Cayman Islands 120
Ocho Rios, Jamaica 168, 178
Oranjestad, Aruba 50, 52
Other Ports of Call 280
Ottley's, St. Kitts and Nevis 222
Ottley's Village, St. Kitts 225
Oyster Pond, St. Martin/St. Maarten 242
Paget Parish, Bermuda 96, 102
Palm Island, St. Vincent and The Grenadines 247
Pares, Antigua 41
Pembroke Parish, Bermuda 96
Peter Island, British Virgin Islands 262
Petit-Bourg, Guadeloupe 157
Philipsburg, St. Martin/St. Maarten 238, 242
Pointe-À-Pitre, Guadeloupe 157
Ponce, Puerto Rico 196, 204
Port Antonio, Jamaica 168, 182
Port Maria, Jamaica 169
Port Of Spain, Trinidad and Tobago 252, 254
Port Royal, Jamaica 169
Providenciales, Turks and Caicos Islands 256, 257
Puerto Plata, Dominican Republic 140, 144
Puerto Rico 190
Punta Cana, Dominican Republic 144
Reading, Jamaica 183
Rendezvous Bay, Anguilla 35
Rincon, Puerto Rico 204
Rio Grande, Puerto Rico 204
Roseau, Dominica 133, 134
Runaway Bay, Antigua 44
Runaway Bay, Jamaica 170
Samana, Dominican Republic 145
San Fernando, Trinidad and Tobago 253
San German, Puerto Rico 197
San Juan, Puerto Rico 197, 205
San Nicolas, Aruba 52
Sandys Parish, Bermuda 98, 105
Santiago, Dominican Republic 140
Santo Domingo, Dominican Republic 141, 145
Scarborough, Trinidad and Tobago 252, 253

Siloah, Jamaica 170
Smith's Parish, Bermuda 98, 105
Soufrière, St. Lucia 231, 233
Southampton Parish, Bermuda 98, 106
Spanish Town, Jamaica 170
Spanish Wells Island, Bahamas 66
Speightstown, Barbados 86
Stella Maris, Bahamas 76
St. Barthélemy 211
St. Croix, U.S. Virgin Islands 268, 272
St. David's Parish, Bermuda 105
St. Eustatius and Saba 217
St. George's, Bermuda 97
St. George's, Grenada 150
St. George's Parish, Bermuda 97, 105
St. John, U.S. Virgin Islands 269, 274
St. John's, Antigua 42, 44
St. Kitts and Nevis 219
St. Lucia 226
St. Martin/St. Maarten 234
St. Peter, Barbados 86
St. Pierre, Martinique 188
St. Thomas, U.S. Virgin Islands 270, 275
St. Vincent and The Grenadines 243
Tortola, British Virgin Islands 261, 262
Trelawny, Jamaica 183
Trinidad and Tobago 248
Trois-Ilets, Martinique 188, 189
Turks and Caicos Islands 255
Utuado, Puerto Rico 201
Valencia, Venezuela 281
Venezuela 280
Virgin Gorda, British Virgin Islands 261
Virgin Islands, British 259
Virgin Islands National Park, U.S.
Virgin Islands 269
Virgin Islands, U.S. 264
Walkers Cay, Bahamas 76
Warwick Parish, Bermuda 107
Willemstad, Curaçao 126, 129
Willikies, Antigua 45
Young Island, St. Vincent and
The Grenadines 247

Capture the moment...

Tips for successful photographs

Know your camera, and be sure it's in good working order. Before going on a trip, shoot a roll of film so you won't have any surprises when it really counts. Use film best suited to your purpose; camera shop personnel can help you choose the right kind. Then, follow the instructions that come with it.

♦ Compose your picture. Try framing it with a foreground feature (a fence or tree), making sure that parts of the subject are not being cut off. Get close enough so that your subject won't be dwarfed in an expanse of background.

♦ When taking close-ups of people, have them stand against a simple backdrop, and be sure they do something other than stare stiffly at the camera.

♦ Mid-morning and mid-afternoon, when the sun's angle creates definite but not overpowering shadows, are the best times for general photography. Pictures taken during the shadowless high noon hours tend to be flat.

♦ If the weather turns bad, take pictures anyway. Rain and fog can add a special magic to your efforts.

Bed & Breakfast Lodgings Index

Some bed and breakfasts listed below might have historical significance. Those properties are also referenced in the Historical index. The indication that continental [CP] or full breakfast [BP] is included in the room rate reflects whether a property is a Bed-and-Breakfast facility.

Bermuda

Accommodations

Astwood Cove	Warwick Parish	107
Aunt Nea's Inn at Hillcrest	St. George's Parish	105
Barnsdale Guest Apartments	Paget Parish	102
Loughlands Guest House	Paget Parish	103
Marley Beach Cottages	Warwick Parish	107
Oxford House	Hamilton	100
Rosemont	Hamilton	100

Martinique

Accommodation

Fregate Bleue Inn	Le Francois	189

Puerto Rico

Accommodations

At Wind Chimes Guest House	San Juan	205
Casa del Caribe	San Juan	205
El Canario Inn	San Juan	206

Trinidad And Tobago

Accommodation

Alicia's House	Port Of Spain	254

Virgin Islands, U.S.

Accommodation

Pink Fancy Hotel	St. Croix	273

Country Inns Index

Some of the following country inns can also be considered as bed-and-breakfast operations. The indication that continental [CP] or full breakfast [BP] is included in the room rate reflects whether a property is a Bed-and-Breakfast facility.

Bermuda

Accommodation

Royal Palms	Hamilton	100

Curaçao

Accommodation

Avila Beach Hotel	Willemstad	129

Dominica

Accommodation

Reigate Hall Hotel	Roseau	134

Jamaica

Accommodations

Datura Villa (Reading)	Montego Bay	173
Ivor	Kingston	172

Puerto Rico

Accommodations

Horned Dorset Primavera	Rincon	204
Parador La Hacienda Juanita	Maricao	203

St. Kitts And Nevis

Accommodations

Old Manor Estate & Hotel	Gingerland	223
Ottley's Plantation Inn	Ottley's Village	225
The Golden Lemon Inn and Villas	Dieppe Bay	225

Restaurants

Golden Rock Dining Room	Gingerland	223
Miss June's Cuisine	Jones Bay	223
Nisbet Plantation Dining Room	Newcastle	224

St. Lucia

Accommodations

Anse Chastanet	Soufriere	233
Candyo Inn	Castries	231
The Green Parrot Inn	Castries	231

St. Martin/St. Maarten

Accommodation

Hotel Captain Oliver	Oyster Pond	242

The Bahamas

Accommodation

Graycliff Hotel	Nassau	72

Turks And Caicos Islands

Accommodations

Salt Raker Inn	Grand Turk	257
Turks Head Inn	Grand Turk	257

Virgin Islands, British

Accommodation

Tamarind Club Hotel	Tortola	263

Virgin Islands, U.S.

Accommodation

Hotel 1829	St. Thomas	275

Historical Lodgings & Restaurants Index

Some of the following historical lodgings can also be considered as bed-and-breakfast operations. The indication that continental [CP] or full breakfast [BP] is included in the room rate reflects whether a property is a Bed-and-Breakfast facility.

Aruba

Restaurant

Chez Mathilde .... Oranjestad   55

Barbados

Restaurant

Bagatelle Great House .... Bridgetown   90

Bermuda

Accommodations

Aunt Nea's Inn at Hillcrest .... St. George's Parish   105
Greenbank & Cottages .... Paget Parish   103
Loughlands Guest House .... Paget Parish   103
Royal Palms .... Hamilton   100

Restaurants

Fourways Inn .... Paget Parish   104
The Frog & Onion Pub .... Sandys Parish   105
The Waterlot Inn .... Southampton Parish   107
Tom Moore's Tavern .... Hamilton Parish   99

Cayman Islands

Restaurant

Grand Old House .... George Town   122

Curaçao

Restaurants

La Pergola .... Willemstad   130
Larousse Restaurant .... Willemstad   130

Jamaica

Accommodation

Ivor .... Kingston   172

Restaurants

Evita's .... Ocho Rios   182
Ivor .... Kingston   173
The Georgian House .... Montego Bay   175

Martinique

Accommodation

Hotel Plantation De Leyritz .... Basse-Pointe   188

Restaurant

Leyritz Plantation Restaurant .... Basse-Pointe   188

Puerto Rico

Accommodations

At Wind Chimes Guest House .... San Juan   205
El Convento .... San Juan   206
Parador La Hacienda Juanita .... Maricao   203

St. Kitts And Nevis

Accommodations

Old Manor Estate & Hotel .... Gingerland   223
Ottley's Plantation Inn .... Ottley's Village   225
The Golden Lemon Inn and Villas .... Dieppe Bay   225

St. Lucia

Accommodation

The Green Parrot Inn .... Castries   231

The Bahamas

Accommodation

Graycliff Hotel .... Nassau   72

Restaurant

Castle Cafe .... Marsh Harbour   72

Turks And Caicos Islands

Accommodation

Turks Head Inn .... Grand Turk   257

Virgin Islands, U.S.

Accommodations

Hotel 1829 .... St. Thomas   275
Pink Fancy Hotel .... St. Croix   273

Resorts Index

Many establishments are located in resort areas; however, the following places have extensive on-premises recreational facilities:

Anguilla

Accommodations

Malliouhana Hotel .... Meads Bay 35
Sonesta Beach Resort Anguilla........Rendezvous Bay 35

Antigua And Barbuda

Accommodations

Rex Halcyon Cove ....Dickenson Bay 43
Royal Antiguan Casino, Tennis,
  Beach Resort .... St. John's 45
St. James's Club...............................Mamora Bay 44
Sandals Antigua Resort & Spa ....Dickenson Bay 43

Aruba

Accommodations

Americana Aruba Beach Resort &
  Casino .... Oranjestad 52
Holiday Inn-Aruba Beach Resort &
  Casino .... Oranjestad 54
Hyatt Regency Aruba Resort &
  Casino .... Oranjestad 54
Wyndham Aruba Beach Resort &
  Casino .... Oranjestad 55

Barbados

Accommodations

Almond Beach Village............................Bridgetown 87
Discovery Bay Hotel ....Bridgetown 88
Sam Lord's Castle Resort......................Bridgetown 89
Sandy Lane Hotel ....Bridgetown 89

Bermuda

Accommodations

Sonesta Beach Resort .... Southampton Parish 106
Southampton Princess Hotel ...... Southampton Parish 106
The St. George's Club .... St. George's Parish 105
Sandy Lane Hotel ....Bridgetown 89

Cayman Islands

Accommodations

Hyatt Regency Grand Cayman ....George Town 121
The Westin Casuarina Resort...............George Town 122

Curaçao

Accommodations

Princess Beach Resort & Casino .... Willemstad 129
Sonesta Beach Resort & Casino.............. Willemstad 129

Dominican Republic

Accommodations

Casa de Campo Resort.......................... La Romana 144
Hotel Casino Bavaro................................. Bavaro 143
Hotel Flamenco Beach.........................Puerto Plata 144
Hotel Golf Bavaro.................................... Bavaro 143
Hotel Jardin Bavaro................................. Bavaro 143
Hotel Playa Bavaro................................. Bavaro 143
Paradise Beach Club & Casino..............Puerto Plata 144
Punta Cana Beach Resort ....Punta Cana 144

Jamaica

Accommodations

Beaches-Negril..Negril 176
Ciboney Ocho Rios-A Radisson Villa, Spa & Beach
  Resort...Ocho Rios 178
Couples...Ocho Rios 178
Goblin Hill Villas at
  San San-Port Antonio .... Port Antonio 182
Grand Lido Braco....................................Trelawny 183
Grand Lido Negril..Negril 176
Grand Lido San Souci...............................Ocho Rios 178
Half Moon Golf, Tennis and
  Beach Club..Montego Bay 174
Holiday Inn SunSpree Resort
  Montego Bay.......................................Montego Bay 174
Renaissance Jamaica Grande ....Ocho Rios 181
Round Hill Hotel And Villas ....Montego Bay 175
Sandals Dunn's River Golf Resort
  & Spa ....Ocho Rios 181
Sandals Inn ....Montego Bay 175
Sandals Montego Bay.........................Montego Bay 175
Sandals Negril Beach Resort and Spa ....Negril 177
Sandals Ocho Rios Resort and
  Golf Club...Ocho Rios 181
Sandals Royal Jamaican ....Montego Bay 175
Swept Away-Negril ....Negril 177
The Enchanted Garden ....Ocho Rios 178
The Jamaica Palace Hotel.................... Port Antonio 183
Trident Villas & Hotel .... Port Antonio 183
Wyndham Rose Hall Golf &
  Beach Resort ....Montego Bay 175

Puerto Rico

Accommodations

El Conquistador Resort & Country Club..........Fajardo 202
El San Juan Hotel & Casino......................San Juan 207
Hyatt Dorado Beach ....Dorado 202
Las Casitas Village....................................Fajardo 203
Ponce Hilton & Casino .... Ponce 204
San Juan Marriott Resort &
  Stellaris Casino...................................San Juan 208
The Ritz Carlton San Juan
  Hotel and Casino ....San Juan 208
Westin Rio Mar Beach Resort &
  Country Club.................................... Rio Grande 204

St. Kitts And Nevis

Accommodation

Four Seasons Resort Nevis .... Charlestown 223

St. Lucia

Accommodations

Ladera Resort ....Soufriere 233
Rex Papillon...Castries 232
Rex St. Lucian...Castries 232
Sandals Halcyon St. Lucia ....Castries 232
Sandals St. Lucia Golf Resort and Spa ....Castries 232
Windjammer Landing-Villa Beach Resort ....Castries 232

St. Martin/St. Maarten

Accommodations

Esmeralda Resort .... Grand Case 239
Hotel La Samanna ....Marigot 241
Hotel Mont Vernon ....French Cul-De-Sac 239
Le Flamboyant Hotel & Resort.....................Marigot 241
Maho Beach Hotel & Casino ....Maho Bay 240

Resorts (cont'd)

ST. VINCENT AND THE GRENADINES

ACCOMMODATIONS

Palm Island Beach Club .... Palm Island 247
Young Island Resort .... Young Island 247

THE BAHAMAS

ACCOMMODATIONS

Abaco Beach Resort & Boat Harbor .... Marsh Harbour 72
Atlantis Resort & Casino............................ Nassau 73
Bahamas Princess Resort and Casino .... Freeport 69
Coral Sands Hotel.......................... Dunmore Town 67
Green Turtle Club........................... Green Turtle Cay 70
Nassau Marriott Resort & Crystal Palace
   Casino .... Nassau 74
Paradise Island Fun Club .... Nassau 74
Pink Sands .... Dunmore Town 67
Port Lucaya Resort & Yacht Club .... Freeport 69
Radisson Cable Beach Resort.................... Nassau 74
Romora Bay Club.......................... Dunmore Town 67
Sandals Royal Bahamian Resort & Spa .... Nassau 75
South Ocean Golf & Beach Resort .... Nassau 75
Walkers Cay Hotel & Marina, Bahamas...Walkers Cay 76

TRINIDAD AND TOBAGO

ACCOMMODATIONS

Le Grand Courlan Resort & Spa .... Scarborough 253
Mount Irvine Bay Hotel & Golf Club .... Scarborough 254

TURKS AND CAICOS ISLANDS

ACCOMMODATIONS

Beaches Turks & Caicos Resort
   & Spa .... Providenciales 257
Ocean Club....................................... Providenciales 258

VIRGIN ISLANDS, BRITISH

ACCOMMODATIONS

Long Bay Beach Resort .... Tortola 262
Peter Island Resort & Yacht Harbour ...... Peter Island 262
Sugar Mill Hotel.. Tortola 263

VIRGIN ISLANDS, U.S.

ACCOMMODATIONS

Best Western Emerald Beach Resort .... St. Thomas 275
Caneel Bay Hotel..................................... St. John 274
Elysian Beach Resort............................. St. Thomas 275
Marriott's Morning Star Beach Resort....... St. Thomas 276
Renaissance Grand Beach Resort .... St. Thomas 277
Sapphire Beach Resort & Marina .... St. Thomas 278
The Buccaneer Hotel .... St. Croix 272
The Ritz Carlton St Thomas.................... St. Thomas 277
Westin Carambola Beach Resort .... St. Croix 273
Westin Resort St. John .... St. John 274
Wyndham Sugar Bay Beach Club &
   Resort.. St. Thomas 278

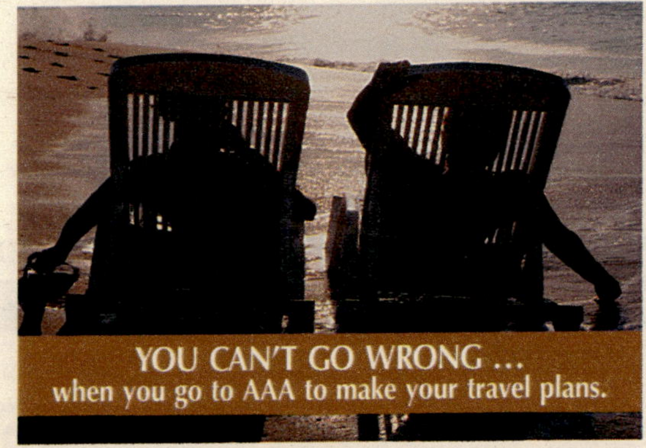

Now You Can Count on AAA for Financial Services Too!

*N*ow, your AAA membership offers even more. Choose from a full range of financial products and services with special AAA member-only rates and features.

AAA Member Select[SM] Prime Access[SM] Credit Card

AAA Member Select[SM] Rewards Credit Card

AAA Member Select[SM] Platinum VISA® Credit Card

Auto Loans & Leasing

Home Equity Loans[1]

Personal Loans

Market Rate Checking

Money Market Accounts

Certificates of Deposit[2]

MAKE THE MOST OF YOUR MEMBERSHIP.[SM]

1-800-680-AAA4

24 HOURS A DAY. 7 DAYS A WEEK.

PNC Bank, FSB, Member FDIC, and its affiliates are the providers of financial products and services for the AAA Financial Services Program. [1]Where available. Home equity loan approval subject to verification of property value. Disbursement of funds subject to receipt of signed loan documents. [2]CDs subject to early withdrawal penalty. Prices and programs subject to change without notice.

Available only through participating AAA clubs.

RED ALERT!

When you pick up a AAA TourBook®, be alert for the establishments that display a bright red AAA logo beside their listing. These establishments place a high value on the patronage they receive from AAA members. They are telling you they're willing to go the extra mile to get your business. Some even offer special amenities designed just for you.

And don't forget to look for the establishments that display the familiar SAVE icon to receive discounts.

So, when you turn to the AAA TourBook to make your travel plans, be on the look out for the establishments that will give you the special treatment you deserve.

Look for AAA Savings on Dining

When using the AAA TourBook® to select places to dine, be sure to look for restaurants with the bright red SAVE symbol beside their TourBook listing. Why? Because these establishments offer special savings to AAA members, ranging from discounts and two-for-one entrees, to a free item with the purchase of a meal.

These restaurants will display the familiar Show Your Card & Save® symbol — your invitation to savings.

So, to enjoy special savings, quality service and a warm welcome, look for the restaurants that value the business they receive from AAA members.

For more information, call or visit your AAA office today.

Let AAA Take the Worry
Out of International Travel
Purchase your foreign travel
at a AAA travel agency and
you'll benefit from AAA's global alliance
with Thomas Cook.

There is an English speaking agent in each of
Thomas Cook's 1,800 offices in over 100 countries,
waiting to fulfill
The Worldwide Customer Promise
to AAA travel agency customers. The promise
entitles you help with the following during your trip,

FREE OF ANY SERVICE CHARGE:
Airline Reservations   Airline Ticket Reconfirmation,
Revalidation or Re-routing*
*performed within ARC & IATAN guidelines
Changes to Travel Arrangements
Hotel Reservations   Car Rental Reservations
Travel Planning Assistance
Emergency Local Telephone Assistance
Peace of Mind Begins at
Your AAA Travel Agency.

AAA
Thomas
Cook
Worldwide Network